Reformation
or
Revolution

A study of modern society in the light of a reformational and
scriptural pluralism

By

E. L. HEBDEN TAYLOR, M.A. (CANTAB), L.TH. (A.T.C.)
Professor of Economics and Sociology
DORDT COLLEGE
Sioux Center, Iowa, U.S.A.

THE CRAIG PRESS
Nutley, New Jersey 07110
1970

Library of Congress Card Catalog No. 77-115822
Printed in the United States of America

TO

MY MOTHER

In deep appreciation and thankfulness to Almighty God for having brought me up "in the nurture and admonition of the Lord," as a boy on the African mission field.

CONTENTS

"Whenever one uses the term 'social question' one means thereby, in the most general sense, that serious doubt has arisen about the soundness of the social structure in which we live, that in consequence public opinion is divided as to the type of foundation on which a more appropriate and more liveable social order may be built. In itself, therefore, the mere positing of the question in no way implies that it must be solved in the socialistic sense. The solution at which one arrives can also be a totally different one. Only this one thing is necessary if a social question is to exist for you: that you realize the untenability of the present situation, and that you realize this untenability to be one not of incidental causes, but on involving the very basis of social association. For one who does not acknowledge this, and who thinks that the evil can be exorcised through an increase in piety, through friendlier treatment or kindlier charity, there exists possibly a religious question and possibly a philanthropic question but not a social question. This does not exist until you exercise an *architechtonic* critique of human society itself and hence desire and think possible a different arrangement of the social structure."

—Abraham Kuyper, *Christianity and the Class Struggle*

"Every type of social relationship has its proper laws peculiar to it, whereby it is ruled. And these laws are different and divergent in each kind of social relationship, according to the requirement of the inner nature of each of them."

—Johannes Althusius, *Politica*

PREFACE

A madman once ran into the market place calling out, "I seek God." The bystanders, typifying the majority of modern Western men who do not live as if they really believed in the living God of the Bible, were vastly amused and said to the maniac, "Why? Is God lost? Has he taken a sea voyage? Has he emigrated?" But the madman cried out again, "Where is God gone? I mean to tell you, we have killed him, you and I. We are all his murderers." Unfortunately, the madman was before his time. The meaning of this parable as related by Nietzsche could not reach his nineteenth century readers. And so the great prophet of modern nihilism tells us the madman went into one church after another and intoned his requiem of the death of God. When asked what he was doing, he replied, "What are these churches now, if they are not the tombs of God." [1] Nietzsche, with the penetration of genius, had fixed upon the great new phenomenon of post-Christian Western society, the gradual fading out of the consciousness of God from the mind of Western man. He has driven Christ out of Christendom and now lives as if God were indeed dead.

What had begun in the second half of the nineteenth century has gone very much further in the twentieth. As a result of this apostasy from God we are faced today with the fateful choice of revolution or reformation. The forces of unbelief have spread out from hotbeds of atheism in Europe to undermine the great Anglo-Saxon democracies. Our English-speaking nations today stand at the cross roads of their destiny. Our situation is remarkably similar to the conditions and climate of opinion which prevailed in Western Europe during the breakup of medieval Christendom in the "waning of the Middle Ages." [2] There is the same disrespect for the authority of government, the same breakdown of marriage and family life, the same scepticism and uncertainty regarding the nature and destiny of human life. In the later Middle Ages this movement of thought was called Nominalism or the "Modern Way"; today it is called logical positivism and language analysis. The universities of America, Britain, and Canada have become "multi-versities" in which all values are held to be relative and scientific method alone regarded as the avenue to truth and blessedness.

Our present revolutionary situation is due to the breakdown of a unified field of knowledge and experience. A great symptom of this spiritual crisis now facing us is the growing drug addiction of our young people. Drug addiction is the symptom of the disillusion of young people with the godless, inhuman, and depersonalized society in which they have had the misfortune to be born. It is an escape from the futility and boredom of modern life and an attempt to find the chemical equivalent of Christian grace and blessedness on the part of people who can no longer find any meaning to their lives. It is a sign of what happens when people live and behave as if God is in truth dead. When love is dead man is dead.

Post-Christian man has created a sterile society in which both God and man are dead. Human life has become meaningless as apostate man finds himself reduced by his own science and technology to a cog in the great machine of nature and of society. The only way of escape lies in a non-rational world of experience, drugs, absurdity, pornography, an elusive "final experience," and ultimate madness. The one freedom left to modern godless man, according to Michael Foucault in *Madness and Civilization*, is the freedom to become crazy.[3]

How did apostate modern man reach this abyss? The origin of the modern apostate humanist outlook upon life may be traced back to the medieval Roman Catholic philosopher and monk, Thomas Aquinas, who first undermined the unified field of knowledge and experience revealed to man in God's Word. Aquinas divided reality up into the two realms of Grace and Nature. In the former he placed God and the supernatural world of angels and the unseen which man could contact only through the sacraments of the Roman Catholic Church and which he studied in theology. In the latter realm of created beings, Aquinas placed all earthly things, including man's body, his social institutions, and natural moral values. Man's will, he taught, is fallen but not his reason. Thus his reason can study the world apart from the ordering principle of Scripture. This autonomy provided the basis for the later secularization of Western art, philosophy, politics, business, and natural science and education. It broke out into the open with Nominalism and its doctrine of a twofold truth and found its political, legal, and academic expression during the Renaissance.

As a result the biblical doctrine of creation became secularized as nature was proclaimed to work like a machine rather than an organism. The divine Creator became the deified image of the creative urge worked in man by his drive for freedom. The idea of God's grace was dying when Filippo Lippi painted the Virgin Mary not symbolically, as had always been the Christian custom, but realistically. He painted a beautiful girl holding a baby. In *Escape from Reason*, Francis Schaeffer points out, "There is something more we need to know about this painting. The girl he painted as Mary was his mistress. And all Florence knew it was his mistress. Nobody would have dared to do this a few years before. Nature was killing grace." [4] Schaeffer believes that grace was dead for Fouquet when, around 1450, this French artist painted the king's mistress, Agnes Sorel, as Mary. He writes: "Everyone knowing the court who saw it knew this was the king's current mistress. Fouquet painted her with one breast exposed. Whereas before it would have been Mary feeding the baby Jesus, now it is the king's mistress with one breast exposed—and grace is dead." [5] Consequently the problems of human destiny had now to be defined in terms not of nature and grace, but of freedom and nature.

By the seventeenth century nature had totally devoured grace, and what was left in its place was man's striving for freedom. However men soon found that their freedom was being threatened by the deterministic and mechanistic image of the world which their natural science was creating. Freedom was now understood as the reversion of man's freedom in Christ. The individual's freedom was no longer seen as dependence upon God and his law but as complete independence and autonomy from God.

As such it soon came into conflict with man's science ideal, since the latter tended to reduce man to a machine. The fight to retain freedom was carried on by the Romantic movement, beginning with Rousseau and Kant. Romantic literature and art express a casting aside of the industrial and scientific civilization as that which restrains and inhibits man's freedom. It marked the birth of the Bohemian ideal. Thus by the beginning of the nineteenth century autonomous freedom and autonomous science stood facing each other in deadly combat. Soon science and technology was to swallow up freedom. In terms of the doctrine of the uniformity of natural causes working in a closed system, the mechanistic view of reality came to include not only physics but everything, including man. Apostate scientists such as Laplace, August Comte, Marx, and Lotze insisted on the complete unity of man's spiritual and physical life, and so freedom disappeared. Neither God nor man's freedom exist any more for Europe's most advanced thinkers in the nineteenth century; everything is now placed in the great machine of Nature. Human values such as love and sympathy for the poor of Europe disappeared as an apostate economic individualism reduced the former peasants and guild craftsmen to slaves of the new factory system. No one better reflected this new attitude towards life than the Marquis de Sade. Schaeffer writes of him in *Escape from Reason*: "He understood the direction that things would have to take when man is included in the machinery. The conclusions he drew were these: if man is determined, than what *is* is right. If all life is only mechanism—if that is all there is—then morals really do not count. Morals become only a word for a sociological framework. Morals become a means of manipulation by society in the midst of the machine. The word 'morals' by this time is only a semantic connotation word for non-morals. What is, is right." [6]

De Sade soon put his new ideas into practice. He argued that man is by nature stronger than woman so he can do whatever he wants with her, beat her, rape her, and even strangle her. What nature decrees in strength must be right. Today sadism is reflected in America's cult of violence on the streets, on her TV and cinema screens, in the death of man in art, music, and life. By making nature independent of God apostate modern man has thus brought upon himself the judgment of God, in so far as he finds that life without God is meaningless, hopeless, and loveless.

On the basis of rationality, logic, and scientific determinism man's life no longer has any meaning to it. Scientific humanism has created a sterile society in which the individual as a person has been reduced to a statistic in the records of big business and big government. His personality has been stripped from him leaving him to fulfill a function in a depersonalized, militarized, technological mass society as an empty husk of a person. Today millions of people are shirking off their responsibilities as parents, workers, citizens, and consumers, and they have surrendered them into the hands of the leviathan state, of the secular labor unions, political parties, and big business. In short, with the death of God they find themselves also dead if not dying in "The Waste Land" of modern society. T. S. Eliot spoke of these people as "The Hollow Men":

> We are the hollow men
> We are the stuffed men
> Leaning together
> Headpiece filled with straw. Alas!
> Our dried voices, when
> We whisper together
> Are quiet and meaningless
> As wind in dry grass
> Or rats' feet over broken glass
> In our dry cellar.[7]

All that is now left for such people to do is to make a non-rational leap of faith into sex, drugs, anything they can think of, because they are now living under the line of apostate humanist despair. They have given up all hope of achieving a rational unified answer to the problems of knowledge and life.

The Christian does not condemn the "hippies" out of hand. He agrees with the hippies' diagnosis of modern society but rejects their solution. Anyone who can gladly accept society as it has become today is even more to be pitied than the "hippies" themselves. Unfortunately the "hippies" themselves are heading toward the same dead end as the dehumanized society they so vehemently condemn.

Both socialist collectivism and hippie and beatnik individualism are based on the same false premise, namely, that man is the master of his own fate and that man is autonomous. The hippie movement is tragic insofar as it is doomed to failure, but its great value is that it gives us the opportunity while there is yet time for reformation and to look at ourselves and see what has become of our utopian revolutionary dreams of "liberty, equality, and fraternity," without God. Our faith in science as man's only savior has brought us to the edge of the abyss. The way of escape does not lie in a nonrational world of "first-order" experiences induced by drugs or by "happenings" but by a return to the true origin of meaning and purpose in human life. Man's happiness cannot be found in pantheism or in surrender to drugs, but only in the service of God and of one's neighbor. For the Christian real happiness only comes from obedience to the Great Commandment as summed up by the Lord Jesus Christ.

Hear O Israel, The Lord our God is one Lord, and thou shalt love the Lord thy God with all thy heart, and with all thy soul, and with all thy mind, and with all thy strength. This is the first and great commandment. And the second is like unto it. Thou shalt love thy neighbor as thyself. On these two commandments hang all the law and the prophets (Matt. 22:37; Mark 12:29-31; Luke 10:25-27).

Likewise the Christian will point out to his unregenerate friends that meaning and purpose for modern man can only be found by returning to the biblical view of human nature and destiny, which locates man's origin in the God who first created and then redeemed him. Only such biblical Christianity can restore dignity and meaning to modern life, because it refuses to divide up human experience between nature and grace, or freedom and nature, or faith and reason. Instead God's Word provides us with a unified field of human experience and knowledge. God's Word alone can provide us with the true ordering principle which gives us our frame of reference and only sure point of departure for all our theoretical and practical life. It does so by working in us a true knowledge of God, of ourselves, and of the law-order of the creation. The Word of God is the power by which the Lord God opens our hearts to "see" things as they really are.

Apart from this revealed framework of creation, radical fall into sin, and equally radical redemption by Jesus Christ in the communion of the Holy Spirit, man's fallen reason darkened by sin uncovers only a meaningless and irrational chance.[8] God's Word alone can put meaning into the facts uncovered by scientific investigation and show us how to use our science to God's glory and the benefit of human welfare and the improvement of man's estate. Without this biblical frame of reference, the data provided by scientific investigation is ultimately meaningless. True knowledge is thus made possible by true religion and arises from the knowing activity of the human heart enlightened through the Word of God by the Holy Spirit. Thus biblical Christianity can play a decisive part in reforming modern life and guide us in the ordering of our everyday experience and scientific activities.

Reformational Christianity can not only provide modern man with a unified field of knowledge for his science, but it can also provide a way out of the false dilemma of individualism versus collectivism, socialism versus capitalism, racism versus integration, for the Bible alone reveals the true basis for society in a cultural unity in diversity. Man's personality can develop only in relationship to God and with his neighbor. The common error of both conservative individualism and socialist collectivism is that both take their starting point in man, whether this be the individual or the group. The biblical view of man in society overcomes this dichotomy in social science. In the light of God's Word we know that God created man for community with his fellow men and as a social being. This means that man does not find his purpose in himself as John Locke supposed, or in the group as Karl Marx supposed, but in the God who created him. The individual and the community are equally called to live in obedience to the laws of their creator.

It is only by such obedience to God's creation ordinances for human society that the present conflicts rending society apart can be resolved. If the individual and the community will occupy their God-given place in a truly Christian society dominated by adventure for God in the context of love and service, their need for drug addiction, civil disobedience and other forms of social deviance will disappear. In such a reformational society young people would once more find a reason to live, and they would not need to take to drugs but they would become busy being "hip" to God's great laws.

In this book we shall describe how men have tried to make their social life independent of God's creation norms for their lives and the tragic results of this apostasy. We shall then suggest a reformational, biblically based solution for the grave problems now facing modern society, especially in the field of industrial relations.

In a very real sense this book must be considered as the sequel to the author's first major work, *The Christian Philosophy of Law, Politics and the State.*[9] While that book was concerned with the principial basis for reformational political and legal action, this one is concerned with the application of the scriptural philosophy of man in society to the fields of labor and industry, and race relations.

It only remains for me to thank my dear wife for her interest, patience, and support. I would also thank my esteemed Christian brothers, Gerald Vandezande and Harry Antonides of the Christian Labour Association of Canada, John Hultink, Bernard Zylstra, and John Olthuis of the Association for the Advancement of Christian Scholarship, the Reverend Louis M. Tamminga and other wonderful members of the Christian Action Foundation, the Reverend Bernard J. Haan, President of Dordt College, as well as the Reverend Richard De Ridder, and my esteemed fellow professors at Dordt College, especially Professor John C. Vander Stelt, the Reverend John B. Hulst, and, above all, my spiritual "father," Herman Dooyeweerd, and "holy uncle," Evan Runner, for their help and encouragement in the writing of this book.

Finally let me thank my editor, the Reverend Rousas J. Rushdoony, and also Gary North of the University of California for their counsel, and above all my dear publisher and mentor, Charles H. Craig, for his patience and guidance.

None of these persons, however, must be held in any way responsible for any of the opinions I have expressed or for any inadvertent errors I may have made.

May the Lord Jesus Christ, once Carpenter of Nazareth and now risen Lord and Savior of the Holy, Universal, and Apostolic Churches of God throughout the world by the Holy Spirit, bless this work and use it to the glory of God the Father and in bringing back peace, joy, and love to the workers and managers of industry, the husbands and wives and their children, and reconciliation between the classes and races of the world. May Reformation rather than Revolution prevail.

Reverend E. L. (Stacey) Hebden Taylor
Department of Economics and Sociology
Dordt College, Sioux Center, Iowa 51250. U. S. A.

Eastertide, 1969

PREFACE NOTES

1. F. Nietzsche, *Die frohliche Wissenschaft* (1882), p. 206.
2. J. Huizinga, *The Waning of the Middle Ages* (Peregrine Books, London, 1965). For recent studies of drug addiction consult Peter Laurie, *Drugs* (Pelican Special, London, 1967) and Alan Bestic, *Turn Me on Man* (London, 1967). Also, D. P. Ausubel, *Drug Addiction* (N. Y.).
3. Michael Foucault, *Madness and Civilization* (Pantheon, New York, 1966).
4. Francis A. Schaeffer, *Escape from Reason* (Inter-Varsity Fellowship, London, 1968), p. 16. Cf. Francis Schaeffer, *The God Who Is There* (Hodder & Stoughton, London, 1968), pp. 15ff.
5. *Ibid.*, p. 16. Cf. Marshall McLuhan, *The Medium Is the Massage* (Bantam, 1967), and his *The Medium is the Message* (Bantam, 1968).
6. *Ibid.*, pp. 38-39.
7. T. S. Eliot, *Collected Poems, 1909-1935* (Faber and Faber, London, 1949), p. 87. Cf. T. S. Eliot, "The Waste Land," in the same collection pp. 61-83.
8. William Barrett, *Irrational Man* (Doubleday Anchor Book, New York, 1962).
9. E. L. Hebden Taylor, *The Christian Philosophy of Law, Politics and the State* (The Craig Press, Nutley, New Jersey, 1966), 650 pages.

In his Cambridge lectures *Christianity, Past, and Present,* Basil
Willey had some very pertinent words for our present condition:

> Berdyaev has suggested that humanism, considered as "the ele-
> vation and setting up of man in the centre of the universe," con-
> tains within it a "self-destructive dialectic"; it first glories in
> human lordship over Nature, then merges man in Nature, and
> finally discovers that it has made him Nature's slave, subject to
> Nature's indifference and determinism. Maritain distinguishes
> between theocentric or God-centred humanism, and the anthro-
> pocentric or man-centred kind, arguing that it is the theocentric
> kind, with its recognition that the centre for man is not himself
> but God, which alone can give man his true position 'on this
> isthmus of a middle state', poised between the natural and super-
> natural worlds. Only by remembering his orientation towards
> God can man even play his assigned part in the natural order with-
> out disaster.
>
> During the last three or four centuries humanism may be said
> to have passed through three well-marked stages, of which the
> last two are stages of progressive de-Christianisation. First you have
> the God-centred humanism of men like Erasmus, Hooker, Donne,
> Milton, or Locke. Next, the man-centered humanism of the
> eighteenth century, of the Encyclopaedists, of Hume, and of
> the idealistic romantic poets and philosophers. At this stage
> morality ceases to be dependent upon supernatural sanctions, and
> becomes either utilitarian—that is, a matter of the consequences
> of actions in terms of well-being or happiness, or a matter of the
> Kantian imperative—that is, of obedience to the law of man's
> own nature. Man is still felt, however, in virtue of his reason and
> imagination, to retain contact with a transcendental order, and
> thus to preserve his traditional dignity and his superiority to the
> purely natural order. Finally you have the positivist stage rep-
> resented by Comte, Mill, Marx and their followers, in which all
> possibility of contact with metaphysical reality is denied, man
> becomes God, and Humanity a religion.
>
> The outcome of all this is what we see around us in the world
> today—the moral and spiritual nihilism of the modern world.
> . . . You cannot continue for ever to stand upon a branch which
> you are sawing away from the parent tree. Without a religious
> basis, humanism can find no grounds for the very values it
> proclaims (pp. 79 to 83).

INTRODUCTION

In his novel, *Two People*, A. A. Milne delightfully sketches for us a certain character named Mr. Pump.

"Mr. Pump," writes Milne, "was not a hypocrite. He was a religious man, whose religion was too sacred a thing to be carried into his business. The tophat that he hung up in his office was not the tophat that he prayed into before placing it thus hallowed, between his feet, even if the frock coat and the aspect of benevolence were the same. He had two tophats, and one hat box for them. On the Monday morning he put God reverently away for the week and took out Mammon. On the Sunday morning he came back—gratefully or hopefully, according to the business done—to God. 'After all,' he said, 'No man can serve two masters at one and the same time.' " [1]

It is not very hard to find plenty of Mr. Pumps in the English-speaking world today with their prayers and piety *one* day a week. The majority of Christians in America, Britain, and Canada are quite willing to serve God with "all their hearts, with all their minds, with all their souls and with all their strength," but of course only for one or two hours a week on the Lord's day in the church building. During the other six days of the week, in their profession, trade, or industry most Americans, Britons, and Canadians don't trouble about their calling as Christians. They have lost all sense of their office and vocation "to have dominion over the earth and to subdue it" for God's greater glory. For such people God is practically dead!

As a result the view is widely prevalent today that the Church of God has nothing worthwhile to offer modern men and women since it is held that the Christian Gospel is largely irrelevant to the way in which life has to be lived in present-day society. Even in the minds of Christian laymen and women there is often no clear connection between the Christian faith they confess on Sundays in the Apostles' and Nicene Creeds and the actual decisions which they have to make in their daily work. Unless people feel that to be a Christian makes some recognizable difference in what they do and feel in the daily occupations which fill the greater part of their working lives and waking hours, they can hardly be expected to regard the message of God's sovereign and saving grace in Jesus Christ as having an important meaning for their earthly lives.

Thus a study of the biblical position and teaching in regard to work in modern society is highly relevant not only to our evangelistic mission in the modern world but also to the way in which our proclamation of the Gospel becomes significant for modern life. Again such a study of the meaning of work in modern society in the light of the Christian philosophy of labor may also prove an important step towards overcoming the divorce between institutional religion and the ways of thinking and behaving of ordinary men and women, which is perhaps the gravest feature of the contemporary "religious" situation. Work is for most people one of the central realities of their lives. When Christians talk with other men about the choices they have to make in their daily occupations, it is clear that in this area of life, as in other areas, the biblical "life-and-world-view" does indeed make a fundamental difference in actual living. Then the gulf between the Church's teaching as it is commonly understood and the realities of daily experience will have been successfully bridged, and the Word of God will no longer appear as remote from modern life as many people today falsely suppose.

Not only does the Church stand to benefit by a rediscovery of the biblical philosophy of labor, but also modern industry and business stand to gain.

A great deal is heard these days on both sides of the Atlantic of the need to modernize American, British, and Canadian industries and businesses so that our nations may the better compete in the world's markets.

Unfortunately such a "scientific" and technical rationalization of

Anglo-American-Canadian industries will never by itself bring about a true spirit of partnership between management and workers without which our industries are doomed to continual frustration, labor disputes, and eventual decay.

What industry and commerce need even more than modernization and rationalization is a new vision of God's holy ordinances or laws for work in modern society and of the true relations which should exist between the so-called bosses and the workers. No Christian can possibly think of industry in terms of the class struggle, nor can he think of work merely in terms of the profits or wages received for it. According to the Bible work is man's proper office and main way of serving God. Both workers and managers are created in God's holy image and therefore they should treat each other with mutual respect as persons and never as mere functions of the economic system. Only when the workers stop feeling that they are nothing more than "hands" and slaves of the machine they operate, only then may we expect them to recover a zest for work. Human labor must never be severed from the *person* of the worker. Manpower is not a mere means of production, only to be considered from the point of view of greater output or profits.

Side by side with this recognition of the human dignity of the worker as created in God's image is the principle of cooperation rather than conflict as God's purpose for modern industry. God's commandment "to love thy neighbor as thyself" also has its consequences for man's social and industrial life. Thus no Christian employer or worker who is obedient to the commandment to love the Lord and his neighbor as himself can compromise with the humanist doctrine of the class struggle. Such a Christian will oppose all those apostate people who would make the class struggle normative for industrial relations. Employers and workers are each other's neighbors because they are called upon to work in the same business undertaking, factory, plant, or shop. The Word of God does not look upon the employer as the enemy of the worker or vice versa, but rather the Bible teaches that *both* employers and employees are cooperators with each other in the great and wonderful human enterprise of executing God's cultural and industrial mandate given to man at the beginning of his history, "to have dominion over the earth and to subdue it" (Gen. 1:28). God's Word teaches that both managers and workers are to be God's priests, kings, and stewards of his material resources, e.g., coal, water, wood, iron, carbon, etc., and that it is God alone who gives to men the power to create wealth (Deut. 8:18). As God's priests and stewards of His holy earth both workers and managers are called to obey His laws for work. Man's priestly "office" in industry is to use things, to manipulate and to manufacture God's raw materials, in order that he may the better offer them up in worship to the Creator and in service to his fellow men. In this priestly task both managers and workers have been called by God to take the raw materials of His creation and to subdue them so that these may the better serve the needs of human society. When thus developed or manufactured, we are called by God's Word to lay our entire industrial product at the feet of Him who is Lord both of nature and of man, and in whose glorious image we all have been created. And so all types of industry and farming are intended by God to be our voluntary love service of the Creator as well as of our neighbor.

As such, work is not primarily a thing one does in order to receive a wage or salary at the end of the week or month but the thing one lives to do. According to God's Word, work is, or should be, the full expression of the worker's faculties, the thing in which he finds spiritual, mental, moral, and bodily satisfaction; and the main means by which he offers his life as a sacrifice of praise, prayer, thanksgiving, and of service to Jehovah God and to his fellow men. Instead of being a drudgery, work should be a delight by means of which we praise and hallelujah our glorious God. George Herbert rightly sensed this hallelujah quality of work in his hymn:

> Teach me, my God and King
> In all things thee to see
> And what I do in anything
> To do it as for Thee . . .
> A servant with this clause
> Makes drudgery divine

Who sweeps a room, as for thy laws
Makes that and the action fine.

As a result of the invasion of men's hearts by Satan and sin, modern industry no longer functions as God commands and intends it to function. Under the domination of sin, work has become cursed, troublesome, tiring, and frustrating. Outside Paradise man remains a worker, but his work and his marriage and family life have become radically deformed by his sin, while his relations with his fellow workers, with his employer, and with other races and classes are no longer based upon cooperation but conflict. In no sphere of modern life are the effects of sin more apparent than in marital, industrial, and race relations. Such effects of man's sin have become written into human institutions and systems as well as ingrained in man's heart.

Unless man turns to God for "a new and contrite heart," his efforts to build up civilization and society are doomed to continual frustration and eventual revolution. The alternative to an inner reformation of modern man's economic, marital, and social institutions is not stagnation and carrying on in the same old way, but revolution, since man moves either towards God or the kingdom of darkness as the law of sin takes hold of his life. At the Protestant Reformation in the sixteenth century many Western men preferred reformation to revolution, and they turned back to God and His Word for guidance. As a result God blessed their efforts to rebuild the crumbling civilization of Europe upon a scriptural rather than a humanist basis.

The only alternative to revolution has always been in a faithful return to God's Word and Law for man in society. Thus the revolutionary spirit of twentieth century unbelief as this has come to be embodied in the so-called "democratic way of life," but which has proved itself to be what Hendrik Hart has called "The Democratic Way of Death," can be attacked effectively only by exposing its roots in modern man's apostasy and then by returning to utter dependence upon the Sovereign God.

The diagnosis of European society given by Groen van Prinsterer in *Unbelief and Revolution* can still be of great help to Christians today in diagnosing the sickness unto death of our society. Groen believed that Europe's apostasy from the God of the Bible had led directly to the French Revolution and the breakdown of true community between men.

The antidote to such unbelief and its revolutionary outworkings in society can only be found in a return of belief in God as the true sovereign of man. Reformation must begin in a return to God's Word as the ordering principle of human life in its entirety. The central principle of life must once more become the Word of God. Only the Bible can provide a sound basis for a reformational way of life since it is the key to knowledge and hence the only foundation upon which to build a true humanism and personalism.

In this book we shall first outline the biblical philosophy of man, society, and science. If they so wish, some readers may come back to this chapter after they have read the rest of the book, since it is more difficult to follow than the rest of the book. Then we shall consider what has gone wrong with work in modern society. This leads us into a consideration of the various attempts Communists, Western humanists, and Roman Catholics have made to put things right. We shall show that none of these proposed solutions can possibly prove successful in practice because each one is a distortion of the truth. Then we shall consider the scriptural basis for a scientific and sociological pluralism as providing the only principial basis for solving the problem of order in modern society. As the first step in reforming society we shall consider what reforms are necessary in the church as an institution and as an organism of society. This will be followed by an examination of the role of the state in the operation of the economy and the necessity for a reformation of the modern business enterprise, as well as of the whole present system of labor relations. We shall suggest that a cultural pluralism alone can provide a solution to the tensions between races in any one society and that the state's duty is to uphold justice between classes and races rather than seeking to impose one particular ideological point of view at bayonet point. The basic principles needed to be applied by Christian employers' associations and Christian labor associations will then be examined and a Christian answer to automation proposed.

Without such a return to the creation structures ordained by God for man's life in society and without such a universally binding structural order for society, practical life is bound to run aground. In his lectures, *The Challenge of Our Age*, Hendrik Hart says:

> If this structural order is denied, on what basis shall society function? If there is a conflict between two people which is brought to court, on what basis shall the judge decide, or what right do the parties have to take it to court, or what is right? Appeals to convention, to experience, to intelligence or to whatever is best, have no lasting basis, have no binding validity. On such a basis, a society is bound to disintegrate.[2]

It is the firm conviction of the writer that only God's Word revealed in the Bible can provide modern society with such a valid basis both for its theoretical and for its practical life. The Bible alone is the great key to knowledge and to our everyday experience of life and hence it alone can provide us with the foundation for a stable and progressive society.

INTRODUCTION NOTES

1. A. A. Milne, *Two People* (Methuen, London, 1947), p. 29.
2. Hendrik Hart, *The Challenge of Our Age* (The Association for the Advancement of Christian Studies, 141 Lyndhurst Avenue, Toronto, Ontario, Canada, 1968), p. 43.
   Also H. Hart, *The Democratic Way of Death* (C. J. L. Foundation, P.O. Box 151, Rexdale, Ontario, Canada, 1968). Cf. Alexis de Tocqueville, *Democracy in America* (edited by P. Bradley, N. Y., 1945), Vol. 2, pp. 318-319.

There is no more hopeful development in the world of humanist scholarship than the growing interest in the crucial role of associative pluralism and the diversification of social power in the structure of liberal democracy. The writer would refer all lovers of freedom in diversity to two most important works upon this subject: Robert A. Nisbet, *Community and Power* (Oxford University Press, New York, 1968), and Robert A. Dahl, *Pluralist Democracy in the United States* (Rand McNally & Company, Chicago, 1968). A long quotation from the latter work will be found at the end of chapter six of this present work. From one point of view this book is an attempt to provide the scriptural foundations for what Professor Dahl and Nisbet are seeking to vindicate in their books from a liberal humanist perspective. Only God's Word can provide us with a sure foundation for both freedom and order in society. In this great task the writer welcomes R. J. Rushdoony's latest work, *The Foundations of Social Order* (Presbyterian and Reformed Publishing Company, Nutley, N. J., 1968). Unfortunately this great study of the Christian foundations of Western civilization was published after I had completed the present book, so I have not referred to it in the text. Also W. Kornhauser, *The Politics of Mass Society* (Free Press, N. Y., 1960), and Frank Tannenbaum, *The Balance of Power in Modern Society* (New York, 1969). Above all, consult Robert A. Nisbet's *The Sociological Tradition* (Basic Books, Inc., New York, 1966), and his *Social Change and History* (Oxford University Press, New York, 1969), which provide the intellectual background for the themes studied in this book. The reader will also greatly benefit from R. A. Nisbet's other work, *Tradition and Revolt*, especially "The Politics of Pluralism; Lamennais," pp. 31-47.

Chapter One

THE BIBLICAL PHILOSOPHY
OF MAN, SOCIETY, SCIENCE, AND HISTORY

(a) *The Influence of Ground-Motives
in the Development of Society*

Shortly after the end of the Second World War, F. S. C. Northrop, Professor of Philosophy and Law in Yale University, published his book, *The Meeting of East and West*, in which he took as his central theme the conflict of ideals and ideologies in the modern world, especially those between East and West, and called for a new and imaginative approach to this intractable subject:

> A new kind of attitude and a new type of scholarship are required. We must open our intuitions and imaginations, even our souls, to the possibility of insights, beliefs and values other than our own; and we must bring scholarship to bear upon the world's problems as a whole, seeing local provincial factors in relation to one another and this whole. Such a scholarship will make mistakes, but these are less dangerous than those which result from ignoring the problem.[1]

Northrop is convinced that there is a problem and that the methods of scholarship are applicable to it. He tells us at the outset what he thinks this problem is and how he proposes to deal with it:

> Each major nation or cultural group in the war and peace of our contemporary world, both Western and Oriental, must be examined and analysed to bring out into the open the particular moral, religious, economic and political doctrine from which it proceeds traditionally. In each instance also an attempt must be made to determine the evidence which led its founders to regard its particular ideology as the correct one. When this is done, certain nations or cultures will probably be found to rest on different but compatible assumptions and ideals; others upon diverse

and contradictory ideals. In the case of diverse but compatible cultures the task will then be that of correctly relating the compatible elements of the two cultures by enlarging the ideals of each to include those of the other so that they reinforce, enrich and sustain rather than convert, combat and destroy each other. Between diverse and contradictory doctrines, as, for example, Anglo-American and Russian economic theory, the problem will be to provide foundations for a new and more comprehensive theory, which without contradictions will take care, in a more satisfactory way, of the diverse facts which generated the traditional incompatible doctrines. It is with this complex, difficult, but interesting undertaking, including the major task of relating correctly the East and the West, that this book is concerned.[2]

Here, plainly stated, were the two assumptions which governed Northrop's whole inquiry, and, once granted, enormously simplified his task. He assumed that each "nation and cultural group" does have a "particular moral, religious, economic, and political doctrine from which it proceeds traditionally"; and that there is a peculiarly close relation, almost an identity, between the moral, religious, economic, and political doctrines of any society, and between all of these and its art. If he could exhibit the precise nature of this relation, he believed that he would have discovered not only a method of interpreting cultures but also a criterion for deciding their value.

Clearly some such criterion is urgently needed, if there is to be any reconciliation of the conflicting ideals, value systems, and ideologies which today threaten to bring about the third world war which will destroy us all. But how can we find a criterion that is not purely subjective?

The difficulty as it presented itself to Northrop is that an ideal, or, to use his own term, a "normative social theory," cannot be verified simply by an appeal to the social facts. These will tell us only how society presently exists, not how it ought to be organized. He asks the question:

> But if correspondence with the social facts is not the criterion of the truth of an ideology, how then can its truth be determined? It would seem that we must have some factual criterion for determining the validity of one social ideal rather than another, and yet the character of any normative social theory is such that the

failure of social facts to conform to it is in considerable part ir-relevant to its validity.[3]

This is the "paradox" of all purely secular social thought, and it is familiar to all students of modern economics, sociology, and political science. Northrop's originality lies in offering a not less para-doxical solution. Normative social theories, he claims, are indeed verifiable, but the facts which verify them are not those of social science. They are those of natural science.

It follows that the relation between the moral, religious, economic, and political doctrines of a society is one of joint dependence on the science of that society, or rather on the philosophy of that society, which is itself based on its science. Thus Northrop writes:

> The normative social theory embodied in the Declaration of Independence and the Constitution of the United States was de-termined in considerable part by the philosophy of John Locke. The manner in which the culture of the Church of England goes back to Hooker and Aristotle is equally obvious. Thus an analysis of diverse cultures shows that whereas the formal and empirical methods of natural science applied to social facts is the correct procedure for determining trust-worthy factual social theory, it is the method of philosophy applied to the verified theory not of social science, but of human and natural science, to make articulate one's philosophical conception of man and the universe, which constitutes the correct method for determining trust-worthy nor-mative social theory.[4]

Northrop's method is most fully exemplified in his chapters on "The Free Culture of the United States" and "Roman Catholic Culture and Greek Science," the former based on the philosophy of Locke and the physics of Newton, the latter on the physics and metaphysics of Aristotle.

It is the conviction of the writer that a solution to the normative problem does not lie in an appeal to the "facts" of natural science, as Northrop supposes, but in recognizing the existence of a pre-theoretical realm of presuppositions, which every sociologist brings to his science, the realm of the assumptions and axioms which he takes for granted before he even begins to sociologize. Western scientists along with Western philosophers have assumed that theoretical and scientific thought in the very nature of the case is an autonomous "neutral" activity based upon a supposed universality of reason. Yet this so-called universality of reason itself contains a great problem. If all philosophical and scientific schools choose their points of departure in reason alone and not in deeper presuppositions, it ought to be possible to convince an opponent in a purely theoretical way that his arguments are true or false. But what actually happens is that philosophers and scientists reason at cross purposes; a scientist of the Thomist school, for example, can never succeed in convincing one of the Kantian or operational school. In reality the universality of reason is itself an uncritically accepted dogma, cloaking diverse supra-theoretical points of departure.

In Northrop's methodology, we see a good illustration of Hegelian logic at work, namely, in his attempt to resolve conflicting points of view in terms of a higher synthesis. He supposes that in such a dialectical line of thinking not a single antithesis can have an absolute character since truth itself is relative. Philosophy then has the task of bridging the antithetical gap between the various value-systems and ideologies of the modern world.

Such a "dialectical way of thought" which already appeared in Greek classical philosophy, does not wish to remain content with synthesizing logically determined opposites such as that between motion and rest. It attempts to reconcile these contrasting theses in a higher unity. This higher unity must then be the synthesis, the union, between thesis and antithesis. Thus Plato, for example, found the higher synthesis of motion and rest in the idea of being; because it can be said alike of both that they really are.

Now it is certainly true that motion and rest often appear together in combination in concrete temporal reality. The antithesis taken in this merely theoretical-dialectical sense is, therefore, nothing but a logical pulling apart of that which in reality belongs together. If you wish to obtain an understanding of motion, it is necessary to distinguish it logically from rest.

However, this logical understanding must not lead to a separation. Such an antithesis must indeed acknowledge a higher synthesis.

The dialectical method of thought, therefore, proceeds on the assumption that the contrasting theses which it wishes to synthesize into a higher unity do not have an absolute, but merely a relative character. The ideas which have been set over against each other then appear, upon more profound reflection, to have a mutual relation in which the one cannot exist without the other. Without anything which is thought to be in rest, no motion could ever be determined and vice versa.

From this it should be clear that such a dialectical way of thought, which by means of logical contrasting theses searches for a higher synthesis, is a valid logical method of thought only as long as it concerns itself with relative contrasting theses. As such it has a mere theoretical character and can, provided it is used rightly, make plain to us that nothing in temporal life is absolute. In so far as Northrop is only concerned with such relative matters we can agree with his method.

However it must be an entirely different case with the antithesis which Christianity has posited in the world. This antithesis can never be taken up into any higher synthesis without at once losing its absolute character. Biblical religion alone claims to reveal to man his origin in the absolute God, Creator of Heaven and earth. As such the Bible can never compromise its claims by admitting another god alongside its God. The biblical antithesis cannot accept a theoretical synthesis between the Christian starting point and the standpoints set over against this one, for it claims an absolute character. As Herman Dooyeweerd says:

> Is it not true that if it is to come to a real synthesis between standpoints which are antithetically set over against each other, a higher starting-point is necessary—one that is elevated above these two opposing camps and which includes both of them? But where would one have to look for this higher starting-point with regard to two opposing religious standpoints, which precisely on account of their religious character raise themselves above the sphere of that which is relative? In philosophy? But philosophy as such is always of a theoretical character and continues to be bound to the relative character of all human thought. In so far as philosophy itself is in need of an absolute starting-point it can derive this only from religion, which even to theoretical thought can provide the only sure ground.[5]

To Northrop's claim to find the starting point in scientific thought itself Dooyeweerd rightly replies:

> Even they who think they have found their absolute starting-point in theoretical thought itself have come to this opinion by an essentially religious drive, which simply for lack of true self-knowledge remains concealed from them.
> For that which is absolute has right of existence only in religion. A true religious starting-point must claim absolutenes, if it is not to dissolve itself in relativism. As such it can never be a mere theory, which by definition always remains bound to that which is relative. Behind all theory and science it drills for the sure absolute ground of all temporal and, therefore, of relative existence. The antithesis which it posits must also be absolute.[6]

The disunity of the modern world thus arises out of basic philosophical presuppositions or ground-motives which have determined the moral, religious, economic, and political doctrines of various modern nations and cultures. Of the power of these ground-motives to influence the development of culture and society Dooyeweerd writes:

> In every religion one can point out such a ground-motive which is operative in human society as a spiritual force. It is the absolutely central force, because out of the religious life-center, it governs all temporal expressions of life and directs it towards the true or pretended origin of existence.
> It determines in the most profound sense the entire outlook on life; it impresses its indelible mark on culture, science, and the social structure of a period. . . . The religious ground-motive of a culture can never be approached from the outlook and personal faith of the individual. It really is a community motive that governs the individual even when he is not conscious of it or even when he does not account for it. But do not be mistaken, it is as such not a possible object of a scientific analysis and elucidation. For the latter never touches the spiritual root of community life, but only its temporal manifestations, not the religious life center, but only its temporally distinguished expressions in feeling, in the way of thought, in artistic expressions, in moral standards, in legal forms, and in faith conception.
> Even science in its point of departure is itself governed by a religious ground-motive. Therefore, it can never stand in a neutral position over against this motive.

In the religious ground-motive the godly or the ungodly Spirit in whose service man has placed himself and is performing his assigned part is directly operative. It is this spirit that establishes community, a spirit which is not governed by man, but by which he is governed. For it is precisely religion that reveals to us our profound dependence upon a higher power, in which we look for the sure ground and origin of our existence and which we can never encounter as masters, but merely as servants. The religious ground-motives acquire their central influence on the historical development of mankind by means of the cultural powers which are successfully able to gain the directing influence in the historical process. The most important spiritual powers that have governed the development of Western culture are the spirit of Graeco-Roman civilization, of Christianity, and of modern humanism.[7]

The religious ground-motive which dominated classical culture and science, Dooyeweerd has termed the "form-matter" motive. The motive underlying modern humanism he calls the "nature-freedom" motive. A third motive is that of "nature" and "grace," introduced by medieval Roman Catholic scholasticism as an attempted synthesis between the biblical motive of "sin" and "grace" and the Greek motives of "form-matter," but which in modern times has also been directed to a synthesis between the Christian and humanistic "nature-freedom" motive.

Under the influence of the Greek form-matter motive the Roman Catholic Church came to think of man as an individual substance of a rational nature. Likewise it took over from Aristotle the Greek concept of nature, so that Aquinas could say that "Grace does not abolish Nature but perfects it." In the Roman Catholic view, man, as a natural being, is composed of a "rational soul" and a "material body." And the "rational soul," defined as the capacity to think logically, is the invisible "essential form" of the body.

Roman Catholics believe that God, at man's creation, added to this a "super-natural gift of grace," by which he would be able to remain in right communion with God. But this "super-natural gift of grace" was lost at the Fall, so that fallen man had to depend entirely on "human nature," with all the weaknesses attached to it. This "nature," which is guided by the natural light of reason, has not been corrupted by sin, and therefore does not have to be restored by Christ. It has only been "weakened" by the Fall. It continues to follow the "law of nature" with which it has been endowed at the creation, and possesses an "autonomy," a relative self-sufficiency, over against the sphere of grace of the Christian religion. "Nature," is only brought to a higher state of perfection by "grace," a grace which flows to it from Christ by means of the priestly hierarchy of the Roman Catholic Church.

It is apparent that this "nature-grace" ground-motive is completely at variance with that of creation, Fall, and redemption. It introduces a split into the creation motive by its distinction between natural and supernatural, and it restricts the effect of the Fall and redemption to the "supernatural sphere." With that the scriptural ground motive has been deprived in the Church of Rome of its integral and radical character. It can no longer lay hold of a man with its full power and absoluteness. It has been broken by the opposition of the Greek conception of nature in its supposed "adaptation" to the biblical account of the creation.

In the Roman Catholic doctrine of the relationship between the soul and the body, it is apparent that no room is left for an understanding of the radical significance of the Fall and of man's redemption by Jesus Christ. For, if the soul of man is not the spiritual root-unity of man's entire temporal existence, but only the rational form of a "material body," what possibility is left of a corruption of man in the roots of his being? God's Word plainly teaches that sin does not originate in our intellectual faculty, but in the human heart, in the religious root of our existence.

Likewise the Roman Catholic view of human society is entirely dominated by the "nature-grace" ground-motive. Its view of society has been borrowed from Aristotle. Man's nature, according to Aristotle, is thought of as a composition of form and matter. In this case "form" is the rational soul, and "matter" is the material body, which comes into being only through the soul. Every creature that is composed of form and matter has become or has come to be. The form principle gives to the process of becoming the direction for the attainment of its proper *telos* or end. Every creature, including man, strives by nature after the attainment of its perfection, in that its "essential form" realizes itself in the "matter" of its body. Man can only achieve his true end in the complete development of his rational nature, which distinguishes him from plants and animals. The "rational law of nature" has been created as part of this "rational nature" and commands him to do good and refrain from evil. Thus man by nature strives after good according to Roman Catholic teaching. Such teaching is diametrically opposed to the biblical revelation of the radical corruption of the human heart (Jer. 17:9; Matt. 15:19; Rom. 3:9-17).

According to Roman Catholic social theory, man, however, cannot attain his natural perfection as an isolated individual. He comes into the world naked and helpless, and he must therefore depend upon society to help acquire for himself the necessities of life. Therefore there has been created in man, in accordance with his rational nature, the social instinct which develops itself step by step in the formation of smaller and larger communities which are interrelated as means to the end, as part of the greater whole.

The lowest in this social ordering of human life is the family, and the highest is the state, in which man's social instinct comes to perfection, since all the subordinate communities only fulfill themselves in the state. The state, therefore, in distinction from the other natural forms of society, is the perfect community. It possesses autonomy or self-sufficiency, since it is the highest and most comprehensive community in the "sphere of nature."

Here also the biblical view of society is in radical opposition to the Roman Catholic view. According to Genesis, God has created everything after its own kind or type. In such a scriptural conception, there is no room for the idea that the state is the perfect community in the natural sphere, which embraces both the individual and the other communities as its parts. For whether or not something is really a part of the whole is determined exclusively by the intrinsic nature of the whole. Thus the city and the county are parts of the state for they have the same intrinsic nature and are ruled by the same intrinsic law of life. For the same reason our hands, feet, and head are really parts of the body, since they are ruled by the intrinsic law of life.

Yet the relationship of the state to the other spheres of life, considered from the scriptural principle of sphere sovereignty, is quite different, for the family, the business, and the golf club differ radically from the state in their inherent structure and nature. Thus the marriage relationship, the family, the school, the church, and the university by their very nature may never be considered parts of the state. For they are principally of a different nature or structural type from that of the state. They each possess sphere sovereignty, the limits of which are not determined by the common good of the state, but by their own inherent nature and law of life.

This does not mean that these social spheres are not bound to the state. But this binding only applies to that which by its very nature belongs to the authority of the state, and not to these remaining spheres. Thus the state may register a marriage, but it may not tell a young lady that she must marry a man chosen by the government. This great principle of sphere sovereignty, which is based upon the scriptural account of creation, requires for its practical application a closer investigation of the intrinsic structure of the various spheres of life. In this book we shall examine the structure of society in the light of the biblical principle of sphere sovereignty.

Unfortunately, in the Roman Catholic view of society it is the Greek nature motive and not the Word of God which controls its thinking about both church and state. According to the Greek conception, the state has its foundation in the rational nature of man. It is necessary to cause the rational form in this human nature to come to its perfect final development or *telos* and to hold in check the principle of matter, that reveals itself in the sensual desires. The state for Roman Catholics is seen as the absolute and total community in the domain of nature, of which all the other spheres are only subservient parts. The relationship between the state and the other natural spheres of life is conceived of as that of the whole to its parts.

The Roman Catholic ground-motive of "nature" and "grace" requires a superstructure of a supernatural character over the natural substructure of human society. Man not only has a natural purpose of life, but a final purpose, by which his reasonable nature can be elevated to the sphere of grace. On this supernatural level, where the eternal salvation of the soul is at stake, the Roman Church calls a halt to the power of the state. The supernatural graces flow into believers only by means of the Roman Catholic institute of the Church. The Church pours this grace into the believer through its sacramental means of grace.

Just as Roman Catholics think of the state as the perfect community in the natural realm, so they think of their Church as the perfect community in the sphere of grace. According to this conception, the institution of the Roman Catholic Church comprises all of Christianity and all of the Christian life. Rome looks for the whole, the total unity of the Christian society in the temporal institute of the Church.

Here also Rome is in radical opposition to the scriptural ground-motive of creation, fall, and redemption. God's Word makes it plain that the real unity of all truly Christian life can be found only in the supratemporal root-communion of the reborn humanity in Jesus Christ. This is the Kingdom of God, which has its basis not in the temporal church institution at all, but in the hearts of all the faithful in Christ. No doubt the church militant here on earth is a temporal revelation of the Body of Christ in its temporal institutional organization as a community of believers. But it does not coincide completely with the Body of Christ. For this reason we should not separate the so-called "visible church" from the "invisible church," since the latter is the religious root of the former. But this temporal manifestation of Christ's Body is not identical with the so-called "invisible church" as the spiritual realm of Jesus Christ, which supersedes time. Rome can make this identification because she believes that the Church in her mystical sense is Christ. But such an idea is contrary to the Scriptures.

As the religious ground-motive governing the development of modern Western culture, humanism arose during the Renaissance. It originated in the religious absolutization of the autonomous human personality combined with a Faustian passion to dominate nature by means of the new science. Humanism asserts the sovereignty and creative freedom of man in this universe. After the Protestant

Reformation had destroyed the unity of medieval Christendom, men concerned for the stability of European civilization sought for a new basis for it other than a common church. Their resort was to reason.

Reason, in this humanistic view, is not identical with the mind or with man's understanding. Reason is not only understanding; it is self-directed understanding. It is understanding which is given direction by a fund of *a priori*, of innate ideas, the *lumen naturale* (natural light) of Descartes. Where for Christians God's Holy Scripture is the light which directs their walk through life, for the rational humanist the Law of God becomes the law within. It is now proclaimed that every man has the truth and the light within his deepest self, and only a universal system of education and universal political suffrage is required to bring this truth out in our lives. The characteristics of these innate truths are universality and necessity, which means that the truth and light which each man has within himself is universally the same. The roots of our seeing the the light and understanding the the truth are everywhere the same.

This religious faith in human reason found expression in a common natural law, a common natural morality, and a common rational core of religious ideas. Thus Herbert of Cherbury spoke in his *De Veritate* of the "common notions" underlying all religions, and Hugo Grotius worked out a new basis for international relations in human reason rather than in God's Will. While acknowledging that man has been gifted with reason by God, Grotius draws the conclusion from this that it will automatically yield good results if man works with his reason, because God created reason good and capable of correct conclusions. And with this the autonomy of reason has been accepted in principle; the law for Grotius becomes a law-of-reason, severed from its divine origin and standard. He writes in *De Iure Belli et Pacis*:

> What we have been saying would have a degree of validity even if we should concede that which cannot be conceded without the utmost wickedness, that there is no God, or that the affairs of men are of no concern to him.[8]

To Grotius this is no final breach with the divine origin of law.

For, God himself having created reason, the law-of-reason conforms to the law as God willed it. This, however, does not render the step he took less decisive; the center of gravity has been placed in human reasoning rather than in God's Word which henceforth becomes the ultimate standard in Western legal and political and economic thought and behavior. In modern humanism man's divine vocation to subject nature and his freedom in Christ thus became secularized. This new nature-freedom ground-motive lies at the basis of the dialectical polarity between individualism and collectivism in modern social and political thought.

Refusing to be directed by the Word of God in their political and social life, Western men for the last three hundred years have instead acted upon the religious presupposition that their rational faculties can produce a common conception of law and social order which possesses a universal validity. This natural law or law of human rational nature is a rational order of human society "in the sense that all men," as Walter Lippman writes in *The Public Philosophy*, "when they are sincerely and lucidly rational, will regard as self evident." [9] Of this new governing concept of Western society, Evan Runner says:

> Humanism was nothing less than an alternative answer (to Christianity) to the fundamental questions of man's life. Instead of seeing man as a religious being (in his wholeness), whose meaning can only be sensed in his covenantal relation to God and His Law, humanism saw man as a rational-moral being, as one who has *within himself*, in his very structure, quite apart from how he stands bofere God, a right reason or proper guide to life, a true knowledge of the Law . Where Christianity sees the possibility of a *two-fold response* (in religious terms obedience or disobedience) to the word-revelation of God, humanism sees the *unity* of all men in their being directed by Reason, which for it, is always and everywhere the same, *the common structure of all men*. . . .
> Humanism always puts fundamental emphasis on "the common." It may be, in the rationalist phase of humanism, the commonness of Reason, or it may be the common *existentialia*, or our common commitment to scientific method in the sense of operationalism. But there is always this peculiar and troublesome thing about humanism: it fails to see the religious commitment

that is involved in its starting-point, and thus identifies its own private and subjective faith with the common, i.e., objective, and public or universal *a priori* structure of Reason. Other men's faiths are subjective, partisan, and private; its own is objective, universal and public. It was a sad day when Christians began to buy that bill of goods and accommodate themselves to the "spirit" of the modern age. For thus there developed the view that a man's Christianity was to be limited to the private sphere of subjective opinion whereas the public order of Europe was to be constructed out of the principles of the universally binding natural law, or the natural light of Reason.[10]

Part of the responsibility for this development must be ascribed to the divisions within Western society caused by the conflict between the Church of Rome and the Churches of the Reformation. No longer able to find an order of universal agreement based on a common confession in God's Holy Scriptures as the ordering principle of Western life, many leading thinkers instead tried to build a stable European society upon such principles as could be acknowledged readily by every nation, creed, and sect. The ancient Stoic theory of universal and necessary truths of reason, a secularized form of natural law theory, offered itself as the only hope of salvation. The foundation of European culture was now asserted to rest in the *a priori* ideas of every man in his capacity as a rational rather than religious being instead of in God's Word.[11]

Just as the Greek form-matter motive has profoundly affected the development of Roman Catholic life and thought about man and society, so the modern humanist nature-freedom motive has determined the direction taken by modern Protestantism. Since the Reformation a tendency has developed in Protestant theology to deny any point of contact between man's "natural" life and God's grace in Jesus Christ.

In the twentieth century this contrast reached its climax in the dialectical theology of Karl Barth. In his famous debate with Emil Brunner called "Nature and Grace" and published in English as *Natural Theology*, Barth explicitly rejected any point of contact between the Christian faith and natural life. "Nature" and "grace" are separated by a fatal line. He had pierced the Roman Catholic synthesis to its central core.

While Rome has accepted the Greek view of nature by accommodating it to the creation motive of the Scriptures, Karl Barth simply turns his back upon the creation motive altogether. For him, it is completely vindicated by the motives of the fall and redemption in Jesus Christ. Barth will have nothing to do with the creation-ordinances which might act as directives for our "natural life." The fall, according to Barth, has so completely corrupted human "nature" that the knowledge of the creation-ordinances has been utterly lost.

Unlike Barth, Brunner accepts the creation ordinances as valid expressions of "common grace," but he depreciates them by viewing them in dialectical conflict with the divine law of love as the "*Gebot der Stunde*" (the law of the present moment). The creation-ordinances, precisely because of their universal character, are cold and formal. They are the realm of the law, which Brunner contrasts with the Christian's freedom in Christ, who is set free from the law. The "law" as the frigid framework, within which God has shut up sinful human nature, must be overcome by the evangelical law of love, which knows no universal norm but only a command for the immediate situation. The creation-ordinances, though given by God, do not as law express the actual will of God, who only reveals Himself in Christlike love. For Brunner the Body of Christ has nothing institutional about it.

For this reason Brunner teaches that the state is a worldly order. It is sinful in its very essence since it is supposed to remain necessarily caught in a dialectical tension with the Christian commandment of love and the idea of true communion. For Brunner, a Christian state is thus a contradiction in terms.

This dialectical theology clearly arises from Brunner's irrationalistic humanist standpoint. Unable to develop a truly scripturally motivated doctrine of society, Brunner uncritically relapses into a synthesis with the modern "nature" and "freedom" motive by accepting in principle the dialectical basic problem of this modern religious ground-motive. Falsely, he supposes he can reduce this basic tension between science and free personality to the "basic antithesis" in the biblical view of creation and the fall. At the back of this synthesis emerges the false contrast between nature and grace, which in Brunner's teaching assumes the form of a dialectical tension between the "commandment of love of the moment" and the law or creation ordinances as such. A wedge is thus driven into the ground-motive of the Holy Scriptures, between creation and redemption, between God's will as Creator and as Redeemer.

(b) *The Problem of the Individual and the Community*

As soon as the individual breaks out of the "closed" condition of primitive undifferentiated tribal society, the problem always arises: how is the individual to be related to the society out of which he has broken free?

Thinkers who make man's reason rather than God's Word the ordering principle of their theorizing have answered this question by falling into the error of individualism or universalism or collectivism. In the history of social thought, there has been a continuous conflict between those views which would make the individual prior to the group of which he is a part and those views which would make the group prior to the individual. In classical Graeco-Roman times, the former view was represented by the school of metaphysical realism or essentialism. The latter view was represented by the nominalistic schools of the Middle Ages. In modern times individualism has tended to be largely psychological. Social groups have been thought to consist of congeries of individuals in their psychical interactions. For this school the actions and decisions of individuals determine social structure and process. Universalistic or collectivistic theories of society, on the other hand, have been associated largely with the irrationalistic, historically oriented idealism which developed out of the teaching of the German philosopher, Immanuel Kant. This historicist type of universalism seeks for some self-sufficient group such as the nation or the state or party in which the individual can discover meaning and purpose to his life. The individual is thought to be embraced in an all-inclusive social group in terms of which he receives his meaning.

1. *Universalism*

In an attempt to overcome the scepticism of the Greek Sophists, which denied the reality of the Greek City-State, Aristotle developed his doctrine of man as a "political animal." The individual is not essentially isolated nor in conflict with the group, as the Sophists, poets, and dramatists had taught; he is essentially related to the city-state, since it is only in such a group that he can realize his proper and true nature or end as a human being. By himself the individual is incomplete. By nature each person strives towards his own self-realization, and since he cannot attain completion in isolation, he is led naturally to attach himself to a group. He is, by reason of his birth, born into a family. His need for self-fulfilment leads him on to membership in his tribe or clan. But these lower societal relationships are not autonomous; only the state can, as the perfectly autonomous community, provide the individual with all that serves the perfection of his rational and moral nature.

Thus the relation between the state and all other societal relationships is constructed by Aristotle according to the scheme of the whole and its parts, of the means to the end, from the "lower" to the "higher." The "lower" relationships, as different kinds of parts of the state, have no goal in themselves, but all exist to serve the interests of the state. Man is by nature a state oriented being, for already in the forming of marriage, family, kinship groups the natural compulsion to form the state is germinating. The state is implicit in the rational-moral nature of man, as the mature form of a plant is in its seed, or the full-grown body of an animal in its embryo.

During the high Middle Ages, Thomas Aquinas carried on the realist tradition, synthesizing elements of the Christian life-and-world-view with that of Aristotle's. Aquinas taught that man only realizes his true "natural" human nature in the state. He viewed the state as the ultimate bond of "natural" human society of which all other associations and communities were only the parts. The state was seen in pagan Greek manner as the totality of all temporal societal relationships in the natural "rational-moral" area of human life. Like Aristotle he believed that all such social relationships are arranged in an hierarchical order with the state being the highest, with the important qualification that it was the highest only within the realm of the "natural." Aquinas looked upon the state as in its turn serving the interests of the church. Man's ultimate end or purpose in life is discovered only in the service of the church. The church was therefore considered to be the total bond of all Christendom, the rule of the realm of grace in its temporal manifestation.

Like Aristotle, Thomas regarded the lower associations of society as related to each other as matter is to form. A lower group is subordinate to a higher group as a means to an end. The individual enjoys only a relative autonomy since he is subject to the state. The state, in its turn, is subject to the church in all matters involving the eternal well-being of the soul. The sufficiency or insufficiency of each group is predetermined in the metaphysical nature of reality. The more inclusive communities have the primacy over the less inclusive communities.

Modern collectivism has two main branches, going back to common roots in European intellectual history; they can be broadly distinguished as those of French rationalism and of German Idealism. In the former tradition we may place Rousseau and Comte; in the latter, Hegel and, in one aspect of his thinking, Karl Marx.

It might be questionable to classify Rousseau as a rationalist, since in many ways he was the fountainhead of Romanticism. However, Rousseau shared in the rationalist conception of a natural order. As Ernst Cassirer has shown in *The Myth of the State* the basic ideas of his political philosophy are largely to be found in the writings of Locke, Grotius, and Pufendorf. Though on the whole he shared Locke's conception of the state of nature as one in which each individual had the right to pursue his interests in his own way, Rousseau treated the problem of unifying such discrete individuals to form a political collectivity as a much more positive problem than did the economically oriented individualists in the utilitarian tradition. Rousseau broke through the Hobbes-Locke dilemma, postulating a factor very different from those they had considered, the famous *general will*. Its difference is made clear by Rousseau's insistence on the distinction between *volonte generale* and *volonte des tous* (will of everybody). The *general will* is generated by a Hobbesian social contract to surrender control of natural rights to an absolute sovereign. The difference is related to the fact that Rousseau's political theory was formulated in the interest of democracy—not as in Hobbes's case of monarchy.

Rousseau found insuperable difficulties in defining an acceptable relationship between his postulated general will and any concrete political institutions which could give expression to it without risking uncontrolled dictatorship by a self-appointed minority or a tyranny of the majority. The difficulties arose from the fact that Rousseau did not consider a basis in societal values and institutionalized norms somehow independent of and underlying the state; he tried to elevate political theory into a general theory of society.

Of Rousseau's totalitarian social philosophy Robert A. Nisbet writes in *Community and Power*:

> What gives uniqueness to Rousseau's doctrine is not so much its severity as its subtle but explicit identification with freedom. What has connoted bondage to the minds of most men is exalted as freedom by Rousseau. To regard the power structure of the State as a device by which the individual is only being compelled to be free is a process of reasoning that sets Rousseau apart from the tradition of liberalism. . . . What Rousseau calls freedom is at bottom no more than the freedom to do what the State in its omniscience determines. Freedom for Rousseau is the synchronization of all social existence to the will of the State, the replacement of cultural diversity by a mechanical equalitarianism. Other writers have idealized such an order in the interests perhaps of justice or of stability, but Rousseau is the first to invest it with the value of freedom. Therein lies the real distinctiveness of his theory of sovereignty.
>
> It is in the bearing of Rousseau's General Will upon traditional society, however, that the full sweep of its totalitarian significance becomes manifest . . . the object of Rousseau's dislike is society, and the special merit of the State lies in its power to emancipate the individual from traditional society. The relationship among individuals that forms the General Will and is the true State is obviously an exceedingly delicate one. It must be unitary and indivisible for its nature fully to unfold. In short, it must be protected from the operations of extraneous channels of constraint. . . . To achieve a pure sovereignty, one which is untrammeled by social influences, one which will encompass the whole

of man's personality, it is necessary that the traditional social loyalties be abrogated. A unified, General Will is incompatible with the existence of minor associations; hence they must be banished. . . .

The proscription of all forms of association except what is identical with the whole being of the State—this is Rousseau's drastic proposal. . . . There is to be no bond of loyalty, no social affiliation, no interdependence save what is symbolized by the General Will. Society is to be an aggregate of atoms held rigidly together by the sovereign will of the State alone.

Nisbet then considers the practical implications of this new apostate humanist social philosophy. For a start it involves the total rejection of Christianity and its replacement by a purely civil religion, for which the sovereign should fix the articles of faith, whose main purpose is the cementing of the social contract.

Respect for the sovereign, allegiance to the State alone, and subordination of all interests to the law of the realm—these are the primary attributes of the civil religion proposed by Rousseau. The symbol of *patrie* is uppermost; religion and patriotism will be but two aspects of the same thing.

The family itself must be radically adjusted to meet the demands of the General Will since morality is essentially a civic condition. "Create citizens, and you have everything you need." For this purpose the state must take over the function of education from parents. The unitary state in fact calls for a remodelling of human nature so that there shall be no irritants to the body politic. Nisbet continues:

It is necessary to inculcate in the minds of the people from infancy the surpassing claim of the State to their loyalty. "If, for example," Rousseau writes, "the people were early accustomed to conceive their individuality only in its connection with the body of the state, and to be aware of their own existence merely as parts of that of the state, they might in time come to identify themselves in some degree with the greater whole." The family should not be granted the all-important duty of education, for too great a responsibility hangs in the balance. The traditional educative function should be transferred from the family to the State, so that, as Rousseau states it, the "prejudices of the father may not interfere with the development of citizens. However, the disintegration of this age-old basis of the family should in no wise create alarm." "Should the public authority, in assuming the place of father and charging itself with this important function, acquire his rights in the discharge of his duties, he should have little cause to protest; for he would only be altering his title, and would have in common, under the name *citizen*, the same authority over his children, that he was exercising separately under the name of *father*, and would be no less obeyed when speaking in the name of the law than when he spoke in the name of nature." In this almost incredible statement is to be observed what is surely the ultimate in the totalitarian absorption of society. Family relationship is transmuted subtly into political relationship; the molecule of the family is broken into the atoms of its individuals, who are coalesced afresh into the single unity of the state. "If the children are reared in common in the bosom of equality, if they are imbued with the laws of the state and the precepts of the General Will, they are taught to respect these above all other things, if they are surrounded by examples and objects which perpetually remind them of the tender mother who nourished them, of the love she bears them, of the inestimable benefits they receive from her, and of the return they owe her, we cannot doubt that they will learn to cherish one another mutually as brothers."

It would be difficult to find anywhere in the history of politics a more powerful and potentially revolutionary doctrine than Rousseau's theory of the General Will. Power is freedom and freedom is power. True freedom consists in the willing subordination of the individual to the whole of the State. If this is not forthcoming, compulsion is necessary; but this merely means that the individual "will be forced to be free" There is no necessity, once the right State is created, for carving out autonomous spheres of right and liberty for individuals and associations. Because the individual is himself a member of the larger association, despotism is impossible. By accepting the power of the State one is but participating in the General Will.

Not without reason has the theory of the General Will been called a theory of permanent revolution. It was Rousseau's subtle achievement to clothe the being of the absolute State in the garments of the terminology of freedom.[12]

In the French tradition of social thought, Rousseau's new note blended with one derived from the conservative thought of writers like De Bonald and De Maistre, who challenged the tradition of the

French Revolution and defended the record of the Old Regime. For these conservatives the greatest crimes of the Revolution were those committed not only against individuals but also against the institutions, groups, and associations of the old society. They saw in the Terror no merely fortuitous consequence of war and tyrannic ambition but the inevitable culmination of ideas contained in the rationalistic individualism of the Enlightenment. In this period, the most significant thinker was Auguste Comte. In Comte's theory the concept corresponding to Rousseau's General Will is that of *consensus* as the essential basis of the cohesion or integration of a society.

According to Comte, the French Revolution was the expression of a spirit which he called metaphysical or critical, and as such it was incapable of rebuilding a social order. The aim which Comte therefore proposed was to establish a social consensus based upon a body of universal beliefs. No society can survive, Comte taught, unless its members have a common scale of values and system of beliefs. These universal, religious beliefs have been destroyed by the metaphysical, critical, and scientific spirit. It is impossible to re-create them in their old form, but it is essential to re-create a system of beliefs which will will serve as the basis of a new order. In other words, the French Revolution having been the agent of destruction, we are now in an essentially economic society lacking any religious basis. Having recognized the rise of industry and the French Revolution, we have now to discover the source of a new order which will regulate and guide the functioning of industrial society.[13]

In making science the essential basis of consensus in his final positive stage, Comte approached the position of Godwin in England and other utopian rationalists. While no Christian can accept Comte's account of the basis of integration and of its workings in society, we can applaud him for having posed a problem which had proved essentially insoluble within the utilitarian tradition. He provided, more directly than Rousseau, a fruitful antithesis to laissez faire individualism.

2. *Individualism*

The ancient world was not altogether given over to universalism. Epicureanism, for instance, was individualistic as well as hedonistic. The later Middle Ages witnessed the breakdown of the great realist and essentialist philosophies and the birth of nominalism. Thus for William of Ockham the concepts of genus and species or the names given to things do not have a real existence apart from the human understanding. All that is known is the individual and the singular, and the process of knowledge is purely intuitional. "This I say," remarks Ockham, "that no universal is existent in any way whatsoever outside the mind of the knower." [14] Such universals are only general concepts which stand for a collection of individuals. Accordingly, nominalism objects to the reification of such abstract concepts as culture, society, the state, etc., as mere abstractions of the concrete individuals whose action and interactions together constitute society and the state. Nominalism supported by the invention of printing and the rise of empirical scientific study and of capitalistic, in place of feudal, methods of production prepared the way for modern individualism.

Perhaps no man has better expressed the philosophy of individualism than Thomas Hobbes. The basis of his social thinking lies in his famous concept of the state of nature as the war of all against all. In this state of nature, before the rise of conventional laws which can act as a restraint, individuals are driven by their own passions, appetites, and inclinations. Hobbes considered the "passions" of the individual to be the ultimate determinants of his action, and he specifically denied that there could be any "common measure" between the passions of different individuals. Perhaps more clearly than any subsequent writer, Hobbes stated the utilitarian postulate of the independence of any one individual's ends from those of any other. He was principally concerned with the implications of this independence of one individual's passions from those of another. By adding the postulate of "equality of hope," and through his fundamental insight that other individuals are important as obstacles or aids to one individual in his gaining the ends dictated by his passions, Hobbes came to his famous proposition: each individual's unregulated attempts to gain his ends would, through all individuals' mutual attempts to "subdue or destroy one another," result in a situation where every man is the enemy of every other man, endeavoring to destroy him by force or fraud or both. This condition of society is nothing but a state of war in which the life of man is "solitary, poor, nasty, brutish and short." [15]

The fear of such a state of affairs calls into action, as a servant of the most fundamental of all passions, that of self-preservation, at least a modicum of reason, which Hobbes thinks of only as a servant of the passions. Man's reason soon teaches him that it is not to his own advantage to remain in the state of nature, so his reason finds a solution to his predicament in the social contract. Reason dictates that he give up some of his rights in order that he might retain something for himself. To obtain a measure of security and peace in which to express some of his passions, the individual must be prepared to surrender some of his rights by joining in a social contract with all other men to live in a civil society or Great Commonwealth. By the terms of this social contract men agree to give up their natural liberty to a sovereign power and authority which in turn guarantees them security, that is, immunity from aggression by the force or fraud of others. It is only through the authority of this sovereign, the great Leviathan, that the war of all against all is held in check and order and security maintained. To this sovereign power and authority Hobbes attributes absolute sovereignty. Law, defined as command, can only proceed from the sovereign. If there are any laws of nature, they are valid only as civil law; "for it is the sovereign power that obliges men to obey them." [16]

From a sociological point of view, Hobbes's type of social contract was most unsatisfactory. Yet he posed the problem of order, that is, of the conditions making a stable society possible, which has never been equalled except by Paul in the first chapter of Romans in his description of godless and apostate men (Rom. 1:18-32). In his work, *The Structure of Social Action*, Talcott Parsons writes:

> Hobbes saw the problem with a clarity which has never been surpassed, and his statement of it remains valid today. It is so fundamental that a genuine solution of it has never been attained

on a strictly utilitarian basis, but has entailed either recourse to a positivistic expedient, or the breakdown of the whole positivistic framework.[17]

In the *Leviathan* Hobbes has broken away completely from the transcendentally sanctioned basis of society, as revealed in God's Word. Instead of "seeing" the state as instituted by God on account of human sin, he depicts it as a non-moral Leviathan, fulfilling the law of nature, which is the preservation of the human race. For Hobbes the biblical explanation for the origin and nature of the state is mere superstition.

Hobbes's social theory must be seen as an application of his faith in reasoning as man's only savior. He had been trained in the new science of Galileo, with whom he had come in close contact on his journeys. In the *Leviathan* he tried to geometrize political and social thought. Thus he tried to reduce all human passions and instincts to phenomena of motion, moving in accordance with the laws of motion. They could then be set in mathematical relations to explain more complicated phenomena.

Hobbes saw in this geometrical method the key by which all reality, including man, could be explained. For this reason he refused to recognize any distinction between man's body and soul. Everything, including man's thought life, must be reduced to bodily movement. So gripped had Hobbes become by the modern science ideal that he saw in such scientific method the only hope for man's salvation. The nature motive dominated his thought completely. And yet he, along with Descartes, saw the new science as the only way leading to man's freedom and salvation.

Of Hobbes's sociological significance Robert A. Nisbet writes in *Community and Power*:

> In the social thought of the seventeenth century all relationships were suspect. Man was the solid fact; all else was ephemeral. As the physical scientists of the day dealt with physical atoms in space and relegated to secondary or subjective status all of those qualities and essences medieval philosophers had accepted as fundamental, so the social philosophers sought to build theoretical systems upon human atoms alone. Relationships of tradition and inherited morality were either expelled from theory or were ra-

tionalized into relationships proceeding ineluctably from man's pre-social nature.

Given originally a pre-political state of nature, a social vacuum as it were, in which the individual was isolated and free, the problem chosen by almost every natural-law theorist was: how did man emerge from this socially empty state of nature and by what means? The answer invariably lay in appeal to some form of contract. Contract, conceived as free agreement among self-interested individuals, became the seventeenth-century rationalist's prime response to problems of social cohesion that had commonly been answered in terms of Christian morality or historically derived status by medieval philosophers.

Ernest Barker has perceptively suggested that the seventeenth-century philosophy of natural law was in certain significant respects a kind of subtle rationalization of the principles of Roman law. It adhered to the same conception of the primacy of the individual and individual will in legal matters. It made relationships of contract fundamental in the constitution of society. And, as in the Roman codes, natural-law philosophy in the seventeenth century gave the political state the position of absolute supremacy over all other forms of human association. Roman lawyers ascribed an essentially derivative role to social groups in the State, and natural-law philosophers similarly ascribed a derivative role to all forms of association lying intermediate to the individual and the sovereign. All the symmetry of design and centralization of function and authority to be seen in Roman law are clearly apparent in seventeenth-century natural law.

All this is fundamental in Hobbes's approach to a scientific explanation of society. The method of geometry never ceased to fascinate his mind, and his conceptual arrangement of individuals, both in the state of nature and in civil society, looks like nothing so much as it does the geometer's arrangement of lines and angles in a geometrical demonstration. For Hobbes, the abstract individual, contract, and the power of the State are fundamental. All else is to be derived rigorously from these assumptions or else discarded. . . .

With the monolith of power that Hobbes creates in the State, there is little room left for associations or groups. Hobbes does not see in these the multifold sources of sociability and order that Bodin had found in them. They are breeding areas of dissension, of conflict with the requirements of the unitary State, not reinforcements of order and justice. He compares associations within the State "which are as it were many lesser Common-wealths in

the bowels of a greater" to "wormes in the entrayles of a nat-
urall man." Economic monopolies of any kind, he detests. . . .
He is suspicious of the universities. . . . Hobbes is not content to
place the family's authority under the strict regulation of the
State. He must also do to the family what earlier legal theorists
had done to ecclesiastical and economic corporations: that is,
individualize them through the fiction of perpetual contract. In
discussing the nature of "Dominion Paternall," he insists that it
"is not so derived from the Generation, as if therefore the Parent
had Dominion over his Child because he begat him; but from the
Child's Consent, either express, or by other sufficient arguments
declared." In short, contract is, in Hobbes's rigorous terms, the
cement of even the family itself. Not from custom, or from
divine law itself, does the solidarity of the family proceed. It
proceeds from, and can be justified by, voluntary agreement,
either express or implied.[18]

With John Locke, the individualistic tradition changed in a way
which can conveniently be described in terms of Locke's difference
from Hobbes in the treament of normative problems. Locke, through
the implicit postulate which Halevy in *The Growth of Philosophical
Radicalism*[19] has called "the natural identity of interests," simply
pushed aside the problem of order as Hobbes posed it. Locke
assumed that natural rights would be reciprocally respected, except
by a minority of "bad men"; and that, on the basis of natural harmony, men could strive to improve their positions, to "appropriate
the gifts of nature," rather than trying to "subdue or destroy one
another," to exchange goods and services to mutual advantage. Locke
contributed almost nothing to analysis of the conditions under
which such a harmony of interests would hold; he merely assumed
that it would occur in the state of nature.

By nature, Locke taught in his *Treatise of Civil Government*, all
men are "free, equal and independent" and no man can be "subjected
to the political power of another without his own consent." [20] In
the original social contract men did not give up all their rights. They
surrendered only so much of their natural liberty as was necessary
for the preservation of society; they gave up the right they had in
the state of nature of individually judging and punishing, but they
retain the remainder of their rights under the protection of the

government they had agreed to establish. They certainly did not, as in Hobbes's theory, set up an absolute and arbitrary ruler. Locke began with the inalienable rights of the individual to life, property, and freedom, which could not be given up by the social contract. Therefore, from the beginning he limited the content of the social contract by not giving it any other purpose than the peaceful enjoyment of the individual's natural rights in a civil state. The individual members of society brought to the sovereign nothing else than their natural competence to defend their natural rights against attack by others. Thus Locke laid the basis for the state of old liberalism: the state conceived of as a limited company for the organized maintenance of the civil freedom rights of life and property. In Locke's social philosophy we therefore witness the reaction of the freedom ground-motive against Hobbes's nature motive which resulted in the destruction of corporate freedoms.

Locke spoke of all people in the state of nature as subject to the law of reason. But this law of reason was given a new content quite different from the organic social principle of medieval Scholasticism. For Aristotle and Aquinas, man is by his very nature a political and social animal. In his essential nature, but not merely as a result of his free consent expressed through a majority vote, he is a political animal. For Locke, on the other hand, the basis for ecclesiastical and civil laws is quite different. Nature is made up of material substances which, instead of entering into the teleological hierarchical order of medieval science, obey the purely mechanistic laws of Newton's physics; thus there is no basis for social laws in nature. As far as Locke is concerned the individual person is absolutely free, independent, and autonomous in this universe, and no principle grounded in nature exists to give the state anything more than a conventional status. Thus for Locke and succeeding liberal rationalists, all men are born free and equal, and the origin and basis of government lies in the consent of the governed. In Locke's opinion man does not enter society because organic relations with other men enable one to express more fully one's moral, religious, and political nature, as had been the case in the classical and scholastic concept of the state. Instead, the state is now thought of as a necessary evil forcing the individual to give up part of the ideal good which is complete independence and freedom in order the better to preserve one's private property.

Locke is, thus, if not the founder, at least the spiritual father of laissez faire economic individualism. Within the tradition of philosophical individualism he was the great theorist of the economic aspects of society—of how, within an assumed natural order, the mutual advantages of association could be attained, especially through exchange, and, eventually, the division of labor. He may in fact be regarded as the principal discoverer of the possibility of mutual advantage in exchange, and of capitalistic conceptions of property, prerequisite to such advantage. He originated the concept of property as founded in the functional necessities of individualistic production as a societal function.

In this theory of the origin and nature of organized society, Locke has replaced the medieval organic and functional theory of society with an individualistic and mechanistic one. For Locke, what leads men to enter community and social life is nothing essential but merely outward economic and political convenience. Society is not organically necessary as Aristotle and Aquinas supposed, but only comes about through a social contract whereby each individual hopes to better safeguard his "natural" rights to "life, liberty and property." For such rationalists the tie uniting individuals in society is thus merely external.

A society formed on such a basis is, of course, not a real community at all, but only a combination, and a selfish one at that, of a contractual character. It did not take long for other rationalists to extend this principle of "contract" to other forms of human community. Thus the marriage relationship came to be regarded as resting on a contract which could be broken at the pleasure of one or both parties. Why should one enter into a fundamental interdependence with another human being if every individual is autonomous and sovereign? Within this apostate individualistic frame of reference, community can never be on the same level of importance as autonomous individuality; but only something subordinate and casual.

However, such a view of the state well suited the needs of the rising class of industrial capitalists, merchant adventurers, and business entrepreneurs, who were seeking to overthrow the restrictions imposed upon them by the old mercantilist control of industry, trade, and commerce. Locke's social philosophy provided the new classes in British societies with an ideology in terms of which they could justify their exploitation of the new working classes. His individualistic idea of the state as only a "night-watchman" was soon allied with the program of the classical school of economists which advocated the unrestricted free play of social forces in business and economic life. In this way economic life became strongly rationalized, and the mercantilist control of industry and trade was allowed to wither away.

Such a rationalistic individualism inevitably leads to anarchical consequences for man's life in society as outraged human nature takes its revenge on the capitalist's and the financier's callousness, indifference, and irresponsibility towards other men's sufferings and poverty. It is largely because of Locke's apostate teaching about the nature of man in society that the English-speaking world, in so far as it has relinquished its Christian basis, appears to be in a state of latent anarchy and collapse.

By the middle of the nineteenth century a fierce reaction set in against this rationalistic individualism. Yet this collectivist reaction in its turn was worked out logically from naturalistic apostate humanist presuppositions. The apostate secular humanist alternative to rationalistic individualism is not free community but primitive tribal collectivism. It is the depersonalized mass man, the man forming a mere particle of the social structure, and the centralized impersonal bureaucratic, automatic, mechanical, totalitarian state, which inherits the decaying liberal democracy. Only where a strong federal system of government together with a strong Christian tradition had prevailed was it possible to avoid this fatal alternative of individualism or collectivism, to preserve a federal, non-centralized, pluralistic, organic structure of the state, and therefore to avoid that abrupt transition from a half anarchic individualism into a tyrannical totalitarianism. The American, British, and Canadian societies of the

English-speaking world, which abhor the way taken by totalitarian Communist Russia and Red China, do not yet seem to have grasped that, if the process of de-Christianization and neutralization goes on much longer within their societies, then they, too, will inevitably go the same way.

Many Christians apparently see no other remedies than socialistic planning and state intervention in business life for the economic malaise and social distress brought upon society by the attempt to apply economic individualism and technical rationality to economic life. It has been claimed that Anglo-American labor movements are merely "functional" associations for the promotion of the workers' welfare, and that they are free from the doctrinaire dogmatism of their Marxist dominated European counterparts. This has been hailed as an advantage opening the way for common action by people committed to various religious beliefs or none. For this reason, no doubt, many Christians have felt justified in supporting the so-called "neutral" labor unions as well as the British Labor Party and the Canadian New Democratic Party.

Yet such belief in functionalism is a typical example of apostate man-centered thinking, since in the Bible men and their organizations never function as such, because man is not a functional being, but a religious being. To surrender on this point is to render the labor movement completely incapable of righting the wrongs created by capitalism. Was not the error of the capitalist precisely that he treated his workers as tools and a function of the economic system? The functionalistic approach of the labor unions is the result of their falling into the same apostate humanistic error for which they so vehemently condemn and denounce the capitalists.

Both capitalists and socialists make the error of not basing their theories of society, and so their activities, upon the right view of man in society revealed in the Bible. Thus conservatives and liberals and socialists stand revealed in their true colors as radical unbelievers who prefer to trust in their own apostate reason, planning, and science than in God's Word as the ordering principle of their lives.

This explains why the socialist movement and its labor unions have been unable to relieve the real distresses of the modern worker, namely his growing depersonalization and atomization into a particle of mass man. The socialists rightly protested against the exploitation and poverty of the workers of a hundred years ago. Yet, they made the same mistake as the capitalists did in viewing the problems brought upon the world by the Industrial Revolution in the field of labor relations entirely from a rationalistic and materialistic point of view. The socialists bitterly attacked the capitalists for their preoccupation with money and profit at the expense of the worker as a person. However, they, too, have become preoccupied with exactly the same thing. They, too, have become obsessed with the idea of obtaining welfare and security for the worker in terms of material possessions, and they, too, adhere to the narrowed down Marxist view of man as only an "economic animal" whose god is his belly.

(c) *The Reformation of Social Science*

The antinomy between individualism and universalism or collectivism in apostate political and social science corresponds to that of mechanism versus vitalism in humanist biology and to that of operationalism versus meaning idealism in the realm of modern semantics. Such contradictions and dilemmas arise from an apostate and therefore false way of "seeing" reality in its true coherence, unity and diversity. Lacking a true "ordering" principle for their sociological investigations in the Word of God, neither individualists nor collectivists are able to explain satisfactorily the true nature of societal relationships.

Apostate modern social science builds its paradigms and models upon the postulate of the neutrality idea and the autonomy of man's reason. It supposes that the nature of man, and in it the nature of all temporal things, finds its center and origin in the human "reason." Yet this reason is in reality nothing other than a composite of our temporal functions of consciousness, functions of the human selfhood, only an aspect of what the Bible calls man's heart. Temporal organic life, the sense of beauty, man's function in historical development, in language, in legal and economic life—all these are also functions of the heart in this sense.

Apostate man, however, falsely supposes that human existence has its origin in reason as man's supposed supra-temporal center, and even that God himself is pure and absolute reason. As a result he comes to identify the findings of his reason in scientific abstraction with the full truth and excludes all naive or integral experience of God's creation as only mere ignorant opinion of the uneducated. At the same time the apostate scholar must still have his absolute, even if this means he must distort what his observation discloses only to be relative. His rational analysis of social phenomena is accompanied by a deeper drive, which in his unregenerate state as a sinner requires a distortion of the very "facts" he is in process of analyzing. Apostate scholars do not always agree on what they thus absolutize. This should not surprise Christian scholars, since oneness of mind and of heart, and community and peace in the world of scholarship no less than in the world of politics and industry can only be the result of God's grace in Christ uniting our hearts and minds in his service as a community of scholars and students joined together by the power of God's Word.

Where scholars are not so bound, nothing is there to prevent them seizing first upon one and then upon another of the many aspects of our created world as being in their view the absolute origin of the other aspects. This is made possible by the very relative character of each of the life aspects; being relative, the other meaning-aspects of life are involved in their very nature. The wholeness of meaning is present universally in a certain way in each aspect of God's creation. It only requires a distortion of this creation-structure to see one aspect as the fulness of meaning required by the heart of all the other aspects.

As a result of this temptation a great variety of scientific "isms" have arisen in the course of the history of science. Man has been conceived of as a rational being, as a producer, as an economic animal, as a symbolizer, as a tool-making animal.

These and other views are all "totality" views about man that arise not from a mere observation and analysis of the positive "facts" presented to our "minds"—if such were the case no conflict between them would be possible. Instead, they arise from the failure of

apostate scholars to "see" the relative aspects of human life as relative and from the resulting tendency to explain all the remaining
aspects in terms of the one aspect that has been religiously absolutized and thus made the deeper source and unity of all the rest,
above all the others, and consider them to be the all-embracing totality which includes the lower relationships as dependent parts.
In contradistinction to all such collectivistic conceptions, individualism absolutizes the individual, claiming that he alone is self-
sufficient and precedes any societal relationship. Individualism
conceives of society only as a function, i.e., as a psychical or
juridical phenomenon. Because of its functionalism, individualism
overlooks the plastic horizon of reality, and thus denies the structure
of individuality of authoritative communities such as the family,
state, or church. It denies the reality of societal relationships and
thinks of them merely as the name given to the arbitrary union between sovereign individuals. Individualism deifies one of the human
subject-functions by refusing to admit that man is made in God's
image along with all other men.

The various schools of apostate modern sociology with their
corresponding "isms" are characterized by this absolutization of a
specific modal aspect of God's creation in a vain attempt to grasp
the nature of human society in the theoretical view of totality.
Such absolutizations cannot be corrected by other absolutizations.
The very problem is how a general sociology may avoid them, that
is to say, from what standpoint a sociological view of the totality of
the different aspects of society is possible.

Herman Dooyeweerd formulates the three transcendental problems
of such a theoretical total view of human society in three questions:
(1) Where is the basic denominator to be found needed for a comparison of the different types of societal relationships, set apart and
opposed to one another in the antithetic Gegenstand-relation of
theoretical thought; (2) How is their mutual relation and coherence
to be viewed? (3) Where do they find their radical unity and totality of meaning, or, in other words, from which starting-point
can we grasp them in the theoretical view of totality? [21] He answers:

From the Christian transcendence-standpoint the radical unity and meaning-totality of all temporal societal structures of individuality is only to be found in the central religious community of mankind in its creation, fall and redemption by Jesus Christ. This starting-point excludes in principle every universalist sociological view, which seeks the unity and all-embracing totality of all types of societal relationships in a temporal community of mankind. Neither a nation, nor the Church in the sense of a temporal institution, nor the State, nor an international union of whatever typical character, can be the all-inclusive totality of human social life, because mankind in its spiritual root transcends the temporal order with its diversity of social structures. . . .

It is only from the biblical Christian transcendence-standpoint that the three transcendental basic problems formulated above can be solved in a way which precludes absolutizations. The basic denominator for a theoretical comparison of the different structural types of human society can here only be the temporal world-order rooted in the divine order of creation. The mutual relation between the social structures of individuality (e.g., family, church, state, etc.) is only to be viewed as that of an inner sovereignty of each structure within its own orbit, balanced by its coherence with the other structures in cosmic time; the latter guarantees enkaptic external functions of any particular social relationship in all the others, insofar as their different structural principles are realized. And this theoretical total view is only possible from the starting point that the different societal structures find their radical unity and meaning-totality beyond cosmic time in the central religious community of mankind.[22]

Only the Word of God written in the Holy Scriptures can provide us with a sure point of departure for our natural and our social science. What God's Word does not do, of course, is to tell us that there are fifteen law-spheres, law-aspects, and modalities in God's creation. This is strictly a matter of analysis. The Word of God merely directs us to take whatever diversity of natural and social structures we find in God's creation as a diversity of the integral fulness of meaning of our religious life. In this way God's revelation of himself as Creator and Redeemer provides us with the great key to a unified field of human knowledge.

Only by accepting God's Word as the ordering principle of our scientific work can we hope to make sense of the vast array of so-called natural and social "facts" around us. God's Word alone can provide us with a true frame of reference and only sure point of departure for all our thinking about his creation. It does so by working in our hearts a true knowledge of God, of ourselves and of the law-order of his creation. The Word of God is the power by which the Holy Spirit opens our hearts to see things as they really are. True knowledge is thus made possible by true religion, and it can only arise from the knowing activity of the human heart enlightened through the Word of God by the Holy Spirit. The biblical motive of sin and grace alone, by its radical grip upon our hearts, can bring about a real reformation of our view of man and of the society and world in which he has been placed by the Creator. Such an inner reformation of natural and social science is the very opposite of the scholastic device of accommodation which first had to destroy the revealed truth that the human selfhood is the central seat of the image of God, in order to replace it by a dualistic conception of man in which the central religious relation of man to his creator is entirely lost.

At the same time we must point out that this biblical reformation of social and natural science does not involve the subjection of science to theology as such. A truly Christian social science must be based on a renewed biblical insight into the divinely established structures of creation and of society and not upon theology as such, which can be of little help in solving sociological problems. For this reason there must be a *directly* biblical and not an indirectly theological reformation of modern political and sociological science. Such a reformation of the basic categories of modern sociology in the light of the scriptural rather than the apostate humanist conception of reality has in fact begun in the work of Herman Dooyeweerd as well as other scholars of the Christian school of thought of the Cosmonomic Idea.

According to Dooyeweerd, God's Word alone can provide a solution to the false dilemma of individualism versus collectivism as well as a proper key to an adequate understanding of the problems affecting man in modern society. Such a key is indispensable if modern society is to be rescued from the dangers with which it is today confronted. While many Christians are dissatisfied with both individualism and collectivism, all they seem able to suggest as the only course open to us to follow is to choose an agreeable compromise position somewhere in the middle. It is Dooyeweerd's firm conviction that Christians need not thus be tied by this false dilemma. He suggests another possibility typified by his biblically motivated principle of the balance of authority and freedom under God and of the sovereignty of the various social spheres.

Taking its starting point in a supposedly neutral and unprejudiced trust in thought itself, apostate social science today is forced to interpret the relationship of the individual to the group and of the group to other groups in the general schema of whole and part. Either the individual is thought to be a part of the group, or the group is thought to be composed of congeries of distinct individuals. On this immanence (earthly) standpoint modern social science is bound to drive itself between the horns of the individualist-collectivist dilemma.

In the light of the scriptural conception of man in society, we realize that the truth lies on neither side. The common error of individualism and collectivism, in typically humanistic fashion, is that they take their starting point in man, whether the individual or the group. The biblical view of man in society overcomes this dilemma. In the light of God's Word, we know that God created man for community, first with himself and then with his fellow men, but as a religious being, not an economic or political animal. The individual and the community are equally called to live in obedience to the laws of the Creator since love is the meaning of human life. God is Love (I John 4:7-17).

The biblical view of man is that in his essential nature man is in community, first with God his creator, and secondly with his fellow man. Thus to man alone is given the gifts of prayer and speech so that he can talk to his God and to his neighbor. Man's life in its inmost essence is conceived of in the Bible as a dialogue and prayer with the Heavenly Father. That man exists not in singularity but in duality is expressed in the biblical account of creation in the statement that "male and female, created He them." The self and the other are like the twin foci of an ellipse, neither of which has meaning apart from the other. Writing of *The Biblical Doctrine of Man in Society*, G. Ernest Wright says:

> The new and responsible individual who is created by God in Christ is not liberated from community in such a manner as would enable us to speak of biblical faith as creating a true individualism over against all collectivism. Man is (in the New Testament) liberated from a false to a true community, and for that reason his first steps in the right direction are to be discovered in conversion. While in modern times we see a rediscovery of community which enslaves man, so that collectivism and individualism appear as opposing concepts, the biblical concentration on God's formation of a people is of such a nature that man, the individual, emerges in society in a manner hitherto unknown. The biblical story must not be interpreted as the progressive emancipation of the individual, but instead as God's action in history to create a community in which the responsible individual finds his true being.[23]

The biblical view of man in society safeguards the rights of both the individual and the group. It does not allow any group to destroy man's individuality, since the individuality of a person created in God's holy image is much deeper than any human community. The full individuality of the person cannot be exhausted within the confines of any earthly association or community, whether church or state. He cannot discover his ultimate and eternal destiny in any supposedly all-embracing earthly group, since he is made for everlasting fellowship with God.

Again careful observation makes clear that groups retain their identity even in spite of changes within their membership, so that the individualist theory of reification must be rejected. Groups have a relatively constant structure which is more than a reflection of the subjective will or activity of any one or even all their members. A truly reformational Christian social science will take both these insights into account when re-building the foundations of modern sociology. Such a program involves a radical break with the immanence stand-point.

According to Dooyeweerd, immanence sociology is forced to

employ the scheme of the whole or the part because it tries to use as a universal method of interpretation what has really only limited validity. It is forced to construe everything within the schema of genus and species. While this method of concept formation may be valid in biological classification, it cannot be used to express the relationships between the various social spheres such as the family, church, industry, state, etc.

If we try to distinguish the state from the family, for instance, by way of genus and species, we are bound to fall into the whole-part scheme. We must then seek the most inclusive social group of which all other groups are members, or we must seek some other basis for relating what are altogether unrelated individual groupings.

Dooyeweerd teaches that neither individualism nor collectivism recognizes the true structure of societal relationships. The dilemma only arises when the structures of individuality are neglected which alone present a basis for the solution of the problem of the relation of the individual to the group. Outside this biblically based doctrine of man in society, apostate scholars are forced to construct human society rationally out of the wills of sovereign individuals or out of some absolutized single community, be it church or state. The principle of sphere sovereignty, he claims, alone presents us with a proper insight into the connection between man and his social groupings, since by this doctrine the individual is never completely defined or absorbed into any one temporal bond whether nation, party, or state. These are limited in the expression of their authority by their own peculiar God-ordained structural principle or norm.

The error of individualism is that it constructs the communities and associations of society out of elemental atomistic relations between individuals conceived of as sovereign agents, with the result that it does not recognize that these groupings also have their own peculiar structural principles.

But collectivism absolutizes one of the many temporal communities, namely the one that is made to embrace all of the others, as the whole which enfolds the parts. This was true of the classical city-state and all modern totalitarian regimes. The error of such universalistic theories is that then this single all-embracing community is given the place of the religious basic community, namely, the Kingdom of God, which transcends time and place. Man cannot thus be enslaved by any such absolutized earthly community since in the center of his personality, i.e., his "heart," man also transcends time. As long as he remains in history, he functions in a multiplicity of equally significant associations and communities as a parent, as a citizen, as a churchman, as an art lover or music lover, as a consumer or buyer, and so on.

The biblical view of man in society alone provides a way out of the dead end humanistic street of individualism versus collectivism, for it alone clearly reveals that man has been created as an individual for life in fellowship with God and his neighbor. The Great Commandment in fact calls man to love God with all his heart and his neighbor as himself. This means that man must not find his purpose and meaning in life in himself, as Hobbes and Locke supposed, or in the group, as Rousseau and Marx supposed, but in the God who created him. The individual and the group are equally called to obey God's laws for society. In fact, it is only by such obedience to God's law that the present conflicts rending society apart at the seams both at home an abroad can be resolved. Both the individual and society will then occupy their God-given place in a world dominated by love and service to God and one's neighbor.

It is only through such love of God and of each other that we become human at all. True personality and true community are two sides of the same wonderful coin. This is the meaning of the greatest and most mysterious text of the whole Bible, namely that "God is Love" (I John 4:8, 16). Love is the meaning and purpose of human life, indeed it is eternal life itself. Therefore the Christian is commissioned to proclaim and demand, on behalf of all men and women, that personal and communal meaning of life which is proper to each, and to oppose everything which obscures or destroys this personal and communal significance of human life. Disharmony and strife are not due, as Northrop thinks, to man's ignorance of natural science, but to man's disobedience to God's law. We must, therefore, break with the superficial dilemma posed by the extremes of both the Left and the Right in modern politics. Until

Christians do so, they will be unable to counteract effectively the secularizing influence inherent in the controversy of individualism versus collectivism. Only by returning to the biblical doctrine of sphere sovereignty and the principle of the balance of authority and freedom under God, can we avoid falling into the trap of justifying collectivism on the basis of the defects of individualism. Christian pluralism is thus the answer to both individualism and collectivism.

(d) *The Antithesis Between Regenerate and Unregenerate Science*

If we accept the biblical doctrine of the fall of man into both original sin and actual rebellion from God, then it follows that *all* human life, including the life of human science and scholarship has been radically affected by sin and that all life, including the life of theoretical thought, must be reformed by God's special saving grace in Jesus Christ in the communion of the Holy Spirit.

Palingenesis, or rebirth by God's grace acting upon our lives, is therefore not confined to the order of religion as such, but in conformity with the scriptural conception of the radical unity of man in his religious root, what the Bible terms the human "heart," it is of immediate importance for the proper exercise of theoretical thought itself.

According to Kuyper there will thus be two kinds of science, determined by a twofold point of departure: the one rooted in the unregenerate heart, the other in the regenerate. Since there are now two kinds of people in the world, due to the fact of regeneration and election, whereby the unity of human consciousness has been broken, there must of necessity be two kinds of science, of which only one can be essentially true. For this reason "the idea of the unity of science, taken in its absolute sense, implies the denial of the fact of *paligenesis*, and therefore from principle leads to the rejection of the Christian religion." [24]

In the broader cultural field there are, of course, certain activities which are not affected by special grace, such as architecture and dentistry. Special grace does not give the Christian a better understanding of such technical matters than the non-Christian, nor does it give any additional knowledge or craftsmanship in any of the arts. In science, for example, the difference between a redeemed person and an unredeemed person does not count when they are engaged in such simple activities as weighing, measuring, or counting, etc. Observation is actually non-abstract in character, and Kuyper maintains that looking through a microscope or a telescope is a form of observation.

But as soon as an attempt is made to interpret the facts thus empirically gathered, and to arrive at "the thought which governs the whole constellation of phenomena," then we may properly speak of science emerging. It is in this field of the theoretical interpretation of the so-called pure "facts" that the impact of special grace and of revelation becomes very great. As C. Van Til points out in *A Christian Theory of Knowledge*:

> The Christian principle of interpretation is based upon the assumption of God as the final and self-contained reference point. The non-Christian principle of interpretation is that man as self-contained is the final reference point. It is this basic difference that has to be kept in mind all the time. . . .
> The non-Christian assumes that man is ultimate, that is, that he is not created. Christianity assumes that man is created. The non-Christian assumes that the facts of man's environment are not created; the Christian assumes that these facts are created. . . . The two types of system differ because of the fact that their basic assumptions or presuppositions differ.[25]

Western science has assumed that theoretical thought in the very nature of the case is an autonomous activity based upon a supposed universality of reason. In his book, *A New Critique of Theoretical Thought*, Herman Dooyeweerd has shown that this so-called universality of reason itself contains a great problem. If all philosophical schools chose their points of departure in reason alone, and not in deeper presuppositions, then it ought to be possible to convince an opponent in a purely theoretical way that his arguments are true or false. But what actually happens is that philosophers and scientists tend to reason at cross purposes. A philosopher of the Thomist school, for example, can never succeed in convincing one of the Kantian school. In reality, the universality of reason is an uncritically accepted dogma, cloaking diverse supra-theoretical points of departure for one's thinking about the cosmos.

According to Dooyeweerd, no scientist can avoid this problem of choosing a point of departure for his thought, and he makes it the central feature of his transcendental critique of theoretical thought. By raising it, he claims that every possible starting point of scientific thought is subjected to a fundamental criticism, for a truly critical attitude of thought does not allow us to choose such a starting point in any one special aspect of reality.

By this Dooyeweerd means that there are as many types of theoretical or scientific thought as there are aspects of the cosmos. In every case there is a synthesis of the logical aspect with one of the non logical aspects as a point of departure. When we take any of these non logical aspects of reality as a point of departure, we then interpret the whole of reality in terms of that one aspect. This is the remote cause of all "isms" in philosophy, biologism, materialism, historicism, rationalism, etc. Not even mathematics is exempt from this necessity of a point of departure for its thoughts. He writes:

> In pure mathematics, the problem immediately arises: How is one to view the mutual relationship between the aspects of number, space, movement, sensory perception, logical thought and symbolical signification? Different schools in pure mathematics such as logicism, symbolistic formalism, empiricism and intuitionism arise in accordance with their respective theoretical visions on this basic problem. These differences are not restricted to the philosophy of mathematics. The famous Dutch mathematician Brouwer, the chief representative of the intuitionistic school, abolished an entire branch of special scientific work which had been built up by the logicist and formalist theories (the theory of the so-called transfinite numbers).
>
> The first three schools, logicism, symbolistic formalism and empiricism, try to reduce the aspects of number and space to the logical, the linguistic and the sensory-perceptual aspects respectively.
>
> Even in logic itself we observe the rise of a great diversity of theoretical schools . . . determined by a theoretical vision of reality.[26]

1. *Scientific Work as Religious Activity*

This means that all the natural sciences as well as the social sciences qua (as) scientific systems of thought are necessarily involved in a prescientific philosophical view as to the relationships and coherence of the several functional aspects of reality, e.g., the numerical, the spatial, the physical-chemical, the biological, the psychical, the logical, the historical-cultural, the linguistic, the social, the economic, the aesthetic, the juridical, the ethical, and the pistical-theological. (See chart of the law-spheres in appendix.)

Dooyeweerd maintains that only the Word of God can provide us with a true point of departure for our theoretical thought and thus enable us to "see" the facts studied in the various sciences in their proper order, structure, and relationships. The facts do not "speak" to us unless we see them in their right order as given at the creation. If the scientist refuses to be taught by the Word of God what this order of the creation is, then he will be forced to substitute some principle of total structuration and explanation of his own devising. Such an apostate thinker will then be forced to seek his ultimate principle of explanation and point of departure in ONE or another aspect of the created universe rather than in the Creator of the Universe. For this reason Dooyeweerd speaks of all non-Christian systems of thought as being immanentistic in character, because they refuse to recognize the ultimate dependence of human thought and science upon God's revelation. As a result, all such immanence philosophy and science, that is, all human thought which takes its origin somewhere in temporal reality and not in God's revelation of himself as Creator of the Universe cannot grasp the intrinsic unity and coherence of all reality but is bound to fall into a false dialectical dualism in which one aspect is played over against another aspect, e.g., matter over against form in the history of Greek philosophy, vitalism over against mechanism in modern biology.

Evan Runner points out in his lectures, *The Relation of the Bible to Learning*, delivered at the first Conference of the Association of Reformed Scientific Studies held in Canada in 1960, that the apostate scholar:

. . . thinks of himself as just this thing here. But since this something that is just here, our temporal existence, exhibits a great diversity of moments or aspects—e.g., the numerical, spatial, physical-chemical, biological, psychical, logical, historical-cultural, lingual, social, economic, aesthetic, jural, ethical and pistical—all these are seen in the light of the Word of God as relative aspects of the religious unity of our life. Apostate man, however, is driven by his religious needs for security and meaning in life to find a substitute to fill in for the true unity and to absolutize one of the relative aspects of life and to elevate it to the place of the heart. . . . He must find an absolute in the relative. He is bound to the creation-structure; he must know himself. At the same time we see him wilfully substituting his lie to replace the Truth. He must have his absolute, even if it means that he must distort what observation will readily disclose to be relative. His rational analysis is accompanied by a deeper drive, which in the fallen state requires a distortion of the very "facts" he is in process of analyzing.[27]

In this tendency to absolutize something which is only relative may be found the origin of most of the philosophical and scientific "isms" which have plagued the history of human thought. All these are totality views about man that arise not from a mere scientific observation and analysis of positive facts presented to our minds—if such were in fact the case there would be no conflict between them—but rather from apostate man's failure to realize that these aspects of his life are relative and not absolute and from the consequent effort to explain all the remaining aspects of reality in terms of the one aspect that has been religiously absolutized and so made the source of unity of all the other aspects. As an example we may refer to Hegel's attempt to take the analytical-logical aspect of reality as his point of departure with the consequence that the whole of reality became for him logicised or idealized. For Hegel the rational alone is the real.

Unlike the apostate scientist who takes his point of departure in one of the aspects of God's creation, the Christian scientist takes his point of departure in the Word of God, which provides him with the ordering principle of his scientific thought. It would be impossible, for instance, for a Christian mathematician to accept a view of pure mathematics as a-priori in the sense that pure mathematics could become emancipated from the modal structure of the mathematical aspects of reality, i.e., the numerical and the spatial which are founded in the temporal order of God's creation. The Christian mathematician accepts the universe as something *given* by God the creator, not as a construct of his own pure rational thought.

There is also a certain a-priori view about scientific models which no true scientific disciple of Christ could accept. For the a-priori theories we have in mind imply a lack of integral coherence between abstract theoretical logical thought and that about which such thought should be concerned, e.g., number, spatial figures, etc., as aspects indissolubly bound up with the other aspects of reality in an integral temporal order. As Dooyeweerd wisely remarks:

> It is impossible to establish a line of demarcation between philosophy and science in order to emancipate the latter from the former. Science cannot be isolated in such a way as to give it a a completely independent sphere of investigation and any attempt to do so cannot withstand a serious critique. It would make sense to speak of the autonomy of the special sciences, if, and only if, a special science could actually investigate a specific aspect of temporal reality without theoretically considering its coherence with the other aspects. No scientific thought, however, is possible in such isolation with "closed shutters." Scientific thought is constantly confronted with the temporal coherence of meaning among the modal aspects of reality, and cannot escape from following a transcendental idea of this coherence . . . even the sciences investigating the first two modal aspects of human experience, i.e., the numerical and the spatial, cannot avoid making philosophical pre-suppositions in this sense.[28]

Dooyeweerd then asks the fundamental question:

> Is it possible that modern mathematics would escape from philosophical pre-suppositions with respect to the relationships and coherence of the arithmetic aspect with the spatial, the logical, the linguistic and sensory ones? Is it permissible to include, with Dedekind, the original spatial continuity and dimensionality-moments in our concept of number? Is mathematics simply axiomatical symbolic logic whose criterion of truth rests exclusively upon the principle of contradiction and the principle of the

excluded middle? Does the "transfinite number" really possess numerical meaning? Is it permitted, in a rationalist way, to reduce the subject-side of the numerical aspect to a function of the principle of progression (which is a numerical law) and can we consequently speak of an actually infinitesimal number? Is it justified to conceive of space as a continuum of points? Is it permitted to designate real numbers as spatial points? Is motion possible in the original (mathematical) sense of the spatial aspect?

This whole series of basic philosophical questions strikes the very heart of mathematical thought. No mathematician can remain neutral to them. With or without philosophical reflection on his presuppositions he must make a choice. The possibility of effecting a separation completely between philosophy and mathematics is especially problematical with respect to so-called pure (non-applied) mathematics, because it is conceived of as an apriori science and its results cannot be tested by natural scientific experiments.[29]

Here Dooyeweerd has inserted a footnote, which reads as follows:

The opinion that pure mathematics would be apriori in this sense, that it may proceed from fully arbitrary axioms, is incompatible with the Christian conception of the divine world-order as the ultimate foundation of all scientific investigation. From our viewpoint the apriori character of pure mathematics cannot mean that the latter would be emancipated from the modal structures of the mathematical aspects which are founded in the temporal order of experience.

The investigation of these structures can only occur in an *empirical* way, since they are not created by human thought and are no more apriori "thought-forms," but rather included in the "modal horizon" of our experience as apriori data. They must be *discovered* in reflection upon our experience of the mathematical aspects. The Kantian conception of the apriori and the empirical moments in human knowledge identifies the "empirical" with the sensory impressions. We have again and again to establish that this sensationalistic conception of the "empirical" is incompatible with our integral (biblical) conception of human experience.[30]

After this footnote Dooyeweerd continues:

Is it not the very task of the philosophy of mathematics to investigate the modal structures of the mathematical aspects on which depend all well-founded judgements in pure mathematics?

Is it possible to separate the task of mathematical science from that of the philosophy of mathematics by saying that the latter only seeks to explain the epistemological possibility of apriori mathematical knowledge, whose methods and contents must be accepted without any critique?

But, by such an attempt at demarcation, mathematics is made a "factum," a "fait accompli," and the possibility of a real philosophical criticism of the latter is precluded.

Such an attitude toward the special sciences may be acceptable in the cadre of a transcendental ground-Idea, in which the Humanistic ideal of science has a foundational function, but, in the light of our transcendental critique of theoretical thought, it must be rejected as false and dogmatical.

It is true that philosophy can only explain the foundations of mathematics, but this does not warrant the ascription of autonomy to mathematical thought, which reaches its focal point in the technique of reckoning, construction, and deduction. Philosophy cannot attribute this autonomy to it, because the mathematician must necessarily work with subjective philosophical presuppositions, whose consequences are evident in mathematical theory itself, as we have explained in the Prolegomena.[31]

The analysis of the basic presuppositions of mathematical science thus described by Dooyeweerd surely reveals that the so-called factual states of affairs with which the scientist deals cannot be regarded as a separate structural element in the creation, so that scientific method may be thought of as concerned only with the so-called "brute facts." The "facts" studied by the scientist are always "interpretative" facts, that is to say, that the scientist always "sees" the various aspects, functions, and coherences of the world around him through the spectacles of his own prescientific presuppositions and initial point of departure. The truly Christian scientist will differ radically from an apostate scholar in that he will "see" these various aspects, functions, and coherences of God's creation in the light of the ordering principle of the Word of God.

It follows that scientific thought and work are fundamentally religious activities in the sense that they depend upon ultimate presuppositions which are accepted in faith. Dr. J. D. Dengerink, writing of this problem with evangelical scholars in mind, points out:

One still frequently finds the conception among Christians and even in more narrowly defined Evangelical circles that, although scholarship is bound to certain external limits by religion and morality, nevertheless in terms of its own inner nature it is a more less neutral, autonomous concern. Even those who explicitly confront the problem of Christian faith and scientific knowledge frequently fall victim to this conception. They accept the premise that facts are facts, and facts are the same for Christians. That can hardly be denied. Christians and non-Christians live and think in terms of the same created reality. But frequently they lose sight of the notion that scientific work consists not in giving a photographic but an interpretative and elucidative account of reality by way of a process of analysis and conceptualization. And they forget that in this process the whole man continues to function in all his particularity, including the religious choice of position which motivates his selection of a certain path in his scientific study. In that light it may not even be correct to speak of faith *and* science. Such a formula may leave the impression that these two are relatively independent magnitudes which man, in this case the Christian, must somehow integrate. It is much closer to the truth to say that scientific work itself, due to its creaturely character, is nothing but a believing, religious activity and that this work of faith and religion can proceed in divergent directions either towards God or away from Him. Varying between different individuals, these two directions and movements are, due to the surd of sin in the lives of Christians, interwoven in a remarkable way.[32]

If scientific work is itself a religious activity, then there can be no conflict between faith and science. What Dooyeweerd terms Kuyper's "great Scriptural conception" is his insight that *all* science is rooted in faith. According to Kuyper faith is the presupposition of every science. Faith is "that formal function of the life of our soul which is fundamental to every fact of our human consciousness." [33] Without believing in oneself one cannot take the first step in the quest of science; it is the starting point of conduct for which there is no empirical or demonstrative proof. All rational demonstration proceeds on unproved axioms accepted by faith. As a matter of fact, all of life proceeds on faith. In every expression of his personality as well as in the acquisition of scientific conviction, every man starts out from faith.

For this reason it follows that the *whole* scale of the Christian sciences, theology included, must be contrasted with the *whole* scale of the non-Christian or apostate sciences, modernistic "liberal" theology included. While formally faith functions in both cases, so that we may say that "Christianity and paganism stand to each other as the plus and minus of the same series," [34] they are at the same time absolutely antithetical to each other, because both proceed from a central religious attitude of the heart, the one Christian, the other apostate.

With regard to this antithesis that characterizes the world in which we live and extends to the realm of scientific and so-called neutral academic thought, Kuyper states that it is not a conflict of faith and science, but a conflict between two different kinds of faith, the one Christian and the other apostate. Thus he writts:

> Not faith and science, therefore, but two scientific systems, or if you choose, two scientific elaborations, are opposed to each other, each having its own faith. Nor may it be said that it is here science which opposes theology, for we have to do with two absolute forms of science, both of which claim the whole domain of human knowledge, and both of which have a suggestion about the supreme Being of their own as the point of departure of their world-view. Pantheism as well as Deism is a system about God, and without reserve the entire system of modern theology finds its home in the science of the Normalists. And finally these two scientific systems of the Normalists and Abnormalists are not relative opponents, walking together halfway, and further on peaceably suffering one another to choose different paths, but they are both in earnest, disputing with one another *the whole domain of life*, and they cannot desist from the constant endeavour to pull down to the ground the entire edifice of their respective controverted assertions, all the supports included, upon which their assertions rest. If they did not try this, they would thereby show on both sides, that they did not honestly believe in their point of departure, that they were not serious combatants, and that they did not understand the primordial demand of science, which of course claims unity of conception. [35]

In spite of Kuyper's radical distinction between apostate and Christian thought, between a degenerate and a regenerate science, he nevertheless, like Calvin himself, acknowledges that pagan thought both ancient and modern reveals many excellent characteristics. The names of Socrates, Plato, and Aristotle are still honored by Christian thinkers, and the philosophy of Aristotle has been an invaluable aid in the training of the Christian scholar. This is explained by Kuyper in terms of the doctrine of common grace first formulated by John Calvin.

How can we account for the good with the bad in the unregenerate? Calvin had asked. Whereas Luther had clung to the idea of a lower earthly sphere in which man is capable of doing much good, Calvin's logical mind could not put up with such a dualism. On the one hand, his deep insight into the terrible consequences of sin did not allow him to admit that fallen man, when left wholly to himself, could produce any good in any domain whatsoever. On the other hand he found it impossible to subscribe to the view of Zwingli, who virtually surrendered the absoluteness of Christianity by teaching that at least certain heathen philosophers who remained utter strangers to the Gospel of Christ participated in God's saving grace. Calvin found the solution for the problem how we must account for the good and the true with the bad and the false in the unregenerate in the concept of Common Grace. He was the first Christian thinker who drew a clear-cut distinction between common and special grace, between the operations of the Spirit of God which are common to mankind at large, and the sanctifying work of the same Spirit which is limited to God's elect (*Institutes*, Book Two, Chapter 3, par. three).

In his great work on Common Grace, Kuyper points out that Calvin's doctrine did not arise out of mere philosophical invention but out of the confession of the mortal character of sin:

> Yet apparently this confession of the mortal character of sin did not square with reality. There was in the sinful world outside the Church so much that was beautiful, so much to be respected, so much that provoked to envy. This placed the formulators of the Reformed Confession before the dilemma: either to deny all this good against their better knowledge, and thus to err with the anabaptists; or to view man as not so deeply fallen, and thus to stray into the Pelagian and Arminian heresy. And placed before that choice, the Reformed Confession has refused to travel

either of these roads. We might not close our eyes to the good and the beautiful outside the Church among unbelievers in the world. This good was there and that had to be acknowledged. And just as little might the least bit be detracted from the total depravity of sinful nature. But herein lay the solution of this apparent contradiction, that also outside the Church, among the heathen, in the midst of the world, God's grace was at work, grace not eternal, nor unto salvation, but temporal and for the stemming of the destruction that lurked in sin.[36]

By means of His common or temporal conserving grace, God maintains the life of all men, relaxes the curse which rests upon them by reason of their disobedience, and arrests the process of corruption and decay, while the Church mediates to men His saving grace in Jesus Christ. Without God's common grace, which thus curbs the effects of sin in human life, there could be no possibility of human science and culture at all and apostate pagan life would collapse in chaos.

Thus man's temporal life with its family, state, marriage, legal and economic relationships is preserved in heathen lands which have not heard the Gospel even when renewing, regenerating grace is not available. Even when men deny God, His goodness and favor enable them to perform civil good, to honor legal contracts, think rational thoughts, compose great music and create great art, to love each other, and to enjoy social graces and virtues. According to Kuyper it is God's common grace which makes human culture and science possible. Human society would have been utterly destroyed if the common grace of the Lord had not intervened. As such common grace is the foundation of culture, since God's great plan for the creation is achieved through common grace. It is not spiritual and regenerative but temporal and material. It is based upon and flows forth from the confession of the absolute sovereignty of God, for, says Kuyper, not only the church but the whole world must give God the honor that is His due; hence the world received common grace in order to honor Him through it. Thus Kuyper upholds the catholic claims of Christianity and urges its validity for all men.

Common grace, although non-saving and restricted to this life, has its source in Christ as mediator of the creation, since all things exist through the Eternal Word. Hence, the point of departure for common grace is creation and the sphere of the natural. But it may also be called supernatural, because it is God's longsuffering mercy to which man as such has no right. As such it is a glimmer of light in the midst of darkness.

While common grace does not change the depraved heart of man, it does restrain him from spending all his energies in building a tower of Babel. And while restraining the downward and destructive tendency of sin, it even enables him to labor alongside the believer in bringing to light the potentialities of God's created universe. The chief task of human culture and science, Kuyper argues, is the development of the potentialities God has placed in his created world. Culture and science is the fulfillment of the great cultural mandate given to man at the beginning of his history. "Be fruitful and multiply and replenish the earth and subdue it and have dominion over it" (Gen. 1:28); and "Keep the garden and dress it." Man's culture and science are thus understood to be the result of a divinely imposed cultural mandate. Culture and science are man's life task and it is through common grace that man can alone fulfill this task. Thanks to common grace the powers of creation come to fruition in spite of sin. This preserving and development of the creation to God's greater glory is the goal of common grace.

2. The Christian Scholar's Ordering Principle of Studies

Both Kuyper and Dooyeweerd have thus made it abundantly clear that scientific work is itself a form of religious activity because human life in its entirety is religion. Man is so created that he is forced to find the meaning of his life either in the God who created him or in some idol or false absolute of his own devising. Both claim that *life is religion*, not that life is religious. Now it may be objected that one cannot say in English that life is religion, and that the structure of the language will only allow one to say that life is religious. To this objection Dooyeweerd would reply that the statement "life is religious" is not what he wants to say at all. He claims that life is religion. It is like the difference between saying that

life is sexual and life is sex. In this second example the statement
life is sexual is true and the statement life is sex is false, and that is
enough to show that there is a difference between having an adjective
and having a noun in the predicate. Dooyeweerd does not want
to say that there is a religious aspect of life, as there is, for instance,
a sexual or an aesthetic aspect (life is beautiful); on the contrary, he
is saying that human life in ALL its aspects is religion. He requires
in the predicate a word coextensive with the subject, and that requires a noun. Life is religion. To say that is at once to reject all
views which identify human life with one or another of its aspects,
as for example, when men identify life with its material aspects
(materialism), or when men say that the essence of man is to be
found in his reason or logical faculty (rationalism) or in morality
(Natural Law); or the Marxist school of thought which identifies
man's life with his tool-making capacity and his socio-economic
functions; or the symbolist school led by Ernst Cassirer which
identifies man with his ability to communicate by means of signs
and symbols (*Essay on Man*).[37] What Dooyeweerd is saying when
he claims that life is religion is that all these other things that have
been noted as having a place in man's life are only aspects of that all-
inclusive life which, as a whole, can only properly be described as
religion.

Religion is man's specific condition. It is what makes us human
rather than animal. It is the ex-sistent condition in which the human ego is bound to its true or pretended firm ground and origin
which is revealed in the restlessness of man in search of the Absolute.
Sharing in the meaning character of all created reality, the selfhood
can find no rest in itself, but restlessly seeks its origin in order to
understand its own meaning, and in its own meaning the meaning of
all created reality.

This restlessness of the selfhood is transmitted to all the temporal
functions in which it is actually operative. In this way scientific
thought as an activity of the selfhood also comes to share in the
restless search for the Absolute. As Dooyeweerd puts it:

> Thought will not be set at rest in the preliminary philosophical
> questions, until the Arche is discovered, which alone gives mean-

ing and existence to philosophic thought itself. Philosophic thought cannot withdraw itself from this tendency towards the Origin. It is an immanent conformity to law for it to find no rest in meaning, but to think from and to the origin to which meaning owes its ground.[38]

If theoretical thought is not able to reach the true absolute Origin of meaning in God, it is forced to raise some aspect of the cosmos to the status of being absolute. In Dooyeweerd's opinion this is the cause of all absolutization of the relative. Every such absolutization of a theoretically isolated aspect of reality to act as root and origin of all the others is basically of a religious nature and a manifestation of the law of religious concentration to which theoretical thought is subjected. Hence Dooyeweerd's definition of religion as "the innate impulse of human selfhood to direct itself towards the true or pretended absolute origin of all the temporal diversity of meaning." [39]

On account of this law of religious concentration, Aristotle's view of man as a rational animal, a being defined in terms of his analytical-logical function, is determined by his view of God as *noesis noesoos*; and Kant's view of noumenal man, as a being qualified by a transcendent moral function, is determined by his moralistic view of God as a postulate of practical reason.

If the selfhood is unable to find the true absolute in God, it is forced to absolutize some aspect of the relative in order to give itself content in the light of the absolutized aspect. In the final analysis religion is absolute self-surrender. The selfhood can only find its own meaning and content in self-surrender to the Absolute God, or in the case of apostasy, to the absolutized relative.

In Dooyeweerd's opinion all theoretical knowledge thus presupposes self-knowledge, while the latter is only possible in religious self-surrender to the one true God or of an absolutized relative aspect of God's creation. The self-knowledge gained in this way is therefore of a religious and not of a theoretical or scientific character. From this Dooyeweerd rightly concludes that theoretical and scientific thought is not self sufficient and the pretended autonomy of scientific thought is therefore exposed as a myth. The content

and direction of theoretical thought are determined by a supra-
theoretical and scientific starting point in which the selfhood parti-
cipates and whence it receives the direction of its activity.

For this reason the Christian scholar must work under the guidance and standards of critical judgment provided in the Holy
Scriptures. If he were to set aside the Word of God as the directing
principle of his life he could no longer claim to apply a Christian
criterion to his studies nor could his own scientific pursuits proceed
in a Christian direction. For the Christian scholar, as for every member of the New Covenant, God's Word is that "arche" or ordering
principle of life the Greek philosophers were forever seeking after;
God's Word is for every Christian the starting point of both his
theoretical and practical activities which governs his life in this
world. It provides him with his Christian principle of interpretation
or *principium*, meaning "beginning," or "origin" for his thinking
and acting in life. Thus the *Shorter Westminster Catechism* asks,
"What rule hath God given to direct us how we may glorify and
enjoy Him?" and it answers, "The Word of God which is contained
in the Scriptures of the Old and New Testaments is the only rule
to direct us how we may glorify and enjoy Him."

According to Dooyeweerd the biblical ground motive or basic presupposition of the creation, fall of man into sin, and his redemption
by Jesus Christ in the communion of the Holy Spirit is the central
motivating and reforming power of every Christian thought or
theory worthy of the name. The Word of God provides those
who accept it with an ordering principle of life that gives order,
coherence, and meaning to all our experience.

For the Christian scholar the Word of God alone is the power
which can inform, i.e., put form and shape into his scholarship.
God's revelation of himself as creator, redeemer and sanctifier revealed in the Scriptures is the power by which He opens up our
hearts to see our human situation in the framework of reality as
it really is by working in us a true knowledge of God, of our
selves and of the law-order and structure of God's creation. The
Word of God thus makes us aware of our place in God's creation

and provides all our science and learning with its proper frame of reference and its only sure point of departure.

Scripture is the Truth of God which reveals to us and makes us see how we stand in relation to God, to our fellow men, and to the world. In its dynamic character God's Word impinges upon our hearts and directs our scientific thinking in the proper direction. Accordingly, although the Scriptures should not be regarded as the source book for the "facts" of science, they would put the set into the scientific saw. The great delusion of scientific humanism is that the saw of science is able to set itself. The Word of God enables us to see the facts studied in the various sciences in their true order, structure, and relationships. The facts do not speak to us unless we see them in their proper order. Thus the Word of God clarifies our view of the world at the outset. It provides us with our archimedean point of departure for all our scientific thought by revealing that we did not arrive on this planet by chance but that God created the universe. When the Bible speaks of creation it does so to reveal to us the central origin, the ultimate source of all reality, and thus it tells us something about reality that man could not discover by means of his own unaided reason. The biblical revelation of creation thus gives us an insight into the "being" or the *Dasein* of reality, viz., its ultimate dependence upon Almighty God. That revelation may never be put upon the same mundane level as the data discovered by research, since in the Christian view this revelation is the very given, the very condition and presupposition of any scientific theories about reality whatsoever. The condition of human knowledge about reality stands on a different level than the effect. This revelatory condition of all human thought and science is what Christians should understand by the claim that the Bible is the Word of God. It is the Word of God because it brings us into touch with the creator or the world and because it makes us see our "place" in God's creation. It is God's Word of Truth about the ultimate nature of things; it tells us who we men are (our heredity); in what kind of location we have been put by God (our environment); and what, in the light of the previous two, we now have to do, namely become reconciled to God through Christ. As such the Word of God is the only true statement by which the nature of our life in this world can be elucidated and its way thus properly directed. As the psalmist says: "Thy Word is a lamp unto my feet" (Psalm 119:105).

What God's Word does not do, of course, is to tell us that there are fourteen or so law-spheres or aspects in God's creation; that is a matter strictly of a scientific analysis. The Bible is not a textbook of science; the purpose and nature of God's Word is not to be scientific but to orient our hearts in the true religious dimension of reality. No less a theologian that John Calvin recognized this truth. To the question, "Is the Bible the final authority on matters scientific?" Calvin replied that when the Spirit of God speaks through the Law and the Prophets He does so not with rigorous exactness, "but in a style suited to the common capacities of man." [40] This of course would not involve the question of miracles, for they are special occurrences for some particular purpose, but for the knowledge of all normal natural happenings Calvin teaches in his great Commentary on Genesis that the study of the phenomena, not of the Scriptures, brings men true knowledge (Gen. 1:16).

W. Stanford Reid, in his fascinating study of *Natural Science in Sixteenth Century Calvinistic Thought*, points out that: "Such an attitude to the Bible and nature meant that Calvin and his followers flatly rejected any form of biblicistic rationalism or mysticism. As Calvin put it: "He who would learn astronomy and other recondite arts, let him go elsewhere." (Comment on Genesis 1:6). . . . It is through the facts of nature that one learns about nature.[41]

Instead the Word of God directs us to take whatever diversity of "modal moments" or aspects we find in the creation as a diversity of the integral fulness of meaning of our religious life. In this way God's revelation of Himself in the Scriptures directs us to the integral creation-order concentrated in man's heart and thus shows us our true place in God's creation. By refusing to accept this ordering principle for their studies apostate scholars have become blind to the true nature of reality. Lacking such a true ordering principle, they are forced to interpret the whole of their experience in terms of one or another aspect which they religiously absolutize instead of in terms of man's covenantal relationship with God. As a result their experience has defied explanation. Yet the reason is not because it has not been given to man "to see" his life and his world, but because apostate scholars have not been standing in the right place to see it properly, that place where all the complex functions of human life assume a meaningful place within the whole creation. That meaningful place is the central place; it is religion; man created and placed before his Creator in a covenantal fellowship with his God to render Him praise and service in his threefold office of God's prophet, priest, and king called to carry out the great cultural and scientific mandate "to have dominion over the earth and to subdue it" in singleness of heart to the Creator's glory.

By describing religion as a "place" we are not referring, of course, to a spatial place, because when we say religion is a place we mean something beyond all merely temporal aspects of reality. Evan Runner points out in *The Bible in Relation to Learning*:

> The word "place" is the bearer of many meanings; it is, as we say, multivocal, as opposed to univocal. It can have any number of modal meanings. For example, when my friend suddenly does something that hurts me I can say that there was no place for such an act, that it was not "fitting." I mean then an ethical "place." I mean that our friendship excludes what he did. Of a musical composition I can hold the opinion that some subordinate motif or part does not belong, does not have a place in the whole. Then I mean an aesthetic "place." . . . besides all these modal meanings of the word "place" there is that fulness or fulfillment of meaning of the word "place" when we speak of place in its central religious sense.[42]

According to the Christian basic religious ground-motive or presupposition the world is not fundamentally the aesthetic "world" or the "world" of science or the "world" of thought or the "world" of sports or the "world" of politics or the "world" of business. These are all "worlds," aspects of man's life in this world, universes of discourse. The world in its deepest sense is the world as it is being re-created and re-formed by Jesus Christ, the world of religion, the world of God's wonderful covenant fellowship with man; the world in which all these other "worlds" or aspects of man's life in God's creation assume their rightful or meaningful place. Nature as such only exists as a functional area of God's creation.

When God asked Adam the question, "Where art thou?" He was not asking, "Behind which bush art thou?" He was saying that He did not find man in the place in which the Lord had put him in the creation. This is the religious meaning of place, and this is what we mean when we claim that man cannot really "see" the world and truly understand the meaning of his life in it unless he stands in his rightful place in God's creation. If man does not stand in this place, then he absolutizes an aspect of creation.

Once we are standing by God's own sovereign grace in this rightful position which is religion, we come to realize the necessity for the reformation of all aspects of modern culture, science, and society. The scriptural ground-motive by which we have become gripped drives us into a struggle with all unreformed elements both in our hearts and in the world around us, not out of any pride in ourselves but out of a deep concern for our fellow man. As Hendrik Hart well puts it:

> The matter of the antithesis is not an inheritance from Hegel nor even an achievement of Kuyper. It is no more than the plain teaching of Scripture with respect to the Christ and the anti-Christ. It seems that in reformed circles this confession of the antithesis is no longer fashionable. We would do well to remember two things before we abolish it. The first is that a denial of the antithesis is a denial of Christ because it is a denial of the anti in anti-Christ. The second is that if we deny the antithetical character of the Spirit of God in relation to every other spirit in the universe we deny the non-believer his chance to realize that he must make a radical turn-about in his life, that he must move in a direction which runs opposite to the one he now follows. The doctrine of the antithesis is not a docrine of pride or of seclusion but a doctrine of love; love for the man whose soul has fallen prey to the spirit of the anti-Christ and who must be made to see that living the life of this spirit is indeed living *anti* Christ.[43]

The Word of God is thus the divine spiritual power which regenerates our hearts and reforms our minds. It is the central ordering principle of the Christian's life and the key to all true knowledge of reality and hence the foundation of a truly Christian culture and society. God's Word alone can provide us with a unified field of knowledge. God's Word alone can make us wise about the conditions of human existence.

(e) The Reformational Understanding of History and Social Change

Before we can study any period of history with any hope of understanding it, we must first define what we mean by history. As Christians we must find our principles of selection of the so-called "historical facts" and ordering principle by means of which to put meaning into such facts in the great scriptural ground-motive of man's creation by Almighty God, man's radical fall into sin, and his equally radical redemption by Jesus Christ in the communion of the Holy Spirit. Only in God's Word can we hope to find an antidote to the modern poison of historical relativism or historicism. In *Renewal and Reflection*, Herman Dooyeweerd writes:

> "Historicism," which allows reality to be absorbed in her historical aspect, is the deadly disease of our "dynamic" age. And no adequate cure will be found against it as long as the Scriptural creation-motif has not completely regained control of our way of life as well as of our thinking. It robs you of your faith in abiding standards; it even preys on your faith in the eternal truth of God's Word. According to historicism all things are relative, all things are *historically* determined, even our faith in ultimate values.[44]

Both the English philosopher of history, R. G. Collingwood, and W. Dilthey, the German philosopher of culture, succumbed to historicism.[45] Having exposed the underlying faith-principles and presuppositions of the various life and world-views which have governed the development of various civilizations and historical societies, they failed to provide a standard by which we could judge which philosophy of life is true and which is false. In his *Essay on Metaphysics* and in his *Autobiography*, as well as in *The Idea of History*, Collingwood suggested that we cannot properly speak of one set of absolute presuppositions as being truer than any other. For since it is the very function of absolute presuppositions to make coherent thinking and historical enquiry possible, it follows that they themselves cannot be established or overthrown by any enquiry. Investigation can never furnish evidence for or against them. And therefore, Collingwood argues, they cannot be judged true or false. The only enquiry which can be made concerning absolute presuppositions or faith principles or ground-motives, as we shall call them, is the enquiry what presuppositions or faith princples or ground-motives are actually adopted by men to guide them at a given time by a given group of thinkers and leaders of a society. And if metaphysics is by definition the science of absolute presuppositions, it must be the history of such absolute presuppositions, for a historical science is the only science of them which is possible.

Dooyeweerd teaches that the only defense against such an uncompromising historical relativism is to realize that historicism is the product of an absolutizing or deification of the historical aspect of reality, as it becomes the object of special research by the science of history. Historicism arises and takes hold on our view of reality whenever the creation motive of God's Revelation in the Bible has ceased to determine and direct our view of reality.

As a result of the abandonment of the biblical creation motive, the historical aspect of reality, in terms of which the science of history investigates the "facts" and events of the past, is identified with history in the concrete sense of "what actually happened in the past" or of what Michael Oakeshott defines in his great book, *Experience and Its Modes*, as "the practical past." The "practical past" may never thus be identified with the historical aspect of reality in terms of which history is today scientifically investigated. The reason is given by Dooyeweerd as follows:

> Concrete events such as wars, famines, revolutions, etc. are a part of concrete reality which functions in principle in all aspects of God's creation without fail. . . . As soon as you identify the historical aspect of reality with that which has happened you forget that concrete history or "the practical past" displays many other aspects which are not themselves of an historical nature. Reality in its broadest sense is then identified with one of the several aspects of creation—the one abstracted by the science of history. Then you become an historicist in your vision of reality and you abandon the scriptural creation-motive.[46]

How then may we distinguish the historical aspect or law-sphere of God's creation from the other law-spheres? Dooyeweerd answers:

> The historical aspect distinguishes itself from the other aspects such as organic life, emotional feeling, logical distinction, etc., not by *what* happens within its realm but by *how* it happens, the manner in which it takes place. For the historian, therefore, the important thing is to discover the modal moment of the historical manner in which a concrete event of the past took place. He needs a criterion to enable him to distinguish the historical aspect from all other modes of reality.[47]

Dooyeweerd finds the modal moment or core of the historical aspect, which guarantees her peculiarity as a "sovereign" science and her irreducibility to any other science in the cultural.

The cultural is the manner in which reality reveals itself in the historical aspect. As used by Dooyeweerd culture refers to all that which owes its existence to human "form-giving," in distinction from that which develops naturally such as a biological organism or a chemical crystal. The design of honeycombs is not a form of culture because it is not developed according to the free choice of design on the part of bees but rather according to the bees' instincts.

The cultural form giving of which historiography seeks to give an account is founded in God's creation and in God's great cultural mandate to man given to him at the beginning of his history to subdue the earth and to have dominion over it. It touches only on the historical aspect of creation, which is subjected to man's cultural formation. As Dooyeweerd makes clear:

> The cultural is the manner in which reality reveals itself in the historical aspect. Usually the word culture is understood to refer to all that which owes its existence to human form giving in distinction from that which develops by virtue of "nature."[48]

Nevertheless this cultural formation is itself merely an aspect of real things, events, etc., and a so-called cultural object such as the American Constitution or Magna Carta functions also in all other aspects of reality which do not bear a cultural character as for example, the numerical, the spatial, the physical, the psychical, the logical-analytical, the lingual, the economic, the aesthetic, and the pistical or faith aspect.

Once we realize that every event of the past functions in all these aspects of reality as well as in the historical-cultural, we need never again become victimized by the relativistic and historicistic attitude.

Only when the biblical motive of creation of the world by God grips our thinking will historicism have lost its control upon our thinking and doing. Only then shall we be in a position to make sense of the "facts" and "events" of the past.

Modern historicism denies the constant structure of the historical aspect itself, in which the divine laws for historical development and cultural unfolding have been enclosed. For the same reason it has no abiding standard by means of which to judge the reactionary and the truly progressive lines of historical development.

What norms then govern the historical aspect?

According to Dooyeweerd's evangelical and scripturally oriented philosophy of history, the norms of history that obtain for the unfolding process of history and culture are (1) historical continuity, (2) cultural differentiation, (3) cultural integration, (4) cultural individualization, and (5) the ground-motive in control of a given culture and society.

Historical Norms and Standards

Dooyeweerd views history as the "opening-up" process which discloses the full meaning of God's creation by making explicit in time the rich modal aspects of God's creation (see chart of the Law-Spheres). In every modal moment of the divine cosmic structure there are given certain principles which should become concretized and emergent in the development of human culture. In a primitive "unhistorical" society and culture, this is not fully accomplished, since the life of primitive man is bound up and identified with the natural, physical, and biological aspects of reality, as is evident in such primitive institutions as totemism, animism, animal art, and tribal organization based upon animal life. As a result of this mytho-poetic identification of himself with nature due to man's radical fall into sin, primitive man had enclosed himself by the natural givenness of reality. That is to say, he did not adequately distinguish between himself and his natural environment. As Henri Frankfort says in *Before Philosophy*:

> The fundamental difference between the attitudes of modern and ancient man as regards the surrounding world is this: for modern scientific man the phenomenal world is primarily an "it"; for ancient—and also for primitive man—the world is looked upon as a "Thou."[49]

As a result of this identification progress and historical development for primitive man became next to impossible, and he became bound by many traditions, superstitions, and tribal mores.

As long as men thus personified natural forces as divine and saw their lives as being embedded in nature they could not develop any sense of the dignity and worth of human nature or conceive of the uniqueness of individuals as persons created in God's holy image. Instead, the individual was constricted by the collectivity of his tribe or clan.

The first step, therefore, for the emergence of both humanism and personalism had to be the emancipation of human thought from primitive superstition and myth. That is to say, before men could discover themselves as individual persons they had to establish a radical discontinuity between themselves and nature; they had to overcome the primitive view which ranged man entirely with nature.

The decisive step in the "opening up" process of human history and cultural differentiation by which this mythopoeic tradition and primitive and ancient collectivism was finally overcome occurred in two societies, namely in ancient Israel, which came under the control of the biblical motive of creation and looked forward to a future redemption by the Messiah, and in ancient Greece. The former established the religious and moral breakthrough, the latter the logical and the scientific. For this reason Matthew Arnold, in *Culture and Anarchy*, in the famous chapter on "Hebraism and Hellenism," wrote:

> Hebraism and Hellenism—between these two points of influence moves our world. At one time it feels more powerfully the attraction of one of them, at another time the other; and it ought

to be, though it never is, evenly and happily balanced between them. The final aim of both Hellenism and Hebraism, as of all great spiritual disciplines, is no doubt the same: man's perfection or salvation . . . their final aim is "that we might be partakers of the divine nature," [50]

Human historical progress and cultural development began to take place when Greek and Hebrew men became open to the higher norms given by God in cosmic structure of creation, beginning with the logical modality or law-sphere. Man had to break through the mythopoeic thought barrier and tribal collectivism into a scientific and religious way of looking at the world before history in the true sense of the word could begin. It is the lasting achievement of the Greeks to have achieved the scientific breakthrough, and of the Hebrews the moral and religious breakthrough. But even when such a breakthrough occurs as in Classical Greece, human sin may still have the effect of opposing the disclosure of the higher aspects of reality in their full religious depths, so that the religious totality of meaning of God's creation was never fully realized by the Greeks throughout their history, while man's rational and logical faculties became absolutized. God was conceived of as the Absolute Nous or Mind.

Dooyeweerd speaks of a meaningful development of culture only when the historical aspect comes into focus. This aspect is the foundation of the entire opening process of the higher modalities and norms. According to Dooyeweerd, culture is the core of this function. Culture, he teaches, is characterized by "form-giving to material which is freely controlled," a form giving according to a free design. He defines the modal moment of the historical aspect of God's creation as "the controlled formation of a given aptitude, structure, or situation to be something which it otherwise would not have been. It is the normative free realization of a thing in the process of culture."

By controlled formation Dooyeweerd intends to convey the idea that every individual does not form history to the same degree. History is primarily formed by the possessors of historical power.

Only by the exercise of such power either over other people or over things can there be a development of a culture.

Without such personal exercise of power a discovery or an invention by means of which we gain control over nature cannot as such, be of history making character. Thus Leonardo da Vinci's discovery of the airplane and the submarine never assumed any historical significance because it remained his private possession. It could have become an effective influence in the making of history only if he had won the support of other people for his invention. But to do that it was necessary to have power-formation and an historical influence which da Vinci had as an artist but not as an inventor or scientist.

Such a use of power in cultural formation is not to be identified with brute force. Misled by this identification many Christians consider it to be unchristian to strive for the acquisition of political power for the purpose of making Christian principles permeate life by means of Christian power organizations.

Such an attitude merely ignores the creation-motive of the Christian religion and makes it impossible to understand Christ's redemptive work in all its full scriptural sense.

The unbiblical nature of this pietistic view should become readily apparent when we remember that God has revealed himself as Creator in the original fulness of power. God is the Almighty One. At creation He gave man the cultural mandate to use his powers to God's glory and the benefit of human need. As a result of the fall the position of power to which God called man took on an idolatrous direction.

Yet Christ the Redeemer revealed himself anew as the One who possesses power in the fullest sense of the word. "All power hath been given me in heaven and earth," Christ told his disciples just before his His ascension into Heaven (Matt. 28:18).

This spiritual power of the gospel differs from the power of the sword of government, and both of them differ radically from the power of science, of art, of love and sex, of industry, etc.

But regardless of the concrete structure in which the historical formation of power reveals itself, it is never brute force. It is always grounded in God's creation, and as such it has nothing demonic about it. Our Lord explicitly calls himself the ruler of the kings of the earth and as the King of Common as well as Special Grace. He rules sovereignly over all the states of this world regardless of whether they acknowledge His sovereignty or not. Christ claims for His service even the power of the sword of government because by means of the sword of justice the earthly state restrains the worst consequences of sin while Christ's Church mediates to men the saving power of the Gospel.

Only sin can place power in the service of the demonic and idolatrous, but this is true of all the other good gifts of God, including our science, our emotions, our legal, educational, and political institutions, woman's beauty, and man's physical strength. Power, in so far as it has been entrusted to man as God's servant, always bears a cultural stamp. It brings with it an historical calling, the task of form giving, of which the bearer of power, whether president, manager, parent, teacher, or even a friend will each one day have to give an account. Every ruler who has ever lived will one day appear before the judgment seat of God.

For this reason power as such may never be used just for the furtherance of one's own personal ambition, as if it were a personal possession. Power has been the driving force behind the cultural development and historical change. The question is: In whose service has it been used, in God's or Satan's, on behalf of one's selfish interest or for the good of the nation and the world?

The formation and exercise of power is subject to essential norms and divine standards, and thus it may not be exercised arbitrarily. Dooyeweerd thus does not agree with historians such as Spengler who conceive of the laws of history as biological laws, so that a civilization once born is bound to grow up, decay, and eventually die. These norms for historical development are of an intrinsically historical nature. For the process of historical development has been placed under certain norms by God himself as the Lord of History as well as of Nature. Both rulers and ruled in each nation are subject to these norms. No nation may claim to be the source of these norms governing its historical development, as the German and English Historical School of the 19th century taught.

The creation motive forces us, as soon as it has taken control of our lives, to recognize that God's Law is sovereign over every sphere of man's life. Man is that being who has been called to obey his Creator. He is created as a responsible being, being answerable to God for all his actions. Unlike the animals, man alone can transgress these norms and directives for his life. The laws governing God's creation up to the logical law-sphere cannot be transgressed; e.g., man cannot transgress the law of gravity. If he jumps off a skyscraper, he falls down rather than up.

In practical life everyone, including apostate liberal humanist historians, sociologists, and lawyers, recognize the relevance and validity of such historical norms as soon as they speak of their opponents as being reactionary. Yet as soon as they call someone else reactionary they are making a value judgment which presupposes the assumption in their minds that they uphold a norm for historical development. It is ironic, to say the least, that the very same "liberals" who teach historical relativism in the lecture room are the very first to brand their conservative political opponents as fascist beasts or right-wing die-hards!

But how do we know that the historical development of a given society or culture is progressive or reactionary? The answer is from the place which God has given to the historical aspect in His creation order.

The distinction between historical and unhistorical, or progressive or reactionary, goes back by analogy to the distinction which we meet with in the logical aspect of reality between a statement which true or false. The historical mode of experience is thus founded in the logical mode of distinguishing our experiences. Without the basis of logical distinction no single historical experience is possible. As an example Dooyeweerd takes the Battle of Waterloo as an historical fact.

> Let us take for example the battle of Waterloo as a historical fact. The famous Austrian economist, Hayek, raised the question whether the work of farmers, who tried desperately to save their crops on the battlefields, also belonged to the battle.
> This question is very instructive. For it proves that our his-

torical mode of experiencing the battle of Waterloo cannot be founded on a record of sensory perception alone. From the sensory viewpoint the work of the farmers took place without a doubt on the battlefield. But, implicitly, we make an analytical, or logical distinction, between the action of persons, whether or not they pertain to the battle as a historical contest of power between Napoleon's forces and those of his allied opponents.[51]

He goes on to point out that the idea of historical develpment is connected with the contrast historical-unhistorical or progressive-reactionary.

> By this contrast we mean that the behavior or program of a leading figure or group is in line with, or contrary to the requirements of historical development. As a clear analogy of the logical relation of contradiction, this contrast implies a normative criterion, so that the concept of historical development must itself have a normative cultural meaning. And since the contrast concerned appeared to be founded in the modal structure of the historical aspect itself, its normative sense cannot be reduced to a merely subjective evaluation of the factual course of history. Rather it must be founded on an objective norm of historical development which implicitly lies at the foundation of the cultural historical mode of experience.[52]

All the aspects which follow the logical aspect have their own normative character in contrast to the pre-logical which are a-normative. Norms are only possible to creatures endowed with the ability to make rational distinctions between true or false, i.e., with the power to think logically.

These norms have been laid down in principle at creation as the principial starting points for human conduct. And as such they demand to be positivized or made concrete by human agents in terms of the historical situation in which they find themselves. This process of giving form to the norms laid down at creation must always correspond to the historical level of development of a given nation or people. For in the process of form giving all the other aspects of human life are intertwined with the historical aspect. This process always goes back to the cultural form giving at a given level of historical development. It is in this sense, for instance, that the basic principles of etiquette call for further development. King Henry

VIII of England used to eat his dinner with his bare hands. Such behavior is no longer considered to be in good taste unless you happen to have returned to medieval conduct. Likewise, the ground rules of language and grammar call for further form-giving in the lingual law-sphere. The English we speak today is vastly different from the English of Chaucer; likewise, the ground rules for economic behavior have developed since medieval times, and the canons for aesthetic appreciation have developed in the structure of modern design, art, and music.

Because of the inseparable coherence between all the later aspects and the historical aspect, it begins to appear, as soon as the creation motive of God's Word looses its hold upon our thinking, as if all forms of social life, language, economics, art, justice, and religious belief are basically historically determined and of historical origin. As soon as we thus absolutize the historical aspect and seek to explain all the other aspects in terms of it, we lose our hold on reality and become the slaves of cultural relativism and historicism. Thus does God the Holy Ghost blind our eyes to the Truth when we refuse to abide in the Truth of God's Holy Word.

Only the creation motive of God's Word which constantly impresses upon us that God created all things after their own kind can prevent us from falling into this relativistic and historicistic trap and error. Again the scriptural revelation that God created everything each after its own kind sharpens our ability to distinguish the various aspects of reality and we no longer seek a monistic answer to the problems of life and of change.

And so, for instance, it becomes impossible that justice in its human formulation can be reduced to history without destroying its nature as justice. The making of history calls for power on the part of those who are called to the task of form giving to the basic principles of culture. The construction of a code of laws, for instance, as is done by such law-givers as Justinian or Napoleon, calls for legal power and competence. But such juridical power cannot be reduced to power in a historical sense. As soon as we attempt to do that, we place justice and power on the same level, thus negating justice. Right becomes might.

The fact that the German Nazi Party taught that a nation proves its right to exist by means of an historical struggle for power and the "survival of the fittest nation," was a typical outcome of an historicistic view of life. "Right is Might" was and still is the basic slogan of the political views of Communism. Such teaching is all the more dangerous since it contains an element of truth in it. For it is true that within the history of the world God's judgments of various nations has been taking place. Thus the Lord of History used the power of Assyria and Babylon to punish Israel and Judah, of the German barbarians to punish the Romans, of the Spaniards to punish the Italian city states at the time of the Renaissance, and of the Allied armies in the Second World War to defeat Nazism. But this never happens in the sense that justice dissolves itself in power.

It is true, however, that within the framework of juridical power the legal aspect of reality coheres inseparably with the historical aspect. Without power in history in the historical sense of military might and the police power, power in the juridical sense cannot exist. "Covenants without the Sword are but words." Nevertheless both of them must be differentiated according to their own inner nature.

Historical development serves, when seen in the light of the creation motive of God's Word to bring the richness of God's creation structures into focus in the cultural aspect of reality and to full differentiated development. For the individual character of the separate creation structures and law-spheres can only come to completion and be made manifest in time in the differentiation of culture.

Historical development simply means this unfolding process by means of the norm of the differentiation of God's higher law-aspects. History is the womb of time which brings forth the richness of His creation structures and makes their existence possible. In this way there gradually emerged out of the undifferentiated closed society of primitive man the state, the Church, university, medieval guild, and modern business enterprise and modern labor union. But this process of coming into being presupposes God's original creation of these creation structures and social ordinances; it is indeed only the fulfillment and realization of the latter in time. And time is itself part of God's creation.

This process of coming into being is thus not something independent over against God's creation but an essential part of God's world plan. Just as the development of a child begins from the still undifferentiated germ cell in the mother's womb, out of which the different organs of the child's body become differentiated, so in human society and history the development begins with undifferentiated social forms such as the gens, tribe, and primitive collectivity. After a lengthy process of development it "opens out" into the differentiated societal structures of modern times. And this differentiation fulfills itself according to its historical aspect by means of a branching off or opening up process of culture in which the power spheres of church, state, science, business, school appear upon the stage of world history. Such differentiation of culture of necessity terminates the absolute and exclusive power of the primitive undifferentiated spheres of life.

The norm of cultural differentiation thus requires that in the development of civilization from a primitive phase, the new forms of association and community must become concretized into new social forms. In man's historical development out of primitive undifferentiated social groupings he gradually found greater freedom in the emergence of separate cultural spheres, e.g., Plato's Academy, Israel's school of prophets, medieval universities, Renaissance artists colonies and workshops, modern businesses, theatres, newspapers. All of these separate cultural spheres are valid concretizations within the temporal world order of the structural principles given at creation. The historical norm of differentiation thus guarantees the individualizing tendency of persons, nations, and societal relationships. As a normative law-sphere this norm requires positivization or specification. It is not possible to determine beforehand what ought to emerge in a given societal relationship. It is up to the cultural leaders and statesmen who possess historical power to formulate the concrete requirements of culture for their own day, but their power must not be exercised arbitrarily. But since the historical sphere is normative, violations of historical norms are possible, and leaders and statesmen may fail to act normatively. Conservative "reaction" against necessary social changes brought about by scientific and technological advance within a given society is anti-normative. Reactionaries praise the good old days and, if they had their way, would roll back the progress of cultural and social advance. By the same token, left-wing revolutionaries are also anti-normative. The revolutionary intentionally breaks with the historical past and disavows the norm of continuity of history. He would dare to sweep the cultural slate clean and start de novo; e.g., the French Revolution, Hitler's New Order, and Lenin's and Stalin's and Mao Tse Tung's New Communist Paradise.

The process by which the cultural aspect of a society is opened up always occurs in a conflict between the guardians of tradition and the propounders of new ideas. The formative power of tradition is enormous, for, in a concentrated form it embodies cultural treasures and wisdom amassed over hundreds of years. Every generation is historically bound to former generations by its tradition. We are all dominated by it to a much greater extent than we often realize. In a primitive closed society its power is nearly absolute. In an "open society," tradition is no longer unassailable, but it has the indispensable function of guarding that measure of continuity in cultural progress without which cultural life would be impossible.

In the struggle with the power of tradition the progressive ideas of new cultural leaders have themselves to be purged of their revolutionary subjectivity and adjusted to the great norm of historical continuity. Even Jacob Burckhardt held to the norm of continuity as a last guarantee against the decline of all civilization.

The norm of continuity demands that cultural form-giving must give due respect to tradition as well as to progress. Progress takes place when the principles contained in the post-historical law-spheres are realized in human society. But this realization must not occur in a revolutionary fashion destroying what is good in the tradition of the past. The past must serve as the basis for the new advance. Thus the invention of the automobile must not be allowed to destroy our respect for the sanctity of innocent human life. Today reformers complain about the execution of murderers but not about the enormous slaughter on America's highways. We have anti-war and anti-execution resolutions in plenty, but one has yet to hear of any for the suppression of the automobile. Why not? Why is the one kind of killing by automobiles condoned and the other condemned? Is it because the pleasure and the profit of the one exceed those of the other? Is it that the moral sense must give way to convenience? Why does this wholesale slaughter of the innocents not distress our progressives at all, while the thought of the execution of a few murderers a year nearly drives them around the bend?

The opening process of cultural life is characterized by the destruction of the undifferentiated and exclusive power of primitive communities. It is a process of cultural differentiation which is balanced by an increasing cultural integration. From one point of view the role of the state in history can be looked upon as a role of integration. The state appears in the arena of history when primitive, feudal, or tribal power-structures are broken up by new cultural forces guided by statesmen and rulers to make place for the state's monopoly of the power of the sword of justice and of political and police power. At this early stage of the state's development it becomes apparent to the new monarchs of Western Europe in the later Middle Ages that political and legal power must no longer be considered the "private property" of those who happen to own extensive territories, but that the ownership of land or other feudal "privileges" must not become the basis for the exercise of political power. Instead the exercise of the latter comes to be seen as a public matter, a *res publica*. We can detect the origins of this legal and political development in the rise of the Roman *Res Publica* on the basis of the earlier tribal political organization in the years 600 to 200 B.C. It is apparent aslo in the rise of the modern nation state at the close of the Middle Ages. The first thinker to refer to it was Jean Bodin. According to Bodin the aim of the state is the maintenance of law and order upon the basis of the king's absolute sovereignty. He defined the state as "the right government of several families, and of what is common to them, with sovereign power." The word "right" in this definition implied that the power is exercised for the common good. Sovereignty he defined as the "absolute and perpetual power in a repub-

lic." Bodin was concerned to distinguish between the French no-
bility's rights to property and their claim to exercise rights of
jurisdiction based upon their feudal land tenure. He insisted that
they are quite different in kind, since the first kind are exercised for
the sake of the second kind. No public office can be a part of any
man's private estate, and whoever exercises rights of jurisdiction
holds a public office. To hold any public office, except the highest,
is to be the agent of whoever holds the highest office in the state,
namely the sovereign himself. Bernard Zylstra points out that we can
see a similar process of political integration at work in the new
nation-states of Asia and Africa. He adds:

> That this mandatory process of political integration—in a sinful
> world—is often accompanied by a severe struggle between feudal
> or tribal power and the new nation-state is tragically illustrated
> today by Vietnam and the Biafran conflicts. Political integration
> can be obstructed by an exaggerated and anachronistic stress upon
> the autonomy of the parts of the state at the expense of the whole.
> This was evident in Germany's and Italy's struggle toward state-
> hood in the early 19th Century.[53]

The opening-up process of culture is characterized by the destruction of the undifferentiated and exclusive power of primitive
communities. It is a process of cultural differentiation which is balanced by an increasing cultural integration. Since August Comte,
Herbert Spencer, and Emile Durkheim, the criterion of differentiation and integration has been accepted by many historians and sociologists to distinguish more highly developed from primitive societies. The process of differentiation was viewed as a consequence
of the division of labor, and an attempt was made to explain it in
a natural scientific manner in analogy to the increasing differentiation
of organic life in the higher developed organisms. The Reformational perspective on historical change does not understand the term
"cultural differentiation" in this pseudo-naturalistic sense. Human
societies are not biological organisms Thus Dooyeweerd points out
that by cultural differentiation he understands:

> . . . a differentiation in the typical structures of the different
> social relationships presenting themselves in human society. A

primitive sib or clan displays mixed traits of an extended family, a business organization, a club or a school, a state, a religious community, and so forth. In a differentiated society, on the other hand, all these communities are sharply distinguished from one another, so that each of them can reveal its proper inner nature, notwithstanding the fact that there are all kinds of interrelations between them. Each of these differentiated communities has its own typical historico-cultural sphere of formative power, whose inner boundaries are determined by the inner nature of the communities to which they belong.

The typical structures of these communities are really structures of individuality, since they are typical structures of an individual societal whole. With the exception of the natural communities such as marriage and family, which have a typical biological foundation, they are all typically founded in historico-cultural power formations, which presuppose the process of cultural differentiation and integration. Consequently, although they cannot be realized before this historical process has started, their typical structures can no more be variable than the modal structures of their different aspects, since they determine the inner nature of the differentiated communities. As such, they must be founded in the order of creation, which has determined the inner nature of all that is present within our temporal world. . . .

In the temporal world-order norms are only given as principles which need a formation by man in accordance with the level of historical development of a differentiated society. The social forms which they assume in this way, are consequently of a variable character; but the structural principles, to which these forms give a variable positive content, are not variable historical phenomena, since they alone make all variable formations of the societal communities possible. Neither the inner nature of marriage, nor that if the family, the state, the church, an industrial community, and the like are variable in time, but only the social form in which they are realized.[54]

The great German Historical school of jurisprudence in the 19th century, led by Karl Von Savigny, started from the absolute individuality of any socio-cultural community, especially the nation-state. It personified the people or nation as the basic denominator of every human society and social activity, thereby proclaiming one temporal human relation as the whole of which all the other societal relations of church, art, science, education, the business firm are but subservient parts. According to Dooyeweerd, this absolutization of the nation-state is completely at variance with the fundamental motive of the Christian religion. Only God can thus claim to be the absolute sovereign. No bearer of authority on this earth is the highest power from which other forms of authority are derived. Ultimate sovereignty belongs only to God.

The historical school of law not only ignored God's ultimate and absolute sovereignty, but it also overlooked the typical structures of individuality which determine the inner nature of the communities, and which, as such, cannot be of a variable historical character. Nevertheless it is true that the process of cultural differentiation and integration is at the same time a process of increasing individualization of human culture, in so far as it is only in a culture which has been opened up and differentiated that individual personality assumes a really historical significance. While it is true that in a primitive closed society such individual personality is not lacking, the power of tradition and custom is such that individuality remains restricted. Innovation is not welcomed in such a closed society, and pressure is continually exerted upon the individual to conform with custom.

As soon, however, as the process of differentiation and integration commences, the individual emerges upon the stage of history as a person in his own right and personal talents become welcomed. It was Burckhardt's thesis that the Renaissance meant the re-discovery of individual personality. He quotes Pico Della Mirandola's famous oration on "The Dignity of Man" in which Pico argued that man's existence precedes his essence, which he makes himself.

It is the state's task of political and legal integration to provide the legal and political framework in which such individuality can express itself. On the basis of the state as a public-legal entity it becomes possible to protect human individuality from absorption into collectivistic power-structures. In the history of Western states the Christian conception of man as created in God's image has been legally safeguarded by such laws as habeas corpus, freedom of conscience and worship; in short, all the civil rights guaranteeing an area of freedom for human personality on the basis of equality. Here lies the historical significance of the American Bill of Rights, adopted soon after the ratification of the American Constitution, and the Universal Declaration of Human Rights adopted by the United Nations in 1948.

According to the Reformational perspective on history, such rights find their foundation in the divine creation order which channels the growth of individual and communal liberties in history. Civil rights, therefore, do not find their source in the state. The state, rather, if it is a constitutional law-state rather than a power-hungry totalitarian state, is the divinely appointed instrument for implementing human rights (Rom. 13). Nevertheless this implementation requires a ripening process. Thus Paul in his letter to Philemon did not advise Onesimus to run away from his master, but to return, but he called upon both to accept each other as brothers for whom Christ died. Some modern liberal Christians have read this letter with surprise and disappointment. They feel that Paul should have seized this opportunity to call for the abolition of slavery. Commenting upon this modern attitude, Emil Brunner points out in *Justice and the Social Order*:

> Paul was by no means restoring his protege to slavery. He had a quite different fate in mind for him, and was striving to obtain it. But what he wanted, he wanted not only for the slave, but for his master Philemon too. The new thing was only to be achieved by a transformation in both. He calls on Philemon to receive his slave as he would receive the Apostle himself, to whom, like his slave, he owes his Christian faith. He wishes to see the relationship between Onesimus and his master based not on justice, but on love, on the love by which Paul is bound not only to the slave Onesimus but also to his master Philemon. . . . The new relationship is to spring from Christian love, the love which unites all three, the whole household, the whole Christian community. . . . What rises before our eyes is the picture of a Christian fellowship of love which leaves far beneath it anything that enters the systems of justice. The institution or order of slavery is dissolved from within and replaced by the order of fellowship in love. . . . The problem of the injustice of slavery fades into the background. Without even being mentioned, it has been solved by something which no claim for justice can achieve, by fellowship in Jesus Christ.[55]

For this reason the content of human rights may well differ in time and place, depending upon the historical situation and the level of human sensitivity to other peoples' sufferings. This gives us a more flexible approach to the problems created by human sin and rapid social change. In the developing Afro-Asian states we simply cannot expect a fully implemented system of civil rights, as we can in the so-called "civilized" Western nations. Until these nations also undergo a great spiritual revolution we cannot expect them to treat individuals with the same concern and respect which Western nations do after a thousand years of prodding by God's Word in the power of the Holy Spirit. Nevertheless, if the age-long hold of tyranny and superstition is to be overcome we must work and pray that the norm of individualization and personal freedom will also be realized in due course in Asia and Africa. The Christian understanding of justice implies that in the long run the state will maintain law and order protecting the rights of minorities against exploitation by majorities The state's main task, in fact, is to integrate, that is, hold the ring and see that no one community or association seeks to ride rough shod over the rights and liberties of other groups or individuals.

The confusion in contemporary sociological thought about such matters as race relations and treatment of minorities arises from the fact that it takes place largely within the conceptual social thinking of Rousseau's apostate social philosophy Rousseau's social philosophy lost sight of the great social spheres of family, church, school, etc., and conceived of society as composed of absolute individuals over against the absolute sovereign state, endowed with a "general will." When the biblical cultural norm of differentiation is taken into account the polarity of individualism versus collectivism is in principle eliminated. This norm requires that as soon as the historical unfolding process has begun the various social structures must be sharply distinguished but not separated from each other, so that each can display its proper character for the enrichment of human culture. *The structure of society, therefore, in the state of cultural and historical differentiation is not individualistic as conservatives suppose nor collectivistic as liberals and socialists suppose, but pluralistic.*

Whenever these great norms governing the unfolding of history are ignored or transgressed then society suffers. Many examples come to mind to prove Hegel's dictum that "the history of the world is the judgment of the world." Whenever men choose to violate these normative principles to which the unfolding process of the cultural historical aspect of human society is subject, then these norms are avenged by social misery, chaos, and upheaval. As Dooyeweerd says:

> It was, an unmistakable proof of the reactionary character of the myth of blood and soil propagated by German Nazism that it tried to undermine the national consciousness of the Germanic peoples by reviving the primitive ethnic idea of *Volkstum*. Similarly, it is an unmistakable proof of the retrograde tendency of all modern totalitarian political systems that they attempt to annihilate the process of cultural differentiation and individualization by a methodical mental equalizing of all cultural spheres; for this equalizing implies a fundamental denial of the value of the individual personality in the unfolding (opening-up) process of history.
>
> So we may posit that the norm of cultural differentiation, integration and individualization is really an objective norm of the historical unfolding process of human society. It is founded in the divine world-order, since it indicates the necessary conditions of this prospective unfolding process, without which mankind cannot fulfill its historical task committed to it by the great cultural commandment. Furthermore, it provides us with an objective criterion to distinguish truly progressive from reactionary tendencies in history.[56]

In the last resort the whole direction which the unfolding process of culture and society displays is determined by the faith motivating the leaders of a given society. The religious ground-motive of the whole cultural development of an historical era manifests itself first of all in the faith of those who are called to mold history. The disclosure of the normative spheres is in the last instance dependent on the disclosing function of faith, which has no anticipatory functions but is a window opening out onto eternity. Among the normative spheres the historical occupies a unique position, for it reveals itself as the foundation of all normative disclosure. Only with historical and cultural development is the disclosure of the higher spheres made possible; e.g., historical consciousness, a differentiated economic life, a deepened conception of law. Dooyeweerd teaches that the disclosure of the normative spheres demands both retrocipations on the historical and anticipations of faith.

In primitive life the restrictive function of faith finds its expression in the absolutization of the pre-logical aspects of reality. Here the forces of nature are deified in such practices as mana, totemism, magic, etc. In civilized communities man creates his idol in the image of the normative functions of his own personality, for example, the Greek deification of man's intellectual functions or *Nous* or the Marxist deification of man's tool-making productive functions. In claiming that man today is "an industrial animal" Ernest Gellner in *Thought and Change* has fallen into the same apostate trap.[57] As a result of all such absolutizations the opening up process of history develops along deformed rather than reformed lines.

In his book, *History and the Gospel*, C. H. Dodd of Cambridge writes:

> At the present time, the existence of the Church has become one of the crucial problems of European civilization. . . . The Church, whether as a stone of stumbling and a rock of offense, or as the headstone of the corner, is destined to be a determining factor in contemporary events.
>
> Whatever part the Church has played in the crises of history, whether negative or positive, whether conservative or revolutionary, it is always a disturbing factor, upsetting human calculations and opening up unforeseen possibilities. It is a standing protest against any conception of history as a closed order, naturally determined. For it witnesses to the creative energies of God in this world, and offers itself to Him as an instrument of His good pleasure. It is in the Church, so far as it realizes its vocation, that history is made, not by us but by the power of God. History is finally to be judged not as a simple succession in time, but as a process determined by the creative act of God vertically from above—if we must use spatial metaphors——and not by the *vis a tergo* of physical and psychological causation. . . . History is "sacred history." Whenever the Gospel is proclaimed, it brings about a crisis, as in the experience of the individual, so also in the experience of whole communities and civilizations. Out of the

crisis (judgment) comes a new creation by the power of God.
. . . The events recorded in the biblical record are presented as a
history of the dealings of God with men. . . . As such, the
biblical history is denominated by German theologians, *Heilsge-
schicte*, that is history as a redemptive process . . . as "sacred
history." [58]

C. H. Dodd continues:

It is important to bear in mind that the same events enter into
sacred and secular history; the events are the same, but they form
two distinguishable series.

The empirical series which is secular history extends over all
recorded time, to our own day, and is still unfinished. In this
series events are linked together by succession in time, and by the
operation of efficient causes, whether these be physical or psychological. . . .

But there is another series into which the historical events may
fall, that which I have called "sacred history," or history as a
process of redemption and revelation. Of this series biblical history forms the inner core. But the Bible always assumes that the
meaning of this inner core is the ultimate meaning of all history,
since God is the Maker and Ruler of all mankind, who created
all things for Himself and redeemed the world to Himself. That
is to say, the whole of history is in the last resort sacred history,
or *Heilsgeschict*.[59]

In terms of this biblical perspective we must therefore view history
not only as the expression of man's reaction to a divinely given mandate but also as the record of God's dealings with the human race.
Dooyeweerd also teaches that no sense can be made of secular history without understanding it in the light of sacred biblical history,
and that it is man's faith either in the God of the Bible or in some
false idol of his own devising which determines whether man's cultural activities will be blessed or come under God's judgemt. He
writes:

When finally the question is asked what is the deepest cause of
disharmony in the opening up process of history we come face to
face with the problem concerning the relationship between faith
and culture and with the religious basic motives which operate
in the central sphere of life. The disharmony in question belongs,
alas, to the progressive line of cultural development, since it can

only reveal itself in the historical opening-up process of cultural differentiation. In a primitive closed culture the conflicts and tensions which are in particular to be observed in modern Western civilization cannot occur. As a consequence of the fact that any expansion of the formative power of mankind gives rise to an increasing manifestation of human sin, the historical opening-up process is marked by blood and tears, and it does not lead to an earthly paradise.

What, then, is the sense in all this endeavour, conflict and misery to which man submits in order to fulfill his cultural task in the world? Radical historicism, as it manifested itself in all its consequences in Spengler's *Decline of the West*, deprived the history of mankind of any hope for the future and made it meaningless. This is the result of the absolutization of the historical aspect of experience; for we have seen that the latter can only reveal its significance in an unbreakable coherence with all the other aspects of our temporal experiential horizon; and this horizon itself refers to the human ego as its central point of reference both in its spiritual communion with all other human egos and in its central relationship to the Divine Author of all that has been created.

In the ultimate issue *that* problem of the meaning of history revolves on the central question: Who is man himself and what is his origin and his final destination? Outside of the biblical basic motive of creation, the fall and redemption through Jesus Christ, no real answer is, in my opinion, to be found to this question. The conflicts and dialectical tensions which occur in the process of the opening up of human culture result from the absolutization of what is relative. And every absolutization takes its origin from the spirit of apostasy, from the spirit of the *civitas terrena*, as Augustine called it.

There would be no future for mankind for the whole process of man's cultural development, if Jesus Christ had not become the spiritual center of world history. This center is bound neither to the Western nor to any other civilization, but it will lead the new mankind as a whole to its true destination, since it has conquered the world by the love revealed in Christ's self-sacrifice.[60]

In this chapter we have sought to establish a scriptural criterion both for the norms of historical change and for man's social structures. Society in all its aspects is a product of *human* cultural formation. Society is not a *natural* but a *cultural* entity. As we have shown, this means that any conception of social change must be rooted in a conception of history, and this, in turn, requires a foundation in a scripturally oriented idea of divine creation. According to God's Word all aspects of reality find their ultimate origin in God's creation (Gen. 1:1; Job 41:11; John 1:3,4; Col. 1:16). Accordingly, human history and culture ought to be the expression of God's cultural mandate, which requires human implementation in the historical unfolding process of culture and society. Man is called by God to make both his own history and his own society. Neither history nor society are the products of an evolutionary process, as apostate historians and sociologists suppose, but rather represent various types of response of man to his cultural task in God's creation. A society will develop harmoniously if man carries out his task in obedience both to God's creational structures and to His historical norms.

Social disorganization will take place whenever these structures and norms are out of harmony with God's will for man and out of balance with each other. If, for example, the norm of differentiation results in social injustice, then it needs re-directing along its proper tendency.

In the history of sociological thought Karl Marx laid all the emphasis upon the structural features of society, while Max Weber emphasized the cultural norms. Marx argued that the ideological superstructure of society was built up on the material basis of a society, and reflected the techniques of production in use at any given period of history, and the mode of production to which these techniques gave rise. Ideology or cultural norms and values he taught could only hasten or retard the process of change, but they could not in the long run stand against it.

Max Weber, on the other hand, maintained that ideological and normative changes were a necessary pre-condition for the rise of modern capitalism, and attributed the emergence of "the spirit of capitalism" to the influence of Calvinism. Weber,that is, tried to refute Marx by explaining economic changes in the modes of production by changes which took place at the Reformation in Christianity. According to Weber the behavior of men in various societies is intelligible only in the context of their general conception of existence. Religious dogmas and their interpretation are an integral part of the world views that render the behavior of groups, including their economic behavior, intelligible. Religious conceptions, as a matter of historical fact, had played a decisive part in determining economic behavior and Weber therefore concluded they must be considered a cause of economic change.

In the light of our reformational sociology we can realize that both men were correct in what they affirmed and wrong in what they denied. Marx was concerned with the importance of structures and Weber with the importance of cultural norms. The former had absolutized the economic aspect of reality and the other the historical. In actual fact social change cannot be understood without reference to both. Culture in general and socio-economic-political structures in particular reflect human ideas and ideals. The political order; the economic order of society; relations between races, employers, and employees; developed and under-developed nations, etc.—all are expressions of man's view of the nature of the universe and of his society, which in turn gives rise to views concerning what validates society's arrangements or "symbols of legitimation."

Men have sought to validate the social order and its cultural norms *within* this world or in a revelation from another. Of the former Ernest Gellner asks in *Thought and Change*:

> Within the flux and uncertainties, the rivalries and oppositions and complexities of *this* world, where is one to seek the firm base, the premise on which one can rest, the criterion to which one may apply? [61]

The answer is that most humanist thinkers in their quest for basic principles have raised some aspect of the universe to the status of being absolute and then sought to explain everything else in terms of it. It is the firm conviction of the writer that we should look outside the universe for the key to its meaning and of the nature of man's life in society. The key can be found only in the biblical revelation.

The reformation for which we are encouraged to work, to pray, and to hope on the basis of Christ's finished work on the Cross, as the years of grace flow on, is not the emergence of a more consecrated type of Christian character than past ages have to show us. There is in this respect no carry-over from generation to generation, but every individual Christian must make a new beginning for himself. It is only insight and understanding of God's creational norms and structures for our lives and societies that are cumulative, and while this means that a new generation of Christians is likely to be confronted with new, and in a sense, more advanced alternatives than were presented to the old, it does not mean that the former is any more likely than the latter to act according to the divine wisdom and knowledge which is hid in Christ Jesus. If today we can see further than our Christian forebears did, it is only because we are standing on their shoulders. What may legitimately be hoped for, as the pattern of the years of grace unfolds itself, is not the emergence of a better race of Christians, but a wider and fuller understanding of the tasks to which God's people must devote themselves in their service of Jesus Christ; not a more scrupulous conscientiousness but an enlarged and better instructed conscience; a conscience enlightened by God's Word in the power of the Holy Spirit.

By what standard does the Christian evaluate the changes which take place in history? How can we tell whether any given change is for the better or for the worse? The word "progress' may be used to connote a continued movement or series of changes in any given direction, as when we speak of our progress on a journey, of the progress of a disease, or even, with Hogarth, of the Rake's Progress.

Must not the Christian be concerned with progress as a movement in the direction deemed most desirable, a continued change for the better? And where else can he find the criterion for such an evaluation except in the Word of God made flesh? The further progress for which all Christians must work and pray can only be that which radiates from the Christian center of history, and this means the progressive embodiment in the life of humanity and of society of the mind that was in Christ Jesus and "a growing up in all things unto Him who is the Head . . . till we all come in the unity of the faith and of the knowledge of the Son of God, unto a perfect man, unto the measure of the stature of the fulness of Christ" (Eph. 4: 13-15).

CHAPTER ONE NOTES

1. F. S. C. Northrop, *The Meeting of East and West* (Macmillan, New York, 1947), p. 10.
2. *Ibid.*, p. 6. Cf. F. S. C. Northrop, *The Logic of the Sciences and the Humanities* (Macmillan, New York, 1948), p. 328ff.
3. *Ibid.*, p. 14. Cf. George A. Lundberg, *Can Science Save Us?* (D. Mackay, 2nd ed., New York, 1962).
4. *Ibid.*, p. 70ff. With Northrop's high claims for natural science should be compared the more modest claims made by J. W. N. Sullivan in *The Limitations of Science* in which he writes: "Science has become self-conscious and comparatively humble. We are no longer taught that the scientific method of approach is the only valid method of acquiring knowledge about reality. Eminent men of science are insisting, . . . on the fact that science gives us but a partial knowledge of reality, and we are no longer required to regard as illusory everything that science finds itself able to ignore" (Mentor Books, New York, 1949, p. 138). Also John MacMurray, *The Boundaries of Science* (Faber and Faber, London, 1939), pp. 72-113.
5. Herman Dooyeweerd, *Renewal and Reflection*, translated from *Vernieuwing en Bezinning* (Zutphen, Holland, 1959), p. 6.
6. *Ibid.*, p. 7. Cf. H. A. Hodges, *Christianity and the Modern World View* (SCM Press, London, 1949), "The Abrahamic Presupposition," pp. 20-29
7. *Ibid.*, p. 8. Cf. N. Macnicol, *Is Christianity Unique?*
8. Hugo Grotius, *De Iure Belli ac Pacis*, Proleg, 11. Cf. Paul Hazard, *The European Mind, 1680-1715* (Penguin Books, London, 1964), pp. 310-312.
9. Walter Lippman, *The Public Philosophy* (Mentor Books, New York, 1956), p. 81ff.
10. Evan Runner, *Can Canada Tolerate the C.L.A.C.?* (Christian Labour Association of Canada, Rexdale, Ontario, 1967), p. 8.
11. Michael Oakeshott, *Rationalism in Politics* (Methuen, London, 1967), p. 3ff.
12. Robert A. Nisbet, *Community and Power* (Oxford University Press, New York, 1968), pp. 145-151.
13. Raymond Aron, *Main Currents in Sociological Thought* (Pelican, London, 1968), Vol. I, pp. 63-109. Cf. Robert A. Nisbet, *The Sociological Tradition* (New York, 1967).
14. In 1 *Sent.* d. 2, q, 8 (U. Geyer, 577), quoted by David Knowles, *The Evolution of Medieval Thought* (Longmans, London, 1962), p. 322.
15. Thomas Hobbes, *Leviathan*, edited by M. Oakeshott (Blackwell, Oxford, 1946), p. 82.

16. *Ibid.*, p. 172ff.
17. Talcott Parsons, *The Structure of Social Action* (The Free Press, New York, 1967), p. 93.
18. Robert A. Nisbet, *op. cit.*, pp. 131-136.
19. Elie Halevy, *The Growth of Philosophical Radicalism*, trans. by Mary Morris (Faber & Groeger, London, 1928), p. 19.
20. John Locke, *The Second Treatise of Civil Government*, edited by J. W. Gough (Blackwell, Oxford, 1946), p. 5ff.
21. Herman Dooyeweerd, *A New Critique of Theoretical Thought* (Presbyterian and Reformed Publishing Co., Philadelphia, 1957), Vol. III, p. 168.
22. *Ibid.*, p. 169. Cf. Robert D. Knudsen, *Sociology* (Westminster Seminary Syllabus).
23. G. E. Wright, *The Biblical Doctrine of Man in Society* (SCM Press, London, 1954), p. 96.
24. Abraham Kuyper, *Principles of Sacred Theology* (Eerdmans, Grand Rapids, 1954), p. 143ff.
25. Cornelius Van Til, *A Christian Theory of Knowledge* (Syllabus, Westminster Seminary, Philadelphia, 1957), p. 27.
26. Dooyeweerd, *op. cit.*, Vol. I, p. 47.
27. Evan Runner, *The Bible in Relation to Learning* (Association for Advancement of Christian Studies, Toronto, 1967), p. 24.
28. Dooyeweerd, *op. cit.*, Vol. I, p. 548. Cf. Rousas J. Rushdoony, *The Mythology of Science.*
29. *Ibid.*, p. 549. Cf. John Rex, *Key Problems of Sociological Theory* (1968), p. 96ff.
30. *Ibid.*, p. 549.
31. *Ibid.*, p. 550. Cf. C. W. Mills, *The Sociological Imagination*, (1959), p. 57ff.
32. J. D. Dengerink, "The Christian and the University," in *The International Reformed Bulletin* (No. 23, Oct. 1965, Grand Rapids, Michigan).
33. A. Kuyper, *op. cit.*, pp. 97-131.
34. A. Kuyper, *Lectures on Calvinism* (Eerdmans, Grand Rapids, 1943), p. 133.
35. *Ibid.*, p. 133.
36. A. Kuyper, *De Gemeene Gratie*, Vol. I, p. 7. Cf. C. Van Til, *Common Grace* (Presbyterian and Reformed, Philadelphia, 1954).
37. Ernst Cassirer, *An Essay on Man* (Doubleday Anchor Book, New York, 1953). Cf. Viktor Frankl, *Man's Search for Meaning* (London, 1964).
38. Dooyeweerd, *op. cit.*, Vol. I, p. 11.
39. *Ibid.*, p. 57. Cf. B. J. Haan, *Scripturally Oriented Higher Education* (Dordt College, Sioux Center, Iowa 51250, 1967).
40. John Calvin, *Commentary on the Psalms* (Eerdmans, Grand Rapids, 1960), in his comment on Psalm 19:4.

41. Stanford Reid, *Christianity and Scholarship* (Craig Press, Nutley, N. J., 1966), p. 69.
42. Evan Runner, *The Bible in Relation to Learning*, p. 28.
43. Hendrik Hart, *The Challenge of Our Age* (Association for the Advancement of Christian Studies, 1968), p. 71.

    For books vindicating the full authority of the Bible as the living Word of God the reader should consult the following:

    Arnold de Graff and Calvin Seerveld, *How to Read the Bible* (Association for Advancement of Christian Studies, 1969).

    Clark H. Pinnock, *A Defense of Biblical Infallibility* (Presbyterian and Reformed, Nutley, N. J., 1967).

    James I. Packer, *"Fundamentalism" and the Word of God* (Intervarsity Christian Fellowship, London, 1963).

    Edward J. Young, *Thy Word Is Truth* (Banner of Truth Trust, 78 Chiltern Street, London, 1964).

    Benjamin Warfield, *The Inspiration and Authority of the Bible* (Presbyterian and Reformed Publishing Co., Philadelphia, 1948), especially the introduction by C. Van Til.

    Cornelius Van Til, *In Defense of the Faith*, Vol. I, The Doctrine of Scripture (den Dulk Christian Foundation, California, 1967).
44. Dooyeweerd, *op. cit.*, p. 45 Cf. K. R. Popper, *The Poverty of Historicism* (1960).
45. The best treatment in English of Dilthey's though is by H. A. Hodges, *The Philosophy of Wilhelm Dilthey* (Routledge & Kegan Paul, London, 1952). For R. G. Collingwood consult his work, *The Idea of History* (Clarendon Press, Oxford, 1946).
46. Dooyeweerd, *op. cit.*, p. 48.
47. *Ibid.*, p. 48.
48. *Ibid.*, p. 49.
49. H. Frankfort, *Before Philosophy* (Pelican Books, London, 1949), p. 12ff. Also Talcott Parsons, *Societies* (Prentice-Hall, New Jersey, 1966), chapter three, Primitive Societies, pp. 30-41, and his *The Social System*.
50. Matthew Arnold, *Culture and Anarchy* (Longmans, London, 1946), p. 90. Cf. Clive Bell, *Civilization* (Penguin, London, 1946), and R. G. Collingwood, *The New Leviathan* (Clarendon Press, Oxford, 1947), Part III. Civilization, pp. 280-342.
51. Dooyeweerd, *In the Twilight of Western Thought* (Presbyterian and Reformed Publishing Co., Philadelphia, 1958), p. 95.
52. *Ibid.*, p. 97. Cf. James H. Olthuis, *Facts, Values and Ethics* (Van Gorcum, 1968).
53. Bernard Zylstra, "Towards a Normative Conception of Socio-Political Change," (paper given at Trinity Christian Colege, Chicago, in January, 1969), p. 4.

54. Dooyeweerd, *Twilight of Western Thought*, p. 102ff. Cf. H. Dooyeweerd, *A New Critique*, Vol. II, pp. 181-330, esp. 259ff.

55. Emil Brunner, *Justice and the Social Order* (Lutterworth, London, 1945), p. 99.

56. Dooyeweerd, *Twilight of Western Thought*, p. 105ff.

57. Ernest Gellner, *Thought and Change* (Weidenfeld and Nicolson, London, 1964), where he writes: In the twentieth century, the essence of man is not that he is a rational, or a political, or a sinful, or a thinking animal, but that he is an industrial animal. It is not his moral or intellectual or social or aesthetic, etc., etc., attributes which make man what he is; his essence resides in his capacity to contribute to, and to profit from, industrial society. The emergence of industrial society is the prime concern of sociology (p. 35).

58. C. H. Dodd, *History and the Gospel* (Nisbet & Co., Ltd., London, 1947), pp. 165-168. Cf. Arnold Toynbee, *Civilization on Trial* (Oxford University Press, 1948), p. 225ff.

59. Herman Dooyeweerd, "The Criteria of Progressive and Reactionary Tendencies in History," (Tomorrow's Book Club, Toronto, 1968), p. 14. Cf. J. B. Bury, *The Idea of Progress* (Macmillan, 1928), pp. 1-27, and J. Baillie, *The Belief in Progress* (N. Y., 1951). For further treatment of the philosophy of history the reader should consult:

Alan Richardson, *History, Sacred and Profane* (SCM Press, London, 1964).

Reinhold Niebuhr, *Faith and History* (Charles Scribner's Sons, New York, 1949.

Oscar Cullmann, *Christ and Time* (SCM Press, London, 1951).

Michael Oakeshott, *Experience and Its Modes* (Cambridge, 1933), a work which R. G. Collingwood described as "not only represents the high-water mark of English thought upon history, but shows a complete transcendence of the positivism in which that thought has been involved, and from which it has tried in vain to free itself, for at least half a century" (p. 159 of *The Idea of History*).

Patrick Gardiner, *The Nature of Historical Explanation* (Oxford University Press, London, 1952).

Norman Sykes, "Some Current Conceptions of Historiography and Their Significance for Christian Apologetic," *The Journal of Theological Studies*, 1950, p. 24.

60. Dooyeweerd, *op. cit.*, p. 14.

61. Ernest Gellner, *Thought and Change* (Weidenfeld & Nicolson, London, 1964), p. 30. Cf. Robert A. Nisbet, *Social Change and History* (Oxford, 1969), for a brilliant critique of contemporary functionalism as well as of Bury's famous *The Idea of Progress*, and of the cultural and social evolutionism upon which they are based.

Chapter Two

THE DEGRADATION OF WORK IN MODERN SOCIETY

The fact that so many people today do not find happiness and blessing in their work would surely suggest that something drastic has gone wrong with work in God's modern world. Why do so many workers today look upon their work simply as a job which they must hold down in order to make ends meet? Why do millions of workers regard such "jobs" as a necessary evil and as "labor in vain" and spend most of their time at work looking at the clock which will tell them when another "shift" is over? Why has work become devaluated and the workers depersonalized?

The answer surely is that the great majority of workers are no longer able to find any meaning in their work. *For the great majority of workers today work has lost its meaning, because it has become divorced from the service of Jesus Christ and their own personal lives and from life in the Body of Christ.* Above all, work in modern society has lost its meaning because modern post-Christian society has been living for the past four hundred years upon a doctrine of man in society which conflicts with the true nature of reality as revealed in the Word of God. In spite of greatly improved working conditions, high wages, and many other incentives, e.g., health and pension schemes, a growing number of British and American and Canadian workers do not feel they are doing something really worthwhile and of any real importance to their communities. And how could they as long as work is estimated in terms of the profits it brings to the shareholders rather than by the worth of the thing that is made? What sense is there in making ladies' stockings that are worn only once and then thrown away? What pride can the Ford or General Motors employee take in producing an automobile with the latest engine design and body streamlining which he knows will be thrown on the scrap heap within five years? What sense can farmers find in producing butter, wheat, and other grains, which will be stored by their governments because to distribute it does not pay? Just think of all the senseless things which are manufactured today! The enormous quantities of newsprint that litter our streets, the scattered hairpins and smashed crockery, and the knick-knacks of steel, wood, rubber, glass, and tin that we buy at Woolworth's and the other chain stores and then forget as soon as we have bought them.

Think of the advertisements imploring us, exhorting us, cajoling us, menacing us, and bullying us to glut ourselves with things we do not really need, in the name of snobbery, slothfulness, and sex-appeal. The advertisements are full of the Ponce de Leon appeal; every day they promote the sale of soap, toothpaste, breakfast cereals, cosmetics, and ladies' lingerie on the specious grounds that they can restore the glow and vigor of eternal youth. As long as gullible people continue to believe such rubbish so long shall we hear and read such things as "Go sweet, go fresh faced, go young, go angel face." The fountain of eternal youth is not to be found in some nationally promoted product as the advertisers claim; it is to be found only in human hearts which have been cleansed of their sin in the Blood of the Lamb whose heart was broken that we might live the abundant life.[1]

And what about the fierce international scramble to find in helpless and backward nations a market on which to fob off all the superfluous rubbish which the inexorable machines of North America and Western Europe grind out hour by hour simply to create employment and make bigger profits? I have known black men in my birth place in Katanga, the Congo, who bought shining white electric stoves to put into their mud huts even though they had no electricity to make them work. Before the last war the Red Indians of my old mission station at Teslin in the Yukon Territory, Canada, were bamboozled into buying a Model T Ford even though no highway was available. In desperation the Indians drove it out onto the ice in wintertime just to see how far it would skid over the frozen Lake Teslin. Likewise poor Eskimos have been sold refrigerators in the Arctic Circle.

We have been so corrupted by godless apostate standards and values that we now think of work as something one has to do to make money, rather than thinking of it in terms of the work done. Instead of asking of an industrial enterprise, "Will it pay?" we should be asking of it, "Is what you make really needed? Is it good?" Instead of asking a worker, "Does you work pay?" we should be asking him "What are the things you make worth?" And of the goods produced in our factories we should not be asking, "Can we induce people into buying them?" but "Are they useful things, well made?" Of employment we should be asking not "How much a week?" but "Will it exercise the worker's skills to the full?"

Imagine the consternation that would be caused at a meeting of the shareholders of Tetley's Brewery if one of the shareholders got up and demanded to know not where the profits went or what dividends were to be paid out, but in a loud and clear voice and with a proper sense of responsibility asked, "Mr. Chairman, just what does go into the beer our company makes?" Because our workers know only too well that such questions will never be asked by the shareholders of the companies for which the work, they could not care less what goes into the beer they produce.

Because their need for status and responsibility remains unsatisfied, our workers remain dissatisfied and discontented. According to Elton Mayo and his School for Human Relations in Industry, this lack of a sense of belonging and of being treated as a person is one of the commonest causes of neuroses in industry and is largely responsible for the social unrest of our times. As Canon V. A. Deman has pointed out in the symposium of lectures delivered during the last war at Dulwich College, published as *Our Culture: Its Christian Roots and Present Crisis*, all forms of 20th century collectivism, whether socialist, communist, or fascist, may be considered as reactions on the part of the Western world's workers to protect themselves against the gale set blowing by the attempts of economists and business men to reduce the workers to the demands of technical rationality, slaves of the machines and maximum profits regardless of the cost in human suffering.[2]

A brief examination of Anglo-Saxon economic and business history during the past three hundred years amply bears out the truth of Demant's statement. Unlike modern monopoly capitalism and international finance, early Anglo-American capitalism was not based upon the irresponsible exercise of economic power by a few over large masses of men. On the contrary, economic life was more or less controlled by a feeling of mutual responsibility between masters, journeymen, and apprentices. By and large, economic and labor relationships tended to be highly personal—between master and craftsman and journeyman and apprentice; laboring together in the same workshop; between buyer and seller living together in the same village or town. The very character of this relation produced some restraints upon the sinful human tendency of the master to exploit his workmen or the seller to cheat the buyer or the workman to produce sloppy goods or services.[3] Following Lewis Mumford's account in *Technics and Civilisation* we may in fact distinguish three technological-industrial complexes—namely, that of the medieval "eotechnic" period, which lasted more or less in various Western nations until the middle of the eighteenth and early nineteenth centuries; the "paleotechnic" phase of the Industrial Revolution, from which we have not yet altogether emerged; and the modern "neotechnic" phase of automation and mass production and consumption, still in process of development.[4]

(a) *Work in the Eotechnic Medieval Age*

In the eotechnic period social organization was upon a feudal basis, the main material of industry was wood, and almost the sole sources of power were wind and water. The craftsman of the time, as opposed to the peasant, was normally a member of a craft guild, working at home for as many or as few hours as he pleased; he was a respected member of his local community, and he took great pride in his work. It is true that his status was fixed from birth, but this was not felt to be a drawback, and it had the great advantage of providing security, freedom from anxiety, and above all a sense of belonging. Moreover, paradoxical as it may appear, social intercourse between classes of different levels was much freer than in the industrial society that later developed. Thus, for example, we read of many true romances where the apprentice boy grew up to marry the master's daughter, e.g., Dick Turpin. Membership in a guild, manorial estate, or village protected the individual throughout his life and gave to each person his own special role to play in society, and above all it gave him a sense of belonging to his community. Thus, while the Middle Ages suffered from plagues, appalling housing conditions, cruelty and superstition, lack of sanitation, in the sphere of human and labor relations conditions were often a great deal better and more satisfying than they have been since. Of the industrial psychology of this period J. A. C. Brown writes in his book, *The Social Psychology of Industry*:

> Although a society in which status is fixed at birth may seem to have many drawbacks from the standpoint of the modern individual, it is likely to be forgotten that it also had many advantages. The anxiety and sense of insecurity which are inseparable from a competitive society with mobile status were avoided, everyone had a secure awareness of belonging. . . . At best, there was an affectionate and obedient attitude not only towards the real family, towards the father substitutes right up the hierarchy; the master of the guild, the lord of the manor, and finally the benevolent authority of the Church.[5]

No doubt it was for such reasons that England during the High Middle Ages was known as "Merrie England" as well as for the reason that the people enjoyed no less than one hundred and fifty "holy-days" or public feast days during the year. Modern sources of power had not yet been tapped, and there were no machines and no labor-saving devices. Yet this was the period when the people of England enjoyed more leisure than they do today, and when real craftsmanship flourished in the land, as the visitor of our glorious cathedrals and beautiful old parish churches may still see for himself. Of the craft guilds of this former era Eric Lipson well wrote in his first volume of the *Economic History of England*:

> The craft guilds had certain qualities which may still afford an inspiration to our own age. . . . The craft guild was admirably designed to achieve its object, the limited production of a well-wrought article. Apprenticeship afforded ample opportunities for

a thorough system of technical training and the inspection of workshops stimulated and encouraged a high standard of craftsmanship. The regulation of prices and conditions of labour tended to protect the journeyman against arbitrary oppression. . . . The control of prices and the quality of wares was intended to protect both the seller and the buyer and to establish rates of remuneration for the craftsmen commensurate with the labour involved. Medieval authorities sought to fix prices according to the cost of production. Convinced that the labourer was worthy of his hire, their principle was to reward him with a recompense suitable to his station. They did not hold to the modern theory of minimum subsistence—the iron law, according to which earnings are forced down to the lowest level at which the artisan can subsist. Instead they seemed to have recognized that earnings should conform to a fit and proper standard of human life.[6]

(b) *Work in the Period of the Industrial Revolution*

The next stage was that of early mercantile capitalism, the domestic stage of industry, and the Industrial Revolution. Business and private affairs in this earlier stage of capitalism at their best tended to be governed by much the same moral and ethical code; a code which was based upon the Protestant emphasis upon the individual's personal accountability to God for both his business and his private conduct. The goal of Puritan Christianity in regard to social matters was the creation of a responsible self-disciplined body of free men and women, a citizenry of independent landholders, small businessmen, and self-respecting journeymen skilled in various trades and professions. R. C. K. Ensor's description of this evangelical motivation of an earlier generation of Anglo-Saxon businessmen deserves quoting:

The essentials of evangelicalism were three. First its literal stress on the Bible. It made the English the "people of a book" somewhat as devout Moslems are, but few other Europeans were. Secondly, its certainty about the existence of an after life of rewards and punishments. If one asks how nineteenth century English merchants earned a reputation of being the most honest in the world (a very real factor in the nineteenth century primacy of English trade), the answer is: because hell and heaven seemed as certain to them as tomorrow's sunrise, and the Last Judgement as real as the week's balance sheet. This keen sense of moral accountancy had also much to do with the success of self-government in the political sphere. Thirdly its corollary that the present life is only important as a preparation for eternity.[7]

The keystone of this mercantile capitalism was a sense of responsibility to the Lord for the conduct of one's business and personal life and a sense of self-reliance upon one's own efforts rather than upon the government. As Lord Lyndhurst once said in some famous words: "My lords, self-reliance is the best road to distinction in private life; it is equally essential to the character and grandeur of a nation." The classic expression of this doctrine of self-reliance was given by Samuel Smiles in his book, *Self-Help*, published in 1859.

Behind this evangelical morality there lay the great Reformation doctrine of the calling of the Christian man or woman to serve the Lord in everyday life as well as on the Lord's Day. From this doctrine of the calling has been derived the moral and spiritual dynamic which brought about the Industrial Revolution. By endowing common labor with Christian dignity and value Martin Luther and John Calvin gave the workers of the Reformed nations a new sense of their dignity and importance. As R. H. Tawney pointed out in *Religion and the Rise of Capitalism*, "Monasticism was, so to speak, secularized; all men stood henceforth on the same footing towards God." [8]

Had our Puritan forefathers not had a high sense of their calling to serve the Lord by a "godly self-discipline" at work, it is doubtful whether our modern industrial Atlantic society would ever have been built, depending as it does upon the need for men's courage, resource, endurance, persistence, precision, judgment, and reliability in dealing with machines. It is thus no accident that the Industrial Revolution took place first in England, Holland, America, and the United States, the homelands of the Reformation, since the workers in these lands had, thanks to their evangelical and reformed upbringing, not only learned how to do an honest day's work but also to rediscover God's world. It is again no accident that the Industrial Revolution took place first in these homelands of Calvinism, for these had been the first to undergo the scientific revolution of the seventeenth century, the prerequisite of any technical progress.

The material potentialities of modern science might have waited in vain for their fulfilment, as had been the case with Greek mechanics in the ancient world, had it not been for the social and intellectual initiative and enterprise of Reformed Christians. This initiative received its moral dynamic from the Reformation. Historians such as Max Weber, M. J. Kitch, and Ernst Troeltsch have proved how much the Industrial Revolution owed to the moral and social ideas of Puritanism which inculcated the duty of unremitting industry and thrift while it discouraged rigorously every kind of self-indulgence.[9]

Other historians such as Stanford Reid of Guelph University and R. Hooykaas of the Free University, Amsterdam, have proved how much the Industrial Revolution in turn depended upon the work of such eminent Calvinistic scientists as Ambrose Pare, Bernard Palissy, Francis Bacon, Isaac Newton, and Peter Ramus.[10] All these men followed Calvin's method of arranging the facts of nature in categories so that they could see resemblances and relationships. Thus they began to develop a form of empiricism, whether in biblical studies, mathematics, the manufacture of pottery, the healing of wounds, or the development of a scientific method. Unlike the medieval schoolmen, these Reformed scientists believed that one must begin with the facts of God's creation if one would discover and understand the works of God's hands.

Such an empirical and experimental approach to God's world meant that these men exercised a considerable formative influence upon the development of physical science. Many have recognized the importance of Bacon in the rise of modern science, but have totally failed to link it to his Calvinistic presuppositions. Moreover, they have failed to see how his views derived from his forerunners such as Petrus Ramus, and were related to the scientific work of other Calvinists such as John Napier and the founding of the first center of British scientific studies by Sir Thomas Gresham in London.[11] The fact is that to a considerable extent the Calvinistic thinkers of the sixteenth and early seventeenth centuries provided the only "scientific method" of the time which met the needs of the technical advances achieved by such men as Galileo, Stevin, and others. They laid down the principles of method later carried further by Huygens, Boyle, and, above all, Isaac Newton. In this way, their Reformed approach to the whole question of nature opened up new fields and directed men into areas of investigation leading to results of which we have not yet seen the conclusion. This Raymond Aron sums up in his *Lectures on Industrial Society* as the emergence of industrial society. "The major concept of our time is that of industrial society. Europe, as seen from Asia, does not consist of two fundamentally different worlds, the Soviet world and the Western world. It is one single reality: industrial civilization. Soviet and capitalist societies are only two species of the same genus." [12]

Following a suggestion of Max Weber's *The Protestant Ethic and the Spirit of Capitalism*,[13] the American sociologist, Robert K. Merton, shows in his essay, "Puritanism, Pietism and Science," available in his *Social Theory and Social Structure*,[14] how the Puritans in England and the Pietists of Europe both greatly assisted the development of modern science, not only by their insistence upon a rational rather than a scholastic understanding of the "order of nature," but by encouraging men to master their material environment. He writes:

> It is the thesis of this study that the Puritan ethic, as an ideal-typical expression of the value-attitudes basic to ascetic Protestantism generally, so canalized the interests of seventeenth century Englishmen as to constitute one important *element* in the enhanced cultivation of science. The deep-rooted religious interests of the day demanded in their forceful implications the systematic rational, and empirical study of Nature for the glorification of God in His works and for the control of the corrupt world.[15]

Merton backs up his thesis first by examining the attitudes of contemporary seventeenth century scientists such as the Puritan Robert Boyle as expressed in his book, *Usefulness of Experimental Natural Philosophy*, and by the Puritan John Ray, founder of modern botany, in his work, *The Wisdom of God*. In the former Boyle maintained that the study of nature must always be to the greater glory of God and the good of man. In the latter book Ray constantly exalted the God who had created such an amazing and beautiful world. In a similar vein Merton shows that John Wilkins proclaimed in his *Principles and Duties of Natural Religion* that the experimental study of nature is the most effective means of begetting in men a veneration for God.

The Puritans also believed that the Christian is called upon to use his scientific discoveries for the improvement of man's fallen estate and for the comfort and welfare of mankind. By thus focussing attention upon the world in which men lived, Puritanism, Merton concludes, had brought about the fusion of rationalism and empiricism, the two values that together constitute the essence of he modern scientific spirit. He writes: "The combination of *rationalism* and *empiricism* which is so pronounced in the Puritan ethic forms the essence of the spirit of modern science. . . . Empiricism and rationalism were canonized, beatified, so to speak."

Merton in the second place supports his thesis by showing the great part played by both the Puritans in England and America and by the Pietists in Western Europe in establishing new educational institutions where the new empirical approach rather than the old scholastic one could be applied. In no institution did the Puritans in England play a greater role than in the Royal Society. He writes:

> Among the original list of members of the Society of 1663, forty-two of the sixty-eight concerning whom information about their religious orientation is available were clearly Puritan. Considering that the Puritans constituted a relatively small minority in the English population, the fact that they constituted sixty-two per cent in the initial membership of the Society becomes even more striking.[16]

Both Puritans in England and the Thirteen Colonies of America and the Pietists in Europe broke with the prevailing methods of education and established their own "Dissenting Academies" as well as new universities.

Of this development Merton writes: "The emphasis of the Puritans upon utilitarianism and empiricism was likewise manifested in the type of education which they introduced and fostered. The "formal grammar grind" of the schools was criticized by them as much as the formalism of the Church.

Merton then refers to the great influence played by such Calvinist scholars as Samuel Hartlib, who sought to introduce the new realistic, utilitarian, and empirical education into England, forming the connecting link between the various Protestant educators in England and in Europe who were seeking to spread the academic study of science. Then there was the great Bohemian Reformed scholar, John Amos Comenius. Basic to the latter's educational philosophy were the norms of utilitarianism and empiricism, values which could only lead to an emphasis upon the study of science and technology, of *Realia* as opposed to *Theoria*. In his work *Didactia Magna* Comenius summarized his views:

> The task of the pupil will be made easier, if the master, when he teaches him everything, shows him at the same time its practical application in everyday life. This rule must be carefully observed in teaching languages, dialectic, arithmetic, geometry, physics, etc.
> The truth and certainty of science depend more on the witness of the senses than on anything else. For things impress themselves directly on the senses, but on the understanding only mediately and through the senses. Science, then, increases in certainty in proportion as it depends on sensuous perception.[17]

The Puritan determination to advance science not only bore fruit in the "Dissenting Academies" of England but also in the universities of Durham founded by Oliver Cromwell and of Harvard, where the new views of Comenius and Peter Ramus were taught instead of the classical science of Aristotle and of medieval scholasticism. Whereas in the older universities of Oxford, Paris, and Bologna the emphasis was still placed upon non-utilitarian classical studies, the Puritan and Pietist academies and universities held that a truly "liberal" education was one which was "in touch with life," and which should therefore include as many utilitarian subjects as possible. As Irene Parker points out in her *Dissenting Academies in England*: "The difference between the two educational systems is seen not so much in the introduction into the academies of "modern" subjects and methods as in the fact that among the Nonconformists there was a totally different system at work from that found in the universities. The spirit animating the Dissenters was that which had moved Ramus and Comenius in France and Germany and which in England had actuated Bacon and later Hartlib and his circle." [18]

Merton then refers to the work of F. Paulsen on *German Education: Past an Present* as well as of Alfred Heubaum, both of whom showed that the Pietists in Germany held similar educational views to the Puritans. Merton says: "The two movements had in common the realistic and practical point of view, combined with an intense aversion to the speculation of the Aristotelian philosophers. Fundamental to the educational views of the Pietists were the same deep-rooted utilitarian and empirical values which actuated the Puritans. It was on the basis of these values that the Pietist leaders, August Hermann Francke, Comenius, and their followers emphasized the new science." [19]

This preponderance of Protestants among scientists has been noted in other countries and has continued to the present.[20] A study of American scientists completed after World War II concluded that the "statistics, taken together with other evidence, leave little doubt that scientists have been drawn disproportionately from American Protestant stock." [21]

Writing in his book, *The Century of Revolution*, the Master of Balliol College, Oxford and a former self-confessed Communist, Christopher Hill, had this comment to make regarding the connection between Calvinism and the rise of modern methods of production.

> Calvinism liberated those who believed themselves to be the elect from a sense of sin, of helplessness; it encouraged effort, industry, study, a sense of purpose. It prepared the way for modern science. . . . The Puritan preachers insisted that the universe was law-abiding. . . . It was man's duty to study the universe and find out its laws. . . . Bacon called men to study the world about them. . . . The end of knowledge was "the relief of man's estate," "to subdue and overcome the necessities and miseries of humanity." Acceptance of this novel doctrine constituted the greatest intellectual revolution of the century.[22]

In his essay on "Protestantism and the Rise of Capitalism," contributed to *Essays in the Economic and Social History of Tudor and Stuart England*, Christopher Hill further elaborates upon the causal connection between Protestantism, economic growth, and capitalism. He does this by demonstrating the connection through the central issue of the Reformation, justification by faith:

> The central target of the Reformers' attack was justification by works. . . . The Protestant objection was to mechanical actions in which the heart was not involved. . . . A Protestant thought that what a man did was less important than the spirit in which he did it. . . . For Christians no action can be casual or perfunctory, the most trivial detail of our daily life should be performed to the glory of God; should be irradiated with a conscious cooperation with God's purposes.[23]

From this central doctrine came two results. On the one hand, says Hill, "It was in fact the labour of generations of God-fearing Puritans that made England the leading industrial nation of the world."[24] On the other hand, however, the individualism of the Protestants meant that while "the Roman Church was able slowly to adapt its standards to the modern world through a controlled casuistry, guiding a separate priestly cast . . . , Protestant ministers had to tag along behind what seemed right to the consciences of the leading laymen in their congregations."[25] Hill concludes that:

> There is nothing in Protestantism which leads automatically to Capitalism; its importance was rather that it undermined obstacles which the more rigid institutions and ceremonies of Catholicism imposed. But men did not become Protestants because they were Capitalists or Capitalists because they were Protestants."[26]

Protestant doctrine, however, Hill says, "gave a vital stimulus to productive effort in countries where Capitalism was developing at a time when industry was small scale, handicraft and unrationalized."[27]

Thanks to this Puritan stimulus, the standard of living of the English-speaking democracies was raised to a level never before reached in the history of mankind. A look at the economic position today of the leading nations of the world soon shows the decisive part played by Protestantism in raising men's physical standards of living consequent upon raising their spiritual standards of living. Taking the income per head of population as given in the British magazine, *The Economist*, 1962, as the best indication of national wealth, we find that the Protestant nations decisively head the list, followed by Roman Catholic and Greek Orthodox lands.

NATIONAL INCOME PER HEAD AND PREDOMINANT RELIGION
(£ Sterling, 1961)

Reformed and Protestant		Roman Catholic and Greek Orthodox		Non-Christian	
1. United States	824				
2. Sweden	575				
3. Canada	546				
4. Switzerland	516				
5. New Zealand	470				
6. Australia	439				
7. Britain	413				
8. Denmark	411				
9. W. Germany	383				
10.				Israel	373
11. Norway	370				
12.		Belgium	368		
13.		France	362		
14. Finland	319				
15. Netherlands	307				
16.		Venezuela	277		
17.		Austria	263		
18.		Ireland	203		
19.		Italy	199		
20.		Chile	179		
21.				Japan	144
22.				South Africa	140
23.		Argentina	135		
24.				Jamaica	133
25.		Greece	130		
26.		Mexico	100		
27.		Spain	97		
28.		Portugal	90		
29.				Yugoslavia	80
30.				Ghana	71
31.		Brazil	48		
32.				Ceylon	44
33.				India	25
34.				Burma	18

The classification is governed by the religion predominating during the main period of economic growth of the country or what W. W. Rostow terms *"the take-off"* period. Rostow gives us the following table of some tentative, approximate take-off dates: [28]

Country	Take-off	Country	Take-off
Great Britain	1783-1802	Russia	1890-1914
France	1830-1860	Canada	1896-1914
Belgium	1833-1860	Argentina	1935-
United States	1843-1860	Turkey	1937-
Germany	1850-1873	India	1952-
Sweden	1868-1890	China	1952-
Japan	1878-1900		

In most cases the religion predominating during this period of industrial "take-off" does not differ very much from the religious affiliation given in the latest censuses. In some nations the Catholic population has grown substantially in the last two generations. Even so, in the United States there are still three Protestants to every two Roman Catholics, in Australia three to one, in Switzerland four to three. In the Netherlands, the Roman Catholics are now almost equal in numbers, and in Canada the Protestants are in a bare majority. (However, excluding Quebec, which has a lower *per capita* income, the Protestants are three to one.) In West Germany there are ten Protestants to nine Roman Catholics, but before the division of the country the ratio was nearer three to two. The distinction between Protestant and Roman Catholic and Greek Orthodox is of course much finer than that which marks them off from non-Christian lands.

Is it purely a coincidence that the Western world and the Anglo-Saxon world, inspired by Christian ideals and morals, the inheritor of a thousand years of biblical preaching and teaching, is prosperous, whilst the two thirds which form the world's hungry billions are mostly found where the Gospel of Jesus Christ, the Bread of Heaven, has not penetrated or taken strong root? Can we divorce Christianity in general and Calvinism in particular from the prosperity of the Western world, and especially of the English-speaking world? Do we not owe God something for our enormous agricultural surpluses? In starving India the land is overrun by millions of cattle and monkeys because they are considered to be sacred. No Hindhu would dare to kill a cow for fear of offending his god, nor can the cattle and the monkeys be driven off the crops from which they consume the food so desperately needed for human beings, because the heathen gods would be upset. Here we have an obvious example of a false religion based upon superstition resulting in bad farming.

Thanks to the powerful influence of God's blessed Scriptures, the saving power of Christ, and the wisdom and science of God, European and North American farmers have stopped all sorts of superstitious farming practices and learned to farm their lands in accordance with God's great scientific laws for the "holy earth." If it had not been for the great Christian monastic orders of the Middle Ages, e.g., the Benedictines and the Cistercians, much of Europe's and Britain's land would have remained forest and bush-land. Thanks to the liberating power of God's Holy Word, Western men stopped living in fear and trembling of the evil spirits, sprites, and fairies whom as pagans they had previously supposed to inhabit every tree and bush. Thanks to the influence of the Bible upon their minds, Western men came to realize that the earth is the Lord's and that it operates according to laws which men are to unveil by means of their science.

If India, Asia, and Africa are ever to raise their material standards of living, it is imperative that the peoples of these lands first raise up their spiritual, moral, and educational standards. What is the use of the Western world sending out modern farm machinery to the pagan peasants of Egypt and India and Africa gripped by the most heathen primitive superstititions, to whom the use of much modern farm equipment is contrary to the will of the false gods and idols they worship? Until such spiritual aid by way of Christian missionaries is first provided, all technical aid is simply a waste of time. Until the process of evangelization and Christian education is undertaken, we cannot expect the Afro-Asians to raise their material living standards. England and Europe had first to undergo the spiritual revolution of the Reformation before they underwent the scientific and then the industrial revolution. In *Asian Drama*, G. Myrdal claims

that nothing less than a revolution, political, social, religious, philosophical, is the precondition of Western-style economic growth in
the underdeveloped world of today.[29]

There is also evidence for the view that the strength or weakness
of management would seem to be related to whether a country is
Protestant. Studies published in America during 1959 by F. Harbison of Princeton and C. A. Myers of the Massachusetts Institute of
Technology, titled *Management in the Industrial World*,[30] compared
the quality of industrial management in the United States, the United
Kingdom, Sweden, Germany, France, Italy, Egypt, India, Chile, and
Japan. The first four all appear to have achieved a high standard of industrial management on a fairly wide scale and have, of course, a high
material standard of living. Standards of management among the other
are reported to be much poorer, and, with the exception of France,
they all have a very much lower standard of living. These weaknesses in management seem to run to a pattern in all non-Protestant
countries, and they are traceable directly to ethical and religious
causes. Managers in these non-Protestant lands are gravely concerned with their authority and the preservation of their preroga-
tives. They prefer docile employees "who will not talk back or
raise questions," rather than employees who are ambitious or efficient.[31] Typical organizational structure is highly centralized and
personal. There is little delegation and consequently much frustration and bitterness on the part of subordinate managers. Key positions are occupied by family members on the basis of family ties and
not on the basis of performance. The family is more important than
the enterprise. Maximum production and performance have little
place in the family plans. "The end supreme and all pervading, is the
family—its economic security, its social prestige." [32] The object of
the business in these non-Reformed lands is to provide a reasonable
degree of wealth for the family, and it is not felt that the productivity
of the enterprise need be pushed beyond this point. All this contrasts sharply with the philosophy of management in the United
States and Britain, where it is generally held to be intolerable that
nepotism and personal interests should stand in the way of a major

enterprise responsible for the employment and standard of living of thousands of workers.

Even non-Christian Japan, which has been most successful in catching up with advanced Western industrial countries, has an income per head only one half of that in Britain. The above authors comment, "Unless basic, rather than technical or trivial, changes are forthcoming, Japan is destined to fall behind in the ranks of modern industrial nations." [33] Writing of France the authors comment:

> Compared to other European countries, France, in the latter half of the Eighteenth Century was rich in the attributes required for an economy based on the exploitation of local resources. . . . One would have had every reason to expect France, in the Twentieth Century, to be a leader in the world's industrial growth and progress. . . . By the end of the Nineteenth Century France was in the grip of a slow and continuous regression in its capacity to produce. . . . Other forces which would normally have exerted pressure for recrystallization of the economic institutions of France remained stubbornly inoperative in an economy of small holdings, an atmosphere of widespread absence of trust and an exalted idea of personal security.[34]

Is it without any significance that in the Roman Catholic Canadian Province, Quebec, as well as in other Roman Catholic lands, the leading executives of the bigger business organizations have tended to be Protestants rather than Roman Catholics? The usual reply made by French-speaking Canadians to this question, when it is raised in discussion, is that until recently the Protestants had the better system of education. But then one is forced to ask why do the Protestants have a better system of education by and large than the Roman Catholics, at least better in such districts as Quebec and southern Ireland? Again the answer goes back to the Reformation. As James Hastings Nichols points out in his classic work, *Democracy and the Churches*:

> Roman Catholic and Anglican education was frankly aristocratic and designed to maintain social and political inequality. The notion of universal education and the common school has been inherited by modern democracy from the Reformation. The history of early public education knows no rival to the schools

of Geneva, Scotland, and New England. The Reformed did not merely believe in the capacities of all men; they took pains to develop them.[35]

H. F. R. Catherwood warns us in his recent work, *The Christian in Industrial Society*, that the English-speaking Protestant nations cannot afford to boast of racial superiority. Whatever greatness they have achieved is due to Jehovah God and His Christ and not to any innate national characteristics or traits. He writes:

> Humanism, the prevailing faith in many of the countries which are still nominally Protestant, may have taken over many of the ethical ideals of Christianity, but it remains to be seen whether, having taken away the theology, the "why" of religion, the ethic the "what" of religion will retain its grip. Only now are we encountering the third generation since the major decline of church-going. If the Christian faith ceased to have any influence in Northern Europe (or North America) but took a firm grip in, say Brazil, which has a growing Protestant minority, then the relative patterns of national prosperity and growth might change quite decisively over a relatively short period. It is, unfortunately, all too easy to imagine the deterioration which could set in here if management and labour increasingly took their tone from their worst elements.[36]

Whenever and wherever Reformed Protestant Christianity has decayed or failed to penetrate you will find ruthless greed, dishonesty, prejudice, passion, and slothfulness at work disrupting life. The writer will never forget seeing colored women in the former Belgian Congo and in the Yukon carrying home water and firewood while their menfolk sat watching them do all the work. Without Christ in control of men's consciences human society and industry falls apart into lawless violence, power with no trace of conscience, the jackboot of tyranny, injustice, and economic exploitation trampling down the weak, the poor, and the sick. When Christ is rejected by a majority of a nation, all defense against the exercise of arbitrary political and economic power vanishes too at the same time. It is the Lord Jesus Christ alone who can subject power to the control of conscience. Except the Lord build a nation's political and economic institutions they labor in vain who build.

Upon being appointed American ambassador to Brazil, Mr. Babson went to say goodbye to the President of the Argentine Republic. After luncheon the two men sat in the sun parlor of the presidential palace overlooking the river. The President was very thoughtful. "Mr. Babson, I have been wondering why it is that South America with all its great natural resources and advantages is so far behind North America." As a guest, Mr. Babson relates in his book, *Fundamentals of Prosperity*, he did not like to suggest any reason, so he replied, "Mr. President, what do you think is the reason?" The President replied, "I have come to this conclusion. South America was settled by the Spaniards who came to South America in search of gold, but North America was originally settled by the Pilgrim Fathers who went there in search of God." [37]

The point of view of the Reformation of seeing all things "*sub specie aeternitas*" not only helped greatly in the development of an inductive method in natural science; it also provided a new moral approach to the use of the things of this world. Calvin and his followers did not see the world as something evil from which man should fly, but rather holding to their doctrine of the sovereignty of God, they believed that God had placed man in this world to exploit its potentialities to the best of his ability that he might glorify God. Under the orders of God, man has the responsibility of developing a material and social culture which would manifest the goodness and the power of God, thus providing man with "the good life." And even though man has sinned in his attempt to claim this world for himself as its true lord, he still has this responsibility and the ability, albeit corrupted, to do so. By virtue of this new moral dynamic, the Calvinists, instead of running away from human culture like so many later pietists, sought to conquer the world for Christ's sake. They sought to glorify God in His Church and to serve Him in His world.[38]

Thus there developed in the lands of the Reformation a new perspective on the world. The old medieval Catholic ideal of asceticism and withdrawal was rejected by Protestant Christians in favor of a new ideal of using and enjoying the creation to the glory of God. This meant use in moderation and in accordance with the righteousness which God demands of His people. It was men endued with this new ideal who provided the driving power of Anglo-American and Dutch capitalism and who were the founders of the economic power of Great Britain, Holland, and America. Thanks to these Puritan merchant adventurers, business men, and entrepreneurs, the standard of living of Britain, Holland, and America was raised to a level never before reached in the history of mankind.

Owing to the propaganda of such socialist historians as the Webbs, the Hammonds, and R. H. Tawney, it has become fashionable to decry these Puritan capitalists and to look upon the Industrial Revolution as an unmitigated disaster. Replying to this caricature of economic history, T. S. Ashton, Professor of Economic History in the University of London, points out that it is perverse to maintain the view that technical and economic changes were themselves the source of the calamity. In his classic little book on *The Industrial Revolution* he writes:

> The central problem of the age was how to feed and clothe and employ generations of children outnumbering by far those of any earlier time. Ireland was faced by the same problem. Failing to solve it, she lost in the "forties" about a fifth of her people by emigration or starvation or disease. If England had remained a nation of cultivators and craftsmen, she could hardly have escaped the same fate, and, at best, the weight of growing population must have pressed down the spring of her spirit. She was delivered, not by her rulers, but by those who, seeking no doubt their own narrow ends, had the wit and resource to devise new instruments of production and new methods of administering industry. There are today on the plains of India and China men and women, plague-ridden and hungry, living lives little better to outward appearance, than those of the cattle that toil with them by day and share their places of sleep by night. Such Asiatic standards, and such unmechanized horrors, are the lot of those who increase their numbers without passing through an industrial revolution.[39]

And we might add without passing through a spiritual revolution such as the people of the Reformation lands passed through during the sixteenth century. When Macaulay compared his own day with the past, it was inevitably to rejoice in the change. Since popular economic history was taken over by the Fabians and socialists, any similar contemporary comparison would equally inevitably be a cause for lamentation. In a very important recent work on *Capitalism and the Historians* it has been proved how the structure of left-wing historiography (the political purpose of which was largely hidden from subsequent generations of school children in English and American schools) depended for its emotional appeal on forgetting Thomas Malthus and his discoveries about population increases in relation to diminishing physical resources as quickly as possible. Actual case studies of the English factory system and the conditions of life of the English workers buttress the conclusions of the authors. Messrs. T. S. Ashton, L. M. Hacker, Bertrand D. Juvenel, and W. H. Hutt have proved that under capitalism the workers, despite long hours and other hardships of factory life, were better off financially, had more opportunities, and led a better life than had been the case before the Industrial Revolution.[40]

It is into this heresy of regarding the operations of "capitalism" as a voluntary process which most socialist historians seem to have fallen. To these writers the growth of population was merely a consequence of industrialism. But this is to neglect the research of the past thirty years which has upset the thesis that industrialism "created" the economic problem.

Economic change means a change of institutions, habits, ideas, and attitudes; it takes place, partially at any rate, because the old institutions, habits, ideas, and attitudes have become ossified or purposeless and obstructive. Behind the change from the defensive social and economic policies of the Middle Ages to the offensive, "individualistic" economic policies of the nineteenth century is one major factor: the consciousness of man's increased power over nature. The age of Malthus was in some respects as short of the indispensable necessities as the age of Aquinas, but it was equipped with better tools and blessed with business entrepreneurs whose vision pierced beyond the contemporary gloom to glimpse the age of plenty beyond. Answering the question, "Why did the first industrial 'take-off' happen in Britain and not in France or elseswhere?" W. W. Rostow writes in his fundamental work, *The Stages of Economic Growth*:

And so Britain, with more basic industrial resources than the Netherlands; more nonconformists, and more ships than France; with its political, social and religious revolution fought out by 1688—Britain alone was in a position to weave together cotton manufacturing, coal and iron technology. the steam engine, and ample foreign trade to pull it off.[41]

Thus the economic primacy of Victorian England cannot be explained entirely in terms of natural resources, James Watt, and a fortunate absence of foreign competition. In the final analysis it was due to the men of wit and infinite resource and courage who felt called by their Reformed faith in the living God to carry out the Creator's cultural mandate "to have dominion over the earth and to subdue it."

(c) Work in the Age of Automation and Mass Production

By the eighteen eighties of the last century the spirit and structure of this early Anglo-American capitalism underwent a profound and revolutionary change as new methods of the organization of capital, new methods of production and distribution were devised and as apostasy triumphed over Christian faith. A whole new collection of business devices and ceremonials were developed in the industrial and commercial world which enabled apostate business men to set aside the moral scruples and Puritan ethic which had formerly governed the lives of their grandfathers and fathers.

Of these legal devices none has been more insidious than the invention of the limited liability company and the modern business corporation. Such business corporations have one outstanding feature; viz., they are completely irresponsible, having neither bodies to be kicked nor souls to be damned. Beyond good and evil, insensible to argument or moral appeal, they symbolized the mounting independence of modern monopoly capitalism and international finance from the old restraints and scruples of Christianity both Roman Catholic and Reformed.

"As directors of a company," wrote William M. Gouge, "men will sanction actions of which they would scorn to be guilty in their private capacity." A crime which would press heavily on the conscience of one man becomes quite endurable when divided among many. "Where the dishonesty or fraud or exploitation has become the work of all members of a business every such business man can now say with Macbeth in the murder of Banquo, 'Thou canst not say I did it.' " [42]

As industry became more mechanized and passed out of the hands of owners of capital into that of the managers of capital, economic life became depersonalized and industry became more autocratic and oligarchic in its structure. In their classic work, *The Modern Corporation and Private Property*,[43] Adolf Berle, Jr., and Gardiner C. Means showed what had taken place by 1925. Nominal powers of decision over the use of capital had become whittled down to *pro forma* annual meetings of shareholders attended by perfunctory, negligible, or cranky minorities. As Burnham so well explained in his book *The Managerial Revolution*,[44] the executive and managerial classes had in effect taken over the *de facto* control of Anglo-American productive processes. As Burnham sees it the technical and industrial society in which we now live is developing into something that may best be described as an administrative or managerial society. He says:

> We are now in a period of social transition . . . from the type of society we have called capitalist or bourgeois to a type of society which we have called managerial. . . . What is occurring today is a drive for social dominance, for power and privilege, for the position of ruling class, by the social group or class of managers. . . . The economic framework in which this social dominance of the managers will be assured is based upon the state ownership of the major instruments of production.[45]

In support of this thesis Burnham points out that a new class in managerial and administrative positions is multiplying in numbers and increasing in power throughout the world. With increasing mechanization in industry and the increasing bureaucratization of society we can therefore envisage a state of things when this new administrative class will outnumber the industrial wage earners. Moreover, while the initial impulse towards the growth of administration comes from the necessity of controlling a force so powerful as mass production, the tendency of administration in accordance with Parkinson's Law is to extend its numbers and its control over the whole of the life of modern industrial society. Even the professions, such as scientific research, medicine, and teaching, are in danger of becoming subject to "technique" and to the central bureaucratic direction and regulation, which such "technique" makes necessary.

By such "technique," Jacques Ellul points out in *The Technological Society*,[46] we should understand not mere machine technology. Technique refers to any complex of standardized means for attaining a predetermined result. Thus, it converts spontaneous and unreflective behavior into behavior that is deliberate and rationalized. Technique as Ellul would have us understand it means nothing less than the organized ensemble of *all* individual techniques which have been used to secure any end whatsoever. He writes: "Technique is nothing more than *means* and the *ensemble of means*." [47] As such, technique has become indifferent to all traditional human ends and values by becoming an end-in-itself. The Technical Man is fascinated by results, by the immediate consequences of setting standardized devices into motion. He is committed to the never ending search for "the one best way" to achieve any designated objective. Our erstwhile means have in fact all become an end, an end, moreover, which has nothing human in it and to which we must accommodate ourselves as best we may. We cannot even any longer pretend to act as though the ends justified the means. According to Ellul, technique, as the universal and autonomous technical fact of our age, is revealed as the technological society itself in which man is but a single tightly integrated and articulated component. The Western world is becoming a progressively technical civilization; by this Ellul means that the ever-expanding and irreversible rule of technique is extended to all areas of modern life: the economic, political, medical, administrative and police powers of the modern state, propaganda, and, above all, warfare. It is a civilization committed to the quest for continually improved means to carelessly examined ends. Indeed, technique transforms ends into means. What was once prized in its own right now becomes worthwhile only if it helps to achieve something else. And, conversely, technique turns means into ends. "Know-how" takes on an ultimate value. Today men look to technique to save them from disaster as once men used to look to God. As Ellul well puts it: "Even people put out of work or ruined by technique, even those who criticize or attack it have the bad conscience of all iconoclasts. They find neither within nor without themselves a compensating force for the one they call in question. They do not even live in despair, which would be a sign of their freedom. This bad conscience appears to me to be perhaps the most revealing fact about the new sacralization of modern technique." He then points out that the characteristics of modern technique, namely, its rationality, artificiality, automatism, self-augmentation, monism, universalism, and autonomy, make it utterly different from the techniques of the past. "Today we are dealing with an utterly different phenomenon." *The Technical Society* is a description of the way in which this new technique is in process of taking over the traditional values of every society throughout the world, subverting and suppressing these values to produce eventually a monolithic world culture in which all nontechnological difference and variety is mere appearance.

The vital influence of technique is, of course, most evident in the economy. Ellul here first points out that technique not only plays a dominant role in production, as Karl Marx recognized, but also in distribution. Ellul remarks:

> No area of economic life is today independent of technical development. It is to Fourastie's credit that he pointed out that technical development controls all contemporary economic evolution from production operations to demography. . . . Even more abstract spheres are shown by Fourastie to be dominated by technical progress; for example, the price mechanism, capital evolution, foreign trade, population displacement, unemployment, and so on. . . . As a result of the influence of techniques, the modern world is faced with a kind of "unblocking of peasant life and mentality." For a long time peasant tradition resisted innovation, and the old agricultural systems preserved their stability. Today technical transformation is an established fact; the peasant revolution is in process or already completed, and everywhere in the same direction.[48]

According to Ellul, technique is producing a growing concentration of capital as Marx foresaw it would. He writes, "Technical progress cannot do without the concentration of capital. An economy based on individual enterprise is not conceivable, barring an extraordinary technical regression. The necessary concentration of capital thus gives rise either to an economy of corporations or to a state economy. . . . This tendency toward concentration is confirmed daily. The important thing is to recognize the real motive force behind it." [49] Ellul claims that the motive force behind this concentration of capital in giant corporations is not to be found in any human, social nor even economic benefits. "What, then, is the motive force behind this concentration?" he asks. The answer he gives is that it is technique alone. Ellul explains the reason:

> A number of elements in technique demand concentration. Mechanical technique requires it because only a very large corporation is in a position at the present to take advantage of the most recent inventions. Only the large corporation is able to apply normalization, to recover waste products profitably, and to manufacture byproducts. Technique applied to problems of labor efficiency requires concentration because only through concentration is it possible to apply up-to-date methods which have gone far beyond the techniques of the former efficiency and time-study experts (for instance, the application of techniques of industrial relations). Finally, economic technique demands both vertical and horizontal concentration, which permits stockpiling at more favorable prices, accelerated capital turnover, reduction of fixed charges, assurance of markets, and so on. . . . The impulse to concentrate is so strong that it takes place even contrary to the decisions of the State. In the United States and in France, the State has often opposed concentration, but ultimately it has always been forced to capitulate and to stand by impotently while the undesired development occurs. This confirms my judgement concerning the decisive action of technique on the modern economy.[50]

The combined effect of all these changes and tendencies then has been to produce an industrial society dominated by "functional or technical rationality." The adjective is necessary to distinguish this meaning of rationality from the belief in the "understanding" as a quality in men which impels them to seek and enables them to apprehend truth and justice. Technical rationality is the capacity of applying means to ends or of organizing actions in order to reach a previously defined goal. It is in the production and distribution of goods and services that technical rationality has today come to exercise undisputed sway, and because of the dominant position of industry in modern society the habit of thinking in terms of technical rationality has spread imperceptibly into other areas of modern life.

In the drive for lower costs and greater output per man hour all the technical skills of industrial engineering and production planning are enlisted. The effort to break down work into simpler operations never ceases. The demands of the competitive market compel management to make new experiments and to employ new methods in the most economical use of capital and labor.

In such an increasingly urbanized, rationalized, and technicized society, controlled largely by impersonal money trusts, the majority of Western workers today spend most of their working hours under the direction of an authoritarian and disciplined business organization. The individual worker in our new age of mass production and of automation tends to become an anonymous, interchangeable unit. Eugen Rosenstock-Huessy, Jacques Ellul, H. Van Riessen, and Friedrich Georg Juenger, in their brilliant expositions of the effects of rationalized production on human beings, have shown how in some particular features the inner essence of this process has been startlingly revealed. It is characteristic of an age of machine production that in some industries it is necessary for some men to work in shifts. Machines tire less quickly than men; they need less prolonged periods of rest. It is they that set the pace, and when they are working at it full stretch it takes three men to keep up with them. The unit of production is no longer one man, but three "shifts." *The person has become an anomymous, interchangeable unit.* He can be represented by a number. In discussing the functional implications of this assembly line method of production Juenger writes in his book, *The Failure of Technology*:

> An invention like the assembly line shows functional thinking to a high degree, for here all the functions of work are lined up within the sequence of lifeless time, and the workmen stationed along the line as functionaries of a work process that has been cut

into pieces. What is the consequence? The worker loses his identity; as a person he loses his individuality; he is only noticeable as
the performer of a function. As a human figure he fades out; and
from the point of view of technical progress it would be desirable if he faded out altogether.[51]

Again, in modern industry payment is usually by the hour. It does
not alter the significance of this fact that in earlier periods payment
was also sometimes by the hour. The point is that it belongs to the
essential nature of modern industry that time is no longer calculated in
terms of the services of *known persons*, but by the hours of labor of
anonymous interchangeable labor forces. The hour for which a man
engaged in building a bridge is paid is not part of his life; it is
part of the several hundred thousand hours required for the building
of the bridge. Working time, that is to say, is disconnected from
the man who does the job and related exclusively to the piece of
work. In other words, a man's work is divorced from his personal
life. The breaking up of the worker's life into a succession of
identical units which he cannot combine into any meaningful scheme
takes from him the power to order his life as a whole. The worker
in the large factory has the feeling of being nothing more than a
number. The growing size of industry is mainly responsible for this
situation. It has resulted in the loss of personal contact with the
company and of any awareness of working together in a common
undertaking.[52]

Economists of the "classical" and even some modern schools of
economic thought have furthered this process of the devaluation of
labor by their definition of labor as a "commodity" along with other
commodities in the general system of production and exchange. As
the opening to his chapter "On Wages" Ricardo states that "Labor,
like all things bought and sold and which may increase or decrease
in quantity has its natural and market value. The natural price is
that price which is necessary to enable labourers, one with another
to subsist and to perpetuate their race without either increase or
diminution." [53]

In his recent work, *Man, Industry and Society*, Rodger Charles
argues with a great deal of justification that it is just this theorem,

that labor is a commodity, which is at the root of so much present-day labor-management conflict. Unfortunately, he points out, not only is it accepted as axiomatic by an old fashioned type of management but also by an equally old fashioned type of trade union leader.[54]

In so far as man in his work is reduced to the position of a mere functionary, who carries out a mechanical task in which he is replaceable by others, and in so far as he is treated as just another "commodity," work loses its personal quality. *It ceases to be a sphere of personal and moral activity. It no longer fosters, as God means it to foster, the growth of personal character, by affording opportunities for personal decision, exercise of judgment, mastery of intractable material, and growth in understanding and skill.*

Given such developments it is not surprising that so many industrial workers today are unable to find any meaning in their work and that they have been reduced to the level of "mass men."

The research work of the Elton Mayo School of Human Relations in Industry has provided us with first hand evidence of this depersonalization of men's labor in modern society. Mayo based his whole analysis of industrial society upon the concept of "anomie," i.e., the lost, forlorn condition of the little man in the vast industrial machine. Mayo found that this feeling of "anomie" acquired its typical character from the new, impersonal method of modern business organization and the so-called "scientific management" of workers introduced by Frederick Winslow Taylor, first at Midvale Iron Works, then at the Bethlehem Steel Company, and the resulting specialization of functions. The atomization of labor, and especially the isolation of a partial function and its resulting fixation, had given the workers at the Hawthorne Works of the Western Electric Company a feeling of being alone in their work, of not really belonging. Mayo discovered something drastically wrong with the social structure of the factory. The workers no longer counted in the formal organization of the plant or within the informal organization; i.e., in their personal relations with the foremen. As a result there had arisen all sorts of social tensions for which Mayo proposed radical new solutions based upon the following discoveries: (1) Work is a group activity; (2) the social world of the adult is primarily patterned about work activity; (3) the need for recognition, security, and a sense of belonging is more important in determining the worker's morale and productivity than the physical conditions under which he works; (4) a complaint is not necessarily an objective recital of facts; it is commonly a symptom manifesting disturbance of an individual's status position; (5) the worker is a person, whose attitudes and effectiveness are conditioned by social demands from both inside and outside the work plant; (6) informal groups within the work plant exercise strong social controls over the work habits and attitudes of the individual worker; (7) the change from the older type of community life to the atomistic society of isolated individuals, i.e., from eotechnic to neotechnic society, tends continually to disrupt the social organization of a work plant and industry generally; (8) group collaboration must be planned for and developed. If group collaboration is achieved, the work relations within a work plant may reach a cohesion which resists the pull towards stasis and atomization.[55]

These results of the investigations carried out in the Hawthorne Works of the Western Electric Company provide convincing evidence that the attempt at scientific management of the workers introduced by F. W. Taylor and other leaders of Time and Motion, as well as the old fashioned view of management towards labor as a commodity, are fundamentally at the root of the workers' discontent, and that management best succeeds when it treats its workers as persons rather than impersonal functions of the productive process and restores a genuine feeling of belonging to a common enterprise by:

> . . . making factory groups so stable in their attitude of group co-operation that men in the groups explicitly recognized that the factory had become for them the stabilizing force around which they developed satisfying lives.[56]

In short, leaders in this particular industry are at last making some attempt to re-create the social bonds which had become disastrously severed through the destruction of community during the later phases of the Industrial Revolution which we have described as the rationalization and scientization of production.

Such an attempt to rationalize and to scientize production was bound to devaluate human labor, since it meant that the workers were made to become the slaves of the machines they operated. When in scientific organization the division into partial labor functions is consistently carried through, then in the case of mass production it will usually be possible to assign a very elementary function to the individual worker: a simple operation that must be repeated with the regularity of clockwork, every minute of the hour, every hour of the day, every day of the week, every week of the year.

Then it was decided to employ technical means in order to integrate these elementary functions into one total process of production. The objects to be processed by such methods of mass production are put upon a moving belt or suspended on moving chains. Sometimes also the workman is himself made into a mobile fixture on a moving platform. The products to which this system of mass production have been applied are today legion: cigarettes, sweets, radios, televisions, cars, refrigerators, pulp and paper, and so on. The devaluation of labor in such endlessly repeated, simple manipulations is further increased when the individual function is itself subjected to scientific analysis and control. It is for this reason that no Christian can accept the present mania in Britain for so-called Time and Motion studies applied to ever increasing areas of British industry, since the price to be paid for such scientific management of men is too high. As the great Christian philosopher of modern science, H. Van Riessen, points out in his fundamental work, *The Society of the Future*:

> The price paid for scientific organization, whenever consistently applied, is the freedom of man in labor, his personal responsibility, the appeal to initiative, to decision, to effort, to skill, and everything over which man disposes in the scope of his freedom. Wherever freedom of work is wanting or means nothing because the features of labor have become so elementary and repetitious that labor as such is devaluated, it no longer deserves to be called by the name of labor.[57]

The conditions of modern mass production have not only reduced the workers to slaves and devaluated their labor, but they have at the same time made it more difficult for men to realize that in their work they are exercising a useful social function. To a shoemaker in a village his function and responsibility are evident; if he fails to make shoes, the community will go unshod. But for the worker in a large mass production factory his contribution to the whole may seem negligible. He is remote from the ultimate use of what he is making, which may be only a tiny part of the completed whole.

Thus the heart of the problem of work in modern society lies in the divorce of work from the service of Almighty God and the worker's own personal life and from life in the community. As Oldham well says:

> Men can be delivered from slavery to the machine only by a revolutionary change in the accepted scale of values in which a primary concern for the welfare of persons takes the place of demonic concentration on technical efficiency and material production.[58]

(d) God's Judgment Upon Apostate Industry and Society

It is imperative for Christian workers to understand that the conflicts which rend modern society and the evils connected with modern methods of mass poduction, though they have in fact been accompaniments, are *not* the inevitable consequences of the coming of the machine. The real source is to be found in apostate modern men's attempt to become independent of God. Behind the technical developments of the past two hundred years lies the whole spiritual process of modern man's attempt to emancipate himself from the control of the Word of God as the ordering principle of his life in this world. Apostate modern man in his drive for independence from the God and Father of Jesus Christ has sought for freedom without any binding moral or religious sanctions by which he understands not only emancipation from political or ecclesiastical absolutism but also complete freedom from God. In addition, apostate modern men have striven for creativeness without responsibility, and they have worshiped the cult of the production of goods and the accumulation of money in the bank as the true content and meaning of human existence. Again, modern "scientific humanists" have striven for power over nature and over their fellow men without any sense of reverence for either their fellow men or for God's creation. As a result of these spiritual tendencies originating from the perversion of the cultural mandate revived at the time of the Reformation, Christians should be able to realize that it was not by some inexorable law of nature that the release of the forces of economic and technical rationality and scientific management brought about the far-reaching social transformation we have described. It brought about the changes which it did because the acquisition by modern men of the new powers released by modern science took place within the context of the modern humanistic drive for complete spiritual autonomy and independence from the Lord Jesus Christ. As Emil Brunner well says:

> It is this context which gave to technics, and also the new science, both a prodigious stimulus and also that direction which has today confronted us with a terrifying problem. Technics has been cut free from the moral and religious context of human life and has become autonomous because its deepest desire was the desire for autonomy on the part of man. From this point of view we can understand why technics acquired such a speed of development and why the tempo was not moderated in order to allow the necessary social adaptations to take place. The furious revolutionary changes in the conditions of life due to the development of technics took place in a period which was very little in a condition to digest, socially and morally, so large a mass of changes. It was not able, that is to say, to bring about the social adaptations and modifications which were necessary if technics were not to become a danger to the life of man.[59]

Thus we cannot hope to understand the nature of industry in modern society if we take account only of those elements in it which meet the eye. As Christians we have to look beneath the surface for the repressed forces which, though they have been ignored, retain their vitality and have exerted a continuous, though often unrecognized, pressure. The dominance of functional rationality and the elevation of technics from being merely a means of improving the conditions of human life to a position where it is regarded as the end and ultimate purpose of human life in modern apostate society has meant that human and social factors in the process of production, distribution, and exchange have been left out of account with the consequent dechristianization and depersonalization of millions of modern workers into so-called mass men or proletariate.

These suppressed forces have in the twentieth century violently asserted themselves and given rise to a social crisis of the first magnitude. As V. A. Demant says: "Our modern industrial society got into its stride under the influence of an abstract theory of human needs and behaviour—namely that men would always act from motives of the maximum economic gain, buying cheapest and selling dearest, irrespective of boundaries of family, class, and nation. In other words the real world of men and women, with their attachments, loyalties, hopes and fears, moral and religious convictions, was supposed to be amenable to purely economic incentives in a free market. . . . This economic 'paradise' hardly got going before society in all sorts of ways started protecting itself against this tendency to dissolve all the realities of social living. All forms of socialism, whether democratic, communist or fascist, are vast measures of 'protection' against the gale set blowing by the attempt to but purely economic rationality into practice." [60]

Thus the problems of modern industry have their root in the fact that labor is not self-disciplined but subject to an alien control in the form of so-called scientific management, and that there is in consequence no responsible exercise of freedom and no meaningful ordering of human activity. The workers have no real responsibility for the conduct of their work. Discipline must in consequence continue to be imposed from without, and therefore to arouse resentment.

In the nemesis which has thus fallen upon the workers, the Christian will detect nothing less than the hand of God coming in judgment upon both capitalists and workers. God himself has brought modern industry into this crisis. He does not allow himself to be neglected. He cannot allow it for our own sakes. Thus He has turned down the dream of independence, the dream of a world without God and of a redemption without Christ, into the nightmare of the mass production factories where the workers and the managers have become slaves of the machines. Such a divine judgment is only too apparent in the nemesis which has overtaken applied science in modern industry. The outcome of such applied science has been slavery, enmity, and hatred. The attempt to become independent of God so that man could master his physical and social environment has resulted not only in man's losing his sense of belonging to God's earth but also in the devaluation of human labor.

For two hundred years men have striven for power over nature and then over each other in order to become independent of God's purpose and law for their lives. As a result they have not only lost all sense of the sacred and sublime in human life, but they have alienated themselves from the very power they had discovered by means of their science and techniques which they have sought to use for their own selfish ends. More and more modern technology and scientific method applied to industry in time and motion studies are reducing the workers to slavery. As with Adam, man's striving for autonomy from God thus reveals the nature and consequence of sin. Science has been able to solve most of our material problems, but only at the cost of creating a moral problem which is insoluble. What shall it profit the human race to control the material universe, if in the process it reduces human persons to the level of mechanical robots and slaves of big business and mass production?

By completely secularizing modern industry and trying to scientize and mechanize all human relationships, the workers now find themselves penalized by God in the loss of their own human dignity as persons at work and in the meaning of their lives. In forsaking God, millions of Western men have been reduced to mass men herded together like ants in our great centers of population as part of the "lonely crowd." [61] In forsaking God, modern humanists have severed their connection with the true basis of their existence as human beings, and they have thereby opened up the way to apostate nihilism, so prophetically foretold by the most honest atheist of modern times, the German philosopher, Nietzsche.[62] The masses now seek satisfaction in such false idols as sports, sex, gambling, alcohol, and automobiles. But as they fail in all this to find true peace of mind, they will eventually land in nihilism. Already many of the

West's leading artists, poets, painters, and thinkers have reached this final stage where human existence is thought to be futile and senseless.

Thus does God punish Western men's apostasy from Him by turning their science, art, philosophy, and industry against them; and by confronting them with the meaninglessness of life apart from Him; and by the loss of all their moral, legal, and political values by means of which alone they could keep control of their science and technology. The living God of the Bible has thus turned the tools of applied and pure science against man by confronting him with the terrible meaninglessness of human life lived apart from Him and His Son.

Post-Christian man has created a sterile society in which he discovers that when he lives as if God is dead, man also becomes dead. Human life has today lost its meaning and purpose as apostate modern man finds himself reduced by his own science and technology to a mere cog within the great machine of nature and society. The only way of escape now lies in a non rational world of experience, of drugs, pornography, and an elusive "final experience," and then ultimate madness. As we saw in the preface to this book, Michel Foucault in *Madness and Civilization* teaches that the ultimate in autonomous freedom is being crazy.[63] It is a great thing to go insane, for then only can you become truly free.

The results of drug-taking and schizophrenia are in fact remarkably similar to insanity, a fact which is well understood by many drug takers, including many thousands of young people in America, Britain, and Canada. *Newsweek* reports that the "hippies" in San Francisco have been using the tune of "We Shall Overcome" to the words, "We Are All Insane."[64] Commenting upon this climax of apostate humanism in insanity, Francis Schaeffer writes in *Escape from Reason*: "Foucault is not too far removed from Aldous Huxley. He is not to be thought of as too isolated to be of importance in understanding our day, and in understanding the end of duality and dichotomy (the split between the rational and the non rational). The logical end of the dichotomy, in which hope is separated from reason, is the giving up of all reason."[65]

On the basis of scientific determinism man as a person finds he no longer has any meaning, and therefore his culture also has become meaningless. The overturning of God's ordering of human society which began during the French Revolution and was continued in the Bolshevik Revolution in Russia has created a society in which man is dead, and he has merely become a statistic in the records of big business and big government. His personality has been stripped away from him, leaving him to fulfill a function in a depersonalized, militarized, and technological mass society as an empty husk of a person. Apostate modern man thus tends to shirk off all his responsibilities as a parent, as a worker, and as a citizen, surrendering them to the state, to his labor union, political party, or his employer. In short, apostate godless man has become emptied of his character as a person created in God's holy image and therefore an individual with eternal significance. Apostate modern man is dead. Thus the Lord God has turned the tables upon man's apostasy and rebellion. He will not allow man to retain his autonomy from Him without suffering loss. As Schaeffer says:

> Any autonomy is wrong. Autonomous science or autonomous art is wrong, if by autonomous science or art we mean it is free from the content of what God has told us. This does not mean that we have a static science or art—it is just the opposite. It gives us the form inside which, being finite, freedom is possible. Science and art cannot be placed in the framework of an autonomous downstairs without coming to the same tragic end that has occurred throughout history. . . . In every case in which the downstairs was made autonomous (i.e., the rational and scientific), no matter what name it was given, it was not long before the downstairs ate up the upstairs (freedom or grace). Not only God disappeared but freedom and man as well. . . . Whenever art or science has tried to be autonomous, a certain principle has always manifested itself—nature "eats up" grace, and thus art and science themselves soon began to be meaningless.[66]

CHAPTER TWO NOTES

1. Vance Packard, *The Hidden Persuaders* (McKay, New York, 1957). Ernest Dichter, *The Strategy of Desire* (T. V. Boardman, New York, 1961).

2. V. A. Demant, *Our Culture: Its Christian Roots and Present Crisis* (S.P.C.K, London, 1947), p. 105ff.

3. A. M. Schlesinger, Jr., *The Age of Jackson* (Eyre & Spottiswoode, London, 1946).

4. Lewis Mumford, *Technics and Civilization* (Routledge, London, 1947), p. 107. *A History of Technology*, edited by Charles Singer, E. J. Holmyard, A. R. Hall, and Trevor L. Williams (Clarendon Press, London, 1955-1965), Vols. I, II, III, and IV.

5. J. A. C. Brown, *The Social Psychology of Industry* (Penguin Books, London, 1962), p. 26.

6. Eric Lipson, *The Economic History of England* (Adam Black, London, 1945), Vol. I, pp. 308-438.

7. R. C. K. Ensor, *England: 1870-1914* (Clarendon Press, Oxford, 1946), p. 137ff.

8. R. H. Tawney, *Religion and the Rise of Capitalism* (Penguin Books, London, 1938), p. 100.

9. M. J. Kitch, *Capitalism and the Reformation* (Longmans, London, 1967), gives the most recent documentation and discussion of the controversy regarding the responsibility for the origin of capitalism. Talcott Parsons, *The Structure of Social Action* (The Free Press, New York, 1967), gives a brilliant summary of Weber's argument in *The Protestant Ethic and the Spirit of Capitalism* (G. Allen & Unwin, 1930).

10. Stanford Reid, *Christianity and Scholarship* (Craig Press, Nutley, N. J.), "Natural Science in Sixteenth Century Calvinistic Thought."
E. L. Hebden Taylor, "The Reformation and Modern Science," in *The Churchman* (Church Book Room Press, London, Summer 1968), p. 87ff.

11. Christopher Hill, *The Intellectual Origins of the English Revolution* (Oxford, 1964), p. 146.

12. Raymond Aron, *18 Lectures on Industrial Society* (Weidenfeld & Nicolson, London, 1967), p. 42.
Ernest Gellner, *Thought and Change* (Weidenfeld & Nicolson, London, 1964), p. 132ff. "Marxist revolutions occurred not as reactions to the miseries of industrialism, but in order to bring them about. The historic role of Marxism seems to be not to lead societies out of the crises of industrial society, but to hlpe them pass over the hump of industrialization. . . . At present it looks rather as if the historic role of Marxism is to diffuse industrialism, and of capitalism to engender those institutions which, if they survive, will preserve some liberty under industrial organisation."

13. Weber, *op. cit.*

14. Robert K. Merton, *Social Theory and Social Structure* (The Free Press, New York, 1967).

15. *Ibid.*, p. 574.

16. *Ibid.*, p. 584ff.

17. *Ibid.*, p. 585ff.
18. Irene Parker, *Dissenting Academies in England* (Cambridge, 1914), pp. 133-134.
19. Merton, *op. cit.*, p. 589ff.
20. *Ibid.*, pp. 590-595 gives a summary of the studies concerned.
21. R. H. Knapp and H. B. Goodrich, *Origins of American Scientists* (University of Chicago Press, Chicago, 1952), p. 274.
    Ely Chinoy, *Society* (Random House, New York, 1967), pp. 406-410).
22. Christopher Hill, *The Century of Revolution* (Secker & Warburg, London, 1961), pp. 92-94.
23. Christopher Hill, *Essays in the Economic and Social History of Tudor and Stuart England*, edited by E. J. Fisher (London, 1961), pp. 16-21.
    Adolph A. Berl, *The American Economic Republic* (Harcourt, Brace & World, Inc., New York, 1963), devotes a whole chapter to "The Value System and the Transcendental Margin," in which he argues that the Protestant Ethic "embodied the driving value system of nineteenth century America. The Protestant ethic has proved far more dynamic in the development of American economics than has perhaps been assumed" (p. 189).
24. C. Hill, *op. cit.*, p. 31.
25. *Ibid.*, p. 27.
26. *Ibid.*, p. 36.
27. *Ibid.*, p. 39.
28. W. W. Rostow, *The Stages of Economic Growth* (Cambridge, 1960), p. 38.
29. W. Vogt, *Road to Survival* (V. Gollancz, London, 1949). Cf. G. Myrdal, *Asian Drama* (Penguin, 1968), 3 vols.
30. F. Harbison and C. A. Myers, *Management in the Industrial World* (New York, 1959).
31. *Ibid.*, p. 164.
32. *Ibid.*, p. 247.
33. *Ibid.*, p. 246.
34. *Ibid.*, pp. 207 and 208.
35. J. H. Nichols, *Democracy and the Churches* (Westminster Press, Philadelphia, 1951), p. 27.
36. H. F. R. Catherwood, *The Christian in Industrial Society* (Tyndale Press, London, 1964), p. 124.
37. J. Babson, *Fundamentals of Prosperity* (Harper, New York, 1930), p. 120.
38. A. Kuyper, *Lectures on Calvinism* (Eerdmans, Grand Rapids, 1961), p. 110f.
39. T. S. Ashton, *The Industrial Revolution* (Oxford University Press, 1952), p. 161.
40. F. A. Hayek, *Capitalism and the Historians* (Editor) (Routledge & Kegan Paul, London, 1954), p. 35ff.

41. Rostow, *op. cit.*, p. 33.

42. Quoted in A. M. Schlesinger, *op. cit.*, p. 335ff.

43. A. A. Berle and G. C. Means, *The Modern Corporation and Private Property* (Macmillan, New York, 1931), where it is said that what the stockholder owns he measures "in a market quotation," pp. 277-278. See Note 29 of chapter eight of my book for Beed's recent criticism of this thesis. J. A. Schumpeter points out in *Capitalism, Socialism and Democracy* (Harper, New York, 1950), that limited liability corporations have led to the divorce between owners and managers of capital. Owners are not responsible for total losses; and they are thus more willing to turn control of the company over to professional managers. But, as Schumpeter shows, this kind of property lends itself to governmental control; the share holder does not resist the substitution of the state's managers for the former managers. Thus private property is no longer the strong barrier it once was against nationalization by the State. Men who are not responsible for their debts will be less concerned with what happens to their indebted private possessions.

44. James Burnham, *The Managerial Revolution* (Penguin Books, 1945). Cf. R. Bendix, *Work and Authority in Industry* (London, 1956), where he documents the subtle changes by which the "entrepreneurial ideology became changed into a "managerial ideology."

45. *Ibid.*, p. 64.

46. Jacques Ellul, *The Technological Society* (J. Cape, London, 1965, and A. A. Knopf, Inc., New York, 1964).

47. *Ibid.*, p. 19ff. Cf. R. Nisbet, *The Sociological Tradition*, "The Rationalization of Authority—Weber and Michels," pp. 141-150.

48. *Ibid.*, p. 150ff.

49. *Ibid.*, p. 154.

50. *Ibid.*, p. 155. Cf. Wright Mills, *The Sociological Imagination*, pp. 165-176.

51. F. Juenger, *The Failure of Technology* (H. Regnery, Illinois, 1949), p. 75.

52. *Contemporay Social Problems*, edited by R. K. Merton and R. A. Nisbet, especially R. S. Weiss and David Riesman's essay, "Work and Automation Problems and Prospects" (Harcourt, Brace & World, Inc., Chicago, 1966), pp. 553-618.

53. David Ricardo, *The Principles of Political Economy* (Everyman, Dent, London, 1960), p. 52.

54. Rodger Charles, *Man, Industry and Society* (Sheed & Ward, London, 1964), p. 25f. Cf. R. A. Nisbet, *The Sociological Tradition*, pp. 21-31.

55. J. A. C. Brown, *op. cit.*, chapter three, "The Work of Elton Mayo."

56. Elton Mayo, *Social Problems of an Industrial Civilization* (Routledge & Kegan Paul, London, 1946), p. 91. Cf. C. W. Mills, *The Sociological Imagination*, p. 92ff.

57. H. Van Riessen, *The Society of the Future* (Presbyterian and Reformed Publishing Co., Philadelphia, 1953), p. 145.

58. J. H. Oldham, "Technics and Civilization," in *The Church and the Disorder of Society* (SCM Press, London, 1948), p. 40.

59. Emil Brunner, "Man and Technics," *Christian News Letter* (London, 1948), Jan. 1948, p. 11.

60. V. A. Demant, *op. cit.*, p. 105. Cf. V. Demant, *Religion and the Decline of Capitalism* (Faber & Faber, London, 1952).

61. D. Riesman, N. Glazier, etc., *The Lonely Crowd* (Doubleday Anchor, New York, 1954).
Francis Schaeffer, *Escape From Reason* and *The God Who Is There* (Hodder & Stoughton, London, 1968).

62. H. Van Riessen, *Nietzsche* (Presbyterian and Reformed Publishing Company, Philadelphia, 1960).

63. Michel Foucault, *Madness and Civilization* (Pantheon Books, New York, 1966).

64. *Newsweek* (Feb. 6, 1967).

65. Francis Schaeffer, *Escape from Reason* (Inter-Varsity Fellowship, London, 1968), p. 71. Cf. A. Lunn & G. Lean, *The Cult of Softness* (London, 1965). Cf. also R. Rosenthal (ed), *McLuhan* (Pelican, New York, 1969), pp. 186-198.

66. *Ibid.*, pp. 23ff., 38, 84.

The reader should also consult Schaeffer's other book, *The God Who Is There* (Hodder & Stoughton, London, 1968), and C. S. Lewis, *The Abolition of Man* (G. Bles, London, 1947), who writes:

> The final stage is come when Man by eugenics, by prenatal conditioning, and by an education and propaganda based on a perfect applied psychology, has obtained full control over himself. *Human* nature will be the last part of Nature to surrender to Man. The battle will then be won. . . . But who, precisely, will have won it? . . . .
>
> At the moment of Man's victory over Nature, we find the whole human race subjected to some individual men, and those individuals subjected to that in themselves which is purely "natural"—to their irrational impulses. Nature, untrammelled by values, rules the Conditioners and, through them, all humanity. Man's conquest of Nature turns out, in the moment of its consummation, to be Nature's conquest of Man. Every victory we seemed to win has led us, step by step, to this conclusion (pp. 42-46).

It is remarkable that a Roman Catholic theologian, Romano Guardini, should also have written along similar lines in his *The End of the Modern World* (Sheed and Ward, London, 1957). He begins by recognizing the achievements of the Renaissance, when modern man came into his own. He also discusses the problems of anxiety:

> Modern anxiety arises from man's deep-seated consciousness that he

lacks either a "real" or a symbolic place in reality. In spite of his actual
position on earth he is a being without security. The very needs of man's
senses are left unsatisfied, since he has ceased to experience a world
which guarantees him a place in the total scheme of existence. When
the limited world picture of the Middle Ages was cancelled out by the
modern picture of a limitless world, God lost His dwelling place; thereby
man lost his proper position in existence. "Where" then is God? (p. 52).
And where is the place of man? It is curious that in the century in which
man has gained the greatest mastery over nature and things, he should
himself feel lost. . . . Man's relations with nature have reached the point
of final crisis: man will either succeed in converting his mastery into good
—then his accomplishment would be immense indeed—man will either
do that or man himself will be at an end (p. 73ff.).

Similarly R. J. Rushdoony points out in *Newsletter* 41 (Jan. 1969):

The death-of-God movement is one of the deepest and most powerful
forces in the modern world. The mistake most people make in trying to
understand it is that they only see its most obvious manifestation in men
like Altizer. But the death-of-God movement is everywhere, and it is
extremely powerful in conservative and evangelical circles. . . . If a man
professes to be a Christian and yet favors the public schools (or statist
schools), and sends his children to them, he is declaring that God is dead
in at least the sphere of education. He is denying the sovereignty and
existence of God for educational life. No less than the sexual offender, he
is saying that God is dead and can be safely disregarded in the area of
education. . . . Our modern economics is the death-of-God economics; it
denies that God exists and governs the sphere of economics by His law.
(Page 1 of his *Newsletter*, published at 22816 Oxnard Street, Woodland
Hills, California 91364.) For a brilliant sociological interpretation see
R. A. Nisbet's chapter on "Alienation" in his book, *The Sociological
Tradition*. Also, cf. G. R. Taylor, *The Biological Time Bomb* (World
Publishing Company, New York, 1968), chap. 1, "Where Are the Biologists
Taking Us."

Chapter Three

THE COMMUNIST THEORY OF LABOR, INDUSTRY AND SOCIETY

(a) *The Marxist Analysis of Industrial Society*

Marxism developed during the nineteenth century in reaction to the laissez faire theories of the classical economist who taught that the true welfare of society would prevail only when individuals could pursue their own private interests without any economic control by the state. As long as the state does not interfere in the free play of economic forces, then it was believed a "natural harmony" or identity of interests would work to bring about the prosperity of all. In this way, civil society had come to be regarded as the free play of economic interests within the juridical frame of the unassailable natural rights of the individual. As Adam Smith had said in *The Wealth of Nations*:

> By preferring the support of domestic to that of foreign industry, the individual intends only his own security; and by directing that industry in such a manner as its produce may be of the greatest value, he intends only his own gain, and he is in this, as in many other cases, led by an invisible hand to promote an end which was not part of his intention. . . . By pursuing his own interest he frequently promotes that of the society more effectually than when he really intends to promote it.
>
> The natural effort of every individual to better his own conditions when suffered to exert itself with freedom and security, is so powerful a principle, that it is alone without any assistance, not only capable of carrying on the society to wealth and prosperity, but of surmounting a hundred impertinent obstructions with which the folly of human laws too often encumbers its operations.[1]

In these famous passages Adam Smith had enunciated the basic principle of modern capitalism—the automatic regulation of industry by reference to market price alone. Smith believed that the fiscal policies of mercantilism had cramped individual enterprise and were holding back the economic growth of Britain. In the first passage we have quoted, Smith was exposing the ineptitudes of the corn bounty; in the other he was exalting private enterprise above paternalism, which allowed monopoly privileges to such trading companies as the East India Company and the Hudson Bay Company. In a famous essay titled *The End of Laissez-Faire*, John Maynard Keynes writes:

> The early nineteenth century performed a miraculous union. It harmonized the conservative individualism of Locke, Hume, Johnson and Burke with the Socialism and democratic egalitarianism of Rousseau, Paley, Bentham and Godwin. . . . The age would have been hard put to it to achieve this harmony of opposites if it had not been for the Economists, who sprang into prominence just at the right moment. The idea of a divine harmony between private advantage and the public good is already apparent in Paley. But it was the Economists who gave the notion a good scientific basis. . . . To the philosophical doctrine that Government has no right to interfere, and the divine miracle that it has no need to interfere, there is added a scientific proof that its interference is inexpedient. This is the third current of thought, just discoverable in Adam Smith, who was ready in the main to allow the public good to rest on "the natural effort of every individual to better his own condition," but not fully and self-consciously developed until the nineteenth century begins. The principle of *laissez faire* had arrived to harmonise Individualism and Socialism, and to make at one Hume's Egoism with (Bentham's) Greatest Good of the Greatest Number.[2]

Smith's conception of man is a typically apostate humanist one. Man is a reasonable and reason-determined being who lives out of his freedom and independence in seeking his own selfish interests to the fullest possible degree. He believed that such enlightened selfishness is the basic motivating force of every human being. It is not without significance that Smith wrote a treatise on *The Theory of the Moral Sentiments* before he turned his attention to the study of economics. In his ethical work he laid the philosophical foundations for the *Wealth of Nations*. Although influenced by Hutcheson's principle of benevolence, Smith was too skeptical a man to rest his ethical views upon unalloyed human kindness. Instead, he argued that we acted as we did out of a regard for the opinion of others. We shape our actions to please an impartial observer, the possessor of an enlightened reason. What we call conscience is the representative within our own breast of the enlightened observer. When we sympathize with a friend in trouble, our criteria are those we conceive will win the approval of this judicious soul. Such an observer of all our actions does not teach universal benevolence. Though he feels the softer human emotions, he expects human beings to pursue their own interest, in ways which violate no ethical canons. It is sympathy which serves as a brake upon a man's egoism. As a rational being man judges his own conduct by what others say and think of it and this keeps his selfishness within bounds.

Applying this faith in human reasonableness to economic conduct, Smith argued that competition in business life has the same mitigating effects on human cupidity as sympathy in one's own private life. The outcome of man's natural sympathy towards others, if allowed to run its course, would be a harmonious and natural order in economic life. The interest of one business man would always be in harmony with the interest of the next one. Indeed Smith was convinced that such competition would ensure that in the long run the price of goods would come to rest at the level of their labor value.

Smith believed that in primitive society "the whole produce of labour belongs to the labourer; and the quantity of labour commodity employed in acquiring or producing any commodity, is the only circumstance which can regulate the quantity of labour which it ought commonly to purchase, command, or exchange for." [3] Smith recognized that property and profits are an imposition upon the workers. There is a note of nostalgia for "that original state of affairs" when the worker had "neither landlord nor master to share with him." [4]

But Adam Smith is hard-headed. His book is devoted not to moral sentiments but to expediency. The way lies ahead, through the increasing productivity that follows the division of labor.

For Smith the state should not intervene in economic life, since everyone bound to the "market" with its healthy competition, would find that his own individual freedom was in harmony with the economic interests of his fellow-men. The market itself would function as the natural force which would, sooner or later, make for equilibrium, since in Smith's system market and competition are equivalent. Competition presupposes factors that are mutually about equal. The functioning of competition in the market place thus presupposes the equality of those engaged in it. Economically engaged people, Smith believed, are equal people.

Smith's ethical and economic teaching is purely immanentistic, since he reduces man to *homo oeconomicus* in order that he could proclaim universally valid "laws" of human behavior in the economic sphere. As such, the father of modern humanistic economics is revealed as being in the grip of the apostate "nature-freedom" ground-motive. In future economic thought *homo oeconomicus* came to replace real flesh and blood men and was used to justify the exploitation of the workers in the new factories rising up all over Western Europe in the nineteenth century. Without this monstrous economic abstraction, the classical economists believed that economic theory could not develop and discover the laws which operate in economic life. Acceptance of this hypothesis enabled economists, however, to find such laws which could then be used against the workers. Marcet's *Conversations in Political Economy* is quoted by M. Dobb in his *Wages* to illustrate this. Her instruction of the unfortunate Caroline brings out very clearly how these new economic laws always worked in favor of the propertied and powerful. Since wages depend on the proportion of capital to workers, nothing must be done to decrease the riches of the rich; no poor-rate which leaves less money available for capital investment, no taxes which diminish the sum from which the wages will be paid. In fact, any effort at taking money from the rich will make the poor poorer; a strange but comforting teaching for the rich. One immediate practical conclusion was that the unions could not raise wages; only an increase in the wages fund could do that.[5] Of this appeal to so-called "laws of nature" J. C. Gill writes in *The Mastery of Money*:

> Too often in the past, men's theories have been represented to be "laws of nature," hindering the proper ordering of society. The factory laws and the humanizing of the scandalous Poor Law of 1834 came about because there were people who valued human life and believed in God, and refused to accept the expert opinions of the political economists of their day. They would not be silenced by them. From then to now, laws and customs have developed which it was forecast, would accomplish the nation's ruin.[6]

In the abstraction of *homo oeconomicus* we find, therefore, more than a fiction; it shows us the power of apostate humanist ground-motives in determining what godless men will "see" around them. In classical economics there is reflected a view of man as the sovereign ruler of his own destiny. Unfortunately the idea of *homo oeconomicus* still rears his ugly head in most modern economic textbooks. In his fascinating dissertation *Vrijheid en Gelijkheid* (Liberty and Equality) A. Kouwenhoven has clearly demonstrated that in contemporary economic literature the same apostate humanist view of man as the master of his own destiny still dominates Western economists as it did the classical economists.[7] They refuse to admit that people today are not really free or equal and that the people are slowly being reduced to slaves of either big business or big government. Such economists can blithely discuss such subjects as poverty, monopolies, labor-management conflicts and yet still talk about the individual's freedom of choice. They must surely know full well that people today are not free in all respects nor that they are equal in various ways. Maarten Vrieze rightly points out:

> This humanist idea of the essential equality of all men as reasonable individuals or units, existing as sub-stances in and by themselves free from any law order which is not fully derived from man himself (either as absolutized "reason" or as a more "positive" law of some kind), continues its existence even when people take notice of factual situations of inequality; the idea then functions as the "ideal" or "norm" according to which the situation must be rectified. And even there where such a conclusion is

not explicitly drawn, the concept shows up suddenly in theoretical reflections. . . . The economist, for example, will make
very clear that he is aware of the concrete differences which
exist in society . . . ,but at the same time he will introduce
standards and yardsticks with which he begins to measure the
economic activities of large numbers of people; he can only
do so upon the presupposition that there is an underlying equality. . . . The humanist has no other means of seeing any order
in the economic phenomena; it escapes his attention—because
his heart is closed for Him who sets them—that there are economic norms in which man functions whatever he does. . . .
It also escapes his attention that there are specific social structures
which qualify the activities of man. It was necessary for humanism, again and again, to pose the premise of the uniformity of economic life: theory building would otherwise have been impossible.
But every time it began to emphasize this uniformity, this visual-
izing of man as a unit which one can manipulate to construct
universally determining laws, resistance came up. The science
ideal kept coming into conflict with the personality ideal, and
this picture has not yet changed in the 20th century.[8]

The powerful principle of self-love and of the identity of interests when used to define social responsibilities, had results which
were wholly evil. In the name of laissez faire economic individualism, employers during the nineteenth century denounced the extension of the Factory Acts, and the enforcement of minimum
standards of sanitation and of safety and care for the women and
children working in the factories of the Western world.

As a direct result of this new economic teaching the former state
control of industry fell into disfavor. According to Eric Lipson:

Henceforth Parliament concentrated its energies upon a commercial policy which was now systematically designed to protect
the interests of the producer and to ensure him the undisputed
possession of the home market; it grew less concerned to control
industry, regulate labor conditions and promote social stability.
in accordance with the change in attitude the old industrial code
was allowed gradually to fall in desuetude. The whole economic
outlook of the eighteenth century was permeated by an encroaching individualism which insisted upon unfettered freedom of action.
. . . Owing to this reversal of roles, the state renounced the right
to dictate to entrepreneurs, the terms on which they should em-

ploy their workfolk, and it exhibited an increasing disposition to tolerate their claims to make their own contract regarding the rates of remuneration, the length of service, the quality and supply of labor, and the nature of the products. . . . Once the state abdicated its authority the relations of capital and labor entered a fresh stage and ceased to be subject to the rule of law. Instead of the general conditions of employment being controlled by a superior power, they were determined according to the respective strength of the opposing sides.[9]

The waning control of the state over industry had its counterpart in the fate which overtook the craft guilds. For centuries the latter had enshrined the principle that industry should be regulated by corporate bodies, and that no one should pursue a skilled occupation who was not a member of one of these bodies. As such the guilds were societal structures which embraced the whole of the individual's life. They were represented in local government, functioned as a private economically qualified trade union, provided contingents to the local militia, and even went so far as to regulate their own police services, festivities, and funerals and kept their own altars in churches.

Membership in such guilds was made legally obligatory, each man being enjoined to belong to some craft whose decisions carried legal status. They owned property and could settle disputes among their members, dealt with questions of hours, wages, quality of workmanship, and apprenticeships. Of these guilds and manors Tannenbaum says:

Membership in a guild, manorial estate, or village protected man throughout his life. . . . The life of man was a nearly unified whole. Being a member of an integrated society protected and raised the dignity of the individual, and gave each person his own special role. Each man, each act, was part of a total life drama, the plot of which was known and in which the part allotted to each was prescribed. No one was isolated or abandoned. His individuality and his ambitions were fulfilled within the customary law that ruled the community to which he belonged.[10]

In other words, in this precapitalist order everyone had tended to enjoy his own specific "place" and society had tended to be based upon status rather than contract. It might be only a humble place, but it was recognized, and conferred rights as well as duties—rights of communal grazing, for example, and the right of the aged to support within the family, or sometimes from the village or the guild. Most workers earned only part of their keep in cash. They had real income from animals, vegetable plots, or in foodstuffs in exchange for skills (cobbler, carpenter, wheelwright) to help ensure subsistence. Above all, labor was not allowed to be sold as a commodity. As Karl Marx pointed out in *Das Kapital*:

> The guilds of the middle ages tried to prevent by force the transformation of the master of a trade into a capitalist, by limiting the number of labourers that could be employed by one master within a very small maximum.[11]

Such a restriction prevented the guild master from changing to a capitalistic entrepreneur. He could only employ workmen in the same craft in which he was himself a master. The merchant could buy every commodity, but he could not buy labor as a "commodity." He was concerned only with the turnover process of the products of the trade.

If an external circumstance made a further division of labor necessary, then the existing guilds would split or form new ones beside the old. But all this took place without the merging of different crafts within the *same* workshop. The guild organization thus excluded, as Marx correctly pointed out, every type of the division of labor which separated the laborer from his means of production and therefore prevented the means of production coming under the sole control of the supplier of capital.

All this changed fundamentally with the coming of large scale factory production. The factory took away the workers' status and put everything upon a money basis; with wages a man could exist; without wages he starved. Children under the new capitalistic organization might be able to earn more than adults; and thus became economically more important than their parents, who either lived on them or starved. Worse still, human labor itself became a commodity along with other commodities in the general process of production and exchange. As Disraeli observed, "Modern society acknowledges no neighbour."

As a result of this industrialization of society, new class distinctions began to appear between the new factory workers in the cities and the owners of the means of production, with the former becoming reduced to "merchandise."

An iron necessity seemed to control these developments. Already, David Ricardo, the great systematizer of the classical school of economics founded by Adam Smith, had established in his *Principles of Political Economy* that the new machines and the workers coexist in a state of constant competition with each other. As the opening to his chapter "On Wages" Ricardo states:

> Labour, like all things bought and sold and which may increase or decrease in quantity, has its natural and its market value. The natural price is that price which is necessary to enable labourers, one with another to subsist and to perpetuate their race without either increase or dimunition.[12]

He goes on to consider how this natural price of labor asserts itself in given circumstances. In the natural advance of society the wages of labor will have a tendency to fall; as population increases, the necessaries will be constantly rising in price because more labor will be necessary to produce them.

As for profits, they had a "natural tendency to fall, for, in the progress of society and wealth, the additional quantity of food required is obtained by the sacrifice of more and more labour."[13] Ricardo accepted the opposition between the workers and the capitalists as a fact. The landlord's share passed inexorably to him. It increased with population. The other two classes fought over what was left. The conditions of conflict were stringent: the national product was invariant and the money which facilitated its distribution was stable in quantity and velocity. Since the landlord's share rose, Ricardo's next proposition had the force of inevitability: "There can be no rise in the value of labour without a fall of profits." In this grim system, "in every case, agricultural, as well as manufacturing profits are lowered by a rise in the price of raw products, if it be accompanied by a rise in wages." The fall of profits diminished the incentive to accumulation of capital. When accumulation slowed, the wages fund shrank and the lot of the worker deteriorated.[14]

Thus when Karl Marx arrived upon the scene he already found most of the ingredients with which to concoct his witches' brew of revolution and upheaval. Marx's economics bore the imprint of Smith's labor theory of value, and Ricardo's theory of class struggle. Although he reduced the major economic classes to two by eliminating the landlords, Marx borrowed a good deal from Ricardo's handling of distribution. Starting with Ricardo's growing doubts about the favorable impact of machinery upon the working class, Marx developed a tremendous indictment of technology in a capitalist society. *Marx united the wish for action with the wish for explanation.* His philosophy of society is thus at once a claim to be a scientific analysis of society in the tradition of the French sociologists such as Saint Simon and August Comte and a call for a revolution to change society. As Raymond Aron well puts it in *Main Currents in Sociological Thought*:

> If it is clearly understood that the centre of Marx's thought is his assertion of the antagonistic character of the capitalist system, then it is immediately apparent why it is impossible to separate the analyst of capitalism from the prophet of socialism or, again, the sociologist from the man of action; for to show the antagonistic character of the capitalist system irresistibly leads to predicting the self-destruction of capitalism and thence to urging men to contribute something to the fulfilment of this prearranged destiny.[15]

In his important study, *Marxism*, George Lichtheim takes issue with such an interpretation. He writes:

> On this reading, Marxism is both a theory of the industrial revolution in its European phase, and an ideology of the socialist movement during the struggle for democracy. While plausible enough so far as it goes, this interpretation falls short of explaining what it was that made Marxism the instrument of total revolution and reconstruction on Russian (though not on German) soil. In particular it overlooks the fact that modern capitalism revolutionised European society only after it had been extensively secularized, i.e., placed on a rational foundation. Late medieval and Renaissance economic development effected nothing of the

kind; while as late as the seventeenth century, the "bourgeois revolution" in England was intermingled with a religious struggle which was certainly more than a sham. It was only in the late eighteenth-century that the dissolution of the traditional religious world-view gave rise to modern secularism, and it was then that the French Revolution proclaimed a totally new conception of politics as the application of rational principles to human affairs. This breakthrough has determined the entire history of nineteenth century Europe, and placed its stamp upon liberalism and socialism alike. These two movements, for all their antithetical views of society, are ideological twins; they arise almost simultaneously from the intellectual crisis at the opening of the century. At first liberalism, through its association with the now briefly triumphant middle class, is better able to exploit the forces unleashed by the industrial revolution; later it is overtaken by socialism which fastens upon the revolt of the proletariat. But the two strains are intermingled from the start, and nowhere more so than in Marxism, which affirms the fulfilment of the common humanist programme.[16]

Marx saw what a totally secularized, urbanized, and "rationalized" capitalist society was doing to the workers who labored in its new factories and mills. Instead of blaming the rootless secularism which was dehumanizing Western civilization, and man's apostasy from God, which had taken place in the French Revolution, he blamed capitalism's division of labor and exploitation of the workers. Refusing to be ordered in his thinking by God's Word, he was forced to absolutize one aspect of human life, namely, production, and then attempt to explain everything else in terms of it. Every aspect of man's life was viewed by Marx through his economic spectacles. Instead of placing the responsibility for the capitalists' inhumanity to their fellow men where it belongs, namely, in the inherent antinomies of apostate secular humanism and the societal relations that became based upon it, Marx proclaimed that capitalist relations of production as such are the sole cause of man's alienation and estrangement. Of this deeper apostate religious motivation of Marx's thought Dooyeweerd has written:

> Since Rousseau and Kant religious primacy had been ascribed to the motive of freedom. But now the religious dialectic again led Humanistic thought to the acceptance of the primacy of the

nature-motive. Freedom idealism began to collapse. Marxist sociology transformed the idealistic dialectic of Hegel into a historical materialism. The latter explained the ideological-super structure of society in terms of a reflection of the economic mode of production. . . .[17]

The basic error of Marxism is not that it assumes a historical-economic substructure of aesthetic life, justice, morals and faith. But it separates this conception from the cosmic order of meaning-aspects, and assumes it can explain the aesthetic conceptions and those of justice, morals and faith in terms of an ideological reflection of a system of economic production.[18]

In the Preface to *A Contribution to the Critique of Political Economy*, Marx summarized his sociological conception as a whole:

The general conclusion at which I arrived and which, once obtained, served to guide me in my studies, may be summarized as follows. In the social production which men carry on they enter into definite relations that are indispensable and independent of their will; these relations of production correspond to a definite stage of development of their material powers of production. The sum total of these relations of production constitutes the economic structure of society—the real foundation on which rise legal and political superstructures and to which correspond definite forms of social consciousness. The mode of production in material life determines the general character of the social, political and spiritual processes of life. It is not the consciousness of men that determines their existence, but, on the contrary, their social existence determines their consciousness. At a certain stage of their development, the material forces of production in society come into conflict with the existing relations of production, or— what is but a legal expression for the same thing—with the property relations within which they had been at work. From forms of development of the forces of production, these relations turn into their fetters. Then comes the period of social revolution. With the change of the economic foundation the entire immense superstructure is more or less rapidly transformed. In considering such transformation the distinction should always be made between the material transformation of the economic conditions of production which can be determined with the precision of natural science, and the legal, political, religious, aesthetic or philosophic—in short ideological—forms in which men become conscious of this conflict and fight it out. . . .

In broad outlines we can designate the Asiatic, the ancient, the feudal and the modern bourgeois methods of production as so many epochs in the progress of the economic formation of society. The bourgeois relations of production are the last antagonistic form of the social process of production—antagonistic not in the sense of individual antagonism, but of one arising from conditions surrounding the life of individuals in society; at the same time the productive forces developing in the womb of bourgeois society create the material conditions for the solution of that antagonism. This social formation constitutes, therefore, the closing chapter of the prehistoric stage of human society.[19]

This passage contains all the essential ideas of Marx's economic interpretation of history, with the sole exception, which we should note, that neither the concept of class nor the concept of class struggle figures in it explicitly.

According to Marx we can best follow the movement of history by analyzing the structures of societies, the forces of production, and the relations of production, and not by basing our interpretation on men's ways of thinking about themselves. There are social relations which impose themselves on individuals exclusive of their preferences, and an understanding of the historical process depends on our awareness of the supra-individual social relations. Again, in every society there can be distinguished the economic infrastructure and the superstructure, the former consists of the relations of production, while the latter of the legal and political institutions as well as religions, ideologies, and philosophies.

(b) *The Communist Manifesto*

In *The Communist Manifesto* Marx added to the above analysis of society a coherent theory of social change in terms of the idea of the class struggle. "The history of all hitherto existing society is the history of class struggles." [20] In modern times Marx detected two such struggles—the struggle between feudalism and the bourgeoise, ending in the victorious bourgeoisie revolution in Britain in 1689 and in France in 1789, and the struggle between the bourgeoisie and the proletariat destined to end in the victorious proletarian revolution. In the first struggle a nascent proletariat is mobilized by the bourgeoisie in support of its own aims, but is incapable of pursuing independent aims of its own; "every victory so obtained is a victory for the bourgeoisie." Thus every step the bourgeoisie has taken so far has advanced politically until today it has obtained complete mastery over society making use of the state as its "executive committee."

The *Manifesto* emphasizes the revolutionary part the bourgeoisie has played in history in its relentless drive to make the "cash nexus" the only bond between men. They have dissolved all other freedoms for the one freedom which gives them command of the world market—freedom of trade. As a result the only tie it has left between man and man is self-interest and "callous cash payment." It lives by exploitation, and its unresting search for markets means an unending and profound change in every aspect of life. It gives a "cosmopolitan character to production and consumption in every country." It compels the breakdown of national isolation; as it builds an interdependent material universe, so it draws as a common fund upon science and learning from every nation. It means the centralization of government, the supremacy of town over country, the dependence of backward peoples upon those with more advanced methods of production in their hands.

The *Manifesto* describes with savage eloquence how the development of bourgeois society makes the workman a wage-slave exploited by the capitalist. The latter spares neither age nor sex. He makes it increasingly impossible for the small producer to compete with him; on every side economic power is increasingly concentrated and the little man, in every category of industry and agriculture, is driven into the dependent condition of the working class. By improving and increasing the means of production the bourgeoisie has not only created the instrument that will bring about its own death, but it has called into being the men who will wield these weapons—the modern working class.

The proletariat develops at the same rate as the capital development of the bourgeoisie They are the modern working class "who live only as long as they find work and who find work only as long as their labour increases capital." [21]

As industry has developed, the proletariat has also grown in number and become concentrated in great masses of population living in the new industrial cities and towns. As their wage keeps fluctuating because of improvements made in the instruments of production, and as they are subjected to ever more severe forms of exploitation, the result is that in sheer self-defense the workers are compelled to fight their masters. They form unions, ever more wide, which come at last to fight together as a class. They fight for guaranteed wages but are successful only occasionally. "The real fruits of their battle, lie not in the immediate results, but in the ever expanding union of workers." [22] If the battle sways backwards and forwards, with gains here and losses there, the consolidation of the workers as a class hostile to their exploiters has one special feature which distinguishes it from all previous struggles between rulers and ruled: the working class becomes increasingly self-conscious as a class. If at first it struggles within the framework of the national state, it soon becomes evident that this struggle is but one act in a vast international drama. A time comes in the history of capitalism when its existence is no longer compatible with society. It cannot feed its slaves. It drives them to revolution in which a proletarian victory is inevitable.

According to the *Manifesto* the bourgeoisie by its very nature must fall. The working class upon whom it is dependent for its own existence will eventually be denied conditions under which it can exist. Every form of society has been based on the struggle between the oppressor and the oppressed. But in order for such a condition to continue the oppressor has to prevent the slave from sinking into such a state that he has to feed him instead of being fed by him. "The modern labourer, instead of rising with the progress of industry, sinks deeper and deeper below the conditions of existence of his own class." [23] The result is poverty which develops far more rapidly than population or wealth. Thus it becomes evident that the bourgeoisie can no longer be the ruling class in society because "it is incompetent to assure to its slaves their slavery." [24] The existence of the bourgeoisie is dependent on the formation and increase of capital, capital on wage labor, and wage labor on competition between laborers for employment. Modern industry drives the laborers to combine into one class, thus digging the grave for the bourgeoisie.

In this second, more fundamental struggle of history between the bourgeoisie and the proletariat Marx recognizes the presence of a lower middle class—the small manufacturer and shopkeeper, the artisan, the peasant—which plays a fluctuating role between the bourgeoisie and the proletariat, and a "slum proletariat" which is liable to "sell itself to reactionary forces." [25] But these complications do not seriously affect the ordered simplicity of the main pattern of revolution.

The proletariat is in fact the only truly revolutionary class of all the classes opposing the bourgeoisie. Since they experience the same type of submission and exploitation in all lands they have been stripped of all national character. "Law, morality, religion, are to him so many bourgeois prejudices, behind which . . . lurk in ambush . . . just as many bourgeoisie interests." [26] As the working class comes to power so it will have to destroy all "previous securities for and insurances of individual property." [27] The proletariat is therefore a movement in the interest of the immense majority which cannot raise itself up. The class struggle of capitalism will be replaced by "an association in which the free development of each is the condition for the free development of all." [28]

The pattern of revolution described in the *Manifesto* had been framed in the light of Marx's reading in modern English and French history, the works of French and British economists of the so-called classical school, and of Engel's study of factory conditions in England. The English bourgeois revolution, winning its victory in the seventeenth century, had fully consolidated itself by 1832. The French bourgeois revolution, more suddenly and dramatically triumphant after 1789, had succumbed to reaction only to re-emerge once more in 1830. In both countries the first revolutionary struggle of the modern age, the struggle between feudalism and bourgeoisie was virtually over; the stage was set for the second struggle, between bourgeoisie and proletariat.

The events of 1848, coming hard on the heels of the *Manifesto*, did much to confirm its diagnosis and nothing to refute it. In England the collapse of Chartism was a setback which none the less marked a stage in the consolidation of a class-conscious workers' movement. In France the proletariat marched shoulder to shoulder with the bourgeoisie in February, 1848, as the *Manifesto* had said it would, so long as the aim was to consolidate and extend the bourgeois revolution. But once the proletariat raised its own banner of social revolution, the line was crossed. Bourgeoisie and proletariat, allies until the bourgeois revolution had been completed and made secure, were now divided on opposite sides of the barricades by the call for proletarian revolution.

The first revolutionary struggle was thus over; the second was impending. In Paris, in the June days of 1848, Cavaignac saved the bourgeoisie and staved off the proletarian revolution by massacring, executing, and transporting the class-conscious workers. The pattern of the *Communist Manifesto* had been precisely followed. As L. Namier, who was no Marxist, put it: "The working classes touched off, and the middle classes cashed in on it."

> The June revolution (as Marx wrote at the time) for the first time split the whole of society into two hostile camps—east and west Paris. The unity of the February revolution no longer exists. The February fighters are now warring against each other—something that has never happened before; the former indifference has vanished and every man capable of bearing arms is fighting on one side or other of the barricades.[29]

The events of February and June, 1848, had provided a classic illustration of the great gulf fixed between the bourgeois and proletarian revolutions.

According to Marx the proletarian revolution would be led by the Communist Party, which would act as the revolutionary vanguard. As such the new program of International Communism stood for: (1) the overthrow of capitalism, (2) the abolition of private property, (3) the elimination of the bourgeois family and the replacement of home education by social education, (4) the abolition of all classes, (5) the overthrow of all existing governments, and (6) the establishment of a communist order with communal ownership of property in a classless, stateless society.[30] To accomplish this program the *Communist Manifesto* announced that the Communists would have to change all traditional ideas in religion and philosophy. Since it puts human experience upon a new basis, it will be forced to change the ideas which are their expression. Concluding it stated:

> The Communists everywhere support every revolutionary movement against the existing social and political order of things. . . . They openly declare that their ends can be attained only by the forcible overthrow of all existing social conditions. Let the ruling classes tremble at a communist revolution. The proletarians have nothing to to lose but their chains. THEY HAVE A WORLD TO WIN. WORKING MEN OF ALL COUNTRIES, UNITE! [31]

The overwhelming impression which the *Communist Manifesto* leaves on the reader's mind is not so much that the proletarian revolution is desirable (that, like the injustice of capitalism in *Das Kapital*, is taken for granted as something not requiring argument), but that the revolution is inevitable. For successive generations of Marxists the *Manifesto* has not been a plea for revolution—that they do not need—but a *scientific* prediction about the way in which the revolution would inevitably happen combined with a prescription for the action required to make it happen.

The reason for this conviction is the Marxist dogma of "Economic Determinism," that is, man's effort to survive. Communists are convinced as a matter of religious faith that everything men do— whether it is organizing a government, establishing laws, supporting a particular moral code, or practicing a particular religion— is merely the result of their desire to protect whatever mode of production they are currently using to secure the necessities of life. Further, Communists believe that if some revolutionary force changes the mode of production, the dominant class will immediately set about to create a different type of society designed to protect the new economic order. Thus the *Manifesto* says:

> Does it require deep intuition to comprehend that man's ideas, views and conception, in one word, man's consciousness, changes with every change in the conditions of material existence? . . . What else does the history of ideas prove than that intellectual production changes in character in proportion as material production is changed? [32]

In the *Handbook on Marxism* we read:

It is not the consciousness of men that determines their existence but, on the contrary, it is their social existence that determines their consciousness. At a certain stage of their development
the material productive resources of society come into contradiction with the existing productive relationships, or, what is but
the legal expression of these, with the property relations within
which they had moved before. From forms of the development of
the productive forces, these relationships are transformed into
their fetters. Then an epoch of social revolution opens. With
the change in the economic foundation the whole vast superstructure is more or less rapidly transformed. In considering such
revolutions it is necessary always to distinguish between the
material revolution in the economic conditions of production,
which can be determined with scientific accuracy, and the juridical, political, religious, aesthetic or philosophic—in a word, ideological forms wherein men become conscious of this conflict
and fight it out.[33]

The essence of Marx's teaching is its claim to have a scientific
character. It arose by reaction from the "utopianism" of the early
socialists, who constructed ideal socialist societies out of the wealth
and ingenuity of their own fertile imaginations and did not consider
it necessary to concern themselves with the question how these
ideal societies of the future were to be evolved out of existing
societies. Marx's method was fundamentally historical; all changes
in the destiny and organization of mankind were part of an ever
flowing historical process. He made the basic assumption that society
would in the long run always organize itself in such a way as to
make the most effective use of its productive resources. He started
from an analysis of existing society in order to show that the capitalist order, once instrumental in releasing and fostering an unprece-
dented expansion of the productive forces of mankind, had now
reached a stage in its historical development where it had become a
hindrance to the most effective use of these forces. It was therefore
bound, in compliance with Marx's initial postulate of economic
determinism, to yield place to a new social order which would once
more permit and promote the maximum use of productive resources.

This new order was "socialism" or "communism" (which he distinguished in his later writings as the initial and final phases of the society to come). Marx's conception was thus both scientific and revolutionary. Most of his writings were directed not to convince his readers that the change from capitalism to socialism was desirable, but to convince them that it was inevitable—though given his original postulate, the two conceptions were implicitly identical. His conception was revolutionary in the sense that he believed that the change required by the replacement of the bourgeoisie by the proletariat as ruling class could only be accomplished by revolutionary violence. His conception was scientific in the sense that he carried to theoretical completion the unification of the previously separated sciences of politics and economics. What Marx had done was to merge both politics and economics in the new science of sociology, a term which he does not seem to have used, but which Auguste Comte invented in his life time. According to Marxists, politics and economics are ultimately a matter of the structure of society, which is in turn a result of the relations between men set up by current methods of production. The tragedy is that Marx should have chosen the economic aspect of human life as the ordering principle of the social sciences. The whole philosophy, religion, and morality of communism today is characterized by this absolutization of the economic aspect of life. As Engels states it: "The final causes of all social changes and political revolution are to be sought, not in man's brains, not in man's insight into eternal truth and justice . . . but in the economics of each particular epoch." Instead of defining man in terms of his relation to the God who had created him, Marxists identify man's life with his tool-making capacity and his socio-economic functions. As Marxists see him man is not to be understood as *homo religiosus* as the Bible teaches but as *homo economicus*. Instead of believing that man is a sinner in need of redemption from the guilt and power of his sin by the death of Christ, Marxists ascribe all the wrong that men do to factors beyond their voluntary control. They blame the existence of evil upon the existence of private property. It is for this reason that both Marx and Engels advocated a change in the economic structure of human society as the only way by which men could save themselves. Only by abolishing the right of the capitalist to control the means of production and to live off the "surplus value" of the workers' labor can the workers of the world become truly free. Out of the capitalists' control of the means of production had blossomed class struggle, greed, pride, imperialism, and war.

As such communism should be thought as a substitute religion for Christianity. Instead of finding its ultimate security and salvation in God, communism finds it in withdrawing the means of production from the control of individual owners. From that alone it expects salvation to come; in that it finds its ultimate certainty in this world. For when private propery and private ownership of the means of production have gone, then, says communism, war will be abolished, and righteousness and peace will prevail upon the earth as never before, and the exploitation of the workers will cease. In their opinion this climax to world history is inevitable, since it rests upon two fundamental laws which Marxists claim to have discovered, namely, dialectical materialism and historical materialism.

The basic thesis of dialectical materialism is described in official communist textbooks as follows: "Matter, nature, is eternal, infinite and unlimited." That means that matter exists always and everywhere. There is nothing in the world that does not originate from matter. With this thesis, it is obvious that communism principially and absolutely denies the existence of God, the Creator of heaven and earth. According to Communists, man is not created by God, but God is created by man; the product of misconception on man's part. As Lenin explains it:

> Marx said, "Religion is the opium of the people"—and this postulate is the corner stone of the whole philosophy of Marxism with regard to religion. Marxism always regarded all modern religions and churches, and every kind of religious organisation as instruments of that bourgeois reaction whose aim is to defend exploitation by stupefying the working class. . . .
> The roots of modern religion are deeply embedded in the social oppression of the working classes. . . . "Fear created the gods." Fear of the blind force of capital—blind because its action cannot be foreseen by the masses—a force which at every step in life threatens the worker and the small business man with "sudden,"

"unexpected," "accidental destruction and ruin, bringing in their train beggary, pauperism, prostitution, and deaths from starvation —this is the TAP-ROOT of modern religion." [34]

Communists do not deny that spiritual life exists, but they insist that such spiritual life is nothing but the offshoot of matter. A thought, for example, is a spiritual thing, but it is, according to communist doctrine, the product of the brain, "generated" by matter.

Dialectical materialism teaches that this matter is not at rest but rather in ceaseless motion. Matter generates higher levels of organization of energy. It is in process toward higher stages of development. This process occurs dialectically; that means it is subject to the law of opposites. Thus electricity is characterized by a positive and negative charge. Atoms consist of protons and electrons which are unified but contradictory forces. Communists conclude that everything in existence contains two mutually incompatible and exclusive but nevertheless equally essential and indispensable parts or aspects. They suppose that this unity of opposites in nature is the thing which makes each entity auto-dynamic and provides the constant impetus for movement and change.

As Communists conceive of it, matter is in a process of movement governed by the laws of negation and of transformation, which causes it to reach higher levels of organization. Originally there was nothing but lifeless matter. By way of a dialectical process living matter developed from this. Life came into existence not as the result of any creative act by God but by chance. Here, in short, we have nothing else than the theory of evolution and the chaos cults of the ancient Near East, dressed up in dialectical clothes.[35]

If Communists appeal to dialectical materialism to explain the origin of nature, they turn to historical materialism to explain the development of human society. In principle Communists believe that the same laws that hold good for the total development of the world hold also for the origin and development of human society. Accordingly, human society too is shaped by a development or process determined not by any divine ordinances but by the principle of matter. For the Communist, history is not the record of God's dealings with men, but the record of the material forces of production in use at any given time. The character of every society in history has been determined by the state of material technological factors that have been utilized by given societies in the production of goods.

For example, when in a particular society the techniques available are as yet rudimentary and manual labor predominates, then, Marxists teach, a society is necessary in which private ownership of goods and persons is the rule. Such a society existed under feudalism. As soon as technology advances, however, and steam and electrical power replaces manual and water power, then society is forced to change its social structure to one of capitalism instead of feudalism.

Today, the Marxists believe, society has reached a point at which the productive forces available make it necessary to change from capitalism to communism. The latest phase in technological change requires the *common* rather than the *private* ownership of property. Under communism the state will simply wither away.

The reason for this is that Communists believe that private property had led the owners of capital to invent the state as a necessary instrument of social control of the workers. According to the *Communist Manifesto*, the state is "nothing more than a committee for the administration of the consolidated affairs of the bourgeois class as a whole." When the workers had become exploited to the point where there was danger of revolt, the dominant class was forced to create an organ of power to maintain "law and order," that is, a system of laws to protect the private property and advantages of the exploiting class. This new order, they teach, is the state.

Thus Engels writes in *The Origin of the Family, Private Property and the State*:

"The state, then is . . . simply a product of society at a certain stage of evolution. It is the confession that this society has become hopelessly divided against itself, has entangled itself in irreconcilable contradictions which it is powerless to banish." [36]

Thus the state is designed to postpone the day of judgment. The government is the "instrument of power"—an unnatural appendage to society—which is created for the express purpose of protecting the privileged class and the private property it possesses from the just demands of the exploited class. Marxists teach that when the private ownership of the means of production and distribution has been abolished the state will no longer be necessary, since there will be no one left to coerce and it will therefore gradually wither away. As class distinctions based upon private property rights disappear and production has been taken over by society as a whole, the coercive necessity for the state will disappear. As Engels put it:

"The government of persons is replaced by the administration of things and the direction of the process of production." [37]

This whole movement towards classless society is inevitable and irrevocable, since it is guaranteed by the irrevocable law of the dialectical progress of matter. Matter must strive with ironclad necessity to generate the highest and most perfect society—the classless society of pure communism.

Under communism or the collective ownership of the means of production and exchange, the workers' labor would no longer be treated as a "commodity" to be bought and sold. That objective is the whole import behind Marx's famous theory of surplus value which has been so much criticized by twentieth century economists. Marx was determined to give back to the workers what he considered had been so unjustly taken away from them. Classical economists had set up as the norm of economic life the freely competitive market, to which each individual was supposed to bring the product of his own labor to be exchanged for equal value, and in which the freedom of exchange produces at once the greatest number of goods and services and a substantially just distribution. Against this Marx set the ideal of the planned socialist economy as "an association of free individuals who work with jointly owned means of production, and wittingly expend their several labour powers as a combined social labour power." [38] Marx's idea was a society in which production is regulated consciously to supply commodities where needed and in the quantity needed and in which each receives according to his needs and gives according to his abilities. He writes:

> Only when production will be under the conscious and pre-arranged control of society, will society establish a direct relation between the quantity of social labour time employed in the

production of definite articles and the quantity of the demand of society for them.[39]

Thus the true productive unit is society itself, the "collective laborer works belongs to the capitalist, and a bourgeois economics division of labor. But the mechanism with which the collective laborer works belongs to the capitalist, and a bourgeois economics construes the increased productivity gained by cooperation as the productivity of capital rather than labor. Marx's economics tried to construe it in terms of human relations instead of cash nexus. Under the conditions that exist these relationships are, for the worker, stultifying and depersonalizing. The perfection of the collective worker is purchased at the cost of narrowing specialization in its parts, the individual workers. As Marx puts it:

> It [manufacture] transforms the worker into a cripple, a monster, by forcing him to develop some highly specialized dexterity at the cost of a world of productive impulses and faculties. . . . To begin with, the worker sells his labour power to capital because he himself lacks the material means requisite for the production of a commodity. But now his individual labour power actually re- renounces work unless it is sold to capital.[40]

This result Marx believed to be at once an instrument of exploitation and a necessary stage in economic development. The coexistence of socialized production and capitalistic appropriation is the underlying contradiction which drives contemporary society toward the association of free individuals and the classless society of the future.

In Marxian economics the distribution of wealth is really a question of social policy to be adjusted to the requirements of production, and any adjustment is compatible with the system if it does not give rise to differences of economic class.

Both Marx and Engels envisaged a transition period between the revolution which would usher in the final socialist society and communism when the state would disappear. This they called the dictatorship of the proletariat, in which the working classes would be led by the Communist Party in destroying the existing bourgeois control and ownership of the means of production, convert these means of production into public ownership, and eventually bring in the classless society. For Communists the voice of the Party is in fact the voice of God, just as for the Jesuits the voice of the pope is the voice of God.

(c) *The Marxist Concept of Trade Unions*

For this reason Engels and Marx regarded the trade unions as promoters of treason to the revolution that would usher in the perfect society of communism. To them every bargain between capitalist owner and trade union was a betrayal of their hope of social warfare. Instead of accepting industrial discord and strife between management and unions as indicative of a natural movement for remedial adjustment, Marxists choose to escape from the requisite conflicts by abolishing the industrial system in which they arise. Communist revolutionaries suppose that if they can only be freed from these particular irritations and disputes they will escape from all of them. For Marx the great aim was a world in which such irritations and disagreements will never again arise. Refusing to accept the biblical truth that sin resides in the human heart rather than in outward institutions as Christ most clearly taught when he said: "From inside, out of a man's heart, come evil thoughts, acts of fornicating, of theft, murder, adultery, ruthless greed, and malice, fraud, indecency, envy, slander, arrogance and folly; these evil things come from the inside and they defile the man" (Mark 7:14-23); the Communists instead see evil to reside in institutions. By refusing to overthrow the capitalistic order of production the trade unions were standing in the way of Marx's coming Utopia, and therefore the trade unions had either to be captured and taken over so that they would serve the cause of revolution, or they had to be destroyed. To the Marxists the trade unions' effort to retrieve the older system of guilds or to reform the new was obstructionist. The acceptance of the world here and now by the trade unions Marx and Engels found especially galling. To them the trade union leader was a "petty bourgeois," a "misleader," and a "traitor." The trade union stood in the path and blocked the way to the communist heaven on earth.

Ever since Marx's time Communists and socialists have always tended to consider themselves superior to the trade unionists, and their parties were conceived as standing outside and as acting on the trade unions from above. The Communist Party is to lead and inspire the workers' movement so that in due course they join in the coming class revolution. Communists even today are so sure of their ends, so certain of the inevitability of their objectives, that the labor leader who opposes their meddling is condemned as an enemy of the working class.

The Communists will raise up the working class by creating the dictatorship of the proletariat. In Russia, therefore, which is the model of all revolutionary movements and Communist Party objectives, "not one important political or organizational question is decided by any state institution in our republic without the governing instruction of the central committee of the party." [41]

The trade unions have to be captured because, as Marx taught, "the general tendency of capitalist production is not to raise but to sink the average standard of wages." [42] Trade unions are a misguided and wasted effort because "they are fighting with the effects but not with the cause of those effects. . . . They are applying palliatives, not curing the remedy." Trade unions must aim at the larger goal which Marx defines as "the abolition of the wage system." [43] This theme runs through Marx's writing whenever he touches on the trade unions.

Engels shared Marx's view. The trade unions are not sufficient for the purpose of the revolution. He said that "something more is needed than trade unions and strikes to break the power of the ruling class." [44]

In 1879 Engels criticized the English trade union movement because it had devoted its energies to the "strike for wages and shorter working hours . . . as an end in itself." The remedy for this preoccupation with the practical and the immediate was to "work inside of them to form within this still quite plastic mass a core of people . . . who will take over the leadership . . . when the . . . impending breakup of the present 'order' takes place." [45]

This was Engels' prescription for the American Knights of Labor, and the idea of "boring from within" and capturing the leadership of the labor unions has been applied by both Communists and Socialists wherever they could. They are still doing it, and have been doing it in America since the 1930's. By the end of the 1930's Communists controlled twenty-one of the international unions affiliated with the CIO. Similarly the E.T.U. was found in Britain to have been infiltrated and then taken over by the Communists. In Canada the Communists took control of the International Sea Farers Union. In Italy they control nearly half the trade unions. For the Communist, then, the trade union is not important as a method of collective bargaining and hence of providing strength to the workers in their bargaining with management, but only as a political and economic tool to further the revolution.

Such a view of the labor unions was taken over by Lenin and elaborated into a working technique. In 1900 he declared, "Isolated from Social-Democracy, the labor movement becomes petty and inevitably becomes bourgeois; in conducting only the economic struggle, the working class loses its political independence; it becomes the tail of the other parties and runs counter to the great slogan: 'The emancipation of the workers must be the task of the workers themselves.' "[46]

It is just this, of course, that the Communists have prevented first in Russia and wherever else they have seized power. As the dictatorship of the proletariat has developed and functioned under dictators Lenin, Stalin, and Khrushchev, the trade unions have been first captured by the Communist Party and used, and then emasculated of all independence of action. The workers' organizations in Russia have no other use or power than that which fits in with the political and revolutionary aims of the Communist Party. In Russia the trade unions function as organs of the Communist Government by means of which it maintains an iron control of the workers. Under Soviet Communism the labor unions do not plead the cause of the workers before the employer, but they plead the cause of the Great Employer—the state—before the employees.

(d) *The Soviet Treatment of Labor in Russia*

Under Stalin the state directed labor. Industrial businesses signed contracts with the collective farms, by which the latter were obliged to send, if necessary by force, specified numbers of men and women to work in the great new factories that were going up in the towns and cities.

A great deal is today known about this forced labor in the Soviet Union from former prisoners now living in the West, and from Soviet writers such as Alexander Solzhenitsyn, about the ritual of arrest, confession, and sentence, and about the life of prisoners and camp organization. It is known that there were four major waves of mass arrests: the "dekulakisation" of the early 1930's, directed against recalcitrant peasants, particularly the better-off kulaks or "tight-fists"; the Yezhov terror of 1936-38, involving army officers, party officials, scientists, and business managers; the deportation of middle-class people from the Baltic states and other newly annexed areas in 1940 and 1941; and the post-1945 arrests of ex-prisoners of war and of people from the occupied areas. In addition, a more or less continuous process of arrest provided a kind of groundswell; throughout the Stalin period citizens from national minorities were particularly liable to arrest; and the ordinary worker might find himself behind the wire as a result of indiscipline or indiscretion—in the early 1950's it was possible to get five years for drunkenness.

How many people were confined in such forced labor camps? Estimates have varied from less than one and a half million to more than seven million forced laborers within the borders of the U.S.S.R. Dr. Jasny reached a figure of three and a half million, but his critics claimed that this estimate could be reduced or much increased without doing violence to the figures of the 1941 NKVD Plan. In his book, *Forced Labour and Economic Development*, S. Swianiewicz has suggested that figure of seven million is more probable. As a former forced laborer in Soviet Russia, Swianiewicz has tried to answer questions such as how did this terrible system arise, what was its rationale, and what function did it play in the Soviet system as a whole? [47]

His explanation of the emergence of the system during the first five-year plan and its perpetuation in the late 1930's and 1940's is Marxist. Given the predominance of the idea of what the author terms "explosive planning," it followed that incomes in the expanding industrial sector must rise more rapidly that the supply of industrial consumer goods and agricultural products, which were receiving less priority. From this arose "the perils of the wages-goods gap." According to Swianiewicz the introduction of forced labor had two results advantageous to the industrialization process. First it mobilized peasants into industrial and building labor at a time when they were not prepared to leave their villages voluntarily. Stalin aimed at securing by decree of the state the reserve of manpower for industry which in Western countries had been created by the chronic and spontaneous flight of impoverished peasants to the towns. Secondly, depressing the standard of living of the prisoners helped to reduce the demand for scarce food and consumer goods.

This explanation surely needs more evidence to support it. Were the authorities who ordered the expulsion of the kulaks motivated by the need for cheap labor rather than by their wish to break the opposition of the peasantry to collectivization? Isaac Deutscher in his classic work on *Stalin* answers that it was both. He says:

> Rapid industrialization at once created an acute shortage of labour, and that meant the end of laissez faire. This was, in Stalin's words, the "end of spontaneity" on the labour market, the beginning of what, in English speaking countries, was later called the direction of labour. The forms of direction were manifold. . . .
>
> Forced labour, in the strict sense, was imposed on peasants who had resorted to violence in resisting collectivization. They were treated like criminals. . . . As the number of rebellious peasants grew they were organized into mammoth labour camps and employed in the building of canals and railways, in timber felling and so on. "Re-education" degenerated into slave labour, terribly wasteful of human life.[48]

When Swianiewicz tries to account for the perpetuation of this system of forced labor into the later 1930's and beyond he is more illuminating. In his account, the driving mechanism at this stage was the combination of scarcity of manpower with the inability of the government to direct labor and to organize the labor market. The scarcity of manpower was due to the fact that most unproductive labor had already been removed from the villages. The inability of the government to direct labor was due not to a belief in freedom but to "the lack of disposition in the population to cooperate with authority." Here Swianiewicz contrasts the social experience of Russia where "the peoples of what is at present the Soviet Union passed neither through the school of democratic citizenship nor through that of trade unionism," with that of Western Europe, which has "produced not only the individualsm of the capitalisic entrepreneur but a disposition for cooperation in matters concerning the national community." He might also have pointed out that the workers of the Protestant nations had also learned a dedication for work sadly lacking in Orthodox lands. As Max Weber well said, "The Puritans wanted to be businessmen; we are condemned to it." The worker in Soviet Russia is condemned to fulfill a narrow social function within vast and anonymous groups, without the possibility of a total flowering of the personality which was possible in Puritan society. However, we can accept his conclusion that legislation controlling the movement of labor was less effective in the U.S.S.R than in Britain during the war. The forced labor system of Soviet communism thus becomes, on Swianiewicz's hypothesis, a very large periphery to the free labor market, and serves to adjust the distribution of labor to the priorities of government.

To explain is not to justify. Swianiewicz seeks to show that even considered purely in economic terms the cost of maintaining the machinery of coercion was so great that no net gain to the government may have resulted. However, he neglects to point out the disciplinary advantages which the known existence of the labor camps must have produced in the free labor sector of the Russian economy.

When Stalin boasted that in Soviet Russia labor "had from a disgraceful and painful burden been transformed into a matter of glory, valor and heroism," his words must have sounded like mockery to the millions of inmates of the forced labor camps.

They did not sound so to those more fortunate workers to whom the great Five Year Plans for the enforced industrialization of Russia spelled social advance. Industrial labor and technical efficiency came to be surrounded with unusual glamor, which made them attractive to the younger generation. The press, the theatre, the film, and the radio extolled "the heroes of the production front" the way famous soldiers and film stars were extolled in Western lands.

Perhaps the most important aspect of Stalin's labor policy was his fight against equalitarian trends. He insisted on the need for a highly differentiated scale of material rewards for work, designed to encourage skill and efficiency. In a famous speech on industrialization given in 1934, Stalin decried the demand for equalization of wages and salaries as a "reactionary, petty-bourgeois absurdity worthy of a primitive sect of ascetics but not of socialist society organized on Marxian lines." He claimed that Marxists were no levellers in the popular sense; and he found support for his thesis in Marx's saying that even in a classless society workers would at first be paid according to their efforts and not according to their needs. As a result of this policy throughout the thirties, the differentiation of wages and salaries was pushed to extremes, with managers receiving ten to twenty times the wages of ordinary workers. A wide gulf came to separate the vast mass of unskilled and underpaid workmen from the privileged "labor aristocracy" and bureaucracy. These highly paid and privileged managerial groups came to be the main props of Stalin's regime.[49] They had a vested interest in it. Stalin himself felt that his dictatorship was the more secure the more solidly it rested on a rigid hierarchy of interest and influence. It is no doubt for this reason that James Burnham claimed in his book, *The Managerial Revolution*, that "The Russian Revolution was not a socialist revolution but a managerial revolution." [50]

In this type of "managerial society" the labor unions would appear to function as mere aids of the managers in the direction of labor and production. According to the Rules of the Trade Unions of the U.S.S.R., the labor unions are "a school of management and a school of communism." All their activities take place under the guidance of the Communist Party. Victor Kravchenko, in his evidence before the Committee on Unamerican Activities of the House of Representatives, stated that "the local Communist Party organization elects one of its suitable members to become president of the trade union. . . . The union's job is to see that strict discipline is maintained, that there will be no strikes, that the workers work for wages established by the central government, that the workers carry out all the decisions, resolutions, et cetera, of the party. . . . If the worker leaves his job in one factory and goes to another without the permission of his director he will be prosecuted under the law for violation of the law prohibiting unauthorized change of employment. This law refers not only to laborers but to any kind of employee." [51]

From this evidence of a former Soviet official it would seem that labor unions are still very much a tool in the hands of the Soviet Government and of the "managerial class" which has succeeded the old capitalist class as rulers of Russia. Their central task is to help strengthen the economy by speeding up production. Officially there is only one labor union in Russia, of which the highest body is the U.S.S.R. Congress of Trade Unions.

Thus the end result of Marx's so-called scientific materialism has been the creation of a collectivist society in which the spiritual lot of the workers has not been improved and in which "production governs all." The underlying tendency in Russian communism is to subordinate everything to production, including man, who becomes merely an instrument of production, and including all spiritual values, whose mission is becoming more and more simply that of providing pretexts in favor of yet more production. Marx had believed that the self-alienation of man, present in a capitalistic society because the means of production are not under his control, would be abolished as soon as these means had become the property of the community. In the Russian variety of communism, where the worker in theory "owns all," he actually owns nothing. According to the Word of God man is indeed alienated from reality, but the cause of this alienation does not lie in private property, but in man's fallen sinful nature, though his redemption from the power and guilt of sin does have social consequences.

(e) *A Christian Critique of Communism*

Before condemning communism we must always bear in mind that it is a product of our Western civilization, which thought it could disengage human freedom and human society from God's law. It was not Karl Marx who discovered Economic Man. Long before Marx appeared on the Western scene the pursuit of wealth and power had become the governing factor in Western life. Egoism had become absolutized. Speaking of the post-Renaissance era, R. H. Tawney once observed that it was:

> . . . the period of a revolution which was to set a naturalistic political arithmetic in place of theology, substitute the categories of mechanism for those of teleology, and turn religion itself from the master interest of mankind into one department of life.[52]

Likewise, Basil Willey tells us:

> The Middle Ages condemned usury as unnatural, contrary of Scripture and to Aristotle; and it also condemned in the names of Scripture and Nature, precisely "that effort to achieve a continuous and unlimited increase in material wealth which modern societies applaud as meritorious." The centuries following the Renaissance liberated the acquisitive impulses, also in the name of Nature, and severed economic ethics from control by any comprehensive conception of the ultimate purpose of human (not to say Christian) living. . . . The Law of Nature, which in the Middle Ages had been a check on unregenerate impulse, had now been transformed into a sanction for laissez faire, and free competition for the spoils of the world.[53]

Communism is the first modern attempt to replace over the confused activities of economic man "*a comprehensive conception of the ultimate purpose of human living.*" But it makes a disastrous identification of man with economic man, and as a result it reduces man to the level of one of his functions. What Marx did was to provide a philosophical justification for what he found already going on in the world of his day. Unfettered by any religious or moral scruples, the apostate humanists of the eighteenth and nineteenth century acceped the dictation of so-called natural economic laws as the ultimate standard of their lives. Since the Word of God was no longer providing the ordering principle of human life and no longer providing guidance concerning human relations in work and industry. These new entrepreneurs were led to treat their fellow men in this area of human life, not as sons of God, but as economic agents.

If Marx did not invent economic man, neither did he discover the class struggle. The Industrial Revolution had introduced into industrial and commercial relations an essential strife. The new economy assured a necessary conflict of interests between those of the producer and those of the consumer. That this conflict of interest was necessary was supposed to be an economic law. Like the laws of nature, no moral denunciation could be accepted as relevant. In the same way it assumed, in the words of Ricardo, that "Labour, like all things bought and sold and which may increase or decrease in quantity, has its natural and its market value. The natural price is that price which is necessary to enable labourers, one with another, to subsist and to perpetuate their race without either increase or diminution." [54] For the poor laborer the economic laws could promise no redress. The whole laissez faire economic system was built upon this supposition; and for generations after the repeal of the Combination Acts, the trade unions had to fight bitterly against the assumption that improvement in the wages and conditions of the workers would eventually destroy the whole economic edifice upon which a modern industrial nation's material welfare now depended. That assumption was that the strong and the fortunate were entitled, nay, compelled, to live at the expense of the weak and the unfortunate. It generated that particular form of class antagonism which became so characteristic of laissez faire industrialism. In this way the Industrial Revolution prepared the way for Marx's doctrine of the class war as essential to the very structure of reality. What he did was to push back to their ultimate philosophical foundations the ideas which were governing the economic world of his time. For this reason, Lester De Koster has argued in his recent book, *Communism and Christian Faith*,[55] that laissez faire capitalism has no real defense against Marx, for the roots of his own system, in part at least, are to be found in this same apostate economic philosophy. Laissez faire economic philosophy is thus no answer to the challenge of scientific materialism and its attendant Marxist sociology.

Marxism maintains that the successes of capitalism must be ascribed to the great technological progress which Marx himself could not foresee. De Koster, however, points out that of even greater importance than such technological advances have been the "moral and religious considerations" which have exerted a significant influence in modern economic life. Capitalism has not gone the way Marx predicted because it has not gone the way of classical economics. Classical economics proceeded from the assumption that happiness would increase with the extended distribution of property and the satisfaction of human wants. It did not take the factor of human sinfulness very seriously and thus paved the way for the Marxist critique of the callousness and brutality of laissez faire capitalists. Orienting himself to classical economics Marx showed that the unlimited operation of the laws of supply and demand had led to the exploitation of the weak by the strong. His prediction that such exploitation would one day result in revolution by the proletariat was not fulfilled in the Western world because the operation of self-interest was in the long run outweighed by considerations of humanity, morality, and justice. New social techniques and social-economic legislation were the methods by which the Western world achieved the amelioration of the working classes.

According to De Koster, Christians must therefore not only oppose Marxism and socialism but also the economic individualism of the classical school of economics. For "moral and religious considerations" are of essential significance for economic relations. Unless the Spirit and Law of God take control of the economic activities of Western men, then their societies may expect to go the way of Russian and Chinese society. More and more Christians must therefore be persuaded to give concrete expression to their Christian principles in their economic and business life. A so-called economic law may not be a pretense for the continued existence of an ethically unacceptable situation. If the economies of Britain and North America cannot be subjected to the divinely established norms governing the relations between man and God's creation and man and man, then Marx's prophecy of revolution in the West may yet be proved correct.

"Christian Anti-Communism," De Koster concludes,

> . . . must be guided by Biblical directives. This requires that we
> acknowledge that communisma rose as a result of sins committed
> by our forebears in economic, social and political relations. More-
> over there must be the realization that the totalitarian character of
> the communist threat is here to teach us that God demands of us
> that we subject our whole way of life and attitudes to His di-
> vine standards of justice and love revealed in the Holy Scriptures.
> The command to love our neighbor must become concrete not
> only in our personal lives but also in the institutions and structures
> of society. We are anti-communists because God cannot have
> fellowship with atheism. But this also includes Western atheism
> and apostate humanism. The Word of God must become a con-
> structive social power in the affairs of men.[56]

While commending De Koster for his criticism of Marxism it
must be pointed out that he wants to find a solution to Marx's econo-
mism in a Christian moralism. De Koster should have made it clear
that to overcome Marxism we must discover a Christian *political*
order as well as a Christian *moral* order. It is not only necessary
to provide moral guidelines for economics and politics, but also to
discover how these Christian values and norms may become positivized in the economic and political realm, and this requires a Christian view of the structures of society.

Further, it must be pointed out that Marx's doctrine of the
"withering away of the state" not only rejects the "body politic" but
really eliminates the aspect and function of justice from reality. If
there is no aspect of justice in the modal order of reality, then there
is no room for the social institution of the body politic. Lacking a
true understanding of the creation ordinances, which include that
of the state, Marx was unable to see the necessity for the state's role
of integrating justice between the various sovereign spheres of society. Instead of advocating that the state should be abolished,
Marx should have called upon Western governments to fulfill their
proper task. The state sins not only by usurping authority, but also
when it does not make use of all the authority given to it. At the
same time, the power of the state should be constantly limited by
that of all the other spheres of society, i.e., family, church, industry,

education. Government as an *office* under God is an institution of divine origin, quite independently of whether the persons of the government fear God. The common grace of God lies in His creation of the governmental authority itself, and therefore we must obey it, but only within the God-ordained limits of its powers. Thus the state takes its place not *above*, as the Roman Catholics teach, but *alongside* the other spheres. To try to abolish the state, as Marx set out to do, is therefore to undermine God's common grace in instituting the ordinance of government. As long as men remain sinful, so long shall we need the state to restore harmonious legal relationships amongst men when these have been disturbed by by evildoers (Rom. 13:1-10).

Again it must be pointed out that the Marxist idea of the administration of things, replacing the government by other men, results in the depersonalization of men and women. Things do not function socially, legally, economically except through the intervention of men, who are fundamentally religious beings created in God's holy image. Behind Marx's teaching at this point the Christian can detect the influence of the science-ideal of modern apostate social doctrine, which reduces man to the level of his physical and chemical and biological functions. Refusing to accept the revelation of the Scriptures that man is created in God's image and is called to live as God's office-bearer on earth, Communists are forced by their so-called "scientific materialism" to view the individual in sub-personal functional terms as an economic animal whose god is his belly. The Marxist belief in functionalism is a typical example of apostate humanist thought. Men and their institutions never function as such, because man is not a functional being; he is *homo religiosus*, religious man, not economic or political man, called to serve his Creator in all his actions.

Unlike Christianity, which derives everything from God's creative will and plan for the world, the Communist derives everything from a material process. For the Marxist, the universe is not the creation of God and subject to His purpose, but rather it is regarded as self-creating and self-sustaining. To the question: Which is the primordial element in the universe, spirit or nature? the Marxist answers: Nature. In Marx's own words, "Nothing exists outside nature and man."

In his Gifford Lectures the former Archbishop of Canterbury, William Temple, points out that there is a sense in which Christianity is also materialistic, but not in the Marxist sense:

> It may safely be said that one ground for the hope of Christianity that it may make good its claim to be the true faith lies in the fact that it is the most avowedly materialist of all the great religions. It affords an expectation that it may be able to control the material, precisely because it does not ignore it or deny it, but roundly asserts the reality of matter and its subordination. Its own most central saying is: "The Word was made flesh," where the last term was, no doubt, chosen because of its specially materialistic associations. By the very nature of its central doctrine Christianity is committed to a belief in the ultimate significance of the historical process, and in the reality of matter and its place in he divine scheme.[57]

The living God of the Scriptures is not an idea, but a Being, a Person. And the Word of God holds out to men the promise not simply of the salvation of their souls, but of the redemption of their bodies "in a flesh that shall be incorruptible." Like Marxism, Christianity rejects idealism, that false philosophy which would absorb matter in mind and affirms with Hegel that "the rational alone is the real." But, unlike Marxism, the Word of God teaches that the material universe is the creation of the one true God, and that both matter and spirit are created for God's greater glory. Thus the Christian philosophy of life avoids the pitfalls both of materialism and of idealism. It denies that the ultimate reality can be reduced to ideas or to matter. It does not deny the reality of matter, but subordinates matter to man's spiritual and moral purposes. It is in the sacraments that the peculiarly Christian conception of the relationship between spirit and matter is best exemplified. It is the spiritual utilization of a material object for a spiritual purpose. As William Temple has expressed it: "In the sacrament, the order of thought is spirit first and spirit last, with matter as the effectual expression or symbolic instrument of the spirit." [58] Religion is the direction taken by man's earthly life. Life is religion, not politics or economics.

Nowhere does this intimate relationship between matter and spirit find greater expression than in the Christian liturgy or service to God of the Lord's Supper or Holy Communion, when we offer up to God our gifts of bread and wine and of money. These offerings are representative tokens of the Church's use of God's bountiful gifts of creation with which he has blessed and enriched us for the benefit of our human needs. They symbolize, in the face of the world's selfishness and greed, the witness and sacrifice of the faithful in Christ, to the end that all men may have a just and equitable share in the wealth of the earth's material goods, and that hunger and want, insecurity and anxiety for the basic necessities of life be banished from all the peoples of the world.

Our offerings of bread and wine and money not only represent God's gifts to us, both material and spiritual, but also all the effort and work that has been necessary to earn that bread in the sweat of our brow. We give to the Lord the elements of bread and wine for him to bless and return to us. The offering of bread and wine, not of wheat and grapes, means that we are offering back to God all the work and labor of our daily lives. The bread that we win in the sweat of our brows is offered to God that it may become the Bread of Life for the nourishment of our hearts (John 6:33-51). The offerings we make to our God are made not merely in the *natural* forms in which God has given his gifts to us, but in *manufactured* forms, representative of our work and labor, and hence of all the political, social, and economic organizations of our lives. God's work in the redemption of the world thus becomes directly related to our daily work since it is only through our efforts in the workaday world of business and industry that God's will can be done on earth as it is in heaven.

Again we must take issue with the unbiblical Marxist explanation for the origin of evil and injustice. The Word of God locates evil in man; Marx and Engels find its origin in the institution of private property. The Bible regards evil as a defect in man's will due to his original fall into sin and to actual sin; Marxism regards evil as residing primarily in the institution of the private ownership of the means of production. The Word of God regards *all* men as sinners, but Marxism regards the proletariat as the innocent victims of a system for which they are in no way responsible. Where Christianity attributes perfect innocence to Christ alone, the Marxist attributes perfect innocence to the working class. Where one looks to Christ alone for redemption, the other looks to revolution. The price demanded for redemption from evil in Christianity is repentance and a new way of life lived in obedience to God's law and revealed purpose for man given to him in the Bible. The price demanded for redemption from evil in communism is enlistment in the cause of the proletariat under the direction of the Communist Party. Where one finds redemption from sin through the outpoured blood of the Lamb of God who taketh away the sins of the world, the other finds salvation through the outpoured blood of the capitalists and a change of ownership or control of the means of production.

Now it is true that the capitalists have often abused their privileges at the expense of the poor. Anyone who has lived in the West Riding of Yorkshire, as I have, has only to look at what William Blake called "those dark satanic mills" to see what the coming of the Industrial Revolution must have meant to the poor workers who were treated literally as mere "hands" and functions of the new machines. But having admitted this it must also be pointed out that the struggle against the injustices, exploitation, and inhumanities of the early generation of industrial capitalists actually started in Christian circles long before the *Communist Manifesto* of Karl Marx appeared. One has only to think of the great Christian philanthropists such as Lord Shaftesbury, Richard Oastler, John Wood, and Parson Bull of Bierley who defended the oppressed workers and children of England, led the great "Ten Hours Movement" to limit the hours of work in the new factories, and helped in securing the passage of the Factory Acts which provided for inspectors to enforce the new regulations governing conditions of employment in the factories.[59]

In a speech delivered at Amsterdam in 1948 Emil Brunner pointed out that:

> ... the trade union movement and co-operative movement, which has done far more for the common man and the actual improve-

ment of social conditions that doctrinaire Marxism, was brought
into being for the most part by Christian men and women, and
has been publicly advocated by leading Churchmen, amongst
others. . . .

It is said that the Church has no right to come forward
against communism since it was silent in the struggle against the
injustices of capitalism. . . . Since when has past neglect and
guilt been a reason for keeping quiet about a new and much
greater injustice? Viewed as a whole, the Church has brought
upon itself a great deal of guilt through its lack of understanding
and interest in the struggle for the liberation of the proletariat.
Can it possibly atone for this guilt by once again keeping silent
when man is being sacrificed to the Leviathan of communism . . . ?

There is no good reason which could justify Christians and the
Church standing aside in the spiritual struggle against communism.
The total-state of communism means the denial not only of human
rights, of human dignity, of the human person and freedom,
but the complete denial of the sovereignty of God, who alone
has a total right to a man, but who, whenever this right is recognized, makes a man free and not a slave. It is also impossible to
separate communism from the total-state. The total acquisition
by the State of economic life—and *this* is modern communism—
leads of necessity, whether man intends it or not, to the total-
state; and conversely Lenin was right when he saw that communism can only be realized and maintained by means of the all-
powerful state. . . .

The total-state of communism is the Leviathan of our age, a
frightful demonstration of dehumanized humanity. It is not for-
tuitously connected with atheism but necessarly so. Further, it
is the necessary consequence of atheism, which is its essential
presupposition. The man who is both a Christian and a communist—in the sense of contemporary communism—is an oddity.
He does not realize what he is doing when he thinks he can ally
himself with the product of radical godlessness without betraying
his faith. . . . Totalitarian atheistic communism is an indivisible
entity which can only be either completely accepted or totally
rejected.[60]

While the Christian recognizes the duty of the state in protecting
the weak against exploitation, he can never recognize the right of
the state to absorb all of the individual's life the way modern communism does. Further, the Christian cannot accept the simplistic

Marxian teaching that evil lies solely in the institution of the private ownership of the means of production, or that a change of ownership will ever provide the cure. What is needed is a change of heart. It is untrue that there are two kinds of people: those who are capitalists and wicked, and those who are poor and good. It is sheer stupidity to suppose that all evil resides in the rich and that all goodness is the property of the poor. Of this communist moral bifurcation H. Van Riessen observes:

> It is easy to go astray in our judgment. The wrath of socialism may have been justly brought down upon a great deal of injustice, but socialism, in its turn, was all too ready with its scheme of the wicked capitalists and the noble proletarians. Such a generalizing scheme is generally unfair; it is even dangerous. We might flatter ourselves with the vain hope that once the account with the capitalist is settled, everything will henceforth go right. Fortunately experience has now taught many socialists to discard this dual classification; human wickedness is no longer the exclusive property of the capitalists. That is a gain of the twentieth century. Nevertheless, the original socialistic antithesis of capitalists and proletarians is not simply a tenet of socialists; it is deeply rooted in popular opinion. It reveals itself repeatedly in conversation, writing, and social planning.
>
> What we forget is that the industrialists, who rapidly rose to prominence, were men subject to like passions as we. The difference is that they were exposed to a great temptation, to which many succumbed. They were tempted because there was no counter balance to their growing power and riches. They took full advantage of the situation, ignoring all other values. There was no bridle to their enterprise other than market and competition. And in their greed for gain they were blind to all forms of human distress about them.[61]

The Communists do not take into account that all men are sinners and in need of the redeeming grace of God in Christ; the poor as well as the rich. Their view of evil, mistaking the symptom for the cause, inevitably gives them a wrong idea of its cure. If it is indeed true that ownership corrupts, it will obviously make no difference simply to change ownership from private to public bodies, since the temptations to abuse of power will become even greater if men can hide behind the cloak of bureaucratic anonymity.

By attributing absolute righteousness to the proletariat, and hence excommunicating all other social classes from the human race, communism leads in practice to the most brutal and ruthless suppression and extermination of its opponents. The Communist thinks of his enemy as an enemy of the human race, and this explains why he does not call the extermination of his opponents murder, but the liquidation of unsocial elements. On the other hand, though not always practiced by Christians, the commandment of Christ that we should love our enemies is central to the ethical teaching of the Gospel. Though we may hate his ideas and battle against them, we must love him as a person, desiring his salvation even as we desire our own. The Christian loves the communist sinner even though he may detest his communistic sinfulness, e.g., cruelty, deception, and lust for power.

The biblical conception of man alone is realistic, for it neither overrates man's motives nor underestimates his potentialities. If man is a sinner, he is also potentially called to "be a saint" (in the N.T. sense of one set apart or consecrated for God's service in the world). Though defaced by both original and actual sin, there remains in every man the image of God his creator. The Marxist denies not only that man is sinful but that he is created in the image of God. Human nature is rather conceived by him as the product of society, as the image or reflection of social conditions and changes in the system of production. That is why the Marxist believes that if you change social conditions, you can create a new human being.

Lastly, the Marxist ascribes the changes brought about in history to changes in the methods of production. According to the Reformed viewpoint, changes in history are ultimately due to the orientation of a man's heart, either as it listens to God's law and obey's God's ordering of the world, or as it absolutizes one of the aspects of God's creation and pursues false gods and idols. Thus religion rather than economics has been the driving force of history and of human cultures, as Arnold Toynbee has made clear in his monumental *A Study of History*. Toynbee writes:

> If religion is a chariot, it looks as if the wheels on which it mounts towards Heaven may be the periodic downfalls of civiliza-

tions on earth. It looks as if the movement of civilizations may be
cyclic and recurrent, while the movement of religion may be on
a single continuous upward line. The continuous upward movement of religion may be served and promoted by the cyclic movement of civilizations round the cycle of birth, death, birth.[62]

If culture is merely the form taken by a religion and change is due
to a man's heart orientation, it follows that it will be necessary to
have an insight into the "modal order" of God's creation as a prerequisite to a proper understanding of man's social institutions.

We may conclude this reformational critique of communism
with some profound observations made by Gary North in his *Marx's
Religion of Revolution*:

> Marx began with the assumption that the labor theory of value
> is operative in capitalist economic affairs. A good must contain
> an equal quantity of human labor with any other good if an ex-
> change is to take place. Prices, therefore, should be in direct pro-
> portion to the quantities of labor contained in the respective
> products. This theory in turn led Marx to formulate the idea of
> surplus value; the presence of unpaid labor in the process of
> production gives the capitalist the power to exchange equals for
> equals and still reap a profit (assuming the validity of his erroneous
> minimum subsistence wage concept). The surplus value issue
> raised still another problem; how could profits be equal on all
> equal capital investments if the only source of profit is living
> human labor? Would not the firm using more living labor in the
> production process reap far greater profits than a firm using
> machinery extensively? Yet this obvious conclusion stood in ab-
> solute contradiction with the economic facts. And if, as Marx
> finally had to admit, all capitals do return equal profits on equal
> capitals invested (in the long run) then the original presupposition
> of the Marxian system is destroyed; factors of production other
> than human labor time apparently create value and are therefore
> entitled to a return. Constant capital is obviously receiving an
> equal return with labor under these circumstances; the capitalist's
> profit does not depend strictly on the quantity of living labor
> present in the productive process. Hence the labor theory of value
> collapses under its own weight. . . .
> Nevertheless, the vision by which Marx and his followers have
> held cannot be refuted by a step-by-step dissection of his econo-
> mic system. Communists have never held to the system merely
> because of its particular insights into the nature of capitalist

production and distribution. The system is held in faith because it promises a better world for secular, apostate men. Marxism fulfilled the needs of 19th century industrial men who were ready to destroy the system under which they lived. It provided an aura of scientific infallibility in an age which worshipped science. It simultaneously appealed to a side of man's nature which is never wholly absent; his desire for total destruction of the present. Men want to escape from history since they believe that it is history which has limited them. Their world is filled with uncertainty, scarcity and death; that this has been the result of man's apostasy and disobedience to God is something which they dare not admit. If they did it would demand repentance. Throughout history, the cosmology of chaos has appealed to such men, for it offers the promise of total liberation from the bondage of time. Liber, in fact, was a Roman god of chaos, and it is from his name that we derive the word "liberty." Thus, the popularity of the hammer as a revolutionary symbol; it is the means of shattering the present world order. Marxism, in combining the two myths of scientific infallibility and revolutionary action, offered hope to those who sought to escape from history. This is the essence of Marx's religion of revolution; it is the same appeal which has dominated all the chaos cults as far back as recorded history extends.[62]

CHAPTER THREE NOTES

1. Adam Smith, *The Wealth of Nations* (Routledge, London, 1895), pp. 345, 492.

2. J. M. Keynes, *The End of Laissez-Faire* (Hogarth Press, London, 1926), p. 10.

3. Adam Smith, *Wealth of Nations* (Everyman edition, London, 1948), Vol. I, p. 41.

4. *Ibid.*, p. 57. Cf. Joan Robinson's discussion of Smith's theory of value in *Economic Philosophy* (Pelican, London, 1962), p. 29ff.

5. Quoted by Maurice Dobb, *Wages* (Cambridge University Press, 1959), p. 100. Cf. Maurice Dobb, *Studies in the Development of Capitalism* (G. Routledge & Sons, London, 1947), especially chapter one, where Dobb discusses the nature of capitalism.

6. J. C. Gill, *The Mastery of Money* (Industrial Christian Fellowship, St. Katharine Cree, Leadenhall St., London, E.C. 3, 1958), p. 16.
   Also J. T. Ward, *The History of the Factory Movement* (Macmillan, London, 1962).

7. A. Kouwenhoven, *Vrijheid en Gelijkheid* (J. H. Kok, Kampen, 1964). He writes: Philosophic thought in modern times has had a fundamental

effect on economic thought. John Locke based the natural right to private property on the work performed by the individual; in combination with the scholastic idea of the value substance, incorporated in the goods, this natural-law concept laid the foundation for the objective theory of labour value. This is where Adam Smith comes in. In his view, competition— which should have a similar mitigating effect in economic life to that of sympathy in the moral life—should ensure that in the long run the price of goods comes to rest at the level of their labour value. Linking up with the Schoolmen's metaphysical concept of substance, Adam Smith saw la- bour as the ethical justification of economic value. He tried to project this idea onto the plane of modern society with its characteristic division of labour. Ricardo, too based his theories on labour bestowed upon the good as the only source of economic value. Marx built on this: the ob- jective labour value theory, derived through Smith and Lock from the scholastics, was the starting point of his views on surplus labour (p. 250).

8. Maarten Vrieze, *Introduction to Economics* (Syllabus used at Trinity Christian College, Chicago, 1967), p. 15.

9. Eric Lipson, *A Planned Economy or Private Enterprise* (Adam Black, London, 1944), p. 152ff.

10. Frank Tannenbaum, *The True Society: A Philosophy of Labor* (J. Cape, London, 1964), p. 30. Cf. Nisbet, *The Sociological Tradition*, pp. 47-106.

11. Karl Marx, *Capital*, trans. from the third German edition by S. Moore and E. Aveling (G. Allen & Unwin, London, 1946), p. 295.

12. David Ricardo, *The Principles of Political Economy and Taxation* (Every- man edition, London, 1948), p. 57.

13. *Ibid.*, Vol. I, p. 120.

14. *Ibid.*, Vol. I, p. 115. Cf. Robert Lekachman, *A History of Economic Ideas* (Harper & Row, New York, 1959), for a good summary of the teaching of the classical economists.

15. Raymond Aron, *Main Currents in Sociological Thought* (Pelican, London, 1968), Vol. I, p. 115. Cf. Raymond Aron, *18 Lectures on Industrial Society* (Weidenfeld and Nicholson, London, 1967), pp. 31-57.

16. George Lichtheim, *Marxism* (Routledge, London, 1967), p. 402.
Cf. Gary North, *Marx's Religion of Revolution*, The Doctrine of Creative Destruction (Craig Press, Nutley, N. J., 1968), which examines Marx's thought in the light of a scriptural perspective upon life. It is the best Christian study of Marxism that has yet appeared. Also John Plamenatz, *Man and Society* (Longmans, London, 1968), Vol. II, chapters 5 and 6; Karl Popper, *The Open Society and Its Enemies* (Routledge, London, 1966), Vol. II (pp. 81-212); and J. L. Talmon, *Political Messianism* (Secker & Warburg, London, 1960).

17. Herman Dooyeweerd, *A New Critique of Theoretical Thought*, Vol. I, p. 210.

18. *Ibid.*, Vol. II, p. 293.

19. Karl Marx, *A Contribution to the Critique of Political Economy* (International Library Publishing Co., 1904), p. iii.

20. *The Communist Manifesto*, edited by Harold J. Laski (G. Allen & Unwin, London, 1948), p. 125.

21. *Ibid.*, p. 133. Cf. Abraham Kuyper, *Christianity and the Class Struggle* (Grand Rapids, 1950).

22. *Ibid.*, p. 137.

23. *Ibid.*, p. 134.

24. *Ibid.*, p. 140.

25. *Ibid.*, p. 138.

26. *Ibid.*,, p. 150.

27. *Ibid.*, p. 152.

28. *Ibid.*, p. 153.

29. Francois Fejto, *The Opening of An Era, 1848*, (Methuen, London, 1948). Edited by Sir Lewis Namier.

30. *The Communist Manifesto*, p. 152.

31. *Ibid.*, p. 168.

32. *Ibid.*, p. 150.

33. E. Burns, *A Handbook of Marxism* (Gollancz, London, 1935), p. 117.

34. Lenin, *Lenin on Religion* (Lawrence & Wishart, London, 1947), p. 16ff. For the effect of this teaching in the persecution of Christians read Richard Wurmbrand, *Tortured for Christ* (Hodder & Stoughton, London, 1967), and his great study titled *God's Underground* (Hodder & Stoughtan, 1968). Also Michael Bourdeaux, *Religious Ferment in Russia* (Macmillan, London, 1967).

35. Gary North, *Marx's Religion of Revolution*, p. 97ff.

36. F. Engels, *The Origin of the Family, Private Property and the State* (C. H. Kerr, Chicago, 1902), p. 206.

37. F. Engels, *Anti-Duhring*, trans. by E. Burns (International Publishers, New York, 1935), p. 315. Cf. R. Nisbet, *The Sociological Tradition*, "The Uses of Power—Marx," pp. 132-141.

38. Marx, *op. cit.*, Vol. I, p. 52.

39. Marx, *op. cit*, Vol. III, p. 221.

40. Marx, *op. cit.*, Vol. I, p. 381.

41. Quoted from Lenin in Max Eastman: *Marxism, Is It Science?* (New York, 1940), p. 232.

42. Karl Marx, *Selected Works*, "Value, Price and Profits" (International Publishers, New York, 1939), Vol. I, p. 337.

43. *Ibid.*, p. 337.

44. Quoted in A. Lozovsky, *Marx and the Trade Unions* (International Publishers, New York, 1942), p. 49.

45. Karl Marx and F. Engels, *Selected Correspondence* (International Publishers, New York, 1942), p. 450.

46. Quoted in Karl Marx, *Selected Works* (New York, 1942), Vol. II, p. 11.

47. S. Swianiewicz, *Forced Labour and Economic Development* (Oxford University Press, 1965), p. 49ff.

48. I. Deutscher, *Stalin, A Political Biography* (Oxford University Press), 2nd ed., 1967), p. 335ff.

49. *Soviet Planning, Essays in Honor of Naum Jasny*, edited by Jane Degras and Alec Nove (Oxford, 1964).

50. James Burnham, *The Managerial Revolution* (Pelican, London, 1945), p. 185ff. Cf. Milovan Djilas, *The New Class* (Praeger, New York, 1957).

51. Quoted in W. Cleon Skousen, *The Naked Communist* (Ensign, Salt Lake City, 1961), p. 315. Cf. Chinoy, *Society*, "Class in a Classless Society," pp. 184-188.

52. R. H. Tawney, *Religion and the Rise of Capitalism* (Penguin Books, London, 1938), p. 23ff.

53. Basil Willey, *The Eighteenth Century Background* (Chatto & Windus, London, 1949), p. 16. Cf. E. Victor Morgan, *A History of Money* (Penguin Books, London, 1965), p. 177ff.

54. David Ricardo, *op. cit.*, p. 57.

55. Lester De Koster, *Communism and Christian Faith* (Eerdmans, Grand Rapids, 1962. Cf. John C. Bennet, *Christianity and Communism* (Association Press, New York, 1949), p. 21ff.

56. *Ibid.*, p. 257.

57. William Temple, *Nature, Man and God* (Macmillan, London, 1949), p. 478.

58. *Ibid.*, p. 492. Cf. A. G. Hebert, *Liturgy and Society* (1958).

59. E. L. Woodward, *The Age of Reform* (Clarendon Press, Oxford, 1946), p. 142ff.

60. Emil Brunner, *Communism, Capitalism and Christianity* (Lutterworth, London, 1950), p. 21ff.

61. H. Van Riessen, *op. cit.*, p. 96ff.

62. Arnold J. Toynbee, *A Study of History*, abridged by D. C. Somervell, (Oxford, New York, 1957), Vols. VII ro X, pp. 87-108. Cf. John Rex, *Key Problems of Sociological Theory* (Routledge & Kegan Paul, 1968), Chapter VII, p. 115ff., where he writes: "What we have to be aware of, however, is the suggestion that knowledge of the thesis and antithesis is sufficient to give us knowledge of what the synthesis must be. . . . All that a revolution settles is that the formerly subject group will be able to create a new social order. It does not entirely settle the question of what that social order will be" (p. 134).

63. Gary North, *op. cit.*, p. 170ff.

Chapter Four

THE WESTERN HUMANIST THEORY
OF LABOR, INDUSTRY, AND SOCIETY

(a) *Tannenbaum's Account of the Origin
and Nature of Trade Unions*

In his important book, *The True Society, A Philosophy of Labor*,
Frank Tannenbaum argues that trade unionism is the "counter-
revolution both to the Industrial Revolution and to the liberal and
laissez faire philosophy of economic individualism and the right of
each man to fend for himself. He begins his work with these striking words:

> Trade-unionism is the conservative movement of our time. It
> is the counter-revolution. Unwittingly, it has turned its back
> upon most of the political and economic ideas that have nourished
> western Europe and the United States during the last two cen-
> turies. In practice, though not in words, it denies the heritage that
> stems from the French Revolution and from English liberalism.
> It is also a complete repudiation of Marxism. . . . In tinkering with
> the little things—hours, wages, shop conditions and security in
> the job—the trade union is rebuilding our industrial society upon
> a different basis from that envisioned by the philosophers, econo-
> mists and social revolutionaries of the eighteenth and nineteenth
> centuries.[1]

Briefly Tannenbaum's view is this: industrialization and the factory system completed the destructive process that began with the
enclosure acts in Britain and emigration to the United States from
European peasant communities, by which everything that gave the
mass of mankind a sense of belonging to a community was lost. In
this intolerable situation the formation of trade unions was not a
considered policy, but the inevitable outcome of man's need to be-

long to a group, and the only group to which he could belong was that related to his job. He writes:

> Thus the social atomization resulting from the payment of an individual money wage was in time to be defeated by the fusing of men together functionally, and this functional coalescence became the firm foundation upon which the trade union grew, and which, in fact, made it inevitable.
>
> The original organizer of the trade union movement is the shop, the factory, the mine and the industry. . . . The union is the spontaneous grouping of individual workers thrown together functionally. It reflects the moral identity and psychological unity men always discover when working together, because they need it and could not survive without it. . . . The theory which insisted that labor was a commodity like any other made collective action the only means of asserting the moral status of the individual. The trade union was the visible evidence that man is not a commodity, and that he is not sufficient unto himself. . . . In terms of the individual, the union returns to the worker his "society." It gives him a fellowship . . . and life takes on meaning once again because he shares a value system common to others.[2]

As members of a local spinning or weaving association in a mill town, men recreated for themselves a "status" that they had once enjoyed in the old manorial village or town guild. Later, the power of organized labor was discovered, but this arose because trade unions existed.

At first trade unions were opposed by the vested interests of capitalism in Britain, Canada, and America. Associations of men were considered to be contrary to the "natural order" and so they were opposed with all the means at the disposal of those in authority. Unions were thus considered to be in "restraint of trade" and declared to be illegal in England by the Combination Acts of 1799 and 1800, and in America in 1867 a judge ruled that the actions of a labor union were "an unwarranted interference with the conduct of the employer's business. . . . In the natural possession of things, each man acting as an individual, there would be no coercion. It is simply not the right of workingmen to control the business of another."[3]

Only gradually, after much strife, was the workers' right to form associations recognized in Britain and North America. In 1871 the

British Parliament passed the Trade Unions Act, which gave the labor movement protection at common law and allowed registration with friendly societies. A further act passed in 1875 allowed "peaceful picketing and excluded from indictment as a conspiracy any agreement or combination to take any action in furtherance of a trade dispute unless such an action by an individual would have been punishable as a crime." This measure meant that, at long last, the unions had become recognized, if rather grudgingly, as an essential social institution. In 1906 the Trade Disputes Act was passed under which, among other things, the unions could not be sued for damages arising out of an act committed by or for them. In 1913 they were allowed to devote funds to political purposes. In America full legal recognition of the labor movement did not come until July, 1935, with the passage of the National Labor Relations Act, otherwise known as the Wagner Act. Its enactment marked a major change in governmental policy. Although there had been periods in the past when the Federal Government had revealed a favorable attitude toward labor, the passage of the Wagner Act revealed not only governmental favor but a willingness to form a partnership with labor.

The Wagner Act provided for the establishment of a new National Labor Relations Board of three experts empowered to supervise and enforce the principle that employees had the "right to self-organization, to form, join, or to assist labor organizations to bargain collectively through representatives of their own choosing, and to engage in concerted activities for the purpose of collective bargaining or other mutual aid or protection." To carry out this principle, the act stipulated that representatives of the majority of workers in a bargaining unit should have the power to speak for the whole. The board was empowered to determine what was the appropriate bargaining unit through supervised elections. It was also given authority to prohibit "unfair" employer practices: interference with employees in the exercise of guaranteed rights; support of company unions; use of hiring and firing to encourage membership in a company union; refusal to bargain collectively with the representatives of the employees.[4]

According to Tannenbaum every trend of modern industry ac-
centuates man's need to acquire status in his working group; it is
intolerable to be one of 50,000 "workers" employed by some great
corporation. But he does not think it is an individual status. The
theory of human equality, which produced the French Revolution
and inspired so much English liberal thought, became meaningless
with the factory system. The trade unionist's status is not something
personal to himself, but status conferred through membership in his
union. Such a power to confer status is derived from the modern
union's power of collective bargaining and legal right to enforce
membership as a condition of employment. He writes:

> As long as the union can limit the number of workers it will
> admit, and insist upon membership as a condition of receiving or
> keeping a job, it can control the workers within the industry.
> The courts, under the common law, have upheld the right of the
> unions to exclude new members on the grounds that they are vol-
> untary associations. But they are voluntary associations with
> compulsive powers over both the employer and the worker. They
> are, in fact, private lawmaking bodies whose rules affect the lives
> of millions of human beings and thousands of industrial plants.
> This is evidenced by the more than fifty thousand collective labor
> agreements existing in the country. The unions that sign these
> contracts acquire an influence over the activities of their mem-
> bers which in time circumscribes their daily lives and redefines
> the privileges of men who, under the law, are equal to each other.
> Without intent or plan, the trade union movement is integrating
> the workers into what in effect amounts to a series of separate
> social orders. It is re-creating a society based upon status and
> destroying the one we have known in our time—a society based
> upon contract.
>
> If membership in a union is essential to an opportunity to work,
> and if every union has rules of admission, apprenticeship, dues,
> initiation fees, promotion, wages, retirement funds, and social
> benefits, then every union becomes in effect a differentiated order
> within the community endowing its own members with rights
> and immunities, shared only among themselves. Moreover, a
> member finds it increasingly difficult to leave his union, because
> the penalties for desertion are severe. These penalties include
> the loss of a job, the impossibility of securing other employment
> in the same industry, the loss of seniority and possible promotion,
> and the surrender of accumulated retirement, sickness, and old-

age benefits. A new body of rights and disciplines, which greatly change the substance of a free society, has come into being. A single bargaining agency collects dues (its own form of taxation) from the worker, without his consent, through the check off, and has enforceable union security provisions so that the worker must end by being a member of the union. In the spread of such industry-wide agreements we have the marking of a new social design in which status rather than contract is the governing rule.[5]

Civil courts in Britain, Canada, and the United States have been dealing with an increasing number of cases where the expulsion or exclusion of a worker by a trade union has indeed threatened his livelihood because of the practice known sometimes as the closed shop and sometimes as compulsory trade unionism. This was an important element in the case of *Rookes v. Barnard*. Rookes was a draftsman employed in the B.O.A.C. design office at London Airport. He had belonged to a trade union, but resigned because he was dissatisfied with its policies. The union was very anxious to preserve a closed shop in the design office and tried, without success, to persuade Rookes to rejoin. So the union officials told B.O.A.C. that unless he was removed from his job the other men working in the design office would come out on strike.

A strike would have been a breach of contract by each of the men who took part in it, since a special agreement existed by which the union had undertaken that no strikes would take place, and this undertaking had been made a condition of every employee's individual contract. Nevertheless the union officials threatened a strike, and in the face of the threat B.O.A.C. gave way. They gave Rookes notice, and for a long time afterwards he was out of work.

Rookes brought an action against the three union officials—including the local branch chairman, Mr. Barnard—who had been most prominent in securing his dismissal.

Sachs J. ruled for the plaintiff by ruling that the defendants had combined to threaten to break contracts, which he regarded as an unlawful act constituting the tort of intimidation. Since it was admitted that the acts complained of were done in furtherance of a trade dispute, it was also necessary to decide that they were unprotected by sections one and three of the 1906 Trade Disputes Act.

Section one protects acts done in furtherance of trade disputes unless they would be actionable if done by one person. Sachs J. ruled that the tort of intimidation was such an act. Section three says acts furthering a trade dispute are not actionable "only" on the grounds that they constitute an inducement to breach of contract, "or" because they are an interference with the trade, business, or employment of another person. Sachs J. decided that since the acts complained of were unlawful on the additional grounds that they amounted to intimidation, section three afforded no protection.

The Court of Appeal reversed this decision, and Rookes appealed to the House of Lords for redress. The House of Lords reversed the decision of the Court of Appeal and accepted the arguments of Sachs J. in the lower court, and decided that the union officials had used unlawful means and that Rookes was entitled to damages. Lord Reid, who gave the leading judgment, said:

> Threatening a breach of contract may be a more coercive weapon than threatening a tort, particularly when the threat is directed against a company or corporation. . . .[6]

In a more general way one might say that just as society cannot exist unless there are rules which forbid the use of violence, so it is also necessary that there should be rules to enforce the keeping of promises, and that breaches of contract should be regarded as wrongful. In principle, therefore, it does not seem unreasonable to say that people should not use threats to break their contracts as a means of causing loss.

At present it is impossible to estimate precisely how far this judgment may affect the right to use strike action to enforce the closed shop, but it depends largely on how far strikers avoid its effects by giving legal notice to terminate their contracts of employment. If—as has been thought up to now—the usual period of one week's notice will normally be sufficient, the effect will not be very drastic. If, however, some of the other *obiter dicta* were to be followed, all strikes in breach of procedure, and even some that were not, would be involved.

The trade unions in Britain are now demanding a revision of trade union law to protect their right to strike. It seems likely that legislation will in fact soon be passed by the new Labor Government to safeguard the position of the unions. But the importance of *Rookes v. Barnard* is that for all ordinary purposes the law will remain as the House of Lords has decided. Outside the field of industrial relations people will still not be able to use threats to break their contracts as a means of causing loss to others.

The restriction of a worker's freedom to choose whether or not he wishes to belong to a union, taken sometimes to the point of persecution as in the case *Huntly v. Thornton*, has aroused much public anxiety. Yet the British trade unions, like their American counterparts, are equally anxious to preserve the practice of the closed shop, claiming wherever they can claim that it is a legitimate and necessary device in their efforts to protect their members.

(b) *The Arguments for and against the Closed Shop*

In his important work, *The Closed Shop in Britain*, W. E. J. McCarthy deals with the practice of the closed shop at length. He begins by dismissing some of the quibbling definitions which the unions themselves apply to the practice in its varying degrees, when they describe some of the milder applications, for example, as "100 percent trade unionism." His own all-embracing definition is:

> a situation in which employees come to realize that a particular job is only to be obtained and retained if they become and remain members of one of a specified number of trade unions.[7]

Within this, he recognizes various types of situations, such as that where an employer is free to recruit workers provided that they subsequently join the union; that where the employer must choose among existing members; that where the worker must first join the union before he can obtain a job; and that where the union itself supplies the required workers. . . . His statistics show that about 3,760,000 workers in Britain are subject to the closed shop in one or another of its forms—that is, about one in six. Most of them are in the manual occupations. So far from the closed shop being on the decline, as some students have supposed, it is in fact increasing:

> The practice is not an historical relic, affecting a small minority of trade unionists; it is an increasingly common contemporary

phenomenon. Yet the nonunionists' position is not equally intolerable throughout industry. The practice has not been pursued with similar vigor wherever the habit of organization has become settled and accepted.[8]

McCarthy then analyzes where and why the closed shop is likely to develop as a union practice, the most usual reasons being to protect craft status or to maintain wages and other conditions where a proportion of the labor employed is casual. Speaking of the functions of the closed shop he suggests that it is used (1) to increase and maintain the numerical strength of the union, (2) to enhance the union's internal strength by enabling it to exercise discipline over its members, by threatening exclusion of all members who do not obey the union's rules, customs, and leadership, and (3) to use the exclusion threat to force would-be entrants to obtain prior acceptance by the union. Summarizing his own argument regarding factors affecting demands for the closed shop, he writes:

> The closed shop pattern cannot be explained simply by reference to its relative disadvantages to employers, or in terms of union solidarity. It should be viewed as a device which unions want to assist them in dealing with particular problems concerned with organizing, controlling or excluding different categories of workers. By helping to overcome such problems it adds to the effectiveness of the sanctions unions impose on employers and aids them in their task of job regulation. The determination and resolution behind most demands for the practice depends on the extent to which unions feel that they face problems that are insoluble without its aid. . . . If there are no such problems or workers are unaware of them, closed shop demands are not likely to rise; unless of course, past problems have given rise to a closed shop tradition. But no matter how necessary the closed shop may be, the crucial factor which finally determines whether or not most groups obtain the practice is whether or not they can muster sufficient power, without its aid, to impose it unilaterally, or to make it worth the employers' while to concede it.
>
> Similar considerations govern the maintenance of the practice. So long as unity and solidarity are preserved; so long as technological or market developments do not result in the erosion of the union's bargaining position it will endure and in time probably become part of the unquestioned assumptions of both sides of industry. But the development of such a situation, and in the

last resort its continuance, depends on the fact that it is appreciated that, if challenged, the great majority of unionists would defend the closed shop. If they or their leaders allow membership to fall sufficiently, the closed shop concession may be withdrawn, or it may be impossible to impose it unilaterally any longer. If strikes are called too often, or last too long, members may return to work or drop out of the union, and the closed shop may be powerless to stop them, indeed it may collapse.[9]

According to McCarthy the closed shop in Britain is prevalent in the following groups:

(1) Skilled "craftsmen," where the need has usually been for the craft qualification shop.

(2) Lesser skilled trades where the labor pool closed shop operates, e.g., seamen, dockers, wholesale market workers, film and television technicians, semiskilled newsprint workers, fishermen, etc.

(3) The great majority of remaining trades affected by the closed shop in which the worker has to join the union after taking up the job, e.g., building workers, engineering workers, miners, etc.

(4) Process workers employed in the iron and steel industry.

(5) Workers in entertainment affected by the closed shop, e.g., musicians.

(6) Workers covered by the employer-initiated closed shop, e.g., the employees of the Co-operative Shops and Societies.

McCarthy has found that the closed shop is not prevalent in the following groups: (1) non-industrial civil servants, (2) teachers, (3) sections of the industrial Civil Service, (4) firemen, (5) footplate workers on the railways, (6) clerical and administrative workers in nationalized industries, (7) electrical workers in nationalized undertakings, and (8) boot and shoe operatives.

Although McCarthy is inclined to set aside the usual trade unionist's justification for the closed shop—that union members resent non-members' sharing protection and wage benefits for which they do not work—he nevertheless concludes that it is a justifiable device in the unions' fight to protect their members against employers. Without it, he implies, the scales would be weighted too heavily against the worker; with it, unions can insist on their voice being heard and industrial democracy thereby flourishes. But he admits that some changes in the law would be desirable to control the unions' power to expel members in such a way as to deprive them of their livelihood. Thus he says:

> I would argue that while the closed shop should continue to be recognized as a lawful and "legitimate" trade union objective. the actual imposition of the exclusion sanction requires some degree of justification in each specific case. In short, I think it ought to be plausible to argue that it was *functionally necessary*. This implies:
>
> (a) that the enforcement of the closed shop results in certain benefits to those who combine to impose it;
> (b) that its enforcement was necessary in order to secure this result;
> (c) that the benefits resulting outweigh the losses suffered by those who are damaged as a result of its enforcement.[10]

McCarthy then discusses various proposals for reforming current malpractices connected with the closed shop in terms of his pragmatic criterion of functional necessity. Among these he includes restrictions on the right to exclude non members as well as restrictions on the right to exclude ex-members; certain changes in the procedural rules and constitutions as well as in the substantive rules of unions; and reforms in the admission rules and electoral rules. Apparently, as a typical modern pragmatist, the thought never enters his head that to reform something which is in principle false and evil is merely to add insult to the injury already suffered by the victims of such falsehood and evil. No Christian would deny that "workers still need to combine to match the power of employers." [11] The fundamental issue is not whether the state should or should not recognize unions but whether the state should give to one union the exclusive right to bargain on behalf of *all* employees of a given firm. McCarthy seems to think the state can and should, provided each closed shop can justify its monopoly control of the bargaining rights of the workers in terms of functional necessity. But this is to beg the fundamental issues at stake. In advocating such a criterion for deciding such a problem McCarthy has revealed himself as a typical Anglo-Saxon pragmatist. Whatever seems to work must be good, and whatever is useful must be true. Whether deliberately or through ignorance McCarthy makes no mention in any part of his book of the pluralistic structure of the Dutch trade unions. He takes it simply for granted that in Britain *all* the workers should, and ought to be made to join, the one existing trade union in any given plant or shop. For McCarthy as well as for Tannenbaum the modern trade union is religiously neutral and therefore non-discriminatory.

In fact, trade union leaders never tire of pointing out that their organizations are open to everyone, regardless of his religious convictions. The diversity of their members' religious commitments is said to be possible because unions do not concern themselves with religious beliefs. The unions are based upon the humanistic premise that religious values and principles need play no part in the aims and actions of the labor organization. This does not mean that the individual trade unionist may not hold private religious beliefs. It simply means that the unions, as organizations, are supposedly neutral with respect to the various religious beliefs of their members. The unions, like the modern American and British political parties, seek to establish organizational unity above religious diversity.

The modern unions jealously guard their claim about their unity based upon this religious neutrality. They are aware that their so-called nondiscriminatory character is based upon this neutral unity. On the basis of this neutrality, trade union leaders, in league with many legislators, have decided that objections to the closed shop and compulsory membership in a labor union are invalid. Against this background it can be understood that the Ontario Labor Relations Board, in stating its reasons for refusing to certify a local affiliated with the Christian Labor Association of Canada, compared workers who object to membership in a "neutral union" with persons "who because of their faith, object to receiving blood transfusions or joining the armed services." [12]

This demand that every worker in one plant or shop must have his rights defended before management by one union is an expression of the modern Anglo-Saxon humanist view that in public matters there must be no division in the community. Ever since the defeat of the Puritan attempt to establish a society based upon the Word of

God as the ordering principle of human life, Anglo-Saxon humanists have tried to order public affairs according to a principle common to all "rational creatures." This principle is man's free sovereign reason. Society should be guided in its actions only by those moral laws accessible to the reason and conscience of unregenerate men rather than by the Word of God. As Martineau, writing of the Cambridge platonist Ralph Cudworth, puts it, "All men have the same fundamental ideas, to form the common ground of intellectual communion and of moral co-operation." [13] This rationalistic belief in the commonness of reason laid the foundations for the modern secular humanist belief in the possibility of community apart from a common allegiance to Almighty God. Henceforth society shall be based upon a common reason rather than upon a common faith.

As a result of this belief in reason as the new oracle of man, human life in Anglo-Saxon civilization has become split into two realms, the private or personal and the public or common. The individual is granted a great measure of religious freedom, but this must be limited to personal concerns of home and church. On no account must religion be allowed to enter the "market place," where men deal with the real issues of life such as education, government, labor and industry, recreation, and press. These activities must be withdrawn from so-called "sectarian" influences so that the "common spirit" of the community may prevail. This is the spirit of reason, of common sense and pragmatism.

In his home and church the Anglo-Saxon may rightly differ on specifically religious matters. He may thus subscribe to Roman Catholic, Jewish, Protestant, or atheistic doctrines and views. But outside his home, church, or club he must abide by the "public philosophy" of the community. As Walter Lippmann neatly puts it:

> The toleration of differences is possible only on the assumption that there is no vital threat to the community. Toleration is not, therefore, a sufficient principle for dealing with the diversity of opinions and beliefs. It is itself dependent upon the positive principle of accommodation. The principle calls for the effort to find agreement beneath the differences.[14]

In the realm of public life it is presumed that men can meet and work together upon a common neutral ground. Neutralism is the view that men can live wholly or partly without taking God's Word and Law into account. Those who pay homage to the fiction of neutrality maintain that many segments of society are merely technical. It is then taken for granted that a business corporation, a labor union, a school, or a government can be run by making exclusively factual, technical decisions which have no relation to one's private religious opinions. It is in terms of this neutralism that trade union leaders justify their demands for the closed shop. They argue that a trade union's activities are in fact limited strictly to the regulation of the technical, factual, and organizational aspects of employer-employee relationships. Writing in the *Canadian Churchman* for April, 1965, union leader William Reader clearly states this view:

> In religion, the unions are necessarily neutral. If religion were to be the basis for organization, in view of the diversity of religious beliefs among workers, the result would inevitably be a multiplicity of unions. This does not mean that a neutral trade union ought, by definition, to be irreligious, or unreligious. A trade union is neutral from the religious point of view, if, as such, it professes and adheres to no single religious group in preference to all others.

Such a concept of religious neutrality is based upon the humanist assumption that man is independent and autonomous. Believers in neutrality deny God's authority over all or a part of life. For such neutralists a labor union need not be subject to the Word of God. It is assumed that union affairs are outside the "religious" realm. No consistent Christian could accept this neutrality concept since if he accepted it, he would be conceding to the apostate humanist that God's authority and ordinances for human work are irrelevant. The Lord God demands to be honored just as much at the bargaining table and the work bench as He does at the altar and the pulpit. By insisting that Christians refrain from applying their Christian principles in the daily concrete situations of their lives at work, the union leaders are in reality interfering with the Christian worker's freedom to make their work an offering and a prayer to God. Under such specious claims to neutrality, the big international unions in

North America and the big unions in Britain are in effect demanding of their Christian members that they forget about God as soon as they punch in for work. As a member of such a neutral union the Christian worker must put aside any idea that his faith in Christ as Lord and Savior of the whole of his life should make any difference to the choices with which he is confronted at work, e.g., to go or not to go on strike. On the contrary he is to allow his conduct at work to be guided by no other consideration than that of the selfish interests set by the majority of the non-Christian members of his union. In short, the Christian is forced by the governments of America, Britain, and Canada to place the desires of his or her union leaders above the declared law of God. The voice of the union "boss" is to become for him or for her as well as for the "unbelieving believers" the voice of God himself.

As an example of what such "neutrality" and its attendant compulsory unionism involves in practice for Christian workers, let us consider what happened to Mrs. Mary Ellen Benson, a member of Local 35 of the United Papermakers and Paperworkers Union. Mrs. Benson was fined five dollars for being absent from a union meeting held on Sunday. Mrs. Benson would not pay the fine because she was attending divine worship at her local church, and she believed she had the right to choose how she would spend her leisure time. The union sued Mrs. Benson in court when she refused to pay the fine. The judge ruled that the union had indeed the right and power to assess the fine and ordered her to pay five dollars to the union and five dollars in court costs. "I thought the Constitution gave us the right to freedom of worship," she said afterwards. When asked why she did not leave the union Mrs. Benson pointed out, "I cannot quit because then I'd be out of a job. I think I know something about right and wrong, and I think this is all wrong." [15]

This gross infringement of the liberties of the individual won at such great cost by our Puritan ancestors from tyrannical governments and classes is certainly wrong, but it is imperative that everyone understands exactly where the wrong lies. For it was not the enforcement of the union's membership rule that Mrs. Benson attend a union meeting on a Sunday morning that was wrong. Without such attendance at meetings no union could properly function and flourish. The real wrong in the Benson case does not lie with the union to which she belonged. Although private associations such as labor unions are committing a grave sin when they refuse to obey the Lord's law for rest on the seventh day, this does not mean that they have no *civil* right to do so. In a free and pluralistic democratic society such as ours has today become, such organizations have a perfect right to hold their meetings on Sunday, and they may insist on faithful attendance at these meetings by union members. The real wrong in the Benson case, as in the Rookes case, is the fact that she, as a member of a private association, had been robbed of her freedom to leave that organization upon penalty of starvation. And it is the Federal Government which deprived Mrs. Benson and many thousands of other Christian workers of this right to work and to join the union of their own free choice by allowing organized labor and management to include clauses in collective bargaining agreements which require workers to join or support by their dues a certain union as a condition of employment, even though the union may not be the organization of these workers' own free choice.

In Ontario in 1962 two Christian workers lost their jobs because they refused to support the National Union of Public Employees. Mr. Bonvanie and Mr. Dehaan were not allowed to refrain from supporting by their dues this particular union without losing their employment by the Ontario Government. Even though they favored Christian principles of work and had good Christian reasons for not supporting the socialistically inclined N.U.P.E., they were "fired." Of course, Christian workers are free. But the exercise of this freedom always has as its bitter result that they become unemployed. A worker today in America, Britain, and Canada is free to join the union which enjoys exclusive bargaining rights at the shop where he works. But he is not free to work there unless he joins the union and pays union dues. He is free either to join and work or not to join and starve. The exercise of his human right of freedom of association leaves him without job or income. The fringe freedom he enjoys to resign his job only underscores the injustice of present arrangements. The closed shop and compulsory unionism and the compulsory deduction of union fees from the worker's wage mean an abridgement of the civil rights of those citizens who cannot with a clear conscience join what is legally supposed to be a neutral union, but is in fact an essentially non-Christian secular humanist union, and often even a socialist one. This is a curtailment of the worker's right to work. Under present Anglo-American labor legislation the worker is free to work only if he sheds himself of his Christian convictions and abides by the decisions of the unbelieving majority. But that is precisely the injustice of the present arrangement, for his fellow non-Christian worker, although he is no better as a citizen, no more law abiding, no more loyal to his country, no more industrious at work, does not have to leave his humanistic religious convictions at the door of the closed shop.

It is the American, British, and Canadian governments' failure to protect their Christian citizens from being coerced into supporting so-called neutral unions which give rise to such abuses of power as these have been experienced by Mrs. Benson, Mssrs. Bonvanie, and De Haan in Canada, and Rooke in England. Such compulsory union membership as a condition of employment in the modern factory or workshop and such compulsory financial support of the neutral union are evils that threaten all our most cherished civil liberties. Let no one in England think that what happened to Mrs. Benson in America cannot happen in England, for the same situation still exists here in spite of the recent decision in the *Rookes v. Barnard* case. A number of members of the Plymouth Brethren have already lost their employment in England because they refused to support the secular trade union. In thousands of firms on both sides of the Atlantic the decision over hiring and firing has passed out of the hands of the managers, to whom it rightfully belongs, into the hands of union bosses.

Such compulsory trade unionism has inevitably led to abuses and corruption amongst the unions' leadership. In his important book, *Power Unlimited—The Corruption of Union Leadership*, Sylvester Petro deals with the corruption of some of the great American trade unions. The immediate occasion of his book was the information and evidence provided by the McClellan Committee appointed by the Congress to examine "improper activities in the labor relations management field," and which held hearings from 1957 until 1959.

The main theme of Petro's book is that power unlimited has led to corruption unlimited. Big labor has been granted special privileges by the Wagner Act, which has given it virtual control over America's economy. He describes in detail how unwilling employees were organized from the top by stranger picketing and secondary boycotts and compulsory unionism. Stranger picketing is used to gain control over employees by putting pressure, through picketing, upon the employer and results in forced union membership The secondary boycott is used to make customers and suppliers quit dealing with the employer upon whom the union is making demands. Through the use of these coercive weapons the big unions have been able to establish monopoly control over their members and industry. Petro further shows how terrorism, especially during the Kohler strike, and physical force were used to intimidate workers and in organizing recruiting campaigns; and how violence and mass picketing have made a complete mockery of the process of collective bargaining.

As a result of such union practices, it has become almost impossible for the Christian worker in North American industry to practice his religion at work. Worse still, by joining such unions as the Teamsters and International Seafarer's Unions, the Christian worker is forced to indulge in such disgraceful and wicked practices as having to intimidate his fellow workers by the use of violence in mass picketing. Petro lists the causes of corruption in the big unions as follows:

> The causes of corruption in the badly run unions are (1) the dragooning of vast numbers of workers into trade unions by violence and coercion; (2) the use of further violence and coercion in the form of job control to silence their complaints; (3) the consequent domination of national conventions by local henchmen of the top union dictators; and (4) the rubber-stamping, always pursuant to democratic *forms* of the manipulations of the mighty. Attendance at local union meetings is as small as it is in many unions because dragooned workers have no real interest in attending in the first place, and because it is safer to stay away. . . .

Those members who insist upon "putting in their two cents" soon learn better.

Statutory insistence upon democratic forms will not correct these conditions. Only excision of the special privileges which draw the looters and their bullies to trade unions will do the job.

Unions can become genuinely voluntary associations if the law will but withdraw the special privileges of compulsion which they have enjoyed.[16]

Yes indeed! The time has most surely come for a complete overhaul of our Anglo-Saxon labor legislation. The time has indeed come to withdraw the special privileges given to union leaders of compelling workers to join unions in which they do not believe. The natural and proper function of a trade union is to represent those workers who want collective representation in bargaining with their employers over terms of employment. This function is perverted the moment a union claims the right to represent employees who do not want representation or conduct political activities which have nothing to do with the terms of employment. To force Christian workers into socialistically inclined trade unions makes complete nonsense of their claim to be "neutral." The fact that so large a segment of our labor organizations have now identified themselves with the aims of socialism and openly or covertly support political parties which proclaim socialism as the answer to all human ills is indisputable proof of the presence in their midst of a basic philosophical and religious outlook and commitment upon life.

The time has come to restore our historic freedom for workers to associate, or not to associate, with men of a similar persuasion, as each man's conscience dictates. As we have seen, millions of workers in America and in Britain and Canada are today required by law as a condition of employment to join the union that is the legally recognized bargaining agent at the place where they work. Such labor agreements deny to these workers the right to decide for themselves what union they will join, or indeed whether they will join at all. The exercise of their freedom not to join involves, as we have already seen, the loss of their livelihood. Our governments allow these dictatorial practices to continue and they have even enacted laws permitting this tyranny.

Union leaders often advance the so-called "free rider" argument in defense of compulsory payment of union dues. The contention is that a man ought not to enjoy the benefits of a union's activities unless he contributes his fair share of their costs. We are unaware, however, of any other organization or institution in the English-speaking world that seeks to enforce this theory by compulsion. The Red Cross benefits us all, directly or indirectly. Would the union leaders of America, Britain, and Canada make donations to the Red Cross compulsory? Certain unions and their apologists would be well advised to keep quiet about the free rider argument, for some of the big unions today have become the real "free riders."

It is one thing to say that a man *should* contribute to an association that is supposedly acting in his best interests; it is quite another matter to say that he *must* do so. No doubt a man ought to join a union if it is a good union that is serving the best interests not only of all its members but of society as well. Most men will give support to a union provided that it is deserving of such support. There will always be some men, of course, who will try to sponge off other people, but let us not express our contempt for some men by denying freedom of association to all our citizens.

The question boils down to this: not the fact that workers refuse to share in their financial responsibilities as union members, but *why* they refuse to carry their fair share. In the case of Christian trade unionists in Canada and America the answer is because many do not look upon the labor movement as a kind of business institution, but they view it as a result of one's life-and-world view. It is not that they object to paying their union dues. It is their objection to the secular humanist basis of the so-called neutral labor union. For such Christian workers to support the neutral labor union would be like betraying one's own country in war to the enemy. It is treason to the Lord Jesus Christ to join any organization which deliberately excludes the Savior of the world from its activities.

To ask the Christian worker to join the humanist union is like asking the atheist to go to church. How can anyone support something that is contrary to his deepest convictions and loyalties? For this reason the writer believes that the arbitrary ruling which forces

Christian workers to support neutral trade unions as a condition of employment and which thus takes no notice of their conscientious objections, violates the most sacred of all freedoms, i.e., freedom of conscience.

The only satisfactory answer to the "free rider" problem lies in the introduction into the Anglo-Saxon labor relations field of the Western European system of proportional representation, under which it would be possible for workers to join the union of their own choice. The worker would then be made aware of his duty with regard to that freedom, and this would result in a stronger and really free labor movement.

Unions will become genuinely free associations only when the governments of America, Britain, and Canada withdraw the special privileges of compulsion and the closed shop which many unions presently enjoy. That is one way in which unions now guilty of socially destructive abuses may become and stay clean. Union members would then have the opportunity to become their own guardians. By such free unionism the workers themselves would be enabled to put a stop to the corruption and graft going on in industry. As long as the union bosses can force workers to join their organizations they will have no incentive to act responsibly. Once the workers can choose to belong or not to belong to a union, depending upon how the union leaders behave, then the pressure to stamp out malpractice and corruption would become irresistible. Only then will the workers have an effective shield with which to defend themselves against exploitation—they can refuse to pay union dues to those who abuse their position as union leaders.

(c) *The Humanist-Pragmatic Basis of the Secular Labor Union*

In the opinion of the writer the big so-called neutral unions have broke away from faith in God's Word as the ordering principle of their union activities, and as a direct result they have been reduced to pursuing purely man-centered materialistic objectives based upon a functional doctrine of work. The struggle for power and status has today replaced the struggle for justice and social righteousness based upon obedience to the Lord's ordinances for man in society as the dominating motive in the big unions' struggle with the big companies. By rejecting God's law for human work revealed in Holy Scriptures, many secular unions have become just as materialistic and spiritually decadent as many big business corporations.

While the trade unions of the English-speaking world were struggling for recognition, and as long as they were obviously the representatives of the "under-dog" and the "have-nots," many union leaders were inspired with a high moral purpose derived from their Puritan and evangelical reformed background, which guided their union activities. According to R. T. Wearmouth in his study of *Methodism and the Working Class Movements of England, 1800-1850,*

> From the very beginning of the trade union movement among all sections of wage earners, of the formation of Friendly Societies, and of the later attempts at adult education, it is men who are Methodists, and in Durham County especially, local preachers of the Primitive Methodists, whom we find taking the lead and filling the posts of influence. From their ranks have come an astonishingly large proportion of trade union officials, from checkweighers and lodge chairmen up to county officials and committee men.[17]

In many other cases union activity was motivated by conscious Christian convictions, and many American, British, and Canadian unions obtained their initial moral impetus and dynamic from Christian laymen who sought to stem the worst consequences of the industrial and financial exploitation of the working classes set in motion by the attempt to apply principles of technical and economic rationality to the processes of industrial production. Union leaders of the last century rightly refused to accept the attempt of the new breed of capitalists to treat the workers as mere "hands" or functions of the machines they were expected to operate.[18]

Today, however, the big neutral unions would seem to have shifted their ground. Instead of battling for social justice and the dignity of the worker as created in God's image, they themselves have become a privileged group in modern society. Today it has become unmistakably clear that the two divisions of society into employers and employed and into the well-to-do and the poor do not coincide;

and that it is with the claims of the employed workers of the big unions, not with those of the poor, that the bigger unions in Britain and North America are most concerned. The original moral dynamic which inspired many trade union leaders of the previous century has now directed its energies elsewhere. The urge to reduce social inequality and achieve social justice for *all* members of society no longer counts as a practical force in wage and salary claims; and with this lack of concern for social righteousness, the chief justification of the labor movement in the English-speaking world has disappeared.

And so it is that the big international and national unions now fight for such things as better wage differentials and fringe benefits for their own membership. The important aspect of any wage is now considered to be not so much its absolute level, but how much it differs from the wage paid to someone else; that is to say, the emphasis is today more upon achieving inequality of remuneration than equality. The vital questions for the modern trade union leader are not as they once used to be, "Will this give my members a butter or a margarine standard of living?" but "Are my members keeping their distance above their inferiors in this and other industries?" In short, the emphasis upon wage differentials symbolizes the great fact that the Anglo-Saxon humanist labor movement has sold itself out to the prevailing pagan, pragmatic, and acquisitive social philosophy of post-Christian humanist society. The unions have joined the humanist bandwagon! Deplorable though it may be to have to admit, it is clear that most unions today are being motivated either by individualistic or collectivistic values, capitalist or socialist, the principles of which may, superficially considered, appear different, but which in reality are both founded on the same apostate humanistic presuppositions about the nature of man in society.

Pragmatic humanism takes for granted that human reason, not God's Word, is the source of all truth; man is considered to be the measure of all things. For the pragmatic humanist such as William James and John Dewey this world is all there is to reality and thus it follows that there can be no valid standards of thought, conduct or reality other than those which are the products of the human mind, which change as the human mind changes. For both men absolute truth is a figment of the logicians, and it is of no importance in practice. Every belief is simply a truth claim. By acting upon the belief we test it, and if the consequences which follow from adopting it are good, if they promote the purpose in hand and so have a valuable effect upon life, the truth of the claim is validated. Hence, man makes his own truth just as he makes his own reality, and the truth of the beliefs he holds and the reality of the objects he perceives being equally relative to his purposes. As William James puts it:

> The "true," to put it very brieflly, is only the expedient way of thinking, just as the "right" is only the expedient way of behaving. Expedient in almost any fashion; and expedient in the long run and on the whole, of course.[19]

Given this operational or instrumentalist theory of truth the task of science is not to discover truth or to read the Creator's thoughts after him as these have been expressed in the Book of Nature. Science is simply an instrument which man uses to maintain social practices and to help realize his practical goals. The question of whether science is true or not is completely unimportant, unless it somehow affects the question of whether it is useful. That is the decisive factor for the pragmatist, and if anyone still wants to use the term "truth" he can say that whatever is useful or works is true.

By the same token pragmatism denies the existence of any objective absolute values such as goodness or beauty. According to Dewey moral standards are like language in that both are the result of custom. Values can only be described, claims Dewey, in the context of ends to be attained and means to be obtained for the realization of the envisioned ends. He writes in his work, *Theory of Valuation*: "The measure of the value a person attaches to a given end is not what he says about its preciousness but the care he devotes to obtaining and using the means without which it cannot be attained." [20] Thus he wants to make values empirical facts, to be measured by the intensity of the desire, the degree of activity caused by the end in view.

If pragmatism is a philosophy of expediency, it is no less a philos-

ophy of adaptation. By aid of his science, man must adjust himself
not only to his natural but also to his social environment.

The Christian philosopher, S. U. Zuidema of the Free University,
Amsterdam, in a penetrating lecture on "Pragmatism" delivered at
Unionville, Ontario, in 1960, said of this pragmatist emphasis on
adaptation:

> It strikes me that "adaptation" is a key word of all pragmatists.
> It points out how free man in his contingent environment can
> prevent being trampled upon and may attain an ever "smoother"
> relation which is profitable for himself and his needs. But no less
> striking is the fact that this word "adaptation" has a twofold usage
> and is used for two *different* ways of human conduct. It refers
> one time to the conduct which accommodates itself to circum-
> stances and another time to the conduct which accommodates
> circumstances to it. The pragmatist uses both meanings indis-
> criminately and does so rightly in so far as both point to a conduct
> which directs itself according to the econmic norm of "efficiency."
> Pragmatism is therefore also a form of economism, a universaliza-
> tion of the economic norm to a basic law of man's being.[21]

In terms of this perspective we can now understand the real
significance of Tannenbaum's definition of the trade union as "the
spontaneous grouping of individual workers thrown together func-
tionally," and we can also understand why McCarthy was forced by
his unstated pragmatist presuppositions about human life to justify
the practice of compulsory trade unionism precisely in the *economic*
terms of "functional necessity." Several dominant traits of the secular
trade unions can be traced directly to their humanist and pragmatic
presuppositions about man's nature and destiny.

In the first place there is the primacy ascribed by the secular
labor union leaders to human needs. Two leading trade union leaders
explain that men have certain economic, psychological, and social
needs which must be satisfied. According to Clinton Golden and
Harold Ruttenburg in their book, *The Dynamics of Industrial Democracy*,

> Labor unions are indispensable in the fulfilment of these needs
> because they can be satisfied only through group relations. Unions
> are peculiarly adapted toward this end, since they serve workers as
> a means of self-expression, as a socially integrating force, as a

provider for economic benefits, and as an instrument for participation in the productive process. Management by itself, through
individual relations with workers, cannot satisfy all three needs,
nor can unions alone. The joint efforts of both are required to
provide workers with a well rounded environment, a happy,
prosperous, and secure life.[22]

Walter Reuther spoke in a similar vein when he described the
trade union movement as follows:

> This is a crusade, a crusade to gear economic abundance to
> human needs. We plan to take management upon the mountain
> top and we would like to give them a little more of the vision we
> have. We would like to show them the great new world that can
> be built if free labor and free management and free government
> and free people can cooperate together in harnessing the power
> of America and gearing it to the basic needs of the people.[23]

The spirit pervading the American labor movement can perhaps
best be seen at work in the views advocated by Samuel Gompers,
who has been called, "the chief architect of the modern American
trade union movement." He was born in London, England, but
emigrated, at the age of 13, to New York City, where he obtained
work as a cigar maker. He became active in the local Cigarmaker's
Union, where he came under the influence of socialism as taught by
the refugees from Europe. The constitution of Gomper's Cigarmakers Local stated that "we recognize the solidarity of the whole
working class to work harmoniously against their common enemy—
the capitalist."[24] Gradually Gompers came to change his mind about
socialism, deciding that the most effective way for the American
working classes to obtain what they wanted was through economic
methods in the "existing order" by working through the trade
unions, which could solve problems, rather than through the government, which could not. On this issue he came into conflict with
Daniel De Leon. To Gompers the trade union movement was an institution in its own right; to De Leon, as to all other socialist radicals,
it was either an instrument of the class war or it was nothing. As
another socialist, Karl Kautsky, put it, trade unions are important
only as they lead to social revolution. They are important "as militant organizations, not as organizations for social peace." This is

due to the fact that up to the present they have proved "at most only a nuisance to the employers." [25] Another socialist declared that "the only difference between the socialists and the trade unionists . . . is that . . . the former clearly realize this ultimate goal (the end of capitalism) . . . the latter do not." [26] For the socialist doctrine of class warfare Gompers substituted a natural class feeling, "a group feeling, one of the strongest cohesive forces in the labor movement."

Whatever may have been Gompers' attitude as to ultimate ends, he refused to allow any socialist dreams of a coming millennium to stand in the way of fighting for what small gains could be attained at the moment. This pragmatism is well expressed in the words of one of Gompers' contemporary unionists, Adolph Strasser, president of the Cigarmakers Union, spoken before a Senate committee in 1883:

> We have no ultimate ends. We are going on from day to day. We are fighting only for immediate objects—objects that can be realized in a few years.[27]

Samuel Gompers' insistence upon rather strict adherence to a policy of organization based on national craft or trade unions, upon frugality in money matters, and upon avoidance of radical economic theories, enabled him with considerable success to bring the pressure of organized labor to bear on such practical demands as the eighthour day, the Saturday half-holiday, federal child labor legislation, the restriction of immigration and alien contract labor, and workingmens compensation. Under his leadership the American labor movement reverted to the type of old-line pragmatic unionism followed in Great Britain for many decades after the collapse of Chartism.

Gompers summed up the goal of this pragmatic unionism as "more," or "more, more more more, now." That is it—the unlimited "improvement of the existing order." According to his interpreter, Louis Reed, "The question of the day after tomorrow, of the trade union of the future he never asked nor answered." [28] Speculating as to what might have been Gompers' ideal society, Reed suggests:

> Industry must become a coordinating and self-governing whole. In this self-government labor must share. Then this democratic

industry must become conscious of itself and its real purpose, and produce for use, not solely for profits." [29] "Industrial democracy or economic democracy, means the development of a government in industry, in which the workers shall participate through their union." [30]

This objective became the long term goal of the labor movement. The exercise of rights, of the inalienable rights guaranteed by the Constitution, now became enlarged to include the right to a job and the right "to have a voice in determining the conditions of employment." So "in American society, where status depends so clearly upon ownership of property, an improvement in social position is most readily achieved when the right to property is expanded to include the right to a job." [31] Gompers wrote that whatever or whoever controls the economic power directs and shapes the development for the group and the nation." [32] Thus the labor union for Gompers existed to improve the situation of the working man, and to raise him to a position of equality with the managerial class, to a position of sharing the economic power, a position of self-government in industry.

The labor historian John R. Commons gives us this interpretation of the meaning of the American labor movement:

> As long as the wage-earning class accepts the existing order and merely attempts to secure better wage bargains, its goal must eventually be some form of the trade agreement, which recognizes the equal bargaining rights of the organized employees. Its union is not "class-conscious" in the revolutionary sense of Socialism, but "wage-conscious" in the sense of separate from, but partners with the employing class.[33]

The Constitution of the A.F.L.-C.I.O. will tell us even more:

> We seek the fulfillment of the hopes and aspirations of the working people of America through democratic processes within the framework of our constitutional government and consistent with our institutions and traditions. . . .
> We pledge ourselves to the more effective organization of working men and women; to the securing to them of full recognition and enjoyments of the rights to which they are justly entitled; to the achievement of ever higher standards of living and working conditions.[34]

These various rights are construed as natural rights. Thus the beginning of the preamble to the constitution of the United Auto Workers Union of 1955 asserted:

> We hold these truths to be self-evident . . . that all men are created equal, that they are endowed by their Creator with certain inalienable rights, that among these are life, liberty, and the pursuit of happiness. That to secure these rights, governments are instituted among men, deriving their just powers from the consent of the governed.

For the labor movement, man is by nature, by mere virtue of being a man, entitled to certain "natural rights." A man has the right to live; to live the worker depends on wages; for wages he has to work; therefore he has a right to work and to earn wages. Thus, wage-earning becomes the main interest of the labor movement. Workers combine in a trade union to assert their natural rights. They unite to get "more and more here and now," more wages for less work. Work has thus become an economic matter, a means of satisfying the the economic needs of the workers.

(d) *A Christian Critique of Secular Trade Unions*

It is thus abundantly clear that the leaders of the North American labor movement consider the fulfillment of man's needs on a purely horizontal level. Man's desires and goals are directed to this life exclusively. His destiny is within himself and within this world. Life and work are completely secularized, and God and His service are considered to be irrelevant. The majority of North American trade unionists do not recognize that man's real purpose and true fulfillment consists in the obedient service of his Creator. They have no eye for the biblical doctrine that man is created in God's image and that as such he is an office bearer of Jehovah in the creation and responsible to God. As we have seen, man does not work merely to obtain a living, but in order to carry out the great cultural mandate to have dominion over the earth and to subdue it for God's greater glory. Work is the service and worship of either the one true God of the Scriptures, or it becomes inevitably the worship and service of mammon. Man is called to serve God in his work as he is called to serve Him in all other areas of life. Economic work is one kind of work, but it too is service of the one true God. In his economic activities man is not just a wage-earner and a consumer, but a servant. Whether an employer or an employee, his primary purpose is still service.

For these reasons the writer finds it hard to understand Tannenbaum's claim that whereas "the Socialists and the Communists operate with general ideas, and are given over to large plans for the establishment of social 'harmony' the trade union movement seems to have no rational basis. It lacks a doctrinal foundation. It has no theory, and it offers no explanation of the beginning and the end of things." [35] So far from this in fact being the case, it is clear that the trade union movement in Great Britain and North America has succumbed to the prevailing naturalistic ethic of Anglo-Saxon pragmatism and humanism which is strictly confined by the limits of the natural. Since this materialistic ethic has no transcendent values to attach itself to, it focuses the maximum of significance upon temporal prosperity and temporal adversity. There is no escape from an ethic grounded in worldly well-being except by means of the biblical ethic, which reaches out to the supernatural.

The false ethic of the pragmatist attempts to disguise its materialistic criteria by masquerading as a mental reality superior to life at the physical level. Thus pragmatic psychologists speak of the well-organized or completely integrated personality, and posit ideals of behavior to which such personalities will conform. It is tempting to believe that the concept of the harmonious personality well adjusted to its environment gives us an ideal superior to the temporal and the physical. But the theorizing of the pragmatic philosophers and psychologists, if pressed to its logical conclusions, invariably proves that this is not the case. Their idea turns out to be the glorification of the natural and the physical. Thus the concept of the harmonious personality compels us to ask with what the personality is in harmony. We shall be told that it is in harmony with its environment. But this is a deterministic and natural ideal. We demand the right to judge our environment.

But by what standards does the personality which is wholly in harmony with its environment judge that environment? Plainly, the pragmatist idea of a self adjusted to its environment is not an ideal at all. If the environment is bad, the Christian personality will surely be at war with it. Some of the greatest saints and heroes of the Church of God were utterly at loggerheads with the various social environments in which they lived. We can scarcely claim that our Lord Jesus Christ himself achieved that specious kind of mental health which is defined in terms of a harmonious relationship between the self and its environment. Had that wonderful Christian misfit, Florence Nightingale, been born in our generation, a child guidance clinic no doubt would soon have put an early stop to all her nonsense.

The modern jargon of the pragmatic sociologists and psychologists devoted to the humanistic cult of adjustment to one's environment can be reduced in every case to complete nonsense. The truth is that all the terms in which the pragmatists today define mental health and social well-being—harmonious, integrated, fulfilled, organized, fruitful, and adjusted—are relative and therefore inadequate. They all demand some objective point of repose. The self must be in harmony with something organized and integrated to some end, fulfilled to some purpose, and fruitful of some definite fruit.

The self, in short, must be good in relation to some overriding purpose which is served by man during his life on earth. And this purpose will either reckon with man as created in God's image and subject to God's law revealed in His Word, or it will ignore his eternal destiny and define man in purely physico-economic, psychological terms. If this purpose takes no account of man's supernatural vocation and responsibility to Almighty God, then it can only provide standards of judgment upon human actions and human character which are ultimately materialistic and naturalistic.

The good personality is good because it brings good to others or to itself. Strictly within the limits of the natural and the phenomenal world open to scientific investigation and inquiry, this good can be defined only in terms of material prosperity, animal sexuality, and physical well being. If we press far enough the relative jargon of the pragmatists, we shall in fact arrive at these ultimates as the root ideal for human life in the twentieth century—physical health, comfort, material prosperity, and adjustment to one's social and economic environment. All the talk about integration, inner harmony, fulfillment, and adjustment turns out on closer analysis to be merely an elaborate disguise for a purely pagan, pragmatist, and humanistic ethic devoted to physical health, material comfort, and the worship of the Almighty Dollar. And then we have the audacity to blame the Russians for adapting themselves to their communistic environment!

This is not to deny that working conditions and just wages are important. They concern God's requirements for justice and righteousness in human interrelationships. However, they must always be seen within the framework of the biblical view of man. The union's secular view of man's needs thus narrows and confines his real perspective on human life, and the modern humanist trade union movement must be held partly responsible for the secularization of our Atlantic society. In seeking to improve men's working conditions, the secular unions have forgotten that man does not live by bread alone, but by every word that proceedeth from God. For the men of the Bible, as we have seen, the first concern is not the wages or the profits one receives or makes, but the quality of the work rendered to God. Whenever the vision of man as God's steward, prophet, priest, and king is lost, then there appears upon the scene of human history the autonomous sovereign individual with rights. Then there is every good reason for demanding more and more wages *ad infinitum*, and there is no other purpose to work than to make a mere living. According to the Christian view the criterion for improvements in man's working conditions is that they shall always increase his ability and capacity to serve God and his neighbor. Work is a form of worship of, and prayer and service to, Jehovah God, and without this ideal, work loses its true meaning and proper purpose. Man's first need in life is not to fill his empty belly, but his empty heart and to be redeemed from the power and guilt of sin through Christ's redeeming grace, love, and power. Without such a redemption of the whole man in all his activities, life remains limited to this world and cannot really flourish. As the Lord said, "I am come that men may have life and have it in all its fullness" (John 10:10, NEB). H. Van Riessen puts it very well in these words:

. . . where God is denied and materialistically man's perspectives are limited to the earth . . . man's horizon grows narrower, doubt and disillusionment appear when in actual practice reality turns out to be the very opposite of his ideals. The earthly perspectives are incapable of rousing his enthusiasm, because they are not genuine perspectives. Then everything is meaningless, for man can only await death. Man is abandoned to himself. He experiences the loneliness of being forsaken by God, and is now also lonely among men. He has no standards and can follow no meaningful course of action. In other words he is confronted with nihilism, and his agony and anxiety drive him to the masses. . . . Within the crowd of the masses man seeks his lost security. He desires collectivity and equality, for freedom is an intolerable burden and the transfer of responsibility is a relief.[36]

(b) *The Unions' Faith in the Abilities of the Natural Man*

The belief in man's inherent goodness and innate ability is a second trait of the unions' pragmatic humanist basis. This belief is more often assumed than stated openly, but it is set forth by Walter Reuther in a discussion about democracy. He says that "the intrinsic soundness and rightness of the ordinary person is the firm base of confidence."

Tommy Douglas, leader of the Canadian socialist New Democratic Party, wrote about the basic philosophy of the N.D.P., and stated that the N.D.P. is grounded upon faith in "(a) the essential moral nature of man, (b) the equality of all men, and (c) the power of human reason and common sense." [37]

In view of the close relationship existing between the N.D.P. and the secular trade union movement in Canada, it may be assumed that this statement of belief is endorsed by the trade unions. Douglas' clear-cut statement does not reflect the teachings of the Word of God. If man is essentially good, then the Genesis account of man's fall into sin is not true, and Paul is not proclaiming the truth when he declares that "there is no difference; for all have sinned and come short of the glory of God" (Rom. 3:23).

Socialists would have men put their faith and trust in their own reason, planning, and scientific method applied to man's social life instead of in God's own appointed method of salvation through the

person, life, and work of the Lord Jesus Christ. Such socialists as
Tommy Douglas in Canada, Harold Wilson in Britain, and Walter
Reuther in the United States would have men look to the power
of human government rather than to the power of God's Word
and sacraments to provide men with security, peace, and plenty.
For the biblically motivated Christian, at any rate, the state, so far
from being the supreme instrument of human emancipation and of
human perfectibility, is a strait jacket to be justified at best as God's
appointed instrument of common grace. Its function is to restrain
the worst consequences of human sinfulness by upholding justice and
maintaining law and order while the Church of Christ gets on with
the business of proclaiming the saving gospel of Jesus Christ.

To preach as the socialists do that man is essentially good at heart
and that human nature does not need cleansing by the blood of
Christ is to imply that Christ's atoning death was unnecessary. No
Christian could thus dare to dishonor the Lord Jesus by thus esteem-
ing His work of reconciliation to be of no importance. Human
nature can be restored to its original state of righteousness only by
being first cleansed in the blood of the Lamb of God who taketh
away the sins of the world. Those who prate of human goodness
outside of Christ are blind to the fact that human goodness can be
restored only in Christ. His words "Without me ye can do nothing"
are in striking contrast with the belief in man's inherent goodness
and power.

The humanist belief in man's goodness fosters a spirit of pride and
self-sufficiency. And this pride rings through union leaders' boastful
claims about the accomplishments of their organizations. Thus Walter Reuther waxes very eloquent when speaking about what the trade
unions have done. In a speech recalling the achievements of Phil
Murray and the labor movement, he stated that Phil Murray, "that
great man . . . brought sunshine, and into their old age a sense of
security and dignity." [38] In describing the task of the labor movement he said:

> We can stand with them and work with them. We can march
> with them in building that brave new world that we dream of,
> that world in which men can live in peace as neighbors, that

world where people everywhere can enjoy a fuller measure of
social and economic justice, a world that you and I and men of
good will everywhere can shape in the image of freedom and in
the image of justice and in the image of brotherhood.[39]

Similarly Claude Jodoin, president of the Canadian Labor Congress, addressing a labor seminar in Hamilton, said:

> If workers today have decent wages, vacations, pension plans,
> insurance, and other benefits, they have them because of trade
> union activity.[40]

Likewise the *Canadian Labour*, official journal of the Canadian
Labour Congress, in its 1961 Christmas editorial bluntly claimed that
"the lessons of brotherhood and cooperation that Christ taught are
implicit in the work of the labour movement which strives to ensure
that 'the meek shall inherit the earth.' " In December, 1960, *Canadian
Labour* proudly stated that the modern labor movement had made
great strides in banishing poverty and unhappiness and in abolishing
unsatisfactory conditions, and that "the present is far superior to
the past, but there remains much to be done."

Given their humanistic post-Christian presuppositions, it is not
really surprising that these secular labor leaders should pay so much
tribute to what man has done and can achieve in reliance upon his
own ability and reason. Rather than recognizing man's dependence
upon his Creator and his need for a Savior, these men continually ignore God and His Anointed One. They refuse to acknowledge that
God is the giver of all good things and that the earth is the Lord's
and the fullness thereof. Instead they boast in their hearts, "My
power and the might of mine hand hath gotten me this wealth"
(Deut. 8:17). It is time that these men take to heart the Word of
God given to man in the Book of Deuteronomy: "Thou shalt remember the Lord thy God; for it is he that giveth thee power to
get wealth, that he may establish his covenant" (Deut. 8:18).

The pride of some union leaders may also be detected at work in
their defense of compulsory union membership. The proponents of
compulsory unionism claim that the workers owe allegiance to the
unions because the unions have provided men with the necessities of
life. An advocate of the closed shop went so far as to say that "all

workers owe it to themselves and to their country to join a Brotherhood or Union and to pay dues willingly. . . . Life is a friction
with our fellow human beings. Activity in the life of your local
is living as it is planned in the democratic way of life." [41]

In such claims there would seem to be no awareness of that fact
that for all that modern man possesses and has, he is utterly dependent upon the common grace of the Lord, whose sunshine and rain
fall upon the just and the unjust, and whose providence undergirds
every moment of each man's life so that not one hair falls from his
head without God knowing it. Here we find a gross overestimation
rather than a wrong estimation of the union's role.

Perhaps this overestimation reaches its apogee in current trade
union apologetic with the words with which Tannenbaum closed his
apologia for the labor movement:

> The trade-union is our modern "society," the only true society
> that industrialism has fostered. As the true society it is concerned
> with the whole man, and embodies the possibilities of both the
> freedom and the security essential to human dignity.[42]

In these words we find an absolutization of a human institution just
as dangerous as the Marxist absolutization of the economic aspect
of life and the class struggle. Lacking the true ordering principle
for his philosophy of labor in the Word of God, Tannenbaum was
forced by his positivistic and pragmatic sociological method to stay
with the so-called facts; that is to say, he adjusted his thinking and
analysis to what there was about him. But in doing so, let us be sure
to observe, he lost hold of the facts. For in every so-called positive
"fact" of human society, including a trade union, there is not only
some inescapable structure of creation ordinances (e.g., one cannot
set up a form of trade union that is not somehow bound to the structural requirements of a trade union as a form of human association),
but also the degree of conformity to or deviation from God's creation norm (which is a divine command, a norm, not a structural
law in the sense of the laws of nature studied by the natural scientists)
which has been operative in the cultural-forming-activity of the men
who built the modern trade unions and labor associations. When a

man's eyes are closed to this fact, whether he be a self-confessed
humanist or Christian sociologist, he is, in a fundamental sense, blind
to the integral meaning of the Holy Scriptures, and without their
light he will not be in a position to see any social fact for what it is,
including a trade union fact. If Tannenbaum wishes to call such
blindness sticking to the facts, well and good, provided we all know
that "sticking to the facts" means this sort of positivistic and pragmatic blindness.

In absolutizing the trade union as the "true society" Tannenbaum
forgets that even our modern technological society reveals a multiplicity of true human bonds in industry, but also in the churches,
families, schools and universities, farms, and political parties. If
these are not true human communities or associations, what else does
Tannenbaum think they are? And as Petro has proved, even in the
trade unions themselves there is often precious little true society,
since the unions are often led by racketeers. Does Tannenbaum consider James Hoffa and his thugs good examples of human friendship
and community? For this reason we believe that Tannenbaum has
gone much too far in claiming that the trade union is the only true
society there is today.

Tannenbaum's absolutization of the modern labor union would
seem to reflect the earlier socio-economic theories of the European
syndicalists and of the Fabians and guild-socialists in England. In
addition to ideas derived from Marx, the European syndicalists continued to carry forward ideas drawn from other socialists such as
Proudhon and also ideas drawn from anarchists like Bakunin and
Kropotkin. The cornerstone of syndicalist doctrine is the inevitability of the class struggle and the need of the proletariat to perfect its
own appropriate forms of collective organization and social institutions. "Events," says one author, "have not fallen out quite as Marx
in his revolutionary mood anticipated. It has begun to appear as
though in his prognostications, he had not reckoned with all the
conditions. And syndicalism is one of the forces which go to restore
faith when it had fallen in need of being restored." [43] For in its crude
form syndicalism was a revolutionary doctrine. G. D. H. Cole explains their doctrine in his book, *The World of Labour*:

The Syndicalist interprets Marx's saying that "the emancipation of the workers must be the act of the workers themselves" as meaning that emancipation can only come to them organized as workers. . . . Class they hold as a natural division, "party," artificial and intellectual. They quote with appreciation the words of Nietzsche, "the State is the coldest of masters. . . ." Wherever there is a people it does not understand the state, it detests it.[44]

The Syndicalists were, however, ready to use the state where it existed, but they made use of political democracy only the better to destroy it. Thus the syndicalists were quite outside the Marxist tradition in denying the value of political action. For this reason they tended to rely on direct action, the general strike, and other forms of violence as distinguished from organized political revolution. The weapon of these direct actionists was to be the general strike, and their ideal a community-owned monopoly controlled by those employed in industry. According to Cole the social general strike has as its purpose not attaining some particular economic or political goal, but "the complete overthrow of capitalist society and the substitution of a new order."[45] Like the guild socialists, they looked forward to a pluralist form of industrial organization and to the producer's control of industry achieved through the direct action of the unions in the general strike.

In England the Fabians led by G. D. H. Cole advocated guild socialism rather than syndicalism as the only cure for society's ills. The defects of Syndicalism were obvious and real enough. A modern critic states them thus:

> Syndicalism must meet the challenges—that the trade unions cannot take over industry by themselves and they cannot therefore expect to be allowed to run it for themselves; that if the State nationalizes an industry it does so primarily in the national interest and not in the interest of the workers in that industry— which would be the main aim of the unions if they had sole control; that the trade unions do not have the technical, administrative and commercial experience to run large-scale industries, and that the trade union government of industry might be no more democratic than capitalist authoritarianism.[46]

The guild socialist tried to skirt around these these difficulties by emphasizing decentralization, giving as much power as possible to the individual workshop, and suggesting that the industry should be owned by the nation and only handed over to the guilds to be operated under charter—the state protecting the consumer through its power over prices and wages. Peaceful evolution to this happy state was also predicted. According to Cole:

> It seems clear that the thing to aim at—whether we can attain to it or not—is not an early revolution, but the consolidation of all the forces on the lines of evolutionary development with a view to making the "revolution" which in one sense must come, as little as possible a civil war and as much as possible a registration of accomplished facts and a combination of tendencies already in operation.[47]

To this end a policy of encroaching control of industry by the workers themselves was advocated. "By encroaching control is meant a policy directed to wresting, bit by bit, from the hands of the possessing classes, the economic power which they now exercise, by a steady transference of function and rights from their nominees to the representatives of the working class." [48]

With Marx, the Fabians and the guild socialists shared both the theory that value is created corporately by society more truly than by individuals singly and the moral conviction that any institution, private property included, must be justified by its social utility. They shared with Marx an apprehension about the human consequences of industrial exploitation of the workers, but they also shared with William Morris an admiration for the moral qualities of craftsmanship. For this reason their plans for a decentralized organization of industry in guilds, and a correspnding diminution of political power, belonged to the ideology of craft-unionism and were not Marxian at all. Tannenbaum, together with the guild socialists, seems to identify the modern trade union with the medieval guilds and both look to the modern trade union to "recreate the bonds of community" torn apart by the industrial revolution. Such an identification betrays a complete lack of insight into the historical development of Western social institutions and a disregard for what we described in the first chapter of this book as the opening up process of history which discloses the higher modal aspects or law-spheres of God's creation. As we pointed out, in every modal moment of the divine cosmic structure there are given certain principles or norms which should become concretized in the development of human society.

In man's long development out of the undifferentiated state of primitive society the enclosed structures of such a society became broken up to make room for the emergence of the separate cultural spheres. All these separate cultural spheres are valid concretizations within the temporal world order of the structural principles given at creation. The historical norm of differentiation thus insures the unfolding of the individualizing tendency of persons, nations, and societal relationships. Yet in the historical aspect of creation, as a normative sphere, these principles require positivization or specification. They must be concretely applied in all human relationships which have an historical aspect. It is the duty of the cultural leaders who possess historical power to formulate the concrete requirements of culture and society for their own age, but their power is not to be exercised arbitrarily. They must act in accordance with the divinely established norms of both continuity and differentiation.

The norm of continuity requires that cultural form-giving must give due respect to tradition as well as to progress. Progress takes place when the principles contained in the post-historical law-spheres are realized in human society. But this realization must not occur in a revolutionary fashion, destroying what is good in the new advance.

The norm of differentiation demands that in the development of society from a primitive phase, the new forms of communal and associational relations between individuals must be concretized into new institutions and social forms.

Now since the historical aspect is normative, violations of historical norms are possible, and leaders in business and political life may fail to act normatively in accordance with the structural principles and ordinances of the creation.

It would for this reason be retrogressive for modern men to return to a social form of organization based upon the lines of the medieval guilds. The opening process of human culture itself points this fact out, since the guilds were still part of the undifferentiated medieval society, where the guilds often performed a mixture of industrial, legal, and political functions. Dooyeweerd points out:

Especially when in the later Middle Ages the craft guilds had aqcuired great political power and in the towns the progress of social differentiation began to reveal itself, these guilds displayed very complicated structural interlacements. Repeatedly we find the following differentiated structures in them interwoven with each other:

1. the structure of a private, economically qualified trade union;
2. that of a coercive organization with a public legal sphere of competence derived from the city government, connected with an economic monopoly and the so-called guild ban;
3. the structure of a part of the political organization of a town on a military basis;
4. the structure of an ecclesiastical organized group with an altar and church services of its own. . . .

The structures mentioned here are in their turn interwoven with all kinds of features peculiar to an undifferentiated community; the guild as a fraternity, with its common meals and guild feasts, with its duties of mutual aid and assistance in all kinds of circumstances.[49]

It is difficult for modern man to understand the nature of the medieval guild and of the organic social system of which it was an integral part. Medieval society was characterized by the preeminence of the small social group. From such organizations as family, guild, village community, and monastery flowed most of the cultural life of the age. Unlike modern society, which is based upon contract, medieval society was based upon status. In the Middle Ages, Jacob Burckhardt has written, "man was conscious of himself only as a member of a race, people, party, family, or corporation—only through some general category."[50] The reality of the separate, autonomous individual was as indistinct as that of centralized political power. Both the individual and the State were subordinated to the immense range of association that lay intermediate to the individual and ruler and that included such groups as the patriarchal family, the guild, the church, feudal class, and manorial village.

In his *Community and Power*, Robert A. Nisbet explains the organic social philosophy underlying medieval social institutions as follows:

"All who are included in a community," wrote Aquinas, "stand in relation to that community as parts to the whole." The im-

mense influence of the whole philosophy of organism and that of
the related doctrine of the great chain of being, which saw every
element as an infinitesimal gradation of ascent to God, supported
and gave reason for the deeply held philosophy of community.
Whether it was the divine Kingdom itself or some component
mundane association like the family and guild, the whole weight
of medieval learning was placed in support of the reality of social
wholes, of communities. . . .

The centrality of community was much more than a philosophical principle however. Whether we are dealing with the family,
the village, or the guild, we are in the presence of systems of authority and allegiance which were widely held to precede the individual
in both origin and right. "It was a distinctive trait of medieval
doctrine," Otto von Gierke writes in *Political Theories of the
Middle Ages*, "that within every human group it decisively recognized an aboriginal and active right of the group taken as a
whole." As many an institutional historian has discovered, medieval economy and law are simply unintelligible if we try to proceed
from modern conceptions of individualism and contract. The
group was primary; it was the irreducible unit of the social system
at large. . . .

Within the town were innumerable small associations, the guilds
—organizations based first upon occupation, to be sure, but also
upon sacred obligations of mutual-aid, religious faith, and political
responsibility. Here, too, in these urban social organizations we
are dealing with structures of authority and function which long
resisted the later efforts of businessmen and political rulers to
subjugate or destroy them. . . .

The larger philosophy of community unquestionably had its
influence, but the major reason for the profound hold of the family
and the local community and guild upon human lives was simply
the fact that, apart from membership in these and other groups, life
was impossible for the vast majority of human beings. . . . The solidarity of each functional group was possible only in an environment
of authority where central power was weak and fluctuating. As
Ernest Barker has written, the medieval state "abounded in groups
and in the practice of what we may call communal self-help because
it was not yet itself a fully organised group. When it became
such it asserted itself and curtailed the rights of groups with no
little vigor." It is indeed this curtailment of group rights by the
rising power of the central government that forms one of the
most revolutionary movements of modern history.[51]

The modern trade union cannot perform all these guild functions in the highly differentiated state now existing in modern society, and it is anachronistic on the part of Tannenbaum to suggest
that they do or can. For one thing the modern unified state has a
monopoly of armed power in modern society which cannot today
be distributed to such non state associations as labor unions. Again
no one in his saner moments really believes that the labor union can
or should assume the function of a church or school. The opening
process of the historical aspect of God's creation as it has developed
in Western society implies (1) the destruction of the undifferentiated social bonds of the medieval guild, (2) the development of
the unification and centralization of political authority and the power
of the sword of justice in the state, (3) the advance of the civil
rights of the individual, and (4) a harmonious development of all the
voluntary institutions and associations outside of the state. It is precisely owing to these four factors that only in the modern state does
one find trade unions. Thus Tannenbaum's attempt to identify
the modern trade union with the medieval guilds betrays a lack of
insight into the historical development of Western society and a
confusion with respect to the structures of human bonds as we find
them in modern life. He is trying to close what has been "opened."

At the same time we would agree with Tannenbaum in his view
that "trade unionism is the conservative movement of our time.
It is the counterrevolution. Unwittingly it has turned its back upon
most of the political and economic ideas that have nourished Western Europe and the United States during the last two centuries." [52]
From this point of view the trade unions may justly be accused
of trying to break the historical norm of differentiation by trying
to hold fast to the norm of continuity, and they are thus guilty of
holding back the opening process of the historical aspect of reality.
If Tannenbaum is correct, by the turn of the twenty-first century
membership in a particular trade union may be as important a
hereditary right as membership in a medieval guild. Already in one
or two craft unions which control apprenticeship strictly it is desirable, if not necessary, to have had a father or grandfather in the
craft. Even now, expulsion from a trade union may mean something

like a sentence of industrial death. Appeal procedure is cumbersome and often unsatisfactory, and unless a union has broken its own rules, the courts may be unable to intervene. Tannenbaum admits as much when he writes:

> The union is a new "society" in which membership has become essential. . . . This new society has a logic and needs of its own, and it lays down conditions and establishes disciplines for both. The worker cannot get any kind of job he wants. He cannot even learn any trade he wants to, because apprenticeship may be limited, the books of the union may be closed, the initiation fees may be high, or the union may discriminate against him by forcing him to pay for a permit to work without offering an opportunity to become a permanent member. His career in the job he gets is circumscribed by the seniority rules. The amount he earns is defined for him, his freedom of movement is circumscribed by the fact he may not be able to enter another industry, or get the same kind of job in another place. . . . If he leaves his union he will lose his job. He must carry out its policies even if he objects to them. His freedom of speech and of criticism is restricted by the fact that local leaders are in a position to do him injury in ways he cannot escape, or for which he cannot find redress because recognition of these grievances has not as yet become part of either the written or the common law, except in his organization. . . .
>
> A union now has powers of "governance" over the lives of its members. . . . Yet it has no adequate common or written law to order the relations between the individual member and the union. . . . The courts have not wished to interfere in the affairs of a private association and have limited their cognizance to those areas where the member was denied orderly procedure and adjudication as determined by the constitution of the union itself.[53]

The only remedy for this new version of "bastard" feudalism within our society that Tannenbaum can suggest is a system of industrial law and industrial courts to protect the individual from injustice by his union. "The new experiences," he writes, "call for a new judiciary, aware of the special questions that need to be dealt with, but free from the costly and time-consuming practices of the ordinary courts." [54]

In principle Tannenbaum can have no objection to the coercion of the individual worker, for, as a good pragmatist, following in the footsteps of John Dewey's teaching in *Human Nature and Conduct*,[55] the question whether a man should be compelled to join and to stay in a labor union against his will is not a matter of principle, but an experimental matter to be decided scientifically by concrete consequences. Since, however, the coercer and the victim will obviously place different evaluations on the consequences, it becomes a major question how such concrete consequences can determine what ought and ought not to be done.

Tannenbaum, by his pragmatism, has landed himself within the camp of the totalitarians. Just as the medieval absolutization of the earthly church ecclesiastical institution resulted in papal totalitarianism, so Tannenbaum's absolutization of the social institution of the labor union has resulted in his justification for this new form of social totalitarianism. If it is true that the labor union is indeed the one perfect and "true society," then no doubt such economic and social domination of the individual worker by the labor union may be justified.

No Christians, however, should subscribe to such a doctrine, since they believe that no earthly institution or association can thus swallow up the individual. God alone is absolute sovereign of the consciences of men. No particular bearer of authority on earth is the highest power, from which other forms of authority are derived. No community or institution, not even the union, must absorb the individual completely. Only the Kingdom of God should absorb all of men's interests. And the Kingdom of God should not, in the collectivist sense, be identified with any temporal organization. According to the biblical teaching a community is characterized by the relationship of authority and obedience. But this authority is always limited, being defined by its own structural principle or creation ordinance. Within human society, therefore, there is no organization such as the state or a labor union which is the whole in which other societies are but parts. Judged by the criterion of the biblical doctrine of sphere sovereignty, of which we shall write later, Tannenbaum thus shows himself to be lacking in a coherent view of man in society, since he favors communal relationships at the expense of individualized relationships. While we would agree with him that economic individualism has tended to depersonalize human beings, we would not agree that the pendulum should now be allowed to swing so far in the other collectivist direction that the individual is submerged altogether by the group of which he is a part. A balanced view of human society will seek to find a harmony and balance between the needs and rights of the group and the needs and rights of the individual, between communal and intercommunal bonds, and between the state and other communities and associations of human society. A true society will thus be pluralist, not syndicalist.

Tannenbaum rightly recognizes the great role played by modern trade unions in defeating both the ambitions of economic individualism and of state collectivism and of the police state. But it seems that in place of the leviathan state he would like to establish the leviathan cooperative business enterprises and to abolish the state altogether and so return to a form of guild socialism. Yet this very antistatism itself developed into Laski's theory of economic monism of the Russian communist variety.[56]

While the Christian also objects to the totalitarian state, he, unlike the guild socialists, the syndicalists, and now Tannenbaum, recognizes that the state, as a divinely ordained institution of the creation order, cannot be eliminated from this world as long as the powers of sin and darkness continue to thwart God's purpose for man. Attempts to do so, as in Marx's doctrine and prophecy of the "withering away of the state," and as in the anarchism of the syndicalists, must inevitably result in the substitution of the state's qualifying function of justice and law with another function, that of economic power, and that, as the Soviet experiment has proved, can only lead to an even greater totalitarianism.

It would thus appear that before we can profitably discuss the nature of a trade union and of its proper function in society, we must first discuss the nature of society as a whole and of the way in which its various institutions and associations should cohere. One's view of a trade union is inevitably determined by one's view of society itself. One's view of society in turn depends upon one's view of man's nature and destiny. Tannenbaum's attempt to discuss the

nature and function of the modern labor union and to work out a
philosophy of labor purely in terms of his functional and pragmatic
doctrine of work, and his avoidance of the ultimate issues have
prevented him from giving us a clear insight into the basic issues and
problems involved. It is the claim of the Roman Catholic Church
that it does indeed develop its philosophy of labor and its doctrine of
work and labor relationships in terms of its larger philosophy of man
in society, and it is therefore the Roman Catholic philosophy of
labor we shall now consider.

CHAPTER FOUR NOTES

1. Frank Tannenbaum, *The True Society, A Philosophy of Labor* (Jonathan
   Cape, London, 1964), p. 3.
2. *Ibid.*, p. 60.
3. Neil W. Chamberlain, *Source Book on Labor* (McGraw-Hill, New York,
   1958), p. 13.
4. Joseph Rayback, *A History of American Labor* (Macmillan, New York,
   1959), p. 342.
5. Tannenbaum, *op. cit.*, p. 140.
6. W. E. J. McCarthy, *The Closed Shop in Britain* (Blackwell, Oxford,
   1964), p. 249.
7. *Ibid.*, p. 3.
8. *Ibid.*, p. 79.
9. *Ibid.*, p. 146.
10. *Ibid.*, p. 261.
11. *Ibid.*, p. 258.
12. *Ontario Labour Relations Board, File No. 20576-60*, Nov. 13, 1961, p. 17.
13. Evan Runner, *Christian Perspectives, 1960* (Pella, Iowa, 1960), p. 151,
    quoting Martineau, *Types of Ethical Theory*, Vol. II, p. 446.
14. Walter Lippmann, *The Public Philosophy* (Mentor Books, New York,
    1956), p. 132.
15. *The Guide* (Christian Labour Association of Canada, June/July, 1962),
    p. 2.
16. Sylvester Petro, *Power Unlimited—The Corruption of Union Leadership*
    (The Ronald Press, New York, 1959), p. 288.
    Cf. William J. Keating and Richard Carter, *The Man Who Rocked the
    Boat* (Victor Gollancz, London, 1956), for an account of corruption in
    New York docks and waterfront.
    For British trade union malpractices see also:
    Eric Wigham, *What's Wrong with Our Unions?* (Penguin Books, Lon-
    don, 1962).

C. H. Rolph, *All Those in Favour* (London, 1963).
For Canada see:
Pat Sullivan, *Red Sails on the Great Lakes* (Toronto, 1958).

17. James Hastings Nichols, *Democracy and the Churches* (Westminster, Philadelphia, 1951), p. 67 quoting.

18. Sidney and Beatrice Webb, *The History of Trade Unionism* (Longmans, London, 1894 and 1897).
    G. D. H. Cole, *A History of the British Working-Class Movement, 1789-1937* (London, 1938); also *The World of Labour* (Bell, London, 1913).
    Henry Pelling, *A History of British Trade Unionism* (Penguin, London, 1963).

19. C. E. M. Joad, *Guide to Philosophy* (V. Gollancz, London, 1946), p. 453 quoting William James.

20. Remkes Kooistra, "Facts and Values," *Christian Perspectives, 1963* (Guardian Publishing Co., Hamilton, 1964), p. 43.

21. S. U. Zuidema, "Pragmatism," *Christian Perspectives, 1961* (Guardian Publishing Co., Hamilton, 1961), p. 144.

22. C. S. Golden and H. J. Ruttenburg, *The Dynamics of Industrial Democracy* (New York, 1954), p. 22.

23. K. B. Shippen, *This Union Cause* (Harpers, New York, 1957), p. 171.

24. Samuel Gompers, *Seventy Years of Life and Labor* (Dutton, New York, 1957), p. 95.

25. Karl Kautsky, *On the Morrow of the Social Revolution* (20th Century Press, London, 1907), pp. 34-35.

26. Morris Hilquit, *Socialism in Theory and Practice* (New York, 1909), p. 240.

27. H. U. Faulkner, *American Economic History* (Harper, New York, 1943), p. 467, quoting Strasser.

28. Louis Reed, *The Labor Philosophy of Samuel Gompers* (Columbia University Press, New York, 1930), p. 16.

29. *Ibid.*, p. 49.

30. *Ibid.*, pp. 44, 47, 53.

31. *Ibid.*

32. *Ibid.*

33. J. R. Commons, S. Perlman, and P. Taft, *History of Labor in the United States, 1896-1932* (Macmillan, New York, 1951), p. 15.

34. Quoted in Chamberlain, *op. cit.*, p. 70.

35. Tannenbaum, *op. cit.*, p. 81.

36. H. Van Riessen, *op. cit.*, p. 175ff. Cf. T. S. Szasz, *The Myth of Mental Illness* (1961).

37. *Saturday Night Magazine* (Toronto, May 12, 1962), p. 15ff.

38. Henry M. Christman, *Walter Reuther, Selected Papers* (Macmillan, New York, 1961), p. 45.

39. *Ibid.*, p. 58.
40. *Canadian Labour* (Montreal Offices of the Canadian Labour Congress, Dec. 1962).
41. Chamberlain, *op. cit.*, p. 571, quoting.
42. Tannenbaum, *op. cit.*, p. 198.
43. J. W. Scott, *Syndicalism and Philosophic Realism* (Adam Black, London, 1919), p. 33.
44. G. D. H. Cole, *The World of Labour* (Bell, London, 1913), p. 86.
45. *Ibid.*
46. H. Clegg, *Industrial Democracy and Nationalization* (Blackwell, Oxford, 1951) p. 5.
47. G. D. H. Cole, *Guild Socialism Restated* (Parsons, London, 1920), p. 187.
48. *Ibid.*, p. 196.
49. H. Dooyeweerd, *op. cit.*, Vol. III, pp. 671-672.
50. Jacob Burckhardt, *The Civilization of the Renaissance in Italy* (Phaidon Press, London, 1950), p. 81.
51. Robert A. Nisbet, *Community and Power* (Oxford University Press, 1968), p. 81.
52. Tannenbaum, *op. cit.*, p. 169.
53. *Ibid.*
54. *Ibid.*, p. 175.
55. John Dewey, *Human Nature and Conduct* (Holt, New York, 1922), p. 200. For a brilliant critique of Dewey's philosophy from a Reformed point of view consult Hendrik Hart, *Communal Certainty and Authorized Truth* (Swets & Zeitlinger, Amsterdam, 1966); also H. Hart, *The Democratic Way of Death* (C. J. L. Foundation pamphlet, 1967, obtainable from P. O. Box 151, Rexdale, Ontario, Canada).
56. For a Reformed critique of Laski's political and social philosophy consult Bernard Zylstra, *From Pluralism to Collectivism* (Humanities Press, New York, 1968). Also Harry Antonides, *The Freedom to Work, Some Thoughts on Christian Social Action and the Basis of Secular Trade Unions* (C.L.A.C. pamphlet, Rexdale, 1967).

Chapter Five

THE ROMAN CATHOLIC PHILOSOPHY
OF LABOR, INDUSTRY, AND SOCIETY

(a) *The Principial Basis of Catholic Social Philosophy*

Within the past seventy years four great Popes have written on a wide variety of human concerns such as family life, political life, liturgical life, and social and economic life. Among their writings they submitted for urgent universal considerations four documents on economic and social matters, and these papal encyclicals, as they are called, provide the basis for the modern Roman Catholic theory of labor. Given their titles in English these encyclicals are:

1. "Revolutionary Matters" (*Rerum Novarum*) by Leo XIII in 1891.
2. "Forty Years After" (*Quadragesimo Anno*) by Pius XI in 1931.
3. "To the Church Hierarchy in the United States" by Pius XII.
4. "Mother and Teacher" (*Mater et Magister*) by John XXIII in 1962.

Pope Leo XIII saw the evils of his day stemming from the French Revolution. In the opening paragraph of *Rerum Novarum* he says:

It is not surprising that the spirit of revolutionary change, which has long been predominant in the nations of the world, should have passed beyond politics and made its influence felt in the field of practical economy. The elements of conflict are unmistakable: the growth of industry and the surprising discoveries of science; the changed relations of masters and workmen; the enormous fortunes of individuals and the poverty of the masses; the increased self-reliance and the closer mutual association of the working population; and finally a general moral deterioration.[1]

Then the Pope goes on to identify the evidences that social injustice is accompanying this revolution as follows:

(a) By the end of the nineteenth century workers' unions were almost completely wiped out.

(b) No alternative protection for working people was being established.

(c) The individual worker was a helpless victim in the new uncontrolled competitive market.

(d) New forms of interest-taking were being developed.

(e) A relatively small number of influential men were gaining complete control of industry and commerce, even on an international level.

(f) In all these new ways of doing business and dealing with workers, neither individuals in business nor leaders in government wanted any advice or comment from religion. They in fact denied that moral principles had anything to do with economics.

Then Leo XIII sets out to suggest in broad outline the way in which a solution is to be found which squares with the traditional principles of natural justice and natural equity:

(1) Both in private life and public life men must accept the moral standards of the Gospel and respect the dignity of man as a child of God, created with an immortal soul and as a temple of the Holy Spirit, and an adopted brother of Christ. Man shares through grace the very life of God himself and he is called to eternal union with God. Consequently, "no one may with impunity outrage the dignity of man, which God himself treats with great reverence, nor impede his course to that level of perfection which accords with eternal life in heaven" (*Rerum Novarum*, 57).

From this dignity flow the basic rights of man, which include the right to life itself, the right to live as befits a human being, the right to a job, and the right to a living wage. For this reason Leo rejected the notion of a limited wage fund available for the needs of workers. On the contrary, they have every right to share equitably in the wealth they help to produce. He says:

It is incontestable that the wealth of nations arises from no other source than the labour of workers. Equity therefore commands that public authority show proper concern for the worker so that from what he contributes to the common good he may receive what will enable him, housed, clothed, and secure, to live his life without hardship. Whence it follows that all those measures ought to be favoured which seem in any way of benefiting the condition of workers (*Rerum Novarum*, 51).

In these famous words Pope Leo XIII laid down the great principle that a proper share of the wealth of nations must go to the workers whose labor produces this wealth. He does not, of course, accept the Marxist concept that labor is the sole source of production. This is evident elsewhere in the Encyclical when he rejects socialism. But he does hold that labor is entitled to a proportionate share of the national wealth, a share that permits workers to live as befits human beings.

(2) At the same time workers must labor conscientiously and take pride in the fruits of their labor. They must respect the employer and his property.

(3) Leo recognized that the right of workers to join together in labor unions, but he insisted they must see to it that such unions represent their cause without violence and rioting, and they must repudiate leaders with evil principles. He argued that it is "a right of nature" that permits man to form private societies and the state "has been instituted to protect and not to destroy natural right" (*Rerum Novarum*, 72). Moreover, the workers may also determine the type of association they wish to have. "Furthermore, if citizens have the free right to associate, they must also have the right freely to adopt the organization and rules which they judge most appropriate to achieve their purpose" (*Rerum Novarum*, 76).

(4) Employers must respect the human dignity of workers. It is a denial of their dignity to consider workmen as mere sources of muscle and power from which to make money. It is a repudiation of the worker's relationship to God to countenance working conditions and working hours which are a detriment to his physical and moral welfare and which prevent him from carrying out his religious duties. It is a veritable iniquity towards employees to take advantage of their need for wages to impose work unsuited to their health,

their age, or their sex. Above all, to underpay, to defraud, and to conduct or permit usurious practices would be sins against the workers that cry to heaven for vengeance. . . . Finally, the employer must refrain from treating the unions or associations formed by workers as revolutionary and subversive societies. Labor associations are the natural right of a citizen. Leo had strong words about excessive hours of work.

> Assuredly, neither justice nor humanity can countenance the exaction of so much work that the spirit is dulled from excessive toil and that along with the body sinks crushed from exhaustion. The working energy of man, like his entire nature, is circumscribed by definite limits beyond which it cannot go (*Rerum Novarum*, 59).

(5) The relations of employers and employees are so significant to the common good that one rightly assumes that the government will direct its interest and its authority towards encouraging and promoting good labor conditions. Laws are needed to act as guideposts to both sides and to act as sanctions when necessary. The Pope urged that public authorities therefore safeguard the rights of workers.

> Rights indeed, by whomsoever possessed, must be religiously protected; and public authority, in warding off injuries and punishing wrongs, ought to see to it that individuals may have and hold what belongs to them. In protecting the rights of private individuals, however, special consideration must be given to the weak and poor. For the nation, as it were, of the rich is guarded by its own defenses and is in less need of governmental protection, whereas the suffering multitude, without the means to protect itself, relies especially on the protection of the state. Wherefore, since wage workers are numbered among the great mass of the needy, the State must include them under its special care and foresight (*Rerum Novarum*, 54).

Leo does utter one word of caution, holding that "the law ought not to undertake more, nor should it go further, than the remedy of evils or the removal of dangers requires (*Rerum Novarum*, 53). This is in accord with the Roman Catholic principle of subsidiarity, about which we shall have more to say. Excessive or extreme state intervention leads to undue centralization of political power and leads to totalitarianism. When Pope Pius XI discussed this problem he was more specific in terms of the protection offered. "These laws undertake the protection of life, health, strength, family, homes, workshops, wages and labour hazards, in fine, everything which pertains to the condition of wage workers, with special concern for women and children (*Quadragesimo Anno*, 28).

(6) One of the key contributions of modern papal social teaching to the industrial field has been its promotion of labor-management harmony rather than the class struggle. Leo XIII pointed out that:

> It is a capital evil . . . to take for granted that one class of society is of itself hostile to the other, as if nature had set rich and poor against each other to fight an implacable war. . . . The two clasess mentioned should agree harmoniously and should properly form equally balanced counterparts to each other. Each needs the other completely; neither capital can do without labour nor labour without capital (*Rerum Novarum*).

Pope Pius XII asserted:

> In the economic domain management and labour are linked in a community of action and interest. . . . Employers and workers are not implacable adversaries. They are cooperators in a common task. . . . Both parties are interested in seeing to it that the costs of national production are in proportion to its output. But since the interest is common, why should it not manifest itself in a common outward expression (May 7th, 1949).

Perhaps the strongest expression came from Pope Pius XI:

> In actual fact, human society now, for the reason that it is founded on classes with divergent aims and hence opposed to one another and therefore inclined to enmity and strife, continues to be in a violent condition and is unstable and uncertain. But complete cure will not come until this opposition has been abolished and well ordered members of the social body—industries and professions—are constituted in which men may have their place, not according to the position each has in the labour market but according to the respective social functions which each performs (*Quadragesimo Anno*, 82-3).

(7) Pope Leo believed that employers, workers, and governments would continue to struggle in vain to work out peaceful, just relations in industry and the economic order in general, unless they first

turned to Christianity with its gospel of peace and the grace to live that gospel. For this reason they must all abandon the idea that the sphere of industry and commerce and social and political ethics are somehow neutral areas of life outside the competence of religion. Either religion supplies the enlightenment and grace which modern men so desperately need, or modern society will walk blindly and tragically to greater conflict and sure disaster.[2]

Of this famous Roman Catholic Bill of Rights and Duties in the Economic Order the great Reformed philosopher and statesman, Abraham Kuyper, wrote in a footnote to the published version of his speech on "The Christian Religion and the Social Question," delivered in Holland in 1891:

> It must be admitted to our shame, that the Roman Catholics are far ahead of us in their study of the social question. Indeed, very far ahead. . . . The action of the Roman Catholics should spur us [Protestants] to show more dynamism. . . . *The Encyclical of Leo XIII gives the principles which are common to all Christians, and which we share with our Roman Catholic compatriots.*[3]

The root of all the evils in the modern world, Pope Leo XIII thus suggests, is the threatening divorce of the natural from the supernatural world, between the realms of nature and of grace. As his biographer R. Fulop Miller writes in *Leo XIII and Our Times*:

> All the utterances of Pope Leo . . . have in common a basic idea —that it must again become possible, as it was in the thirteenth century , to resolve all apparent contradictions between reason and faith, between the striving after temporal ends and the higher ordination to a divine end . . . and thereby to re-establish that harmony between the two that had been achieved in the *Summa Theologica.*[4]

In studying the Roman Catholic view of labor it is essential that we keep this emphasis upon principle in mind. Unlike the secular Anglo-Saxon pragmatic and empirical approach to reality, the Popes' social teaching and the resulting Catholic Action are derived from what J. Husslein in his *Social Wellsprings* aptly terms "social wellsprings" or principles. The Roman Catholic philosophy of labor is a principial philosophy, not a pragmatic one.

Let us then examine the Roman Catholic application of its principles both in theory and in practice. In the encyclical *Rerum Novarum* we meet primarily with principle, in *Quadragesimo Anno* with theory, while Catholic Action attempts to apply it in practice. As such *Rerum Novarum* may be considered as the prologemena and *Quadragesimo Anno* the statement of Roman Catholic social philosophy.

Like his great contemporary Abraham Kuyper, Pope Leo XIII pinpointed the true origin of the modern "social question" in the spirit of the French Revolution as it had come to manifest itself in the revolutionary movements of the closing years of the nineteenth century. The Pope would have agreed with Kuyper's brilliant analysis:

> The French Revolution . . . produced its evil not so much in this, that it threw the Bourbons from the throne . . . but rather through the complete change it produced on the sense and philosophy of life of the nations. In the Christian religion lay the principle that the subjection of all to God creates the tie which joins authority and freedom—the French Revolution casts out the majesty of the Lord and tries to build up an artificial authority based on the free will of the individual. . . . The Christian religion taught us to understand life on earth as a subordinate part of an eternal existence—the French Revolution denied and opposed everything which fell outside the horizon of this earthly life. The Christian religion spoke of a lost paradise, a state of purity from which we fell, and for this reason called us to humility and conversion—the French Revolution saw in the state of nature the criterion of the normally human, incited us to pride, and put, in place of conversion, liberalization of man's spirit. Moreover, the Christian religion has, as fruit of divine pity, brought into the world the pity of a love springing from God—the French Revolution placed over against that the egoism of the passionate struggle for possession. And, to touch on the basic point, which lies at the heart of the social question, the Christian religion sought personal human dignity in the social relations of an organically associated society—the French Revolution destroyed that organic tissue, broke these social bonds, and finally, in its work of atomistic trifling, had nothing left but the monotonous self-seeking individual, asserting his own self-sufficiency.

This is the pivot on which the whole social question turns. The

French Revolution, and so, too, present day Liberalism, is anti-social, and the social need which now disturbs Europe is the evil fruit of the individualism which was enthroned with the French Revolution.

Here then the die was cast. It could not happen otherwise that out of this wrenching loose of everything that held our human life together in human dignity, there must of iron necessity be born first a deep-seated social need, then a widespread Social-Democratic movement, and finally for every people and nation a nettling social problem. . . . Neither the social question . . . nor the Social Democracy which now threatens the public order . . . would ever have assumed . . . such ominous directions if the French Revolution had not brought about such a complete change in the consciousness of the nations, the classes and the individual.[5]

As Kuyper saw it the social question of his age had arisen out of man's apostasy and rebellion from God since the days of the French Revolution. He correctly interpreted the collectivist theories of the socialists and Marxists as the inevitable reaction against the individualistic theories of the French revolutionaries; he writes:

The common characteristic of all the forms and degrees in which this imposing movement expressed itself, is in the rising of the community-feeling, feeling for social justice and for the organic nature of society, against the one-sidedly developed individualistic form which the French Revolution and its corresponding economic school of laissez-faire had impressed on society.[6]

At the same time Kuyper believed that socialism and communism were not only opposed to the principle of the French Revolution, but that they were its inevitable fruit. He explains:

This apparent contradiction results from the fact that the individualistic character of the French Revolution is only a derived principle. It is not the root principle, from which it borrows its dynamic. For the French Revolution, the root principle is its God-provoking "no God, no master" or, if you will, humanity emancipated from God and his established order. From this principle there develops not one line but two. First, the line along which you make up your mind to break down the established order of things, letting nothing remain but the individual with his own free will and imaginary supremacy. But alongside of this there develops also the other line, at the end of which you are tempted to push aside not only God and his order, but also now deifying yourself to sit on God's throne, as the prophet said, and create a new order out of your own brain. This last, now, is what Social Democracy (socialism) does. But in doing this, it is so far from letting go of the individualistic starting point that it rather would found the social structure it wants to erect, by way of universal suffrage, on the sovereignty of the people, and thus on the individual will. . . . The starting point of the Social Democrats as well as of the Liberals is individualistic, in the individual person, and thus in the Pelagian free will.[7]

According to Kuyper the modern dilemma between collectivism and individualism, socialism and conservatism is thus a false one, since both have accepted the apostate humanist doctrine that the source of power and authority over men is to be found in the will of man rather than in the will of God, and that man's reason rather than God's Word should henceforth become the ordering principle of human society. Both socialists and liberals had reacted against the practical results of the French Revolution. Yet neither party had repudiated the rationalistic ideas of the Enlightenment, which had brought Europe to the brink of disaster. All the leading statesmen of Europe had remained "enlightened" and the theories of Rousseau, Voltaire, Diderot, St. Simon, and Auguste Comte had become the common property of both groups. The only point where there was any disagreement was in the area of the practical and in the means to realize the utopian ideals of the Enlightenment.

Kuyper called upon the Reformed Christians of Holland to break with this false choice between liberal and conservative, socialist and individualist, because both liberalism and conservatism and socialism and individualism are united in their common apostate humanistic presuppositions about man in society and the possibility of achieving community between men upon the basis of a "common reason" rather than a common faith. Kuyper brought into the open the fundamental issue in modern economics and politics: will men and nations accept God's authority, law, and sovereignty over their lives, or will they make their own reason sovereign? He writes:

The first article of any social program which will bring salvation must remain: "I believe in God the Father Almighty, Maker of Heaven and earth." This article is today being erased. Men will no longer recognize any God in statesmanship. Not as though men did not find the poetry of religion charming; but because whoever says I believe in God thereby also acknowledges that there is an ordering of nature by God, and an ordinance of God over our conscience; a higher will, to which we as creatures have to submit ourselves. Today, everything must be a free creation of human art. The social structure must be planned only according to whim and caprice. And therefore God must go, so that with no natural bond to restrain them, men can turn every moral ordinance into its opposite, and undermine every fundamental of human association.[8]

Why should the Pope concern himself with such mundane matters as the condition of the working class and the social inequalities between the classes? As supreme guardian of religious truth is he not going beyond his jurisdiction? Roman Catholics will answer that the Pope is fully entitled to pronounce upon such mundane matters because fundamental *moral* issues are involved and hence the reference to the "general moral deterioration" mentioned by Leo at the end of the opening paragraph of his encylical. Acording to Roman Catholic doctrine the Church is not only the official teacher of divine revelation but also the custodian of the nations' morals. As such the Church is the official moralist which decides on the morality of all human acts. Thus Leo says:

> We affirm without hesitation that all the striving of men will be in vain if they leave out the Church. It is the Church that proclaims from the Gospel those teachings by which the (class) conflict can be brought to an end, or at least made far less bitter; the Church uses its efforts not only to enlighten the mind, but to direct by its precepts the life and conduct of men.[9]

To understand this claim of the Pope to have jurisdiction over public affairs involving moral issues, we must briefly consider the social philosophy of Thomas Aquinas, since Pope Leo based his own teaching upon a Thomistic foundation, as he himself announced in his encyclical *Aeterni Patris*, issued in 1879.

(b) *The Thomistic Theory of Human Society*

Aquinas' view of human society is entirely dominated by the Roman Catholic ground-motive or basic religious presupposition of "nature" and "grace." As he himself put it: "Grace does not abolish nature but perfects it."

Nature, conceived as form and matter in the Greek sense, became for Aquinas the autonomous basis of supernatural grace. By means of his doctrine of the eternal law of God, with its subjective counterpart in the natural law, Aquinas sought to accommodate the Greek-form-matter motive with the biblical nature-sin motive. Through the natural law the creation, in its essential nature, has a subjective part in the eternal law of God. According to Aquinas, the point that distinguished the rational creature from the irrational was the former's ability to reason and therefore to perceive the eternal law of God, that is, the divine ordering of things. Man, through natural law, shared in the eternal law of God and consequently was, by employing his natural reasoning faculties, in a position to know good and to know evil "The impression of the divine light in us" propels this natural law that is implanted in us, and this natural law enabled man "to be in possession of the natural principles of his actions." In a different place he held that "natural law was nothing less than the participation of the rational creature in the eternal law." [10] Such a synthesis of biblical and Greek ground-motives implied a distinction between a natural and a supernatural sphere of thought and action. Within the sphere of nature a relative autonomy was ascribed to human reason, which Aquinas supposed to be capable by its own unaided light of discovering the natural truths about the universe and of man's social life within it.

Christ, the Word of God made flesh, was now no longer seen as the new root of the creation, as the great reformer of true nature, but as existing in the supernatural realm with God and His angels, making contact with man by means of the sacraments of the Church. "Nature" concentrated in "reason" was declared self-sufficient and autonomous in her own sphere, the temporal world order. Aquinas, in fact, made the natural reason of man independent of God's written revelation. Learning, morality, political life, and "natural theology" were therefore, as autonomous areas of natural reason, practiced in an Aristotelian manner. But in addition to this intrinsically pagan idea of "nature," a "supra-temporal" area of grace was constructed which transcends natural reason and can only be apprehended by the light of God's revelation. In his study of *A History of Political Thought: The Middle Ages*, Walter Ullman of Cambridge University writes:

Aquinas himself considered at all stages of his mature writing that there were always two levels on which any discussion on political topics ought to proceed. This two-tier system was indeed an imperative necessity if the Aristotelian welter of ideas was to be accommodated within the Christian structure. The traditional gulf between nature and grace was bridged by Thomas. There was no ambiguity in his thought about the efficacy of nature itself and of natural law—both did and could operate without any revelation or grace or divine assistance because they followed their own inherent laws and these latter had nothing to do with grace. But— and this was the great step forward—whilst in the traditional doctrine there was a sharp contrast between nature and grace, in fact a very real dichotomy, with Thomas there was none of it; with him contrast and dichotomy gave way to a hierarchy of different orders, so that the two opposites were to be seen as two hierarchically differently placed orders, the one the natural, the other the supra-natural. Hence, so far from being hostile to each other, nature and grace were to be viewed as complementary. This was the meaning of the often quoted statement of Thomas that "grace does not do away with nature but perfects it."[11]

The Christian view of the Fall now had to be accommodated to this pagan conception of "nature" as well. The scriptural view of the "heart" as the religious root and center of human nature had to be abandoned in favor of the Aristotelian concept viewing "reason" as the origin of human nature. The "heart" became identified with the temporal psychical function, now considered the stimulant of the will. Thus Thomas could no longer admit that human nature is depraved in its very root because of the falling away from God of the heart in rebellion and apostasy. Instead, he taught that "nature" was not completely spoiled by sin, but merely "wounded," that is, the supra-natural gift of grace had been lost.

The idea of nature as an element that contained its own force and its own principles of operation enabled Aquinas to declare that this or that phenomenon was "according to nature," "above nature," "contrary to nature," and so on. Setting out from Aristotelian premises, Thomas had no difficulty in applying them to society and its government. As Ullmann points out:

> The Aristotelian teleology regarding the operations of nature and the idea of the State as a product of nature reappeared in the Thomist system; and so did the Aristotelian definition of man as a "political animal," which Thomas improved by designating man also as a social animal, so that his definition was expanded to man being "a political and social animal." [12]

Man's nature, according to Aristotle, was taken to be a composition of form and matter. In this case, "form" is the rational soul, and matter is the material body. Every creature that is composed of form and matter has become. The form principle gives to the process of becoming the direction for the attainment of its own particular "telos" or end. Every creature that has become thus strives by nature after the attainment of its own proper end or purpose in life, in that its "essential form" realizes itself in the "matter" of its body. Thus a plant strives by nature to develop from its seed into a perfected plant, the embryo of an animal to the finished animal form. According to Aristotle, in the case of man his natural perfection consists in the complete development of his rational nature which distinguishes him from plants and animals. "The rational law of nature" has been created as part of this rational nature and it impels man to do good and to refrain from evil. Man therefore "by nature" naturally strives after the good.

Aristotle's doctrine culminated in his view of the state as the supreme community of citizens, which was a product of nature, the result of the working of the laws of nature, and not the result of any agreement, social contract, or convention, as the Sophists had claimed it to be. The laws of nature which brought forth the state were to Aristotle germane to man himself. He was born with them and they determined him to live in the state, without which he could not exist, and within which he could achieve his own perfection. Man was thus by nature a political animal. The state, to him, was the consummation of all other natural unions, such as the family, the village, the town, etc.

The state is in fact the highest form of community. All other societal relationships, such as marriage, family, blood-relation, vocational and industrial groupings, all these are merely lower components which serve the higher. The state is grounded in the "rational-moral" nature of man. Nature working through the vehicle of human will and reasoning not only brought forth the state, but also determined its path. Since nature willed "the good," Aristotle argued, and since the state was the supreme expression of all human associations, it followed that the state aimed at the highest good.

The instrument by which this aim could be achieved was, for Aristotle, the law, that is, the articulated will of nature pronounced by the citizens. Man cannot realize his natural perfection in isolation, but only within the community. Marriage and the family are the first "lower" necessities of life, the "next higher" are fulfilled by the village community. But these lower societal relationships are not autonomous; only the state can, as the perfectly autonomous, self-sufficient and independent community, provide man with all that serves the perfection of his "rational-moral" nature. In the *Politics* of Aristotle we read:

> When we come to the final and perfect association, formed from a number of villages, we have already reached the polis— an association which may be said to have reached the height of full self-sufficiency; or rather (to speak more exactly) we may say that while it grows for the sake of mere life . . . it exists, when once it is fully grown, for the sake of the good life (and is therefore full self-sufficient).
>
> Because it is the completion of associations existing by nature, every polis exists by nature, having itself the same quality as the earlier associations from which it grew. It is the end or consummation to which those associations move, and the "nature" of things consists in their end or consummation; for what each thing is when its growth is completed we call the nature of that thing, whether it be a man or a horse or a family. . . .
>
> From these considerations it is evident that the polis belongs to the class of things that exist by nature, and that man is by nature an animal intended to live in a polis. He who is without a

polis, by reason of his own nature and not of some accident, is either a poor sort of being, or a being higher than man.[13]

Thus Aristotle constructs the relation between the state and the other societal relationships according to the scheme of *the whole and its parts*, and of the goal and the means, from the "lower" to the "higher." The "lower" relationships as different kinds of parts of the state have no goal in themselves, but all must serve the state. Man is by nature a state-oriented being, for already in the forming of marriage, family and kinship groupings the natural compulsion to form the state is germinating. By nature the state for Aristotle thus exists before the individual. The state is implicit in the rational-moral nature of man, as the mature form of a plant in its seed, or the full-grown body of an animal in its embryo.

Based on the rational faculty of man's nature, the state is defined by its purpose; namely to care for the general welfare. According to Aquinas' conception, it is in this natural purpose that the immediate basis for civil authority lies. For without such authority the state community cannot exist. If then the state has its origin in nature, then so does civil authority. Accordingly Aquinas taught that political institutions are an aspect of "natural" morality, that is, they can be justified on a purely human plane, independently of religious values.

For Thomas, man and Christian became conceptually different notions. Man was a natural product, and as such demanded attention. His naturalness was his hallmark, and as a member of human society he was a social animal. Ullmann points out:

> The complement of man in organized society was the citizen. The citizen was man writ large. The citizen was, to Thomas, no longer the subject, the *sub/ditus*, who simply had to obey superior authority. It was Aristotle's definition of a citizen as one who partook in government which supplied the solvent and which made possible the release of the (inferior) subject from (superior) authority. For, sharing in government was precisely what was denied to the subject (of the theocratic church-state), nor had he any share in the making of the law which was given to him. The important point here is that Thomas, by absorbing Aristotle's ideas, effected in the public sphere not so much a metamorphosis

of the subject as the rebirth of the citizen who since classical times had been hibernating. It is impossible to exaggerate the significance of the emergence of the concept of the citizen; his rebirth was of crucial importance. . . . Moreover the distinction drawn by Aristotle between man and the citizen reappeared in Thomas' system:

It sometimes happens (he said) that someone is a *good citizen* who has not the quality according to which someone is also a *good man*, from which it follows that the quality according to whether someone is a good man or a good citizen is not the same.

The significance of this statement does not need any comment. It was the denial of what for want of a better term we have called the totalitarian point of view. It was a major step forward towards a new orientation. What applied to the one need not necessarily apply to the other. The citizen—political man—answered the description of a being different from mere man. Thereby the spectre of splitting up man's activities begins to be discernible, and herewith the subjection of man to different sets of norms and postulates (political, religious, moral, economic, etc.).[14]

This sharp conceptual contradistinction between man and citizen was to be of crucial importance; it broke down the monolithic structure, it broke down the oneness or wholeness point of view, and considered the individual person from at least two angles, the political and the moral. And, when once the implications of this dichotomy were understood, the consequences also followed: first, the separation of the Christian from the citizen, and from the man; and later ensued the further categorization into social, economic, cultural, etc., norms, each with its own set of principles. It was nothing but the atomization of man's activities.[15]

By dividing up human life into two realms of nature and grace, Aquinas thus undermined the unified field of knowledge and experience revealed by God to man in the Holy Scriptures. Knowledge of the natural sphere for Aquinas could be obtained by man's "natural" reason, which had remained uncorrupted by the Fall of man into sin. Only man's will had fallen, not his reason. From this incomplete view of the biblical fall has flowed the most serious consequences, including the Social Question with which Pope Leo XIII was so concerned. Man's intellect became autonomous or independent of God's holy Word. This autonomy, in the course of the following centuries, was to provide the basis for the secularization of

Western philosophy, law, politics, art, business and economic life, and, above all, Western science and education. Upon the basis of this autonomy first provided by Aquinas, European life, intellectual, artistic, scientific, and economic, became free of God's law and separated from His revelation. As a result there soon came to be felt no need for a distinctive Christian philosophy of society and the state. After Aquinas the tendency towards complete secularization increased until it reached its apostate climax in the French Revolution in 1789 and the Bolshevik Revolution in 1917.

The idea of the "natural" social and political nature of man led Aquinas to assert the necessity of the full and harmonious integration of the individual in the community. Thus he writes:

> The goodness of any part is to be considered with reference to the whole of which it forms a part. So, all men being a part of the city, they cannot truly be good unless they adapt themselves to the common good. Nor can the whole be well constituted if its parts be not properly adapted to it.[16]

Aquinas in fact sees the state as the absolute and total community in the domain of natural society, of which all the other social spheres can be but subservient parts. In other words, the relationship between the state and the other natural spheres of life is conceived of by Aquinas and most subsequent Roman Catholic thinkers as that of the whole of its parts. The individual citizen as such has no meaning or value apart from the whole community of which he is a part. According to A. P. D'Entreves:

> There is no doubt that Aquinas conceives of the State as an organism, of the individual as subordinate to the community, and of the common good as the supreme value to which all others are instrumental. He repeats and endorses the Aristotelian statement, that the family and all other groups differ from the city not only in size, but "specifically," and derives from it the conclusion that "the common welfare is different in nature from that of the individual, just as the nature of the part is different from that of the whole." [17]

At the same time Aquinas did not at all advocate the cause of state absolutism, as later apostate humanists were to do with their theories of the indivisible and inalienable sovereignty of the secular state. He pointed out that the prince has authority only so long as he governs according to the moral law. He is "under God and law." The action of the state is delimited by objective rules of justice which ensure the respect of the fundamental demands of the Christian conception of human personality.

When Aquinas teaches that the individual and the "lower" spheres of life are parts of the state, he also adds the proviso: insofar as they are of the same order. This means to begin with that the supernatural order in its sacramental superstructure, of which both the individual and the institution are a part, is withdrawn from the jurisdiction of the secular authority, which Aquinas limits to the natural domain of life. As Aquinas himself puts it:

> Man is not formed for political fellowship in his entirety, and in all that he has . . . but all that a man is, and can do, must be directed by God.[18]

Aquinas thus delimits the authority of the state over the individual by objective rules of justice and morality which ensure that he will obey God.

The Roman Catholic conception of the state is not only opposed to political totalitarianism, but it is also opposed to the centralization of all power in the state. It conceives of the state as being built from the bottom up, in a step-by-step ascent from the lower to the higher communities. A higher community must not concern itself with what a lower community can do satisfactorily by itself.

Out of this doctrine there has developed the celebrated Roman Catholic principle of subsidiarity or supplementation which received official expression in the encyclical *Quadragesimo Anno* of Pope Pius XI as the guideline for the delimitation of the task of the government with respect to the regulation of business life. According to this principle, the state is to provide for the common good only that which neither the individual nor the activities of the lower communities can provide. The principle of subsidiarity is expressed as follows in *Quadragesimo Anno*:

> It is an injustice, a grave evil, and a disturbance of right order

for a larger and higher organization to arrogate to itself functions which can be performed efficiently by smaller and lower bodies. . . . Of its very nature the true aim of all social activity should be to help individual members of the social body, but never to destroy them.[19]

In his fundamental work *Christian Democracy in Western Europe 1820-1953*, Michael Fogarty compares this Catholic principle of subsidiarity with the Dutch Reformed doctrine of sphere sovereignty.

The Catholic and the Reformed (notably Dutch Reformed) Churches express in slightly different terms an essentially similar idea about social structure. Catholics speak of the "principle of subsidiarity." . . . For the Reformed churches the corresponding principle is that of "sovereignty in one's own circle," or "the special task and vocation of each group."

There is obviously a difference of accent. The Protestant conception underlines the separate and exclusive responsibility of the individual and the small group, though only with defined limits and subject to the vocation of service to others. The Catholic phrasing stresses rather the inclusion of these small units of society in greater wholes, within which however they have a sphere of autonomy on which they have a right to insist. But in practice the two conceptions come to much the same thing. There is work to be done at every level of social organization from the individual to the international community, and the responsibility for what can be done at lower levels must not be allowed to gravitate to the top. Every social unit or group has a sphere of work which it can do efficiently in the interests not only of its members but of society as a whole, and this sphere must be defined and reserved for it. A higher authority may of course insist that some subordinate group live up to its responsibilities. . . . It may "direct, watch, stimulate and restrain," as the encyclical goes on to say. But only in the last, extreme resort may it take over its subordinate responsibilities and discharge them itself. A phrase sometimes used to cover this whole conception, from both the Protestant and Catholic side, is "autonomisation"; the "autonomisation," that is of individuals and social groups. It can also be described as "horizontal pluralism"; a policy which insists on the independence, rights and responsibilities of each individual or group which can show that it has a legitimate sphere of its own; independence firstly as against others on the same level of social organization, and secondly as against those at other and particularly higher levels.

Horizontal pluralism is defined primarily as a way of helping the growth of human personality. It offers the greatest number of openings for leaders to develop and show their ability; and for effective participation by the rank and file. It avoids the dangers of both "massification" and "atomisation":

The danger of massification is not merely that the individual is swallowed up in the mass. . . . It is also that he is simultaneously isolated within the mass. He hesitates to open himself to others. He tries to ensure that only superficial contacts develop between himself and others; his neighbours; contacts based on common interests, or public events which affect his group, his class, . . . his workmates as a whole. But he loses the true warm contact with other human beings. He and his neighbour slip by one another, not knowing the reality and basis of each other's life, or the reality of each other's need [20] (*Evangelie en Maatschappij*, Dutch Protestant Trade Unions, November 1953, pp. 154-155).

While commending Fogarty for this excellent exposition, we must disagree with his assertion that the Catholic doctrine of subsidiarity and the Reformed doctrine of sphere sovereignty are "essentially similar." On the contrary, they are fundamentally divergent, since the Catholic principle is derived from the Thomistic conception of the "reasonable nature" of man. As Dooyeweerd points out:

It is the Greek concept of nature which here comes to the fore. This concept of nature . . . is the result of the Greek form matter motive, i.e., the religious motive of Greek culture.

The "reasonable law of nature" teaches that man only depends on those necessities of life for which he cannot provide as an individual. The same law of nature teaches that a lower community, like the family or business, is only dependent on the higher (ultimately the state) for those interests of the community of which it cannot take care itself. This then is the content of the famous principle of supplementation. . . .

This does not alter the fact that Thomism views the individual as well as the lower communities in the "natural domain," as parts of the complete state.

It is precisely against this essentially Greek view of society that the scriptural principle of sphere sovereignty is opposed. . . . According to this scriptural principle God created everything after its own kind. That which possesses a completely different character of its own can never as such become part of a whole, of which it differs principially in its own kind.

The insight into the inner structures and the proper peculiarity of the differentiated spheres of life (i.e., the church, the state, the family, the school) is precisely foreign to Thomistic social science. It distinguishes the communities only from the next object to which they are subservient in their co-operation with the natural perfecting of man. In this, to give some examples, the marital community . . . is understood by Thomas as a "legal institution founded in human nature, subservient to the propagation of the human race."

Is the inner character and law of life of the marital community in this way in any sense encountered? How, then, can we judge the marital relation when husband and wife can no longer expect children . . . ? Is the marital relationship really characterized, in its inner nature, by understanding it as a legal relationship? Would not marriage become a hell if the legal point of view were the dominant consideration? [21]

In accordance with its religious ground motives of nature and grace Roman Catholicism requires as an essential element of its social science a superstructure of grace to complete the substructure of nature. As Aquinas put it, *"grace does not abolish nature but perfects it."* Man is not only called to perfect his reasonable nature, but he is also called to elevate himself to the realm of grace. For Aquinas there is natural law and there is revealed truth, but of both of them the Church, God's voice on earth, is the interpreter, natural law only differing from revealed truth in that man could have come to it even without divine revelation in the Scriptures. But, things being as they are, the Church stands to uphold it. Therefore it follows that though the individual has indeed rights against the state, he has no rights against the Church. As Thomas argues in *De Regimine*, behind the *humanum regimen* there is always the *divinum regimen*. In this world the powers of *rex* and *sacerdos* are committed separately, the one to earthly kings, the other to priests, and principally to the Roman pontiff. But the different value of the ends necessarily implies a subordination of the one power to the other, of the *regnum* to the *sacerdotium*. Hence it follows that to the Supreme Priest, the successor of Peter and Vicar of Christ," all kings in Christendom should be subject, as to the Lord Jesus himself." For Thomas the

Church has an inherent right to declare when the prince's rule was in violation of the moral law.[22]

Just as the state is the perfect community in the "natural" realm, including its parts and all other natural spheres of life, so also is the Church of Rome in the realm of "grace," the whole of Christian society in its supra-natural perfection, the perfect community of Christendom. According to this medieval conception of "the *corpus christianum*" (the body of Christ) the ecclesiastical institution of the visible Roman Catholic Church comprises all of the Christian life. Rome looks for the whole, the total unity of the Christian society, in the temporal institution of the church.[23]

From this claim of the Church of Rome to have a final authority over the state and over the individual citizens and to represent the total community of the Christian life follows the demand that the other natural communities of society shall be directed by Catholic principles of individual and social conduct. For the good Roman Catholic, therefore, the Christian family, the Christian school, and Christian social action and the Christian state must act and live in accordance with the decisions and policy of the Roman Catholic hierarchy. This does not mean that Rome denies the "natural basis" of these spheres of life. As long as they move in the natural realm they may enjoy autonomy and make their own decisions. But as soon as moral issues or problems emerge then the Church must intervene since she reserves for herself the binding explanation of the natural law.

In the light of this brief summary of Roman Catholic social philosophy we can now understand why it was that Popes Leo XIII and Pius XI in their famous encyclicals not only offered directives for the specific Christian aspect of the "social question," but they also explained in these letters the dictations of the "natural law" and the "natural moral law" as these affected Christian social action. As Pope Pius XI said in *Quadragesimo Anno*:

> It is the moral law alone which commands us to seek in all our conduct our supreme and final end, and to strive in our specific actions for those ends which nature has established for them.[24]

What then does the Roman Catholic Church teach about sócial issues? It teaches that we must use natural reason rightly, and reason teaches us that "every man has by nature the right to possess property as his own." [25] Humanity must remain as it is; "there will always be differences and inequalities of condition in the State." [26] The Church concerns itself to incline the rich to generosity and the poor to resignation, and labors for the reconciliation rather than the conflict of classes. The "first and most fundamental principle" of social policy must be the inviolability of private property. "The chief thing to be secured is the safeguarding of private property by legal enactment and policy. Most of all, it is essential, in these times of covetous greed, to keep the masses within the line of duty." [27] Property must also be protected from excessive taxation by the state. The class structure of rich and poor is divinely ordained and unchangeable. However, this does not mean that there has to be class conflict. "Each requires the other, capital cannot do without labor, nor labor without capital." [28]

For Leo, the relationship between employer and employee is a moral one, and hence "religion, whereof the Church is the interpreter and guardian, is exceeding powerful in drawing rich and poor together." The Church teaches that the work should be honest and conscientious and the employer should not treat his workers as chattel and should pay his men a just wage.

Leo justified social legislation within carefully defined limits, taking a position very similar to that of the more moderate group of Protestant social reformers in the English-speaking world. He advocated Sunday rest, the regulation of the work of women and children, and maximum hours for at least some types of men's labor. He urged the ideal of a living family wage instead of "free" wage contracts, but he did not suggest actual legislation for a minimum wage. The regulation of hours and working conditions, generally, he considered, could be better handled by boards within industry than by the state directly. Here, of course, he was setting forth "guild" conceptions of industry. He defended the association of workmen as a natural right which the state could not abrogate, and he especially recommended the type of association in which the employers and employees were members. Such corporations should provide for religious duties. They should also attempt to prevent unemployment and should create funds for emergencies such as sickness, accident, and old age.[29]

"Finally," says Leo, "employers and workmen may themselves effect much . . . by means of . . . institutions and organizations. The most important of all workmen's associations are unions."[30] Leo is here still dealing with principles; Pius XI will elaborate these into a practical program which Catholic Action will then execute. But the basis has been laid in *Rerum Novarum*, which, we have showed, is derived from the Thomistic doctrine of human society.

(c) *The Catholic Program for Social Action*

On the fortieth anniversary of *Rerum Novarum*, Pope Pius XI issue an encyclical titled "On Restoring the Christian Social Order," but more commonly known, as all encyclicals, by its first words, *Forty Years After*. In it Pius "gratefully recalls" Leo's famous letter, and notes that many of its injunctions have had a beneficial influence in church and modern society.

Pius further states that "new needs of our age and the condition of society have rendered necessary a more precise application and a more certain amplification of Leo's doctrine." [31] Pius then says:

> But before proceeding to discuss these problems we lay down the principle long since clearly established by Leo XIII that it is our right and duty to deal authoritatively with social and economic problems. . . . For the deposit of truth entrusted to us by God, and our weighty office of declaring, interpreting, and urging in season and out of season the entire moral law, demands that both social and economic questions be brought within our supreme jurisdiction, in so far as they refer to moral issues.[32]

In these words of Pope Pius XI we clearly see that for Roman Catholics the whole "social question" hinges upon "the entire moral law." As E. T. Gargan puts it, "What is wrong is not the structure but its misuse." [33] As Roman Catholics view things, it is not the structure of modern society that is at fault, but man's abuse of it. The structure is for the Roman Catholic always "natural," but the direction of human affairs must be guided by supernatural norms. *For the Calvinist, life is religion; for the Roman Catholic, life is morality.* As a result Roman Catholic social reconstruction turns out to be no true reformation of society at all but at most a re-direction of things as they are naturally given, or a superaddition of Catholic morality and social science to the social structures as they stand. The Roman Catholic does not, from a scriptural sense of the structure of reality, reform or attempt to reform the state, but rather he largely accepts it as it has gradually developed in the historical experience of the Western nations. He seeks a solution by thinking of the Roman Catholic Church as a supernatural *addition* to the *natural* civil so-society in which the Church finds itself. Thus Roman Catholic re-form proceeds largely by way of synthesis and accommodation of Roman Catholic social theory and unredeemed human institutions. Such a method of cultural accommodation of course finds its origin in the Thomistic nature-grace ground motive. Of Aquinas' attempt at synthesis H. Richard Niebuhr writes in *Christ and Culture*:

> In his theories of man's end, of human virtues, and of law, as well as in other parts of his practical philosophy and practical theology, Thomas combined into one system of divine demands and promises the requirements cultural reason discerned and those which Jesus uttered, the hopes based on the purpose in things as know by the cultivated mind and those grounded on the birth, life, death and resurrection of Christ. The whole effort at synthesis here is informed by, if not grounded on, the conviction of which Trinitarian doctrine is a verbal expression; namely, that the Creator of nature and Jesus Christ and the immanent spirit are of one essence.[34]

This "nature-grace" way of thinking about man in society is for the Roman Catholic not just a method of getting things done but a basic frame of reference or religious ground motive which determines the way a Roman Catholic thinks and behaves. It is thus a religiously orientated view of the whole meaning of life and may therefore be considered a faith commitment which becomes the governing princi-ple of all practical action.

For this reason Pope Pius XI approaches the question of social order from a moral rather than a religious standpoint. He appeals to men of all races and classes to unite on the basis of the one universal natural law by appealing to their natural reason. Given his Thomistic presuppositions, he is forced to "reconstruct" in this moralistic way by appealing to the natural moral law rather than to the Word of God directly. Thus he renews the Church's plea to all men of good will to meditate on the solutions he proposes. He begs the more "reasonable" leaders of industry, labor, education, and government to influence the economic order along the following lines:

(a) To use their rank and their initiative to convince all sectors of the economy, including agriculture, that they are interdependent, and that no one of them can live without the others.

(b) To set out to create a spirit of partnership in which industry, labor, agriculture, science, education, and government will combine their efforts for the betterment of all. As a means of proving their sincerity he recommends a return to some form of the guild system of earlier times, a vocational system grouping together those in the same field and then binding the vocational groups into regional and national councils. The Pope sees the development of this kind of coordination as the one way to ensure partnership and equity within each of the sectors of economic enterprise and between the sectors.

The Pope makes use of the Latin *ordo* when speaking of this vocational system of grouping together those in the same occupation. This word *ordo* has been translated into English as "occupational group," "vocational group," "functional group," "guild," "estate."

Husslein speaks of the conception as follows:

> Cicero speaks of the Order of Scribes and of the Senatorial Order. . . . Similarly we can speak of the Order of Agriculturists, the Order of Miners, the Order of Physicians, the Order of Builders, the Order of Steelmen, if we so desire. But the point is that precisely so the Holy Father would have his word *Ordo* employed.[35]

By means of such professional and vocational guilds or estates the Pope hoped to solve the problem of the class struggle. Thus in the Order of Builders, the contractors as well as the Italian ditch diggers would all be in it together. It is by such means they must organize, and thus create a "sovereign sphere.' Von Nell-Breuning describes this Catholic "sphere sovereignty" in his work, *Reorganization of Social Economy*, as follows:

> Here it is a question, as in the case of social order in general, of the rights of member societies toward society as a whole and vice versa. Since member societies are societies in the true sense of the word, having their own purpose, there follows first of all that all the legal conditions peculiar to each social organization will in their case exist to be effective, valid by themselves, and independent of a superior social authority investing them with their original and therefore social rights of individuals. This is the natural right of self government which is an attribute of the members societies for the sake of realizing their special purpose and the fulfillment of their own vital tasks (Principle of Autonomy).
>
> This autonomy, however, cannot be absolute, but is subordinate to the moral end, and therefore, to the whole society. According to the law of unity of authority within society, it follows that the supreme authority which must care for the common good of the entire society, must also possess the right to supervise the activity of member societies, to regulate the indispensable contributions of the member societies toward the society as a whole, and to intervene against violations of the public welfare committed by member societies (Principle of Intervention).
>
> The order of social authorities itself is in conjunction with the order of special objectives within the general social objective; the good to be realized by member societies within the framework of public welfare will be greater, the more they participate in the social authority. As a result, we have a subordination and a superordination of the multifarious authorities in society which we designate as the Principle of Hierarchy.[36]

As we have already seen, the Roman Catholic theory of society also requires the Principle of Subsidiatry as the corollary of the Principle of Hierarchy. It means that since each "order" or member society takes care of a particular good, and since all together aim at the common good, each member society is a part of the whole in an ever higher gradation of authority. The state, concerned as it is with the common good exclusively, is the highest (natural) rung on this ladder of authority. Von Nell-Breuning believes that only by means of such a social system can modern society avoid class conflict; He writes:

The present economic regime discloses two classes with opposing interests. . . . The obvious solution is the substitution of corporative orders for the different trades or industries, in each of which orders both classes are embraced, capital and labor, employer and employee, cooperating in common council and common efforts for the good of the common trade or industry, and at the same time keeping in view the entire good.[37]

This doctrine of the corporative state has become the Roman Catholic social ideal; the state governs a hierarchy of societal relationships where each is part of the greater whole, i.e., the state which directs all human activities towards man's natural purposes. But since "grace does not abolish nature but perfects it," the state in Roman Catholic social theory must itself operate in accordance with the dictates of the natural moral law as this is declared and defined by the Roman Catholic hierarchy. The state exists by the grace and favor of the Church, but since the Church is not concerned with technical matters, it allows the state a large measure of practical autonomy. As Husslein explains the doctrine:

The Church is not concerned with technical questions. These she leaves to experts. Nor is she concerned with political questions as such, but only in so far as they come under the moral law.[38]

By means of this doctrine of the corporative state Pope Pius XI hoped to thwart the socialist and communist parties' efforts to win the allegiance of the working classes of Europe. In *Quadragesimo* he stated unequivocally that it is impossible for a Catholic to be both a sincere socialist or communist and a true member of the Roman Catholic Church. As things turned out his encyclical was used by the Fascist parties of Europe to justify the rule of a clique of industrialists over industry without the inconveniences of trade unions and parliaments. Under Mussolini's Fascist dictatorship the national control of industry rather than self-government in industry became the essence of the matter. Both in theory and in practice the Fascist state is above syndicates and corporations, and the tendency developed for the new organized orders of industry to become merely administrative arms of the ministry of commerce for a more highly centralized control of industry by the government. Under the Fascist version of the corporative state both workingmen and employers lost their independent organizations, and received in return equal representation on the new boards appointed to govern industry. In his encyclical the Pope expressed some qualifications about Mussolini's exploitation of the guild system as possessing "an excessively bureaucratic and political character." [39] In general, however, the Pope felt that the Fascist corporative system had proved its ability to settle industrial conflicts by state action and in the "repression of socialist organizations and efforts." J. H. Nichols rather unkindly but no less truly points out that "Virtually every Fascist revolution of the next decade was to fly the flag of *Quadragesimo Anno* and its corporative state." [40]

No doubt it was this experience which prompted Pope John XXIII, in his great encyclical *Mater et Magister*, to demand a far greater participation by the workers in the industries in which they work:

> We hold as justifiable the desire of the employees to participate in the activity of the enterprises to which they belong as workers. It is not feasible to define *a priori* the manner and degree of such participation, since these depend on the specific conditions prevailing in every enterprise—conditions that can vary from one to another. . . . But we think it fitting to call attention to the fact that the problem of the participation of the workers is an ever-present one, whether the enterprise is private or public; at any rate, every effort should be made that the enterprise become a community of persons in the dealings, activities and standing of all its members. This demands that the relations between the employers and directors on the one hand, and the employees on the other, be marked by appreciation, understanding, a loyal and active cooperation and devotion to the undertaking common to both, and that the work be considered and effected by all members of the enterprise, not merely as a source of income, but also as the fulfilment of a duty and the rendering of a service. This also means that the workers may have their say, and make their own contribution to, the efficient running and development of the enterprise. . . . The demand for workers to have a great say in the conduct of a firm accords not only with man's nature, but also with recent progress in the economic, social and political spheres.[41]

Provided the principle of unity and efficiency of management is ensured, Pope John felt that the desire of workingmen to share actively in the life of the firm where they work is a legitimate one, and one which must be satisfied to the degree and in the manner permitted by the actual situation. He thus taught:

> A humane view of the enterprise ought undoubtedly to safeguard the authority and necessary efficiency of the unity of direction, but it must not reduce its daily co-workers to the level of simple and silent performers, without any possibility of bringing their experience to bear [on the running of the enterprise] and entirely passive in regard to the decisions that regulate their activity.[42]

As technology advances, greater skill will be required of workers, and this in turn will require that greater educational and training opportunities should be afforded to these workers. All this serves to create an environment in which workers are encouraged to assume greater responsibility in their own sphere of employment (*Mater et Magister*, 96).

Up to this point, John XXIII had not advanced too far beyond the teaching of his immediate predecessors. The next observations he made, however, involved a far greater recognition of the proper role of labor in the modern world. He noted the development of labor unions in recent time, approving the idea of collective bargaining, and the great part these unions had played in avoiding the class struggle. Consequently these workers should now "be given the opportunity to exert their influence through the state, and not just within the limits of their own spheres of employment." In other words, Pope John wanted unions to achieve their objectives by means in addition to collective bargaining. Thus he said:

> The reason for this is that the individual productive concerns, regardless of their size, efficiency, and importance in the state, form but a part—an integral part—of a nation's entire economic and social life, upon which their own prosperity must depend. Hence, it is not the decisions within the individual productive units which have the greatest bearing on the economy but those made by public authorities and by institutions which tackle the various economic problems on a national or international basis. It is therefore very appropriate, or even necessary, that these public authorities and institutions bring the workers into their discussions, and those who represent the rights, demands and aspira-

tions of the workingmen; and not confine their deliberations to
those who merely represent the interests of management (*Mater
et Magister*, 97-99).

Economic decisions by political bodies on a national or international level are public matters, not private actions by the owners
of property. Hence workers, and the unions that represent them,
participate as a matter of right in deliberations that so deeply affect
their welfare. On this public level, their interests are coordinate with
those of management, whereas on the company level workers' claims,
while real and substantial, are necessarily subordinate in economic
matters.

(d) *Roman Catholic Temporal Action*

While the Popes have provided the social theory by which men
should be guided in their social life, it is the task of Catholic Action
and of the "lay apostolate" to carry it out. Michael Fogarty calls
this the "sphere of strategy" or of "middle principles." He says:

> There is a difference here between the Catholic and the protes-
> tant views, due to differing conceptions of the nature and au-
> thority of the Church. But this difference is more apparent in
> theory than in practice. To summarize, define, and teach the
> broader principles of political and social conduct, those most im-
> mediately following from revelation and the natural law is seen
> even by Protestants as the business in the first instance of the
> trained theologian or philosopher, and in the second of Christian
> Action movements, more or less formally under the official
> Church's control. But to decide how these principles can best be
> carried into effect in a given political, economic or social environ-
> ment is seen even by Catholics as primarily and essentially the re-
> sponsibility of the lay Christian Democratic movements. And
> this covers the long-term strategic judgments as well as day to
> day tactics.[43]

In 1951 and again in 1957 a World Congress for the Apostolate
of the Laity was held in Rome. The idea that the Roman Catholic
layman is also an apostle or servant of Jesus Christ in some sense was
not new, but it had tended to become forgotten. Then, thanks to the
great Liturgical Movement which has now been operative in the
Roman Church for the past hundred years, a new emphasis has come

to be made on the common priesthood of all the faithful and an insistence on the social responsibility of the Christian.[44] Then Pope Pius XI in *Quadragesimo Anno* gave the laity its charter of action, calling upon it to join with the clergy in the Christianization of modern society.[45] The purpose of both Congresses was to search for the best methods and principles which would render the work of the lay apostolate effective in the conditions of post-Christian society. In his address to the First World Congress, Cardinal Gracias stated:

> Every good Catholic is an apostle. The mother who teaches her children, the father who does neighbourhood evangelization, or simply shows exemplary conduct are acting as apostles. But this apostleship is derived. The Church hierarchy is the true apostolate. It was to the twelve that Christ gave the apostolic mandate, not to all the believers, and the twelve handed down their jobs; Peter to the Pope, the others to the cardinals and bishops.[46]

Thus the Church of Rome does the "official," the Roman Catholic layman the "unofficial" apostolic work. The Church cannot handle all the work, and hence the laity must help the clergy. "Catholic Action," said Pius XI, "is the participation of the laity in the hierarchical apostolate." [47] In his pamphlet *What Is Catholic Action*, J. Newman points out that such participation never means that the layman takes over the official work of the clergy, but that he can do work on behalf of the clergy, at the clergy's request. This is the more official participation. He can also engage himself in unofficial participation such as neighborhood evangelism. The lay apostolate arises from the fact that every Catholic by virtue of his baptism and confirmation is in some way a priest. But such priesthood is subordinate to that of the clerical priesthood. As the encyclical *Mediator Dei* made plain, the layman is not a priest, save in a spiritual or metaphorical sense, since of himself he does not possess or enjoy the true power of the priesthood to celebrate the Mass.[48]

At the point that laymen organize to carry out the hierarchy's social and political directives we have a special form of the lay apostolate, namely Catholic Action, and when such organized groups concern themselves with social problems, we find Catholic

social action. They can be study groups, or perhaps welfare organizations, or educational groups.

In an appendix to his work *True Humanism*, Maritain distinguishes
between three distinct planes of such Catholic action. First there is
the spiritual plane, when the Catholic acts as a member of the Mystical Body of Christ. He writes of this plane:

> Whether it be in the order of liturgical and sacramental life,
> of the work of the virtues or of contemplation, of the apostolate
> or of works of mercy, our activity has its determining object in
> eternal life, in God . . . the service of the redemptive work of
> Christ in ourselves and in others. This is the plane of the Church
> itself.[49]

Then there is the second plane of activity, which Maritain defines
as the temporal one, when Catholics act "as citizens of an earthly
city, engaging in the affairs of humanity's earthly life." Of this
plane he writes:

> Whether it be in the intellectual or moral order, scientific and
> artistic or social and political, our activity, while all the while, in
> so far as it is right, being turned towards God as its final end, has
> as its determining end a good which is not eternal life, but one
> which is generally concerned with the things of time, the work
> of civilisation, or of culture. This is the plane of the world.
> These two planes are clearly distinct, as the things which are
> Caesar's and the things which are God's. . . . They are distinct,
> they are not separate. . . . They are different, but the one is sub-
> ordinate to the other; the temporal as such needs to be vivified
> by the spiritual.[50]

Maritain then distinguishes between "acting as a Christian" in the
world and "acting as a Christian as such" by which he means that
"we must not only act as Christians and as Christians as such, as living members of Christ, on the spiritual plane; we must also act as
Christians, as living members of Christ's body, on the temporal one.
Otherwise the weakness and abstention of Christian energies in the
things of time will result in the abandonment of the world into the
hands of other energies who do not labor for its good." [51] With this
may be compared Edmund Burke's famous words: "All that is necessary for the triumph of evil is that good men do nothing."

Maritain then suggests that there is a third plane of activity, which is intermediate between the other two. Of his plane he writes:

> This intermediate plane is that of the spiritual as inflected to the temporal one, the plane of the spiritual where it joins the temporal. . . . On this third plane as on the first the Christian acts and appears before men as a Christian as such and to this extent commits the Church. . . . It is on this third plane as on the first that the laity is called by catholic action to collaborate in the apostolate of the teaching Church. It is on this third plane that they exercise a catholic *civic* action . . . when they intervene in political affairs in the defense of religious interests. . . . The whole work of catholic action is done on the first and on the third plane.[52]

Elsewhere, in *Scholasticism and Politics*, Maritain expressly states that Catholic action does not and cannot take place on the second plane, i.e., the temporal or worldly plane. He says:

> On the temporal level, our action . . . if it is what it ought to be . . . will be an action proceeding from Christian inspiration, yet it will not present itself as specifically Christian. . . . On the spiritual level . . . it will have as its object the expansion of the Kingdom of God in souls, as specifically Christian (the Christian apostolate). . . . It is on the first and on the third level of the Christian's action—on the level of the purely spiritual and on that of the spiritual uniting with the temporal in the name of spiritual values—and only on these two levels, that Catholic action is accomplished, because this is, by definition, an apostolic action.
>
> Catholic action does not remain on the purely spiritual level of itself, it demands passage to the lower level. . . . Christian social action is par excellence in its mode of action. In what sense is this so? . . . Let us not forget that the social, the economic, and the political, are intrinsically dependent on ethics, and that, by this title, for this formal reason, are concerned with eternal life, and therefore with the pastoral ministry of the Church.[53]

Pius XII confirmed Maritain's teaching when he remarked that "it is self-evident that the apostolate of the laity is subordinated to the ecclesiastical Hierarchy," [54] but that lay organizations may enjoy a certain measure of autonomy. The answer of autonomy lies in a distinction between guiding directives and actual activity.

If the Roman Catholic hierarchy has not given specific directives,

then by definition it follows, Maritain writes, that there can be no
Catholic Action but only action by Catholics:

> Where this Catholic action on the world is not itself directed to
> apostolic ends . . . there is, of course, action by Catholics but no
> Catholic action as such. That is why economic and professional
> works—cooperatives, social insurance, trade unions and the like—
> no matter how Christian their inspiration may be, do not enter
> into the concept of Catholic action.[55]

Maritain's teaching received official approval at the Second Vatican Council in the decree *De Ecclesia*, which states:

> The economy of salvation demands that the faithful should
> learn to make a careful distinction between the rights and duties
> they have undertaken as members of the Church's flock and those
> which belong to them as members of Human society. They must
> make efforts to harmonize both sets of rights and duties, bearing in
> mind that they must be guided by the Christian conscience, no
> matter what the temporal activity in which they are involved, for
> not even in temporal business can any human activity be removed
> from God's control. In our day there is the greatest need that
> this distinction and this harmony should be seen in the clearest
> possible light in the manner in which the faithful act, if the
> Church's mission is to be able more fully to correspond to the
> special conditions of the world today.[56]

In practice, this distinction concerns two different but complementary forms of apostolic activity, both of which are quite indispensable to the Church's mission to the world. On the one hand
Catholics believe in Catholic Action under ecclesiastical patronage
and concerned with the spiritual apostolate of the Roman Catholic
Church in the modern world. On the other hand they believe in
action by Catholics not directly subject to the hierarchy, which
takes place on the natural level, where they can only do what their
hands find to do. As Maritain well puts it:

> The social is by nature concerned with the second level, the
> level of the temporal, on which we act as members of the earthly
> city, and on which we ought to act in a Christian manner, on our
> own responsibility, at our own risk and peril, but not professedly
> as Christians sent by the Church.[57]

The full implications of this vital distinction have recently been clarified by Paul Crane, S.J., in his article, "Reflections on a Failure," in the December, 1965, issue of *Christian Order*, and by B. A. Santamaria in *The Price of Freedom*. Here is what Crane says:

(1) The object of any Catholic Social Movement is to influence evolving society in a Christian direction.

(2) The essential instrument of influence can only be the active group of dedicated Christians working within society itself. Without this type of group action no Catholic Social Movement will prove effective. The object of such a movement must be to build up a network of these groups.

(3) The unity of these groups is forged on the basis of uncompromising and shared allegiance of members to the truth of Christian principles.

(4) To work effectively such groups must pursue concrete and defined objectives which fit into a pattern of positive reforming activity.

(5) The long term effectiveness of these groups will be maintained to the extent that they are (a) well serviced by a paid secretariat, (b) coordinated within a strategic network by a competent authority, (c) constant and uncompromising in their dedication to Christian principle and the need for its application.

(6) The activity of these groups does not fall within the sphere of Catholic Action properly so called. It represents rather the action of Catholics. As such, it should not be placed under episcopal jurisdiction. The organized Church, as such, is not involved in the activity of these groups It is Catholic laymen who are involved, along with other Christians, in their working environment. Their activity should merit at least the active sympathy not only of right-thinking Catholics, but of all men of goodwill.

(7) Misunderstanding of the nature and purpose of these groups is bound to cause friction within the Church and between the Church and secular society. The prospect should be faced with equanimity, and a firm resolution on the part of authority within the Church never, for the sake of appearance of peace, to suppress the efforts of those who give their lives to the pursuit think, is what our Lord meant when he said that he had come to bring not peace, but a sword.[58]

From this excellent statement it follows that Catholic Action and

Action by Catholics must be understood as a function of the Roman Church's doctrine of the "antithesis" between God and the powers of darkness. But, as Dooyeweerd reminds us, this antithesis is understood by Rome entirely in the light of its religious ground motive of nature and grace. As such Rome views the antithesis on the one hand as the attempt to separate nature from the faith of the church and on the other hand as the refusal on the part of unbelievers to place the social institutions of the natural world, i.e., marriage, family, school, etc., at the service of grace and its main channel, the clerical hierarchy. As Dooyeweerd says:

> "Nature" and "grace" cannot be separated according to the Roman Catholic view. He who thinks the "natural life" to be sovereign places himself over against Roman Catholicism in an irreconcilable antithesis.[59]

Dooyeweerd then points out that this carries with it consequences in the realm of Catholic action. In a predominantly Roman Catholic country the Roman Catholic naturally will not need to form a specifically Roman Catholic political party or labor union. But in a country with a strongly mixed population he will have to accept the antithesis in these realms.

Thus Pope Pius XI declared:

> Whenever the laws of the country . . . make it impossible for Catholics to form Catholic unions or political parties, under such circumstances, they seem to have no choice but to enrol themselves in neutral trade unions.[60]

In accordance with this directive the Pope ruled on February 2, 1926, that the Mexican Roman Catholics could not form a political party which calls itself Catholic. Dooyeweerd quotes a Dutch Roman Catholic writer on this subject who wrote during the last war as follows:

> One may conclude that wherever the enemy of the church is in control, and is willing to war against the church with its power, and carry with it with all fierceness, if there seems any reason for it, in such a case a Roman Catholic political party would only make things worse and this is undesirable. . . . In a country which has little anticlericalism a Catholic party would promote

this anticlericalism. This would do more damage than good.
. . . On similar grounds one must conclude that a Roman Catholic
political party in Mexico or for that matter in France or England
or the U.S.A. would be undesirable.[61]

However, this writer maintained his thesis that "a Catholic political party in principle is the right thing wherever the state does
not acknowledge the ecclesiastical power." [62]

Rome further teaches that if and when the formation of a Catholic
political party or labor union is inexpedient or impossible, then the
Catholic must belong to a Catholic action labor group. Hence, we
find Catholic trade unions in Quebec, but not in the U.S.A., and a
political party in the Netherlands, but not in Canada. Nevertheless
the ideal remains to bring all areas and aspects of modern society into
subjection to the Roman Catholic hierarchy. Thus Catholic Action
seeks wherever possible to bring pressure upon governments, legislative bodies, and the press to realize the social philosophy of the
papacy. Roman Catholics demand freedom in the English-speaking
world to bring in the Roman Catholic utopia. Louis Veuillot's famous proposition about religious liberty aptly sums up the Roman Catholic attitude toward liberalism and democracy in general.
"Where we Catholics are in the minority, we demand freedom in
the name of your principles; where we are in the majority, we deny
it in the name of our principles." [63]

In no field of modern society has Catholic Action achieved greater
results than in the field of building up Catholic trade unions. In
Holland and Flanders the Christian unions are today the largest, and
probably come close to an absolute majority, while the Socialist
unions come second, and the Communists a bad third. In France
and Italy the Communist-controlled unions come first, but unions
under Christian Democratic leadership now have a majority. In
Germany, Austria, and Switzerland the socialist unions come at the
top. Christian trade unionists are in these lands a minority, but
strongly enough organized and well enough represented in certain
trades and industries to count for a good deal more than the Communists. In Switzerland there are independent Catholic and Protestant unions. In Germany there have for some years been separate

Christian clerical workers' unions. On the whole, it is in Germany and Austria that Christian influence in the trade unions has made least progress since the First World War. It may not have much diminished, but can scarcely be said to have increased. Elsewhere, including Switzerland, the increase has been clear and great.[64]

According to Michael Fogarty these Catholic trade unions define their attitude towards socialists as follows:

(1) The Socialists, and particularly the Marxists, saw the right development of society as leading towards public ownership and national planning. The Christian movements accepted some degree of this but aimed primarily at a decentralized order based on industrial self-government. Firms should be autonomous (and therefore independently owned), with workers' participation in management, ownership, and profits. Industries or professions should be self-governing, on the basis of collaboration between freely organized trade unions and employers' associations. Special attention should be given to the basic unit of social and economic life, the family.

(2) The Socialist road led through class war and revolution. At this time the Socialist movements included not only Social Democrats in the modern sense, but also what would now be called Communists, and in some countries . . . substantial bodies of anarchists. The Christians' aim on the other hand might be described as collaboration through conflict. Employer-worker collaboration was possible and indeed necessary, though it could become effective only if each party was ready and able to stand up for its own views and interests.

(3) For the Socialists the forces which counted in society were basically *material* (the economic infrastructure) and in no way supernatural, and reflected themselves in massive class movements. The objective was to win the class war. The Christians, as trade unionists, were not likely to underestimate the importance of economic factors or of social classes. But the decisive factor, whether as means or aim, was for them the *quality of individual personalities*. As Cardinal Faulhaber was later to say, "the soul of culture is the culture of the soul." And the Word of God was their guide, with

its message on the supernatural as well as the earthly destiny of man.[65]

Fogarty points out that both Catholic and Protestant unions in Europe today are run by the workers themselves. As early as 1900 most of those concerned with the Christian workers' movements had become convinced that effective cooperation between classes could best be achieved only if each class stood firmly on its own feet. It took rather longer, in fact down to 1912, to secure equally general support for the corollary that standing on one's feet might on occasion entail fighting for one's rights, if necessary with the aid of a strike.

(e) *The Roman Catholic Doctrine of the Right to Strike*

Today neither Catholic unionists nor Catholic theologians see any objection in principle to strikes, provided that the usual conditions for a "just war" are fulfilled. Gerard Tremblay of the Confederation of Catholic Workers in Quebec stated that "The National and Catholic syndicates never objected in principle to a just strike. . . . For the strike is based on the right of legitimate defense, and upon freedom of work." [66] The bishops of Australia in 1947 said that "Under modern conditions, the right to organize in trade unions and the right to strike, under certain defined conditions, are inseparable."[67] The bishops of Quebec in 1950 noted that certain categories of workers perform services so essential that they are forbidden by law to strike. The bishops held that under these circumstances there should be compensating methods which are adequate to obtain justice and redress of grievances. "The law should, for example, provide for compulsory arbitration, adequately safeguarded in regard to impartiality, effectiveness, and promptness of decision."[68]

According to Roman Catholic doctrine the conditions that make a strike permissible are the same as those for a just war. These are: a just cause; failure of bargaining and conciliation; expected results proportionate to the sacrifice involved; and the use of lawful and morally sanctioned means.

The first requirement, calling for a just cause, does not mean that only matters of strict justice warrant a strike. Between demands of justice and those that involve injustice there is a wide area of claims based on equity and fairness. If the dispute is over wages, for example, the Roman Catholic moralist would say that a strike is justified if the employer is making extraordinary profits and paying substandard wages. He would say that a strike is unjust when workers, already paid wages above the industry average, strike for still more and drive an employer to the edge of bankruptcy.

Should Christian workers strike for better wages in an industry already paying them a living wage but which has had several years of unusually good profits? Suppose these profits resulted from better market conditions and not from any increased productivity on the part of the workers? Is this unusual surplus to be given to the stockholders, who are already receiving a good return on their investment, or should the workers also demand a share? Strict justice casts little light on this problem. Yet there would seem to be a case in equity and fairness in giving the workers a share in these additional returns. John F. Cronin believes that "One might even justify a short strike to enforce this demand." He points out that political strikes are in a different category.

> In a democracy, it is not normal to use economic pressure to secure political demands. Secondary and sympathy strikes also create problems. May workers strike to help their fellows in a competing plant where a strike has already taken place? They may if they have a direct interest in the result, since they may have reason to fear that failure of one group to get its demands will lead to similar pressures on them later on. But it would not be fair to go out just as a demonstration of sympathy, when no direct interest is involved. Jurisdictional strikes often involve problems of justice. They may be permitted when an employer arbitrarily disregards established rules and customs. But they do not seem fair when the employer is the innocent victim of a dispute between two unions.[69]

Then there are the cases envisaged by the house of bishops of Quebec, in which the public interest could not tolerate a strike. Cronin believes that "generally speaking, doctors, nurses, firemen and police should not strike." But where such strikes are prohibited he suggests that "there should be alternate methods for a just settlement of grievances." [70]

A second condition recognized by Roman Catholic moral theologians for a morally permissible strike is the use of normal means for settling disputes before a strike is called. There should have taken place a reasonable period of negotiation. If this fails, Catholics believe in calling in conciliators to try to mediate the dispute. They have therefore worked, wherever possible, to establish public and private agencies to establish such a service.

Cronin is not too happy about the use of arbitration or labor courts to settle disputes over the negotiation of contracts. He says:

> No one doubts the value of these devices when used to interpret or to enforce a contract previously agreed upon. But they suffer serious deficiencies when used in the negotiation of claims and interests that arise when a new contract is being discussed. Arbitration is a judicial procedure, whereas claims and interests are not usually matters of strict right.
> To cite an example, a union may wish to promote employment in an industry by securing pensions that would permit long-term employes to retire at the age of sixty. It might also ask that workers be given a ten-week vacation after ten years of service. These may be laudable innovations, but a judicial body would be hard put to reach any decision on them. A further difficulty with arbitration is that it entrusts to outsiders decisions that may vitally affect the future of a company. An ill-considered wage increase, for example, might bankrupt the firm. In spite of these limitations, however, compulsory arbitration may be a lesser evil where strikes are forbidden.[71]

A third condition recognized by Catholic moralists as justifying a strike is that the expected results should be proportionate to the sacrifices involved, not only for the workers, but also for the public. Strikers must have a sufficiently good reason for declaring a strike. This reason must be proportioned to the importance of the evils which always result from a strike: loss of time, harm done to industry and family budgets. Again, Catholic trade unionists believe that strikers must have some hope of success. They must weigh with caution possibilities of success or failure. "Labor leaders who provoke a strike when they are about certain that it will not succeed work directly against the best interests of the labor class."

The final condition recognized by Roman Catholics to justify Christians striking is that morally acceptable means must be used in carrying out a strike. Consistently with their great respect for propery rights, Catholic trade unionists forbid sabotage in all its forms. Similarly, unlike apostate humanist trade unionists, Catholic unionists respect the rights of non-strikers and even of their employers. As Cronin points out:

> It certainly would be unfair for workers to leave a steel mill, without first taking the steps necessary for a proper cooling of the furnaces. Strikers in a food store should make provision for the orderly sale of perishable goods. No matter how bitter may be the resentment of the workers against an employer, it is not legitimate to destroy his machines or damage his property. Even worse is the use of violence, as may happen when strike-breakers are imported.[72]

While admitting the right of picketeers to use persuasion (peaceful) to stop non-strikers working, no reputable Catholic unionist would resort to violence to the person, which is everywhere condemned.

With these principles surely no Reformed Christian can disagree. As long as sin infects the hearts of employers and employees, provision must be made for the civilized regulation of industrial disputes. Even as Christians work for harmony and cooperation in industry and try everything in their power to promote a peaceful settlement of disputes, they cannot close their eyes to the fact that sometimes the strike weapon is the only instrument which the worker can use to bring unjust and tyrannical employers and companies to their senses. As such strikes are the price exacted by man's inhumanity to man and the direct outcome of human sinfulness. As long as sin continues to exist in modern industry, so long will strikes continue to occur.

(f) *Catholic Action at Work in Western Europe*

At first the Catholic unions of Europe were greatly divided over what form their relationship should take with the Catholic bishops or clergy. What was to be the working relationship of the Catholic union to the Catholic Church? Members of the Clerical Workers' Union of France, for example, were required in the early days to be members of a religious guild. The German Catholic unions on the other hand insisted on the principle of interdenominationalism. Denominational unions might be more or less formally under the authority of the clergy. They were under it very formally in the case of the Italian unions at least until 1902. The Dutch Catholic unions are today the most denominational in Europe. The Protestant unions in Holland and the Catholic unions in Switzerland set out to be interdenominational, but ended up by being confined to one denomination or group of denominations alone.

The debate ran on for many years, down to the First World War, its storm centers being Germany, where the "trade union controversy" of these years became one of the landmarks of the whole history of the Christian workers movements. Fogarty points out that "The debate as a whole did more than any other to clarify the distinction between Catholic Action and Christian Democracy." Agreement crystallized in the end, about 1914, round three principles:

(1) There should be what will be called here "Workers' leagues": in Germany or Holland they would be called "class" or "Stand" organizations. Their business is primarily education and personal formation, for which orthodox doctrine is particularly important, and which is therefore of special interest to the Churches as such. Such leagues accordingly belong properly to Christian Action. They should be organizations of laymen, but under the authority or at least—as it is more correct to say in the case of Protestant bodies—under the very marked influence of the clergy and the Churches as such.   (2) Trade unions on the other hand are concerned chiefly with matters of economic and political. technique, which are only indirectly and as regards principles the responsibility of the official church. Their effectiveness also depends— much more than that of the leagues . . . —on the support of the mass of workers, many of them by no means strong believers, whose confidence rests on their conviction that the union is not only a strong but an independent advocate of their interests. Unions therefore belong to the field of Christian Democracy, and can and should have a much slighter official connection with the Churches than the workers' leagues. Unions of Catholics or of

Protestants are acceptable, but so are interdenominational unions or even, as in Britain or America, formally neutral unions. . . . Christians should however join only unions which *in fact* base their policy on the Christian revelation and the tradition of the natural law, and in which the Christian point of view can be effectively expressed.

(3) The work of friendly societies, cooperative societies, and similar services might at first sight be classified with that of the unions. In practice however it is often convenient to draw a line between services connected with work, such as vocational training, which are best administered by the unions, and other services of use to the workers and their families irrespective of their trade, which are best administered by the workers' leagues.[73]

By the early twenties these principles were being applied according to two different patterns.

(1) The Catholic workers in Holland, Belgium and Switzerland gave definite form to federated Christian Workers' Movements embracing leagues, unions and services alike. In these federations each constituent movement retained and retains a high degree of autonomy. All have some direct link with the official Church, inasmuch as chaplains are appointed. But in the case of the trade unions the chaplain's role has come to be a very limited one. Of this federated Christian Workers' Movement Fogarty suggests that the outstanding fact about them is that though each individual movement is autonomous, "they are woven together so as, along with neighbouring movements outside the federation, to create for their members a complete frame of life, specifically and outspokenly Christian." [74]

At this point the reader is requested to look at Table 1 in the Appendix, which outlines the system as it operates in Belgium.

(2) In Germany, France, Italy, and among Protestants in Switzerland, and in the end Holland, this tight type of organization has not met with much favor. Here the unions by the nineteen twenties became not merely autonomous within a wider Christian Workers' Movement but entirely independent, and their link with the Churches became much more tenuous. In Germany the unions came to be interdenominational, and in France and Italy they became what Fogarty describes as "a-confessional." The Dutch Protestant movements followed a rather different pattern, with the result that their trade unions became in practice denominational

and they maintain a liaison committee between the unions and the workers' leagues (Table II of Appendix).

(g) *The Catholic Organization of Industry*

In the field of work, as everywhere, both Catholic and Reformed laymen in Western Europe are chiefly interested in human personality, and so in building up the cooperative, self-governing, industrial communities which seem to them most likely to favor its development. Their ideas about industrial organization center chiefly around two problems, those of industry-wide organzation and of workers' participation in the firm.

As we have already seen, concern for industry-wide organization has been one of the main features of Roman Catholic economic policy and philosophy. "The principal part" of the Encyclical *Quadragesimo Anno*, so Pius XII wrote in 1952, is that which "contains . . . the idea of the corporative professional organization of the economy as a whole." What this "corporative professional organization" means in practice can best be seen in the Dutch scheme of "Statutory Industry Councils," whose parentage is acclaimed with equal enthusiasm by Calvinists and Catholics alike. The scheme is usually known as *P.B.O.*, from the initials of its Dutch title (*Publiekrechtelijke Bedrijfsorganisatie*).

The scheme grew out of the conviction that people living together in a certain geographical space have common interests and need common services; and thus they can properly be called a community and ask for the public law of the state to make special provision for their needs. The Dutch came to realize under the inspired propaganda of Professor J. Veraart, that the body of owners, managers, and workers engaged in operating a given set of processes, or in turning out a given product, also have enough duties and interests in common to justify speaking of them as a "community" and equipping this community with legal power to manage its common affairs. After tremendous debate as to the best way this should be done the *Industrial Organization Act of 1950* was passed.

Under the Act, Industry Councils can be set up for firms operating similar processes; cotton spinners, for example, and Commodity

Councils for those who contribute to the supply of a particular product; from cotton spinners, for example, through to piece-goods. Commodity Councils have a government-appointed chairman. Otherwise, council members are appointed by the appropriate employers' organizations and trade unions. Non-manual workers are guaranteed a place on the trade union side. Ministries may send representatives to the Council meetings, but these have no vote. Councils may be given power to regulate a vast range of matters including:

(1) Registering the businesses with which each is concerned and collecting from them a levy and any necessary information, subject to safeguards against the publication by a council of business secrets.

(2) Production and distribution, including such aspects as mechanization, rationalization, standardization, management methods, and competition. This covers price fixing, or the prevention of price fixing. Wages, working conditions, and welfare schemes, recruiting and training programs, schemes covering redundancy.

(3) Social, economic, and technical research.

A Council may not make any order which is an "impediment to fair competition." Nor may it regulate such matters as business reserves and investment, nor the establishment, expansion, and closing of businesses. Its decisions can be suspended or annulled by the government "in so far as they are contrary to law or the public interest."

It is not intended that all the powers under the Act should be available in every industry or commodity group, nor that all Councils should have the same constitution. Each industry or commodity group is to have a scheme tailor made to suit its own requirements. These are worked out under the supervision of a national Social and Economic Council also set up by the Act. This, as the Act is careful to insist, is in no way a separate "economic Parliament." It is, like the industry and commodity councils, an advisory body to which may be delegated powers to execute certain aspects of government policy. One third of its members are appointed by employers' associations, one third by trade unions, and the remaining third by the government.

Fogarty points out that:

P.B.O. builds on the foundations of a wide range of industry wide activities which have grown up in Holland over the years. The Dutch system of unemployment pay, for example, seen through British or American eyes, looks more like an industry-wide guaranteed wage scheme than a scheme of State social insurance. It is indeed a major contribution passed into law primarily through the Christian parties and social movements, to the idea of the industry as a community with a collective responsibility for all those who work for it.[75]

The idea that people working together in the service of consumers constitute a "natural" sovereign sphere, responsible to and for all its members and also the wider community of which it forms part, has been extended by Catholic and Calvinist Christians to the individual firm as well as to the industry or "commodity group." Both wings of Christian democracy in Western Europe believe that management and workers have common interests and joint responsibility. This should eventually, they insist, be reflected in joint control of the firm. For only full industrial democracy, with not merely a consultative but a decisive voice for all, can provide full opportunity for the development of the personalities of the workers and the widest chance for the workers to take responsibility and develop their power to lead. But by joint control the Christian workers' movements mean literally "joint" control and honest cooperation between managers and workers, not a step towards total victory in the class war. For they do not dispute the right of investors to earn such profits as the Catholic theory of the just price permits, nor the responsibility of managers towards consumers and shareholders as well as workers.

A statement by the International Union of Social Studies on Workers' Control summarizes the official Roman Catholic view on the subject:

(1) There is in general no absolute or "natural" right to joint control of industrial decisions of any kind.

(2) But joint control is in modern conditions often very desirable, for the usual reason of promoting the growth of human personality and opening up new opportunities of leadership and responsibility.

(3) Each contributor to a firm's activities brings with him
needs and interests which others must respect. Any decision
which involves solely the interests of a given individual or group
is a matter solely for that individual or group. A decision exclusively affecting the value of a firm's capital assets, for instance, is
a matter exclusively for those who provide these assets. But decisions which affect the rights and interests of two or more groups
are a legitimate matter for joint control.

(4) No formula or set of formulas can yet be said to have
proved definitely the best. For the moment, therefore, what is
needed is the greatest possible amount of experiment under varying conditions.[16]

In his book *L'Avenir de l' Entreprise—un Patronat qui S'Engage*,
J. Zamanski, the Chairman of the French Catholic employers' organization, was able to suggest dozens of schemes in firms of all
shapes and sizes, ranging from elementary joint consultation to fully
shared control. The Christian Democratic parties have been largely
responsible for the Works Council laws now in force all over
Europe; in France from 1945-1946, in Austria from 1947, in Belgium
from 1948, in Holland from 1950, in Germany (the most far-reaching of all) from 1951 and 1952.

Within the firm, the Christian Democratic movements agree that
the authority and personal responsibility of top management must
be preserved, or even strengthened. The main initiative in policy-
making within the firm, as well as the main responsibility for execution, must rest with the top management. Managers must certainly
follow a policy in the interests and with the consent of their con-
stituents, inside as well as outside the firm. But they themselves must
take the lead in making it.

But this does not mean that the industrial manager should behave
like an autocrat. In the opinion of the Catholic trade unionists,
effective leadership implies readiness to consult on an equal footing
with the various interests concerned, and to accept the decisions at
which they as a group arrive. Top managers should be bound by
decisons reached at the level of the firm as well as of the industry or
the nation. In some firms this has resulted in the workers' councils
obtaining the right to nominate members to the boards of com-

panies, e.g., German coal, iron, and steel firms. In others this has resulted in various schemes of profit sharing. Outside Germany and Austria, where joint-control has made the greatest strides, it is more usual for laws establishing works councils to give the councils more restricted powers:

(1) The right to elect a council, and to meet management on specified occasions.

(2) The right to supervise, and often to administer, their firm's welfare work.

(3) Varying responsibilities for "personal" matters such as dismissals, appointments, or works rules; that is, matters most directly affecting the personnel.

(4) The right to be informed about the technical and economic progress of the business, and to discuss it. This in some countries includes the right to send in an accountant to establish and to report and advise on facts about the firm's economic position.[77]

While seeking to establish more harmonious relationships between managers and workers in these various ways, the Christian Democratic and Catholic Action movements still recognize the existence of classes, with distinct ways of life and separate interests which they are entitled to develop and defend. The growth of human personality requires not merely that each individual find a role and status in society appropriate to him, but also that he enjoy a certain measure of security. One of the main foundations of security, as the Christian movements see it, is to belong to a class of people like oneself, among whom one feels at home, and to know that this class is organized and indispensable enough to be a power in the land.

Class organization is seen as having value in industrial relations. Christian Democratic movements may sometimes fear trade union interference with self-government in the firm. But none today would claim that it was possible to build mutual confidence and cooperation in the firm or industry without trade unions and employers' organizations. *For mutual confidence is impossible without mutual respect, and this must be based not only on character and common ideals but on organization and strength.* One of the last serious challenges to this principle from a Catholic source came in 1924. As a result of disputes in the textile industries in the north of France, the Catholic employers appealed to Rome to condemn the Christian trade unions. The reply published in 1929 reaffirmed the value of class cooperation but at the same time made clear that in the view of the Roman Congregation concerned:

(1) Trade unions, entirely independent of the employers, are necessary.
(2) The defense by these unions of "legitimate economic and temporal interests" is entirely justifiable.
(3) This defense may quite properly be carried on in collaboration, from case to case as conditions demand, with other, non-Christian, working class organizations.
(4) A special value of separate class organizations lies in their potentialities for education—hence the special importance of keeping them on a Christian basis.[78]

If the purpose of organizing the members of a social class is first of all to give them a sense of security, it is also essential that the labor organization should be run *by*, as well as for, the members of that organization. There was a time when the idea of the "mixed guild" prevailed, and when no Christian workers' organization was complete without its middle or upper class patrons. That day is over, and the International Federation of Christian Trade Unions has for many years been the most tenacious defender of the whole trade union world of the principle that class organizations must be fully independent and democratically run. It has the distinction of being the only major trade union body never to admit the right of the state or party-controlled "trade unions" to rank as genuine organizations of the working class. Others, including the T.U.C., have for instance been prepared to admit the Soviet "trade unions" to the International Labor Organisation; but never the I.F.C.T.U.

The Christian Trade Union International (I.F.C.T.U.) has helped the Christian trade union movement to expand overseas by opening two regional offices for Africa and one for Latin America. A Catholic trade union movement was started in Canada in 1912 by the Workers Federation of Chicoutimi, Quebec Province. By the end of the nineteen forties it had overcome its teething troubles, built up a membership of 80,000, and become the dominant labor organization in French Canada. Shortly after the Second World War the

Dutch Protestant unions dispatched an organizer to Canada, and as a result of his work a number of Christian locals were founded, resulting in the formation in 1952 of The Christian Labor Association of Canada. The French and Belgian Christian trade unions have built up substantial memberships in North and Central Africa and Madagascar. A Christian trade union movement appeared in Vietnam just after the war, grew rapidly, and by 1953-1954 was the biggest and best organized in the country.

Roman Catholic Temporal Action has thus exerted a tremendous influence in the formation of Catholic political parties, workers, movements, and trade unions in the homelands of Latin Christianity. Thanks to the successful efforts of the Catholic laity the Roman Catholic philosophy of labor as defined by papal encyclicals has been translated into reality in Western Europe.

(h) *Catholic Action at Work in America*

Until 1908 the Roman propaganda supervised American Catholicism as a mission field, and at the time of the First World War half of America's Roman Catholics were still in foreign language churches. Only in the period between the wars, with mass immigration ended did the Roman Church gain sufficient ground in the struggle to unify and organize its vast invasion of America to be able to turn from internal problems and try to shape American society as a whole towards Roman Catholic goals, including its political and economic objectives.

J. H. Nichols writes in *Democracy and the Churches*:

> The significant development of American Catholicism has taken place under Pius XI and Pius XII since World War I. The tremendous expansion of so-called "Catholic Action" under these leaders has made American Catholicism a stronger sociopolitical force than any other American denomination. . . . No other Church or group of Churches exerts such influence on American education, popular culture, labor, or even possibly American politics, local and national. The Catholic Church looms up less as a religious than as a cultural and political force, because of the new quasi-political character of Catholic Action. This type of mobilization of the laity builds on a higher proportion of people who

are not at all devout, but merely social and political Catholics. They are willing to accept the hierarchy as their bosses in constructing an efficient power bloc.[79]

The new era of Roman Catholic influence and power in the United States began with the conversion of the emergency National Catholic War Council to the National Catholic Welfare Conference in 1919 as the coordinating administrative general staff of American Catholicism. Up till then policies on social issues, for example, had varied from diocese to diocese. Now an integrated nation-wide policy was possible. Annual meetings of the Roman Catholic bishops began in the same year. The results of these developments must not be judged in numbers. As Nichols points out:

> The significant results of the American Counter Reformation are rather strategic. With the techniques learned in supporting or fighting European totalitarianism, Roman Catholicism in this generation made a systematic attack on the ganglia of American culture and social control, the schools, press, radio, movies, courts, police, military, labor movement, foreign service, as well as political parties, especially on the municipal and state level. With many of these new developments Protestantism had not come to terms and neither had a policy nor agencies to influence them. Rome had both. . . .
> Because of the superior organisation of the Roman Church . . . and because of its sociological location among the less advantaged groups, the Roman leadership found much more popular support among its laity and exerted more actual influence in political and economic life. This was true in legislation and also in such voluntary social organizations as trade unions and cooperatives.[80]

Typical of the new attitude of Roman Catholicism toward American society as a whole was its new social philosophy, as this had become defined in the great papal encyclicals. It was this new philosophy of labor and industry which gave it the edge over all Protestant groups in America by enabling it to claim to speak for the common working class people of the large American cities. Thus American Catholicism must be held largely responsible for F. D. Roosevelt's success in the presidential elections of 1932, 1936, and 1940.

In no field did American Catholicism exert a greater influence than in the field of labor and industrial relations. Led by John A. Ryan, who had achieved fame by his first book, *A Living Wage; Its Ethical and Economic Aspects* (1906), and R. A. McGowan, the National Catholic Welfare Conference Department of Social Action came to exert more influence upon the course of American labor legislation and policy than all the Councils for Social Service of the Protestant Churches put together. It was Ryan, in fact, who drafted the famous 1919 Bishops' Program for Social Reconstruction, called by F. L. Broderick, "perhaps the most forward-looking social document ever to come from an official Catholic agency in the United States." [81]

The program called for minimum wage legislation; insurance against unemployment, sickness, disability, and old age; a sixteen-year minimum age limit for working children; legal enforcement of the right of labor to organize; a national employment service; public housing; no general reduction in wartime wages, but a long-term program for increasing them, not only for the good of workers, but also to bring about a wider distribution of purchasing power, as the means to prosperity; prevention of excessive profits and income through a regulation of rates of interest which allow the owners of public utilities only a fair return on their actual investment, and, through progressive income taxes on inheritance, income, and excess profits; participation of labor in management and a wider distribution of ownership through cooperative enterprises and worker ownership in the stock of corporations; effective control of monopolies, even by the method of government competition if necessary.[82]

All of the proposals contained in the Bishops' Program, except for the proposal of labor participation in management, subsequently became fact. The program reflected the papal philosophy of the corporate state, and it served as a vehicle for the democratic principles of labor organization and collective bargaining, while it opened up vistas for employers of the elimination of competition within a given industry. Roosevelt's New Deal and especially the Wagner Act and the Social Security Act embodied many of its proposals. Ryan acclaimed the Wagner Act as "probably the most just, beneficent, and far-reaching piece of labor legislation ever enacted in the United States." [83]

In 1938, to Ryan's delight, Roosevelt called for and Congress enacted a public works program and primed the pump further through building a two-ocean navy. That same year also saw passage of the Fair Labor Standards Act, which eventually set up a minimum wage of forty cents an hour and a maximum work week of forty hours for certain businesses engaged in interstate commerce. The Act did not go so far in wages, hours, or coverage as Ryan had wished, but its passage marked a triumph for Roman Catholic labor philosophy. In 1940, partly as the result of work by Ryan and Mc-Gowan, the United States Roman Catholic bishops issued a statement on "The Church and the Social Order," which warned against industry's abuse of power and stressed the legitimacy of unions and strikes when necessary as a means of bringing about a greater equality in union-management relations. The bishops called upon business and industry to provide "not merely a living wage for the moment, but also a saving wage for the future against sickness, old age, death, and unemployment."

After Roosevelt's death in 1945, Ryan wrote an article for the *Review of Politics* in which he said that the National Labor Relations Act, the Fair Labor Standards Act, and the Social Security Act "have done more to promote social justice than all the other federal legislation enacted since the adoption of the Constitution."

No less striking than this American Catholic program for the reconstruction of modern society was the technique with which Catholic Action set out to control the shaping of American labor. Such a method of action had been laid down by Pope Pius XI. While admitting the right of Roman Catholic workers to join secular trade unions, the Pope pointed out the necessity for taking certain precautions:

> Side by side with these unions, there should always be associations zealously engaged in imbuing and forming their members in the teachings of religion and morality, so that they in turn may be able to permeate the unions with the good spirit which should direct them in all their activity (*Quadragesimo Anno*, 35).

Under direct orders from Pope Pius Roman Catholic seminaries began instructing all candidates for the priesthood in "the intense study of all social matters." [84]

In addition, the Pope insisted there must be provided specifically Catholic associations for Catholic union members, in which they would receive Catholic moral training in its social and political bearings.

In 1937 the Association of Catholic Trade Unionists (A.C.T.U.) was organized in America to form a disciplined elite within the labor movement. Chapters soon appeared in many industrial cities, each supervised by a priest. This Catholic Action group works inside the unions today as a Catholic pressure group. At present A.C.T.U. work is largely confined to fighting Communist infiltration of the so-called neutral unions, and its successes have been scored chiefly because the overwhelming majority of labor union members in the United States are also anticommunist.

Catholic Action in America also conducts labor schools which perform notable educational service in the practices of union government, public speaking, economics, and Roman Catholic social doctrine.

The influence of this coordinated penetration was soon apparent, especially in the C.I.O., where the Catholics made themselves the main opponents in the war against the Communist infiltration of American labor unions. Of this Catholic and Communist penetration of the American labor movement, J. H. Nichols writes:

> Between these two authoritarian disciplined minority pressure groups it began to be increasingly difficult for the American movement to have any genuine liberal democratic development. Catholic Action was using the anti-Communist issue and Communist methods to establish itself in the strategic centers of American labor, and from there to propagandize its whole antidemocratic "corporative state" program. Rome was effectively fighting Communism in American labor and providing leadership in widening labor's share of industrial control. In both regards Protestantism was quite ineffective.[85]

The educational work of the N.C.W.C. Social Action Department included a great variety of conferences as well as publications. After 1922, for example, the "travelling universities" of the Catholic Conference on Industrial Problems opened for scores of two-day sessions in a variety of cities. At these conferences theologians, economists, employers, trade unionists, and government experts engaged in discussion on concrete problems. The Roman clergy were provided with more extended courses, in the priests' summer schools of Social Action, which were organized in ten dioceses. As a result a tremendous change in the attitude of the Roman Catholics in America on social action was effected within a generation.

As a result of this Catholic Action, by 1962, when the first Roman Catholic President of America was elected in the person of John F. Kennedy, the Roman Catholics of America, in terms of the conversion and shaping of society, state, and culture, were exerting more influence in American life than all the Protestants of the nation put together, even though they outnumbered the Catholics by three to two.[86]

How can we explain this? The fundamental difference lies in the church discipline exercised in the two religious systems. The Roman Catholic type of discipline is more external and superficial and easier to maintain. It rests, as we have seen, on clerical authority and control of laymen. The self-interest of the Roman clergy is thus enlisted in the effort to maintain discipline. Rome wants its own schools, hospitals, welfare agencies, press, lawyers, diplomatic agents, labor unions, and political party—all the organs of its own Christiana *societas perfecta.* In short, Roman Catholics in America as in Western Europe are organized as Roman Catholics and not as mere citizens of the respective countries in which they happen to live.

Unfortunately, the great Protestant denominations of the English-speaking world have become an undisciplined and individualistic body of men and women. Each Protestant today tends to follow the dictates of his own reason rather than the Word of God. In this sense each Protestant has made himself his own pope. Until Protestants recover Calvin's system of church discipline, they can never hope to match the Church of Rome in influencing the cultural developments of their respective nations. As J. H. Nichols well says:

> A disciplined church has more influence than a church that does not seek to shape its corporate witness by the will of God. . . . What was left of Protestant discipline was democratic, but some had so long avoided measuring their decisions in prayer and dis-

cussion together under the judgment of the living God (of the Scriptures) that there was fear that in putting their professed faith to the test they would discover it was no longer there.[87]

In the providence of Almighty God the Christian Reformed Churches of Holland, America, and Canada have recovered such a discipline, and as a direct result they have once more begun to influence the cultural development of their respective nations, especially in the sphere of labor relations. It is therefore to this Reformed philosophy of labor we shall now turn.

Before doing so let us take heed of the somber warning with which Nichols concluded his great study of *Democracy and the Churches*:

> From the viewpoint of Western culture, or the world as a whole, there were three religious and political blocs to be distinguished. The Roman Catholic world was, save in so far as it had adopted protective coloration in the English-speaking countries, politically authoritarian and dogmatically antiliberal. Marxist countries shared the same formal pattern. Each bloc attempted to define the issues so as to carry with them the Puritan democrats. It was "Democracy against Fascism," or it was "Christian civilization against atheist Communism." It is extremely important both politically and religiously that in this tension Puritan Protestantism retain a very distinct sense of its unique tradition and refuse to be hoodwinked by either of these slogans. Whatever temporary alliances might be expedient, Puritan Protestantism is responsible to God alone and can yield its conscience to no infallible interpreters—neither to a party (in Moscow) nor to a hierarchy (in Rome).[88]

CHAPTER FIVE NOTES

1. *Industrial Relations Seventy Years After Rerum Novarum* (Proceedings and addresses of the Catholic Social Life Conference held in Halifax, Nova Scotia, October 13-15, 1961. Published by the Social Action Department of The Canadian Catholic Conference, 90 Parent Ave., Ottawa, Canada), p. 3.

2. J. F. Cronin and H. W. Flannery, *Labour and the Church* (Burns and Oates, London, 1965), pp. 11, 24, 37, 59, 75.

3. Abraham Kuyper, *Christianity and the Class Struggle* (Piet Hein, Grand Rapids, 1950), p. 14 note.

4. R. Fulop-Miller, *Leo XIII and Our Times* (Longmans, Green & Co., Lon-

don, 1937), p. 81. Cf. A. R. Vidler, *A Century of Social Catholicism* (Faber & Faber, London, 1964).

5. A. Kuyper, *op. cit.*, p. 33ff.

6. *Ibid.*, p. 38.

7. *Ibid.*, p. 41.

8. *Ibid.*, p. 44.

9. *Industrial Relations Seventy Years After Rerum Novarum*, p. 39.

10. Aquinas, *Summa Theologica*, 1,a; 2, ae,qaue 91, art 1 and 2. quoted by A. P. d'Entreves, *Natural Law* (Hutchinson, London, 1957), p. 39.

11. Walter Ullmann, *A History of Political Thought: The Middle Ages* Pelican Original, London, 1965), p. 181.

12. *Ibid.*, p. 175.

13. *The Politics of Aristotle*, trans. by Ernest Barker (Clarendon Press, Oxford, 1946), p. 4ff.

14. Ullman, *op. cit.*, p. 176.

15. *Ibid.*, p. 169.

16. Quoted in A. P. d'Entreves, *Aquinas Selected Political Writings* (Blackwell, Oxford, 1948), p. 119.

17. *Ibid.*, p. xviii of The Introduction.

18. A. P. d'Entreves, *Medieval Contribution to Political Thought* (Oxford University Press, 1939), p. 29, quoting Aquinas.

19. Quoting Pope Pius XI in M. P. Fogarty, *Christian Democracy in Western Europe, 1820-1953* (Routledge & Kegan Paul, 1957), p. 41.

20. *Ibid.*, p. 41ff.

21. Dooyeweerd, *Renewal and Reflection*, p. 115.

22. D'Entreves, *Aquinas, Selected Political Writings*, p. xx.

23. Dooyeweerd, *A New Critique*, Vol. III, p. 510ff.

24. Quoted in J. Husslein, *Social Wellsprings* (Collins Bruce, Milwaukee, 1942), Vol. II, p. 192.

25. *Ibid.*, Vol. I, p. 200.

26. *Ibid.*, p. 186.

27. *Ibid.*, p. 189.

28. *Ibid.*, p. 178.

29. *Ibid.*, p. 197.

30. *Ibid.*, p. 195.

31. *Ibid.*, Vol. II, p. 191.

32. *Ibid.*, pp. 191-192.

33. *Leo XIII and the Modern World*, edited by E. T. Gargan (Sheed & Ward, New York, 1950), p. 71.

34. H. Richard Niebuhr, *Christ and Culture*, p. 130.

35. Husslein, *op. cit.*, Vol. II, p. 208.

36. Von Nell-Breuning, *Reorganization of Social Economy* (Bruce, New York, 1936), p. 209.

37. *Ibid.*, p. 210.
38. Husslein, *op. cit.*, Vol. II, p. 192.
39. *Ibid.*, p. 213.
40. J. H. Nichols, *op. cit.*, p. 197.
41. *Industrial Relations*, p. 17ff.
42. *Ibid.*
43. M. Fogarty, *op. cit.*, p. 24. Cf. F. Boulard, *An Introduction to Religious Sociology* (Darton, Longmans and Todd, London, 1960).
44. Ernest B. Koenker, *The Liturgical Renaissance in the Roman Catholic Church* (University of Chicago Press, 1954), p. 71ff.
45. Husslein, *op. cit.*, Vol. II, p. 189.
46. J. Newman, *What Is Catholic Action?* (Newman Press, Westminster, 1958), p. 1.
47. Husslein, *op. cit.*, Vol. II, p. 198.
48. Koenker, *op. cit.*, p. 78ff.
49. Jacques Maritain, *True Humanism* (G. Bles, London, 1946), p. 288.
50. *Ibid.*, p. 288.
51. *Ibid.*, p. 292.
52. *Ibid.*, p. 294ff.
53. J. Maritain, *Scholasticism in Politics* (Macmillan, New York, 1940), p. 203.
54. J. Newman, *op. cit.*, p. 20.
55. Maritain, *op. cit.*, p. 198.
56. *De Ecclesia, The Laity*, para. 36 of the Decrees of the Second Vatican Council.
57. Maritain, *op. cit.*, p. 208.
58. Paul Crane, S.J., "Reflections on a Failure," in *Approaches* (Anglo-Gaelic Civic Association, 50 Crockford Park Road, Addlestone, Weybridge, Surrey, England), midsummer edition, 1966.
59. Dooyeweerd, *Renewal and Reflection*, chapter three.
60. *Ibid.*, p. 126.
61. *Ibid.*, p. 127.
62. *Ibid.*, p. 128.
63. J. H. Nichols, *op. cit.*, p. 88.
64. Fogardty, *op. cit.*, p. 211.
65. *Ibid.*, p. 191.
66. H. A. Logan, *Trade Unions in Canada* (Macmillan, Toronto, 1948), p. 591.
67. J. F. Cronin and H. W. Flannery, *op. cit.*, p. 44.
68. *Ibid.*, p. 45.
69 *Ibid.*
70. *Ibid.*, p. 46.
71. *Ibid.*
72. *Ibid.*, p. 47.
73. Fogarty, *op. cit.*, p. 195.

74. *Ibid.*, p. 196.
75. *Ibid.*, p. 61
76. *Ibid.*, p. 66.
77. *Ibid.*, p. 76.
78. *Ibid.*, p. 78.
79. J. H. Nichols, *op. cit.*, p. 245.
80. *Ibid.*, p. 246.
81. Cronin & Flannery, *op. cit.*, p. 147.
82. *Ibid.*, p. 152.
83. *Ibid.*
84. Nichols, *op. cit.*, p. 252ff.
85. *Ibid.*, p. 249.
86. Cronin & Flannery, *op. cit.*, p. 147.
87. Nichols, *op. cit.*, p. 249.
88. *Ibid.*, p. 279.

A NOTE ON THE FRENCH WORKER-PRIEST MOVEMENT

We have not dealt with this movement in our own text, since it failed and it was banned by Rome as well as the French bishops. However, we would draw the reader's attention to two important books on the subject. First, there is Emile Poulat's *Naissance des Pretresuvriers*, which deals with the origins of the movement. Poulat has provided for the first time the full background to the movement, and he confines himself to what led up to it.

It was the publication of the book called *La France Pays de Mission?* in 1943 that concentrated French religious opinion on the gravity of the Church's task in establishing contact with proletarian society. The authors, Abbe Godin and Abbe Daniel, gave facts and figures to justify their thesis that France had become a mission country needing reconverting to Christ. Abbe Godin in particular was consumed with a sense of urgency. He had been closely connected with the Young Christian Workers, and increasingly he had come to realize the need for a special group of priests who would identify themselves with the workers of the industrial suburbs in Paris, not through a parochial structure, but in a mission which would seek to penetrate a society wholly estranged from the Church's traditional ministry. In September, 1943, Cardinal Suhard, the archbishop of Paris, had been so impressed with Godin's book that he ordered the publication of 100,000 copies of it, and he gave his full support to the new initiative of a Mission de Paris which he launched with these words: "The primary object of the Mission to Paris is to convert the heathen. Its secondary object is to demonstrate to the Christian community, that it needs to adopt a new attitude." A few days later, on January 17, 1944, after the inauguration of the mission, Godin died. Yet he remains the key figure to an understanding of the worker-priest movement, though he never lived to see it come to birth.

Godin was far from alone. And Poulat provides much unfamiliar material to justify his claim that *La France Pays de Mission?* was only the culminating point of a movement that both in the efforts of individual priests and in the multiplying agencies of Catholic Action had reflected over many years a profound evolution in the French Church's conception of her missionary task. And, above all else, there was the experience of the war, the fall of France, the millions of French prisoners of war, and later the terrible experience of forced labor and the concentration camps. What might have seemed an academic discussion was transformed by the experience of national humiliation and universal suffering into something very real. For the French clergy were conscripts, and in the German concentration camps they were to be confronted with what had hitherto been a reality far removed from their experience—the almost total estrangement of the workers of France not merely from the practice of religion but from the very sense of religion itself.

Even more crucial was the experience of deportation, when priests who were involved in the Resistance or who had otherwise earned the hostility of the Vichy Government or its German masters went off into captivity and in many cases to death in the concentration camps. An identity in suffering, often with those who had no extrinsic share in their faith, gave to many priests a deep sense of the tragedy of the loss of contact between the Church and the common people of France. Deprived of all privilege, they were just men among men, and found new, often unlikely, ways to exercise a fundamental ministry of compassion. And when, in 1942, the German authorities began the massive movement of French forced labor into German factories, there arose a challenge which was magnificently met. Many priests, with forged papers and with no outward sign of their priesthood, went to Germany with the workers just as the prophets of old had gone into capitivity with the people of Israel. They shared the workers' toil and their agony and established clandestine groups of Catholic believers which in turn drew others who had hitherto thought little of the Church and had never in any case considered priests as other than comfortably-off strangers. Nothing is more moving in Poulat's book than his account of this hidden work of devoted priests of God—in Berlin, Dresden, Frankfurt—forced to improvise, deprived of all the usual helps and sanctions of an ordered clerical life. As one of them wrote:

> Canon law, liturgy; we have had to drop them. All that architecture which piety and human respect have over the centuries built round the body of Christ. . . . That Christ who many of us have touched with our fingers, Christ the worker who has been sent into forced labour alongside us.

Pere Dillard, a distinguished Jesuit economist who had once dined with President Roosevelt in happier days before the war, found in this direct contact with a world that had hitherto been simply a matter of statistics and sociological research a terrible revelation of the truth:

> My Latin, my liturgy, my mass, my prayer, everything that makes me separate, a curious phenomenon, like a pope or a Japanese bronze—a stray specimen left of a race that will soon disappear.

It was no longer a case of a few enthusiasts who had become aware of the pastoral problems presented by the loss of faith among industrial workers in a Paris suburb. A whole generation of young priests and seminarians (for they too had been rounded up for forced labor) returned to France profoundly affected by the years of shared work and suffering with the ordinary working people of France. And their return was not easy. The adjustment to wearing a cassock and living the middle class life of the conventional French priest seemed a return to the wrong kind of status quo. Yet such were inevitably the pressures of clerical life that very soon it became a matter of business as before. But not for all. And the emergence of the worker-priest movement owes much more, as Poulat makes clear, to this tragic and yet invigorating legacy of the war than to any conscious response to the findings of the religious sociologists or indeed to the changing moods of the theologians.

Perhaps this was the essential weakness, a certain impatience that looked for drastic remedies, and remedies that sometimes were applied without enough regard for the true facts of the case. The easy relationship under the stress of captivity, the necessary improvisation and indifference to law, could not automatically be transferred to life in the settled structures of France itself. It is the great merit of Poulat's magnificent book that he relies entirely on the testimony of the men themselves—but his evidence suggests enough to show how certainly strain and misunderstanding on the part of the French hierarchy with the worker-priests were bound to follow.

If Poulat describes the origin of the movement, Gregor Siefer has given us an excellent account of its decline and collapse. In *The Church and Industrial Society* (London, 1964) Siefer shows clearly why the worker-priest movement failed, due largely to a fatal uncertainty of purpose. As the priest-workers grew closer to the society they sought to redeem through their presence, they were confronted with the responsibilities of the worker as such. They were inevitably caught up in the conflicts of class warfare always so powerful in France; they could hardly refuse to take their place in a common struggle with the workers if their solidarity with the workers was to be no more than a patronizing gesture. Hence the participation in 1948 of some priest-workers in World Peace Movement demonstrations, the embarrassments that followed from the Holy Office's condemnation of communism in 1949, and, above all, the arrest of two worker priests in 1952 during the demonstrations in Paris against the new N.A.T.O., C-in-C, General Ridgway.

Again, many priests had become union leaders and their increasing identification with the aims of the workers led to a questioning of many of the features of usual priestly life. Accusations multiplied; priests had given up saying Mass, they never wore clerical dress, and they were even accused of infidelity to the celibacy by which they were bound.

By 1954 the movement had reached a crisis. On January 19, 1954, the French bishops issued a letter to the worker-priests insisting on a choice of alternatives: "either you rely on your own judgment and refuse obedience to Christ, or you believe with all your soul in Christ, even if your own lives, and those of your forsaken brothers, the workers, are thereby broken. The real problem is one of faith."

Such is the dilemma confronting the Roman Church. Rome cannot really accept the idea that is the workers' own responsibility to redeem the milieu that is their own, and if the priest—as priest—assumes a function that is not properly his, this is to impose, by a strange irony, a clericalism in reverse. Until Rome recovers the great Reformation doctrine of the priesthood of all believers in Christ and the doctrine of the calling, there is no way out of the dilemma which she has brought upon herself by her deviation from the religion of the New Testament.

Chapter Six

THE SCRIPTURAL BASIS FOR
A SCIENTIFIC AND SOCIOLOGICAL PLURALISM

(a) *Life Is Religion*

While Pope Leo XIII was voicing his protests against the social injustices of his times and advocating a solution to the social question along moralistic Thomistic lines, his contemporary Abraham Kuyper also began to deal with these same problems in the light of his Reformed and scripturally directed philosophy of man in society. Thanks to his genius Kuyper came to see the social question facing modern Western society within a much larger context than either his own Calivinist predecessors such as Groen van Prinsterer, De Costa, and Bilderdyk, or recent Roman Catholic leaders.

Unlike the popes, Kuyper could not accept the Roman Catholic bifurcation of reality into the temporal and spiritual or the natural and super-natural, the higher and lower spheres of life. *Instead, following the biblical teaching, he understood the spiritual as the religious direction of man's temporal life.* Out of the heart of man Kuyper saw arise all the issues of life. The heart is the concentration point, the religious root of man's entire temporal existence. Out of it arise all his deeds, thoughts, feelings, and desires. In his heart man gives an answer to the most profound and ultimate questions of life, and in his heart his relationship to God is determined.

According to Kuyper man is not to be defined, as Aquinas taught, as an individual substance of a rational form, nor will he accept the Thomist teaching that the soul is the form of the Body. Instead of any such temporal qualifying functions, Kuyper teaches that man is to be defined in terms of his "heart" in which all temporal functions are transcended and concentrated. Man alone of all created beings transcends time, since he alone is created in the image of God. Kuyper therefore rejects the Thomistic idea that man is a mixture of two substances, an "individual substance of a rational form," since the problem as to what causes the mixture to become one substance remains unanswered. Moreover, in the Thomistic conception, the soul as a rational substance does not transcend time. It is a complex of normative spheres abstracted from the temporal nexus of meaning. While recognizing that there is a distinction between the human heart and the human body, Kuyper refuses to accept any dualism. The "heart" refers to the direction taken by man's "bodily" life, i.e., his temporal activities.

Human existence, though it functions in all aspects of God's creation, is not qualified by any of these, since it transcends the modal diversity in its religious center, which in the profound biblical language is called the "heart" of man, out of which arise all the issues of human life. As the Scriptures tell us, "As a man thinketh in his heart so is he" (Prov. 23:7) This individual religious center of human existence is the human selfhood in its primary religious relation to its Divine Creator which has been perverted by man's radical fall into sin, but which is restored by man's radical redemption by Jesus Christ as the new spiritual root of mankind. Kuyper's greatest pupil, Herman Dooyeweerd, expresses this Reformed view of the relationship between the religious center of the human selfhood and the aspects of human experience as follows:

> When one asks (the sciences which are concerned with the study of man): "What is man himself, in the central unity of his existence, in his selfhood?" then these sciences have no answer. The reason is that they are bound to the temporal order of our experience. Within this temporal order human existence presents a great diversity of aspects, just like the whole temporal world, in which man finds himself placed . . . every special science studies temporal human existence in one of its different aspects.
> But all these aspects of our experience and existence within this order of time are related to the central unity of our consciousness, which we call our I, our ego. I experience, and I exist, and this I surpasses the diversity of aspects, which human life displays within the temporal order. The ego is not to be determined by any aspect of our temporal experience since it is the central ref-

erence point of *all* of them. If man would lack this central I, he could not have any experience at all.[1]

Dooyeweerd stresses that this central human selfhood must not be viewed as a metaphysical substance. As the individual concentration point of human existence and experience it is nothing in itself, i.e., apart from the three central relations which, according to the order of creation, determine its meaning. These are, firstly, the relation of the human selfhood to its divine Origin in whose image man has been created and upon whose service of love man should concentrate all his temporal functions according to the central commandment of love. Secondly, there is the central communal relation to the persons of one's fellowmen as image-bearers of God, whom man should therefore love as himself in accordance with the central commandment. Thirdly, the human selfhood is related, as central individual reference point, to the temporal world in which man finds himself and which he only transcends in the religious center of his selfhood. Since the first relation embraces the second and the third, Dooyeweerd speaks of the human ego as the *religious* center of human existence which, as the central seat of the image of God, has the innate religious impulse to direct itself to the Absolute. In the state of sin this impulse takes an apostate direction by absolutizing that which is only relative, with the result that man in this state has lost the real knowledge of God as well as genuine self-knowledge and a true view of reality, since the latter two are dependent on the first.

The direction taken by the human heart is determined by its acceptance or rejection of God. The human "heart" can never remain neutral. It loves God or it is hostile to him. It is renewed by God's grace in Jesus Christ or it continues to live in apostasy. For this reason Kuyper was compelled to reject the Roman Catholic teaching that faith is a super-imposed gift of God to the "natural" man. Faith is an essential aspect of human nature and thus no duality can ever divorce it from nature. Religion is therefore common to all men. No man can claim to be constitutionally devoid of the *semen religionis* which God, together with the *sensus divinitatis*, has implanted in every man. The religious organ is to be found, not in a part of our being, for example, in our intellect, will, or feelings, but in our whole being, at that point where all the human faculties are drawn together in a unity. As Kuyper puts it: "The heart is to be understood not as an organ of feeling but as that point from which God acts and from which he acts on the understanding." [2]

From this it follows that there is no aspect of our existence which can be considered to be indifferent or neutral to religion. God is absolute sovereign, all life belongs to him and is created by him according to its own proper law and nature. The sovereignty of God over the whole cosmos and over *every* aspect of human life is thus the keystone principle of the Reformed philosophy of life.

Everything created has been furnished by God with an unchangeable law for its existence. These laws or ordinances of creation we may call laws of nature, provided that by this term we mean, not laws originating in nature, but laws imposed upon nature. From this doctrine of God's sovereignty over all aspects of creation, Kuyper and Dooyeweerd have developed the conception of sovereignty in each sphere, applying it especially to their view of the temporal social spheres of human society.

(b) *The Scriptural Framework for Science*

According to both Kuyper and Dooyeweerd all truly scientific thinking about God's creation must take its point of departure in the biblical ground motive or basic presupposition of the creation of the cosmos by Almighty God, man's fall into radical sin in his "heart" and his equally radical redemption by the Lord Jesus Christ in the communion of the Holy Spirit. This biblical ground-motive operates through the Spirit of God as a dynamic power in the religious root of man's temporal existence, namely in his "heart." It brings about of necessity a radical change in the direction of one's life and thus of one's attitude towards everything that exists as well as in one's vision of the temporal world. As Augustine pointed out, the logic of Christ provides those who accept Him as their Lord and Savior with a radical revision of their first principles as the only valid presupposition to an adequate cosmology, anthropology, and sociology. The basis for the revision of classical naturalism and humanism, Augustine held to lie in the *logos* of Christ, conceived as a revelation to man, not of new truth, but of truth as old as the hills. As he once said, "I believe in order that I may understand." [3] Unfortunately for mankind, Augustine never carried through his program of reforming the basic categories of classical science in the light of the ordering principles of God's Word. As a tragic result, Western civilization continued to develop along lines unreformed by the Word of God. An attempt was made at synthesizing the classical view of man in society with the biblical view, with disastrous consequences for Western culture. As a direct result of this medieval accommodation between "nature" and "grace" there was no longer felt any need for a distinctive Christian philosophy of law, politics, economics, and society. The social sciences as well as the natural sciences were in fact abandoned to the influence of the pagan Greek ground-motive of "form" and "matter" in their external accommodation to the Christian philosophy of man in society. After Aquinas had fused the teachings of Aristotle with those of Scripture, the tendency increased to elucidate the first principles of social and natural science without any reference whatsoever to the principles of God's Word for human society. Why bother with God's revelation if the human reason can discover the principles governing "natural" human society as Aristotle had believed it could? If man can of his own rational faculties and by means of his scientific method build a successful social and legal order, why bring religion into life? From Aquinas' incomplete view of the biblical fall there has flowed the most serious consequences. Man's intellect was viewed as autonomous or independent of God. This so-called autonomy provided the basis for the secularization of Western philosophy, law, politics, art, science, and, above all, Western education. As a tragic result "nature" began, so to speak, to eat up "grace" and Christ, as it were, was driven out of Christendom.

While Aquinas himself never drew such unchristian conclusions, it did not take long for his successors at French, German, Italian, and British universities to do so. Such a process of the secularization of the social sciences or the humanities as they were then called inevitably developed out of the distinction first drawn by Aquinas between the order of faith and the order of natural reason.

One of the great tragedies of the Protestant Reformation was the failure of the Reformers to reverse this secularizing process in Western legal, economic, and social thought by developing a social and natural science in the light of a scriptural view of reality. The Reformers did not bring about any radical revision of first principles in the spheres of political science, economics, and sociology for the simple reason, as August Lang showed in his essay, *The Reformation and Natural Law*,[4] that they were so involved in the theological disputes, religious controversy, and the very struggle for survival that they simply did not have any time left in which to develop a truly scriptural view of society.

Luther confused matters by his doctrine of the higher and lower realms. Calvin did bring the two realms of grace and nature together, but he did not bring out the full implications in his scriptural insights as these applied to such matters as politics and economics. The main error set in during the second and third generation of the Reformation, when a new Protestant accommodation with Aristotelianism took place in the thinking of such men as Melancthon, Thomas Beza, and then later, during the seventeenth century, in the work of the Dutch Reformed theologians and American Puritans such as Roger Williams and Jonathan Edwards. Pierre de la Ramee (Peter Ramus) did attempt to provide Protestants with a new logic, which he set forth in his famous work, *Dialecticae libri duo*, which substituted a simple logic for the complicated Aristotelian logic taught in most European universities. But this new method did not bring about any inner reformation of science.[5] Of this failure of the Reformation to reform Western science Dooyeweerd says:

> In the domain of science, the Reformation had, by the grace of God, a great opportunity to effect a basic reform of university instruction in the countries which had aligned themselves with it. Quite unfortunately the Reformation did not take hold of this opportunity. The magnificent program of Melancthon for the reform of education was not at all inspired by the biblical spirit. On the contrary, it had a humanistic philological spirit, which was accommodated to Lutheran doctrine and which gave birth to a

new scholastic philosophy. The latter, in turn, prepared the way for the humanistic secularization at the time of the Enlightenment. In Calvinistic universities Theodore Beza restored Aristotelianism as the true philosophy, adapting it to Reformed theology.

This Protestant reform of scientific knowledge cut a miserable figure when it again took up the dualistic maxim: "For faith one must go to Jerusalem; for wisdom one must go to Athens." It was equally discouraging to see in the seventeenth century the celebrated Reformed theologian, Voetius, protesting as a champion of Aristotelianism against the innovations of Descartes. The truly biblical spirit which had inspired John Calvin's *Institutes of the Christian Religion* was conquered by the scholastic spirit of accommodation, which had been imbibed from the anti-biblical motive of nature and grace. It was the driving force of this dialectical motive, the heritage of Roman Catholicism, which stunted the force of the Reformation and which for more than two centuries eliminated the pssibility of a serious adversary to the secularization of science.[6]

It was to combat such a secularization of science that Abraham Kuyper founded the first truly scripturally oriented Reformed university in the world, namely the Free University of Amsterdam, which was founded in 1880. In the great address Kuyper delivered upon the official opening day of this first truly Reformed University Kuyper significantly delivered a speech which he called *Sovereignty in Its Own Sphere*.[7] He needed the principle suggested in this title as a basis for the elimination of state-monopoly in Dutch higher education. However, Kuyper placed his argument for the right of Reformed Christians to establish their own university in a larger setting. His social conception was part of a life's effort to revitalize and renew the reformational biblical outlook on man's life in this world. Kuyper found his immediate inspiration in Calvin's teaching. When he presented the substance of his thought in the Stone Lectures at Princeton University in 1898, he chose as the title of his lectures: *Calvinism*.[6] He insisted that the significance of the sixteenth century Reformation could not be confined to the ecclesiastical affairs of the church institution if it were to remain a potent force in modern culture. Instead, he took up the reins of cultural leadership and formation where Calvin had left them and brought Christ back into everyday modern life.

Kuyper realized that the social problems facing his age were not just limited to the relations between church and state, as Pope Pius XIII supposed, but also with the mutual relationships between all social institutions. How does one distinguish social institutions from each other? he asked. He answered only by observing the diversity of authority. To Kuyper social friction arises when the authority proper to one social sphere goes beyond itself to control another social sphere and hence cause life in both spheres to suffer the damage resulting from such a conflict. It has occurred repeatedly that those in authority in one social sphere have interfered with the office-bearers in another social institution. In this way the states and churches of Europe have more than once intruded into each other's affairs. Whenever this happened, things have gone wrong in the practical conduct of affairs. One has only to think of the struggle for power during the Middle Ages between the emperors of Germany and the medieval popes. As Kuyper saw it, social problems are fundamentally problems involving the *structure* or "set-up" of the social spheres. If social harmony between church and state, state and education, state and industry is to prevail in modern society, then it is necessary to understand the true nature and origin of social institutions. As a true Calvinist, Kuyper finds the true nature and origin of social institutions in the sovereign plan and purpose of the Sovereign God of the Scriptures. That is to say, he grounds his social and political doctrine in God's creation ordinances and law structures, rather than in Aristotle's doctrine of the reasonable nature of the so-called "natural" man. For Kuyper there is no "natural" sphere of life somehow apart from God, but there is only God's creation as it unfolds itself in history.

As both Kuyper and Dooyeweerd see it, a true knowledge of reality is only possible in the light of a true knowledge of God provided in the Bible. If a person does not have this knowledge of God within his heart, then he cannot hope to know the truth about God's works in creation in their full coherence, unity, and diversity. The truth about the structures of creation is bound up with the truth about the Creator. For both men, God is the ground of all that exists and therefore the source of all truth. Christ as the perfect revelation of God is the fulness of the meaning of Truth. Apart from this trancendental basis and fulness of truth in Christ the Logos of God, the a priori temporal dimension of truth has no meaning or validity. In other words, it is only by accepting God's special revelation in the Bible that we can hope to understand the meaning of any fact in the world. Facts are what they are in the last analysis only by virtue of the place and function they occupy in God's sovereign plan and purpose. Every fact is a God-created and a God-interpreted fact.[9]

Apostate humanistic science has tried by its own "scientific method" to give man command of the so-called "facts," but without a scriptural framework for their interpretation these "facts" only remain disintegrated bits of information that in themselves are not real knowledge but only what Michael Oakeshott calls in *Experience and Its Modes*[10] "arrests in experience." Only when they become integrated into the fullness of our personal experience of God, each other, and the world can they enter into our knowledge of reality. The question of knowledge thus has everything to do with the question of meaning. Unrelated "facts" as such have no meaning. Before facts can become part of our knowledge, they need to be related to each other in terms of some basic ordering principle and framework of interpretation or total view of the world. Brute facts simply do not exist. They only become meaningful in an order; they can only speak to us when they have been *structured*. To know anything worthwhile about "facts" one must first have an awareness of order. Facts require norms and structural principles for their existence and a frame of reference for their adequate interpretation.

Kuyper and Dooyeweerd teach that all truly scientific thought must take its point of departure in God's Word rather than in man's fallen reason before it can become truly scientific. God is the inescapable premise of all valid human thought. Man either faces a world of total chance and brute factuality, a world in which no fact has any meaning or relationship to any other fact, or else he accepts the world of God's creation, subject to his sovereign law. Only on this presupposition, Dooyeweerd holds, is a valid natural and social science possible.

For this reason they would agree with R. J. Rushdoony, who writes in *The Mythology of Science*[11] that "the non-Christian is able to formulate and discover only because he operates on secretly Christian premises while denying that faith," as well as with Robert Reymond's judgment that "No fact is truly known unless its createdness in the biblical sense is owned by the scientist." [12]

The Book of Genesis reveals that man has been called to be a scientist as well as a worker in God's creation as part of his great cultural mandate. Thus Adam was given the task of "naming" everything in God's creation, i.e., to classify it (Gen. 2:19-20). Such intelligent predication would have been impossible unless God existed as the reference point and ground and origin of all meaning.[13] *God's Word alone can provide man with a unified field of knowledge.*

In the light of this scriptural perspective upon science we can understand the problematics and dilemmas of apostate contemporary natural and social science, especially in the fields of sociology, economics, and political science. On the one hand the empiricists try to reduce the meaning and structure of social "facts" to mere factors of heredity and environment and to find in the verification principle the only criterion of truth.[14] Under the influence of their apostate faith in science as man's only savior, many modern sociologists have supposed that they could establish and examine social relationships as pure "facts" apart from any normative view starting from the order of God's creation. Thus Emile Durkheim tried to look for "things" in the social world which he could classify into species in the same way that biologists classify plants and animals.

It is in fact very difficult to find an empirical characteristic which might serve to demarcate the social law-sphere of God's creation from the other aspects. Even Durkheim himself recognized this in practice, for his own definition of the social involves a complex theoretical complex. According to him social facts are to be distinguished from other kinds of fact by the fact that they are external to the individual and exercise restraint over him. It is this coercive feature of society which Durkheim saw as its chief characteristic. For Durkheim sociology is the study of such social facts, which he defined in his *Rules of Sociological Method*[15] as ways of acting, thinking, and feeling general in a society, which exert coercion upon the individual to conform. Clearly this definition does not tell us by what empirical characteristics social facts may be recognized, though by confusing the perspective of the scientist with that of the observed participant (who can distinguish the social from the non social in this way?) Durkheim gives us the impression that it does. But even he recognizes that it is unsatisfactory, for he goes on to give a second definition of a social fact as, "every way of acting, which is general throughout a given society, while at the same time existing independently of its individual manifestations!"[16] But this definition is no more satisfactory than the first, for, though in its first part it seems to offer an empirical means of differentiating the social from the non social, Durkheim insists that this alone would be an insufficient characterization of the social. Everything therefore turns on the second part of the definition, but here we are faced with a metaphysical conception which Durkheim claims to have avoided in his search for an objective "neutral" approach to his subject. For this reason the writer would agree with John Rex's statement in *Key Problems of Sociological Theory*[17] that "Durkheim's attempt to provide a purely empirical criterion of the social is a failure. And this is not surprising. For the fact of the matter is that the actual data with which sociology is concerned, and which it seeks to explain, consists of human behavior and the products of human behavior, the same data with which psychologists, economists, and historians have to deal. The difference lies not in the data, but in the different theoretical frame of reference, in terms of which the data are interpreted. It was Durkheim's great merit as a sociological theorist that he saw and insisted upon the distinctiveness of sociological, as contrasted with psychological explanations. Unfortunately, however, his empiricist bias as a methodologist prevented him from clarifying the true nature of the difference."[18]

While Durkheim tried to explain human society in modes of thought derived from biology, the German scholar Max Weber tried to do so in historical and logical categories. According to Weber, in whose analysis of the fundamental concepts of sociology the notion of "action" plays a central part, the defining feature of human action is its "meaningfulness." Thus in his famous definition he writes in *The Theory of Social and Economic Organization*, "in action is included all human behavior insofar as the actor attaches a subjective meaning to it." [19] Weber distinguishes between four types of action: (1) Rational action in relation to a goal. (2) Rational actional action in relation to a value. (3) Affective or emotional action. (4) Traditional action.[20] Weber thus starts with a frankly subjective approach to sociological theory unlike Durkheim, who claimed to be objective in his approach. He defines rationality in terms of the knowledge of the actor rather than of the observer, as Durkheim does, and he conceived of sociology as a comprehensive science of social action, which would render man's social, economic, and political behavior in societies past and present more intelligible. As a methodological device he made use of his famous "ideal" types to make social action more intelligible. Weber distinguished his ideal type sharply from Durkheim's notion of the average type and insisted that its purpose is not descriptive but explanatory. He also insisted that it is a construction of the scientists, rather than something which emerges in a simple way from the facts.

Weber's Ideal type is related to his notion of comprehension of social action, in that every ideal type is an organization of intelligible relations within a historical reality or sequences of events. Again, the ideal type is related to a characteristic of both modern society and modern science, namely a process of rationalization. The construction of ideal types was an expression of Weber's attempt to render the subject matter of history, economics, and sociology more intelligible by revealing or constructing its internal rationality, or meaning. Finally, the use of such ideal types helps us, Weber claims, to obtain a better comprehension of man's past and present experience. According to Raymond Aron in *Main Currents in Sociological Thought*, Weber used his ideal types to designate three kinds of concepts. Aron lists these as follows:

1. First, ideal types of historical particulars, such as capitalism

of the Western (European) city. These two examples represent a species of ideal type, namely the intelligible reconstruction of a global and particular historical reality, global since the term *capitalism* designates a whole economic regime; particular since according to Weber capitalism as he defines it has been fully realized only in modern Western societies. The ideal type of a historical particular remains a partial reconstruction since the sociologist selects a certain number of traits from the historical whole to constitute an intelligible reality. . . .

2. A second species is that of ideal types which designate abstract elements of the historical reality, elements which are found in a large number of cases. In combination, these concepts enable us to characterize and understand actual historical wholes.

The difference between these two kinds of concepts will be clearly seen if we take capitalism as an example of the first species and bureaucracy as an example of the second. In the first case we are designating an actual historical entity unlike any other, whereas in the second we are referring to an institution, or an aspect of political institutions, which does not cover a whole regime and of which one finds many examples at different moments in history. These ideal types of elements characteristic of society occur on various levels of abstraction, of which I shall indicate only three.

First, such concepts as bureaucracy or feudalism. Second, the three types of domination, rational, traditional, and charismatic. Each of these is defined by the motivation of obedience or by the nature of legitimacy claimed by the leader. . . . The third and highest level of abstraction is the level of the types of action: rational action with reference to goals, rational action with respect to values, traditional action, and affective action.

3. The third species of ideal types includes those that constitute rationalizing reconstructions of a particular kind of behavior. For example, according to Weber, all propositions in economic theory are merely ideal-typical reconstructions of the ways men would behave if they were pure economic subjects. Economic theory rigorously conceives economic behavior as consistent with its essence, this essence being defined in a precise manner.[21]

The "ideal" type is for Weber neither a judgment of value nor one of fact. It is a pure hypothesis on the basis of a large number of social facts. It is a historical and logical construction, and therefore not a structural principle governing sociological data.

Dooyeweerd points out in his *New Critique of Theoretical Thought* that such types cannot really give us any real understanding of the inner nature of the state, of a university, of a church, of an industrial enterprise. The reason being that none of these social institutions can be identified with the variable and changing factual relationships in which their internal structural types are realized in the course of history. The structure of individuality of all these social structures has been laid down in principle at the beginning of the creation and they urge themselves upon man and cannot be changed by him. "This is why the real structural principles of human society can never be replaced by constructed "ideal types," in the sense of Max Weber." [22] Weber's "ideal" types in fact reflect his basic historicism, that is, his tendency to explain all the other aspects of God's creation in terms of the historical aspect, which he then absolutizes.

As long as social scientists hold to such a conception of "ideal" types they preclude themselves from obtaining a real insight into the basic problem of sociology, namely, that of discovering a total view of human society. Lacking such a total view or ordering principle, they are forced to interpret social phenomena in terms of one particular aspect of reality, such as biology or history or psychology, which they then deify. According to Dooyeweerd, it is this lack which accounts for the emergence of the various schools of apostate modern sociology.

Such apostate scholars tend to suppose that the nature of man, and in it the nature of all temporal things, finds its center and root in the human "reason." Yet, as Dooyeweerd has shown, this reason is in reality nothing other than a composite of our temporal functions of consciousness, functions of our self, only an aspect of our heart in the full scriptural sense. Temporal organic life, sense of beauty, man's function in historical development, in language, in legal, economic, and social life—all these are also functions of the human heart in this profound biblical sense.

Fallen man, however, falsely supposes that human existence has its origin in "reason" as man's supposed supra-temporal center, and even that God himself is Absolute Reason. As a result, he comes to identify the findings of his reason in scientific abstraction with the "whole" truth and excludes all naive or integral experience of God's creation as mere ignorant opinion.

At the same time, apostate scholars must still have their absolute, even if this means that they must distort what their observation discloses only to be relative. Their rational analysis of social phenomena is accompanied by a deeper drive, which in their unregenerate state as sinners requires a distortion of the very facts they are in process of analyzing. As we have seen in the case of contemporary sociology, apostate scholars do not agree on what they thus absolutize. The various schools of modern sociology are characterized by this absolutization of a specific modal aspect of God's creation in their attempts to grasp the nature of human society in a theoretical view of totality. Such absolutizations cannot be corrected by other absolutizations. The very problem is how a general sociology may avoid them, that is, to say from what standpoint a sociological view of the totality of the different modal aspects of God's creation is possible.

According to Herman Dooyeweerd, only the Word of God can provide the scholar with a sure point of departure for his theoretical life. Only by accepting God's Word as the ordering principle of his scientific work, can the scientist hope to make any sense of the vast array of the facts around him. God's Word alone can provide him with a sure frame of reference and point of departure for all his thinking about reality. It does so by working in the human heart a true knowledge of God, of one's self, and of the Law-Order of the creation. The Word of God is the power by which the Holy Spirit opens up the human heart to "see' things as they really are. True knowledge is thus made possible by true religion, and it can only arise from the knowing activity of the human heart being enlightened through the Word of God by the Holy Spirit. The biblical motive of creation, fall into sin, and redemption by Jesus Christ in the communion of the Holy spirit is thus the key to the knowledge of God and of the self which alone can open to us the revelation of God in the Scriptures and in all the wonderful works of His creation.

In the light of this scriptural perspective upon science we can now understand the problematics and dilemmas of contemporary social science. On the one hand, the school of empiricists have tried to reduce the meaning and structure of social facts to biology. On the other hand, the functional and historical schools of Max Weber, Talcott Parsons, and Robert K. Merton have sought to explain social behavior in terms of action theory and of ideal types.[23] This conflict in sociology between empiricist and historical and functionalist corresponds to that of vitalist and mechanist in modern apostate biology. It only arises from an apostate and therefore false way of "seeing" social reality. Without a true ordering principle in God's Word, empiricists, functionalists, behaviorists, idealists, and historicists are unable to explain satisfactorily the behavior of man in societies past or present, or the relations which should exist between the various communities and associations of human society. Instead, they tend to reduce the social aspect of creation to historical, logical, psychological, and biological modes of explanation.

(c) *The Reformed Doctrine of Sphere Sovereignty*

(1) *Sphere Sovereignty in Science*

Such reduction in science can be avoided only by understanding the biblical doctrine of sphere sovereignty. The expression "sphere sovereignty" stems, as far as we know, from Abraham Kuyper. When Kuyper first used this term he mainly conceived of it in terms of God's creation ordinances for practical societal institutions, such as the church as an institution, the state, the school, university, and industry. In his view there is no one social institution such as the state of which all the others are merely parts. On the contrary, each social structure has been instituted by God to carry out its own specific task, and it derives its authority over the individual directly from God and not from any other social institution. By "spheres," therefore, Kuyper understood exclusively societal institutions. He conceived of these spheres not modally but regionally, because he did not distinguish clearly between sovereignty and autonomy. In spite of this limitation, the real scriptural character of his view should be recognized. The diversity of authority in the social spheres is in direct correlation with the diversity of authority. It does not find its origin in arbitrary human choice as apostate social scientists have supposed, but in the wealth of God's creation activity.

Had it not been for Kuyper's practical sociological pluralism, the struggle for educational freedom, which still remains undecided in the English-speaking world, would never have been achieved in the Netherlands. Thanks to Kuyper's doctrine of sphere sovereignty, the Dutch electorate was persuaded to grant full educational freedom to Christians as well as socialists and humanists.

It remained for Kuyper's successors at the Free University to draw out the full scientific and philosophical implications of his greatest doctrine. Thanks to the work of Dooyeweerd and D. H. Th. Vollenhoven, it is now recognized in Reformed circles that sphere sovereignty operates socially, ontically, and epistemologically. The diversity of authority in the social spheres is paralleled by the modal diversity of the great modal spheres or law-aspects studied by science.

Kuyper lived in the high noon of positivism in science. This tendency in Western thought, in common with the rationalist tradition of the seventeenth century, overrated mathematics and physics as the ideal sciences towards which all others should seek to approximate. Along with this similarity, however, there also emerged a difference, which should not be neglected. Descartes and Leibniz had limited themselves to the study of subjects below the analytical law-sphere. (See Chart at the end of this book.) For this reason, the thinkers of the *Aufklarung* or Enlightenment who developed an intense interest in subjects above the analytical law-sphere, such as history, language, social communication, the state, ethics, and theology, saw no possibility for including these fields or subjects in science or for ascribing them to Kant's "practical reason."[24]

The positivists such as August Comte and Spencer, who also shared such broadness of interests with the men of the Enlightenment, rejected the solution of expanding the boundaries of science beyond the mathematical and physical so as to include these newer social sciences. Instead, they demanded the positivization of the social studies. Thus Comte in his *Cours de Philosophie Positive* spoke of the law of the three stages of human evolution and the necessity for a new classification of the sciences.[25] The law of the three stages consists in his assertion that the human mind passes through three phases. In the first, the mind explains phenomena by ascribing them to beings or forces comparable to man himself. In the second phase, that of metaphysics, the mind explains phenomena by invoking abstract entities like "nature." Finally, in the third phase, man is content to observe phenomena and to establish the regular links existing among them. He abandons the search for the final principle behind the facts and confines himself to establishing the laws that govern them.

But this transition from the theological age to the metaphysical age and thence to the positive age does not occur simultaneously in all the varied intellectual disciplines. In Comte's thinking, the law of the three stages has no precise meaning unless it is combined with the classification of the sciences. For it is the order in which the sciences are ranked that reveals the order in which the intelligence becomes "positive." The positive method was adopted sooner in mathematics, in physics, and in chemistry than in biology. There are reasons why positivism is slower to appear in disciplines relating to the most complex matters. The simpler the object of study, the easier it is to think positively. Writing of this analysis of the development of "positive" science, Raymond Aron says in his *Main Currents of Sociological Thought*:

> The combination of the law of the three stages and the classification of the sciences leads to Auguste Comte's basic formula: the method which has triumphed in mathematics, astronomy, physics, chemistry, and biology must eventually prevail in politics and culminate in the founding of a positive science of society, which is called sociology. . . . Comte's sociology was meant to resolve the crisis of the modern world, to provide a system of scientific ideas which will preside over the reorganization of society.[26]

While Comte was surely correct in demanding the inclusion of disciplines relating to man in society within the domain of science, he was in error in supposing that the methods which had proved so successful in natural science would prove equally valuable in the study of human society. Instead of relating the diversity of subject matter dealt with by such disciplines as history, law, ethics, economics, sociology, and theology to a diversity of methods of research, Comte called for one method, namely, the mathematical-physical method of observation, classification, and measurement in terms of causal laws. Inspired and driven by his faith in the modern humanist science ideal, he became blinded to the great diversity of God's modal law-spheres and the consequent need for a multiplicity of areas of research. As such Comte has been described by F. A. Fayek in *The Counter-Revolution of Science* as guilty of the methodological fallacy of scientism. Scientism is, briefly, the illegitimate extension to the treatment of the social sciences of the methods which have succeeded so well in the natural.[27] It is assumed without question that these methods are universally appropriate. Hence, as Hayek puts it, "the scientistic, as distinguished from the scientific, view is not an unprejudiced but a very prejudiced approach which before it has considered its subject, claims to know what is the most appropriate way of investigating it." [28] But in fact Hayek claims there are radical differences between the subject-matters of the natural and social sciences. For example, the natural sciences make a distinction between appearance and reality. The stick in water *looks* crooked, but, says physics, *is* straight. The fire seems to have heat, but, says science, this heat is nothing but the rapid movement and collision of non hot molecules. This habit of distinguishing between appearance and fact has gone so far that the language of contemporary science is no longer able to describe the appearances of things except in so far as they can be expressed mathematically.

It follows that what man thinks about—namely, the external world of things—constitutes for the physicist an initial obstacle to his inquiry which has to be overcome; it is never a datum *for* his inquiries. Now contrast the social sciences; these deal not with the relations between things but with the relations beween men and things and, still more, with the relations between men and men. Hence, for them, what matters is not so much what things are "as what the acting people think they are." This is not merely to say that the social as opposed to the natural sciences deal with "the phenomena of individual minds" and not directly with "material phenomena"; it is to insist that the data of the social sciences "cannot be defined in the objective terms of the physical sciences, but only in terms of human beliefs." Hayek illustrates his argument with examples.

Neither a "commodity" or an "economic good" nor "food" or "money" can be defined in physical terms, but only in terms of the views people hold about things. Economic theory has nothing to say about the little round discs of metal as which an objective or materialist view might try to define money.[29]

Is it not then obvious, Hayek asks, that to apply the methods of the natural to the social sciences is to extend them to a subject matter with which they may be wholly unfitted o deal?

While welcoming Hayek's insights regarding the difference between natural and social science, the writer cannot accept the humanistic philosophy underlying Hayek's own position. Just as Comte is driven by the science ideal of the modern nature-freedom ground motive, so Hayek himself is in the grip of the personality pole of this selfsame motive. No more than the positivists can Hayek accept the existence of a structural unity in diversity of created reality. The very idea of structure, given to "nature" apart from man's creative freedom, is something which all humanists, whether idealist or positivist, must reject. For both wings of apostate humanism man through his reason or through his autonomous freedom must create this structure for himself.

Until Hayek accepts the creation structures given by God, he will not be able to account adequately for the diversity of the subject matter of the various scientific disciplines. The diversity of methods in science arises not in the human reason, as Hayek supposes, but in the diversity of God's great law-spheres.

In *Renewal and Reflection* Herman Dooyeweerd points out:

The created reality displays, in the order of time, a great multiplicity of aspects or modes of being in which its religious root breaks open into a wealth of colors, just as the unbroken light is broken up into the gamut of colors of the rainbow when it passes through the prism.

These modes of being are the aspects of number, of space, of movement, of energy, of organic life, of psychical life, of logical differentiation, of historical cultural development, of symbolic meaning, of social relations, of economic value, of aesthetic harmony, of law, or moral worth, and of the assurance of faith.

These aspects of reality constitute the provinces of research of the differentiated professional sciences, of mathematics, of the physical sciences, of biology, of psychology, of logic, of history, linguistics, sociology, economics, of aesthetics, jurisprudence, of ethics, and of theology. Each of these sciences views reality only in one of its aspects.

Suppose for a moment, that science without the light of a true knowledge of God and of self directs itself upon the investigation of these various spheres of reality. That science would then be in a position similar to a man who views the colors of the rainbow without having knowledge of the unbroken light which is broken up by a prism into these colors. These colors seem to blend. Would such a man, if he were to ask himself where the different shades of color originate, not be inclined to proclaim one color gamut as the origin of all the others? And would he then be able to discover the exact mutual relation and coherence between the colors? And if he were not able to do so, how then would he be able to become acquainted with each one of the color-gamuts as to their own inner character?

If he is not color blind, he will indeed continue to distinguish, but he will take as a starting point the shade most striking to him and view all the others as shades of the absolutized one.

Such is the man who believes to find in science the basis and starting point for his view of temporal reality. Repeatedly such a man will be inclined to identify a certain aspect of reality, e.g., that of organic life, or that of emotion, or that of the historical cultural development, with the total reality and to reduce all other aspects to the various modes of revelation of that one, absolutized aspect.... Take modern "materialism," for example, which traces the whole temporal reality back to the movement of material particles. Or take the modern naturalistic philosophy of life, which views everything in the one-sided light of the organic development of life. In truth, it is not science as such which drives man towards such absolutizing, but the idolatrous, religious ground-motive which has taken hold of his thought processes.

Science can only teach us reality in the theoretical explanation of its many aspects. It teaches us, as such, neither the knowledge of the more profound unity, nor the origin of these aspects. It is religion which motivates us to search for this unity and origin because it compels us to concentrate all that is relative upon the absolute ground and origin of all things, because it continually drives men to the knowledge of God and self.

As soon as an idolatrous ground-motive takes hold of us it compels our thought to absolutize that which is relative, and' to deify that which is created. On account of this, false religious prejudices obscure our conception of the *structure* of reality.

He who absolutizes created reality according to one of its aspects can no longer comprehend any one of its aspects in their own inner character. He has a false view of reality which, however, in no way prevents him from discovering various important moments of truth. However, these moments of truth are taken up by him into a false total view of reality. As a matter of fact, it is exactly in this false view of reality that they become the most dangerous and poisonous weapons of deception.[30]

These sovereign law-spheres are the ways in which created reality exists, and so Dooyeweerd calls them modes or modalities. Since these never appear as separate entities but are always aspects of individual things, he calls them law-aspects. Since they appear only with things existing in time, he calls them functions. They are not to be confused with Kant's so-called transcendental postulates or categories of human thought. And thus they are irreducible and may not be brought back to more basic modes, as is done, for example, in rationalism, in which the aspects which are higher than the analytical are considered as mere constructions postulated by the human mind. Similar reductions can be found in historicism, in which all reality is subsumed under the category of historical modes of thought or biologism or Marx's dialectical materialism.

Since these aspects are "ontic" (existing apart from man's mind), they cannot be reduced to each other, and thus we can rightly speak of the relationship of these aspects or law-spheres as "sovereign in their own orbit." Each law-sphere has a status rooted in its divinely instituted nature, which cannot be infringed upon without harm and falsity resulting since each sphere of existence has received from the Creator its own peculiar nature and has been created "each after its own kind." The capacities of one sphere may not be transferred or appropriated by another sphere. This constitutes its modal sovereignty, in virtue of which each modal sphere is equal, with its own distinctive part to play in the great economy of creation.

At the same time these various spheres of the creation function in an unbreakable coherence with each other within the framework of the cosmic order given and upheld by God. Thus the scriptural principle of sphere sovereignty not only teaches us the mutual irreducibility, but also the indissoluble interrelatedness and mutual coherence of all aspects of reality in the order of temporal becoming. No aspect is a thing cut off from the other aspects; in each aspect we find a modal expression of the integral and radical character of the religious fulness of meaning of created reality.

As an illustration we may give the "aesthetic" aspect of a concrete work of art. A painting or a symphony cannot exist without a number of parts. Yet that number is not number in the sense of arithmetical number, but an aesthetic mirroring of the aspect of number; the parts are still aesthetic parts. There must also be aesthetic space, movement, economy, etc.

This creation *principle of sphere-universality* is what has supplied whatever grounds apostate scholars have been able to adduce ·for their attempts to find the whole meaning of reality in what is actually but one aspect. Yet the mirroring of all the sides is not the same thing as all the sides. It is here, therefore, that all the "isms," e.g., materialism, historicism, psychologism, legalism, moralism, and aestheticism arise and find a specious legitimacy, but ultimately flounder. Each seems to have something important to say for itself; yet in the light of a scriptural framework of science is seen in fact to be only an apostate religious distortion of the religious fulness of meaning, of reality. Only when the scriptural ground-motive completely directs our thinking can we hope to "see" reality in its true nature and structure by showing us both the inner character of each law-sphere and its coherence with all the other spheres.

The modal spheres do not, however, exist only in horizontal dependence of each other, and vertical dependence upon God. They exhibit, Dooyeweerd teaches, an order of increasing complication in accordance with the order of the succession of the spheres in the temporal coherence of meaning. Because immanentistic apostate philosophy could not grasp this idea of a cosmic order of modal spheres, and thus necessarily eliminated the temporal order and inter-modal coherence of the spheres, it cannot offer a satisfactory account of the relation between the different aspects of reality, and tends to "see" it merely as one of increasing *logical* complexity. But the modal spheres may never be identified in this way with the so-called "categories of thought" or with any arbitrary theoretical delimitation or reduction.

Each law-sphere is characterized by a certain specificity, a modal moment or kernel which guarantees it irreducible specific meaning. Thus the faith modality is characterized by the modal moment or kernel of transcendent certainty regarding the Origin of all being and meaning, the ethical modal moment by love of one's neighbor, the juridical by retribution, the aesthetic by harmony, the economic by thrift or economy, the social by social intercourse, the linguistic by symbolic signification, the historical by the cultural process of development of human society, the analytical by theoretical distinction, the psychical by feeling and sensation, the biological by organic life, the physical by energy, the kinematic by movement, the spatial by extension, and the numerical by discrete quantity. This irreducibility does not imply that a law-sphere exists in and by itself. It is, rather, an aspect of empirical reality whose modal meaning can only reveal itself within the inter-modal meaning coherence with all the other aspects. Each modal sphere is a refraction of the religious fulness of meaning; consequently, the temporal order of the modal spheres must be expressed in each sphere. Each sphere has a modal moment, irreducible to that of any other, which safeguards its orbital sovereignty. But surrounding the modal moments are a number of *analogical* moments, some of which refer back to the modal moments of preceding or substratum spheres, others to the modal moments of succeeding or superstratum spheres. The first are called modal retrocipations, the second modal anticipations. Both analogical moments are qualified by the modal moment of their sphere.

The retrocipatory moments are constitutive of a modality. The anticipatory moments are regulative; they open up and deepen the meaning of the aspects. The fundamental concepts of a science are formulated by the analogies between the modalities which "precede" the particular science being studied, e.g., in the case of the juridical modality the numerical through to the aesthetic law-spheres and the juridical modality itself.

In the study of jurisprudence Dooyeweerd thus distinguishes between the concept of justice and the idea of justice. The former is formulated by discovering the analogies between the lower modalities and the juridical modality. The idea of justice is formulated by discovering the relation between law and the higher functions, namely those of ethics and faith.

In its relation to the lower aspects of reality we must thus think of the legal modality in its restrictive funcion. If legal life develops only in relation to these lower aspects, then it remains closed, e.g., the primitive idea of corporate personality and the custom of blood vengeance against the whole clan, family, or tribe to which the individual murderer belonged. But as soon as law develops in relation to morality and faith, then we discover a deepening of legal life, e.g., the principle of equity before the law is a moral deepening of legal rules, so that the individual factor can be given a greater play; the introduction of the notion of guilt and of individual responsibility are both moral refractions upon the law.

From the vantage point of its aspectual structures, reality reveals itself in this way as a modal diversity in intermodal cohesion. In principle, the respective modal spheres determine the border lines between the various special sciences. The elementary basic concepts employed in each science are ultimately oriented to these analogical moments, that is, the points of inter-connection between the modal moment of the aspect being studied and the other modalities.

The following is an example of the modal moment, modal retrocipations and anticipations as exemplified in the analytical logical law-sphere.

MODAL MOMENT: rational distinction
Retrocipations: logical apperception
                  logical thought life
                  logical movement of thought
                  logical thought-space
                  logical unity and multiplicity

Anticipations: logical domination (ruling by systematic
                      theoretical concepts of logical forms)
                   logical symbolics
                   logical commerce
                   logical economy of thought
                   logical harmony
                   logical right
                   logical eros (platonic love)
                   logical certitude.

(2) *Sphere Sovereignty in Society*

Just as in the natural world God has created everything after its
own kind and with its own peculiar nature, so in man's social world
he has ordained that what man constructs in the domain of culture
and history shall have its own peculiar nature and structure. In history and culture we find the institutional embodiments of the created
order. In the Reformed view creation is not a temporal event. It is
the "calling into being" of all things by the Creator. But this refers
to the order of reality, and it does not imply that all things, e.g., the
state, already exist in actuality at the beginning, for history is the
unfolding of God's creation order in time, so that in history the
state, the business enterprise, the labor union appear as the factual expressions of God's creation order. Here Dooyeweerd distinguishes
between (a) the law-side and (b) the subject-side. The state, the
labor union, the business enterprise, etc., were (are) present in creation with respect to the "law-side" but not with respect to the
"subject-side" (i.e., the empirical reality).

Just as our view of reality as a whole will be determined by our
religious presuppositions regarding the origin and nature of this
world, so our view of the peculiar character and mutual relationships
of the different spheres of society will be governed by our initial
religious and philosophical starting point. The scriptural ground-
motive of creation, man's fall into radical sin, and his equally radical
redemption in Jesus Christ alone enables us to understand the various
aspects of society in their true character, mutual relationships, and
coherence.

What then, in the light of this biblical ground-motive, is the true root unity of society? Is it the Church as Roman Catholics believe, or the state as Communists and Socialists believe, or Big Business as capitalists believe, or the individual as anarchists suppose? It is none of these institutions or persons. Instead, Christians believe that Christ alone is the root unity of human society. As Dooyeweerd says in answer to our question:

> It is the religious root-community of mankind, which fell in Adam, but has been restored in communion with God of Christ. With this revelation of the eternal root communion of mankind which is fundamental to all temporal societal relationships the Christian religion places itself in an absolute antithesis with every view of society which absolutizes and deifies any one particular temporal societal form or institution. . . . Only if man understands the true religious root-unity of mankind will he be able to perceive the essential nature, the correct mutual relationships and coherence of the distinct spheres of human society. This relationship is again the relationship of sphere sovereignty which can only reveal itself in an indissoluble relationship of all spheres.
>
> What does the term "sphere sovereignty" mean with regard to temporal human society? It guarantees to each of the social-spheres an essential nature and life principle of their own; and so it has a sphere of original authority and jurisdiction. This authority is derived from God's sovereign authority; it is not derived from the authority of one of the other spheres.[31]

The divine order for human society manifests itself in a great variety of specific ordinances or creation structures. All these ordinances not only find their origin in God, but they are continually upheld by Him in His divine omnipotence and temporal conserving common grace. In Him they find their ultimate purpose. They are the instruments through which God executes His lordship and activates human life along stable ways. In and through these ordinances or social structures the Lord God confronts man. That is to say that they are not a "natural datum" like the laws of physics, but rather they are laid upon man as norms to be realized, actualized, or positivized in history. Or, to put it another way, God calls man into His service as His co-worker in the realization of a righteous, just, peaceful, and holy political, economic, and social order. "The heavens, even the heavens are the Lord's; but he has given the earth to man." These words of the psalmist put the focus on man's function and place in God's creation. Man is God's office-bearer in God's creation. Man is called to be God's steward. As Paul G. Schrotenboer well says:

> In the broadest sense the idea of office refers to man's administration of the entire world which God has given to him to manage. The creation account in Genesis clearly states that God placed man over the world to rule it in obedience to his Maker. . . .
>
> The idea of office refers to the way God uses man to administer the world. Man's office in the world is his stewardship of life, that is, the way he orders his life and all things given him to control. . . .
>
> The office of man is his *position in relationship*. His position, as it relates to God, constitutes him a *servant* who is called to obedience. As it relates to fellow man it makes man a *guardian*, who must bring his charge to maturity. As it relates to the world it constitutes man a steward who must faithfully exercise dominion in the name of God. . . .
>
> God intended that man's life in its entirety would be service. To that service God appointed him, for that service he gave him the gifts he needs and of that service God calls man to give account. Man in office is always considered "before the face of God."
>
> In his relation to fellow men, man the office bearer is a guardian and a member. He is put in charge of others, e.g., as parent, as teacher, as ruler. . . . God has arranged men in a relation of higher and lower. Some rule, others are ruled. . . .
>
> In his relation to the world man is a steward to whom God entrusts the entire creation. He must use it, exercise lordship over it and give God a record of what he does with what he has received. . . . Every man has an office. Being a Christian and an office-bearer are one and the same. Individually and as a group Christians are incorporated in the "body" of which Christ is the head.[32]

According to God's Word, then, human culture is the fulfilment of the great cultural, scientific, economic, and political mandate given to man at the beginning of his history. "Replenish the earth and subdue it, and have dominion over it" (Gen. 1:28).

The social ordinances given by God are laws of structure which determine man's task as office-bearer in God's creation as well as of the various relationships of society in terms of which this task has to be carried out. As office-bearer man functions in a multiplicity of institutions such as the family, the state, the political and legal order as well as the church as an institution. Each of these structures has its own divinely planned order or "set-up," whether or not those who take part in these social groupings acknowledge this order, either in theory or in practice. Each of these social structures stands in God's world with its own specific task to perform, which cannot be arbitrarily changed by man. If he tries to do so, then he comes under God's judgment. A great historian has recognized this truth in his dictum, "The history of the world is the judgment of the world." Arnold Toynbee has counted at least twenty civilizations that have come under God's judgment for failing to obey the laws for their various social structures.

Each of these social groups displays in its broadest outlines a constant structure, and each is subject to its own specific law of structure, which it cannot negate without suffering disintegration and loss. Thus does the living God of the Bible maintain His sovereignty over human society.

The developments within Russia after the Bolshevik Revolution in 1917 are a striking confirmation of this biblical doctrine of society and its divinely given social ordinances. The Communist leaders, in spite of their apostate godless theories of free sex, trial marriage, easy divorce, and the common ownership of property, were forced by the resulting social confusion and breakdown of family and economic and social life to reacknowledge, at least to a certain extent, the intrinsic significance of marriage and family life as well as that of private property and the need for economic incentives. Here in the midst of man's rebellion against God's creation ordinances for human society, something of His righteousness and superior power was revealed.

(d) *Norms and Directives*

The divine act of creation established the order which determines the nature of all "natural" and "social" structures and "facts."

Dooyeweerd expresses this fundamental teaching of the Christian religion in terms of a basic distinction between the "law-side" and the "factual subject-side" of creation. The law-spheres (see chart at end of book), in turn, reflect this distinction; in each modal aspect there is a correlation between modal laws and the respective modal functions of facts subject to these laws (cf. e.g., the different modal sense of physical, biological, sensitive, economic, and juridical facts, etc.) In the pre-analytical aspects the modal laws have the character of "natural" rules; in the analytical and post-analytical aspects they have the character of norms.

Thus plants and stones and animals, though subject to God's law, function according to God's law without being addressed by Him in the same manner as God addresses man. They have no option but to live in accordance with the law of their own created being and nature. Neither animals nor plants function subjectively in the analytical and following law-spheres, but only objectively. Only man functions in these modalities as a person created in God's holy image. For this reason these modalities may be termed normative law-spheres in contrast to the preceding law-spheres which are a-normative (see chart), because the law in these spheres is given to man in the manner of a norm, principle, or directive which requires his obedient positivization in history.

Only in terms of this distinction and within this scriptural frame of reference can we hope to solve the intractable problem of "facts" and of "values" in the social sciences. Within the normative law-spheres "facts" assume axiological qualities which are constitutive for their modal meaning within these aspects. In other words, without values there are no facts in the post-analytical law-spheres. Without the use of structural principles, categories of explanation and postulates we cannot obtain any understanding of any social fact. It is impossible, for example, to explain monogamy merely in terms of custom. Before we can intelligently discuss any marriage custom we must have a prior idea or standard of marriage in our minds in terms of which we can evaluate the particular expression of marriage. Of this necessity for value in social science Dooyeweerd writes:

One has to keep in mind that the factual social relations in human society can never be determined apart from some essential social norms. This implies that the causal explanation is impossible in sociology and economics without applying social norms. By way of example, we wish to maintain that the causal explanation of increasing criminality from factors (such as the wrong kind of social environment, the bad-housing situation, economic crises, etc.), relates facts of an obviously normative character. If one tried to eliminate consistently all normative adjudication, one will discover that one is left with no essential social facts at all.[33]

If being under God's law is what gives meaning to the creation, it follows that facts and values are intimately intertwined and related. Nowhere are there any loose facts that are unrelated facts. A fact is always related to God's law for the creation, whether the fact is a thing, a relation, or an evaluation, and from its relation to God's law it derives its value at all times. It is impossible to ascertain *factual* ethical relations apart from the ethical norms. There is no pure, neutral, objective knowing of the facts. "Brute facts" do not exist. Facts are only meaningful in an order, they speak when they are structured. To know anything about a fact, one must have an awareness of order. As James H. Olthuis points out in his important article "Values and Valuation" in *Philosophia Reformata* (now published in *Facts, Values and Ethics*):

> Valuation is necessary in an establishment of the facts. Facts require norms for their very existence. Norms take on subjective form in facts. Apart from the normative structures, there is no way to acknowledge the constant structures one confronts in reality, such as, state, church and family. The relationship or correlation of fact and norm is explicit, for example, when one talks of a *good* family. But it is just as real, although implicit, when one names a certain group of individuals a family. How does one know that this particular group is a family? There is only one answer: it meets the norm for the family. *Insight* into the facts takes place in the light of norms; therefore, no, light, no sight! . . . In place of facts one could speak of "states of affairs." Facts are states of affairs in which norms have been realized. . . . We ought to talk of economic, or ethical, etc., norms and economic, ethical, etc., states of affairs in which these norms are being realized.[34]

The norms governing man's life on earth form one whole in spite of their great variety. But what makes these norms into one whole, one complex? It is the fact that they can all be traced back to one and the same origin in God's plan for mankind. God has laid down these norms as the directives along which human life should be conducted if it is to be blessed.

Man, however, has been created as a responsible being, and he must therefore from these directives discover the norms that should apply in his daily life; for the Creator gives directives only, not rules for the concrete situations of life. Motivated by the central law of love, mankind is called to the discovery, recognition, and concretization or positivation of the structural laws inherent in the cosmos. The resulting positive laws form the "bridge" between the central command to love God and "thy neighbor as thyself" and the structural law. The normative laws, as distinct from the a-normative, require human recognition and actualization in accordance with man's historical development before they are subjectively binding. All positive human laws derive their validity and their binding force upon the individual conscience from the firmness and steadfastness and truth of the divine law-order faithfully maintained by God the Father in Jesus Christ. Unless human laws are thus anchored to God's law-order, positive law soon is adrift, and sooner or later is dashed to pieces on the apostate rocks of historicism, relativism and subjectivism. Thanks to God's temporal conserving grace this "breaking to pieces" is always hampered, and ultimately defeated, by the presence of the anchor. Without the divine law-giver there can be no valid law.

Before norms can become effective in human life, they must be rendered positive. The element of positivizing is an inherent part of the post historical law-spheres. It is the historical analogy of these spheres underlining the point that positivation depends on the stage of man's cultural development. Olthuis rightly suggests that we should view this 'positivization' as a subjective act in which the *resultant* (the concretized posited law) rather than the formative human will is taken up on the law side. . . . The possibility (as well as the fact) that human 'positivizations' acquire normative status rests as a given in the creation order. It stands as the corollary of the 'built-in' inherent requirement of the norm-laws of creation that they be recognized and concretized *before* they are *subjectively* binding. The glory of man's task as man consists in this fact that he is called to take a free, responsible, spontaneous role in the opening-up of the meaning of creation." [35]

Such positivization does not take place only when the state formulates some new legal ruling such as the abolition of slavery in the United States after the Civil War in three amendments to the Constitution. It can take place when a heathen family adopts a new mode of life after becoming Christian, or when an apostate labor union changes its constitution in accordance with biblical norms of justice. Family, church, industry, as well as the state, all have a law of their own, qualified in each case by the typical characteristics of the community concerned.

Of all the norms which should control the development of human society none has proved of greater importance for human well-being than that of the sovereign spheres of society. Upon its application and concretization in human history has depended whatever personal freedom individuals have been able to enjoy. Throughout history first one social sphere then another has sought to dominate all the others with disastrous consequences for human happiness.

The Bible rejects all theories of society which view social institutions such as the family, the school, the labor union, or the church institution as part of a greater whole such as the state. It teaches that no earthly relationship can embrace or give expression to the religious unity and community of mankind. The basis of all true community between men lies not in the state nor in big business but only in the Lord Jesus Christ, the Second Adam "who to our rescue came." By revealing to us the religious root of mankind in creation, fall, and redemption by Jesus Christ, God's Word has also revealed to us the real meaning of human community, in opposition to all forms of collectivism, individualism, nationalism, church imperialism, and the deification of the state in both ancient classical and modern humanist paganism. Neither the family, the church as an institution, the state, the labor union, nor the business corporation may demand of the individual the absolute loyalty he can give only to God. Instead, each institution and organization of human society is under divine charge to give expression—each in its own unique way—to the radical religious unity and community that alone exists in Jesus Christ.

For this reason neither collectivism nor individualism can do justice to the real nature of social relationships. The dilemma posed by all apostate theories of society can be overcome only in terms of the scriptural conception of human society, in which all societal relationships are related back to their origin and firm basis in Jesus Christ.

In the religious center of his experience alone can man transcend all of the modal structures of individuality. This conception has had profound implications for man's understanding of human society. It inspired the English Puritans to take up arms against King Charles II, who sought to impose upon the people of England the absolutist pattern of government of King Louis XIV of France. It led the Thirteen Colonies to defend their hard-won freedoms against encroachment by the English King and Parliament which, claimed to be omnipotent and sovereign over all aspects of North American life. Thus Rushdoony points out:

> In the American tradition, the word "sovereignty" has a theological connotation; sovereignty is an attribute of God alone. The Constitutional Convention of the United States avoided all reference to the word and concept in framing the U. S. Constitution. In one of the more famous addresses of American history, on "The Jubilee of the Constitution" in New York, April 30, 1839, John Quincy Adams associated concepts of omnipotence and sovereignty as essentially one. The former President declared that the Americans had resisted the concept of Parliamentary omnipotence. "From the omnipotence of Parliament the colonists appealed to the rights of man and the omnipotence of the God of battles." Adams then spoke of "The grossly immoral and despotic doctrine of despotic state sovereignty, the exclusive judge of its own obligations, and responsible to no power on earth or in heaven" as a revival of the old doctrine of Parliament's omnipotence. The concept of sovereignty, he pointed out, was totally alien to the American political tradition. . . . The term "sphere

sovereignty" as used by Dooyeweerd has reference to the sov-
erignty of God and His law spheres over man, not that man has
any sovereignty in various spheres of human action. This distinction is basic and needs to be stressed.[36a]

Such an American fear of entrusting too much power into the
hands of any earthly "sovereign" state can be explained only by the
Puritan doctrine of God's total sovereignty over human life as well
as by its teaching of the total depravity of human nature due to
man's fall into sin. As Lord Bryce pointed out in *The American
Commonwealth*:

> Someone has said that the American Government and Constitut-
> tion are based on the theology of Calvin and the philosophy of
> Hobbes. This at least is true that there is a hearty Puritanism in
> the view of human nature which pervades the instrument of 1787.
> It is the work of men who believed in original sin and were re-
> solved to leave open for transgressors no door which they could
> possibly shut. Compare this spirit with the enthusiastic optimism
> of the Frenchmen of 1789. It is not merely a difference of race
> temperaments; it is a difference of fundamental ideas.[36b]

It is this recognition of God's sovereignty and man's sinfulness
which distinguishes the American Revolution from both the French
and Bolshevik Revolutions. While the latter revolutions were the
political expression of apostate men's arrogant faith in their own
reason, the former expressed the Christian conviction that the state
is limited under God. (See last note at end of this chapter.)

No less a thinker than Alexis de Tocqueville recognized the vital
role which had been played by religion in the development of
American society. The fundamental theme of his great study, *Democracy in America*, is that in the last analysis freedom depends on
the manners and beliefs of the men who are to enjoy it. The decisive factor in these manners is religion. American society was, in
Tocqueville's eyes, the society able to combine the spirit of religion
and the spirit of liberty; and were we to seek a single reason why in
America the survival of liberty is probable while in France its future
is precarious, the answer, according to Tocqueville, would be that
American society combines the spirit of religion and the spirit of

liberty, while French society is torn by the opposition between church and democracy, or religion and liberty.

According to Tocqueville, it is the conflict in France between the modern spirit and the church which underlies the difficulties democracy encounters in remaining liberal and that on the other hand the kinship of inspiration between the spirit of religion and the spirit of liberty is the ultimate foundation of American society. Thus Tocqueville writes:

> I have said enough to put the character of Anglo-American civilization in its true light. It is the result (and this should be constantly kept in mind) of two distinct elements, which in other places have been in frequent disagreement, but which the Americans have succeeded in incorporating to some extent one with the other and combining admirably. I allude to the *spirit of religion* and the *spirit of liberty*.
> The settlers of New England were at the same time ardent sectarians and daring innovators. Narrow as the limits of some of their religious opinions were, they were free from all political prejudices. Hence arose two tendencies, distinct but not opposite, which are everywhere discernible in the manners as well as the laws of the country. Liberty regards religion as its companion in all its battles and its triumphs, as the cradle of its infancy and the divine source of its claims. It considers religion as the safeguard of morality, and morality as the best security of law and the surest pledge of the duration of freedom.[36c]

It was Christianity alone which proved strong enough to break down the ancient classical doctrine of the totalitarian all-embracing sovereign city-state and Roman Empire. As Dooyeweerd points out:

> From the Christian transcendance standpoint the radical unity of all temporal societal structures is only to be found in the central religious community of mankind in its creation, fall and redemption by Jesus Christ. This starting point excludes in principle every collectivist sociological view, which seeks the unity and all embracing totality of all types of societal relationships in a temporal community of mankind. . . . This was the firm starting point from which Christianity by the spiritual power of its divine Master broke through the pagan totalitarian view of the Roman Empire, and cleared the way for a veritable and salutary revolu-

tion of the social world-view. The radical meaning of this Christian revolution would be frustrated by identifying it with the Stoic idea of mankind as a temporal community of an all inclusive character.[37]

From the scriptural point of view there is not one "monistic" radical type of social structure which embraces all the other various social spheres as its parts. The Bible knows nothing of the pagan doctrine of the sovereign state which, as Harold Laski pointed out in *A Grammar of Politics*, "makes of right merely the expression of a particular will, without reference to what that will contains." [38] For this reason the writer entirely agrees with Bernard Zylstra in his study of Laski's political thought titled *From Pluralism to Collectivism* that the "alternative to the pitfalls of both an individualistic conception of the state as well as of a universalistic or collectivistic monism can be found in political pluralism. Max Beloff's statement is as relevant today as it was when he commented on Laski's career: "Clearly, political pluralism is still a vital need nationally, as well as internationally." [39] Zylstra then points out that "A revitalized social pluralism requires a more stable foundation than Laski offered (in his early 'pluralist' phase of thought). His 'quantitative' pluralism must give way to a 'qualitative' conception, based on a general inquiry into the qualitative inner nature of the different social structures inclusive of the state." [40]

Neither collectivism nor individualism can provide us with such an analysis, since both ignore the structures of individuality of the divine order of creation which alone present a solution for the problem of the relation of the individual to the group or other various groups to each other. Outside the scriptural frame of reference for natural and social science apostate thinkers have to construct society rationally out of the wills of sovereign individuals or of some absolutized sovereign social institution, be it church, state, or big business. The principle of sphere sovereignty alone presents us with a proper insight into the connection willed by God for man and his social forms, since the individual is never absorbed into any one temporal bond because he is ultimately responsible to God. These temporal bonds of society are limited in the expression of their authority over the individual by their own peculiar structure of individuality.

The Structures of Individuality

The full significance of sphere sovereignty as a philosophical basis for a "qualitative social pluralism" cannot be grasped apart from Dooyeweerd's theory of the structures of individuality and the "enkaptic" intertwinements between them. He distinguishes the structures of individuality from the individual things of naive or integral everyday experience themselves. The latter are the subjects; the structures of individuality signify the cosmonomic principle of the subjects, the "structural type."

In the structures of individuality, the modal aspects of the creation are grouped to form an individual totality, which as a unity overarches the modal aspects. The modal structures thus lie at the foundation of the individuality structures. This does not mean that the modal aspects assume an identical or an equally important function in the individuality structures. A structure of individuality functions in all the modal law aspects of creation, either as *subject* or as *object*. In the language of the philosophy of the cosmonomic law-idea a thing has a function of subjectivity in all the spheres to which it is subject, but in a later sphere it has a function of subjectivity. Thus the bird's nest has a function of subjectivity in the first three spheres, but a function of objectivity in, for example, the psychological sphere in so far as it can be an object of concern to the bird, or in the aesthetic sphere, if it forms part of the aesthetic structure of a painting or a poem. The tree, again, has a function of subjectivity in the first four spheres, but a function of objectivity in the legal sphere, if it is the cause of a law suit, or in the aspect of faith, if it becomes the object of worship of some heathen cult.

But a structure of individuality is not simply a sum of the different modal spheres in which it has a function of subjectivity. It has an original modal individuality, Dooyeweerd states, situated in its last sphere of subjectivity, which he terms the qualifying function of the structure. This function discloses the anticipatory moments of the structure. So complete is the control of, say the biological function of the tree, that the whole tree reveals an individual structure and internal unity.

It is the biological modality which qualifies a tree, because the last modality in which it functions as a subject is the biological sphere, and it is from this sphere that a tree claims its peculiar nature and original individuality. A tree is clearly qualified by its organic life function, as the function of its internal destination. Under the guidance of this qualifying function the prebiological functions open, in a typical way, their meaning within the internal structure of the tree. Although the numerical, spatial, kinematic, and physical functions maintain their own modal structure or character, since their modal meaning kernel cannot be reduced to that of the biological aspect, they do indeed receive a typical biological qualification within the life processes of the tree. Thus the bio-physical and biochemical processes occurring within the living organism are biologically qualified. Only by means of such an analysis can we avoid the dilemma posed by the controversy between vitalism and mechanism.

The biological function therefore occupies a cardinal position in the structure of individuality which constitutes a tree a tree and not a rock or star. This defining or qualifying function Dooyeweerd calls the leading or pilot function, since the earlier aspects are typically directed to this function in the structure of individuality of the tree.

However, the reality of a thing is not shut off in any single modality. Thus the structure which constitutes a tree as a thing is also expressed in the higher as well as the lower modalities. In all the postbiological spheres, however, a tree functions as an object. The tree therefore functions in all aspects of temporal creation; but within this total structure of the tree the aspects are ordered or grouped into a particular unique individual whole around the leading or pilot function. This unique grouping around a specific function, Dooyeweerd terms the structural principle or law to which the individual thing is subject and which makes its existence possible. The structural principle of individuality or structural type has constant validity within the temporal cosmos.

Each structure of individuality shows a descending order after higher and lower structural types in which it is gradually more and more individualized. Dooyeweerd refers to the most comprehensive type as the *radical* type of individuality-structure; it embraces all of the entities whose internal structure is qualified by the same modal aspect. On this basis he depicts three radical types of prelogical qualifications: the realm of inorganic nature, the realm of plants, and the realm of animals. Within these "radical-type realms" one discovers a wide variety, first of sub-types, and finally of elementary types which comprise only individual entities An additional distinction, applicable to all individuality structures, is made between *genotypes* and variability types. The former belong to the constant inner nature of an individual whole. The latter do not arise out of the inner nature of the individual entity but out of its intertwinement with entities of another nature.

(e) *The Social Structures of Individuality*

Since man in his temporal existence is not typically qualified by a particular modal function, Dooyeweerd holds that it is theoretically unwarranted to speak of "mankind" as an ontological realm in the way one can speak of a realm of inorganic matter, of plants, and of animals. In the religious center of his existence man transcends all of the modal and individuality structures. Zylstra points out that such a conception of man "has profound implications for one's view of the temporal social spheres. Because of its biblical starting point 'the philosophy of the cosmonomic law idea rejects sociological 'monism' in a radical manner." [41]

With reference then to plant and animal life we may say that the internal principles of the relevant individuality structures constitute the typical structural "laws" which condition the factual existence of the individual entities as far as their inner nature is concerned. A similar state of affairs obtains in human society, with this fundamental difference, however, that the radical types of the social spheres are of a *normative* character.

This implies that the individuality structures comprised of these radical types, in so far as they concern the invariable inner nature of the social spheres, are normative structural principles. As such they require a process of factual human cultural formation and positivization in accordance with the cultural level of a given society. This process gives rise to the variable social forms in which the structural principles of the social spheres are realized and which differ in accordance with the various cultural areas and the level of historical development of the latter. The Roman Catholic doctrine of Natural Law with its insistence on the recognition of unalterable, external norms, valid at all times and places, not only renders absolute the function of the human reason, but also underestimates the value of man as a culture-forming creature. Our world is subject to continuous change; new social structures emerge as, for example, when capitalism replaced feudalism. Such new social structures require new legal systems. Changes in the historical situation may require the application of new legal principles. When this happens, we do not logically deduce these from the historical givens—as the schools of realism and historicism suppose—but we do discover them in the meaning structure of the legal and economic modality. This does not mean that a certain legal or economic norm is no longer valid; it only means that at different times and places it requires a different formulation. Only in this way can we do justice to the principle of cultural development of the potentialities still hidden in God's creation, which it is one of the tasks of man, created in responsibility, to make explicit in his historical cultural formations. If this requirement is not fulfilled, positive human law can fall into disuse, and it can even become an injustice, when it is no longer the correct embodiment of a legal, economic, or social norm, e.g., changes in the law of property in America and Britain and in the legal status of women before the law since primitive Germanic tribal days when property was collectively owned and women treated as chattels and the slaves of men.

According to Dooyeweerd the structural principles which govern physical reality also define human social relationships and institutions. They are the transcendental conditions of our experience of the variable factual relations which come into existence in history.

Within human society these structural principles are of a normative character.

It is remarkable that one particular aspect always functions in a qualifying and one in a foundational manner for each of the social relationships. (See chart at the end of this book.)

Though every social relationship functions in all aspects of creation, there are always two modal aspects which play a special defining role. We may speak of these qualifying modal aspects as "the typical foundational function" and the "typical leading function."

As an illustration let us take the human family. The family is essentially a typical community of love between parents and their children, but it rests upon the basis of biological sexual procreation upon the part of the parents. The moral aspect of love plays the leading role, and the biological aspect the foundational role, in the internal structural principle of the family. In considering the relationships within the family and its relation to other social units, it is essential that we take the family's individuality structure into account. It's founding and leading functions give a peculiar individuality to all of its aspects. Again, the founding and the leading functions cannot be isolated from each other. The communion of love between husband and wife cannot be separated from their sexual union. In married life the communion of love and sexual union are always interacting, either stimulating and reinforcing the marriage bond or weakening it.

The family has a structure of authority which is peculiarly its own. The responsibilities of a father to his children are different from those of the same father to the childen of his brother or sister. Likewise, the individuality of the family is apparent in the relationships of authority and subordination which pertain within it. According to God's Word, the husband is the head of the wife as Christ is head of the Church. Both have authority over their children (Eph. 6:1; Col. 3:20). However, such authority must be exercised lovingly, and fathers are admonished "not to discourage their children" (Eph. 6:4).

Likewise, the foundational function of the church as an institution is historical, since it rests upon its own historical organizational form

as a Christocracy while its leading function is qualified by faith in the
Triune God of the Scriptures. The labor union too is founded in
history and qualified by moral considerations. Of this we shall write
at greater length.

Dooyeweerd also distinguishes between communities and intercommunal or interindividual relationships. He defines these as follows:

> By "community" I understand any more or less durable societal
> relationship which has the character of a whole joining its mem-
> bers into a social unity, irrespective of the degree of intensity of
> the communal bond.
> By interindividual or intercommunal relationships I mean such
> in which individual persons or communities function in coordina-
> tion without being united into a solidary whole. Such relation-
> ships may show the character of mutual neutrality, of approach-
> ment, free cooperation or antagonism, competition or contest.[42]

A second social category relates to the level of cultural development of both categories of social relationships; here the fundamental
distinction between undifferentiated and differentiated social bonds
is drawn. The process of historical development of human society is
one of increasing differentiation of the social spheres with the consequence that the initial primitive undifferentiated and closed condition of these spheres is broken through.

With respect to the communal relationships, Dooyeweerd makes
two additional distinctions. First, there is the difference between
natural and organized communities. The former, such as the family
in its natural sense, are based on organic life-relations between the
members. These do not need an organized foundation and can be
realized at all times and places in human history, though·in variable
social forms. The latter, however, presuppose a cultural power-
organization in human history. An organized and differentiated
community, such as the state or the church, is therefore bound to
certain historical conditions for its realization.

In the second place, communal relationships can be distinguished
into institutional and non-institutional. This division overlaps the
one between natural and organized communities. The former Dooye-

weerd describes as follows: "By 'institutional' communities I understand both natural and organized communities . . . which by their inner nature are destined to encompass their members to an intensive degree, continuously or at least for a considerable part of their life, and such in a way independent of their will." [43] Examples of this type are the natural family, the state, and the church, but also many undifferentiated organized communities such as sibs, guilds, etc. The individual is usually a member of a family or a state by birth; not by the exercise of any choice in the matter. (See chart at the end of this chapter for The Types of Social Structure.)

For this reason, the family, the state, and the church must never be placed on the same level of authority as the free associations of society. In the unfolding process of Western cultural formation the distinction was drawn for the first time in the history of mankind between the state and society, largely due to the power struggle between church and state. At the Reformation Calvin was thus able to liberate the whole realm of culture from the tutelage of both church and state, by proclaiming the existence alongside church and state of a third realm which he called the sphere of the *adiaphora*, the things indifferent. This belonged to the court of conscience, where no pope or king held sway. This area Calvin did not restrict to a few insignificant matters of taste and opinion among individuals. It included music, architecture, technical learning, and science. In short, Calvin thought of society as the broad field of personal freedom outside of the control of the authoritative structures of church and state in which men and women may associate with each other freely as individuals.[44] Such free associations have in the course of modern history given rise to an innumerable number of associations, clubs, and fellowships, and these also must be recognized as sovereign in their own sphere. As a result of the process of differentiation in these interpersonal social relations, the individual citizen of the Western world has gained a sphere of private liberty in his private life outside of all the institutional communities.

Recognition of the religious unity of mankind in Christ as well as the essentially limited place and function of all such authoritative institutions as church and state alone can guarantee the free development of such an "open society" through which the individual's freedom to respond to his divine calling can express itself.[45] At the same time this development confronts man with the corporate responsibility to develop and integrate every institution and social organization in such a way that they may become expressions, each in its own particular way, of the Body of Christ.

Such a scriptural perspective on human society stands in radical contrast to all forms of contemporary individualism of the right wing and of contemporary collectivism of the left wing of modern politics as well as to the depersonalizing tendencies of the "technological society" so graphically described by Jacques Ellul in his book with this title.[46] The biblical view of freedom excludes in principle both collectivism and individualism, and it alone enables us to see the structural patterns in interlacements between the different types of human relationships. Thus the internal sovereignty of the social spheres alone can provide us with a true basis for a harmonius relation between authority and freedom in human society. Man's service of God as his office-bearer in the creation is the condition of man's freedom.

The sovereignty of these spheres of society does not mean that they exist in splendid isolation from each other. Bernard Zylstra reminds us that if this were indeed the scriptural position it would disregard a "formidable body of social data." He then writes:

> For an observer of the contemporary social scene is immediately confronted with an amazingly complex system of inter-connections between social spheres of intrinsically different inner nature such as the state, ecclesiastical bodies, families, industrial units, educational and scientific institutions, etc. One of the first obstacles which a pluralist social conception must overcome concerns an adequate account of this complexity without resorting to a universalist sociology. In other words, the question is whether the different social spheres can indeed maintain their intrinsic identity in the interweaving processes of modern society; . . . how can the multiple social relationships be adequately accounted for without considering them as *parts* of a more encompassing *whole?* [47]

The sociology of the Cosmonomic Law-idea answers this pertinent question in terms of its theory of "enkaptic interlacement." Briefly stated this means that the social spheres must be considered as existing in close connection with each other. The social forms, in which the internal structural principles of the social spheres are given a factual concrete shape in human history, are the junctures of numerous intertwinements between social spheres of different inner nature. Just as the human body consists of three enkaptically interwoven yet different structures of individuality, e.g., biological, psychical, and pistical (faith), so society consists of numerous enkaptic interlacements of different structures of individuality. The family, for example, is typically interwoven with marriage, but the family is also interwoven with the institution of the state which legalizes it and with the church which blesses it in God's name. The family functions enkaptically within the state, and the church yet still remains intact as a family structure. The marriage ceremony establishes the link between the marriage community and the state without disturbing the inner nature of either social structure. Dooyeweerd rightly insists that this relation of enkapsis between two heterogeneous social spheres must be sharply distinguished from the relation of a whole to its parts.[48] The latter is present, for instance, in the relation between a state and its provinces. But a part-whole relation does not obtain between social spheres of a different individuality structure. That is, if a social bond exhibiting a distinct structure of individuality is bound "enkaptically" within another social bond of a different nature, the former will attain an enkaptic function within the latter, which does not belong to its *inner* sphere. But within its own inner sphere—determined as it is by its particular structural principle—the social bond has "sphere-sovereignty" and maintains its intrinsic typical character. In short, a civil ceremony of marriage enkaptically links marriage to the state without making marriage a function of the state. Likewise, a university may receive grants from the state without becoming its servant, though such a danger always exists. A trade union may be closely connected with a government department in carrying out labor policy, but this does not necessarily involve the subordination of the former to the latter institution. If these social institutions are genuinely seeking to express their own normative internal structural principles, they will maintain an authentic existence which need not be derived from nor beholden to the state. Here, as in the realm of personal freedoms, the condition of corporate freedoms of such associations is eternal vigilance. Unless the will to be independent of state control exists in the human heart, no institution can hope to resist encroachment by the leviathan state. Such a will to freedom has in actual historical experience been found to arise only out of a living faith in the God and Father of the Lord Jesus Christ. This should not be surprising, for did not Christ tells us, "I am the way, the truth and the life" (John 14:6)? Only as we walk in His way, believe in His Truth, and share in His life can we hope to remain free of domination by the apostate forces of darkness which today are seeking to destroy the glorious liberty of the sons of God.

Deep in the fabric of Anglo-Saxon society there is embedded an apostate humanist conviction that religion divides men but reason unites them. Ever since the days of the Cambridge Platonists in England during the seventeenth century there has increasingly taken hold of Anglo-American society a belief in the dogma of the commonness of reason and in the possibility of community between men apart from a common allegiance to the rule of Christ. In this rationalism we have a major historical factor in the rise of the humanist idea of society as being based upon man's sovereign will and reason rather than upon God's. Religion must be confined strictly to men's private lives because it is sectarian and breaks up community between men. Thus in seeking for a basis for human society humanists have sought to find a common ground and field in the non-religious areas of life. Here true unity can be attained and civil liberties safeguarded. All can be satisfied and all can receive equal treatment provided men do not allow their private religious convictions to intrude into the non-religious areas of life.

As an example of this apostate humanist drive to exclude religion from modern life we may cite the *42nd Annual Report* of the American Civil Liberties Union, which clearly states: "The best guarantee of religious freedom . . . is to keep the state out of religious affairs. Neither the public school nor any other agency of government should be used to promulgate any or all religious faith. . . . The practice of religion properly belongs to the church, synagogue and the home." [49]

For the same reason, no doubt, the signers of the recent Marlow "Declaration on Social and Industrial Relations" which included the present Archbishop of Canterbury, A. M. Ramsey, and the Moderator of the General Assembly of the Church of Scotland and the Roman Catholic Archbishop of Birmingham, saw fit to make no mention of their own faith in Jesus Christ as Lord of industry. Instead, these modernistic churchmen also appealed to some supposed common reason and principle of social utility to bind managers and workers together into community. The Marlow "Declaration" in fact states that: "Society is created by man for man. One cannot take from society without giving in return." No true Christian could possibly subscribe to such a doctrine. Society is created by Almighty God for His glory. The "Declaration" also states:

A happy and smooth working industrial partnership requires that
(a) the dignity of man is respected at all times,
(b) there is an effective system of negotiation and consultation using all appropriate methods, and
(c) responsibility is fully accepted individually and collectively.[50]

Such a humanistic faith in man's dignity apart from any recognition that he has been created in God's image and apart from the fact that Christ died for him is a sorry basis upon which to rebuild industry. As J. S. Whale has well written in the *Protestant Tradition*:

If there be no living God, the sovereign Creator and Redeemer in whose image man is made, why should the individual take precedence over the mass; over Party, or Nation or Race? Why should the ant be more important than the ant-heap? Take away faith in the living God who made man for himself, and who overarches the whole human scene in his transcendent sovereignty— and the special status of the individual is gone. That place of honour which liberal philosophy claims for him is his only because Christ died for him. . . . It is precisely in those countries which care nothing for Christ's death that in a very short space of time they come to care nothing for a man's life. . . .

It has become increasingly evident to us that the sacred right of the individual human person is a *sacred* right, but only because it presupposes dogmatic faith in a revelation from on high. The sanctity of the free personality of man is going to depend in the future, as it has done in the past, not on the so-called decencies of man, nor on the benevolent paternalism of the welfare state, nor on the tender mercies of private enterprise, nor on the visionary operations of inevitable progress, but on the vitality of supernatural religion; in short, on the vindication of the Crown Rights of the Redeemer in His Church. Protestants stand for the two ideas of supernatural religion and liberty; for these two ideas in combination; and for the historic conviction that in the long run you cannot have either alone. You must have both together, or neither; since God's service is perfect freedom, and since it is only in freedom that God can be truly served.[51]

Unfortunately, today the apostate humanists are bent on keeping God out of both the public school and the field of labor relations. In North America both the public school and the "neutral" union adhere in principle to majority rule and both fail to honor the rights of the minority. Both offer fringe benefits to the minority; the public school permits those having conscientious objections to be released from class. The labor "bosses" permit those having conscientious objections to the union to seek work elsewhere. Neither gives an answer to the question: How can there be freedom for parents to educate their children according to their religious convictions on an equal footing with non-Christians if their convictions do not agree with those of the government schools? There can only be freedom and justice for all in the realms of civil rights, education, and labor when all men recognize that life is religion and that religion does in fact penetrate all areas of life and will not stay confined within the limits in which the apostate humanists have tried to enclose it.

In *The Politics of Mass Society*, William Kornhauser reminds us that the mere fact of a multiplicity of associations in a society does not necessarily provide the conditions of pluralism that alone can assure the survival of personal and communal freedoms. The population of a society could be organized into a set of associations that merely served the interests of the state as in the case of the Hitler Youth movement. He therefore argues that what is required for a pluralist society is a multiplicity of *affiliations*, wherein no one group is *inclusive* of its members' lives. Thus labor unions have members of various ethnic and religious groups, churches cut across class lines, and political parties draw from a heterogeneous range within the population. Such extensive crosscutting affiliations prevent one line of social cleavage such as class from becoming dominant. In Kornhauser's view the essential condition for a liberal democracy is the existence of a number of autonomous secondary associations which reduces the vulnerability of their members to domination by elites. In other words, it is the pluralist type of society which we have advocated in this chapter to which Kornhauser turns as a protection against any trend towards totalitarian democracy. He writes:

> In summary, a liberal democracy requires widespread participation in the selection of leaders, and a large amount of self-governing activity on the part of non-elites. It also requires competition among leaders and would-be-leaders, and a considerable autonomy for those who win positions of leadership. The basic question arises, what kind of social structure will meet these conditions of liberal democracy? The theory of mass society expounded in the present study implies that social pluralism is a social arrangement which performs this function. A plurality of independent and limited-function groups supports liberal democracy by providing social bases of free and open competition for leadership, widespread participation in the selection of leaders, restraint in the application of pressures on leaders, and self-government in wide areas of social life. Therefore, where social pluralism is strong, liberty and democracy tend to be strong: and conversely, forces which weaken social pluralism also weaken liberty and democracy.[52]

While welcoming Kornhauser's thesis we would conclude this chapter by pointing out that liberty and democracy first require a recognition of God's sovereignty and the will to remain free and independent of enslavement by the state, which the Spirit of Christ alone can provide.

TYPES OF SOCIAL STRUCTURES*

Structural Functional Criterion	Authoritative Communal Relationships	Non-authoritative Social Relationship	Free Social Relationships
Natural Communities	The Immediate Family	The Extended Family	Primitive Barter
Undifferen-tiated Bonds	Clan, Tribe	Guilds or Sib	Tribal Warfare
Differen-tiated Bonds in the process of history			
Qualifying Function			
Faith	Church as an Organized Community	Sectarian Group	Women's Society
Ethical	Masonic Lodge	Labor Union	Red Cross
Juridical	The State	Jurymen	Legal Professional Association
Aesthetic	Marine Band	Orchestra	Concert Audience
Economic	Revenue Department	Business Corporation	Stock Exchange
Social	American Army	Athletic Club	Baseball Spectators
Lingual	Government Information Service	Reuters News Agency	Ham Radio Group
Cultural	Soviet Ministry of Culture	Royal Society (Science Research)	Tourists
Analytical	Soviet Academy of Science	College Faculty	Student Debate

*(Adapted from M. Vrieze's *Introduction to Sociology* syllabus lectures delivered at Trinity Christian College, Chicago, in 1968.)

CHAPTER SIX NOTES

1. H. Dooyeweerd, *In the Twilight of Western Thought* (Presbyterian and Reformed, Philadelphia, 1960), p. 180.

2. A. Kuyper, *Lectures on Calvinism* (Eerdmans, Grand Rapids, 1961), p. 45ff.

3. Augustine, *De Utilitate*, 22-5, also *In Joan Evang.* XIX, 6. "Understanding is the reward of faith. Therefore seek not to understand that thou mayest believe, but believe that thou mayest understand." For a useful treatment of Augustine's epistemology see Charles Cochrane, *Christianity and Classical Culture* (Oxford University Press, New York, 1944), p. 432ff.

4. August Lang, "The Reformation and Natural Law," *Calvin and the Reformation* (Revell Company, New York, 1909), p. 57f.

5. W. J. Ong, Ramus, *Method and the Decay of Dialogue* (Harvard University Press, 1958), p. 142f.

6. H. Dooyeweerd, "The Secularization of Science," in *The International Reformed Bulletin*, Number 26, July 1966 (Amsterdam), p. 11ff.

7. A. Kuyper, *Souvereiniteit in eigen kring* (Amsterdam, 1880).

8. A. Kuyper, *op. cit.*, p. 10ff.

9. Cornelius Van Til, *A Christian Theory of Knowledge* (Syllabus used at Westminster Theological Seminary, 1954), p. 25ff.

10. Michael Oakshott, *Experience and Its Modes* (Cambridge University Press, 1933), p. 78f.

11. R. J. Rushdoony, *The Mythology of Science* (Craig Press, Nutley, N. J., 1967), p. 44. Cf. W. Stanford Reid, *Christianity and Scholarship* (Craig Press).

12. Robert L. Reymond, *A Christian View of Modern Science* (Presbyterian and Reformed Publishing Co., Philadelphia, 1964), p. 25.

13. Richard A. Wilson, *The Miraculous Birth of Language* (Guild Book No. 213, J. M. Dent & Sons, Ltd., London, 1941, for British Publishers Guild), pp. 42-46, for a very fair treatment of the Genesis account by a Professor of English Language and Literature.

14. Talcott Parsons, *The Structure of Social Action* (The Free Press, New York, 1967), pp. 3-122 for a first class account of "The Positivistic Theory of Action." This is one of the most important works in sociology ever written as it reveals the dilemmas and antinomies faced by apostate humanist thinkers in their attempts to explain human society apart from God. He reveals the inner tensions of the modern nature-freedom or science-personality ground-motive as these appear in economic and sociological thought since Thomas Hobbes wrote his *Leviathan* and Locke his *Two Treatise of Civil Government*.

15. Emile Durkheim, *Rules of Sociological Method* (Translated by S. A. Solovay and J. H. Mueller, University of Chicago Press, Chicago, 1938).

16. *Ibid.*, p. 13; cf. R. A. Nisbet, *The Sociological Tradition* (New York, 1966), pp. 1-20.
17. John Rex, *Key Problems of Sociological Theory* (Routledge & Kegan Paul, London, 1968). Cf. *Theories of Society*, edited by T. Parsons, E. Shils., etc. (The Free Press, New York, 1965).
18. *Ibid.*, p. 6ff.
19. Max Weber, *The Theory of Social and Economic Organization* (Translated by A. M. Henderson and Talcott Parsons; Oxford, New York, 1947), p. 110. Cf. Parsons, *Structures of Social Action*, p. 640ff.
20. Weber, *op. cit.*, chapter 1.
21. Raymond Aron, *Main Currents in Sociological Thought* vol. two (Weidenfeld and Nicolson, London, 1968) p. 193f. This book gives the best humanist history of sociology yet written.
22. Dooyeweerd, *New Critique*, Vol III, p. 171. Cf. R. Kooistra, *Facts and Values*, A Christian Approach to Sociology (Christian Perspectives, 1963; Guardian Publishing Company, Hamilton, Canada, 1964), p. 31, for an account of Weber's thought in the light of the Christian sociological viewpoint.
23. For an example of Parsons' approach to sociology, consult his book, *The Social System* (Routledge & Kegan Paul, Ltd., London, 1964), and of Robert K. Merton's approach, see *Social Theory and Social Structure* (The Free Press, New York, 1967), Introduction, p. 5f., where Merton calls for concentration upon "*theories of the middle range*; theories intermediate to the minor working hypotheses evolved in abundance during the day-by-day routines of research, and the all-inclusive speculations comprising a master conceptual scheme from which it is hoped to derive a very large number of empirically observed uniformities of social behavior." In other words Merton is here moving from his prewar idealist position as a disciple of Weber and Parsons to a more pragmatist position which gives up all hope of an all-embracing conceptual framework in sociology, He admits that "a large part of what is now call sociological theory consists of general orientations toward data, suggesting types of variables which need somehow to be taken into account, rather than clear, verifiable statements of relationships between specific variables. We have many concepts but few confirmed theories; many points of view, but few theorems; many "approaches," but few arrivals. . . . I believe . . . that for some time to come, it is theories of the middle range which hold the largest promise." Merton then proceeds to provide us with "attempts to lay out the foundations and framework of the kind of social theory called functional analysis. . . . It is this framework of functional analysis which has variously guided the writing of all papers in this volume." For this type of functional sociology it would appear that society can be analysed without any reference to good or evil. Social life is thus found

resting on institutions which fulfill certain functions for the maintenance of society. And this being all that the sociologist is able to say, according to functionalism, the terms by which he will describe the achievement of the noblest function in society will apply equally to its vilest aberrations. Social stability thus becomes the only accepted value. Is not the stability of evil the worst of all evils?

24. Paul Hazard, *The European Mind, 1680-1714* (Penguin Books, London, 1964). Also Paul Hazard, *European Thought in the Eighteenth Century* (Penguin Books, 1965), p. 301f., "Disaggegation."

25. Auguste Comte, *The Positive Philosophy*, translated by Harriet Martineau, 2 vols. (Trubner, London, 1853), Vol. I, p. 200.

26. Raymond Aron, *Main Currents in Sociological Thought*, Vol. I (Penguin Books, London, 1968), p. 66. Cf. *Theories of Society*, p. 646, for Comte's Three Stages.

27. F. A. Hayek, *The Counter-Revolution of Science* (The Free Press, Glencoe, Illinois, 1952), p. 13ff.

28. *Ibid.*, p. 45ff. Cf. P. A. Sorokin, *Fads and Foibles in Modern Sociology and Related Sciences* (H. Regnery, Chicago, 1956), for a condemnation of positivistic sociology which, he holds, must be redeemed from its bankrupt presuppositions and false methods.

29. *Ibid.*, p. 31.

30. Dooyeweerd, *Renewal and Reflection*, "Sphere Sovereignty" (Available in English in mimeographed form only), pp. 2-4 of this section.

31. *Ibid.*, p. 31.

32. Paul G. Schrotenboer, "Man in God's World," in *International Reformed Bulletin*, No. 31, October 1967 (1677 Gentian Dr., S.E., Grand Rapids, Mich.), p. 12ff.

33. H. Dooyeweerd, Syllabus, 1946-1947 (Amsterdam), p. 134.

34. James H. Olthuis, "Values and Valuation," *Philosophia Reformata*, Jan. 1967 (Amsterdam), p. 52. Cf. *Facts, Values and Ethics* (Humanities Press, New York, 1968), p. 182f.

35. *Ibid.*, p. 50.

36a. R. J. Rushdoony, Introduction to H. Dooyeweerd's *The Christian Idea of the State* (Craig Press, Nutley, N. J., 1968), p. ix ff.

36b. Lord Bryce, *The American Commonwealth* (Macmillan, London, 1893), Part 1, ch. xxvi.

36c. Alexis de Tocqueville, *Democracy in America*, trans. H. Reeve, revised by F. Bowen and ed. P. Bradley (A. Knopf, New York, 1954), Vol. II, Bk. I, chs. 3 and 4, "The Influence of Manners and Religion upon Democratic Institutions in the United States."

37. Dooyeweerd, *A New Critique*, Vol. III, p. 169.

38. Harold Laski, *A Grammar of Politics* (G. Allen & Unwin, London, 4th edition, 1938), p. 44.

39. Bernard Zylstra, *From Collectivism to Pluralism* (Van Gorcum, Netherlands, 1968), p. 206.
40. *Ibid.*
41. *Ibid.*, p. 213.
42. Dooyeweerd, *A New Critique*, Vol. III, p. 177.
43. *Ibid.*, p. 187.
44. Henry R. Van Till, *The Calvinistic Concept of Culture* (Presbyterian and Reformed Publishing Co., Philadelphia, 1959), p. 98.
45. K. R. Popper, *The Open Society and Its Enemies* (Routledge, London, 1966). Cf. *Theories of Society*, edited by T. Parsons, E. Shil, etc., Part Two, "Differentiation and Variation in Social Structures," especially Introduction by Talcott Parsons.
46. Jaques Ellul, *The Technological Society* (J. Cape, London, 1965). This book reaches remarkably similar conclusions to those of H. Van Riessen in *The Society of the Future* (Presbyterian and Reformed Publishing Co., Philadelphia, 1964). Both are Reformed thinkers yet appear never to have heard of each other!
47. Zylstra, *op. cit.*, p. 216.
48. Dooyeweerd, *A New Critique*, Vol. III, p. 627ff. for his treatment of the enkaptic interlacements.
49. Quoted in Paul Schrotenboer, *Freedom and Justice for All* (C. J. L. Foundation, P.O. Box 151, Rexdale, Ontario), p. 5.
50. *The Marlow Declaration* (Marlo, Bucks, England, 1963), pp. 4, 6.
51. J. S. Whale, *The Protestant Tradition* (Cambridge University Press, 1962), p. 265ff.
52. W. Kornhauser, *The Politics of Mass Society* (Free Press, New York, 1968), pp. 230-231.

For a good account of the biblical foundations for the argument presented in this chapter the reader should consult G. Ernest Wright: *The Biblical Doctrine of Man in Society* (*The American Doctrine of the Limited State*, SCM Press, Ltd., London, 1954).

In his *Pluralist Democracy in the United States* (Rand McNally, Chicago, 1968), Robert A. Dahl forcibly argues the case of political pluralism in terms of American political experience. He writes:

> The fundamental axiom in the theory and practise of American pluralism is, I believe, this: Instead of a single center of sovereign power there must be multiple centers of power, none of which is or can be wholly sovereign. Although the only legitimate sovereign is the people, in the perspective of American pluralism even the people ought never to be an absolute sovereign; consequently no part of the people, such as a majority, ought to be absolutely sovereign.
> Why this axiom? The theory and practise of American pluralism tend to assume, as I see it, that the existence of multiple centers of power, none of which is wholly sovereign, will help (may indeed be necessary) to tame power, to secure the consent of all, and to settle conflicts peacefully:

1. Because one center of power is set against another, power itself will be tamed, civilized, controlled, and limited to decent human purposes, while coercion, the most evil form of power, will be reduced to a minimum.
2. Because even minorities are provided with opportunities to veto solutions they strongly object to, the consent of all will be won in the long run.
3. Because constant negotiations among different centers of power are necessary in order to make decisions, citizens and leaders will perfect the precious art of dealing peacefully with their conflicts, and not merely to the benefit of one partisan but to the mutual benefit of all parties to a conflict (p. 24).

The writer would agree with the above statement with the one provision that God and *not* the people is sovereign in society. Only the biblical framework discussed in this chapter can provide an adequate safeguard for both freedom and pluralism. R. J. Rushdoony has also shown that recognition of God's sovereignty is the only foundation of social order in his *The Foundation of Social Order* (Presbyterian and Reformed Publishing Company, Nutley, N. J., 1968), pp. 219-226, where he proves that apostate humanism is the enemy of both freedom and pluralism. In *The Politics of Mass Society*, W. Kornhauser argues that an essential condition for a liberal democracy is the existence of a number of autonomous secondary associations which reduces their vulnerability to domination by elites. Pluralism is for him the answer against totalitarianism (New York, 1960). Also James B. McKee, *Introduction to Sociology* (New York, 1969). "The Conditions for Democratic Order," pp. 462-465, for a good criticism of Kornhauser's thesis. For a discussion of the differences between the American and French Revolutions see R. A. Nisbet, *The Sociological Tradition*, p. 31ff.

Chapter Seven

THE ECONOMIC AND SOCIAL CHURCH MILITANT

(a) *The Case for Christian Economic and Social Action*

"All power is given unto me in heaven and earth. Go ye therefore, and teach all nations . . . to observe all things whatsoever I have commanded you; and lo, I am with you, even unto the end of the world" (Matt. 28:16f.). In these splendid words of the Risen Christ, spoken just before his Ascension and Exaltation into Heaven, Christians received the great commission to win back mankind to God's service. Our Lord here makes the stupendous claim that He is Lord of all lords, King of all kings, and ruler of all things in heaven and earth. That is to say, He claims that He has a share in God's supreme sovereignty and that all authority has been given to Him in heaven and earth.

All authority means the supreme right to appoint to office. Christ, the second Person of the Godhead, possesses absolute sovereign authority. As such our Lord Jesus Christ is the full and complete office bearer, and He is therefore the origin and source of all power exercised on earth. Christ has delegated only partial sovereignties to men. In Him alone all these earthly sovereignties are united in an undivided service of God that involves nothing less than the redemption and reformation of the whole of human life.

Christ only delegates authority to persons occupying various positions in society. Thus parents obtain their authority over their children not from the state, as humanists suppose, but from Christ (Eph. 5:1ff.). Thus the government obtains its authority to exercise the sword of justice over its citizens not from the will of the majority of the people, as liberal democrats suppose, but from Christ (Rom. 13). As the King of common as well as of special grace, the Lord Christ has instituted the "office" of government on account of human sinfulness. As such the authority of all earthly governments is from Christ himself, to whom they are ultimately responsible. While the people may rightly elect their rulers, they must never forget that the ultimate authority of government comes from Christ, which they must obey for conscience sake.

Since Christ alone is supreme, the authority exercised by men is limited. For this reason no single earthly institution can or should exercise a totalitarian, all-inclusive authority over men. Such an all-inclusive authority is given only to Christ as the Second Adam and the head of the new humanity (Col. 1:16). Only Christ possesses absolute sovereign authority and power, and He alone is the origin and source of all authority exercised on earth.

Today many Christians would seem to have forgotten Christ's claim that *all* power has been given to Him in heaven and earth. They seem to have identified power with brute force, and, misled by this identification, they consider it unchristian to strive for the acquisition of power for the sake of making Christian principles and God's creational-structure permeate into the institutions of modern society, by means of Christian social and economic action and Christian organization. For such pietists the question of power may not even be discussed by Christians.

In his influential work, *The Divine Imperative*, Emil Brunner taught that the state is essentially a power organization and therefore under the influence of the demonic. The Christian may speak of love and justice, but as soon as he brings power into the picture he listens to the voice of Satan.

In the same way advocates of the abolition of capital punishment argue that the use of the power of the sword of justice in executing convicted murderers is totally unscriptural, while pacifists argue that no consistent Christian can take part in the exercise of military power.

Such a misrepresentation of the biblical doctrine of power points only to the fact that these modern Anabaptists have forced the scriptural doctrine of the creation of the world by Almighty God into the background of their thinking about power.

Lacking a biblical concept of power, they can no longer understand the redemption brought about by Christ in its full and powerful scriptural sense. For such people Christ has not come to redeem
the *whole* of life but only a part of life, namely a man's private subjective states of mind and feeling. The unbiblical nature of this point
of view becomes obvious as soon as we remember that God revealed
himself as Creator of the world in the original fulness of power.
The Bible teaches that God is the Almighty One (the All-Powerful
One), the original and only source of power, from whom all other
manifestations of power in the universe are derived. There are,
therefore, no limitations to God's power, by which the world
was made; with God all things are possible and nothing is too hard
for the Lord (Mark 10:27; Jer. 32:17; Gen. 18:14). Of course, the
power of God is not thought of in the Bible as capricious; it is always
qualified by God's righteous and holy will.

By the great cultural mandate, "Be fruitful and multiply and replenish the earth and subdue it and have dominion over it" (Gen.
1:28), man is called by God to share in God's power of giving form
to the forces of nature. Just as the Lord God is sovereign over the
creation and has brought forth many wonderful and noble works,
so He has given to man His image-bearer control over the earth as
his dominion. Culture, industry, and science are in fact man's life
task. In this cultural, industrial, and scientific task man has been
called by God to take the raw materials of God's creation and by
means of his art, science, and technique bring out all the possibilities
which are hidden in creation. Thus Faraday was serving God just as
truly in discovering electricity as Luther was in discovering the
great truth of justification by grace alone in his monk's closet.

Unfortunately, as a result of the fall of man, this position of power
to which God had called man took on an idolatrous direction. Instead of using his power for God's greater glory and the benefit
of man's need and the improvement of man's estate, sinful man now
used it and still uses it for his own selfish ends.

But then Christ came. As Redeemer He revealed himself anew as
the One who possesses power in the fullest sense of the term. And

He calls *all.* His disciples to the task of spreading the power of the gospel to all nations.

This power of the gospel of free sovereign grace must never be restricted as it has become restricted by pietistic Protestants merely to the salvation of individual souls. Instead it must be seen to include the *whole* of human life, culture, and science. When Christ saves a person He saves the whole person, not just part of him. Christ changes the whole temporal as well as spiritual direction of a person's life when he changes a person's heart by cleansing him of sin.

Obviously this spiritual power of the gospel differs from the sword power of the state. And both of them differ radically from the power of science, of art, of industry, or the social power of labor unions or radio or television.

But regardless of the concrete situation in which the historical and cultural formation of power reveals itself, it is never brute force as abolitionists and pacifists suppose. It is always grounded in God's creation and in God's original cultural mandate to man to have dominion over the earth. As such the exercise of power, whether politically, economically, artistically, scientifically, or ecclesiastically, has nothing demonic about it.

The Lord Christ explicitly calls himself the ruler of the kings of the earth. He claims for His service even the sword-power of the state, since to Him has been given all power in heaven and earth (I Cor. 15:25).

Only sin can place power in the service of the demonic, but this is true also of all the other good gift goods of God, including life itself, our feelings, our thoughts, justice, sex, business, science, etc. In so far as power has been entrusted to man as God's servant and creature, it always bears a cultural stamp. Power brings with it an historical task, imposed by God on man at his creation; the great task of giving form to the material aspects of God's creation, and of which the bearer of power will one day have to give an account.

Thus the businessman will one day have to give an account before Christ of the use to which he put his powers of leadership and enterprise. The labor union leader will have to account to Christ for the use to which he has put his powers of persuasion and leadership over his union members. Likewise, the father and the mother of the use to which they put their parental powers over their children and the politicians of the use to which they put the authority entrusted to them by Christ in the exercise of the powers of government over their fellow men. Even the artists and the scientists will have to give an account to God of the use to which they put their special powers and gifts. Such a prospect of a future judgment upon all our earthly activities should provide us with the incentive to use our powers and abilities as responsibly and as conscientiously as we can.

Christ not only claims to be the only true source and origin of power, but He also calls upon all His disciples to "be witnesses unto me both in Jerusalem, and in all Judaea, and in Samaria, and unto the uttermost part of the earth," after they "shall receive power, after the Holy Ghost is come upon you" (Acts 1:8).

For this reason we must reject as unbiblical and disobedient to Christ's great commission Karl Barth's repudiation of Christian social action and organization. As Dooyeweerd says of Barth's teaching:

> Culture is bound to human society, which in its turn demands cultural formation, i.e., a controlling manner of shaping social relations between men. All power is derived from God. . . .
> Christ has said that all power on earth and in heaven was given into His hands. The horror of power-formation for the sake of the fulfilment of the Christian task in the cultural development of mankind is, consequently, unbiblical. The Church itself is historically founded in power over men by means of the organized service of the Word and the Sacraments.
> Doubtless, every power given in the hands of man implies a serious risk of abuse. But this state of affairs can only accentuate the normative meaning, it can never justify the opinion that power in itself is an evil.[1]

The question which Barth fails to ask is: To what ends will power in fact be used? For used it will be, either in the service of Christ or of some false god or idol.

In the Great Commission Christ makes it clear that power of *all* kinds must be used in His service. Human life in its integral wholeness is the service of the one true God whom Christ revealed or of the various absolutizations of one or more relative aspects of creation. Christ wishes to rule over *all* aspects of our lives. He did not die on the Cross and rise again just to make us "religious," but to make us new men and women, and to provide us with a new basis for the integration and organization of our lives, and thus to build up a new Christian culture and society.

The formation and exercise of power are not, as has often been supposed, subject to natural laws, but rather they are subject to essential norms and creation principles. And these norms are of an intrinsically historical nature, since the process of historical development has been placed under certain norms by God himself, norms to which nations and their rulers are equally subject. As Christ's Body in the world we are to struggle for nothing less than the redemption and reformation of society as a whole, since "nowhere in all of human life and society," as Abraham Kuyper pointed out, is there so much as an inch of space and time which Christ does not claim, 'It is Mine.' "

The Christian's duty is to make sure that these norms are obeyed rather than violated. To refuse to take specifically Christian action in the economic and social spheres is simply to surrender these spheres into the hands of non-Christians. Whether the Barthians like it or not, all economic and social action is religion in the sense that it serves the cause of either the true God whom Christ revealed, or some false god. Since all human life is lived out of an ineradicable and fundamental religious relation either to the true God or to some false god, all economic and social life must express the belief of those who are engaged in it. This is true even when it is denied; its truth is rooted in the sureness of God's creation ordinances. Thus, the economic and social life of men will disclose the same fundamental religious antithesis of direction that characterizes human life as a whole. In their ultimate presupposition or faith principles, the "ways" of men diverge. Faith, which is the gift of God, thus becomes the wedge that divides humanity. Augustine long ago saw the City of God in this world as the work of God's grace in the hearts and lives of men and as being opposed to the kingdom of darkness which arises out of an apostate faith of a rebellious humanity.

The biblical doctrine of the antithesis refers to the enmity that

God has put between the seed of the woman (the Incarnate Word and all those who are incorporated by grace into Christ's Body) and the seed of the serpent (all those who still live in enmity with God and who persist in their apostasy from Him) (Gen. 3:15). It is this act of God which has determined the history of mankind as Augustine clearly understood. Ever since Christ came into world history a great struggle has been waged between the "children of the light" and the "children of darkness." [2] An opposition exists between human lives lived in apostasy from God and human lives lived in obedience to God. Since this antithesis roots itself in the hearts of men, it does not merely affect the periphery but the whole of men's lives, and this includes their economic and social activities. Not a single aspect of human life lies outside this antithesis between the service of God and the service of Satan. For God is sovereign over His creation, and Christ's kingship extends over the whole of culture. As Henry Van Til well put it:

> The doctrine of the antithesis rightly interpreted holds to a duality in culture corresponding to the duality in the race—a belief-ful culture and an apostate culture; for there is no possibility of reconciliation between Belial and Christ, hence no communion (*koinoonia*), that is, spiritual fellowship. In principle, therefore, the antithesis (between the Christ of God and the world organized apart from Him) is absolute. It admits of no compromise. It permeates to the whole of existence; it leaves no area of life untouched.[3]

For this reason the Reformed Christian believes that, if the Christian religion is to exert any cultural forming influence upon the life of modern society, it simply must live out of its own distinctive political, economic, and social principles.

In his famous inaugural oration at the founding of the Free University of Amsterdam in 1880, Abraham Kuyper gave the first scientific formulation of this Reformed doctrine of the antithesis. He pointed out that this reality, which is observable throughout the history of the world, is rooted in the point of departure that characterizes every system of thought which proceeds from the human heart. Through regeneration a man becomes a new creature in Christ, so that his consciousness is changed, his mind enlightened by the Spirit of God to understand the revelation of God given in the Scriptures. Kuyper drew the conclusion that there are two kinds of people in the world, the believers in Christ and the unbelievers, the obedient and the apostate; hence, also there must of necessity follow two kinds of science, art, politics, economics, labor unions, etc.

Accordingly, no regenerated Christian can escape the dilemma the antithesis sets forth if he or she really takes seriously the universality of Christ's Kingship and the central confession of God's sovereignty over the whole cosmos as Creator. Of this antithesis Dooyeweerd says:

> Many peace-loving Christians . . . do not recognize that this antithesis does not draw a line of personal classification but a line of division according to fundamental principles in the world, a line of division which passes transversely through the existence of every Christian personality. This antithesis is not a human invention, but is a great blessing from God. By it He keeps his fallen creation from perishing. To deny this is to deny Christ and His work of redemption in the world.[4]

The Christian economic and social task is thus concerned with the inner reformation of man's industrial and social life as an aspect of the integral renewal of our whole life in obedience to Jesus Christ.

Christian economics and Christian trade unionism are not a question of details and of piecemeal reconstruction of the economic order but a question of applying Christian principles. Christian economics takes its origin in the Christian's acknowledgment of the total sovereignty of the Word of God over the whole of human life.

For this reason it should be clear why Christian economic and social action can never mean simply a question of getting Christian persons into existing economic and neutral trade union positions. Many Christians think they can best serve Christ by joining so-called neutral business enterprises and labor unions and trying to influence them as best they can. However, the whole point is that Christian economic and social action is not doing things according to the patterns of behavior accepted by apostate humanists; it is doing the will of God as revealed in the Holy Scriptures in the economic and business sphere of human society, exercising our office as God's prophets, priests, and kings to recover the social order for God and His Christ.

Comparing the Gentiles and the Christians, Peter says:

They stumble, in disobeying the Word; to this destiny they were ordained. But you are "A chosen race, a kingly priesthood, a holy nation, a people for God's prized possession," that you may proclaim the mighty deeds of Him who called you out of darkness into His marvellous light—you who aforetime were "no people" but are now "the people of God," who "knew not God's mercy," but now know his mercy.[5]

Commenting on this wonderful passage F. W. Beare writes:

There is considerable boldness in the language which describes the Christian Church as "a race," "a nation," "a people"—when in literal fact it embraced members of many different races and nations. . . . Yet it must be remembered that there was a distinct tendency in the ancient world to think of religion as the essential basis of community, and of common religious observances as the determining feature of nationhood and the one really significant factor of homogeneity. The biological factor was involved only in so far as it was itself conceived to have a religious basis; and the lay state which regards religion as irrelevant to its proper functioning and so leaves it to the discretion of the individual, was undreamed of. Even Rome, which accorded a wide tolerance to private cults . . . and largely removed civil law from the sphere of religion, continued to look upon the official religion as the necessary centre and safeguard of the common life; and the ancient city state was built upon the civic religion, in the rites of which all citizens participated. . . . When men withdrew purposefully and openly from participation in the rites of the official religion, as Christians were bound to do, then they ceased to be members of the community in any effective sense; the old ties of relationship were broken. Negatively, therefore, those who became Christians had no more part in the race or nation of their birth; and positively they formed new ties, and were united in a new community which was less a private brotherhood like those of the mystery religions, than the unifying bond of all existence which we find in the nation or the state. The Romans already regarded the Jews not as one race among many, but as a race apart, and they came in no long time to regard the Christians as a "third race," distinct from the Jews and from the generality of the Empire's inhabitants, loosely designated "Romans." This description of the Christian society by Peter, therefore, was by no means an extravagant image, but a penetrating perception of the true situation and character of the Church.[6]

Are modern Protestant pietists in the English-speaking world known as members of a Third Race, or have they too become a private brotherhood like those of the ancient mystery religions? The great apostle to the Gentile world, Paul, like Peter, also called upon Christians to find a distinctive Christian avenue to deal with the disputes that had broken out among them. Rather than take their troubles and disputes before an unbelieving judge, Paul enjoins us to "suffer loss and injustice" and to find their own Christian solution in terms of the power of the Cross and Resurrection of Christ and to appoint suitable men within the church to settle such disputes in the future (I Cor. 6:1-11).

While Christians cannot leave the world, they must become separated from the motives and habits of apostate heathen Graeco-Roman culture, science, industry, and politics. Their social intercourse must be arrested wherever possible from the corrupting influences of the pagans. Only then will it become possible for Christians to conduct themselves properly as followers of the new way of life Christ began toward "them that are without" (I Thess. 4:12; Col. 4:4-5; I Tim. 3:7; I Cor. 5:13; 6:1-11). According to Paul Christians should form a closely knit community with a style of living and culture all its own. Christians are to unite in order that they may the better build up the Body of Christ. Commenting on Paul's striking description of the Church as the Body of Christ, Calvin Seerveld well says:

> What is the Body of Christ? It is that union of men who profess that they with body and soul, in life and death, are not their own, but belong to their faithful Saviour Jesus Christ out of whom, through whom and to whom they live as their head. The body of Christ is this communion of men called together by the living Word, all those who respond, willing to submit their whole lives openly to Christ's lordship.
> No monolithic, universal ecclesiastical institution is intended. The Biblical mandate to build up Christ's body aims its imperative directly at every single part of that body in its specific work-

ings. Believing teachers, for example, are enjoined to grow together, to study in concert, to mature in uni-versity, so that the
educational eye of Christ's body may get keen vision with depth.
The Lord asks Christian workers, for another example, to edify
one another, that is, to build one another up, to encourage and
help the other believer *in his working capacity*, to consolidate
their resources, to unite, so that the laboring arm in the kingdom
of God be supple and strong—that's logical! That's Biblical.
. . . Building up Christ's body is not a matter of human preference
or not; it is a matter of God's directive. . . .
    United Christian workers are not "separated" from their fellow
man and unbelievers—that's a laugh. We confront them daily.
. . . The question is how are God's workers to confront them?
As individuals secure in their personal faith, doing a silent, honest
day's work in the factory, keeping out of trouble, witnessing
briefly at lunch hour conversations? Does that answer Revelation's call to grow up in Christ's name? I do not mean to play
down personal testimony, but I do challenge the reduction of
"witness" to individualistic testimony. And I call into question the
mean spirit of a current atomistic Protestantism which has no
sense of Christ's lordship over earth, sea, sky and society, which
is content to "save souls" for heaven, and which has made such
inroads in American reformed circles mostly because the rich
Biblical, Reformational directive of "communal witness" has not
been an operating principle in our lives. The Christian is not in
this world alone, but is a member of Christ's body. And the
Christian's task in the world is not to be conceived in terms of
missionary evangelism, but evangelism is to be vigorously carried
out in the context of building up Christ's body. To be fuzzy on
this point is to surrender the deep Biblical insight and focus of a
covenantal faith that is relevant for time as well as eternity. Once
this Biblical injunction to build up Christ's body is lost, with its
intensive orienting power for every saint's creational existence, the
converted fruits of an individual's witness and the church's
preaching have no framework, directive, program to follow to
express the effected salvation of their life—it is the life of man in
its full-orbed reality which is saved, is it not? [7]

The Gospel is precisely the glorious proclamation that the total
life of mankind has in Christ the Second Adam been re-directed to
God in its new Head. Humanity and humanity's life-in-the-world,
i.e., men together, corporately in the totality of their temporal expressions, and in all their manifold relationships and ways of as-

sociating with each other, have, in principle, been saved, are being saved, and will be saved in Christ.

Accordingly, Christian social action is not something individual Christians can do on their own in individual witness and evangelism. The Christian's social and industrial task is part of the divine assignment, part of the cultural mandate to mankind; but it is now a task given to God's chosen people, the men and women of the Third Race, the renewed humanity, to accomplish together out of their new knowledge of the Truth which is in Christ and in the power of Christ's resurrection and His outpoured Holy Spirit. Christian social action is thus an aspect of our building together the genuine community of the Kingdom of God that is sure to destroy all the other false communities of kingdoms of apostate men who serve the principalities and powers of the old world of sin and darkness.[8]

As Christian employers and workers in modern industry we are called to do God's will and to exercise our office according to the will of our Sovereign God as revealed in His Word. In this we are but followers of Christ in the scriptural sense of the term. Christ was the great Ebed Jahweh (Servant of God) who came to do His Father's will; to stand faithful in the office of the Second Adam, to be the servant of God in the whole of his Father's creation. The will of the Heavenly Father, we read in Colossians 1:19, was through himself (Christ) to bring all things whether in heaven or earth back into a right relation to the Father. Everything that has been disrupted and distorted by sin, including both men and their social and political institutions, are to be brought back into obedience to God's ordinances and laws. Here is the cosmic scope of the redemption achieved by Christ on the Cross, the re-creation of God's fallen world (Rom. 8:19-23). This is the coming of the Rule of God, the righted creation which it is every Christian's task in life to serve (Matt. 6:33). Our Lord himself pointed to the parallel between His own work and ours when He said: "As thou hast sent me into the world, even so have I also sent them into the world" (John 17:18).

We are sent into the world to share in Christ's anointing, so that we may become once again a kingdom of priests unto our Sovereign

God. Thus, Christ saves the creation by first restoring his cultural agents to a new obedience. As Henry Van Til well puts it:

> Christ is the transformer of culture, as Schilder maintains, for He is creating here and now in this present evil world a kingdom of truth. For this Calvin gave his full measure of devotion in transforming Geneva from an immoral cesspool to a model of Christian living, according to contemporary witnesses. For if man, the producer of culture, is a restored prophet, priest and king, his culture must of necessity be renewed. For this is the new obedience to which Christ calls his followers since they are in the world but not of the world. Believers as restored creatures are called along with the rest of mankind to engage in cultural activity, in which they present their whole being as a living sacrifice unto God (Rom. 12:2). . . .

> Calvinists, then, under the kingship of Christ confessedly possess a global view of culture as an all encompassing task to bring all things to the obedience of Christ, since he has given the assurance, "All things are yours, and ye are Christ's and Christ is God's (I Cor. 3:22).[9]

Consequently, Christian power formation is inevitable, for it is but the natural outcome of our obedience to Christ our King and of the binding, unifying, and consolidating power of the Word of God which grips the hearts of men and directs them so that they can exercise their office as loyal servants of Jesus Christ.

It is from this scriptural dynamic that Christian power organizations are born. Let it be well understood that the real strength of the Christian organization does not depend on the number of people who support it, or on the amount of money in its treasury, or on the measure of recognition and respect it receives from the secular apostate world. As Gerald Vandezande points out from his own experience as business manager of the Christian Labour Association of Canada for the past ten years:

> The genuine power of the Christian labor organization and the Christian political party is from Jesus Christ Himself to whom all power belongs and who, therefore, sends his anointed servants into the world to demand that human life in its entirety be obedient to the divine law-order. Christian organizations are the concretization, the actualization of the whole-hearted faith-commit-

ment of men and women who earnestly strive to carry out the Lord's command to be his obedient servants in close communion with all who are also rooted in Jesus Christ.[10]

The great Christian philosopher of culture in the Netherlands, K. J. Popma, has likewise spied out the secret dynamic of the Christian power organization. He writes:

> Christ makes of his own a second division in his army of which he is himself the commander in chief and first division. . . . He goes forth, conquering, and carries his own along with him in his victory . . . , links his own to the formation of his power. Therefore it is always worth every effort, therefore it is worth our very life, to establish Christian schools, to strive for Christian politics and a Christian social order, to insist upon Christian scientific pursuits and Christian philosophy. This is worth everything; for sharing in Christ's formation of power makes all human endeavors radiant and glorious amid the poverty of our efforts, the weakness of our attempts and the short-signtedness of our judgment.[11]

While the Reformed Christian thus accepts the necessity for separate Christian cultural formation and separate Christian power organizations, he differs from the Roman Catholic Christian in that he does not think it proper for the clergy or boards of clergymen to direct the non cultic activities and affairs of the Body of Christ in the world.

This is improper for the good reason that such ecclesiastical intervention in the affairs of Christian parents, employers, workers, teachers, etc., would be an infringement upon their respective sovereign spheres. In the Pastoral Epistles neither the state relationship nor the marriage bond nor the family tie is placed under the direct supervision of the Christian clergy as far as their internal organization and their characteristic activities are concerned. When Paul urges the Christians at Corinth to straighten out their differences, he does not say one word about going to the presbyters. The experience of the ecclesiastical imperialism of the papal autocracy during the Middle Ages, as well as of the theocratic presbyterianism of Scotland and the New England states during the seventeenth century, should have warned us by now of the dangers in permitting the Christian clergy and the church as an ecclesiastical institution themselves engage directly in practical politics, economics, and business. The work of the ministry of the Word and Sacraments is surely to instruct the faithful people of God by so preaching the Word of God and showing its contemporary relevance for the world's problems and sins that those Christians who engage in practical life can draw their own conclusions from such principial preaching and teaching for the life of the state, of the factory, and the labor union. Laymen and laywomen are not babes in Christ as the Roman clergy have given others to suppose, but mature persons who have been called to stand firm in their new freedom from sin in Christ (Gal. 4:5).

Christian economic and political organizations are not in themselves mere departments of the Christian ministry or mere functions of the ecclesiastical church institution or the servants of clerical imperialism. Instead, they should grow out of the gifts of the Holy Spirit. Yet even Christian labor unions and employer associations are and must always remain instruments of Christ the King himself. It is none other than Christ himself who sends out His Spirit and qualifies us for our vocation in the world, because He must reign as King of culture, society, and industry until He has put all His enemies under His feet (I Cor. 15:27).

(b) The Church as an Organism and as an Institution of Society

It is imperative that Christians rediscover the New Testament doctrine of the Church. In his various books H. N. Ridderbos has shown that the word *ecclesia* in the New Testament is used in at least two different senses. Usually *ecclesia* refers to the local congregation or to the congregation gathered together for worship. In other instances, however, the word has a much broader meaning, as in Matthew 16:18, for example, where our Lord talks about the Church in the ideal sense of the word, the so-called invisible Church, the people elected and called by God.[12] In the same way Paul refers to the Church in her totality, to the *Universal Church*, which is not to be understood as the union of individual congregations. The universal Church as the new Israel or new people of God or the Body of Christ realizes itself in the life and worship of the local congregations and for this reason the word *ecclesia* can be used (a) for the people of God in general and (b) for the Christian community in a particular locality. The Church, therefore, refers first of all to the *whole* people of God or to the Body of Christ in its totality.[13] In the second place the word *ecclesia* can be applied to the local congregation gathered together for worship, since each congregation is a manifestation and representation of the body of Christ.

At this point, however, we encounter a peculiar difficulty in our thinking about the biblical understanding of *ecclesia*. This is the assumption that whatever Scripture reveals about the Church must apply exclusively to the Church as we know it today, as a distinct communal relationship with a limited place and function in society. The validity of this modern assumption is hardly ever questioned. Yet it is precisely this modern assumption which needs to be questioned and refuted. As Arnold de Graaff points out in *The Educatinoal Ministry of the Church*:

> This question constitutes the major problem of ecclesiology, since it is directly related to the central meaning of the Word of God. It seems quite obvious that the church in its organizational structure as it exists today next to the family, the school, the state, industrial organizations, and numerous other societal relationships cannot possibly embrace *the total* life and witness of the covenant community. But does not Christ make a total claim upon the lives of his people? Does He not regenerate the hearts of the members of His body through His spirit, so that their entire existence is redirected? Does not God's Kingdom embrace all of creation? To whom then is the Gospel addressed? To the church, but to the Church as we know it today with its limited place and function?
>
> The answer we give to this question, implicitly or explicitly, is determinative for our understanding of the Word of God in general, and consequently, for our view of the place of faith and religion in life.[14]

It is obvious that the empirical church we meet at the street corner today differs radically from the local *ecclesia* in the New Testament. During the past two thousand years great changes have taken place in the cultural life of mankind. As a result of a process of cultural differentiation, many functions formerly performed by the family, the tribe, the state, or the church have now been taken over by other social institutions. and organizations. Thus the education of the common people has been taken over by the state from the church in many countries. At the time the New Testament was written the communal life of believers was largely centered around the worship services and the mutual love and care for one another. But since the blessed days of the apostles much has changed. The Christian community has found many ways in which to give expression to its corporate witness and responsibility, e.g., the rise of medieval monasteries, guilds, universities, and a host of Christian societies devoted to various objectives, e.g., the Bible Society, the London Missionary Society, etc. It is in the light of this development that the scriptural references to the church must be understood.

By failing to realize that the Scriptures do not mean by the word *ecclesia* what we today have come to understand by the local church at the street corner the German scholar K. L. Schmidt was led to say in his article on the Church contributed to Kittel's *Theological Word Book of the New Testament*:

> The Church is never triumphant; it is only militant. . . . A triumphant Church would be the kingdom of God, and no longer *ecclesia*. Nor is the Assembly of God in Christ to be described as on the one hand visible and on the other invisible. *The Christian community in any particular place represents the whole body, and is precisely as visible and temporal as the Christian man.*[15]

Likewise L. B. Smedes in his book, *The Nature of the Church and Some Problems in Evangelism*, maintains "Paul gives us no reason to suppose that he is speaking of an organism in distinction from the institution. He refers to one entity, the organism in its living fellowship. He knows only the church." [16]

As a result of their religious and philosophical presuppositions regarding the nature of human society both men find only one kind of church in the New Testament, namely, the institutionalized, organized church as we know it today.

By limiting the word *ecclesia* and its synonyms to the organized church of today, we are bound to misinterpret the Word of God in other important respects. As a result the Bible becomes a "church-book," which becomes limited in its meaning and relevance to man's faith or to the so-called "spiritual realm." The Gospel becomes restricted to the religious aspect of human life and Christ is confined strictly to the church building or the bedroom. On the contrary, as we showed in chapter one, God's Word teaches that life is religion, the service of the one true God or of an idol of man's own devising.

Applying this scriptural insight to the field of ecclesiology means the question of the nature of the church is not one that comes to expression in the locus of theology but of our religious relation to God. It is not an abstract topic for theoretical discussion at all, but one that involves nothing less than our whole view of human nature, origin, and destiny. As soon as one speaks of the church as an institute, i.e., as a structure in society, then one inevitably is led into a view of society as a whole. To refuse to see the whole of life in the light of the ordering principle of God's Word must lead to a distorted view of church, state, and society.

One's conception of the relations between the different institutions and organizations of society is bound to enter in when one seeks to determine the meaning of the New Testament references to the *ecclesia*, or for that matter, to marriage and the family, or to the state. Thus we simply cannot speak meaningfully about the function and nature of today's church without a basic understanding of the development of Western society. As a result one should not be chided for making use of a given philosophical conception of the development of society, for no one can do without such a theory, whether he admits it or not.

What the Christian should be concerned about is whether the religious starting point, upon which these presuppositions concerning the structures of human society are based, is in keeping with the central meaning of God's Word. A view of reality, including the normative process of cultural differentiation or unfolding which is not directed by the scriptural ground-motive of creation, fall into sin, and redemption by Jesus Christ in the community of the Holy Spirit will inevitably distort one's interpretation of the Scriptures and especially the biblical references to the *ecclesia*.

This scriptural ground-motive must not be understood as a static, formal summary of the teachings of the Bible but rather, as a religious ground-motive which directs our whole life along stable paths. In its dynamic grip upon our hearts God's Word opens up a true knowledge of God, of our own selves, and of the law-structures of the creation, including the structure of the church. God's Word provides us with an ordering principle of life that gives order, coherence, and meaning to all our experience. It is the power which alone can inform and put shape into our studies, including the study of the *ecclesia*.

It is for this reason that Abraham Kuyper was able to break through the traditional conception of the *ecclesia* as limited to the institution by distinguishing between the *church as an institute*, by which he meant the organization of the offices, the service of the Word, and Sacraments, and the *church as an organism*, by which he indicated the believers in their mutual relationships in all areas of their lives. In this more biblical conception of *ecclesia* the church remains the people of God, and every element of clerical leaven is rejected.

The Church, according to Kuyper, is not a new creation, but the reconstitution of mankind in Jesus Christ. And as such, as the new humanity, the Church comes to expression in all aspects of life. The believers, united in their common faith in Christ, constitute the people of God, a community of the saints. They do not only function as such within and as members of the institutional church, but they *are* the people of God and the body of Christ, which must necessarily come to expression in all the activities of the community of believers, educational, political, economic, artistic, and so on, and not only in their strictly ecclesiastical life. Wherever there are people of God, there the Church is to be found. Kuyper was aware of the danger and the far reaching consequences of limiting the *ecclesia* to the institutional church. As Ridderbos points out:

> What inspired a man like Kuyper was the calling of the Christian "in every area of life." He stood over against the challenge of the liberal (humanist) supremacy in public life, and also of modern science and culture, and with the intuition of genius and a

mighty faith grasped for the idea of the kingdom of God; and so came to the famous declaration that "there is not an inch in the whole broad terrain of human life to which Christ does not lay claim. . . ." Kuyper could find affiliation with Calvin, for whom also surely not only the soul, nor only the church, but public life as well is the place where the kingship of Christ must be brought to recognition.[17]

Over against the pietistic tendency to withdraw from the world of human culture, science, politics, and industry, Kuyper posed the radical unity of life as service of either the one true God of the Scriptures or of the various false absolutizations of modern life, e.g., scientific materialism, evolutionary biologism, historicism, and relativism. Kuyper proclaimed the absolute lordship of Christ over all of creation. Christ's rule in the hearts of His people must come to expression in all that they do, think, and say in every area of life.

With this view of the Church as the new humanity in Christ, Kuyper had basically overcome the dualistic separation between the sphere of nature and the sphere of grace, between the temporal and the spiritual, the sacred and the secular. Unlike Roman Catholics, Kuyper could not accept the bifurcation of reality into two such realms. Instead, following the biblical teaching that life is religion, he understood the spiritual as the religious direction of man's temporal life.

For this reason we must not think of his conception of the Church as both "organism" and "institute," as two more or less separate entities one of which could then be considered of greater importance than the other. Kuyper never intended any such separation nor that the "institute" should be regarded as of lesser importance than the "organism."

With regard to the relation between the "organism" and the "institute," Kuyper maintained that the variety of the ways in which the *ecclesia* expresses itself may be distinguished but never separated. It would therefore be quite wrong to place the "institute" over against or next to the church as "organism." The *one* body of Christ, the "organism," expresses itself both in the "institute" and in the church as "organism," that is, in all the other spheres of human life.[10] The "invisible" Church as the reborn humanity or the body of Christ is one and reveals itself in the entire "visible" church, in the total life and witness of the people of God, including their worship and the organization of the ecclesiastical offices and services. The emphasis upon the "invisible" Church, the "organism," or the body of Christ, did not lead to any depreciation of the "visible" church, which includes the "institute." It is precisely the "institute" that has a unique and central place in the lives of God's holy people.[18] Through the administration of the Word of God and the blessed sacraments Christ himself would gather His people, transform their lives, and inspire them to whole hearted service of the sovereign God. But since this reformation and renewal of all of human life can only come about through the power of the Word of God, the "institute" can be "nothing more" than an instrument in the service of the "organism." The "institute" can only *administer* the Word of God and the sacraments, but from this administration one may expect to flow the healing, cleansing reforming power of God himself.

It is thus evident that Kuyper used the word "organism" in two different senses: (1) as a synonym for the "invisible" Church or the body of Christ in *all* its "visible" manifestations, and (2) as an indication of the activities of the community of believers *outside* of the sphere of the institutional church with its ecclesiastical offices. Because of this double meaning of the word "organism," Kuyper's terminology is perhaps confusing and should be avoided. Yet his main intention is plain enough and deserves our full support, since the relationship of believers to Christ transcends all communal and social relationships and because the church as we know it today cannot possibly embrace the total life and witness of the covenant community. Ridderbos well says of Kuyper's distinction between "organism" and "institute":

> It is my conviction that this distinction gives expression to an important truth. And that not merely because in this way the visible unity of the church does not have to be sought only in the unity of organization of the offices but also because in this manner the maturity of the church-members can clearly come to light in order to reveal that this, too *without the direct accompaniment of the ecclesiastical offices* is an expression of the body of

Christ. Today there is much discussion of the "neglected office" (i.e., the office of *all* believers) and of the problem of the *laity*. There would be, in my view, less confusion on this issue if it were seen that this office of all believers is not confined within the limits of the institutional church but that it penetrates every area of life. And there would be less need to speak about the *problem* of the laity if the communal activity of the believers in the world were also viewed as an expression, *Gestaltung*, of the church.[19]

Kuyper's distinction indicates a genuine insight into the universal significance of Christ's redemptive work. The kingship of Christ requires nothing less than the reformation and renewal of human life in all its aspects and social structures, and it is the cosmic dimension of His work, its universal blessing revealing itself primarily in the preservation of creation and its structures (common grace) which makes such a reformation possible. By means of his distinction between the new humanity and the institutional church as well as by his refusal to identify the two, and with his conviction that the body of Christ must also come to expression outside the sphere of the institutional church, Kuyper had in principle over the dualism between nature and grace, the church and the world, the sacred and the secular.

It was because Augustine of Hippo did not properly distinguish between the Church as the rule of Christ in the hearts of believers and the temporal church institution, that he came to hold the erroneous view that the state and other social institutions can only become Christian by subjecting themselves to the direction of the institutional Catholic Church. As a result of his identification of the Church in its supra-temporal religious fulness of meaning as the body of Christ with the temporal church institution, Augustine laid the foundation for the medieval view of the Holy Roman Empire, with its secular spiritual sword, under the supremacy of the papacy.

According to this medieval Catholic view the *"ecclesia visiblis,"* as the temporal manifestation of the *"ecclesia invisiblis,"* that is, the supratemporal body of Christ, became identified with the temporal Church institution. This latter spiritual institution was assumed to enjoy the transcendent fulness of power and the all-embracing scope of the *"ecclesia invisiblis."* In this Roman Catholic view

the church of Christ and the kingdom of God coincide; the church
is the realm of Christ, and the Roman Catholic hierarchy is the means
by which Christ exercises his dominion over mankind. The pope in
this Roman system is the vicar of Christ, in whom the kingdom of
God on earth finds its highest representative.

As a result of this mistaken medieval Catholic equation of the visible body of Christ with the temporal church institution, the medieval
dualism between "nature" and "grace" became inevitable. For this
Roman Catholic theory, temporal life belongs to the sphere of nature.
Christ is not the direct King of secular life and culture. The sphere
of faith is separate; it is the sphere of grace. Human society as such
is not a part of the body of Christ, but in its inner structure and nature is worldly and devoid of grace. It has its origin and purpose in
man's earthly existence and, as such, does not lead to eternal life. The
only connection that the sphere of the natural can have with the
sphere of the spiritual is by means of the temporal church institution.
Society can be bound to Christ only through the church institution.
According to Herman Dooyeweerd in *The New Critique of Theoretical Thought*:

> This universalistic conception of the Church institution was the
> erroneous starting point of the scholastic theory of human societal
> structures. It involved a compromise with the classical Graeco-
> Roman view of the State as the perfect whole of human society
> inclusive of the public religion. Fundamentally it was a manifesta-
> tion of the "carnal desire" to deify the temporal Church institu-
> tion, to give the temporal authority of the Church dominion over
> the souls of believers, and to guarantee the temporal Church the
> supremacy over the whole of societal life, including the secular
> government. . . . The "*ecclesia visiblis*," viewed as the hierarchy
> of a sacramental institution of grace, with its monarchical cul-
> mination in the papacy, was as such supposed to transcend all the
> "secular" societal relationships, and to embrace the whole of
> Christian life. In this universalistic conception the Church in-
> stitution is absolutized to the perfect Christian society.
>
> Thomas Aquinas only gave this medieval view a new foundation
> in the scholastic basic motive of nature and grace and adapted
> the former to the Aristotelian metaphysics and politics. The
> dogma of papal infallibility, promulgated in 1870 by the First
> Vatican Council, transfers Christ's absolute authority to the

temporal institution as a hierarchical official organization. The conception of the seven sacraments, as the supra-natural means of grace of the Church institution, is essentially connected with the Roman Catholic view of the supra-natural power of the hierarchically organized clergy. The indispensable requirement for carrying through this conception was the assignment of a real governmental character (not derived from the State) to the official hierarchy.[20]

By understanding the idea of unity in terms of government, rather than unity in terms of a common allegiance to Jesus Christ, the Popes Gregory VII, Innocent III, and Boniface VIII were able to cross the Christian conception of sovereignty with pagan Roman conceptions. The climax of this ecclesiastical absolutism was reached in the claims of Pope Gregory VIII to be the universal Pontiff, to have the sole right to depose bishops, to call General Councils, and to depose the Emperor. Of this papal claim to absolute sovereignty over both church and state Arthur Michael Ramsey, present Archbishop of Canterbury, has written in his book, *The Gospel and the Catholic Church*:

> Either it means a supremacy inherently destructive of the sovereignty of kings and rulers, or else it means that their sovereignty has over against it the Church as a rival state, politically strong enough to hold the balance of power. In either case the view of Church sovereignty has travelled far from the New Testament and from St. Augustine's *City of God*.[21]

The reason for this papal claim to absolute sovereignty is to be found in the medieval identification between Christ and the Church. The Church exists in the union of the natural with the supernatural; this union is the continuation in earthly form of the divine-human life of Christ. And this continuation constitutes the mystical identity of the Church with Christ. According to G. Brom: "The church fathers are as positive as possible in their equating Christ and the church. In Christ the church speaks, and in the church Christ speaks, this is what Augustine teaches. For Gregory the Great says: "Our Redeemer has identified Himself into one person with the church He adopted. . . . More than once in the New Testament the church is identified with Christ, and simply called Christ. . . . The church has the same mission and the same authority." In Roman Catholic thinking this idea of identity is considered to be the essence of all other views of the church which constitutes the foundation of its authority.[22]

For Roman Catholics this supernatural identity with Christ is expressed in the visible unity of the one Holy Roman Catholic Church. The identity of the Church with Christ thus tends to become jurisdictional. This is made clear enough in the papal encyclical *Mystici Corporis Christi* of Pope Pius XII, where the pope writes that when Christ left the earth "He entrusted to the Prince of the Apostles the visible government of the whole society which he had founded." In the jurisdictional unity of Christ with the Church in the pope there lies the essential principle of the living, visible unity of the Church. Without the pope, the external manifestation of the Church's identity with Christ is gone; the body visible would be without the head visible. The identity of the Church with Christ means the unity of the Church in the pope.

As a corollary of this Roman view of the Church's identity with Christ is the corresponding identity of authority. When the pope speaks as pope Christ speaks; when the Church speaks in the pope, the issue is settled. Karl Adam, in his great work *The Spirit of Catholicism*, says:

> When he speaks as pope, as successor of St. Peter, then he speaks as the visible basis and pledge of unity, out of the compact fullness of the Body of Christ, as that principle in which the suprapersonal unity of the Body of Christ has achieved visible reality for the world of space and time. Therefore he does not speak as a despot in his own right, as some absolute monarch, but as the head of the Church in intimate vital relationship to the complete organism of the Church. . . . Yet the pope, in whom this community by Christ's will obtains visible form, rules absolutely *ex sese*, that is to say that in his activity he is in no respect dependent on any member of the Body of Christ, neither on the whole episcopate, nor on the individual bishops, nor on the rest of the faithful.[23]

Given Adam's premises that the visible Church is identical with Christ, it follows that she must be able to speak with the authority of

Christ. Yet it would hardly be possible to state more emphatically than Adam here states that the pope's relation to the Church is qualitatively different from that of every other member or organ; he makes the pope in effect not a member of the Church at all, but an external authority to which the Church is subjected.

In his work, *The Conflict with Rome*, G. C. Berkouwer points out that though Rome makes distinctions between identity and communion with Christ, they cannot be such that truly allow the Church to be subject to Christ as Lord of the Church as long as the pope is held to be visibly identical with Christ. Nor, he says, can the Roman Church be really subject to the criticism of the Word of God.[24]

The Church of Rome teaches an identity with Christ that is prohibited by the nature and office of the Mediator. It is Christ alone who has won the Church's salvation in his sacrifice upon the Cross, and who now reigns over His people. For this reason the organic union of the Church with Christ cannot mean essential identity with either His life or His function.

It is surely required by the analogy of Scripture to infer that in the Pauline language about the Church as the Body of Christ we have a figurative use of language. Our Lord himself never spoke of the Church as His body. But he does use another figure closely related to this image. It is that of the vine and the branches, and no one would attempt to literalize the statement, "I am the vine; ye are the branches" (John 15:5; cf. Matt. 16:18). The Church of Rome seems to have forgotten that analogy is not identity. The literal fact on which Rome bases her doctrine of identity with Christ is the organic unity of the physical body (Rom. 12:4, 5; I Cor. 12:12-27).

Having recognized the figurative force of this biblical analogy we can then ask what is it trying to say? John Murray answers as follows:

> (1) Christ and the church are complementary. We cannot think of a body without a head or a head without a body. Christ is the head of the body (Col. 1:18). Thornton has expressed this graphically when he says: "The Church apart from Christ would be like an empty wine-cup. Christ without the Church would be

like wine which, for lack of a wine-cup, no one could drink" (*The Common Life in the Body of Christ*, p. 310). In like manner Christ's cosmic sovereignty as head over all is his only in relation to the church. He is head over all to his body the Church (cf. Eph. 1:22,23). . . . Christ's mediatorial dominion is ecclesially conditioned and his headship over the Church is conditioned by universal dominion.

(2) The figure of the body implies an organic relationship that exists on an immensely higher plane than anything with which we are acquainted in our phenomenal experience. A supra personal collective such as we have in the institution of the state does not exemplify this organic character and falls far short of what obtains in the mystical body of Christ.

(3) The church as the body derives its life from Christ the head. It is here that the passages in Ephesians are particularly significant (Eph. 1:23; 3:19; 4:13-16). . . . The church is the fulness of Christ in that the fulness resides in him, the fulness of grace and truth (John 1:14), "the treasures of wisdom and knowledge" (Col. 2:3), the fulness of life (John 5:26), the fulness of power (Matt. 28:18) is being communicated to the church. It is not without relevance that the figure of the vine and the branches in the teaching of Jesus, recorded only by John, conveys precisely this truth of utter dependence and communication of life and that in terms of "fulness" it is John who expresses this precise concept when he says: "because out of his fulness we all received grace for grace" (John 1:16).[25]

No Christian would deny that the Rule of the Lord Jesus Christ is *total*. The Kingdom of God is the total renewal in Christ of life in all its structures. Yet the office bearers within the temporal church institution, including the bishops of Rome, possess no such total authority as the popes have claimed for themselves. Such claims are nothing less than an idolatrous deification of a human institution. In his classic work, *The Infallibility of the Church*, George Salmon answers the Roman argument that God would not have left His Church without an infallible guide by first pointing out the silences of the popes for long periods in the face of great problems when infallible guidance would have been most welcome. Secondly, that the teaching which is claimed to be infallibe as often as not has come in response to pressure from fallible quarters. Salmon would have appreciated the *bon mot* of a Roman Catholic lawyer: "When you are infallible, you have to be very careful not to make a mistake," which in spite of its apparent levity may really go to the heart of the matter. Again, Salmon showed how both Popes Liberius and Honorius had taught heresy. If the anathemas of the sixth general council and the confirmatory letter of Pope Leo II ("also Honorius, who did not illuminate this apostolic see with the doctrine of the apostolic tradition but permitted her who was undefiled to be polluted by profane teaching") can be reconciled with the decrees of the First Vatican Council there is no proposition that the human mind is incapable of embracing.[26]

Just before His Ascension and Exaltation into heaven our Lord claimed that He alone possesses all power on earth as well as in heaven (Matt. 28:16), thereby implying that He shares in God's supreme sovereignty and that all authority has been given to Him alone on earth (I Cor. 15:24-26; Phil. 2:9-11).

All authority means the supreme right to appoint to office. As Second Person of the Godhead Christ is the full and complete Office bearer and as such is the origin and source of all power exercised on earth. Christ delegates only partial sovereignties to men. In Him alone and not in the pope all these earthly sovereignties are united in an undivided service of God that involves nothing less than the redemption of the whole of human life.

From this it follows that the office bearers in the church institution obtain their authority directly from Christ and not from the pope nor from the congregation, as some Protestants suppose. As King of Common and Special Grace Christ has instituted the office of government in church and state on account of the hardness of men's hearts. The authority of government in both church and state is derived from Christ. While the people may rightly elect their rulers in church and state, they must never forget that the ultimate authority of government over men comes from Christ alone, which the people must obey for conscience sake (Rom. 13:1-8).

Perhaps the main reason that so many "liberal humanists" do not recognize the Kingship of Christ over modern society is because for over fifteen hundred years Christians have tended to identify the Christian religion and the church with respect to their scope, structure, and intentions. In his book, *The Emperor Theodosius and the Establishment of Christianity*,[27] Noel King has traced this identification back to the Second Ecumenical Council, held at Constantinople in A.D. 381 and 382. The canons adopted at this Council were ratified by the emperor as part of the law of the Roman Empire. On July 30, 381, Theodosius signed a decree giving universal validity to the synod's decrees on faith, as well as to its decisions regarding appointments to episcopal thrones. At an earlier date the emperor had granted this state-church a unique privilege declaring that henceforth all citizens who became renegades into paganism were to be punished by losing the right to make wills. Christianity thus became the religion of the state in the full sense of that phrase.

The distinction between "clergy" and "laity" was introduced into the Church almost entirely under this secular Roman influence. It was taken over from the patterns of civic life in the Roman Empire, and it became entrenched in the reign of Theodosius, when certain privileges and benefits were extended to the clergy of the Christian Church, which had previously been bestowed by the Roman Empire on the heathen priesthood. And at that point it became important to define who was entitled to these benefits and who was not. Hence, the beginning of a *legal* division between members of "the clergy" and the "laity." This tragic division gradually became more and more firmly established during the Middle Ages. Christianity became identified with the "established" Church. Consequently the majority of Western Christians lost sight of any distinction between the significance of the central, religious heart commitment of the believer to the Lord Jesus Christ and the particular place and function of the church as an institution of God's special grace in the totality of life. It came to be supposed that Christianity concerned only the organized activities of the church as an official institution of society. In his article, "Church in Society," John C. Vanderstelt points out: "The inevitable result of this approach is a Christian religion which in self-asserting fashion claims for itself totalitarian, ecclesiastical power over the rest of society. Think, for example, of the Roman Catholic idea of the *Corpus Christianum* during the Middle

Ages. Today it is present in the attitude that all nonecclesiastical organizations become Christian only by virtue of the fact that they are somehow affiliated with or subsumed under a direct or indirect authority of the church." [28]

As long as Christians continue to think of the church institution as the whole which should embrace all other social spheres, the humanist's opposition will continue to be directed against such implicit or explicit church-imperialism rather than against the living God of the Scriptures and of Christ the redeemer of life in its entirety. Not until Christians and post-Christians see the meaning of life as directed toward either God or an idol and false god, can either be genuinely honest with each other. Only when both sides realize that life is religion will it be possible not to be misled by a so-called common ground in "natural" reason devoid of the influence of God or the devil. When this distinction is upheld then there can be no more place whatsoever for any form of ecclesiastical imperialism. Then, instead of offending with the claims of the church, it will be Christ himself who causes the uproar and scandal as He did in Nazareth (Mark 6:3). In his review of H. Blamires' book, *The Christian Mind*, John C. Vanderstelt writes:

> The disappearance of the real Light from the world has all too often been caused by narrow-minded, imperialistic churches and theologies. The world's hostility against such imperialism has forced churches and theologians to retreat. And now they keep this Light for the world under pietism's bushel, and even the latter they hide from the world by placing it inside a church. . . .
>
> We must remember that the world will not forget the position and activities of the Roman Catholic Church during the Middle Ages, and that it required a French Revolution to break the Roman Catholic monopoly. The world will not forget the role in past history of the Anglican Church in the practical affairs of life. Having learned its lesson from history, it will, therefore, resist also any type of Barthianism with its theological ethics, theological jurisprudence, theological aesthetics, theological sociology, etc., etc. In spite of the many differences between Roman Catholics, Anglicans and Barthians, they have all at least this in common that they regard the all embracing Kingdom of God as being synonymous with a Church and a theology. And they all also believe that the collision God has wanted is one which

results from the clash between the Church and the world.

However, this latter collision is not the only and most important one. It is but one of the symptoms that manifest the real clash at the heart level of human existence, where forces of Darkness collide vehemently with powers of Light, where the real fundamental, and biblical antithesis finds its initial and most radical expression, where believers and unbelievers call "a spade a spade."

Roman Catholicism, Anglicanism, Barthianism, and individualistic pietism cannot, by their very nature, provide the real answer for the baffling crisis of contemporary Christianity. Though their attempts are many, their intentions deeply sincere, their zeal undaunted, and their concern profound, nevertheless, their plans and activities are artificial, not in accordance with the creational structure of life and history. Christian politics, Christian education, Christian journalism (and we may add Christian economics and sociology), for example, cannot be arrived at by bringing together for discussion theologians or church officials *and* politicians, educators and journalists (to whom we may add labor leaders and employers and clergy). Blamires sensed this; not views of Christians, but Christian views! Because of the lack of Christian views he feels lonely, at a loss. His urging us to get going and form a community of opinion, penetrated by the light of the Revelation, must evoke our whole hearted response and immediate concretization.[29]

According to Dooyeweerd the only way Christians today can hope to avoid these evil consequences of the medieval synthesis of "nature" and "grace," of Christianity and Classical Culture is to maintain the biblical teaching that the "invisible" church or the Church as the Body of Christ includes far more than the instiutional life of the church. The Church as the Body of Christ includes *all* of temporal society in so far as it derives its life, being, and direction from the Risen, Ascended, and Reigning Christ and employs *all* its energies to advance His Kingdom and rule over the hearts of men. As he writes, the Church ". . . is found wherever the Christian attitude to life expresses itself in temporal form," wherever there are people of God, there the Church is to be found.[30] All human relationships and societal structures, including the institutional church, must be seen in the light of the *religious* unity of mankind. In Adam mankind in its entirety fell away from God, but in Christ the new humanity is restored to fellowship with God, and it is only this *religious* community in Christ that can embrace the whole of Christian life. No single institution or organization can or may encompass all communal relationships and exercise totalitarian control over human life. Christ alone may demand total obedience; and all other authority is delegated to earthly rulers by Christ and is limited in scope. The identification of the institutional church with the fulness of the body of Christ, therefore, must necessarily lead to a collectivist absolutization or deification of the empirical church and ecclesiastical offices. Dooyeweerd says:

> The Christian religion struck a decisive blow at the very foundation of the entire ancient view of human society. Behind all the temporal societal relationships it revealed the religious root of the human race. It disclosed the transcendent religious bond of unity of the latter in the creation, the fall into sin, and the redemption in Jesus Christ, the Head of the reborn human race. . . .
>
> The Christian view did not place a new community (the Church in its transcendent religious sense) on a parallel with, or if need be, above all temporal relationships, as a merely higher level in the development to human perfection. Nor did it project a cosmopolitan temporal community of mankind beyond all boundaries of families, races, and states, in the Stoic fashion.
>
> Instead, it laid bare the religious fullness of meaning of all social relationships, each of which ought to express this meaning-fulness according to its own inner structure. Without this insight into the radical spiritual foundation of human societal life, the differentiation of structural principles of temporal society cannot be understood in its true meaning.
>
> The critical point in any Christian view of this temporal society is the question what position is to be ascribed to the Church, as an organized institution. It is beyond doubt that the latter, in its inner nature, is not to be viewed apart from the Body of Christ in its transcendent religious sense as the radical communion of reborn mankind in Jesus Christ. Nevertheless, it may neither be identified with the religious fulness of the body of Christ, nor with the temporal expression of the latter in those societal relationships which as such have a radically different type from that of the organized Church-institution.[31]

What is at stake here is not merely some "pet" philosophical the-

ory concerning the church, but a fundamental view of human society as a whole, which is motivated by the scriptural view that life
is religion. It is impossible to discuss the nature of the church as
an institution of human society without saying something, if even
only by implication, about society as a whole. As Vanderstelt says,
"It is only within the context of *one* God, *one* Revelation, *one* Christ,
and *one* creation that we can begin to see the place and task of an
integrally religious and creationally undivided mankind which is
subjected to all the creational laws, including those for the historical
development of society; a mankind which is called upon to respond
obediently to the new Law of God's regime in Christ. Only after
we have seen these truths are we able to deal with the nature,
place, and task of the church in society." Any attempt to deal with
the church in and by itself, without considering the structural interrelations of all the sovereign spheres of society in general, inevitably
leads to a "docetic" and "phony" conception of the church, and consequently to a fatal dualism between the church and the world, the
sacred and the secular, the temporal and the eternal.

Most Christian theologians have allowed their view of the church
to be influenced by non-scriptural philosophies and sociologies derived from Platonic, Aristotelian, Hegelian, Marxist, capitalistic pragmatic, existentialist, and process presuppositions about human nature
and society. As a result of this false starting point the majority of
theologians, Catholic, Protestant, and Orthodox, have been unable to
relate the order of redemption to the order of creation. Thus the
very terms most used in ecclesiology, *ecclesia invisiblis* and *ecclesia
visiblis*, have been derived from the metaphysical antithesis between
noumenon and *phenomenon*, i.e., a temporal world and an eternal
world of pure being or form. Such a separation is false in the light
of the biblical doctrine of the unity in diversity of God's temporal
creation.

In *The Divine Imperative*, Emil Brunner distinguishes between the
church as a cultic community and "the Church of faith," which
stands for the older term, "ecclesia invisiblis." In the church as a
cultic community he admits the necessity for a material institutional
form. As an order of man's devising, it should keep its proper

distance from the authority of God's Word. In his work, *The Misunderstanding of the Church*, Brunner claims that what is today called the ecumenical movement is hindering true Christian unity by laying so much stress on an organized unity of the churches. He contends that a misunderstanding about the *ecclesia* of the New Testament lies behind this mistaken effort. He writes:

> The *ecclesia* of the New Testament, the fellowship of Christian believers, is precisely *not* that which every "church" is at least in part—an institution, a something. The Body of Christ is nothing other than a fellowship of persons. . . . The faithful are bound to each other through their common sharing in Christ and in the Holy Ghost, but that which they have in common is precisely no "thing," no "it," but a "he," Christ and His Holy Spirit. . . . As the Body of Christ the Church has nothing to do with an organization and has nothing of the character of the institutional about it.[32]

Paul G. Schrotenboer has pointed out that Brunner's ecclesiology "has severely damaged the truly personal encounter between God and man, by his rejection of the Church as officialdom and an institution. He claims that the only authority the apostles had was their primal witness. . . . His view is situational rather than biblical. He looks at the *situation* of the apostles rather than at the *assignment* which Christ gave them. Brunner's theology has little place for representatives. In fact, his personalism has virtually no room for office at all." [33]

For Brunner the Body of Christ has nothing institutional about it. It consists only of persons, held together by Christ and His Holy Spirit. It might be thought that Brunner is merely contending for the old escape from the problems of disunity which assert that the Church is invisible. This he strenuously denies. Brunner's thought owes much to the thesis developed by Rudolf Sohm in 1909 in his book, *Wesen und Ursprung des Katholizmus*, which distinguished between *Geist* and *Recht* (Spirit and Law). Brunner maintains that what has gone wrong with the church has been the introduction of the idea of law into the spiritual society of the *Ecclesia*. And this began very early, starting even in the New Testament itself; its

conclusion is the Papal Church. For Brunner the *Ecclesia* is the
sphere of actual and realized fellowship in Christ; but it is not—and
cannot be—legally organized. The success of the ecumenical movement depends, according to Brunner, upon a recognition of this. Of
this distinction drawn by Brunner between the church as a legal
institution and the church as a fellowship of believers in Christ,
Dooyeweerd writes:

> The conception implied by this terminology unambiguously
> absolutizes the temporal community of faith to the *transcendent
> root* of the church. The "cult community" as an "empirical com-
> munity" is not conceived of in its only possible sense of a tem-
> poral *community of faith* in its common cult but is opposed to
> the community of faith as the empirical versus the transcendent
> hidden church. This fideistic standpoint falsifies the structure of
> the temporal church-institution. Its consequences are apparent in
> the entire view these writers take of the conception of the Re-
> formers concerning the relation between the *ecclesia visiblis* and
> the *ecclesia invisiblis*.
>
> The background of Brunner's dualism between form and con-
> tent of Church-law is the deeper dualism between "nature" and
> "grace," Law and Gospel. So long as this dualism keeps ruling
> our thought it is impossible to gain an insight into the structure
> of individuality of the temporal church-institution. The con-
> trast Brunner makes between "the Church of faith" and the "cult
> community," replacing the distinction between "*ecclesia invisi-
> blis*" and "*ecclesia visiblis*" (the institution), testifies to a lack of
> insight into the internal structure of the institutional Church.[34]

Brunner's notion of the church arises from his dialectical irrationalistic philosophical starting point in existentialism and personalism.
Refusing to develop a truly biblical doctrine of the church, Brunner
simply uncritically relapses into a synthesis with the theories of the
church of the immanence standpoint of apostate humanism by accepting in principle the dialectical basic problem of the modern
nature-freedom motive. Falsely, he supposes he can reduce this
basic problem to the basic antithesis in the Christian view between
creation and the fall. At the back of this synthetic standpoint
emerges the false contrast between natuer and grace, which in Brunner's teaching assumes the form of a dialectical tension between the

"commandment of love of the moment" and the "law as such." He commits the serious error of confusing the factor of power in the structure of individuality of churches with the subjective way in which churches in this sinful world have abused their power. Of Brunner's basic approach around the dialectics of law and Gospel, of impersonal and personal, world-truths and God-truths, nature and grace, Paul G. Schrotenboer well says in his essay on Brunner in *Creative Minds in Contemporary Theology*:

> Brunner's theology is a grand attempt to synthesize an irrational (reason-devaluating) personalism and the biblical message. . . . The central question is: *Can Brunner bring his personalism and the biblical data into a harmonious unity?* . . .
> It must be seen, however that the deepest stratum of Brunner's theology is situation, rather than biblical. The consideration of concrete existing man is constitutive for his theology; the consideration of man in the prelapsarian and postmortem states is only additive. The latter are limiting concepts which assist man in explaining himself as he is today. Brunner finds man's responsibility more important than his creatureliness. Moreover, creation is not a cosmic or causal event, but an act of God's address. Every man is his own Adam and must be understood from his existential situation. . . .
> In still another way Brunner has severely damaged the truly personal encounter between God and man: namely, by his rejection of the Church as an officialdom and an institution. He claims that the only authority the apostles had was their primal witness. Once again his view is situational, rather than biblical. He looks at the *situation* of the apostles, rather than at the *assignment* which Christ gave them. Brunner's theology has little place for representatives. In fact, his personalism has no room for office at all.
> In reaction to Brunner, we do well not to choose the official instead of the personal. To the contrary, we must maintain that in order to effect the encounter, God instituted the offices in the Church so that, as Jesus said, "he that receiveth you, receiveth me, and he that receiveth me receiveth him that sent me" (Matt. 10:40). The true view of the Christian's office in the world would deliver life from the bane of impersonalism if men would only see the special *place* and *assignment* that God has given them.[35]

The only way out of the false dilemma of choosing for the

"Church of love as against the "Church of organization" is to return to the biblical view of the Church as God's New Israel and the Body of Christ. As long as Christians remember that the Church of God is called into being as the "servant Church" there will be no place for any false "triumphalism." To recognize the Church's basic structure as a communion of God's people, indwelt by God's Spirit, on pilgrimage through this world, is to recover an essential element to ecclesiology.

The institutional church is not called to dominate any of the other forms of the Kingdom of God, as they too are endowed with internal sovereignty. The task of the institutional church is rather to serve God in the way He has prescribed, in harmony with other forms of society.

Since the institutional church is fully integrated in the order of creation and functions within all the modal aspects of reality, it is not higher or superior to any other societal structure. Looked at from the scriptural perspective on reality, all communal relationships are equivalent to one another, since they have a common basis in the "universal" Church and function, each according to its own typical nature, within the creation order. Each societal relationship has its own irreplaceable value and typical structure, but as expressions of the Church as the People of God and the Body of Christ in the different spheres of life they are all equal in rank. The Church as the People of God and the Body of Christ includes all of temporal society insofar as it derives its life from the Lord Jesus Christ and employs its energy to advance His Kingdom and rule over the hearts of men. Thus a Christian marriage, family, state, school, business, or any other Christian relationship which acknowledges Christ as King of heaven and earth belongs to the visible Body of Christ on this earth just as much as does the visible, temporal, ecclesiastical institution. As Dooyeweerd says:

> The *ecclesia visiblis* is not limited to the institutional Church, but in principle embraces all the structures of human society. The only Christian starting point remains the supra-temporal "*ecclesia invisiblis.*" In this religious radical community in Christ all temporal societal structures are equivalent to one another, just as all

the different law-spheres are irreplaceable refractions of the fulness of meaning in Christ, each in its own modal structure.[36]

This does not mean, of course, that the institutional relationships of church, state, and family are not more important and fundamental for human society than the free associations. Yet, considered from the point of view of the all-embracing religious community in Christ, all societal structures are equivalent to one another.

Only the motivating force of the biblical religious ground motive can deliver us from all forms of synthesizing with non-biblical ground motives, such as the Roman Catholic attempt to accommodate the Greek "matter and form" motives in terms of "nature and grace" as well as the Protestant effort to synthesize Christianity with the modern "nature and freedom" motive in terms of Brunner's irrationalistic personalism. Only the scriptural doctrine of sphere sovereignty can give us the true perspective in terms of which to understand the real structures of God's creation, including the structure of the church.

The church, like every other social relationship, functions in all the modal aspects or law-spheres of the creation. Thus the church has the following aspects among others: the mathematical consisting in the unity of the church in the plurality of its members; the historical in that the church as an institution is engaged in giving form to its own internal life; the economic coming to expression in fund raising, savings, and investments, the juridical expressed in the church's canon law and order; the aesthetic consisting in the church's need for her own typically qualified "sacred music" and "sacred art"; the ethical, since the church functions within the moral aspect as a typical community of love among believers in Christ, bound together by their common confession of faith in Him as their Lord and Savior; the analytical, since the church is obliged to give logical form to its reflection upon the meaning of the divine revelation; the lingual expressed in the church's use of various forms of symbolical signification by means of signs, symbols, and sacraments; the psychical, since the church engages in evangelism, sick visiting, and pastoral counseling; the biological, expressed in baptism, marriage, and burial services, as well as the healing and care of the sick; the physical and spatial, since the church occupies and uses buildings consecrated for the worship of God.

The church, then, is not some supra-temporal phenomenon having no contact with other aspects of existence, but a community of believers qualified by their faith in Christ with an individuality structure of its own, yet fully integrated in the temporal world order. It has its own *type* of fellowship, its own *typical* legal ordering and constitution, music, art, financial policies, language, symbols, tradition, education, buildings, and so forth. These moral, juridical, aesthetical, economic, historical, logical psychical, and biological aspects in which the church functions as a communal structure of human society cannot be placed over against the "spiritual" essence of the church, its faith-aspect as Brunner tries to do. There is nothing in the various modal functions of the church as such that is incompatible with its inner nature since every aspect of God's creation is a reflection of the religious fulness of meaning and as Genesis tells is therefore "good" (Gen. 1:31).

As a concrete communal relationship the church thus functions in all the aspects of creation, but always as the *church*, that is, in its own typical manner, never as the state or the school or the business enterprise or the theatre. Its exceptional character as a community of faith in Christ, therefore, should come to expression in all its activities. Its buildings must be church buildings, its music church music, its instruction *catechetical* instruction, its aid and care of the sick and poor an expression of *agape*, its fellowship a fellowship of of the Gospel, and its pastoral counsel and admonition a ministry of the Word of God, not of men. The unique and glorious character of the church must therefore come to expression in every aspect of its life. This individuality structure of the church has so far received little attention among theologians. Yet without such an analysis of the modal functions of creation in which the church operates, many aspects of its life remain unexplained. Dooyeweerd has only laid down the outlines for such an inquiry which needs developing more fully.

(c) *The Church as an Instrument*
     of God's Special Grace in Christ

While it is utterly beyond human power to establish which of the members of the church institution are really Christian and which are so only in name, the ecclesiastical institution in principle can only embrace those who have been included in the New Testament covenant by holy baptism. In comparison, therefore, with the other temporal societal relationships revealing the *ecclesia invisiblis*, the institutional church occupies an exceptional position, since it alone is qualified as a *Christian community of faith*. It is in this sense that the church institution is an instrument of special grace. All its members have a common faith, even though they may differ in nationality, age, knowledge, sex, class, and profession.

The function of faith differs from all other functions of the creation in that it bears a border character. Negatively this means that the qualifying faith function of the church institution does not have any modal anticipations. Positively it means that in the function of faith, all of creation points toward the Origin of all things, toward Almighty God who created and redeemed the world through Jesus Christ. Dooyeweerd points out that "the very unique place of faith in temporal reality is entirely misunderstood if one has not understood its border position between time and eternity. It is the final, the border aspect of temporal reality and, at the same time, the window to eternity. Faith cannot exist without revelation from God. It is its nature to be oriented to that revelation." [37]

Dooyeweerd rejects the Greek view of faith as meaning "holding an opinion, not knowing with certainty" as well as the Roman Catholic conception of faith as a "supernatural gift of grace to the intellect through which the latter can grasp the supernatural values of salvation." As a result of this Catholic view of faith, the faith function of reality simply became a supernatural extension of the analytical thought function. It remains a mere intellectual assent to the doctrines taught by the Roman Catholic Church. In this scholastic conception of faith any insight into the peculiar nature of the faith function within the border aspect of temporal reality is bound to be lost. According to Dooyeweerd, real faith is something different both from uncertain opinion and a mere intellectual acceptance of propositions. He writes:

> The central meaning of faith is ultimate temporal certainty concerning the Sure Ground of our life, being gripped in the heart of one's existence by the revelation of God as the Fountain of all things. There is no real faith . . . which is not oriented to such a revelation of God. Thus, its definition as intuitive certainty or evidence does not touch the root of the faith function. . . .
>
> It is precisely to this indestructable orientation to God's revelation, that the faith function and the faith aspect within which it works owes its border position between time and eternity. The faith function as such is included in the temporal world order. It belongs to temporal life, just as does organic life and life function. . . . The faith aspect is the last in the time order of the aspects. All others anticipate this one. It is, however, oriented to that which transcends time, the absolute basis and origin of all temporal life. . . . On the one hand it points beyond time to the religious root and origin of all our temporal existence and yet it is also indissolubly tied to the modal moments of all other aspects of the creation.[38]

As a community qualified by faith in God's revelation of himself as sovereign creator and redeemer of the world, the church differs from the family or the state. Unlike these social relationships, all the structural aspects of the church point beyond the created reality. Unlike the church the family or the state can be made up of both Christians and non-Christians. The church can only exist as a Christian community of faith pointing directly to the fulness of the body of Christ, the Church in its central religious sense.

At the same time it needs to be remembered that both the family and the state also function in the modality of faith and as such cannot be neutral. A neutral state such as that advocated by secular humanists is only a fiction of their own apostate imagination. A non-Christian state or family also makes a confession of faith. It forces people or children to bow down before the false gods of power, production, and profits. Since the outbreak of the French Revolution the life of most modern states has been pushed in an apostate direction, and a political confession or ideology has been made in the name of the sovereignty of the people, or the dictatorship of the proletariat, or in the omnicompetence of the state itself, or in the goddess of "reason" or "science" and planning.

Unlike the family, which is a "natural" institution founded on the biological function of sex, the church, like the state or the university or the business corporation or labor union, is founded in an organization of historical power. But again, the typical nature of this power of the faith-community differs radically from that of other historically founded institutions and associations. The organization of power upon which the church is based is the power of the Word of God, which immediately points toward Christ's reign in the hearts of His people, to the power of His Spirit. In the institution of the apostolic office and Christ's charge to administer the sacraments and to proclaim the Word of God, our Lord himself has given this faith power its initial organization. As Dooyeweerd puts it:

> The whole temporal Church institution is founded in the historical power of Christ as the incarnate Word. It is the historical power of "the Sword of the Divine Word" which by faith is directly grasped as the revelation of Christ's transcendent fulness of power, of His kingship over the whole world. Christ himself gave this historical power its first provisional organization in the institution of the apostolic office and the sacraments: "Go ye therefore, and teach all nations, baptizing them in the name of the Father, and of the Son and of the Holy Ghost." By His Word through the mouth of His apostles He has ordained the basic structure of the institutional church organization.[39]

The various ecclesiastical offices and functions, which by a process of differentiation and individualization already during the New Testament period arose out of the apostolic office, are all characterized by the power of faith, which refers directly to the fulness of power in Jesus Christ, to His absolute authority and universal kingship. These offices, therefore, must also be thought of as instruments for the effectual working of God's grace through his Word and sacraments.

Among the various societal relationships, however, the church as an institution does occupy a central place in the Christian life, since it is qualified by the function of faith, which determines its entire structure. As such, according to its internal structural law, the church as an institution is an institutional manifestation of God's *special grace* in Jesus Christ. According to its inner nature this community can only embrace Christian believers and their children. In this respect the church as an institution differs from the family or the state, which can be made up of both Christians and non-Christians. The church can only exist as a Christian community of faith pointing directly to the fulness of the body of Christ, the Church in its central religious sense.

Unlike the family, which is an institution of God's common grace, the Church is a manifestation of God's special grace. Dooyeweerd prefers the use of the term "temporal conserving grace" rather than Kuyper's term "common grace" to denote the grace of God in Christ by which the temporal world order is preserved by limiting the consequences of the destructive power of sin. Thus temporal life with its family, state, marriage, economic, and academic relationships is preserved even when renewing, regenerating grace is absent. God's conserving grace alone enables apostate culture to develop and unfold. As Dooyeweerd puts it:

> Insofar as the other societal relationships (other than the empirical church), in their actual reality, are *subjectively* withdrawn from the "*Corpus Christi,*" they fall outside of the "*ecclesia visiblis.*" Only in this respect do they remain enclosed within the *civitas terrena,* viz., in a *subjective* sense. But the conserving grace in Christ preserves and maintains the structural offices of the institutional organizations and communities, and liberates them, at least in principle, from the *civitas terrena.*[40]

According to Dooyeweerd there is no grace or benevolence of God towards sinful man apart from Jesus Christ, the Savior of the world. The grace of God, Father, Son, and Spirit, operates in a twofold manner as conserving and renewing grace, both of which operate throughout the entire realm of human life. There is no question here of reintroducing as it were through the back door the medieval religious ground motive of "nature" and "grace." Life is not divided into two realms of "conserving grace" and "regenerating grace." This Dooyeweerd makes clear:

Particular grace directly concerns the supra-temporal root of mankind, whereas common grace remains restricted to temporal life. . . . Common grace has its root and centre only in Christ as the incarnate Word. We oppose any kind of dualistic theory of specific *"spheres of grace,"* which is essentially nothing but an after effect of the dualistic basic motive of "nature" and "grace."[41]

At this point it may well be asked: "If the Church, as a temporal organized community, is recognized as an institution of particular grace, do not we then run the risk of identifying this temporal institution with the supra-temporal 'Body of Christ'?" And on the other hand, is there not a risk of eradicating the difference between common grace and special grace if, in accordance with Kuyper, we distinguish between the "church as an institution," and the "church as an organism"?

Dooyeweerd replies that we need not, provided that we always bear in mind that there is no grace or goodness of God in this sinful world apart from Jesus Christ. Christ is the sole source of all blessing and the Savior as well as Preserver of the world. He says:

"Special grace" or "particular grace" really refers to the radical change brought about by Jesus Christ in the apostate root of the whole temporal cosmos, which is concentrated in mankind; therefore this "particular grace" bears a radical universal character. Already in the present dispensation this radical change of direction in the root of life must necessarily reveal itself in temporal reality, in its conserving effect as well as in its regenerative operation. Its conserving effect is primarily manifest in the preservation of the temporal-world order by God in Jesus Christ, as the Head of the Covenant, so that the disintegrating effect of the fall into sin in temporal life is checked.

God does not renounce His creation, not even in its subjective apostasy. He maintains the temporal structures, which cannot find their creaturely root, their religious centre, in the spirit of apostasy. . . . Jesus Christ is the "Second Adam" in whom nothing of God's creation can be lost. . . . Outside of Him there is no divine grace, no "common grace" either, but only the manifestation of God's wrath on account of sin. . . . Special grace which we had better call "renewing" or "regenerating grace," only embraces the *"ecclesia invisiblis,"* i.e., reborn mankind. The temporal manifestation of the *"ecclesia invisiblis"* pervades temporal society in all its structures. It is found wherever the Christian attitude to life expresses itself in a temporal form.[42]

By means of his special grace working through the Church as the Body of Christ in all societal structures as well as through the Church as an institution, the Lord is restoring the whole of His creation to its original splendor and glory. Thus the deeper unity between the two modes of God's grace becomes apparent insofar as it expresses the Christian spirit at work, not merely in the cultic community of the temporal church institution, but throughout all areas of human life. This, Dooyeweerd says, is what "Kuyper meant by his view of the Church as an organism, in which he clearly and fundamentally opposed the dualistic separation between "special" and "common grace." [43]

Whether we call it "temporal conserving grace" or, as Rushdoony prefers, "earlier grace" [44] or common grace with Abraham Kuyper surely does not really matter, as long as we hold fast to the idea which these terms suggest. It is God's common grace which alone makes the "antithesis" possible. It is in fact the *condition* of the antithesis. Human society would have been utterly destroyed had the common grace of the Lord not intervened to restrain the rampage of sin.

By His common grace God restrains the perverseness of fallen human nature from breaking out into external acts of violence and wickedness. In a variety of ways, internally and externally, the Lord checks human sin (I Sam. 16:14; II Kings 19:27-28; Acts 7:42; Rom. 13:1-4; II Thess. 2:6ff.). In some instances God ceases His restraining activity upon the human conscience and gives men over to a reprobate mind in order that their sin may work itself out in its utter godlessness and corruption (Rom. 1:24, 26, 28). Even this, however, shows that previously the Lord had prevented their disobedience from running its natural course and that He had held it in abeyance.

Those who would so readily discard this clear teaching of God's Word in order to maintain their righteousness before the heathen would do well to remember that the Old Testament places the whole history of Israel within a setting which is universal. God's dealings with the Chosen Race may be said to begin with the covenant with Abraham. But there was a more ancient covenant. After the deluge had obliterated the first creation, when the ancestors of the entire human race came out into a world reborn, "God spake unto Noah and to his sons with him and said, "And I, behold I establish my covenant with you and with your seed after you, and with every living creature that is with you, the fowl, the cattle, and every beast of the earth with you" (Gen. 9:8-10). Of this Noachian covenant C. H. Dodd of Cambridge writes:

> This passage . . . was written by an author for whom God's covenant with Israel was a regulative fact of history and an assured *datum* for thought. The pattern of this covenant reappears in the report of the covenant with Noah; the divine act of deliverance is proclaimed, and the obligations of the covenant declared. The writer, then, was quite deliberate in emphasizing all through, the complete universality of the primeval covenant—all mankind, every living creature, the earth itself are parties to it (Gen. 9:8-17). This is the covenant under which the stork in the heavens knoweth her appointed place. It follows that the patriarchal and Mosaic covenant was made with men who were already in covenant with God; and that there is, strictly speaking, no man who is without the Law, unless by his own act, since all men inherit the covenant established with Noah and his seed.
>
> Under the terms of the Noachian covenant, God offers to men a guarantee of stability in the order of creation—what science calls, or did call until recently, the "uniformity of nature" (Gen. 9:11; cf. 8,22). In turn He lays upon man certain injunctions and prohibitions. Man is to "replenish the earth"; he is to refrain from manslaughter and from eating the flesh of animals with the blood (Gen. 9:1-7).[45]

It seems likely that the minimum requirements demanded of Gentile Christians in the Apostolic decree of Acts 15:29 represents this Noachian code, which in that case must have been pre-Christian. God's covenant with Noah is a perfect expression of his common grace. St. John speaks in the Prologue to his gospel of the light "that lighteneth *every* man that cometh into the world. The Word as light was in the whole world, yet unacknowledged; the Word as light came to Israel and was rejected. To those, however, who accepted it, it gave the right to become the children of God. In

Christ, therefore, man is confronted with that Word of God, or Wisdom or Law, which is the very law of His creation, the same which was partially disclosed to Israel in the Torah, and is known in some measure to all mankind through conscience, as the Moral Law, a law which our Savior came not to abolish but to fulfill (Matt. 5:17).

Dooyeweerd himself prefers the use of the term "temporal manifestation of the body of Christ in all societal relations," rather than Kuyper's term "the church as an organism." At the same time he agrees that "in this broad sense it also embraces the temporal church institution."

The *"ecclesia visiblis"* in this universal sense must not be identified with the temporal church institution, since the latter remains bound to its specific structural principle as a community qualified by its faith in Christ as Lord and Savior and so could appear in history only when the Word of God was made flesh. The temporal manifestation of the Body of Christ, in its broadest sense, on the other hand, not only embraces all the societal structures of our temporal human life, but made its appearance at the first sign of the great antithesis or opposition between the *civitas Dei* and the *civitas terrena*.

In order that His kingdom may come, the Lord Christ restrains sin by His conserving grace. His kingdom must develop as long as world history continues. His renewing grace works both through His people as a whole in their various "offices" in society and by means of the church as an institution.

For this biblical reason, therefore, Christian education, Christian economic enterprise, Christian trade unionism, and Christian politics can never be achieved merely by bringing together theologians and church officials with secular labor leaders, businessmen, and politicians for weekend conferences. The biblical reformation of society will take place only when God's covenant people realize that their Savior and King calls them to function not only as His people at worship, but also as His servants in the world. As Joel H. Nederhood said at a Fall Rally of the Christian Action Foundation of America in 1967: "Christian Action consists of sons and daughters of the resurrection going out speaking as one voice and acting as one man with reference to politics, to education, the problem of races, and the great social problems that confront us today." [46]

Compare this biblical advice with the teaching of Bishop Wickham in *Church and People in an Industrial City*. The Bishop of Middleton distinguishes among three possible modes of relationship between the church and the world:

(1) The theonomous relationship where the church becomes a reflection of the secular, common society. In such a condition of "theonomy" grace and nature co-inhere and to use Tillich's words, "the ultimate meaning of existence shines through all finite forms of thought and action, and the creations of culture are vessels of a spiritual content." It is a condition where the Church reflects the total life of the Christian community, of which she is the crown and glory, and the community . . . embodies in its life the insights and valuations of Christian faith.

(2) The "heteronomous" relationship, to use Tillich's term, where a "theocratic" church, refusing any adaptation to society, is set within an "autonomous" society which it regards as secular and foreign. In the modern industrial areas of Europe it is one of those characteristics that the massive Roman Catholic Church and the sectarian groups have in common, although it is maintained far less than the theory suggests, since its members cannot avoid the influence of the world in which they are compelled to live.

(3) Then there is the third mode of relationship for which the term a "great church" may be appropriate, called though in a period of recession, to make its witness in a secular society. According to Tillich this is the true role of the Christian Church. It is the situation where the Church is acutely conscious of belonging to the world, subject to the conditions of the world, yet a catalyst within the world which is its only sphere of obedience. It seeks neither to manipulate nor dominate the world, nor to escape from it, nor merely to reflect a voluntarist religious aspect of it, but to understand it, prophesy within it, interpret it, and stain it. This, of course, has been the role of the Church wherever the theonomous relationship has been approximated. It is also the role to be undertaken, in fear and trembling, where society as a whole is not confessedly Christian, but where Christians are free men, men of their age, and members of an autonomous culture. Nor should it be regarded as a weaker role imposed on the Church

by reason of adverse circumstances, but rather as a normative role, implicit at all time, but peculiarly relevant in a world grown for good or ill beyond the stage of pupilage and determined to be master of its own destiny. It defines the Church in its relation with the world neither as a monolithic rock unmoved by the currents of history, nor as an ark for the saved, nor as flotsam and jetsam floating on the surface, but as a deep current itself running in the seas.[47]

The role of the Church as Christ's organism out in the world can never mean this mere "influencing of the influencers" in post-Christian society in the vain hope that they might be tempted to incorporate a fragment of the Christian yeast into the loaf of modern apostasy. It is *not* the views and theories of Christians that God is demanding of His Body but the application of His normative creation ordinances and norms to all areas of human society and that Christians at least live in obedience to God's Word in the concrete situations in which they find themselves. The purpose of Christian action and Christian organization is to concretize such biblical norms and values for human life into the structures and institutions of modern society and to bring them down to earth. In short, *it is the method Christ himself taught us of incarnation rather than fermentation and staining as Wickham falsely supposes.* Christians are to become the salt of society!

Christians may never give in to the temptation to follow the crowds of contemporary apostate men who are so much out of step with God's creational norms and values. We must reject without hesitation every and any suggestion that Christians have the liberty to adopt a way of life which refuses to take its starting point in Christ who is the "Way, the Truth and the Life" (John 14:6). Instead, we should call upon all men "to walk in his ways" (Psalm 119:3) and to run in the way of God's commandments (Psalm 119:32), for His Word is a lamp unto our feet and the only true ordering principle for the whole of human life. Life is religion, the service of the one true God or of an absolutization of one or more aspects of reality. If the idolators refuse to obey God, we must withdraw and form our own Christian organizations, since our culture and way of life is simply the living form taken by our religion.

Abraham Kuyper had a truer understanding of these matters than
the Bishop of Middleton. Kuyper felt an urgent practical need for
an effective influence of the Christian body of citizens upon such
problems as politics, education, and industry. To effect this the
Church had first to be drawn from the cultural isolation into which
it had fallen as a result of its pietism and neutralism. Of prime importance, as Kuyper saw it, was for Christians to see their responsibility in the public and cultural life of the day. He reasoned that
if God concerns himself with that life by means of His common
temporal conserving, restraining grace, then Christians must get to
work that there also the name of the Lord might be glorified. Kuyper felt not only this urgent need but also its great risks. Thus, he
ends the preface to his great work, *Common Grace*, with the following words:

> Spiritual as well as ecclesiastical isolation is anti-Reformed, and
> only then will this work accomplish the purpose I had in view,
> when it has broken this isolation, without which God prevent any-
> one ever being tempted to lose himself in that world; it must not
> control him, but he it, in the strength of his God.[48]

After examining the scriptural basis for such Christian action and
organization in the world in his work *Pro Rege*, Kuyper devoted the
whole of Chapter XIX of Volume III to this subject of Christian
organization. The question naturally arises, Kuyper writes, "whether
the subjects of King Jesus can for this purpose (the organization of
society) unite themselves with those who reject Him in one and the
same organization, or whether it is the requirement of their conviction that they organize themselves independently, call into being
a system of Christian associations, and have to accept a conscious
division between themselves and others in the social sphere also." [49]
Kuyper then remarks that such separate Christian action is already a
fact in the Netherlands, but that does not discharge us from the
task of providing a principial elucidation of the rightfulness for this
separation. He writes:

> There is thus not the least uncertainty on this point. In mixing
> socially danger always lurks for Christians. One so easily allows
> the law to be laid down by society and its worldly form. What

society can get away with, Christians too can so easily permit. One floats along on a stream to which one can offer no resistance. And unconsciously one exchanges the principle of the Christian life for the unpurified principle of worldly society. . . .

It was necessary here deliberately to ground this system of private, separate organizations in Scripture, because voices are still being constantly raised among us which regard this rule as now no longer susceptible of complete application. . . . The influence which emanates from all these (non-Christian) organizations is thus without exception destructive for our Christian confession. One reasons and acts out of principles which are absolutely opposed to ours. If now one allows oneself to enter into such organizations and if one mingles in such organizations with those who are of a wholly other mind, then what they think or judge becomes the starting point of the decisions that are to be taken, and one supports by one's membership what one, in conformity with one's Christian confession, may not support but combat. In such anarchistic socialistic or neutral associations, a spirit is operative which never can or may be ours. The leadership in such organization falls never to us but always and inflexibly to our opponents. They carry out their intention, and whoever of us embarks with them ends up where they want to land but where we may never land. Thus our principle settles down at the point of non activity, loses its position of influence and is pressed into the corner. Mingling with these leaders of another spirit in the organization itself leads always to a bitterly sad fiasco of the Christian principle and prepares the way for their victory and our overthrow.

If one disregards this and yet enters such company, there then arises in addition the danger that evil companionships corrupt good morals. In the organization we are now thinking of material interests are always and invariably in the foreground; the concern is for more power over against the employer and higher wages for one's work. Of course, there is in itself nothing wrong with the fact that everyone stands up for his rights and also attempts to improve his material position. But just for that reason the temptation is so great even for Christians in such organizations to let the end justify the means, to let material interests prevail over spiritual interests, and to float along on a stream which may never be ours.

The spirit at work in such principially unbelieving organizations is so alluring and contagious that almost none of us, once he enters into such company, can offer resistance to it. One absorbs this principle without suspecting it. Especially so because once one is a part of such organizations, one sees one's Christian principle doomed to silence.

In separate Christian organizations there is the prayer, the guid-ance of God's Word, mutual admonition, and one comes naturally, on each occasion, by free spiritual discussions, to test one's own attitude and method on the pronouncements of God's Word.[50]

Does such separate organization of employers and workers into their own Christian associations and unions mean that Reformed Christians are going to isolate themselves from the world and sep-arate themselves from other employers and workers, looking only after their own selfish interests? No! A thousand times no! It is just the contrary in spite of Wickham's sneer about Christian theo-crats. A Christian trade union is not a union of Christians that se-clude themselves from the rest of mankind, as Wickham imagines. On the contrary, it is a Christian organization which stands right in the midst of the world with all its sinfulness, injustice, and cruelty and which devotes itself in word and deed to the cause of social justice for *all* workers. Thus, Christian trade unionism is the *real* trade unionism, for it grows out of the only source of true com-munity known to mankind, namely the love of God revealed for man upon the Cross of Jesus Christ. Only at the foot of the Cross can the present conflicts between capital and labor, between the individual and the group, between the private and the public interest ever be truly resolved and healed. Only when both managers and workers, both the governed and the governors accept God's forgiveness of their sins and live by God's laws and God's Word—only then may we ex-pect true peace with justice to prevail between men. Real community in industry and society is possible only upon a New Covenant basis in which our fellow workers and citizens become mutually recognized as our brothers for whom Christ also died. Only when the workers and managers are first reconciled to God and obey God's law, only then will they become reconciled to each other. Only when workers and managers have first been forgiven of their sins by God will they be enabled by God's grace and help to forgive each other of their trespasses. Without such a spirit of forgiveness and cooperation upon the common acceptance of God's Word as the ordering principle of modern business and industrial life, no peace and progress will come to modern industry. Without such a common acknowledgement of God's sovereignty and God's law, there can be no basis for the maintenance of ordered freedom.

(d) The Structure of Authority in the Church Institution

Dooyeweerd begins his analysis with an inquiry into the typical structure of authority in the ecclesiastical institution. He distinguishes between the authority of the church and state and between an *office* of the church and an *office* of the state. What does he mean by such a term?

Essentially the idea of *office* is derived from the biblical revelation that man has been created by God with authority to develop God's creation in accordance with the great cultural mandate "to have dominion over the earth and to subdue it" to God's greater glory and the satisfaction of human need. Office presupposes a dispenser of all authority and power, one namely who is Sovereign, whose absolute right it is to give man a command. Office means therefore limitation, for the person in office is not himself the Sovereign but stands under the Sovereign's authority. Office expresses the fact that man is placed in God's creation with a special task to perform. By his very being as one created in God's image man is called to serve his Creator in the whole creation. Office is not merely service, but also administration.

Within temporal reality we find a diversity of offices. In order to see the integral unity of these diverse offices it is necessary to turn to the biblical revelation of Jesus Christ as the Supreme Office—bearer in the creation whom we are told is God's Prophet, Priest, and King. All the diversity of offices on earth find their concentration in the office of Christ as Covenant Head of the creation. As such Christ is the full and complete Office bearer, and He is therefore the origin and source of all power exercised on earth. Our Lord has delegated only partial sovereignties to men. In him alone all these earthly sovereignties are united in an undivided service of God that involves nothing less than the preservation and redemption of the whole of human life.

In this way we arrive at the biblical idea of the universality of religion or of life in its totality as religion, which makes it possible to see the difference between the church as an institution of special grace and the central religious rule of Christ over all spheres of human society. Each earthly office bearer is limited to a given societal relationship. For example, the authority of parents does not extend beyond the family, nor the authority of the minister beyond the institutional church. Within society we find a diversity of such "offices" each of which has a limited area of competence. As a result of this biblical insight Dooyeweerd teaches that each societal structure has its own sovereignty of competence which no other structure may infringe upon. Christ has delegated a certain authority to each office-bearer which may not be overstepped with impunity, since each office bearer is directly responsible to Christ himself.

While the authority of the state is primarily ruling over men by means of the power of the sword of justice, the authority of the office bearer in the church institution is not one of ruling but of service. "The ecclesiastic offices are qualified and destined as the instruments of faith for effectuating the absolute authority of the Divine Word and Spirit." [51]

The authority of ecclesiastical office is qualified as service in the community of faith in Christ. This qualification is grounded in the internal structure of individuality of the church as an instrument of special grace. For this reason the juridical structural function of the church institution is also determined by its qualifying function in faith. Church law is concerned with the spirit rather than with the letter of church order. Thus the structure of ecclesiastical authority differs radically from that of the state's authority, being qualified as a *ministerium* in the community of faith, and therefore must be understood as *service* and never as governmental *dominion*. A church that wishes to display a truly scriptural constitution cannot recognize any public legal governmental authority in its internal legal order.

It follows from what has just been said that political forms of civil government may not be taken over by the church without undermining its structure as a church. As Dooyeweerd well says:

The typical political forms of authority, such as monarchy, democracy, and aristocracy, in their different historically founded varieties, e.g., constitutional monarchy, parliamentary democracy, etc., are absolutely incompatible with the structural principle of official ecclesiastic authority.[52]

Both papal monarchy and sectarian democracy deprive the church institution of the authority of Christ. The authority of the church does not lie in the congregation as the Puritan independents supposed nor in the rule of one man as the Roman Catholic ultramontanists have supposed. It is vested in those office bearers who are called by Christ in accordance with the precepts laid down in His Word. *The government of the church is thus Christocratic rather than democratic or aristocratic.* No Christian understood this great biblical truth better than John Calvin. In the third chapter of the fourth book of his famous *Institutes of the Christian Religion* Calvin writes:

We must now treat of the order which it has been the Lord's will to appoint the government of his Church. For although he alone ought to rule and reign in the Church, and to have all preeminence in it, and this government ought to be exercised and administered solely by his word,—yet, as he dwells not among us by a visible presence, so as to make an audible declaration of his will to us, we have stated, that for this purpose he uses the ministry of men whom he employs as his delegates, not to transfer his right and honour to them, but only that he may himself do his work by their lips; just as an artificer makes use of an instrument in the performance of his work.[53]

Whereas in Roman Catholicism the pope makes law and is subject to no man's criticism, in the Reformed churches no one is held to be infallible. Christ alone is the sole head of the Church, and Christ as presented in the Scriptures is the supreme authority and law to which all church officers and leaders must yield obedience. This Calvinistic principle of the exclusive sovereignty of Christ in His Church is the foundation of the Calvinist system of collegial church government known as the presbyterate. No important ecclesiastical decisions are made in Reformed churches by one single office bearer but collegially on the principle that no one individual shall rule in the church in the name of Christ. Calvin stated this principle well: "He (i.e., Christ) attributes nothing but a common ministry to men and to each of them a particular part." [54] Such a system of government by elders or presbyters is derived from the institution of "the elders" in the Old Testament. (Exod. 3:16, 18; 4:29; 12:21; 17:5; 18:12; 24:1; Lev. 4:15; 9:1; Num. 11:16ff.; Deut. 5:23; 22:15-17; 27:1; Josh. 7:6; 8:33; I Kings 8:1; I Chron. 21:16; Ps. 107:32; Ezek. 8:1; Lam. 5:14). Their position as representative of the people and as embodying jurisdictional authority is attested by the fact that they were closely associated with Moses, with the priests, the Levites, and the judges of Israel. They are sometimes called the elders of the congregation (Lev. 4:15; Judges 21:16). John Murray points out:

> The interesting feature is that in many instances these are called the *presbuteroi* and in several cases *gerousia* which means the council of the elders. Now I submit that when we come to the New Testament and find the presbyterate as a governing body in the church of God it is contrary to all reasonable supposition that the Old Testament eldership did not exercise a profound influence upon the institution which appears in such unmistakable characters in the New Testament church, especially when we take account of the continuance of this Old Testament pattern in the synagogue of the Jews (cf. Luke 22:66; Acts 22:5 for *presbuterion*.). . .
>
> The presbyterate is the form of government for the Church of Christ. There are two considerations that have to be borne in mind. First, there was an institution intermediate between the apostolate and the presbyterate. This is exemplified in Timothy and Titus (cf. I Tim. 1:3, 4, 18; 3:14, 15; 4:11-15; II Tim. 1:6, 13, 14; 2:2, 14; 3:14; Titus 1:5, 13). . . . As we survey the charges given the passages cited, both Timothy and Titus appear to act as delegates of the apostle but not without due approbation and ordination by the church (I Tim. 4:14). Next to the apostolate they do exercise functions and prerogatives that are of a more embracive character than those belonging to the bishops and elders in the various churches. The second consideration of importance is that elders were ordained in the various churches concurrently with the ministry of the apostles. Most striking in this respect is Acts 14:23, where, referring to such places as Antioch, Iconium, and Lystra, we read "that when they had ordained them elders in every church, and prayed with fasting, they com-

mended them to the Lord on whom they believed." Thus, as soon
as the churches were established, elders were appointed. And so
we find the eldership to be the local governing body in each
church (Acts 11:30; 15:2-23; 16:4; 20:17; 21:18; Phil. 1:1; Tit.
1:5; James 5:14). The authority of the apostolate lies behind this
institution and in no way does the concurrent exercise of rule
introduce discrepancy. Rule by elders is the apostolic institution
for the government of the local congregation and this involves the
principles of plurality and parity. The inference is inescapable
that this is a permanent provision for the government of the
churches. Since the apostolate is not permanent and since there
is in the New Testament no other provision for the government
of the local congregation we must conclude that the council of
elders is the only abiding institution for the government of the
church of Christ according to the New Testament.[55]

While agreeing with Murray's conclusion, the writer would
point out that many Reformed congregations are no nearer this New
Testament pattern than are Roman Catholic or Anglican congregations. In the New Testament Church the "elders" never assumed
the authoritative status *vis-a-vis* the laity which they have come to
to acquire in the Western world. In the New Testament we look in
vain for the Western distinction between the *ecclesia docens* and the
ecclesia docta; between the clergy, whose privilege it is to teach and
instruct, and the laity, whose duty it is meekly to attend; the lay
theologian was as common in the New Testament Church as he is
rare in the Western world. It was not thought necessary in the New
Testament to wear a clerical collar in order to speak with authority
of the things of God. For modern Western Christianity, on the
other hand—both Catholic and Protestant—the very words "layman"
and "laity" have been severed from their biblical roots and have acquired a purely negative meaning. The layman is no longer one
who through the mysteries of baptism and confirmation has become
a member of a priestly body, the *laos* or people of God. He is considered only in terms of what he is *not* and cannot do. He is an
outsider, a non expert, in short, one who is not a parson or a minister.
As a result the Western layman has come to accept the idea that
his proper role in the worship services of the church is a purely
passive one. He goes to church to hear a service performed for his

benefit by a clergyman, assisted by a select body of men and women all dressed up to look as much like clergy as possible. As to his extraliturgical ministry that is circumscribed by the well-defined frontiers of what is called "church work," i.e., raising money, organizing a club, etc. Our hymns themselves seem to imply that the only activity proper to the layman is as a lay helper or church worker. They have no conception of the laity as itself an *essential part of Christ's apostolate to the world*. The general drift of these hymns is summed up in J. M. Neale's lines describing the virtues proper to bishops, priests, and deacons, then comes the couplet:

And to their flocks, a lowly mind
To hear and to obey.

It seems to the writer that these lines give a fair picture of the general view of the place of the layman in the Church today—to hear and to obey; there is little left of his priestly ministry so vividly described by Peter in the great words: "Ye are a chosen generation, a royal priesthood, an holy nation, a peculiar people, that ye should shew forth the praises of him who hath called you out of darkness into his most marvellous light" (I Peter 2:9). Excluded from any active part in the worship services of the church, deprived of his extraliturgical apostolate, the layman is left to his own private devotions. As a result there has been developing over the centuries a rank spiritual individualism leading to religious subjectivism and sentimentalism. Piety, in the modern sense, has become an inadequate substitute for a ministry involving every member of Christ's Body and embracing every legitimate field of human activity. Something has surely gone wrong. The Son of God did not take our human nature upon himself in order that we might be turned some into parsons and presbyters while others are turn into parishioners and laymen. The apostolic vision of a re-created universe has faded, giving place to a dualistic world, half sacred, half secular. There is no real cure for all this without a recovery of the true sense of the worship services of the church as a corporate action of the whole Body of Christ in any one locality.

We must understand that from the perspective of the New Testa-

ment the whole of Western Christianity, Catholic and Protestant, has
been affected by this tremendous dislocation in the true catholicity
of Christ's Body. The reforms of the sixteenth century are of secondary importance; because, in the classical theological controversies
of the Western churches during the past four hundred years, all the
contending parties have shared the same sub-Christian presuppositions about the place and function of the laity, not only in the liturgy
but in the life of the church as a whole. The Russian theologian
Khomyakov has stated that "Protestants are cryptopapists," by which
he meant that Protestantism originated as a reaction to medieval
papal distortions, and thus inevitably reflects those distortions in its
own attempted reforms. He wrote:

> Once logical self-determination was admitted in principle, no
> bonds, arbitrarily imposed, could survive for long. In this way
> Protestantism, the legitimate but rebellious child of Romanism,
> came into existence. It was the reaction of Christian thought
> against the errors of Romanism, and therefore it was unable to
> spread outside the world which had been subject to the Pope.
> Protestantism transferred the papal infallibility to every man, that
> was all.[56]

Whereas Roman Catholics tend to worship the Pope's reason,
many Protestants have come to regard their own reason as supreme.
While the Romanists advocated the clericalism of the sacrament,
Protestants have often given the impression of upholding the clericalism of preaching. Of this development Mascall writes in *The Recovery of Unity*:

> It must, of course, be admitted that great attempts were made
> in Protestantism to make Christian worship *intelligible* to the
> laity; the restoration of the vernacular is the most obvious indi-
> cation of this. However, to make the laity understand what is go-
> ing on is not the same thing as to give them an integral share in
> the performance. . . . And in Protestantism no less than in post-
> Reformation Catholicism the liturgy is something performed by
> the minister. . . . Thus we get the intolerable verbosity of most of
> the reformed liturgies, in which the minister prays and reads and
> exhorts and preaches, but in which the laity are hardly allowed
> to say a word from start to finish. . . . It would hardly be an
> exaggeration to say that what Protestantism did to the religion

of Western Europe was simply to substitute a clericalism of the
Word for a clericalism of the Sacrament. Whereas the Catholic had been accustomed to come to church to be edified by seeing the priest celebrate the Mass, the Protestant came to church to
be edified by hearing the minister preach the sermon; and the
preaching of the sermon, no less than the celebration of the Mass,
was a purely clerical performance.[57]

Nowhere does the New Testament suggest that the "elders" alone
should do *all* the preaching and *all* the teaching and *all* the administration of the church. If it is true that the New Testament
presbyterate was modelled upon the pattern of the Jewish syna-
gogues, then is it not likely it would have performed similar if not
identical functions? The Jewish elders managed the affairs and
charities of the local Jewish community, represented it in its dealings with the civil power, and exercised oversight in matters of
discipline and of the observance of the Law.

Precisely because the doctrine of the fourfold office has become
such a firm part of the Reformed tradition so that many have come
to regard it not merely as a consequence but as the very content of
the New Testament, we would do well to pay careful attention to
the New Testament on this point. For us it needs no argument that
for the sake of good order a church needs pastors, elders and deacons, and teachers. On good grounds Calvin instituted the Genevan
church in this way. Not very long after him other churches combined the office of teacher with that of pastor. Later the office of
deacon was also merged with that of the pastor. For four hundred
years the tendency has been to professionalize the Reformed ministry with the result that the Reformed Churches no less than the
Catholic Churches now appear in a very different light to that presented in the New Testament. Today's Protestant minister, as to
his place and function in the church, differs in actual *practice* very
little from his Catholic counterpart. And insofar as these two—with
or without special vestments—have come to resemble each other so
closely, they thereby prove how little our present-day churches resemble the church of the New Testament. As Lothar Coenen says:

Whatever else can be said about the offices in the New Testament, one thing is certain; the office of priest has been abolished. The New Testament church knew no priestly function except that which was performed by the whole congregation (I Pet. 2:5) and the Jewish priests that were added to the church played anything but a priestly role. This is connected with the fact that the Christian religion is precisely not a continuation or resumption of a cult; the final, unique sacrifice has been accomplished on the Cross by our only high priest, Jesus Christ.

When our present-day churches, therefore, with their contraposition of the one priest/minister and the many believers (laymen), must of necessity create the impression of engaging in cultic ceremonies, then this is certainly a point on which the New Testament church challenges us to a radical reformation of our thinking.[58]

The distinction between "clergy" and "laity" was introduced into the Church almost entirely under secular influence. It was taken over from the patterns of civic life in the Roman Empire and it became entrenched at the time of the Peace of the Church under Constantine, when certain privileges and benefits were extended to the clergy of the Christian Church, which had previously been bestowed by the Roman Empire on the heathen priesthood. And at that point, it became important to define who was entitled to these benefits and who was not. Hence the beginning of a legal division between members of "the clergy" and the "laity." This gradually became more and more firmly established during the Middle Ages.

When the Roman imperial government lost control of the western provinces of the Roman Empire, the Western Church was left for several centuries in a cultural and political vacuum. She had to use all her spiritual prestige to establish even a minimum standard of order and decency in public life. We can thus understand why she began more and more to magnify her authority, claiming first a measure of independence over against the civil power under Pope Gregory VII and ultimately a right of supremacy over it under Popes Innocent III and Boniface VIII. We can understand too the gradual concentration of power within the Church itself into one center, the medieval papacy. In this way the Church became an effective striking force which was used to further Christian standards of marriage, business, and government in the rising feudal kingdoms of France, Germany, England, and Italy. But this was achieved at a price. It meant that the Church was slowly transformed from a free society of persons into a feudal theocracy under the Pope as God's vicegerent; from a fellowship of the Holy Spirit into a power organization. The fundamental relationships within the Body of Christ were henceforth conceived as relations of authority and obedience.

The grace of God likewise became mechanized, and channelized through the seven sacraments of the Church. The ecclesiastical hierarchy, to whom the sacraments had been committed, developed a monopoly on grace. As Harnack pointed out, in the medieval mind Christ and the historic Roman Church became identified:

> Christ and the Church are really made one, in so far as the Church which administers the sacraments is also, as the mystical body of Christ, so to speak *one* mystical person with Him. This is the fundamental thought of Medieval Catholicism, which was adhered to even by the majority of those who opposed themselves to the ruling hierarchy[59]

Slowly a new plan of salvation began to emerge in which the Word of God became submerged beneath the all sufficient grace which the Roman Church was able to offer its members in the sacramental system. The priest had become a miracle worker on whose sacramental sign the whole Church was dependent.

Unhappily, while the power of the Church in the world, and of the hierarchy in the Church, and of the Pope amid the hierarchy. went on increasing, there was for centuries no effective force to counterbalance it. The masses of the people, ill educated, superstitious, and unfamiliar with the Bible and even with the Latin of the Mass, came to look upon the Church as a great *machine of grace* which went on working independently of them, performing spiritual functions for their benefit, but not needing or inviting active participation. The clergy themselves from their own point of view could hardly avoid seeing matters in a similar light. There was for centuries no body of educated lay opinion which was capable of discharging the function of the laity as an order in the Church. It was from the monasteries and the clerical order that all spiritual initiative had to come, and the great body of the faithful came to be regarded as a docile flock whose only business in the Church was to follow their spiritual guides and to obey them without question.

The inevitable result followed. The unity of the Body of Christ was lost to view, and the word *church* began to be used as if it meant the clergy in contrast to the people. From the eleventh century onwards the laity began to lose all sense of active participation in the priestly and redemptive mission of the Church, and in so doing to lapse into spiritual serfs in the Kingdom of God. The Holy Spirit was thought of no longer as moving freely through the whole Body of Christ, but as canalized through the seven sacraments, and thus in the hands of the clergy. Worse still the Holy Communion, as Gregory Dix has shown in *The Shape of the Liturgy*, came to be thought of as something said for the people by the priest, and not as something *done* by the whole congregation with and through the priest acting together within the High Priesthood of Jesus Christ.[60] The Spirit of Christ was now thought to be localized in the "host" of the Mass rather than dwelling in the hearts of His people. As a result the Word of God written in the Scriptures which witnesses of Christ could no longer fulfil its function as the touchstone for the life and teaching of the Church because the understanding and interpretation of the Bible were reserved for the hierarchy.

The "Church" therefore, in this restricted sense in which it was identified with the Roman hierarchy, was no longer effectively under judgment. On the contrary, the Roman see, the pinnacle of the whole structure, could now say of itself that it "judges all and is judged of none." This growth of clericalism in the Western Church is today coming to be recognized as being one of the gravest symptoms of that medieval distortion of Christian life and truth which underlies all our later Western divisions and controversies.

If we are to abolish clericalism we must return to the biblical doctrine of the ministry. In the Old Testament, indeed, the priesthood was vicarious in the sense that the priest did on behalf of the people what they could not do; there was one tribe in Israel which was priestly, and eleven that were not. But in the New Testament this kind of division is utterly abolished. There is one mediator be-

between God and man, the High Priest, Jesus Christ, and no priestly caste within His Body. The entire Body is a royal priesthood, and every member has his share in that priesthood by virtue of his baptism. The ordained ministry, within the New Covenant, is not a vicarious one, but a representative one. It is commissioned and set apart, to exercise in the name of the whole Body, Head and members alike, the ministry which belongs to the whole. What is given to the ordained minister is formal authority to preach, and proclaim in the name of the whole Church what every member has not only the right but the duty to proclaim. He is given formal authority to exercise the ministry of reconciliation and forgiveness which belongs by right to every member of the healing community. He is given formal authority to lead and preside at the celebration of the Lord's Supper, which is the con-celebration of the whole people of God. For in this sense every celebration of the Holy Communion is a lay celebration. The celebrant is the entire people of Christ, of which the bishop or presbyter is merely "the president." Every minister of Christ's church should be looked upon as the servant of the servants of God. The ministry of the church must once more be understood in its New Testament sense, as the ministry of the servant, in direct extension of the ministry of the Son of Man, who came not to be ministered unto but to minister (Matt. 20:25-29).

It is imperative that we do see it this way round—that the clergy are the servants rather than the superiors of the laity. As Hans Rudi Weber has well said: "The laity are not the helpers of the clergy so that the clergy can do their job, but the clergy are the helpers of the whole people of God, so that the laity can *be* the Church." [61]

At the same time we must be careful not to define the laity in opposition to the clergy, which is itself a by-product of clericalism. As persons who have been freed from their bondage to sin by Jesus Christ and who now share in His royal anointing, both the "layman" and the "clergyman" are members of the *Laos* or People of God. As a royal priesthood and the community of the Messiah, the Church as a whole is called by God to testify to Christ's triumphs and administer God's care and love for the world, for such is her reasonable service. Christ himself endows His people with the gifts of His

Spirit, enabling them to live as a devoted people, renewed in knowledge after the image of their Creator. In this regard Arnold de Graaff rightly reminds us that this is what should be understood by the term the "priesthood of all believers." He says:

> These expressions are somewhat confusing, since they may induce one to think of some general *ecclesiastical* office. But if it is used in this limited sense, then we need another term to indicate the general office of being man. It is better, therefore, to speak of a general and a special ecclesiastical office and to reserve the term "office of believer" for the general office of being man. For to be a Christian believer is nothing more or less than to be *genuinely human*, renewed after the image of our Lord and Redeemer.[62]

Such a distinction will help us to avoid the fatal error of limiting the layman's activities to purely "religious" activities within the church as an institution. It is in the world that the people of God are called to serve Him in building up His Kingdom. For the Church as Christ's Body is God's instrument for reclaiming the world for the Kingdom. The ministry of the laity is the ministry of God *both* within the structures of the Church *and* within the structures of the world. Considering the activities of the "laity" in terms of a view of the church as only an institution poses insoluble problems and such an ecclesiology cannot possibly do justice to the "world" or "cosmology."

Evangelical pietism has encouraged the view that specifically Christian work is evangelistic work rather than reforming all aspects and areas of life. It refuses to accept the vocation to the "secular" everyday world of business, politics, teaching, etc., as something which a Christian could have, as it were, for its own sake and in its own right. The best that most evangelicals can say of the world is that it must be used and turned into occasions for evangelism, and the only reason why a converted Christian should take a "secular" job is that in it the Lord might use him for pulling a few brands from the burning. Essentially, seen like that, a secular job is looked upon as a poor second best. If you are a fully committed Christian according to pietism you will become engaged in full time evangelism. The only Christian work such pietism recognizes is ecclesiastical work in the church institution. The world outside the church institution, in short, become something essentially mundane and beyond redemption since it is considered to be "neutral." Of this terrible bifurcation of life into the sacred and the secular, Calvin Seerveld well says:

> This engaging religious perspective does not discern the full will of God as revealed in the Scriptures. The mistake of such thinkers is to ascribe to the structural ordinances of creation a being independent of God's absolute lordship in Jesus Christ. . . . The shortsighted sin to such thinking—who is ever free from it altogether?—is that it admits Jehovah's rule over only part of reality, over man's "heart," motives, valuation, but not over all man's actions; Christ's lordship is restricted in a personalized, humanistic manner, and whatever is conceived by these thinkers as not peculiarly human deeds is declared off limits for God; that is neutral terrain.
>
> This point is not negotiable, I think, for a Biblically Reformational Christian; nothing in creation is neutral before Jesus Christ. . . . If all creation is struggling, groaning, waiting for the day of redemption of us who sinned, if all things are from Christ and through Christ and to Christ, on what grounds, on what biblical grounds? can one doubt and deny that whatever our human hands bring forth also falls directly under the sway of His sceptre. . . . All human production—a philosophical critique, an art object, a clean swept street, or a fish dinner—all of it can be and is to be done as unto Him, who Himself cleaned feet and ate fish. This biblical point of Christ's cosmic totalitarian compass is not negotiable to a Reformational Christian perspective.[63]

In this great campaign to recapture all structures and aspects of human life for Jesus Christ the clergy's function is to build up the body of Christ in His name and through His Word, so that God's people may be fully equipped to serve their Lord in their daily lives in the world. It is also to preach the gospel to the poor, to heal the broken hearted, to preach deliverance to the captives of Satan, sin, and darkness, and to administer the great sacrament of our salvation which Christ himseilf ordained.

In a paper for *Youth and the Gospel* given recently in Holland the Rev. F. J. Pop has given a good review of the various forms in which the apostolate of both clergy and laity can find expression today. Here follows an abbreviated report of his enumeration.

(a) *Apostolate by proclamation.* This relates to all ways in which the truth of the gospel is told and people are called to faith and repentance. This is done by:
  (1) Meetings: street preaching, special church missions, mass rallies, campfire talks, debating sessions, etc.
  (2) The written word: propagation of the Bible, periodicals, calendars, folders, etc.
  (3) Visiting: often in combination with the written word.
  (4) Instruction: Sunday school for unchurched children, courses, Bible study clubs, etc.
  (5) Radio, television, and film.
  (6) Plays: stage, pantomime, etc.

(b) *Apostolate by service,* as practiced by:
  (1) Service in disaster areas.
  (2) Service in underdeveloped countries.
  (3) Service where the need is insufficiently met by the state: aged people, lonely people, invalids, marriage and family problems, etc.
  (4) Assistance to adults in adult education, use of spare time, guidance of engaged and married people.

(c) *Apostolate by signs and wonders.* By this is meant signs of God's power manifested in faith healings, prayer, the laying on of hands, exorcism of evil spirits, and sudden deliverance from addiction.

(d) *Apostolate by exemplary existence.* Christians must show to others what it means to live in the peace, power, justice, joy, and love of God's Kingdom. The emphasis falls on the way of behavior (I Pet. 3:1-7).

(e) *Apostolate by social and political action.* This concerns not so much the individual but groups of Christians acting together in Christian trade unions, political partices, and academic and educational movements.

(f) *Apostolate by participation and identification.* One thinks of the French worker priests who identified themselves with their fellow workers in industry. The Church must become known as the caring-community.

(g) *Apostolate by dialogue.* By "dialogue" we should not understand the conversations that occur in the forms mentioned under (a), that is, conversations whose purpose is to convince the other. In true dialogue the Christian, for example, engages in conversation with humanists and Communists to find out why they think as they do and to give his reason for the faith in Christ that he possesses. This means having a thorough knowledge of the contents of one's own religion so he can defend it in discussion.[64]

CHAPTER SEVEN NOTES

1. Dooyeweerd, *A New Critique of Theoretical Thought*, Vol. II, pp. 246-247. Cf. Karl Barth, *Against the Stream* (New York, 1954), p. 20ff.
2. Reinhold Niebhur, *The Children of Light and the Children of Darkness* (Nisbet, London, 1945).
3. Henry Van Til, *The Calvinistic Concept of Culture*, p. 213.
4. Dooyeweerd, *op. cit.*, Vol. I, p. 524.
5. Ephesians 4:7, 12-16.
6. F. W. Beare, *The First Epistle of Peter* (Blackwell, Oxford, 1947), p. 92.
7. Calvin Seerveld, *Christian Workers, Unite!* (C.L.A.C., Rexdale, Ontario, 1962), p. 14ff.
8. G. B. Caird, *Principalities and Powers* (Oxford, 1956), p. 2ff.
9. H. Van Til, *op. cit.*, p. 213
10. Gerald Vandezande, *Must Christians Form Power Organizations?* (C.L.A.C., 1964), p. 8.
11. *Ibid.*, quoting from Popma.
12. Herman Ridderbos, *The Coming of the Kingdom* (Presbyterian and Reformed Publishing Co., Philadelphia, 1962), p. 334.
13. Herman Ridderbos, *Paulus: Ontwerp van zijn Theologie* (Kok, Kampen, 1966), p. 367.
14. Arnold H. de Graaff, *The Educational Ministry of the Church* (Judels and Brinkman, Delft, Holland, 1966), p. 59ff.
15. K. L. Schmidt, "The Church," in *Bible Key Words; The Church* (Harpers, New York, 1951), p. 66.
16. L. B. Smedes, *The Nature of the Church and Some Problems in Evangelism* (Christian Reformed Publishing Co., Grand Rapids, 1958), p. 10. Cf.

Rt. Rev. J. W. C. Wand, *The Church, It Nature, Structure and Function* Morehouse-Gorham, New York, 1948), p. 43, for a good Anglican definition. "The Church is an organism rather than an organization."

17. H. Ridderbos, "The Church and the Kingdom of God," in *The International Reformed Bulletin* (No. 27, October, 1966), p. 9.

18. A. Kuyper, *Encyclopaedie der Heilige Godgeleerdheid* (Kok, Kampen, 1909), Vol III, p. 204.

19. H. Ridderbos, "The Church's Mission Today," *International Reformed Bulletin*, Nos. 20, 21, 22, Jan., Apr., July, 1965, p. 27.

20. Dooyeweerd, *New Critique*, Vol. III, p. 510ff.

21. A. M. Ramsey, *The Gospel and the Catholic Church* (Longmans, London, 1956), p. 163. Cf. B. Jouvenel, *Sovereignty* (Cambridge University Press, 1957), p. 174ff.

22. Quoted by G. C. Berkouwer, *The Conflict with Rome* (Presbyterian and Reformed Publishing Co., Philadelphia, 1958), p. 267.

23. Karl Adam, *The Spirit of Catholicism* (Sheed & Ward, London, 1929), p. 39ff.

24. Berkouwer, *op. cit.*, pp. 24-37.

25. John Murray, *The Nature, Unity and Government of the Church* (Banner of Truth Trust, London, 1965), p. 7.

26. George D. Salmon, *The Infallibility of the Church* (John Murray, London, 1952). Cf. Bishop Butler's reply in *The Church and Infallibility* (Sheed & Ward, 1953).

27. Noel King, *The Emperor Theodosius and the Establishment of Christianity* (SCM Press, London, 1958).

28. John C. Vanderstelt, "The Church in Society," in *International Reformed Bulletin* (No. 34, July, 1968 at 1677 Gentian Drive, Grand Rapids, Mich. 49508, U.S.A.), p. 20.

29. John C. Vandersteld, *The Christian Mind*; an analysis of Harry Blamire's recent book (*International Reformed Bulletin*, No. 16, 17, Jan., April, 1964), p. 26ff.

30. Dooyeweerd, *New Critique*, Vol. II, p. 525.

31. *Ibid.*, p. 214ff.

32. Emil Brunner, *The Misunderstanding of the Church* (Lutterworth, London, 1952), p. 10ff.

33. Paul G. Schrotenboer, "Emil Brunner," in *Creative Minds in Contemporary Theology*, edited by P. E. Hughes (Eerdmans, Grand Rapids, 1966), p. 12ff.

34. Dooyeweerd, *New Critique*, Vol. III, p. 509.

35. Schrotenboer, *op. cit.*, p. 121.

36. Dooyeweerd, *op. cit.*, p. 534.

37. Dooyeweerd, *Reflection and Renewal*, p. 200.

38. *Ibid.*, p. 205.

39. Dooyeweerd, *New Critique*, Vol. III, p. 537.
40. *Ibid.*, p. 535.
41. *Ibid.*, p. 523.
42. *Ibid.*, p. 524.
43. *Ibid.*, p. 525.
44. R. J. Rushdoony, Review of E. L. Hebden Taylor's *The Christian Philosophy of Law, Politics and the State*, in *The Westminster Theological Journal* (Nov., 1967, Vol. XXX, No. 1), p. 100.
45. C. H. Dodd, *Natural Law in the Bible* (*Theology Reprint* No. 17, from May and June issue of *Theology*, 1946), p. 6ff.
46. Joel H. Nederhood, "Are We Big Enough for Christian Action?" (Christian Action Foundation of America, Box 185, Sioux Center, Iowa 51250, U.S.A.), p. 3.
47. E. R. Wickham, *Church and People in an Industrial City* (Lutterworth, London, 1962), p. 229ff.
48. A. Kuyper, *De Gemene Gratie* (Kok, Kampen, 4th ed., 1902), Vol. I, p. 7.
49. Abraham Kuyper, *Pro Rege, Het Koningschap van Christus* (Kok, Kampen, 1911), Vol. III, p. 184ff.
50. *Ibid.*, pp. 189-191.
51. Herman Dooyeweerd, *The New Critique*, Vol. III, p. 543.
52. *Ibid.*, p. 545.
53. John Calvin, *Institutes of the Christian Religion* (Eerdmans, Grand Rapids, 1949), Vol. II, p. 316.
54. *Ibid.*, p. 377ff.
55. John Murray, *The Nature, Unity and Government of the Church*, p. 12ff.
56. Quoted by Sege Bolshakoff, *The Doctrine of the Unity of the Church in the Works of Khomyakov and Moehler* (S.P.C.K., London, 1956), p. 190ff.
57. E. L. Mascall, *The Recovery of Unity* (Longmans, Green & Co., London, 1958), p. 5ff.
Cf. Augustin Cardinal Bea, *The Unity of Christians*. Edited by Bernard Leeming (G. Chapman, London, 1963), and his other more recent work, *The Way to Unity After the Council* (G. Chapman, London, 1967). Both books give us the clearest statement of the Roman Catholic position on reunion that has yet appeared. The Cardinal regards the problem of disunity as something that can be resolved only by the action of God himself, or by men consciously acting and thinking within the will of God. It is not something, like a dispute between nations, which can be settled by a carefully contrived political treaty. It concerns revealed truth, of which he thinks the Roman Church alone is the custodian. His essential conviction is that, provided the desire for unity were allowed free expression across the hardened barriers of the centuries so that the divided could meet in unobstructed charity, the Roman position could be ex-

plained, understood, and accepted. For the Cardinal reunion thus means the submission of all other churches to Rome.

58. Lothar Coenen, "The Challenge of the New Testament Church," in *The Church's Mission Today*, p. 17.

59. Adolf Harnack, *History of Dogma* (Boston, 1903), Vol. VI, p. 200.

60. Gregory Dix, *The Shape of the Liturgy* (Dacre Press, London, 1954), p. 546ff.

61. Quoted in *The Layman's Church*. Edited by T. Beaumont (S.C.M. Press, London, 1965), p. 17.
    Hendrik Kraemer, *A Theology of the Laity* (Lutterwort, London, 1958). *The Layman's Place in History*, edited by Stephen Neil (S.C.M., London, 1964).

62. De Graaff, *op. cit.*, p. 76ff.

63. Calvin Seerveld, *Christian Workers, Unite!* (C.L.A.C., Rexdale, Ontario, 1964), p. 12.

64. Quoted in *The Evangelism and Service of the Church in an Estranged World* (*The Reformed Ecumenical Synod*, Grand Rapids, 1966), p. 6ff. Cf. James H. Olthuis, "Must the Church Become Secular?" in *Kingdom, Church and Secularism* (*International Reformed Bulletin*, Jan. 1967).

Chapter Eight

THE REFORMATIONAL CONCEPTION
OF THE BUSINESS ENTERPRISE

As we have seen in chapter six, Reformed sociology teaches that the doctrine of sphere sovereignty alone presents us with a proper insight into the connection willed by God between man and his social structures, since the individual is not allowed by this doctrine to be absorbed by any temporal bond. God alone is the absolute sovereign of the bodies and consciences of men, and He demands that we obey Him against all earthly authorities, whether civil or ecclesiastical, whenever they claim absolute power, especially the power to control men's thinking on questions of conscience. No bearer of authority on earth is the highest power from which other forms of social authority are derived. Sovereignty belongs only to God, while He delegates limited authority only to the various social spheres, so that these must be understood as coordinately rather than subordinately related.

This scriptural sociological pluralism means that every social unit or group has its own God ordained sphere of work to perform, which it must be allowed to carry out without interference by another social institution. The state may, of course, insist that the family, school, or labor union live up to its social responsibilities. But only as a last resort may the state interefere and take over some other sphere's responsibilities and discharge them itself. Thus, for example, the state must never interfere with family life, since the husband's authority over his wife and children is not derived from the state but from Christ himself (Eph. 5:23). Likewise, we must recognize that the church is not the state. There is scarcely anyone today who advocates that it should become one. But just as truly, the principle of sphere sovereignty requires that we also recognize the principial structural difference between the school and the state, and between a labor union and the government.

There is a close parallel between compulsory trade unionism and the public school which is suggested by public tax revenue. In each case the apostate humanists claim that both school and union are agencies of the government. The school they see as the proper function of the state, to be used by the state to "brainwash" its citizens for its military, economic, and political purposes. Such people have failed to see that the public school has a character all its own, distinct from either the state or the church. While both church and state have legitimate interests in the school, as is true in turn of the church and school regarding the state, in no sense should the law of the state do violence to the functioning of the school according to its true nature. Parents have a God given right to educate their children in terms of the perspective of their own life-and-world view. When the government infringes upon this God given right, then the door is opened to totalitarianism.

Failure to understand the sovereignty of the various spheres of society and to recognize the specific tasks of the various associations and communities of society inevitably leads to all kinds of inequalities and injustices. In no case has this been more true than in the violent intervention by the state in the operation of the modern economy.

(a) *The Role of Government in the Operation of the Economy*

How big should the government become? What part, if any, should it play in the operation of the modern economy? How much should it tax and spend of the people's money? In answer to these questions there are today four major schools of thought—(1) the Roman Catholic, (2) the laissez faire school of non intervention, (3) the collectivistic school of violent intervention, and (4) the Reformational school.

The influential school of laissez faire English liberals during the nineteenth century taught that the primary function of the state was merely to set up and enforce certain "rules of the game" under which private enterprise could then be counted upon to get goods efficiently produced and distributed. To the question, "Why should the government intervene at all in business affairs?" Adam Smith had one answer: because the benefits of enlightened self-seeking can be obtained only if competition channels these efforts to the common good. Seldom do merchants gather together, he wrote, that their talk does not turn to means of getting higher prices for their produce. Without competition among sellers, more consumer spending may mean high profits and not more products. It is the job of the government, representing all the people, to see to it that such competition prevails. It was in the name of competition that Adam Smith argued in *The Wealth of Nations* for a relaxation of the paternalism of the Mercantilist State and for the abolition of the corn bounty and trading companies such as the East India Company and the Hudson Bay Company privileged by law. Smith believed that the automatic regulation of industry by reference to market price alone rather than by the whims of impersonal government bureaucrats would increase the nation's wealth. Fiscal regulations had cramped private enterprise and brought about evil consequences which were no part of the national intention, as patently in his generation as war-time price controls did in our century.

The great laissez faire economists such as Smith, Ricardo, Mill, Marshall, and Jevons did not dispute the need in a free enterprise society for some rules of fair play in economic life as in personal behavior. Without common consent to eliminate fraud, to respect property ownership, and to honor contractural promises, business dealings would be carried on under a great handicap. They agreed that it is the function of government to establish and to enforce these basic rules and laws against murder, theft, arson, and fraud to enable men to live securely together. Among Adam Smith's disciples "laissez faire" never meant that the government should do nothing, but rather that it should leave economic affairs alone within a framework of basic moral and legal rules of the game. For economic individualism that government governs best which governs least, as far as the day to day operations of the market are concerned. As Rushdoony says: "Laissez faire was set in the context of a Deistic natural law faith, but, more basically, it was a recognition of God's absolute laws, His sphere laws for economics. Gresham's law is operative today, as it has been from the beginning of history." [1]

At the other extreme, Communists and Socialists argue that all productive resources of society should be owned by the government, and that the production and distribution of goods and services should be handled by the state by means of "planning." Human society must be governed by specific planning so that it can develop without the disturbance of depression and unemployment. If the planners have their way nothing will be left to chance, to improvisation, and individual initiative. For collectivists society must be treated as a scientific problem. It can then be analyzed, and from this analysis a prognosis of the future can be drawn. On such a basis a scientific plan will then be introduced assuring human welfare and security and equality for everyone. In *The Society of the Future*, H. Van Riessen points out that such planning will, of course, require the control both of society as a whole and of the individuals composing it in such a way that the plan will not be disturbed. Personal individuality will eventually have to be more or less determined by the planners, if their plans are not to be disrupted. Thus wages, prices, rents, social security, production quota, choice of job, migration, birth rate, and even recreation will all have to be directed from the top if planning is to succeed.

Planning envisions much wider perspectives than merely managing the currency and setting production quotas, for it cannot hope to succeed if confined simply to economic life. The population, for example, will have to be induced psychologically to accept the plan. It will therefore become necessary to include the spiritual aspects of life in the planning process in order to convince the people that they should fully support the plan. It is therefore inevitable that education and the public control of all the media of modern communication will have to be included within the powers of the planners. Even the churches will have to fall into line with the wishes of the planners and adjust their programs to it if they wish to survive in a collectivistic society. In his profound and frightening study of *The Technological Society*, Jacques Ellul says:

When a society becomes increasingly totalitarian, it creates more and more difficulties of adaptation and requires its citizens to be conformist in the same degree. Thus this technique [of social adaptation] becomes all the more necessary. I have no doubt that it makes men happy in a milieu which would normally make them unhappy, if they had not been worked on, molded and formed for just that milieu. What looks like the apex of humanism is in fact the pinnacle of human submission; children are educated to become precisely what society expects of them. They must have social consciences that allow them to strive for the same ends as society sets for itself. Clearly, when modern youth are fully educated in the new psychopedagogic technique, many social and political difficulties will disappear. Any form of government or social transformation becomes possible with individuals who have experienced this never-ending process of adaptation. The key word of the new human techniques is, therefore, *adaptation*.

The new pedagogical methods correspond exactly to the role assigned to education in modern technical society. The Napoleonic conception that the *Lycees* (schools) must furnish administrators for the state and managers for the economy, in conformity with social needs and tendencies, has become world-wide in its extent. According to this conception, education no longer has a humanist end or any value in itself; it has only one goal, to create technicians.[2]

Collectivism in short is the mobilization of society for unitary action in accordance with the demands of modern technique. The human mind will be made to conform to the much more advanced brain of the machine. Man will sacrifice his freedom in order to increase his material security. Every aspect of life will become technized and politicized, even love and marriage will become functions of planning and technical control.

According to Dr. John Platt, a bio-physicist at the University of Michigan and director of the university's Mental Health Research Institute, population will be managed by mass produced contraceptive agents in foodstuffs. He told the annual conference of the American Institute of Planners in 1967 that such a technique might control the population explosion twenty to thirty years sooner than present available methods.[3] Couples wishing to have a baby would have to obtain permission to buy drugs to offset the contraceptive drug in the food. He said that the technique was beyond reach technically as well as politically at the moment. But the process, once perfected, could be as simple as putting vitamin D in milk or adding iodine to salt. Other scientists in California have advocated treating the nation's water supply with similar drugs.

At present, thank God, these planning techniques have not yet been put into practice in the English-speaking world as some of them have been in Communist lands. In his textbook on *Economics,* G. L. Bach points out that "Today, the United States stands as one of a minority of the world's nations with a basically private enterprise, capitalist economy. Communism is the economic pattern for far more of the world's population than is the private enterprise system we know. The U.S.S.R. and China alone account for over a billion people, one of every three human beings alive." [4] Nevertheless these same collectivistic tendencies are advancing in the free part of the world, since collectivism appears to so many of our liberals and apostate humanists as a remedy for elements in our societies which everyone agrees are impediments to full freedom, e.g., depressions, unemployment, poverty in the midst of plenty.

It is vital that we all realize before it is too late that collectivism and freedom are real alternatives—if we choose one we cannot have the other. And collectivism can be imposed upon a gullible electorate with an appearance of not destroying continuity with our historic traditions of limited government and the rule of law, only if enough Americans, Britons, and Canadians lose or forget their love of personal freedom under God. Today as never before in our history the price of our liberties is eternal vigilance. Although most Christians may reject the totalitarian end of the road planning, the more they champion planning or socialism as the cure of all society's present ills, as many "liberal" churchmen have been doing in America and Britain and Canada for a generation, the less possibility they will leave themselves and others for a final resistance to and escape from all the bitter consequences.

At present many American Christians seem to have adopted a middle position between economic individualism and collectivism. They believe in the virtues of a free, private enterprise economy, yet make no stand principially against the growing power of the Federal Government. The growth in government expenditures at all levels—federal, state, and local—has been fantastic, reaching $243 billion in 1967. Of this vast amount, defense spending and social security welfare payments accounted for about two thirds of all federal, state, and local government spending.

From a Reformational point of view, what should the public sector do? Who should pay the taxes, and who receive the benefits?

Economic individualists such as Murray Rothbard in *Man, Economy and the State* argue that "each man, in pursuing his own self-interest furthers the interest of everyone else," and that continued violent intervention by the state in the private sector will bring the nation down in ruins.[5] Rothbard can make such a claim because he looks at the function of government from the point of view of the individual whom he thinks of as sovereign in this universe. Such a sovereign individual must be allowed his full freedom to exercise his "natural" rights, especially his rights to private property. By such civil rights laissez faire individualists therefore mean the freedom to acquire property or to sell it or to make contracts with regard to it. In this context of natural law social theory, equality is thought of in terms of each member of society having equal rights to property regardless of whether one's property is large or small. Such a view is derived from the teachings of John Locke, the philosophical progenitor of the old liberalism.

Locke began his social theory with the inalienable rights of each man to his life, liberty, and property. Thus Locke declared that "the great and chief end . . . of men uniting into commonwealths, and putting themselves under government, is the preservation of their property." He defined a man's property as "his life, liberty and estate,"—in other words, himself and his natural rights as a whole, not only his property in its ordinary sense. According to Locke, by nature all men are "free, equal and independent," and no man can be "subjected to the political power of another without his own consent." [6] Any number of men may agree together to incorporate themselves into a body politic, but in Locke's view of the social contract men do not give up all their rights. They surrender only so much of their natural liberty as is necessary for the preservation of society; they give up the right they had in the state of nature of individually judging and punishing, but they retain the remainder of their rights under the protection of the government they have agreed to establish. The state is thus in principle a limited state. Man's natural rights could not be surrendered even by the social contract. Thus, from the beginning, Locke limited the content of the social contract by not giving it any other purpose than the peaceful enjoyment of natural civil rights in a civil state. The individuals brought to the ruler nothing else than their natural competence to defend their natural rights through self-direction against attack by others. Thus, Locke laid the basis for the constitutional state of the old liberalism. The state is a limited company for the organized maintenance of individual freedom and rights of property and life.

Another assumption of contemporary economic individualists such as Rothbard and L. von Mises is that of the natural identity of interests between men. In his work, *The Structure of Social Action*, Talcott Parsons points out that "This is the device by which it has been possible for utilitarian thought, with few exceptions, for two hundred years to evade the Hobbesian problem of order." [7] Both Rothbard and von Mises assume as a basic postulate of their thought that the market processes of capitalism do a better job of expressing people's desires on how the productive resources of society should be used in each case than any government can possibly do. It is the people's desires rather than the planners' wishes which should carry the most weight.

The allocation of resources through the private economy, according to W. H. Hutt, occurs primarily in response to consumers' money demands for goods and services. He calls this "*consumers' sovereignty.*" By means of each dollar the consumer spends he votes for whatever goods or services he wants produced. In this way he exercises his economic democratic rights.[8]

Economic collectivists such as J. K. Galbraith prefer "*citizens' sovereignty*" to such "*consumers' sovereignty,*" since in the market place, voting for resource allocation is on a *one-dollar-one-vote* basis, whereas in the public sector, in a democratic country, it is on a *one-person-one-vote* basis. Thus, in the private sector the rich man has many more votes than the poor man. In the public sector a democratic system attempts to give each citizen equal voting power, regardless of whether he is rich or poor.

In *The Affluent Society*,[9] Galbraith argues that the prevailing laissez faire individualist distrust of the governmental process has led to a serious under-allocation of resources to the public sector (leaving national defense aside). In the world's richest economy, we allocate less than 15 percent of our net national product (about $100 billion out of about $700 billion in 1967) to satisfying all non defense collective wants through governmental services.

Galbraith maintains that the American economy is so rich we can readily afford more and better public services, that we need them badly, and that indeed the alternative is generally wasteful civilian consumption just to keep our economic system going. Yearly model changes on automobiles, plush night clubs, and mink coats are symbols of conspicuous consumption, meeting demands developed if not created by advertising. Yet America's public services are barely adequate. Half the nation's most able youths still do not go to college. The great cities are marred by slums and their streets jammed. The police forces and local governments are often peopled by incompetent individuals, so poorly paid as to be constant targets for graft. All this, Galbraith argues, reflects a basic social unbalance in the affluent American economy.

It is obvious from this brief summary of his thesis that Galbraith looks at the function of government from the point of view of society as a whole rather than of the individual. He stresses equality rather than freedom as the fundamental social value to be pursued. Equality is understood by Galbraith and other collectivists as the right of *all* citizens to a fair share in the goods and services of the economic system.

From the Reformational perspective the point to be noted is that the economic collectivist no less than the economic individualist are basically united by their common immanence humanist standpoint. Both approach the problem of the role of government in the economy in the light of their apostate humanist presuppositions about man in society. But whereas the collectivist absolutizes the community, the individualist deifies the sovereign single individual. The socialist looks to the government to integrate people's economic activities, the capitalist looks to the price system and the free market to do so. One stresses freedom, the other equality.

The difference in fundamental presuppositions between individualist and collectivist is reflected in the difference in emphasis each ascribes to the role of government in the economy. In the case of laissez faire individualism the government's function is determined by the ground-motive of freedom, in the case of the socialist collectivist the function of the state is determined by the ground-motive of science, and the ideal of the freedom of the community receiving expression in the scientific distribution of all available resources of the society to everyone equally. The collectivist looks to the government to create order in the economic relationships within society. The individualist expects the natural identity of interests and competition to provide the integrating factor required. The laissez faire school thinks that the freedom of the individual must be the criterion of the state's intervention in the economic process always coming to a halt at the point where the individual's freedoms and civil rights are being infringed upon. The collectivist thinks that the public interest must take precedence over the private interest and that the good of the whole body politic must come before the good of the individual.

A solution to this liberal-socialist dilemma concerning the role of the state in the operation of the economy is not possible until we first discover the structure of the state and the particular place of the authority of the state within this individuality structure.

According to the scriptural principle of sphere sovereignty it is only in terms of God's ultimate sovereignty that the function of the state can be properly understood. The state is ordained by God to maintain the external public legal relations between the social spheres. For this reason neither individualism nor collectivism is acceptable to the consistent Christian who recognizes only God's sovereignty in this world and rejects any claim to sovereignty on the part of the individual or of the collectivity as idolatry. The Christian considers that the choice between individualism and collectivism is the product of the apostate humanist's attempt to understand society apart from God's creation ordinances for it. Immanence (this worldly) thought is unable to resolve the contradictions inherent in this dilemma because of its false starting point. Only God's Word reveals that man is created as an individual person and as a member of society and that both are responsible to God. The role of the state in the operation of the economy can be understood only within the scriptural conception of society as a whole and of the individuality structures laid down at creation. As Maarten Vrieze says, "Economic theory cannot say a word about the standpoints of socialism and of classical liberalism or about the role of government in the national economy unless it recognizes the norm principles which are driven into a specific positivation direction by each of these movements."

What then is the structure of the state? What role has God assigned for it to play in the operation of the economy?

According to Dooyeweerd, the state is grounded in history and rests upon the historical formation of power. The state does not arise in history until in the process of cultural differentiation, "the power of the sword" is separated from the undifferentiated organization of primitive society and is concentrated in a government." [10]

To recognize the foundational function of the state, it is not enough to say that it rests upon the historical formation of power, since the same can be said of other structures such as the church, the business enterprise, or the labor union. Historical power is a modal concept which can be predicated of a number of social structures of individuality. The typical foundational function of the state is to be found in the internal monopolistic organization of the power of the sword over a given geographical and cultural area.

From this definition of its basis it is evident that the state exists by the grace of God on account of human sinfulness, so that together with its coercive power the state is a characteristic institution of God's common, temporal conserving grace. The Roman Catholic view, which grounds the state in the sphere of the natural, does not do justice to the terrible fact of sin. In both Old and New Testaments, the organized power of the sword is emphatically related to man's fall (Rom. 13:1-13; I Pet. 2:13; Rev. 13:10; I Sam. 12:17-25; 24:7, 11; 26:9-11; II Sam. 1:14-16). The governmental authority thus exists because of human sinfulness and is not the result of any social contract between individuals in a distant mythical past.

The fact that the state is based on the power of the sword must not be interpreted naturalistically, since the foundational function is but a part of the state's structural principle, in which power is normatively related to the state's leading function, which is justice. The qualifying or end function of the state is jural and the state is typically qualified as a juridical relationship. We may define the state as a public legal community of government and subjects on the historical basis of a monopolistic organization of power within a given geographical area. Such a definition places the state's "might" in direct coherence with "right."

The leading function in the structure of the state must be characterized by this integration of justice, otherwise it lapses into a tyranny. A mere power-state which disavows justice as its leading function is nothing else but a band of thugs. On the other hand, the state cannot continue to exist if law and justice are separated from their historical basis in power.

The state is ordained by God to maintain the public legal relations between all the other sovereign spheres of society. The state is the legal integrating factor of society. Does this mean that the Reformational view of the state is a totalitarian one? The answer is in the negative, because this integration does not make the other associations and communities within society intrinsic parts of the state, as in Roman Catholic social theory, but a public legal community arises, whose purposes are limited by its leading function of justice.

In the territorial legal community of the body politic all the specifically qualified juridical interests should be harmonized in the sense of a truly public legal retribution against lawbreakers and integrated into the public interest. The term "public interest" must never be used as a slogan for any sort of political program designed to collectivize society, but must always be juridically qualified, since its use may never warrant an encroachment upon the internal sphere sovereignty of the non political societal relationships such as family, school, church, and industry.

We must see this "public interest" in the context of all God's holy ordinances and "offices." Only then can the limitation of what the public interest constitutes be balanced successfully against the private interest. For the limits of both the public and the private interest can be found only in the divine institution of the various offices of human life. In each of these offices God maintains His sovereignty and authority in a particular way that is appropriate to each office.

In each office man is to recognize the sovereignty of God according to the order and authority that God gave for that office. The authority of each office-bearer is qualified by the structure of each particular social relationship involved. Thus the authority of the father over his children is different from the authority of the employer over his employee or of the church eldership over the individual church member. In the state we find a peculiar situation in this respect. While in all other social relationships the authority of the office-bearer is qualified by and stands under the control of the function peculiar to that relationship, e.g., the family authority under the control of moral love, and the authority of the local church under the aspect of faith, in the structure of the state the authority finds its qualification in justice itself. The father exercises his authority in the family and this means ethical justice. But the office-bearers in the state exercise their authority in accordance with the requirements of justice. Thus the specific divinely imposed task of the government is to establish the legal framework for all the other spheres. It is from this typical leading function of the structure of the state that we discover an insight into the extent and limits of the state. The state's task is to maintain the public order of justice in which individuals and the societal relationships in which they find themselves and fulfill their vocation are publicly protected and respected in their various authorities. The state's duty is to regulate, according to the criterion of the legal public interest, every citizen's and every social sphere's *external* relations to all the other spheres, so that individuals and social institutions may flourish and grow in peace (I Tim. 2:1-3). The "public" interest here being understood more in the sense of carrying out God's justice for the various realms of society rather than in any socialist sense of the welfare state. The state is not the whole of which all the other spheres are only its subservient parts.

For this good reason Dooyeweerd teaches that the modal moment of the juridical aspect of the state is judgment, the well-balanced harmonization of a multiplicity of interests. The public law of the state must therefore seek to maintain harmonious relationships between *all* the interests within its territory. No single interest within the borders of the state can be ignored. This harmonizing process consists in the weighing of the various interests of society against each other in the scales of justice so that each receives its just and proper due, based upon a recognition of the sphere-sovereignty of the various social spheres.

As such the state must never interfere in the *internal* law of the family, church, university, labor union, or business enterprise. The government's task is to regulate, according to the criterion of the public legal interest, every social sphere's *external* relations to the other spheres. The *internal* law of these social spheres is beyond the state's jurisdiction. The authority of the government ceases where that of another divine "office" begins.

However, all these social spheres have an external as well as an internal juridical function. A church, for example, is affected by a noisy factory, so that the latter is rightly prevented by law from interfering with public worship on the Lord's Day. The government must try to harmonize such external legal interests, but it must also respect the internal sovereignty of the other social relationships and promote justice as a whole by utilizing public law in order to balance the external legal relations of all societal relationships. According to its own nature the state touches on every social sphere but always in its own typical public legal manner.

By means of their principle of subsidiarity Roman Catholics are able to maintain the idea of private enterprise, because their social theory does give the first responsibility to the lower organs of society such as family and industry for the sake of realizing their own special purpose and the fulfillment of their own vital tasks.

At the same time the Roman Catholic principle of intervention requires that the state possesses the right to supervise the activity of the lower organs of society, to regulate the indispensable contributions of the lower organs toward society as a whole, and to intervene against violations of the public welfare committed by lower organs of society.

Such a claim of the right of the state to intervene is based upon the principle of hierarchy and its philosophic hierocratic (priestly) view of society in terms of the higher and lower organs of society of which the state is considered to be the highest and the all-embracing whole, subject in its turn to the Roman Catholic hierarchy.

The great value of the doctrine of subsidiarity lies in the fact that it enables Roman Catholics to lay stress upon the "autonomy" of the lower organs of society before the activity of the higher ones step in. Thus the principle of subsidiarity, like the principle of sphere sovereignty, acts as a bulwark against socialist or collectivist totalitarianism. It does so by developing the arrangement of society from the "bottom up" and not from the "top down," so that the authorities ultimately must leave the task of "arrangement" as much as possible to the private individuals and lower organs of society.

The great defect of the Roman Catholic principle of subsidiarity lies in the fact that there is no *intrinsic* limiting principle for the intervention of the higher organ (the state) in the lower organs (e.g., family and industry). Thus there is no real *principial* safeguard against dictatorship. The principle of subsidiarity still ultimately looks upon industry and family life as parts of the greater whole which is the state, whereas the principle of sphere sovereignty alone of all social theories maintains that such spheres are irreducible to any other sphere.

(b) *The Reformed Critique of Catholic*
    Solidarism and Syndicalism

Judged by the principle of sphere sovereignty the Roman Catholic economic policy of solidarism or industry-wide organization along the corporate lines suggested by Pope Pius XI in *Quadragesimo Anno* must be rejected. Writing of this tendency towards the horizontal organization of industry in Western Europe, H. Dooyeweerd says:

The increase of collective bargaining stimulated the idea that employers and labourers should try and find new horizontal forms of organized cooperation. The aim was to give expression to their solidarity in taking to heart the common interests in the different branches of industrial life and to strengthen the communal bonds between employers and labourers in the separate industrial undertakings.

It was especially the Christian conception of social solidarity which inspired this idea, frankly in opposition to the Marxian dogma of class struggle. In different countries it has exercised a salutary influence upon the integrating tendencies in modern industrial societal relationships. Nevertheless, it must be granted that this movement of Christian solidarism had not completely emancipated itself from the universalistic-romantic view of human society, current in the so-called Christian-historical trend of thought of the Restoration. Especially the conception of an entire branch of industry as a "natural community," which was considered as an autonomous and "organical" part of the "national whole," revealed an after effect of this romantic view, which could eventually be synthesized with the Aristotelian view of society.

It was overlooked that a branch of industry necessarily displays a correlation between organizational-communal and intercommunal or interindividual relationships, and that the latter can never be transformed into the former. It was further overlooked that a national community can never encompass the internal industrial relationships, notwithstanding their enkaptical intertwinement with national life.

This universalist (collectivist) misconception resulted in the erroneous idea that a public legal organization of industrial life was to be considered as a natural development of the true inner nature of the different branches of industry, as "natural communities." From an organic view of society, it was concluded that the horizontal organizations of these industrial branches could lay claim to a public legal competence *on their own account* by virtue of an "historical right," consequently a competence not derived from the legislator. Here we meet with the appeal to the medieval guilds, whose public legal autonomy preceded the rise of the modern State as a *res publica*. . . .

This "organic view" was readily accepted by the movement of

Christian solidarism both in its Roman Catholic and Protestant trends. In the Netherlands the Protestant Christian league of trade unions interpreted the principle of sphere sovereignty of industrial life in this sense. But in this way this principle was completely misunderstood since it was viewed apart from its structural foundation in the temporal order of reality. It was overlooked that medieval political autonomy, so long as it was viewed as a subjective right of the guilds, only suited to an un-differentiated society and that a public legal authority is never to be derived from the inner nature of a private organization of industrial life in its different branches. Here, too, it appears that a collectivist denaturization of the genuine Christian idea of social solidarity necessarily leads to an eradication of the struc-tural principles of the different types of societal relationships.

A public legal organization of industrial life, as it was intro-duced in the Netherlands by the Public Industrial Organization Act of 1950, can as such never belong to the inner sphere sover-eignty of industry and agriculture as economically qualified sectors of the societal process of production. Within a state's territory any public legal authority exercised by organs composed of rep-resentatives of organizations of employers and trade unions, is derived from the legislator. A public legal organization means an organization of the industrial and agricultural branches which is typically qualified by the leading juridical function of the state. The organs of such an organization may have a delegated auton-omy, whose limits are completely dependent on the public interest in the previously defined sense. But any confusion of this auton-omy with the inner sphere sovereignty of the economically quali-fied private industrial and agricultural relations must lead either to a deformation of public legal authority, or to an absorption of free industrial and agricultural life by the political sphere of the state.[11]

For this reason P.B.O. and other industry-wide organizations must never be allowed to become avenues of centralized planning by the state for the internal life of industry and the labor unions. Again, such industry-wide horizontal organizations as P.B.O. must not be al-lowed to become means by which industry and the trade unions realize their own private economic interests by means of the sword power of the state. If they are allowed to do so, there is a grave danger that some form of syndicalist guild socialism may yet develop in modern society.

The two great, mutually exclusive, contemporary opponents of a free society as we have known it are collectivism and syndicalism. Both recommend the integration of society by means of the erection and maintenance of monopolies; neither finds any virtue in the diffusion of power. But they must be considered mutually exclusive opponents of a free society because the monopoly favored by syndicalism would make both a collective and a free society impossible.

In a certain sense syndicalism is an even greater threat to our liberties than socialism in its Western versions. Syndicalism and the so-called corporate state of Roman Catholicism would not only destroy our historic Anglo-American-Canadian freedoms; but they would also destroy any kind of orderly existence. Syndicalism rejects both the concentration of overwhelming power in the government and the wide dispersion of power which is the basis of freedom. Syndicalism is a contrivance by means of which society is disposed for a perpetual civil war in which the parties are the organized self-interest of functional minorities and a weak central government, and for which the community as a whole pays the bill in monopoly prices and disorder. The great concentrations of power in a syndicalist society such as that advocated by Tannenbaum are the sellers of labor organized in functional monopoly associations. All monopolies are prejudicial to freedom, but there is good reason for supposing that a management-labor monopoly along the lines suggested by Tannenbaum would be most dangerous of all, and that a society in the grip of such a monopoly would enjoy less freedom than any other sort of society. The consumers would certainly suffer as the syndicalist industrial groupings fixed prices to suit their convenience rather than the general public.

As we have already seen, the secular trade union monopolies have shown themselves more capable even than big business of attaining really great power, economic, political, and even military. Their appetite for power has proved insatiable, and producing nothing they encounter none of the productional diseconomies of undue size. Once grown large, they are exceedingly difficult to dissipate and impossible to control. Appearing to spring from the lawful exercise of the right of voluntary association, they enjoy popular support however scandalous their behavior. Business monopolies, on the other hand, are less dangerous than labor monopolies because they are less powerful. They are precariously held together, they are unpopular, and they are highly sensitive to legal control. Taken separately, there is no question which of the two kinds of monopoly is the more subversive of freedom. But, in addition to its greater power, the trade union monopoly is dangerous, because it demands big business monopoly as its complement. There is what Simons calls in his *Economic Policy for a Free Society* "an alarming identity of interest" between the two kinds of monopoly; "each tends to foster and to strengthen the other, fighting together to maximize joint extractions from the public while also fighting each other over the division of the spoils." [12]

Indeed, the supposed conflict of capital and labor (the struggle over the division of earnings) has become in Western Europe and North America merely a sham fight (often costing the public more than the participants), concealing the substantial conflict between the producer (business and labor, both organized monopolistically) and the consumer. Such syndicalism therefore has some claim to be considered the main adversary of freedom and of the Reformed principle of sphere sovereignty.

The Reformed sociologist admits the right of the government to assist industry but not to direct its day to day activities. Thus, he would welcome government legislation to assist depressed areas. In such a case the state is merely carrying out its public legal integrating function by weighing the interests of all the factions in the nation so that it may arrive at a just balance.[13]

Industry-wide organizations such as P.B.O. can really function only as organs of the public legal coordination and integration between the state and industry. It must be recognized that all such industry wide organizations are really governmental organs and not organs of industry, and therefore the decision of such nationwide industrial councils must be subject to public legal norms and not to economic norms.

In practice the socialist attempt to make use of P.B.O. in Holland as an instrument of centralized state planning of the economy has failed because in the years since P.B.O. was established, in 1950, industry has developed along its own lines in accordance with its own sphere sovereignty.

Dooyeweerd teaches that the principle of sphere sovereignty needs to be applied dynamically to meet the changing needs of modern society. But it should not be rejected in favor of a so-called guided economy and planning if we wish to retain our freedoms. For, although the state functions necessarily in every modal aspect, including the economic one, its leading function is the juridical and legal; and all its economic activity must be in accordance with its purpose as public legal community. He writes:

> The entire development of modern Western political and economic life has resulted in abandoning the old liberal policy of "*laissez-faire, laissez passer.*"
>
> In itself this thought of ordering is congenial. But it may bring on all the dangers of the totalitarian idea of the absolutist state, if it is not subject to the control of the structural principle of the body politic. The economic integration of the State's population within its territory by means of a political ordering of non-political economic industrial life should remain under the leading of the juridical idea of public interest. The structure of the State necessarily requires this typical leading so that the internal sphere sovereignty of the economically qualified societal structures will be safeguarded.[14]

The state should properly take cognizance of economic and business life by providing public legal protection in its commerce and business enterprises. As H. Van Riessen puts it:

> The protection and development of this sphere affects *demands* and *conditions* valid for other spheres. The state may properly develop and maintain national conditions favorable to an equitable commercial life, e.g., the guarantee of the value of its currency. The state exceeds its function when it interferes in economic life by determining individual conditions affecting credit that properly belong to the individual decision of the enterprise concerned. The digging of canals and public power projects, such as the Boulder Dam concern national *conditions* affecting the economic life but also have a broader reach. For the digging of canals and the reclamation and cultivation of inundated territory, e.g., are

not limited solely to economic life; they enable life in all its rich variety of facets and relationships.[15]

Neither Dooyeweerd nor Van Riessen advocates the return to laissez faire conditions. Instead they think of the relation between the state and economic life analogously. The state ought not to regulate and direct economic life in such a way that it places its own authority above the authorities proper to the economic sphere. At the same time they are convinced of the necessity of the government developing and maintaining favorable national and local conditions in which the economic sphere may properly flourish. In borderline cases of distress, emergency, or injustice, they believe the state ought to act protectively to put matters right.

For both Reformed sociologists the government is properly exercising its function of integrating justice and the public interest when it upholds the wage rate and protects collective agreements about conditions of work. Similarly they favor governmental protection of the frequently powerless employees from economic exploitation by gigantic combines, cartels, and monopolies. This involves the regulation of labor conditions, which are, in any case, a matter of social concern and they should not therefore be controlled by impersonal rationalistic economic considerations of profit alone. Both men favor social legislation, e.g., minimum wage laws, since it is part of the state's integrating function to prohibit gross social inequalities.[16]

For the same reason they believe that all monopolies or near monopolies are impediments to the free development of the economic sphere of society as well as to individual liberty. They have no illusions about monopolies. As Christian sociologists they know that no individual, no group, association, or union can be entrusted with too much power, and that it is mere foolishness to complain when absolute power is abused. It exists to be abused. And so they would encourage the growth of arrangements which will discourage its existence. In other words, they recognize that the only way of organizing the enterprise of getting a living so that it does not curtail men's freedom is by the establishment and maintenance of effective competition. Since monopolies are often the creation of the state, they do not think it beyond the capacity of society to build upon its already substantial tradition of creating and maintaining competition by law. But they also recognize that any confusion between the task of making competition effective and the task of organizing the enterprise of getting a living and satisfying human needs will prove fatal to freedom. For to replace by political control the integration of activity which competition provides is at once to create an even greater monopoly and to destroy the diffusion of power inseparable from freedom.

Dooyeweerd and Van Riessen are insistent that the structural boundaries between the authority of the employer and of the government must be maintained, for industrial life according to its own peculiar nature is not a part of the function of government. The application of the principle of centralized planning on the part of the government must necessarily regulate industrial life as part of the life of the state.

Dooyeweerd holds that industrial life is the result of a process of economic differentiation during the course of history, by means of which it has come to develop its own inner nature and its own principles. This is the principle of free economic enterprise qualified by capital and labor, which must not be absorbed by the state if society is to develop in freedom as God has ordained. For this independent function of free enterprise is inseparably related to the principles of risk and mutual competition. And the profits earned are wholly justified when we consider the services which free enterprise offers to human society. According to Dooyeweerd and the Reformed economists of the Free University such as De Kooy and De Roos, the only efficiency to be considered is the most economical way of supplying the things men desire to purchase. The formal circumstance in which this may be at its maximum is where enterprise is effectively competitive, for here the entrepreneur is merely the intermediary between consumers of goods and sellers of services. Of course there is always the danger of the abuse of the profit motive, but this is not the primary feature of free enterprise, and it may be curbed. The regulation of the profit motive or the regulation of prices by the government must not, however, involve the removal of the business entrepreneur from our society, since freedom of business enterprise depends upon spiritual liberty and responsibility. As soon as industry becomes a branch of the state as under communism, then this freedom comes to depend upon the centralized planning of the government experts, and thus would entail a usurpation of power by the state. Moreover, citizens have a God given right not to be economically directed and controlled by the government.[17] It is ironical to say the least, that while such centralized planning is increasing in Western societies, the Communists are being forced to revert to free enterprise. T. P. van der Kooy thus points out:

> An extremely important phenomenon, to which I want to call attention, is the contemporary tendency to reform the methods of the planning of production in the Soviet Union and its satellites. The present discussion among economists in those countries—in which the labor value theory seems to be subjected to a thorough revision, and the economic function of the profit motive is given attention—plays an important role in this tendency. . . . Is it perhaps not possible that in a country, where historic materialism is adhered to, a change in the economic system demanded by an economic necessity may not also bring about over a period of time a change in ideology? [18]

According to Reformed economics a government may not incorporate the internal legal life of industry or commerce, even if a program of guided economy aims at decentralization. For then the agreements between enterprises and businesses based on private law, in respect to prices and production, would have to disappear to make room for a determination of prices based on public legal rules. In such a state controlled system there would no longer be any room left for the principle of risk and free economic enterprise. The responsibility for the development of economic life would then rest upon public administrative organs, which these could efficiently exercise only if they came to enjoy a complete totalitarian control of the national and even the international market and the regulation of all the means of production, distribution, and consumption. While recognizing a need for a stringent control of certain features of modern big business and of international cartels and business combines, and that the public interest may demand that private capital gains and deadly monopolies should be curbed, Dooyeweerd and the Reformed school of economists do not believe that it would be possible to fit the internal life of industry and commerce into the strait jacket of a centralized public law without eventually enslaving the whole population and arresting further economic growth.

(c) The Reformed Conception of the Business Enterprise

Having established the right of the private business enterprise to develop along its own lines without constant intervention by the state, it is at the same time vital to point out that in the Reformed view the business enterprise must behave responsibly first towards God then to its own workers, shareholders, and the consumers. The Christian employer no less than the Christian worker are equally called to live by God's creation norms for the economic sphere, and by means of their industry to glorify God and serve their neighbors. For this reason we must reject H. F. R. Catherwood's moralizing approach to this subject in his chapter on "The Christian as an Employer" in the book *The Christian in Industrial Society*. He writes:

> The Christian should aim to be the sort of person who inspires a high standard of behaviour, but he should combine this with a sympathetic nature so that those who get into a mess can come to him more easily. . . .
> On the job, the Christian will want to keep as high a moral standard as he can. Christian doctrine makes it perfectly clear that there are certain rules of conduct in our relations to each other which help those relations. The Christian employer, personnel officer or welfare officer will try to see, so far as possible, that within the factory gates those rules are kept and that employees while on duty are sober, moral and responsible in their behaviour to each other.[19]

Of course no Christian could object to this statement of the conduct required by the Christian employer, but it does not get down to the basic problems facing modern management and workers. For such Protestant pietists no less than for Roman Catholics, the problems facing modern industry are moral ones. Everything else will solve itself when this big question has been solved. *That industry and labor involve primarily a proper recognition of the places of the management and the workers within the framework of the business enterprise is simply not seen.* The principle of sphere sovereignty and the principle of the balance of authority and freedom are essential in understanding the structure of the economic sphere.

First it must be clearly understood that the economic aspect of reality or law-sphere is one peculiar to itself, and it must not become absorbed by either church or state. What then constitutes the modal moment of the economic sphere? What distinguishes it from all other aspects of reality? The answer is the demand to save. Thus to act economically means to obtain a maximum of useful effect with a minimum of effort. The modal moment of the economic sphere thus consists in the saving of calculated values. Stated more simply, it consists in the thrifty use of resources and it has been defined as the science of scarcity. As Dooyeweerd explains:

> The foundational scientific meaning of the word "economy" is the sparing or frugal mode of administering scarce goods, implying an alternative choice of their destination with regard to the satisfaction of different human needs. . . .
> Economy demands the balancing of needs according to a plan, and the distribution of the scarce means at our disposal according to such a plan. In this fundamental sense the term is used in the science of economics.[20]

For this reason management may be defined as a free private association of employers qualified by the economic function. As such management is called in the first place to produce goods or services as efficiently as possible and to make the most use of limited resources.

By contrast the workers in a given business enterprise are morally and socially qualified. But against the doctrines of economic individualism the economic and the social are not to be separated. Thus, every worker has a right to a just wage, decent conditions of work, vacations, and an old age pension.

However, order has to be maintained and affairs must be regulated so that some are called to "manage" and others to work. Hence, in economic life management and labor need each other. Apostate capitalists failed to recognize this community of interest between managers and owners and their workers, and as a result they tended to reduce their workers to mere factors in the process of production and to economic chattels. Quite rightly the workers reacted against this depersonalization as an outrage to their humanity and as an affront to their human dignity. Emil Brunner points out that this apostate capitalist attitude towards the workers arose out of the individualistic conception of property. He writes in *Justice and the Social Order*:

> It is the standpoint which has been called the "master in the house" view of property, and it is shared by many, though fortunately no longer by the majority, of employers in Switzerland. The working class is right to revolt against it; but not right when it condemns and attacks every employer and capitalist as *ipso facto* one who shares that view. Employers and capitalists are right in defending themselves against such an assumption; they are not right in inferring an unqualified right of disposition from their property in the means of production. For this "master in the house" standpoint infringes on the order of economic life as an organic whole, which is the order laid down in the creation. It is first and foremost the employer who should realize that he, the master, is the servant. . . . It is true that industry needs competent and responsible leadership. It is true that economic democracy in any formal sense would be the ruin of industry; it is true that the organic union of all in the economic community does not mean "equal rights of self-determination" for all, but, like the family, implies a certain hierarchy of competence and responsibility. But that hierarchy does not abolish a coresponsibility on the part of the worker proportional to his capacity and output. By paying the workers their contractural wage, the employer has not fulfilled his duty to them, for work is not a commodity that can be bought, but a service whereby a communal relationship is established.
>
> The idea of a community of labour and organization is a necessary inference from the Christian view of the relationship established by labour. Where there is a just order of labour, employer and worker do not confront each other as exploiter and exploited, but as members of a labour community in which the welfare of the one is the welfare of the other. Properly understood the welfare of the "firm" is the welfare of the workers, and vice versa.[21]

According to the Reformed view, there must be recognized a just balance between the authority of the management and freedom on the part of the workers as men and women called to fulfill their task of service of Almighty God in industry and farming. When this balance is distorted it is no wonder that one side begins to eye the other with suspicion and hatred. When the laborer is but a part of the machinery of production, instead of production being geared to the worker, it is no wonder that work becomes a curse for him. If the workers join together in the "closed shop" and take it upon themselves to decide who shall be "hired" and who "fired," the relationship between management and worker becomes even worse. When workers take upon themselves the function of management, the efficient ordering of the business enterprise collapses into anarchy.

The question as to who should bear responsibility in the business enterprise thus depends upon one's view of the nature of the business corporation. According to P. Borst there are two main conceptions:

(1) The business enterprise is the exclusive property of an individual or corporation who has concluded agreements with a number of other people according to civil law. On this view industry is an object of ownership and the responsibility for the concern falls exclusively on the owner.

(2) The business enterprise is not an object of ownership, but is itself a subject, an independent being; industry is normally formed out of the organizational relations of an independent body, usually a limited company. The employers and the workers are functionaries; the shareholders are not owners of the business, but "post-creditors" and as such bear no direct responsibility for policy.[22]

Most views of the business enterprise fall between these two extremes. The choice we make between these two views will, Borst says, be decisive for the definition of responsibility in industry. If industry is no more than a part of the property of a particular person, then that person is responsible for what he does with his own property. Direct responsibility will rest exclusively with him.

If, in contrast, the business enterprise is a more or less independent institution that exists outside the legal person of the "owner," then we obtain a divided responsibility resting upon the different "functionaries in the concern": the manager, shareholders, workers. This responsibility exists towards the concern itself, towards the industry as a whole, and towards the consumers. Such a view of coresponsibility in industry, Borst suggests, has arisen out of the doctrine of the public trust which has long given legal standing to an organized group. The business enterprise from this standpoint is thus viewed as a trust not only for the interests of the shareholders, but also as an implied trust for the workers.

What will be the responsibility of the workers in this second type of business enterprise? To what extent should the workers participate in the *economic* affairs of the business enterprise?

Borst points out that we cannot answer this question until we first define exactly what is meant by "participation in management." He distinguishes three senses in the meaning of this phrase: (1) the right to be informed, to be told the facts, (2) the right to advise, and to be consulted, and (3) the right to decide jointly.

It is also necessary to distinguish three forms of joint-decision: (1) joint voting, that is, to share in making decisions, for example, where the shareholders, the management, and the workers each has one third of the voting power on all matters connected with the future policy making of the firm, (2) unanimity, that is, no decision can be made without the cooperation of all parties (a type of veto-right), and (3) right of appeal, that is, any party which cannot agree with the proposed course of action should have the right to appeal to an impartial body outside the firm to make the final decision, e.g., an arbitration board established by the government.

By what principle should the Reformed Christian be guided in answering the question whether labor should be given a share in the management of economic affairs? Borst answers by saying:

> The ground for participation in management, that is for the responsibility of the workers, is association in a common task. The original royal function of man, laid upon him at the creation, wherein his likeness to God's image finds expression, that of being the lord of creation has been destroyed by sin. Work became a curse. One sees this in modern industry; the worker is estranged from his work, he has become a tool, he lacks all interest, he feels no more responsibility, he is a willing tool for massification. The

worker no longer inquires after God, and no longer finds the way to his Creator.

In conflict with all this the Christian trade-unions strive again for the restoration of work as a blessing, and to restore the dignity of the worker created in God's image. New responsibility must be laid upon the worker; participation in management will restore to the worker the legal status which belongs to him in industry according to Christian principles. It will connect him again to his work and his fellows in the concern; it signifies a new community in the concern and in the work. The relationship between boss and men is not simply that the boss operates living instruments, but that both categories form a community of people with a common task, which thus gives to the worker certain obligations as well as rights. . . . Given such participation in management the workers will work better and produce more. . . . It will combat abuses which undermine the institution of private property and so prevent the state taking over all industry.[23]

Borst is very careful to point out that *shared* responsibility does not necessarily mean *equal* responsibility. Management, shareholders, and workers have each their own responsibility, which is defined by the nature of their position and their function. He agrees that the business enterprise requires an hierarchically organized administration. There must be authority and leadership, just as on a ship or in the army. He therefore rejects any syndicalist or socialist ideas of worker control of industry. The Communists at first tried out such ideas and rejected them when they proved a fiasco, almost bringing down the Soviet economy in ruins.

He points out correctly that "political democracy is a different thing from social democracy" and that "relations in a business are totally different from those in a trade organization." The business enterprise must form a unity without any dispute for leadership. In the light of these structural principles Borst draws the following conclusions regarding the participation of workers in management:

(1) The workers should be informed and consulted on all matters concerning the daily running of affairs. However, joint decisions in the daily running of affairs is not possible owing to the hierarchical character of industrial management.

(2) The workers should also be kept informed regarding ex-

ceptional matters such as expansion, reorganization, amalgamation, closing down of the firm.

(3) Joint voting leads to a tripartite system, whereby shareholders and management and labor share policy making among them. This is generally impossible and even detrimental.

(4) Joint decisions in the sense of unanimity being required (the veto-right of the workers) are also undesirable since the workers are seldom well enough informed to make the right choice.

(5) Workers should be given the right of appeal to an independent tribunal whenever their rights are ignored or their livelihood is threatened by gross mismanagement or when they are unjustly treated. By means of such an impartial court of appeal a way out is found whereby the worker does not usurp the employer's function and yet can obtain redress in all really grievous cases.

(6) In the final analysis it is the attitudes which prevail between management and workers which are decisive. The question of responsibility in industry and the participation of workers in management is not decided by formal regulations and decisions. It is the attitude and the atmosphere or spiritual climate in which these principles are realized that is decisive. Such an attitude will be formed and nourished by one's view of the purpose of the business enterprise, which will in turn be determined by one's total view of the nature and purpose of human life.[24]

It is therefore a basically religious problem with which modern industry is today faced. Unless both workers and managers are agreed that Jesus Christ alone is sovereign over industry and alone can empower men with His grace, love, and light, there does not seem to be much future for it. Without such a common allegiance to Christ, the Master Carpenter, American, British, and Canadian industry must soon grind to a halt in a welter of strikes, recriminations, and mud slinging. It is not more government intervention that we need in modern industry, but more Christ intervention. He alone can provide modern industry with the dynamic to work without which it must soon retrograde as industry did in the later Roman and Byzantine Empire. It is not better personnel management and technical rationalization that industry needs today, but a new vision amongst both workers and employers of God's holy ordinances for work and of the true Christ-centered relations which should exist between the "bosses" and the workers.

The workers in post-Christian Western society are today being exposed to the temptations of an apostate humanist economic system which promises them an almost unlimited improvement of their material position but which, at the same time tends to make them slaves of big business or big government. What shall it profit the big corporations of the world to make fantastic profits if in the process the managers and the workers lose their souls?

Resistance to this demonic system is only possible if enough Christian workers and employers vigorously sponsor such structural changes in modern industry that our workers regain their dignity as persons created in God's image and redeemed from the power and guilt of sin by the Lord Jesus Christ; bear for their part responsibility in the regulation of their firms' business life, and in so doing realize again the significance and purpose of their labor.

In opposition to the brutal depersonalization with which both an apostate capitalistic individualism and an apostate socialistic collectivism threaten our Western world no less than the Eastern and African worlds, all those who recognize Christ as their only Lord and Savior have the duty to show that the criticism of the Holy Gospel of God upon our apostate industrial and social order is far more radical than any Communist critique, and that a real recovery and reformation of the violated social and industrial relationships is not to be attained in any other way than by a return to God's structural norms and principles for the world of management, industry, and work.

These great directives for the proper conduct of industry have been broken by man's extravagance, dishonesty, greed, and exploitation of his fellow man. Instead of developing the economic sphere of life in accordance with God's creation norms, men have tried to become independent of God, and as a result there emerged that modern monstrosity known to mankind as *homo oeconomicus*, economic man, that is, the business man or worker with no religious or moral scruples who works solely, entirely, and completely for his own

maximum profit, utterly disregarding the rights of his fellow men.
The laws governing the conduct of the economic law sphere are
norms. The Reformational philosophy of man in society distinguishes between normative and a-normative spheres of reality (see
chapter six, section (d) of this book and the chart of the cosmonomic idea in the appendix). By this we mean that the subjects of
the numerical, spatial, physical, biological, and psychical law spheres
have no option but to obey the correlative laws for their spheres.
Thus a stone must fall down if thrown up into the air. From the
analytical sphere onwards, however, the laws become norms or
standards for human conduct. Although these norms have been
laid down by God in principle in the structure of each sphere, they
must be discovered, explicated, applied; that is, positivized. The
laws of justice or love, for example, do not contain a precise formulation of their meaning in each concrete instance. By the same token
these norms can be disobeyed and violated. As we have seen in our
study of the economic development of society, the norms of the
economic sphere have been constantly broken, for example, by
men's extravagance, dishonesty, greed, and exploitation of their fellow men. Instead of developing the economic sphere of life in accordance with God's creation norms, men have tried to become
independent of God, and as a result there emerged *homo economicus*, that is, economic man with no religious or moral scruples, who
worked solely for his own maximum profit and gain, completely
disregarding the rights of his fellow men. Of this apostate economic
development Dooyeweerd writes:

> The rationalized and absolutized idea of free interindividual
> relations dominated the entire industrial sector of Western society
> and gave it an extremely individualistic and merciless capitalistic
> form. . . .
> The process of unlimited one-sided technical rationalization
> in economically qualified industrial life sharpened the contrast
> between the interests of labor and capital to a real class-struggle.
> Labor was viewed apart from the human personality as a market
> ware. . . . Family and the kinship-life of the workers were de-
> natured by the encroachment of the impersonally rationalized
> industrial labor-relations. . . .

Such individualistic tendencies in social development form an irreconcilable antithesis with the Christian idea of free inter-individual relations. The civitas terrena (city of earth) revealed itself in this individualistic process of disintegration, and Christianity was doomed to decay whenever it thought of making a truce, or concluding a peace-treaty with this kingdom of darkness.[25]

Let these words of Dooyeweerd serve as a solemn warning to all Protestant Christians in the English-speaking world who have allowed the Church of Jesus Christ to become the kept woman of a godless, apostate, economic individualism. Let us all strive for a Christian economic system which will seek to realize God's creation norms for the business enterprise. Unless Christians take such action they can expect to undergo God's judgment along with the rest of the godless capitalists and labor unions, for God is not mocked (Gal. 6:7).

While it is desirable that Anglo-Saxon employers should themselves, of their own free will and in free agreement with the workers, make the modern business enterprise a true community interest; where they will not do so then the state should step in and restore justice to the economic system. It is imperative that the employers abandon the "master in the house" attitude and treat their workers as persons and as fellow brothers for whom Christ also died and behave as God's stewards and office bearers.

The limited liability company is the backbone of Anglo-American-Canadian industry and economy, and in the eyes of the Common Law the business enterprise has a corporate personality; that is, as George Goyder puts it in his important work, *The Responsible Company*, "the company is something distinct from the totality of its shareholding." [26] In practice the shareholders alone are considered to be the "company," and the directors who sacrifice their interest to any other consideration such as the workers' welfare are running considerable risks. Their position is secure provided they produce a profit that statisfies the shareholders. Of the duty of the directors to the community and the workers there is in the articles of association of the company no mention. It is of course true that in its trading operations certain obligations have to be met which in practice usually secures for them their most elementary rights. The wage must be paid and the Acts to protect public health and safety must be obeyed. But there is no trace of anything in the company's legal obligations which suggests that the workers are in any degree participators in the enterprise; no hint of any sort of a "natural industrial community." Anyone who thinks that such a legal basis for the limited liability company is capable of producing the right attitude in industrial relations is surely being a little optimistic. There is a great deal of truth in Goyder's assertion that "beneath the facade of central wage demands there is a profound but unformulated conviction that the present system is unjust and unnatural." [27] While not following Goyder all the way in his analysis of the exact nature of the injustice here in question, we would agree that it is being unreasonable to expect any sort of real cooperation between management and workers, as long as the elementary form of the business enterprise by its legal articles of incorporation as an association expresses so brutally the lopsidedness of modern Anglo-American-Canadian capitalism. The situation has been exacerbated by the increasing size of the average business corporation; the remoteness of the legal owners from its operations leads to a weakening of what little responsibility they may still feel. On the other hand, this division between ownership and control could be beneficial if the legal framework obliged the directors and managers and shareholders to give due recognition to the rights of the workers and to allow them a measure of participation along the lines Borst has suggested. Where the professional managers accept the Christian charter for management they can exercise a wise leadership which secures the human rights of their employees. Unfortunately there is not a large enough number of such Christian managers in Anglo-American-Canadian industry who are even aware of such a Christian approach to their workers, and if their attention were drawn to it by legislation which they ignored at their peril they could be persuaded to give the matter the attention it deserves.

The problem of the responsible business enterprise has been carefully studied by George Goyder, whom we have already quoted above. He is himself an experienced industrialist, and so cannot be accused of impractical idealism. Goyder is, as the name of his book suggests, concerned with the totality of the responsibilities of the company—to the community as a whole as well as to the individual employed by him. Goyder has no regrets about being himself a capitalist. "The primacy of the profit motive in industry is not in question. It is generally agreed that survival is the first duty of any man of business and survival for the business man means profit." [28] He then writes:

> Any reform of Company Law must be careful to safeguard the unity of the directors and their freedom of action. . . . The problem is to make power responsible, not to hamper it or to subject it to detailed restrictions. There must be freedom to grow, freedom to lead, freedom to make mistakes. Leadership and initiative do not usually result from balance of power (between management and workers). They require the command of power, the giving and the acceptance of responsibility. . . . I do, however, object to the attitude of certain management circles which finds it convenient to deny any connection between productivity and the social purpose of the enterprise. . . . Industrial organization, as it grows bigger and more complex, must seek to redeem the worker's sense of participation by making the company itself capable of human attachment and loyalty. . . . The task is to find a way of giving working men their associational rights and at the same time ensuring that the company remains efficient, while rendering to the community and the consumer what in justice belongs to them. . . .
> To this end, what is in question is the ultimacy and not the primacy of the profit motive. . . . A person who makes money his final goal is rightly regarded as suffering from a diseased mind. Ordinary people value money for what it brings in amenities, in leisure or power, and men's motives are legion. . . . But in industry and particularly in the large impersonal company that we have seen as being typical, profit is turned from a proximate or *primary* goal into an *ultimate* one. This is to make industry a battlefield of irreconcilable interests. It is to falsify the purpose of industry and to take away its power to command the loyalty of men.[29]

As a first step towards a healthier state of economic affairs Goyder suggests putting a "General Purposes Clause in the Memorandum of Association" of the bigger public companies, for in fact many firms, successful, profitable, and efficient, in England and in America, already possess such a clause, placed there by the initiative of a Christian management. The obligation should not, according to Goyder, be placed on the private, limited-liability company; this is probably wise—until at least by slow degrees the majority of the public companies have digested the change.

The clauses contained in the memorandum should, he suggests, cover the following:

(1) Making the company economically viable, providing adequately for its future and paying fair and reasonable dividends to its shareholders.

(2) Providing goods and services of the highest quality and lowest price consistent with its responsibilities under (1) above and (3) below.

(3) The interest of the employees, viz., providing the best possible conditions of employment for all those in the company, with reasonable opportunity for advancement and security of employment subject to (1) and (2) above.

(4) That in all matters in which the company's activities affect the community it should act so far as possible in the same manner as a responsible citizen could reasonably be expected to act in the same cirmumstances.

To make sure that firms carried out these provisions Goyder suggests that a social audit—taking place at intervals of three or five years—should be conducted by qualified outsiders having the duty of looking over the pricing policies of the company as they affect the consumer, the labor policies as affecting the workers, and finally, the community policies pursued by the firm.[30]

(d) *The Necessity for Christian Employers' Associations*

Unless some such reforms of the modern business enterprise are undertaken soon along these lines, the Western world may yet find itself faced with the prospect of big business corporations and state controlled enterprises taking over the complete control from its duly elected governments and legislatures. Great corporations such as

General Motors, Lockheed, Imperial Chemical Industries, Du Pont, Ford, and the rest are becoming equal in power to, if not in some respects above, the state. Those who work for them even in a minor capacity are more than mere employees. As William H. Whyte, Jr., showed in his disturbing book, *The Organization Man*,[31] they are a new species of priesthood who do not merely work for their organizations, but "belong" to them as medieval monks once belonged body, soul, and spirit to their monasteries.

In his recent BBC lectures, now published as *The New Industrial State*,[32] John K. Galbraith emphasizes what he believes to be the almost unassailable power of the "mature" corporations. The old-fashioned economic picture of the free play of the market and consumer sovereignty no longer applies to a world of giant corporations, in which people increasingly serve the convenience of organizations which were meant to serve *them*. Instead, the scale of modern organizations, the complicated technologies involved, say, in producing a car, the long time scales needed to plan a product, and the vast sums of money involved in financing large scale production has led to a different state of affairs.

In this the managers of the giant corporations are largely free from control by their shareholders unless things go very badly wrong; retained profits make them largely independent of financial sanctions; sheer size enables them either to make their own parts and accessories or to exercise great pressure on their suppliers, and by and large they do not compete with each other on price. According to Galbraith, the great corporations have grown much larger than is necessary to enable them to produce efficiently or market successfully. Their growth beyond the points of their technical and marketing optima has occurred in order to enable them to plan effectively. By this he means that they must be large enough to prevent interference from rivals who might frustrate their plans and also to offset contingencies. In a sense these giant corporations have become autonomous planning units, independent to a large extent of social control. The larger they grow the more effective their planning.

Various consequences are said to flow from all this. Not only is the day of the individual entrepreneur over, but even the directors of a modern big business corporation only nominally manage or direct operations. Galbraith repeatedly insists that the stockholders can exercise little influence on the conduct of a corporation unless they are prepared to exercise the ultimate sanction of selling out. This point was hammered home by Peter F. Drucker in *The New Society* in 1951 and by Adolf A. Berle in *Power Without Property* in 1960 (see note for this reference).[33]

Galbraith next points out that such concerns, in the way they conduct their affairs, have little in common with small and medium-sized undertakings. For one thing, whereas the latter are usually managed by the persons who own them, in the giant companies ownership and control are divorced. Their shareholders can exert little control over the conduct of business. The formulation of policy and its execution are in the hands of a body of professional experts whom Galbraith terms the technocracy. In this respect the great private corporations bear a close resemblance to the public corporations or other forms of public enterprise. It is the sum of the specialists' particular judgments which now makes the policy and decides whether a product is feasible and whether it will sell. It follows that an economy dominated by such concerns is likely to operate very differently from the old-fashioned capitalistic economy. Whereas Adam Smith's "economic men" made individual decisions which they could carry out *individually*, Galbraith's technocrats merely drop their little pinch into the pot, making decisions which have to be carried out *corporately*. In this situation it will become increasingly difficult to fix responsibility.

According to Galbraith, the great business corporation in the expanding sector of the economy which it dominates has abolished "economic man" and the maximization of profit. Vertically organized, the giant corporation now controls its own supplies, and their price, and sells to the public what it decides the public will buy. In this new economy, the sovereignty of the consumer, as proclaimed and cherished by the classical economists, has become illusory, and the discipline of the market once exerted over producers has been virtually destroyed. It is futile, states Galbraith, to deplore these changes. They are inevitable concomitant of technical and commercial progress, however incompatible they may be with the kind of market described in the textbooks. So the economic theorist tries to avert his eyes from the changes, because to acknowledge them would oblige him to jettison most of his science.

Central to Galbraith's argument is his claim that the market as a guide to production has been replaced by planning by giant companies themselves or, where the task has exceeded their powers, by state planning. The entrepreneurs, who in the old days stood at the center of the economic process, have been replaced by groups of managerial and technical specialists who in collaboration control policy. The criterion that governs their policy is not the maximization of profits but the increased security of the companies and the continued expansion which enhances that security. The power of the groups in control of corporate undertakings is increased by the practice of "plowing in" profits, which relieves them of dependence on outside investors for new capital. Their power is further strengthened by their research establishments, which are the source of most additions to technical knowledge.

The dethronement of the sovereign consumer means, in Galbraith's opinion, that the productive activities of the giant corporations, who produce among them half the total of goods and services consumed in the United States, are no longer undertaken in response to demands that originate with him. By advertising and other means the consumer is persuaded to buy what is good for the company to produce. In denying the reality of consumer choice, Galbraith leans heavily upon the example of General Motors. As this truly gigantic concern produces more than half the automobiles sold in America, he insists that what it produces in any year *is* the fashion. The consumer is told to take it and like it.

In the large corporations prices are not set by the "higgling of the market," that is to say, by competition among several producers, but by each company itself with reference to the earnings at which it has chosen to aim in order to satisfy its ambitions for growth. The conditions of this monopoly or oligopoly which makes it possible for these giant corporations to fix their prices are deplored by economists still bemused by the supposed virtues of the free market. Yet,

Galbraith argues, it is absurd for governments to attempt, by administrative or legal measures, to re-establish competition in place of this system of price fixing, since, in view of the heavy long-term investment required for modern industrial production, the risks inherent in competitive pricing, as in consumer sovereignty, are too heavy for the producer to bear.

All these tendencies have inevitably, according to Galbraith, been strengthened by the enlargement of the economic functions of the state. The modern state spends a high and ever-growing proportion of the national income. Collective demand by public bodies acting on the consumer's behalf has grown at the expense of individual demand. The government itself, or its agencies, operates a growing section of the economy and in greater or less degree tries to regulate the rest. Since the great corporations in America need to plan ahead, while in the U.S.S.R. the state increasingly finds it does not pay to interfere too much with firms, Galbraith suggests that the industrial systems of communism and capitalism are growing increasingly similar. The public corporations of the Soviet Union today closely resemble the giant corporations of America in the actual way they operate. For instance, the members of boards controlling Soviet nationalized industries are subjected to as little supervision from the Soviet Supreme Council as the company directors from their "capitalist" shareholders. The conflict between modern private capitalism and a planned economy has indeed become a sham fight. It would therefore, argues Galbraith, be recognized for what it now *is*, were it not that the modern corporation has evolved historically from the old system of entrepreneurship with which, however, it now has little connection.

What conclusion should Christians reach about Galbraith's thesis? Before we can reach a decision it should be pointed out that G. C. Allen has published a powerful rejoinder against Galbraith's thesis in his *Economic Fact and Fantasy*.[34] Allen admits that "up to a point Galbraith's interpretation of industrial trends echoes that of many economists of this and earlier generations. Few would deny that the operation of the economy has been profoundly affected by the two factors he stresses, namely, the rise of the giant industrial company and the enlargement of the state's economic functions. But when he goes beyond this point in deploying his argument it is more difficult to agree with him." [35]

Allen demonstrates with facts and figures, first, the importance to the modern economy of the vast number of small and medium-sized companies still making good profits, yet formed and managed entrepreneurially. "Even where large scale production has undoubted advantages, small and medium-sized firms often have a role to play in producting specialities. . . . Some small firms at particular moments in history are enterprising newcomers on the way up. In a society where technology and demand are constantly changing, such firms find opportunities as innovators. . . . Large scale businesses are not always infused with a pioneering spirit. Experience shows that such firms have often been sceptical of the possibilities of new products, so that it has been left to determined and imaginative entrepreneurs, starting in a small way, to launch new industries. The history of the early development of the motor car, the safety razor, and the jet engine testifies to this truth. . . . Can it be doubted that if we had had to rely entirely on large established producers for innovations, industrial progress would have been largely retarded? Genius is not always easily accommodated in planned programmes of development. Large size is sometimes attended by rigidity." [36]

In the second place, Allen reminds us that there is such a thing as leadership which can be vitally important whatever the size of the corporation. "The rise of large firms to their present stature," he points out, "can usually be attributed to one or to a very few men of remarkable business capacity. . . . That managerial responsibilities are widely diffused has not robbed the entrepreneurial function of its constructive part in industrial growth. Ultimately this function is discharged by individuals of exceptional talent and not by groups. . . . Throughout the last 70 years most of the major industrial achievements have been associated with a few remarkable men. Consider the part of Kessler and Deterding in the evolution of Shell, of Sir Hugo Hirst and Sir Edward Holden in the development of GEC, of Royce and Johnson and later Lord Hives in the successive phases of Rolls-Royce's history, of William Morris in the birth and growth of what is now the British Motor Corporation." [37]

In the third place, Allen points out that there is often competition between even big firms, which are by no means immune on occasion to market forces as their fluctuating profits records show. He writes: "Even when an industry is dominated by a single firm, its position is seldom unassailable for long, since, its markets are liable to attack from large firms hitherto engaged in other industries. Galbraith did not discuss this important possibility. . . . The ambitions of the several giants may serve to provide consumers with alternative sources of supply. . . . Modern technology has led to a rise in the size of firms, but it has also widened the area of competition both by cheapening communications and transport and by increasing the number of substitutes for existing products. The notion that the economic history of modern times shows a steady progression from highly competitive markets to monopoly is remote from the truth." [38]

Finally Allen argues that the consumer's sovereignty has been strengthened rather than weakened by his increase in income. He writes: "As his income rises, the consumer finds himself able to choose among an ever-increasing variety of goods and services. His demand becomes less stable and predictable than in the days when he had barely enough to satisfy his basic needs. One might hold, therefore, that much of industry's investment in persuasion is directed toward off-setting the tendency for consumer demands to become increasingly fickle. It represents an effort to bring more order or stability into a market situation where producers are vulnerable in the sense that the alternative choices before consumers are being constantly enlarged. . . . A glance at the industrial history of recent decades will show that, despite the exertions of established industries to strengthen their grasp over markets, changes in technology and demand have exerted devastating effects even on large and powerful producers. The old transport industries and the manufacturers who served them have fallen back before the advance of the motor car and the aircraft. The old textile producers have given place to the manufacturers of synthetic fibres. . . . In the face of these vast changes in the structure of demand and production, it cannot be asserted that the consumer has been content passively to accept what producers have preferred to give him. Many of the changes occurred in spite of the entrenched positions of powerful, established firms." [39]

In addition to Allen's arguments it can be pointed out that developing technology does not always work in favor of the giant firms, as Galbraith supposes. Why are Americans now able to shave with stainless steel razor blades? Because a small scale English firm got a toe hold in the United States and forced a near monopoly to do something it had resisted doing for years.

In a rather testy note on the Edsel affair, Galbraith insists that this case is so frequently quoted only because it is so rare and untypical. Yet this does not alter the fact the the promotion of the Edsel automobile was the most massive, expensive, and complex exercise in manipulating consumer choice ever undertaken in the history of American business, but it still prove a catastrophic failure. The consumers' resistance to the efforts of the "hidden persuaders" carried a lesson that was not lost on those whose business is to sell automobiles, not fancies. Consumers as well as corporations can become sophisticated.

The biggest concern, unless supported by the coercive power of the state, is always vulnerable to innovation. Even the state cannot protect a market. The size and monopoly position of the British General Post Office has not protected that institution from losing more than eighty percent of its customers for telegrams since the end of the Second World War.

Of course, it could be argued that Allen is talking mainly about the relatively undeveloped British economy, and Galbraith about the mature American one. Nevertheless this writer thinks that Allen has made some severe dents in Galbraith's argument. Like so many theses sweeping in their scope, it tends to sweep the inconvenient exceptions under the carpet.

Perhaps the best way is to regard Galbraith as a prophet, describing not precisely things as they are today but things as they are liable to become tomorrow.

In this role much that he says is illuminating. It is true as he says that there is increasing puzzlement over capitalism without control by the capitalists and socialism without control by society. While shareholders may not be able to control or change the new managerial elite running their property, in Britain (where the so-called "public sector" of the economy in 1967 took or controlled 50% of the national income) the boards of her innumerable state and public bodies, services, and agencies are under even less supervision of their owners (the British public) than any big or small enterprise's directors are by theirs. He does not note, still less emphasize, that much so-called "institutional investment" is indirectly (e.g., through investment trusts and clubs, unit trusts, pension funds, insurance companies, etc.) voluntary and involuntary *individuals'* saving and investment at one remove; and that in many cases the individuals concerned can, and do, back out if dissatisfied.

If Galbraith's description of affairs today should prove after all to be a description of the structure of business life fifty years from now, one can only hope that by then his repeated reminders that economic goals are not the only goals of society, and that the industrial system is only part of a balanced human life, will have been taken to heart. If not, then the prospect for human liberty and happiness does not seem to the writer particularly good.

Just as human freedom is threatened by the tendency of labor leaders to absolutize the labor union as the one "true society," so it would seem to be threatened by the increasing tendency of the leaders of big business to absolutize the giant corporation as the perfect pattern of economic production. A spokesman of this tendency, Peter F. Drucker, writes in *The New Society* as follows:

> To Henry Ford the machine was the new and the important element of modern society. But in reality the new factor is not a mechanism but an *institution;* the modern large enterprise. In every industrial country the enterprise has emerged as the *decisive,* the *representative,* and the *constitutive* institution. . . . The *decisive* character of the enterprise is displayed in its role in the economic process. The great majority of the people do not work for one of the large industrial enterprises. Yet their livelihood is directly dependent upon them. . . . The enterprise determines economic policies and makes the economic decisions. A small

number of big enterprises sets the wage pattern and establishes the "going wage" of the economy. . . . It is the big enterprise which establishes the pattern of union-management relations. It is the big enterprise at which government control and government regulation of industry aim. Finally, the big enterprise establishes the social pattern of the plant community. . . .

The large industrial enterprise is also the *representative* institution of an industrial society. It determines the individual's view of his society. . . . It actually represents the new organising principle of an industrial society in the purest and clearest form. . . . The enterprise is the mirror in which we look when we want to see ourselves.

The big enterprise is the true symbol of our social order. Its internal order and its internal problems are considered the distinctive order and the pressing problems of an industrial society even by those who are not apparently affected directly. It is also the place where the real principles of our social order become clearly visible. Above all, in the industrial enterprise alone can the problems of our industrial society be tackled. The structure that we shall build in the industrial enterprise, the solutions we shall find—or fail to find—for its problems will thus decide the structure and the solutions of industrial society altogether.

The enterprise exists in essentially the same form in every industrial society no matter how organised; it is thus the *constitutive* institution. The industrial enterprise arises from the needs of industrial life rather than from the beliefs or principles underlying political organisation.

One symptom of the autonomy of the enterprise is the process known in America as the "divorce of control from ownership." With but few exceptions, all the very large enterprises in America are no longer controlled by the stockholders. . . . Even in those few big corporations where ownership is still concentrated, the actual control is increasingly exercised by professional managements.

The enterprise is an *autonomous institution*. It does not derive its power and function from the motives, purposes or rights of its owners. . . . It does not derive its structures, aims and purposes from the political or legal organisation of society. It has a "nature of its own and follows the law of its own being. Historically, the enterprise of today is the successor to the firm of yesterday. Legally, the enterprise is a creature of the State, and nothing but a legal fiction. In nature and function, however, the enterprise is *sui generis*.[40]

In this passage Drucker has landed himself within the camp of the modern collectivists. Just as the medieval absolutization of the church institution resulted in papal totalitarianism, so Drucker's absolutization of the social institution of the business enterprise has resulted in his justification for this more modern yet no less deadly form of economic totalitarianism. Lacking an ordering principle in God's Word for his analysis of the place and function of big business in modern society, Drucker is forced by his pragmatic method to stay with the "facts" around him, but in doing so he has lost hold of the true facts because he lacks any norms or structural principles in terms of which to evaluate them correctly.

If it is true that the big business enterprise is indeed the *decisive,* *representative*, and *constitutive* institution of modern society, then no doubt its economic and social domination of the workers and consumers may be justified.

No Christian, however, worth his "salt" (Matt. 5:13) could possibly subscribe to such an interpretation of the "facts" since he believes that it is God's great structural principles or norms for human society and not any business executive's lust for power over his fellowmen which should be the decisive and constitutive factor in the organization of man's social and economic life.

God's Word teaches that no earthly institution can be allowed to become the whole of which the other social structures are only the parts. God alone is the absolute sovereign of the social organization-types to which he has delegated only partial authority necessary to carry out its function in society. No particular bearer of authority on earth can be thought of as the constitutive power from which all other forms of social organization or authority are derived. No institution, be it a church, the state, labor union, or big business enterprise must absorb the individual completely nor dominate society. Only God's Kingdom should thus absorb all of men's interests and it should not become identified with the sole interest and consideration of any *one* temporal social organization.

As we have shown in the previous chapter, a scriptural view of human society requires a respect for the sovereign sub-spheres of society. While social institutions are characterized by a relationship of authority and obedience, this authority over the individual is always limited, being defined by its own structural principle. Within human society, therefore, there is no institution such as the labor union or the big business enterprise which is the whole of which other institutions are only the parts. Judged by this biblical principle of sphere sovereignty or areas of authority, Drucker no less than Tannenbaum shows himself to be lacking a coherent view of man in society which balances authority and freedom, since he favors organizational relationships at the expense of individual relationships.

A coherent view of society will seek to find a balance between the needs and rights of the group as well as the needs and rights of the individual, between the rights of the producer and those of the consumer, between the rights of management and those of the workers, between the public legal interest and the private interest.

Drucker rightly recognizes the great role played by modern big business in providing society with the benefits of mass production. But unfortunately, like Tannenbaum he appears to be advocating a form of the corporate state of Fascism in which big business is given the legal right to dominate all other social institutions.

Such a totalitarian claim to direct human affairs must be firmly resisted from which ever quarter it comes, either labor union or big business, since God's Word teaches that God has entrusted such absolute power to Christ alone (Matt. 28:18). Since Christ alone is supreme, the authority exercised by men is limited. For this reason big business may not claim to exercise totalitarian authority over society any more than big government. As the Second Adam Christ alone possesses such absolute sovereignty over men.

Whenever earthly authority and power is divorced from its divine origin and placed in a purely secular context, it provides no safeguards against injustice and exploitation. Once men locate sovereignty in the will of one social institution they lose sight of the true ordering of human society, which then becomes distorted. No earthly authority is safe unless it recognizes and is rooted in and limited by the sovereignty of Christ. It is only Christ then who can protect the freedoms of persons against encroachment either by big labor union, big business enterprise, or big government. We can choose to be governed by God in the labor union, in the business enterprise, or in politics, or we can condemn ourselves to be ruled by tyrants in all three realms.

The time has surely come for Anglo-Saxon Christians, both Catholic and Reformed, to establish federations of Christian employers who will seek to make Anglo-Saxon business enterprises truly responsible organizations. Such Christian employers' organizations have been operating successfully in Western Europe for fifty years. Thus French Roman Catholic employers are organzed today into the French Christian Employer's Center (C.F.P.C.); the Dutch Roman Catholic employers have formed the "General Association for Catholic Employers" (A.K.W.V.). The Belgian Roman Catholics have joined together to form a Belgian Federation of Catholic Employers (F.E.P.A.C.). The Protestant Christian employers of Holland have established the Christian Employer's Association (C.W.V.).[41] (See Table Five of Appendix.)

What these Christian employers' movements understand by their function today is illustrated by an article with that title by A. C. J. Rottier which appeared in the Bulletin of the International Association of Roman Catholic Employers (U.N.I.A.P.A.C.), founded at Antwerp in 1924.

Not so long ago, says Rottier, the employer was thought of as an individual, as a dictator, and as concerned essentially with the direction of his firm. He might also have incidental attributes, such, for instance, as supplying capital or starting a firm. Within the firm his function was thought of primarily in economic terms and from the angle of profitability. Today his position has completely changed. Inside his firm the employer is expected to discharge a range of "social" functions connected not merely with making profits but with the welfare of all engaged in the firm: selection, training, safety and health, a family wage, etc. Even more important, he has now to realize that the firm has become the most important unit in the social structure as a whole. He has therefore to think in terms of full employment and inflation, of the balance of payments, of national investment policy as well as the welfare of his own firm. And he has to recognize, fit in with, and play his very important part in shaping the norms of the society surrounding him. This requires that he become no longer a dictator but a constitutional leader, taking account of and in many respects formally bound by the views of others; notably of trade unions or the government. Constitutional leadership is not easy, since there are many interests to reconcile even within the firm—those not only of capital and workers, but also of technical and supervisory and managerial grades. Often interests have a different degree of pull at different levels. Thus P.B.O. gives a heavy weight to labor, whereas capital has a strong position under company law. A further complication is that the "employer" is often no longer one person. Managerial responsibility in a modern firm is spread over a group of officials, not concentrated in one man; and so, still more is the responsibility for making, notably through P.B.O. or employers' associations, management's contribution to the welfare of society as a whole. The employer today, in short, must be a man of wide views, a group leader rather than an individualist, capable of collaborating at many levels in an enterprise where many interests are concerned. And the employer's position has to be justified by his ability to reconcile and lead. He can claim no right to dictate. No doubt he is entitled to claim the degree of authority needed to carry out his duties, but this is always within and subject to the wider whole. And if he fails in his task, says Rottier, society will rightly call him to account:

> Employers claim to play a leading part in economic life, or rather in both economic and social life. They must now either abandon this claim or accept all those obligations which this role of leadership implies.[42]

Fogarty points out this Catholic approach:

> This is essentially the same ideal as emerges from modern management literature; the ideal of the manager as a professional man, who admits and understands his responsibility to every section of the community, and is skilled in extracting a coherent policy from all the maze of influences—the many "moral systems," in Chester Barnard's phrase—in which he is involved.[43]

The difficulties at first encountered by the Christian Employer's

Association in Holland (C.W.V.) are described by the Calvinist A. Borst in his pamphlet, "Hold the Fort!" which gives the Association's view of its aims and problems. Christian principles, says Borst, cannot have their full impact unless they are lived out in a visible community; one visible in each area of life.[44] To give them effect requires organized power. It must be power organized specifically on the basis of God's absolute sovereignty over all. Not much good has come of the "little grains of salt" who have tried to add savor to the "neutral" organizations. There is a whole range of issues on which the Protestant employers' organizations differ from the "neutral" bodies, which, whether or not they contain Christian members, are in effect "liberal," i.e., independent of God's will and His creation norms. Examples are schemes for works councils, for making collective agreements legally binding, for insisting on proper qualifications for those who propose to set up small businesses, or for paying family allowances or discouraging the work of married women. On all these matters, and on schemes for industrial self-government, the Protestant employer's organizations are in favor, the "liberal" organizations against. The Protestant organizations have also a special role to play inside their church. Being specifically Reformed, they are well placed to keep the official Church informed about economic needs, and to collaborate with other Protestant social organizations—especially the trade unions and political parties—and so promote good will among Christians and reduce conflict. And the prestige of each Protestant group in its own field is increased through belonging to the Protestant social movement as a whole. In that sense the presence of the C.W.V. in its own field helps the work of other Protestant groups in theirs, just as their presence in their fields helps that of C.W.V.

But to define these principles of Protestant Social Action is one thing; to get them accepted and recognized is another. He points out that many Dutch Protestant employers before the last war were influenced by Barthian theology as well as sheer reaction and insisted, as so many Anglo-American-Canadian Christian business men still do, that business is business, with its own laws which can be observed as well by a neutral as by a Protestant organization. For such Protestants the business enterprise functions only in the economic sphere.

Yet a little reflection must surely convince them that the business enterprise functions in all the aspects of God's creation. Thus the business enterprise has the following aspects amongst others: the mathematical, consisting of the unity of the firm in the plurality of its members as well as in its accounting procedures; the spatial aspect, since it is located at a definite place; the biological and physical, the psychical coming to expression in the esprit de corps of the workers; the logical, since a firm whose affairs were conducted illogically would soon go bankrupt; the historical, since the firm is founded in history; the lingual, expressed in the use of special business signs; the social, expressed in the firm's public relations with society as a whole; the economic; the aesthetic, expressed in the harmonious working together of all employees of the company; the juridical, expressed in the firm's use of commercial and company law; the moral, since a firm whose workers were not hard working, honest, and loyal would suffer loss; and finally, the aspect of faith. The business enterprise no less than the Church as an institution functions in the faith-aspect of God's creation. Not only a Christian business but also a non-Christian business as well functions in the modality of faith. Unbelief as such or secularism is only another form of misdirected faith and a wrong employment of faith, the worship of the Almighty Dollar instead of Almighty God. The secular business enterprise seeks its final authority in a lie rather than in Christ. As such it invites the judgment of God upon itself. It will either serve and advance the cause of Christ, or it will be opposed to Christ. Let all Christian employers and managers and directors arise out of their slumbers and with God's help make the Lord Jesus Christ the managing director of their concerns. Then it will be said of them as it was said of Joseph of old: "The Lord was with Joseph and he prospered" (Gen. 39:2-4).

CHAPTER EIGHT NOTES

1. R. J. Rushdoony, Review of E. L. Hebden Taylor's *The Christian Philosophy of Law, Politics and the State* in *The Westminster Theological Journal* (Nov. 1967, Vol. XXX, No. 1, Philadelphia), p. 101.
2. Jacques Ellul, *op. cit.*, p. 348.
3. Quoted in *The Daily Telegraph*, Oct. 1967 (London, England). Cf. R. J. Rushdoony, *The Mythology of Science*, for further examples, especially his chapter on "Man in 1984."
4. G. L. Bach, *Economics* (Prentice-Hall, New Jersey, 1968), p. 560.
5. Murray N. Rothbard, *Man, Economy and the State* (D. Van Nostrand Company, Inc., Princeton, N. J., 1962), Vol. II, p. 766. The whole chapter on "The Economics of Violent Intervention in the Market" is worth close study.
6. John Locke, *The Second Treatise of Civil Government* (Basil Blackwell, Oxford 1946), p. 62.
7. Talcott Parsons, *The Structure of Social Action*, p. 97.
8. W. H. Hutt, "The Concept of Consumers' Sovereignty," *Economics Journal* (March 1940), pp. 66-77. Hutt originated the term in an article in 1934. For a criticism of the concept see Murray Rothbard, *Man, Economy and the State*, p. 561.
9. J. K. Galbraith, *The Affluent Society* (Houghton Mifflin, Boston, 1958).
10. H. Dooyeweerd, *The New Critique*, Vol. III, p. 379ff.
11. *Ibid.*, pp. 597-598.
12. H. C. Simmons, *Economic Policy for a Free Society* (University of Chicago Press, Chicago, 1948), p. 157. Cf. Frank H. Knight, *Freedom and Reform* (Harpers, New York, 1947).
13. H. Steenkemp, *Dutch Protestant Social Legislation* (Amsterdam, 1957). Cf. B. Goudzwaard, "Economische Politiek als Beginsel- Politiek," *Anti-Revolutionaire Staatkunde*, (32 Nov. Dec. 1962).
14. Dooyeweerd, *op. cit.*, p. 483.
15. H. Van Riessen, *op cit.*, p. 80.
16. K. Groen, "Dooyeweerd and Governmental Organization of Industry," in *Jurisprudence Essays* (Kok, Kampen, 1951), p. 77.
17. Dooyeweerd, *Renewal and Reflection*, pp. 193-215.
18. T. P. van der Kooy, "Communism and Christian Faith," in *The International Reformed Bulletin* (No. 15, Oct. 1963), p. 10. Cf. Paul A. Samuelson, "New Trends in Iron Curtain Economics?" *Economics*, p. 788.
19. H. F. R. Catherwood, *The Christian in Industrial Society*, p. 98.
20. Dooyeweerd, *New Critique*, Vol. II, p. 66.
21. Emil Brunner, *Justice and the Social Order* (Lutterworth, London, 1945), p. 155.

22. P. Borst, *Responsibility in the Industrial Enterprise* (Free University lecture delivered in August 1963).
    Cf. Bob Goudzwaard, *The Christian and Modern Business Enterprise* (C.L.A.C. at 1058 A, Albion Road, Rexdale, Ont., 1968).
23. *Ibid.*, p. 4.
24. *Ibid.*, p. 5.
25. Dooyeweerd, *New Critique*, Vol. III, p. 595ff.
26. George Goyder, *The Responsible Company* (Blackwell. Oxford, 1961), p. 20. Also G. Goyder, *The Future of Private Enterprise* (Oxford, 1951).
27. *Ibid.* p. 22.
28. *Ibid.*, p. 72.
29. *Ibid.*, pp. 87, 38, 39, 57, 72.
30. *Ibid.*, p. 89.
31. William H. Whyte, *The Organization Man* (Doubleday Anchor Book, New York, 1956.
32. John K. Galbraith, *The New Industrial State* (Hamish Hamilton, London, 1968).
33. Peter A. Drucker, *The New Society* (W. Hienemann, London, 1951).
    Adolf A. Berle, *Power without Property* (Macmillan, London, 1960.
    In the *Journal of Economic Studies* (Aberdeen University), Summer No. 2, Vol. 1, 1966, Clive S. Beed of the University of Melbourne writes on "The Separation of Ownership from Control." In this important article Beed takes apart, with scholarly apparatus plus more than five pages of references, the hypothesis first advanced by Berle and Means in *The Modern Corporation and Private Property* (1932), which we have already discussed in chapter two of this book. Beed tries to prove that the popular Berle and Means thesis is, and was, widely wide of the mark; that the nineteenth century entrepreneur often had "sleeping partner" shareholders backing him and without control; that both majorities and minorities of shareholders in modern companies frequently change the managements (especially through dissatisfied institutional shareholders who step in); and that mergers, bigness, etc., far from being beyond competition and far from fixing prices and production and profits *a priori*, lead rather to intensified competition, price cutting, and losses due to failure to meet the market's requirements. Beed claims that Berle and Means have never statistically or with any other objective and scientific data been able to verify, or even quantify, their thirty-six-year-old hypothesis. Beed concludes on Berle's and Means's hypothesis about a growing separation of ownership of capital from its control:

> The issue of the total or partial separation of ownership from control is far from resolved, mainly because passive control may never exhibit itself in an active manner. That such exhibition is lacking does not disprove its existence, but quantification of it becomes impossible. Were

the limitations of the Berle type method and results sufficiently in the minds of its users to preclude *non-sequitur* conclusions about reality, no argument need be made. Generally such is not the case and it has been the concern of this article to demonstrate the lack of adherence to the principles of the scientific method in the works of its chief exponent" (p. 40).

In the opinion of this writer, Beed's own arguments do not disprove the existence of a tendency operating in the modern economy towards a separation of ownership of capital from its control. Beed ignores the technological impetus toward the concentration of capital. As Jacques Ellul points out in *The Technological Society*, "Technical progress cannot do without the concentration of capital. An economy based on individual enterprise is not conceivable, barring an extraordinary technical regression. The necessary concentration of capital thus gives rise either to an economy of corporations or to a state economy. A concentration of enterprise corresponds to this concentration of capital. This fact can hardly be denied today, especially in view of the power of these enterprises. . . . In the United States in 1939, 52 percent of all industrial capital was held by one tenth of one percent of the total number of enterprises; and in 1944, 62 percent of all workers were employed in two percent of American enterprises (Cape, London, 1965, p. 154).

34. G. C. Allen, *Economic Fact and Fantasy* (Institute for Economic Affairs, London, 1967), p. 1.
35. *Ibid.*, p. 11.
36. *Ibid.*, pp. 13-14.
37. *Ibid.*, pp. 15-16.
38. *Ibid.*, pp. 18-20.
39. *Ibid.*, pp. 22-25.
40. Peter Drucker, *The New Society*, pp. 11-19.
41. M. Fogarty, *op. cit.*, pp. 232-263 for an account of these Christian employers' movements in Western Europe since 1880.
42. Quoted in Fogarty, *ibid.*, p. 235.
43. *Ibid.*, p. 236.
44. A. Borst, *Hold the Fort* (C.W.V. Amsterdam, 1939), p. 3.

A Christian Businessmen's Associations has recently been formed in Ontario dedicated to the furtherance of the principles discussed in this chapter.

Chapter Nine

THE REFORMATIONAL UNDERSTANDING
OF LABOR AND RACE RELATIONS

(a) *The Reformational Conception of the Labor Union*

In our story of the Anglo-Saxon pragmatist-humanist theory of labor relations in modern society, we saw that such positivistic sociologists as Frank Tannenbaum and W. E. J. McCarthy were forced by their pragmatic sociological method to stay with the so-called facts; that is to say, they adjusted their thinking and analysis to what there was about them. But in doing so they lost hold of the facts. For in every so-called positive "fact," including a trade union, there is not only some inescapable structure of the creation ordinances (e.g., one cannot set up a form of trade union that is not somehow bound to the structural requirements of a trade union as a form of human association), but there is also a degree of conformity to or deviation from God's creation norm for the labor union, which has been operative in the cultural-forming activity of the men who built the modern trade unions.

Lacking a true ordering principle for human society in God's structural creation ordinances for human society, and without any proper insight into God's creation order, it is not surprising that there has developed a levelling tendency in modern man's experience of and insight into the nature of the various associations and institutions which together constitute human society, with the tragic result that we look upon these social bonds as pressure groups, interest groups, and functional groups. Nowhere has this levelling tendency been more apparent than in the field of labor relations. Thanks to the influence of collectivistic theories of the state, the defenders of compulsory trade unionism claim that the union is at least a quasi public legal institution. That is, even as the government has the right to compel, so also the union has the right to force the men who work in the shop or factory to join the union and pay dues as a condition of employment.

We shall not be able to reject this totalitarian claim unless we see it as an unjustified attempt on the part of a *voluntary association* of workers, which makes up only a segment of society, to grasp the power of the sword of government. In claiming to be the only "true society" the "neutral" unions have exceeded their just bounds. Freedom for all the workers in modern society is possible only upon the basis of the recognition of the autonomy of the various spheres of life. Compulsory trade unionism is in effect governmental power exercised by a private organization. No Reformed Christian questions the necessity for labor unions in our modern industrial world. But the Reformed Christian does dispute the right of neutral unions to dictate to Christian workers the terms on which they may accept employment. The great problem today, as Sylvester Petro has made abundantly clear in his book, *Power Unlimited—The Corruption of Union Leadership*, is the excessive power of the big international labor unions. It is here that the Reformed theory of human society can make an invaluable contribution. As Bernard Zylstra points out in *Challenge and Response*:

> Power in human hands is a dangerous weapon. A union must have power, but where are its limits? That question can only properly be answered when we have a religious interpretation of power. In a man centered universe, it is extremely difficult to bind power within boundaries. In a God centered universe, any human manifestation of power is limited. This is the essence of the Christian principle of sphere sovereignty which implies that social organizations are related to each other in a coordinate fashion and not in a hierarchical or subordinate way. It is typical that in an environment where men have no deep respect for the Creator, they do not know the limits of their might. The extreme form of social disharmony or unrighteousness is totalitarianism in which all human functions are part of the state. Totalitarian tendencies are also in evidence when unions try to control press, politics, and education. A Christian labor union must oppose such tendencies by a balanced view of its task. Unionism can be most

effective in achieving a better place for the worker by minding its own business. That business concerns economics not politics.[1]

It is because modern post-Christians have failed to "see" the specific task of the various associations of human society that today we find so much injustice and inequality in modern industry. A voluntary association of workers has no *moral* right to compel membership in its organization as a condition of employment. Compulsion must be reserved only for the state, which is an involuntary structure.

The Reformed Christian distinguishes between authoritative societal relationships which are institutional in character and do not owe their existence to human initiative and free societal relationships into which men may enter freely for a variety of purposes. The former possess an internal communal character that is to a certain degree independent of the interaction of its members and is marked by authority, e.g., the immediate family, the church, or the state. The institutions of marriage, the family, the state, and the church are established by God as part of His divine ordering for human happiness. According to divine prescription, marriage binds the parties together for their entire life, and one is born into a family, a church, and a state without making any choice. The apostate humanist attempt to explain these relationships as a voluntary association of self-sufficient individuals is thus false, betraying the desire to become independent of God and to achieve religious certainty in the sovereign individual. Free societal relationships, in contrast, are of an external character and they are much freer. Dooyeweerd therefore defines a community as "any more or less durable societal relationship which has the character of a whole joining its members into a social unity, irrespective of the degree of the intensity of the communal bond."[2] An association is either an interindividual or intercommunal relationship, "in which individual persons or communities function in coordination without being united into a solitary whole. Such relationships show the character of mutual neutrality, of approachment, free competition or antagonism, cooperation or contest."[3] In an association, individuals are coordinated next to each other without the relation of authority, as for example in the case of a buyer or seller. Dooyeweerd holds that each community or association is characterized by two functions, a *foundational* and a *leading* function. An insight into the proper connection between these two tells us what the structural principle of the community or association is.

For this reason the church, state, and society must never be placed on the same level of authority. Church and state are both authoritative societal relationships but society is not, since it is defined as the broad field of personal freedom, outside of authoritative social relationships, in which men associate with each other as equals and freely organize together. Such free societal relations have in the course of the unfolding process of history given rise to innumerable associations between free men and between free societal relationships, and these must be seen as sovereign in their own sphere. From the organization of free persons, such various free societal relationships as the universities and the trade unions have sprung into existence. These relationships have been historically grounded since they originated through positive formation on the basis of a specific power. A business, for example, is formed on the basis of the power of capital.[4]

With this Reformed doctrine of sphere sovereignty we may compare the political pluralism advocated by John Neville Figgis in his influential work, *Churches in the Modern State*. Thus Figgis writes:

> The State did not create the family, nor did it create the churches, nor even in any real sense can it be said to have created the club of the trades union, nor, in the Middle Ages, the guild or the religious order, hardly even the universities: they have all risen out of the natural associative instinct of mankind, and should all be treated by the supreme authority as having a life original and guaranteed.[5]

In this pluralism Figgis stands midway between F. W. Maitland, who introduced Gierke's theory of the reality and autonomy of the personality of the various associations of society to the English-speaking world of scholarship, and Harold Laski, who used Gierke's doctrine of the autonomy of the non political and lower political associations in his "pluralist" phase of political thought to defend the freedom of industrial groups from control by the state.

Maitland pointed out that the emergence of such free societal associations as the medieval universities and guilds posed a problem for political thinkers because the state was the only association clearly recognized in the classical theory of Natural Law. The state, it was supposed, arises according to the will of God for the ordering of society, the restraint of the evil tendencies of men, and the furtherance of human well-being. The state and the individual were the two entities with which classical, political, and legal thought was exercised. Hence there was the combat "in which the Sovereign State and the Sovereign Individual contended over the delimitation of the provinces assigned to them by Natural Law, and in the course of that struggle all intermediate groups were first degraded into the position of the more or less arbitrarily fashioned creatures of mere Positive Law, and in the end were obliterated." [6] Natural Law, in fact, found no place for the Corporation; hence, "the Corporation could find a place in Public Law only as a part of the State and a place in Private Law only as an artificial Individual." [7]

Gierke sought to justify the existence of these Corporations or free societal associations in terms of his famous theory of group personality. For Gierke every true human association becomes a real and living entity animated by its own individual soul; of all such leagues, state organized nations are the greatest, and the corporate spirit, the People-spirit, is the very core of the separate personality which each possesses.

As Gierke himself explains his theory:

> The development of law lies in human action. But the subject of this action is not individuals, but communities. The individual man who cooperates in the process always acts as a component member and in furtherance of a human community.[8]

According to Gierke, then, a corporate body is, or can be, a real person or a real super person. As such he conceived of the different types of human associations as full *organisch-gegliederte* personalities, i.e., as persons with a spiritual organic expression, to which he ascribed a separate soul or spirit in the will of the corporation, and a separate spiritual body in the organization. Thus, he coordinated the corporate persons with natural persons, as living beings. In Gierke's view, each such corporate grouping of society is independent and autonomous. Autonomy, says Gierke, is the power of a properly organized association, which is not a state, to make a law for itself. The law which is thus established is, in the true sense of the term, objective and binding, and must be clearly distinguished from mere subjective law. It may, in other words, be properly described as legislative. In Germanic law many associations have had this power, subject always, however, to the limitation that it must not conflict with the law of any higher authority, especially the state. Autonomy was thus a fruitful source of law in the Middle Ages.

Unfortunately, Gierke's theory of autonomy and of the essence of human organized communities does not really discover the inner structural principles of the latter because of his metaphysical collectivistic theory of organized communities which seeks the substance of the latter in a common or general will. Dooyeweerd points out, "The most Gierke could attain to on the ground of this theory was a formal juridical autonomy for the internal law of the *Verbande* (organized association). There could be no room for a real juridical sphere sovereignty." [9]

Since neither Gierke, Maitland, Figgis, nor Laski had any real idea or belief in God's creation order, they looked upon the independence and autonomy of social bonds from the empirical rather than the normative structural side of reality given at creation. As a result they were unable to point to the normative qualifying functions of social bonds or human associations which alone enable us to distinguish one type of social bond from another.

As long as modern sociologists remain entangled in the dilemma of collectivism or individualism they will never be able to understand the structural correlation of communal and intercommunal or interindividual relationships. This is even the case with Gierke, who was fully aware of the fundamental differences between these two kinds of social relations. As Dooyeweerd suggests, "The coordination of individual persons and collective persons led Gierke to a sharp division between 'private law' and 'public law.' But when we detach this coordination from its speculative metaphysical foundation and reduce it to a separation of external and interindividual and internal communal relations, it appears to be in conflict with the structural coherence between them." [10]

Neither collectivism nor individualism recognizes the true structure of societal relationships. The dilemma only arises when the structures of individuality, which alone present a basis for the solution of the one and the many, are neglected. The principle of sphere sovereignty alone presents us with a proper insight into the connection between man and his social forms, since the individual is never defined or absorbed into a temporal social bond. These are limited in the expression of their authority by their structural principle.

The error of individualism is that it constructs the communities and associations of human society out of the elemental atomistic relations between individuals conceived as sovereign agents with the result that it does not recognize that these communities also have their own peculiar structural principles. But collectivism absolutizes one of the many temporal communities, namely the one that is made to embrace all the others as the whole which embraces and enfolds the parts. This was true of the classical city-state and of all modern totalitarian regimes and of the neutral labor unions in their attempt to become the "only true" society. The error of such collectivistic solutions is that then this single all embracing community is given the place of the religious basic community, the Kingdom of God, which transcends time and place. Man cannot and must not thus be confined by any such absolutized earthly community, be it a church, the state, or a labor union, since man in the center of his personality, his "heart," also transcends time, while as long as he remains in history, he functions in a multiplicity of equally significant communities and associations.

The biblical view of man in society can alone provide a way out of the dead end apostate humanistic street of individualism versus collectivism, for it alone clearly reveals that man is an individual created together with other men to live in such communal groups as families, churches, and states. Man's personality can develop only in fruitful relations with God and with his neighbor. Man is

called by God to love the Lord with all his "heart" and his neighbor
as himself.

The common error of individualism and collectivism, in typically
humanistic fashion, is that they take their starting point in man,
whether that be the individual or the group. The biblical view of
man in society transcends this dilemma, since it reveals to us that God
created man for community with his fellow men and as a social
being. This means that man does not find his purpose in himself as
the economic individualists such as John Locke supposed nor in the
group as the economic collectivists such as Karl Marx supposed, but
in the God who created him. The individual and the community are
equally called to live in obedience to the divine ordinances and structures laid down by the Creator. As Brunner well says:

> Opposed to all forms of collectivism, as well as to individualism,
> stands the Christian conception of the individual and the com-
> munity in all its inward consistency and completeness. It is not
> a synthesis, still less a compromise, but the original unity. The
> other conceptions stand revealed as fragments torn out of it. For
> the Christian understanding of the individual and the community is
> not human wisdom, but the wisdom of God manifested in creation.
> It is the justice which befits the human being as an individual and
> in community because it is in accordance with the creative plan
> of Him Who created individuals and communities alike. . . .
>
> In the Christian understanding of man, a communal structure
> based on a contract is neither necessary nor possible. Communities
> are just as much established in the divine order of creation as
> the independence of the individual. They are innate in the God-
> created individual with his capacity and need for completion.
> Their prototype and standard is the family founded on mar-
> riage. . . .
>
> The absorption of the individual in the collective whole is just
> as impossible in Christian thought as the construction of the com-
> munity on the basis of a social contract. The independence of
> individuals is just as much God's creation as the community
> founded on their diversity. The dignity of man, which is his by
> reason of his creation in the image of God, is not bestowed on him
> by the community. He brings it with him, so to speak, into the
> community. It is given him direct by God, by that divine call
> which makes him, the individual, a responsible person. It is be-
> cause the individual is directly responsible to God that he pos-

sesses an independence transcending all community. A human person is more than marriage, more that the state (more than a trade union), . . .

There will be human beings when marriage and the State (and we may add trade unions) are no more. Man alone, not marriage not family, not the State, is predestined to eternity. The State, marriage, and all institutions are there for man, not man for them. . . .

The Christian view of the relationship between individual and community may be formulated thus: fellowship in freedom, freedom in fellowship.[11]

It thus becomes the primary duty of the Reformed theory of the labor union or trade union to discover the internal structural principle of the labor union as this is founded in the creation ordinances. The normative structural principle of the labor union rests upon God's will and purpose for man in society and not upon the will of the state or the "general will" of the people.

What then is the structural principle of the labor union which distinguishes this particular form of free human association from all other societal relationships? How may we best define a trade union? The answer is by discovering its foundational and leading functions. Dooyeweerd defines the internal leading function of a trade union, in its typical coherence with the foundational function, as

a moral bond of solidarity between the labourers typically founded in their organized historical vocational power to elevate labour to an essential and equivalent partner in the process of production.[12]

The modern trade union is grounded in history and rests upon the historical formation of economic power. It does not arise in history until in the process of differentiation a division of labor has taken place and a distinction arises between the ownership and the control of the means of production. In the precapitalistic form of domestic industry trade unions could have no place since each man tended to possess his own instruments or tools of production. Lipson has shown that the fundamental trait of capitalism is the wage system under which the worker sells, not the fruit of his labor, but the labor itself. The wage system did not arise in industry on account of the introduction of machinery. Lipson finds the origin of the wage system in the divorce of the workers from the ownership of the material on which they worked. He continues:

> When the material became the property of a capitalist em-
> ployer, he thereby secured the right to dispose of the finished
> product, and the manual craftsman was transformed from an
> independent producer into a labourer working for hire. This
> change of status was attended with momentous consequences;
> it created the basis for the perennial struggle between capital and
> labour. The antagonism of these two forces was not the outcome
> of the "Industrial Revolution," as it is often supposed. . . . In one
> form or another "labour unrest" has manifested itself in industry
> for five hundred years. The workman's labour is a perishable
> commodity; he cannot withhold it for any length of time or
> he will starve. Hence there easily arises the possibility of exploita-
> tion, and from the fifteenth century down to our own day the
> energies of the working classes have been absorbed in the effort to
> establish and maintain a "standard of life." The conflict of capital
> and labour was fought out over three main grievances—low
> wages, payment in kind, and unemployment.[13]

Lipson then points out that the British government took over the function of regulating wages and maintaining the "standard of life" of the working community between the end of the Middle Ages, when this function had been performed by the medieval guilds, and the nineteenth century when the exercise of this right fell into dis-favor thanks to the influence of the laissez faire teachings of the classical economists. For nearly two hundred years the great Stat-ute of Apprentices, passed in 1563, governed this state regulation of wages and conditions of work.[14]

Under the influence of a growing economic individualism, fostered by the development of capitalism, the state began to assume a differ-ent attitude towards labor problems, especially those relating to wages, unemployment, and technical training—with the consequence that the industrial legislation of the sixteenth century was allowed to fall into disuse. Lipson holds that it was "this change of public policy" which "was one of the factors in the rise of trade unionism"; another factor being the increasing difficulty of attaining master-ship of a craft. The change in attitude on the part of the government forced the workers to shoulder responsibilities which had hitherto been the province of the state alone and to rely upon their own efforts for the maintenance of the "standard of life." Lipson believes that this development "transformed the relations of capital and labor, which were no longer shackled by an external authority, but were left free to determine, according to their strength, the rates of wages and the general conditions of employment." [15]

Only by combining together into trade unions were the workers able to meet the new owners of capital upon anything like an equal basis. As Tannenbaum well puts it, "The employer became the catalytic agent that crystallized the workers into a self-conscious group" and the social atomization resulting from the payment of an individual money wage was overcome by the fusing of men together in labor unions."

The great tragedy is that the trade unions fell under the evil influences of the selfish greed of the capitalists, and instead of seeing their associations as qualified by the leading function of morality they tended to see it qualified by the economic function. As W. F. De Gaay Fortman says: "There is the fact that the spirit of capitalism, with its unlimited stimulation of self-interest and with its scorn of all moral considerations in the economic sphere of life, has had its destructive effect on the working classes. Countless workers have learned the doctrine of unrestricted self-interest from their employers and how they did learn it!" [16] In other words, the workers themselves succumbed to the pernicious apostate humanist doctrine of economic individualism and of the worship of *homo economicus*. Instead of seeing their work as man's worship and service to God and their neighbor they saw it as a means of self-gratification. Instead of seeing the trade union as a necessary association of workers called into being by the economic unfolding process of history, and therefore to be qualified by moral and human considerations, the workers have seen the trade union as an instrument of the class war by means of which they can obtain a bigger share of the productive cake.

(b) *The Necessity for Christian Labor Associations*

For the Reformed Christian, at any rate, the labor union is the response of the laboring body of Christ to God's call to share in the great cultural mandate to have dominion over the earth and to produce goods and services that human needs may be satisfied. Thus, Christian trade unions are principially distinguished from all so-called neutral humanist unions by reason of the fact that the Christian worker is looked upon as *homo religiosus* and not as *homo economicus*. The Reformed Christian locates the dignity of the worker as well as of the employer in man's place in the creation as servant of God and not in his own so-called "natural rights." Both employer and workers are called to serve God in the industrial realm and thus the class struggle is in principle rejected. But this does not mean that the workers do not need to become organized into their own labor associations. It does mean that such Christian labor associations are not going to become exclusively concerned with such purely material considerations as higher wages, shorter working hours, and better material living standards obtained by wielding the strike weapon. Christian trade unionists together with Christian employers are concerned to reverse the process of secularization in industry today which has resulted from the service of the false gods of mammon and *homo economicus*.

Unlike the Roman Catholic labor or employers' associations, which are expressions of Catholic Temporal Action, and therefore in principle, if not always in fact, subservient to the higher organs of state and church of which in Roman Catholic social theory they are considered to be only a part of the greater whole, the Reformed labor and employers' associations are in principle as well as in practice *directly* responsible to Almighty God and to His Kingdom norms. Thus, it must be clearly understood that when we state that *a trade union is a voluntary association morally qualified and founded upon the historical vocational power to elevate labor to an essential and equivalent partner in the process of production*, we understand the word "moral" not in any Roman Catholic sense of natural law discernible by the human reason, but in the sense of God's moral commandments revealed to us in His Word and Law.

The Christian Labor Association of Canada, therefore, speaks of its basis as the Christian principles of social justice and love as taught in the Bible. It further speaks of its aim as the organization of workers in trade and industrial unions, "for the purpose of propagating, establishing, and maintaining justice in the realm of labor and industry, and promoting the economic, social, and moral interests of the workers through the practical application of Christian principles in collective bargaining and other means of mutual aid or protection." It defines these Christian social principles as "basic concepts for just and charitable relationships among men which are taught in both the Old and New Testament of the Bible, and are given expression in society through adherence to ethical and moral standards that reflect such social principles." Moreover, it points out that in the field of labor "these principles have bearing especially upon the dignity of human beings and their equality before God; their rights in regard to sharing in the benefits of creation resources and cultural progress; relationships of men among one another and responsibilities toward each other and to society as a whole." [17] A full statement of the Principles and Practices of the Christian Labor Association of Canada is given at the end of this book as Appendix No. 3, and the reader should read them for himself.

From this it will be obvious that the Reformed Christian trade unionist is not opposed to the idea of labor associations as such but only to the apostate direction taken by the so-called humanist "neutral" unions. Above all he wants to make the Word of God the ordering principle of his economic as well as personal and private activities. As he sees it, it is the very honor of the Lord's good name which is at stake in economic and industrial life.

For this reason the Protestant trade union movement has always promoted collective labor agreements between management and workers, since it sees in this a realization of its goal for a worker to have his own responsibility and of its goal to effect joint consultation and cooperation with the employers. The advantages of a collective labor agreement are summarized by De Gaay Fortman, a leading Dutch Protestant trade unionist, as follows:

(1) It should be seen in the first place, as evidence of the employers' recognition that, in settling wages and other labor conditions, the workers have rights equal to theirs. Cooperation

between employers and laborers has stimulated a greater harmony in the same industry.

(2) It brings about stability in labor relations so that labor conflicts are avoided and a regular process in production is promoted.

(3) Although it maintains its civil law character and expires periodically, it does, however, have strongly durable character, for where once labor relations planning has been begun by means of collective agreements, cooperation between employers and workers toward agreement as a rule continues.

(4) It has vigorously strengthened the confidence of the workers. Through collective agreements they have learned how it feels to have a share in the responsibility and to be able to reach something. Numerous collective agreements have grown to be real law codes, in which not only fair wages have been established, but also old age pensions funds, improvements of the rules of dismissal, vocational training, organs of cooperation in the undertakings and holidays.[18]

In the opinion of the members of the Christian Labor Association of Canada, founded in 1952, the time has come for all Christian workers in the English-speaking world to join forces in striving to establish a Christian organization of labor and industry, which is not the same as unions and business organizations, consisting exclusively of devout Christians. These faithful followers of Christ are simply trying to establish a condition of industrial and labor organization which will give the maximum opportunity for men and women to practice their Christian faith at work as well as in the home, and to restore dignity and meaning to their lives by resisting the abuses and injustices of the "neutral" unions and by establishing conditions of work such that all workers may in freedom work with direct responsibility to God as His stewards, prophets, priests, and kings.

The Christian trade unionists in both America and Canada are fully conscious of the necessity of organizing labor unions to combat the injustices of monopolistic and competitive capitalism and to eliminate low wages and poor working conditions which unfortunately still exist, but they are determined to make it possible for Christian workers to practice their religion at work by basing their union activities upon the sound biblical principles of work. In the opinion of these gallant soldiers of Christ, the solution to the problems facing us in the field of labor relations is not to be found in the present neutral trade union habit of combatting one injustice by another, nor in the present use of violence, intimidation, secondary boycotts, stranger picketing, racket picketing, mass picketing, and strikes to attain labor's ends. Two wrongs have never yet made one right. Neither will peace and prosperity come to industry and agriculture by the use of such methods. Prosperity will come to our nations only when we eliminate the present injustices prevailing in labor relations in our industries by the application of Christian principles of mutual cooperation between management and workers and by giving both employers and employees a sense of belonging and of loyalty to a common enterprise in which each has its proper and vital role to perform. Ways must be found to improve the industrial climates of our countries, enabling men and women to play their full part in industry and commerce and to restore a sense of responsibility and true community in these fields. Just as the strength and good morale of industry is of the highest importance to the very survival of the Anglo-Saxon democracies, so the conduct of industry affects the moral welfare of all those engaged in it. Both sides of industry must become more and more directed by God's law and norms for human work so that the Spirit of Christ can grow to full stature in both managers and workers, and the Risen Christ can express himself through each and all.

(c) *The Case for Union Pluralism in Modern Industry*

Given the pluralistic and multi-religious character of society today, Christians should not only seek to establish their own employers' and labor associations, but they should also unite to secure the enactment of right to work laws in the labor legislation of their respective nations. Most nations of the English-speaking world today guarantee complete freedom of religion to all their citizens and treat all citizens equal before the law. Such freedom is of the utmost importance for the continuance of our free existence as persons. But such freedom of religion should not only mean freedom to attend the church of one's choice, but also the freedom to practice what each citizen believes to be in accordance with his deepest convictions regarding fundamental issues. Freedom and justice for *all* the citizens of a nation must involve, among other things, the right to work with the religious differences between citizens kept intact, the right to work under fair and equal conditions, the right to work without having humanistically oriented unions allowed by the law of the land to force their brand of secular pragmatic-humanist trade unionism upon Christian workers and without having to leave one's religion and worship of God at the factory or shop door.

At present, industries in Britain and North America, in most cases, have their workers represented by only one union and cooperation between unions within the same shop or industry is not considered to be the Anglo-Saxon way. Only one faith, that of pragmatic-humanists, is allowed to structure and to determine labor policies. The demand that every worker in one concern or plant must have his rights defended before management by one union is an expression of the Anglo-Saxon view that in public matters there must be no division in the community. This is a result of the demand for unity at all costs—even at the expense of a Christian solution to labor problems. A Christian trade union is allowed to exist but it must fit the existing legislative pattern laid down in Canada by the infamous Rand decision. On January 29, 1946, Justice I. C. Rand awarded the International Union, United Automobile, Aircraft and Agriculture Implement Workers of America (U.A.W.-C.I.O.) the right of the compulsory checkoff of union dues from the wages of all workers at the Ford Motor Company at Windsor, Ontario, whether they were union members or not. Rand gave his reasons as follows:

> I consider it entirely equitable then that all employees should be required to shoulder their portion of the burden of expense for administering the law of their employment, the union contract; that they must take the burden along with the benefit. The obligation to pay dues should tend to induce membership, and this in turn to promote that wider interest and control within the union which is the condition of progressive responsibility. If that should prove to be the case, the device employed will have justified itself. The union on its part will always have the spur to justify

itself to the majority of the employees in the power of the latter to change their bargaining representatives.[19]

The Rand formula only adds insult to injury. It makes the Christian worker support with his dues secular humanist organizations in which he cannot possibly join because of his religious convictions. It is a blatant example of taxation without representation. Would Rand compel Christians also to support a synagogue?

Because of the division of men in their basic convictions about human life, there is an antithesis between them that affects not only their ecclesiastical institutions but also their economic organizations. For Christian workers to organize their own trade unions is simply to indicate that they can have no part in today's secular unions, for their Christian principles must lead them to build their own forms of labor life. Thus, in industries, where there are workers with contesting life-and-world views, justice requires that there must be provided by law a pluralistic rather than a unitary method of representation so that all workers may enjoy the freedom to live out of their own convictions. For this reason all lovers of the Lord Jesus Christ who wish to witness for Him at work must demand of the American, British, and Canadian governments that changes be made in the existing legislation in the field of labor laws to permit plural representation in labor contracts. The present practice of granting exclusive bargaining rights to one so-called "neutral" union for *all* the employees in any given plant or shop must be abolished. In a free and "open" society such a practice is most unjust. The state should not delegate the power of the sword to any one particular association of workers, but it should recognize and protect the emergence and growth of a variety of voluntary free associations, including labor unions. When, for example, a Christian labor organization is formed as a result of the desires of a number of Christian workmen, such a formation should not be hindered by the state, but on the contrary it should be made possible and even encouraged. The role of the state in such an instance is not that it forbids or commands such a formation, but that it provides the legal possibilities and conditions for such a formation. Unless such spontaneous and free associations of this kind are possible, we are in effect living in a closed rather than an open society. Indeed, the very survival of freedom in the English-speaking world depends upon such spontaneous and free activities of the people. A Christian labor organization should no more be discriminated against by the state than a church or Christian school. *Men may be born into the state and the family without any choice in the matter, but to my knowledge no one has ever yet dared to suggest that men are born into secular neutral trade unions.* For these reasons Christians should agitate for the adoption of plural representation of workers in accordance with their life-and-world views in collective bargaining at their places of work.

In a report submitted by the Reverend David F. Summers to Bishop H. R. Hunt of Toronto Diocese, it is claimed that such a system of plural representation of workers in the process of collective bargaining is something peculiarly of Dutch origin and that it would not work in Canada. Summers points out that in Holland organizations of industry and labor are established on religious or ideological lines. Each employers' and employees' organization starts from certain premises concerning the most desirable social order, from which are derived rather specific ideas about the respective responsibilities of management, capital, labor, and government. The Dutch organizations are concerned not only with wages, hours, and conditions of work, but also with political, cultural, and ideological matters. As W. F. de Gaay Fortman explains it:

> The idea that lies at the base of this relationship is as follows: every employers' organization and every trade union starts from certain premises concerning the most desirable social order. Each of them wants to make the structure of industrial life conform to certain cherished ideals about the relation of the state to industry, about the respective responsibilities of management, capital, and labour, and about the relation of nationalized sectors of industry to private sectors. The trade unions are concerned not only with attaining material improvements for the workers; they seek also to give them an independent, responsible place in the industrial process. Apart from this, they take an increasingly active interest in the cultural development of their members. In all this work, they start from premises of a religious or ideological nature. The patterns of society derive their forms from the philosophy of life on which they are based.

This way of thinking has led in the Netherlands to the founding of Catholic and Protestant employers' and trade unions alongside those which call themselves general. Given the existence of organizations with a religious base, the other, "general" organizations also tend to take on an ideological cast.[20]

In the conduct of collective bargaining:

(1) Representatives from the central organizations of Catholic, Prottestant and neutral management groups plus a few unaffiliated groups meet with . . . .

(2) Representatives from the three central trade union groups (augmented by a few independent groups), and

(3) Representatives from the Dutch Government.

Wage rates and social security matters are discussed, and policies are agreed to at national, industry wide levels. So, too, at the plant level the various ideological groups meet first separately and then jointly to work out the application of the general pattern. Local working conditions that are too specific to be dealt with at a higher level are discussed by local committees representative of all the groups concerned.

Comparing this Dutch pluralistic system with the unitary Canadian one, Summers said in his report to Bishop Hunt:

The differences between the Dutch and Canadian systems of collective bargaining are immediately apparent. In our industrial relations the plant or shop is the basic unit. Each employer deals with his own employees, so it is at this level that the cooperation of all employees is required. Our system is posited on an approach which would make it difficult if not impossible for employer and employee groups of the Dutch pattern to operate effectively. One bargaining unit of employees is represented by one union which is chosen by democratic vote of the employees concerned. Our law makes no provision for two or more organizations to represent the employees concerned, nor does it allow for these to be proportionately represented by a bargaining committee—a proposal the C.L.A.C. has put forward. Indeed, certification expressly forbids such an arrangement. Industry wide bargaining, though suggested by a few unionists, is not well received as an idea, and does not exist in practice in Canada.

The C.L.A.C., in beginning from the premises of the Dutch system described by Fortman, and attempting to operate within the framework of our Labour Relations Act, has run into some very difficult problems. It is posed with a dilemma which can only be resolved by a considerable alteration in their approach or a radical change in our legal provisions. Either system is workable, but a mixture of the two contains elements of contradiction which make any apparent compromise unworkable.[21]

Summers then continued in his report to argue in favor of retaining the present North American labor relations legislation which expressly makes it impossible for more than one union to represent the workers. In reply, let it first be pointed out that Christian influence in industry is likely to be strong only to the extent that Christians are a strong and organized force, made up of workers and employers soaked in Christian principles, and in a *legal* position to demonstrate their principles in action. Such organized witness counts far more than all the pietistic moralizing in the world. One could accept Summer's plea for Christians to remain within existing neutral labor unions if the unions had not become so blatantly socialistic or pragamatic in their aims and objectives. Summers objects to the Christian Labor Association because of its religious orientation but he does not express similar objections against the humanistic coloring of the neutral trade unions. However, he is less than fair when he accuses the C.L.A.C. of seeking to use the union meeting as a forum for the conversion of people to Calvinistic theology. On the contrary, the C.L.A.C. welcomes every worker who desires to apply "the Christian principles of social justice and love as taught in the Bible." The organization is not limited to people who are committed to a certain theological position, but it is open to all who "pledge to uphold the Constitution and by-laws of the C.L.A.C." Nor is the C.L.A.C. an organization under the direction of Reformed clergymen, but an organization of the workers themselves. Any worker is free to join, provided he can support its aims and objectives.

On this very matter of supposed religious discrimination the C.L.A.C. has won a resounding legal victory against the Ontario Labour Relations Board which had for so long refused to certify it as a *bona fide* legal bargaining agents for its Christian workers because of its supposed discrimination. On May 2, 1963, Chief Justice J. C. McRuer quashed the O.L.R.B.'s refusal to certify the C.L.A.C. In his judgment McRuer pointed out:

> In my view the Board made a grievous error in the application of judicial principles by placing on the applicant for certification an onus to establish that the present union as reconstituted does not discriminate on the basis of creed because an officer in the union as previously constituted gave evidence on which the Board based a finding of discrimination. To accept such a principle of judicial determination would place on any union that had been discredited by its officers at a previous hearing the onus of proving that it was non-discriminating in a subsequent application. This would leave it open for irresponsible officers to completely discredit a union and shift the onus of proof in all future applications. There is no legal basis on which the Board could place on the applicant any special onus in the case.

The Chief Justice concluded by saying:

> In this matter the Board erred in the discharge of their judicial duties. They were doing worse than giving a decision in the "teeth of the evidence," and thus acting unjudicially and in a manner not authorized by the statute.[22]

McRuer then proceeded to examine the C.L.A.C.'s constitution to see "if there is anything in it to support a finding that the union discriminates within the meaning of the relevant statutes." He referred to the statement made by the Labor Board's counsel who had said during the hearing "he was hard put" to point to anything in the constitution on which one could have found a decision that the union discriminated against a person because of his creed. After reviewing the meaning of the word "creed," the judge examined the C.L.A.C.'s constitutional provisions to see "if it discriminates against any person because of its creed" and he concluded that the Labour Board "misconstrued" its clear language and the law.

To the Board's objection and contention that the requirement and practice "that every meeting held in the interest of or under the auspices of the C.L.A.C. shall be opened and closed with prayer, with Scripture reading and the singing of an appropriate hymn at the option of the presiding officers," were inconsistent with the obligation not to discriminate, Justice McRuer said:

It cannot be said that in law a requirement that the meetings of a trade union must be opened with prayer makes the trade union discriminatory within the meaning of section ten of the Labour Relations Act or section Four of the Fair Employment Practices Act. Prayer is a supplication for divine guidance. It is true that it is a recognition of a supreme being. However, the Legislature that passed the Labour Relations Act opened its sessions the day the Act was passed with prayer. Likewise the Parliament of Canada opens its daily sessions with prayer. The British National Anthem, used as the Canadian National Anthem, is a prayer. The Bill of Rights, Statutes of Canada 1960, chapter 44 affirms "that the Canadian nation is founded upon principles that acknowledge the supremacy of God." The oaths of Her Majesty's Judges and Ministers together with the oaths of office of all public officials, all acknowledge the supremacy of God.

Prayer is not a subscription to any creed in the sense that the word is used in the relevant statutes nor is the practice of singing hymns and psalms at the meetings of the union a subscription to a creed. Psalms as sung and hymns, are merely poetry set to music and for the most part they are prayers. If I supported the Board's refusal to certify the union on the ground that its members engage in prayer, read passages from the Bible and sing psalms and hymns at their meetings, the result would be that a union that required no standards of ethical or moral conduct and opened its meetings by reading from Karl Marx and singing the Red International might be certified but one that permits the practices here in question could not be. I do not think that this was the intention of the Ontario Legislature nor do I think that the express terms of the relevant statutes prevent unions from engaging in devotional exercises of the character set in the constitution of the applicant from being certified.[23]

It would thus appear that Justice McRuer has a truer understanding of these matters than does the Reverend David Summers, Executive Secretary of the Religion and Labor Council of Canada. What ulterior motive did Mr. Summers and Bishop Hunt conceal when they refused the writer's request for help for the Christian Labor Association in its struggle against the Ontario Labour Relations Board in 1962? Can it be that Bishop Hunt and Mr. Summers would rather see the C.L.A.C. destroyed than survive?

After examining relevant sections of the Constitution and its statement of principles and practices Justice McRuer concluded that he could discover no evidence of unlawful discrimination:

> My conclusion is that neither the Constitution nor the declared practices and principles of this union bring it within the prohibitions of the relevant statutes. It is not to be overlooked that the statutes do not prohibit discrimination, but only discrimination on certain stated grounds. All trade unions discriminate against members who will not subscribe to certain doctrines or beliefs of trade unionism. In the broad sense these could be called creeds, but they are not creeds as I construe the meaning of the word "creed" in the statutes. . . . As I have emphasized, what is prohibited is certification of a trade union that "discriminates against any person because of his creed." This is a restrictive clause and must be interpreted accordingly. My conclusion is that the Board erred in three main respects:
>
> (a) In coming to its decision it resorted to evidence that was given before the Board at hearings of applications for certification by the same union in 1954 and 1958 when the union was differently constituted. . . .
>
> (b) The Board misinterpreted the meaning of the statute as applied to the Constitution and by-laws of the union.
>
> (c) There was no legal evidence on which the Board could base its findings that the union was discriminatory within the meaning of the statute.
>
> An order will go quashing the order of the Board with costs.[24]

Against the necessity for Christian labor organizations it has been argued that Christians would do better to witness in secular unions. To this the reply is of course Christians in neutral organizations can and do meet other Christians for discussion at the level of principles. But, being involved to the extent that they are with non-Christians, they are not so steeped in Christian principles as people who belong to the Christian labor unions. It must be pointed out that the various institutional expressions of the Christian life-and world view depend on and support one another. In this regard, writing of the Dutch situation, Fogarty well points out:

As Dutch Christians of all denominations traditionally insist, the various institutions of Christian life depend on and support one another. The press supports the unions and the unions support the party, and so on: all combining to ensure that members' political, economic, and social decisions are taken against a thoroughly Christian background. Each influence gains in strength from its combination with others. And this argument also works in reverse. Breaking away from the Christian parties may be the thin edge of the wedge. Those who take the first step may take others, to the non-Christian trade unions or press or schools, and the whole Christian environment of decisions then breaks up.[25]

While not denying that there is need for small numbers of highly trained apostles and specialists to live amongst and penetrate neutral or humanist organizations, it is also necessary to remain aware of the danger that even specialists may fail to maintain a genuinely Christian line in a "neutral" or even anti-Christian environment. The most striking example of this was the collapse in 1953 of the first phase of the worker-priests' movement in France. Worker priests were launched into a largely pagan environment subject to highly organized Marxist influence. Many of them had little opportunity of maintaining contact with their base. A number as a result were penetrated by their environment instead of penetrating it, and the Pope rightly had to stop the dangerous experiment.[26]

For these reasons it is imperative that Christians strive to establish their own distinctive Christian organizations, and to do so they must first establish a system of plural representation of workers in collective bargaining. Naturally, the introduction of such a multiple bargaining system would not work if it were not accompanied by a genuine sense of cooperation and a mutual respect for differences in fundamental values and viewpoints. Such conflicting viewpoints might not seem to be conducive for much cooperation. But that is exactly why the development of independent Christian organizations is so necessary if the Christian workers in America, Britain, and Canada are ever to enjoy the freedom to serve God in their jobs. With a willingness to cooperate on the part of neutral and Christian workers much could be achieved. Many of the more technical problems related to collective bargaining could be tackled together. There are undoubtedly areas of activities which lend themselves to such cooperative efforts between workers of differing life-and-world views. Yet this need not interfere with the independence of the various organizations. Each organization could work for the realization of those goals it considers desirable. Thus, the possibility of the development of various organizations in accordance with the deepest wishes and convictions of different people would be made possible. Such an opening up process would be of great advantage to the people directly involved and to the development of a truly free society.

It might be further objected that such a proposal would make for a cumbersome and more complex labor relations situation, and should thus be rejected. In reply, let it be said that our entire democratic system is equally complex and exactly for the same good reason, viz., because it gives an opportunity for different people to seek to realize divergent aims and values in life. The burden of freedom is heavy, as Eric Fromm has explained in his *Fear of Freedom*. But the burden of slavery is much heavier because in totalitarian and "closed" societies, such as Red China and Soviet Russia, the attempt is made to reduce each individual person to a part of the uniform whole. Yet such uniformity is deadly to the human spirit, and what is more, it can never achieve real community between men. The human person was not created by God for such experiments in "social engineering," and the state cannot create real community among *all* its citizens by compulsion. That is why attempts to do so such as that advocated by Rousseau in the "Social Contract" never will meet with success.

What would such a system of plural representation involve? First, let it be pointed out that it would not mean that the employer would have to bargain separately with each union and conclude separate and possibly different collective labor agreements. Such an arrangement would indeed be cumbersome and impractical. It is essential that the same wages and conditions should apply to all employees of the same employer; otherwise the employer might be tempted to play one group of workers off against the other.

The system would involve a representative council or works

committee being elected in each place of employment where different unions would be allowed by law to exist and to recruit their members. Such a council would be composed on the basis of the relative membership strength of the total number of workers in any given shop, plant or works. This council, in consultation with its own groups of employees, could then work together in framing policies and in bargaining with the employer about conditions of work, wages, etc. This would require that the multiple groups should reach agreement among themselves before a bargaining session with the employer takes place. Each group could also provide whatever service would be required, e.g., the processing of agreements for its own members. This arrangement would solve the problem of the one union incurring expenses and providing benefits for non members. An added advantage would be that some workers who presently have no voice in the affairs of their employment would be enabled to join in union activities. Above all such a system of plural union representation of workers in one plant or shop would keep each particular union competitive and on its toes. The union which rendered the best and most efficient service to its members would tend to obtain the greatest number of workers.

If such a principle of proportionate representation of workers could be enacted into existing labor legislation, it would greatly reduce the internecine struggles for power between the bigger unions; for example, the struggle for power between two unions for the right to represent the employees of the International Nickel Company in Sudbury, Ontario. Those who favor the Communist-led union over the United Steelworkers of America could belong to the Mine-Mill organization. The others would be free to join the Steelworkers. Such a method of plural representation would give all the workers a real choice and they would not be forced, as they now are, to accept the decisions of a union which obtained representation only by a small majority. Only by such means of plural representation can the existing pluralistic character of post-Christian Atlantic society be adequately and justly reflected in the field of labor relations. Only by such a method of union representation will there be freedom and justice for *all* workers, including Christian workers.[27] Such industrial pluralism alone can reform the present deformed labor relations presently existing in the American, British, and Canadian economies.

In support of this principle of plural union representation of workers in one plant or shop, Evan Runner in a speech titled "Can Canada Tolerate the C.L.A.C." concluded with this appeal to the humanist leaders in government:

The majority of western men today are not Christian believers. The error of the rationalists was that they continued to hold on to the medieval idea of a single monolithic society. And T. S. Eliot is still thinking along these lines. Instead of his *Idea of a Christian Society* we would propose that we develop a Christian idea of society, where the fact of a plurality of faiths (including the rationalist's faith in *ratio* or the scientist's faith in operationalism) is recognized. . . . Toleration is really possible to the greatest degree only in a pluralist society. We Christians no longer wish to impose *our* views on others who do not agree with us. We simply do not wish the *humanist dogma* to be imposed on us. We want each faith to be free to organize the several areas of life struggle, at least those where the crucial struggles of a particular era are concentrated. This has been the Achilles' heel of the humanist society. Humanism made what it called Reason absolute, and permitted it to set the limits of toleration. It failed to see its view of Reason as a kind of religious commitment, and in fact identified its own private, partisan, sectarian and subjective faith with the universal and necessary rational equipment of human beings. It saw its own faith as axiomatic and of the very structure of scientific method, thus as public, universal and objective, in contrast with the Christian faith and other faiths as private and subjective. This was simply to secure to the humanist faith an apparently impregnable position in human culture and to make its own impregnability the criterion and measure of toleration. As Walter Lippman, speaking for humanism, put it in his book *The Public Philosophy*: "Originally it (the meaning of freedom) was founded on the postulate that there was a universal order on which all reasonable men were agreed; within that public agreement on the fundamentals and on the ultimates it was safe to permit and it would be desirable to encourage dissent and dispute." For the organization of contemporary society we Christians find such a position intolerant and intolerable.

We appeal to the humanists in our society not to allow an old dogma to get in the way of true humanity. There have always been a large number of people in Anglo-Saxon countries who consider themselves beyond any particular ideology or system of belief and wish to see squarely the existing states of affairs. We appeal to all such to recognize the characteristics of absolute religious commitment in the old rationalism, to acknowledge that it will be impossible to remove the plurality of faiths that at present exist, and to work with us towards a truly pluralist and humane society.[27]

(d) *The Reformational Understanding of Race Relations*

Of all the intractable problems now facing mankind none is more serious than that of the relations between the different races and nations of the world. In the last book he wrote before his assassination Martin Luther King said in *Chaos or Community*:

> There is the convenient temptation to attribute the current turmoil and bitterness throughout the world to the presence of a Communist conspiracy to undermine Europe and America, but the potential explosiveness of our world situation is much more attributable to disillusionment with the promises of Christianity and technology. . . .
> Once the aspirations and appetites of the world have been whetted by the marvels of Western technology and the self-image of a people awakened by religion, one cannot hope to keep people locked out of the earthly kingdom of wealth, health and happiness. Either they share in the blessings of the world or they organize to break down and overthrow these structures or governments which stand in the way of their goals.[28]

In spite of some moves toward a just solution of the problem, the main trend of the twentieth century has been toward racist solutions of intergroup problems. Never in the world's history has there been so much mass slaughter, expulsion of minorities, and division of territory along ethnic lines as during the past sixty years. Among various apostate humanist solutions proposed and used we distinguish the following.[29]

(1) *Annihilation or Genocide*

Looking at the most wicked of the apostate humanist solutions, we find that carried out by the Nazi Party of Germany under Hitler's leadership. Between coming to power in 1933 and their defeat in 1945 by the Allied armies of the West and Soviet Russia, the Nazis destroyed more than five million Jews, with a brutal and scientific efficiency. Hitler looked upon the Jews as a kind of germ infecting the body politic and thus justified his terrible final solulution. Another example of mass extermination occurred in the Hindu-Moslem dispute over the partition of India in 1948, a conflict which resulted in the death of over three million people. Such a method of solving racial disputes no Christian could ever contemplate, since he believes that God has created *all* men of every race, color, and nation under heaven in His own holy image. As the Book of Acts puts it, "God that made the world . . . hath made of one blood all nations of men for to dwell on all the face of the earth, and hath determined the times before appointed, and the bounds of their habitation" (Acts 17:24, 26). God did not originally create several independent human races or nations. He created one human pair, from whom have descended all the nations of the earth. All men as creatures are, therefore, brothers, related to one another by ties of blood and common creaturely origin. Moreover, God ordained that the human race should live in accordance with His Law. Legally, morally, and spiritually the several nations and peoples of the world have been given a common law, the law of God, which binds them together and should determine their relationships. On the basis of this common law, genocide is prohibited as an affront to the majesty of the creator, and because man is made in God's image (Gen. 9:6).

(2) *Expulsion and Partition*

A less barbarous solution to the problem of race relations also much used in our terrible twentieth century has been partition and expulsion. Owing to nationalism, the idea that a nation should be composed of those who share a similar ethnic and lingual background has been especially popular in recent times.

A mass shifting of population has resulted from the attempt to make political boundaries coincide with ethnic groupings. People whose families have lived in certain areas for hundreds of years suddenly found themselves declared undesirable aliens and they were forced to move elsewhere. Examples of this solution may be found in the expulsion of the Greeks from Turkey and of Turks from Greece, the partition of Palestine into a Jewish state and an Arab state after the Second World War—with the expulsion of over a million Arabs—the division of Ireland into a Roman Catholic part and a Protestant part, the partition of India between Moslems and Hindus. Proof that no group is secure against the effects of such a policy is seen in the fate of the Germans living outside the boundaries of Germany. Over ten million Germans were ordered, after World War II, to leave areas in Central and Eastern Europe where their families had lived for centuries. It is possible that white minorities may one day be expelled from parts of Africa.

During World War II both Russia and the United States forced ethnic groups to move from one part of the country to other areas. The Russians broke up the Volga German Republic and transported its inhabitants to Siberia. The United States placed thousands of West Coast Japanese in detention camps located hundreds of miles from their homes. Little is known of the ultimate fate of these Volga Germans, whose ancestors had been invited to Russia by Peter the Great. The United States eventually reversed its policy and allowed the Japanese to live where they wished when the government realized that they were entirely loyal.

(3) *Segregation and Discrimination*

This type of solution to the problem of race relations, though much less brutal than the methods just described, is even more widespread. In a great many countries the attitude toward members of subordinate groups is that they should be allowed to function only in a way that serves the interest of the dominant group; in other words, discrimination. The essence of discrimination in this sense is a practice that treats equal people unequally, in that members of different ethnic groups do not have the same opportunities to compete for social rewards.

The practice of segregation implies that contacts between the subordinates and the dominant group will be confined to those which are essential for the direction of the subordinates in their labors. Subordinates may come into contact with the dominant group as household servants or as workers in farming and industry. However, purely social contacts are greatly restricted, or, if possible, altogether eliminated.

The segregation-discrimination pattern is probably most perfectly developed in the traditional Hindu caste system of India, in which the occupations that people may perform are carefully defined by one's caste, intermarriage is taboo, eating at the same table as a member of a different caste forbidden, and separation is the rule in most social relations. Ely Chinoy points out in *Society*:

> Indian society is usually divided into four inclusive castes—the *Brahmins*, or priests, the *Kshatriya*, or warriors, the *Vaisya*, or merchants, and the *Sudra*, or peasants. There are, in addition, the *outcasts* or *untouchables*, those who have been expelled from their caste, either in their own persons or in that of their ancestors, for violations of the rigidly enforced codes of caste behavior. In 1931, the most recent date for which figures are available, approximately 6 percent of India's Hindu population were Brahmins, just over 70 percent belonged to other castes, and over 20 percent were untouchables.[30]

In Southern Africa there have been three distinct approaches to the problem of race relations: (a) the South African approach of separate development or apartheid; (b) the Rhodesian approach of multi-racism, and (c) the Portuguese approach of full integration.

The strange thing is that all three approaches have evoked the concentrated hostility of the United Nations and so-called world public opinion. Thus the impartial observer can only conclude that race is not really the issue at all, but merely the ogre created to whip up emotion and trouble in the councils of mankind.

What, then, is South Africa's real crime? The answer must be that she has dared to call in question that great sacred cow of our revolutionary age, the godless dogma that sovereignty over the individual resides in the general will of the majority rather than in the revealed will of Almighty God written in the Holy Scriptures.

It is tragic that many Christians in America, Britain, and Canada have condemned South Africa and Rhodesia in identical terms, that is, the necessity for majority rule and the sovereignty of apostate man's rational will rather than in terms of a Christian doctrine of culture, government, and society. After twenty years experience of working with black Christians in Rhodesia the Venerable A. R. Lewis, Archdeacon of Inyanga, Rhodesia, writes this comment upon this issue:

A Christian, presumably, should be concerned with the actual merits of the case. Is there anything specially Christian, or morally imperative, about the "majority rule" which is demanded at once or in the very near future? Since majority rule is probably an impossibility, if not strictly a contradiction in terms, it would perhaps be better to speak of "universal adult male suffrage." That is what is meant. This has only to be stated for it to become obvious that there have been Christian societies in the past, as there are Christian societies today, conducted on quite different lines. Britain herself had a limited and qualified franchise until quite recently, and this at a time when she was more, not less Christian than she is now. It is simply untrue to suggest that a just and Christian society must practice universal adult male suffrage, though of course in some circumstances it may do so. One would suppose that the welfare of the majority and the protection of minorities ought to be the primary Christian concerns. If this is so, much of the criticism directed against Rhodesia (and we may add South Africa) might be more relevantly levelled at the new black-ruled one party states and military governments. . . .

If it is true that an essential difference between Britain and Rhodesia concerns the "sixth principle" advanced in negotiation by Britain—that any settlement must be acceptable to the people as a whole—two questions must be asked at once. Why does this principle not apply to black-ruled states? And, since it has been accepted long ago by the Rhodesian government anyway—are we not back, in practice, at the demand for one man one vote? Is it not assumed that the majority must decide what is good for the people through the ballot box?

This assumption takes no account of the fact that the ballot-box is a western device which is not the natural mode of self-expression for non-western peoples. . . . It overlooks the practical consequence of forcing this device on simple semi-literate communities; the demagogue can get himself into power by threats and extravagant promises; and once in control can establish a

tyranny which it may be impossible to bring down without violence. This is a demonstrable fact, and Rhodesians are entitled
to ask British Christians to take it into account. It is noteworthy
that those churchmen who stridently demand "one man one
vote" now are usually either not in Rhodesia at all, or are in a
position to depart hastily if they wish when the bloodshed begins.
Unlike the ordinary African they have no stake in the country.[31]

(4) *Assimilation*

The solution which most appeals to apostate "liberal" humanists
is full racial and cultural integration. In *Race and Ethnic Relations*
Brewton Berry defines assimilation as follows:

> By assimilation we mean the process whereby groups with dif-
> ferent cultures come to have a common culture. . . . Assimilation
> refers to the fusion of cultural heritages, and must be distinguished
> from *amalgamation*, which denotes the biological mixture of ori-
> ginally distinct racial strains. It must be distinguished, too, from
> *naturalization*, a political concept denoting the act or process of
> admitting an alien to the status and privileges of a citizen.
> Americanization, of course, is simply a special case of assimilation,
> and refers to the process whereby a person of some foreign
> heritage acquires the customs, ideals and loyalties of American
> society, just as Europeanization, Russianization and Germaniza-
> tion denote a similar process with respect to these cultures.[32]

The classic example of the assimilation of disparate cultural and
ethnic groups into a common society is seen in the integration of
European immigrants in the United States. Such immigrants came
from a number of national cultures with a wide variety of languages,
customs, dietary habits, family patterns, and general attitudes towards life. The first reaction of immigrants was usually to settle
in ethnic colonies, either in small towns or in urban neighborhoods.
Often they viewed the United States as a temporary refuge where
they might stay until an unfriendly political regime in their European homeland had disappeared, or until they had saved up enough
money to retire in comfort in their homelands. Many immigrants
did spend their entire period of sojourn in ethnic colonies surrounded
by fellow nationals, and a considerable number were able to return
to Europe as they had planned. The majority of immigrants, how-

ever, remained in the United States, and either they or their descendants moved out of the ethnic colonies as their assimilation progressed to such an extent that their European background became only a faint memory.

In the opinion of American "liberals" it is unfortunate that non-white Americans did not become as easily integrated into the common humanistic society. Instead, the prevailing pattern in America has been the integration of Caucasion immigrants and the segregation of other groups. The "liberals" have therefore embarked upon the dangerous policy of forcible assimilation of whites and non-whites. On May 17, 1954, the Supreme Court, in *Brown* v. *Board of Education*, held that segregation in state public education was inherently discriminatory and unconstitutional. In a companion case, the Court struck down school segregation by federal authorities in the District of Columbia. These rulings at one stroke transferred the legal sanction and moral authority of the nation's basic law from the segregationist forces to the civil rights advocates and unleashed a Pandora's box full of troubles, of which the black students' riots at America's "Ivy League" universities and colleges in 1969 are only a harbinger of worse troubles to come.

The black students are rightly demanding all-black studies departments on college campuses along with other forms of black separatism. They do not wish to see the American Negro suffer the same fate of extinction as the Maoris of New Zealand, whose culture has been killed by kindness. Negroes in America were from 1619 to at least 1868 deprived of their African languages, culture, and identity. Black college students today want desperately to find that identity.

Black colleges have to date been the most successful in rediscovering African culture and in giving to black students a collective self-assurance and a sense of cultural unity. Well over 50 percent of Negroes who attend college, however, go to predominantly white institutions. Such black students in white colleges perceive their loss and demand that black studies be added to the curriculum. They are calling for separate dormitories and autonomous racial schools within colleges and universities. Of these demands the Rev. Robert

F. Drinan, S.J., Dean of Boston College Law School and a close observer of the civil rights scene, writes:

> The New York Times termed this phenomenon "a militant black withdrawal into campus ghettoes" and called it "a disease." This type of misleading rhetoric does not take account of the profound apartness and lack of self-identification which the Negro student feels on a predominantly white campus.
>
> The fact is that black students, almost always confined to a separate and unequal world prior to their coming to an all-white campus, should be expected and encouraged to harmonize their past experiences with their present training.
>
> The excruciating nature of the search for identity which confronts the black student on a white campus can be only dimly perceived by a white observer. This writer, recently talking to a Negro student from Virginia at one of New England's prestigious colleges, asked him how he liked it. He replied "Most of the time I wish I had gone to Fisk or Tuskegee or Morehouse. It would have been easier there to find out who I am."
>
> That poignant statement illuminates the depth of the frustrations which prompts appeals for black dormitories and cries for all-Negro departments.[33]

(5) *Cultural Pluralism*

It is also a classic argument for cultural and ethnic pluralism. Of all the methods considered so far cultural pluralism would seem to be the one most in line with the scriptural view of race relations. The great Council of Jerusalem ruled that it would be an infringment upon the Christian's newly found freedom in Christ to enforce cultural and racial integration between Jewish and Gentile Christians by requiring circumcision of the latter as a condition of membership of the Universal Church (Acts 15). It was laid down that Gentile Christians should continue to live according to their own cultural laws, customs, and ceremonies. As Adolf Schlatter says in *The Church in the New Testament Period*:

> The chief result of the agreement between St. Paul and the Jerusalem Church was that in the Church the Jews and the gentiles were not assimilated, but each kept their own traditions unimpaired by any attempt at uniformity. Thus the Church became heir to both traditions. Having taken over from the Jews their

Scriptures and their ethic, the Church was no less open to the priceless contributions of their Greek tradition.[34]

It is the failure to distinguish between assimilation and integration in the sense of equal rights before the law which is responsible for most of America's present racial troubles. As Sir Mark Bonham Carter, Chairman of Britain's Race Relations Board, said in *The Sunday Telegraph* on July 30, 1967:

> The Americans never made up their minds about what they were trying to achieve. Until very recently assimilation and integration were almost interchangeable words. Here the present Home Secretary's first statement on race relations made it quite clear that the Government's policy was not a flattening process of assimilation, but integration, which he defined as equal opportunity, accompanied by cultural diversity in an atmosphere of mutual tolerance.[35]

The idea of human equality before the law should not lead us to overlook the differences between individuals as well as between groups and races. Injustice has often occurred in the past by treating unequals in an equal manner as by treating equals in an unequal manner.

America is surely mature enough to allow full freedom to each of her various and wonderfully diverse cultural groups to develop in accordance with their own deepest aspirations. Why should the "liberals" seek to push their philosophy of drab uniformity down the throats of other groups? *Only by means of cultural pluralism can freedom now be preserved in America.* If Switzerland and Canada can make such a policy work, surely it is not beyond the wit of Americans to do the same.

In Switzerland, Protestants and Catholics have been able to live agreeably together under the same government, while speaking German, French, and Italian. Since the Swiss citizen does not feel that his religious loyalty or his ethnic identification is threatened by other Swiss, he is free to give a complete allegiance to the Swiss nation as a common government which allows for the tolerance of distinctly different cultural groups. Canada, with the division between the French and the English, and Belgium, with a division between the

French and the Flemish speaking population, are other examples of cultural and ethnic pluralism. The different groups who make up a pluralistic society in these nations frequently engage in a struggle for influence, but the essential idea is that national patriotism does not require cultural or racial uniformity, and that differences of nationality, religion, language, and race do not preclude loyalty to a common national government and are in fact to be welcomed.

In America both the Indian and Jewish segments of the population have rightly resisted attempts to become assimilated into the great American "melting pot." The Orthodox Jews in America, who constitute the majority of Jews, certainly are not assimilationists. Rabbi Milton Steinberg believes that most assimilatory efforts in the past have resulted only in the dejudaizing of the Jew without winning for him gentile acceptance. Nor does he believe in Jews withdrawing from active participation in public life. "I do not now envisage, nor have I practiced, withdrawal from the general life of America." He insists, instead, that one may remain loyal to Jewish religion and tradition without its militating in the least against full participation in the common political life of the nation. He calls this "cultural dualism," and says of it:

> Any program for the Jewish group must meet a twofold test of acceptability—the welfare of the Jewish group, and the welfare of America. . . . America is best served by its Jews when they strive to exploit the special resources of their group.[36]

Do Jews and Negroes need to be assimilated to escape minority status? And do they want to be assimilated, to be forced to give up their own cultural identity? James B. McKee answers these questions in his *Introduction to Sociology*. He writes:

> To suggest assimilation into the majority culture is to imply the superiority and desirability of the cultural ways of the majority, and to denigrate the contrasting cultural life of the minority. But a new sense of appreciation of the diversity of cultures, a new value orientation to ethnicity suggests to some that the loss of diversity through assimilation will lessen the cultural richness of America.

But the crux of pluralism lies, not in whether the majority sees the preservation of diversity as a cultural asset, but whether the minority group sees it as a viable and meaningful objective. The Jewish community has long accepted pluralism as a dominant value, for it constitutes a way in which the Jewish group can maintain its own integrity, while continuing to have an equality of life-chances in that society. Perhaps more significantly, the new Negro objective of a black community, the often aggressive rejection of the goal of integration of the "white liberal" leadership of civil rights, the explicit call for separatism by some militant leaders, and the new pattern of cultural preference for things black and African, suggests that a racial version of pluralism may be emerging as a new and significant aspect of American race relations.[37]

In view of the failure of the "liberal" policy of forcible assimilation of different ethnic groups in American society and the confusion of assimilation with the political principle of integration in the sense of providing justice for all, let us pray that all Americans come to realize and to accept the advantages of a policy which openly accepts unity in diversity. Such a cultural and ethnic pluralism is in fact the only one in accordance with God's revealed will in the Bible, and so the only policy that will really work.

(e) *The Scriptural Basis for Cultural and Ethnic Pluralism*

The Church of Jesus Christ both as an institution and as an organism functions in the social modality of God's creation. Inherent in the life of faith is communion with God and with our fellow believers. This fellowship is of a spiritual nature and it must not be reduced to social intercourse in the ordinary sense, in which it is subjected to the peculiar norms of chivalry, conviviality, tact, and fashion. It does, however, point back to the modal moment of the social aspect and binds the faith aspect to it.

In the social sphere the church as the Body of Christ is qualified by its faith in Jesus Christ as the Lord and Savior of human life in its entirety and not by any rationalistic doctrine of "liberty, equality, and fraternity," apart from Him. It is at this point that Christians who accept the Word of God as the ordering principle of their lives will part company with many "liberal" and modernist

Christians as well as ecumenists. Beguiled by Harnack's reduction of Christianity to the universal fatherhood of God and the brotherhood of man, these persons seem to think that the Kingdom of God is pretty much equivalent to the moral, legal, and political unification of the whole human race. For them religion has become only a new aspect of moral activity with the result that the Kingdom of God has become stripped of the eschatological transcendence that belongs to it in the Gospels, a purely present and mundane commonwealth.

It is not, therefore, surprising to find such liberals, ecumenists, and modernists ardent supporters of the present attempt now being made in certain quarters to bring about full assimilation of races within the states of the English-speaking world. Such an attempt is no doubt motivated by the best intentions. Unfortunately, the road to hell has been paved with good intentions and the present campaign to bring about togetherness without God is no exception. *It is not only impossible but anti-Christian to try to bring community be-between races by compulsion.*

In *The Basic Ideas of Calvinism* H. Henry Meeter says in this regard:

> Although all nations form a racial unity, there is also, according to Scripture, a definite place for such natural group formations as distinct nations. This important fact must not be overlooked. Had the human race remained sinless, there would have arisen in the organic life of men larger and lesser groups, each with its own cultural task and sovereignty in its own sphere commensurate with the task assigned to it. Sin, which has disrupted human life generally, has also worked havoc with the cultural demand of God to each of these groups, that they subdue the earth and accomplish the special task assigned to each of them. Instead of the unity which God had intended that organic groups should attain through diversity, each developing its own distinctive task, *there arose an attempt at uniformity without distinctiveness.* The classical biblical example of such godless uniformity is given to us in the story of the erection of the tower of Babel on the plains of Shinar. Had this project been executed, there would have arisen a godless world-empire, in which the subjugation of the earth and the development of the diversified talents of men and cultural

tasks generally would have been retarded greatly, not to say defeated. . . .

There are two basic factors inherent in the very nature of things which affect the way in which the several peoples of the earth should live together. . . . The unity of the human race obliges them to live together as members of one family, but the distinct characteristics, the tastes and cultural tasks of the several nations and peoples call for a corresponding independence and sovereignty in their own spheres. This their God-given cultural duties demand.[38]

If Americans now accept religious pluralism as the condition of peaceful relations between different churches and sects, why can they not accept cultural and ethnic pluralism as well, as the only workable solution to the problem of race relations. Why be ashamed of being born white or black? Why not accept the fact gladly and then work to build up pride in one's own race so that each race can make its own distinctive contribution to one's own country and then to mankind as a whole. As C. H. Dodd said in his lecture, *Christianity and the Reconciliation of the Nations*:

> The New Testament ends with a glowing picture of the destination of human history. There is a vast concourse before the throne of God, from every nation, tribe, people and language, and there is the Holy City, with all the nations bringing their glory and honour into it, and walking in the light of the city where night never falls. . . .
>
> From this passage at least we may safely deduce that Christianity recognizes the grouping of mankind according to nationality, race and language as a fact of history falling within the divine purpose, but not as an ultimate fact about man, since it is to be transcended as history reaches its goal.[39]

Although all nations form a basic unity in terms of a common descent from Adam and Eve, there is also, according to Scripture, a definite place for such natural groupings as distinct nations and races. This important fact must never be overlooked. In the poem of Deuteronomy 32 we read:

> When the Most High gave to the nations their inheritance
> When he separated the sons of men,

He fixed the borders of the peoples
According to the number of the sons of God.
For Yahweh's portion is his people;
Jacob is his allotted inheritance (Deut. 32:8-9).

Commenting on this passage in *Principalities and Powers*, G. B. Caird says:

Each nation, that is to say, has its own angelic ruler and guardian, except Israel, which comes under the direct sovereignty of God. The Deuteronomist does not seem to have been disturbed by the knowledge that the pagan nations worshipped their angelic rulers in the place of God. These rulers had been allotted to them by God alone and, provided that Israel was not seduced by their worship, the order of God's providence was not disturbed.[40]

The Scriptures suggest that before the Flood mankind was not divided up into races, but was one race with a unity of speech (Gen. 11:1). It was also united in its purpose of defying God's command to fill the whole earth. Instead, mankind resolved "to build a city, and a tower, whose top may reach into heaven" (Gen. 11:4). The Lord's verdict upon this attempt to achieve world peace and unity apart from Him by domination and exploitation (Gen. 10:9), was to "go down, and there confound their language that they may not understand one another's speech," and to scatter them "abroad thence upon the face of all the earth" (Gen. 11:7-9). In the Table of Nations we are told that this division of mankind into different language groups took place in the days of the patriarch Peleg (Gen. 10:25).

In the course of time this linguistic difference between the descendants of Noah was reinforced by ethnic differences. The Scriptures do not explain how and when these ethnic differences appeared. What God did was to change mankind's habits and tastes, as well as speech, so that these people no longer desired to live together. They were now living in distinct worlds of thought. Hence one went out in one direction, another in a different direction. This fact is clearly indicated by the genealogies of Genesis 10 and 11. In a fascinating article, "Racial Dispersion," R. Laird Harris points out that: "race is a physical term. *The A.S.A. Symposium* quotes Boas's definition that race is the 'assembly of genetic lines represented in a population.'" In terms of this genetic definition Harris then writes:

> We need not adopt the view that has sometimes been expressed that the three sons of Noah were black, yellow, and white. If they were so, what were their wives? Rather we would say that in these six people were all the genes which have separated out into the modern races. . . . Shem may have had the genes for kinky hair and yellow skin, Ham for white skin and Mongoloid eyes, etc. But the genes we would have to say were all there whether in evidence in the body characteristics or not.[41]

The racial differences that exist today, according to W. Smalley, were probably brought about by mutations that "occurred in small, isolated groups which, because of their small size and isolation at rather extreme positions in the Europe, Asia-Africa land area, inbred the new factor. Both cultural and environmental selection could have operated." [42] Negroes are considered by anthropologists to have migrated from Southern Asia into Africa in comparatively recent times. According to Genesis 10, descendants of all the three sons of Noah were living in Western Asia after the Tower of Babel. Therefore it is impossible to say from which son or sons of Noah the Negroid and Mongoloid peoples have descended. In his work, *Mankind So Far*, Professor William Howell says that the Australian aborigines probably reached their island continent "at roughly the time that the Indians were going to America, perhaps 10,000 B.C." [43] In discussing the problem of the original distribution of Negroes and Nigritoes, Howells has this to say:

> They are doubtless "newer" races than the Australian, because they specialized, particularly in hair. . . . Their final outward spread, however, would have been recent, because the Negritoes would have needed true boats to arrive in the Andamans or the Philippines. The Negroes would have made their Asiatic exit still later, with a higher (Neolithic) culture, and probably also with boats. A relatively recent arrival of Negroes in Africa should not shock anthropologists. . . . And there are no archaeological signs of pre-Neolithic people in the Congo at all, and it might have been empty when the Negritoes and the Negroes came.[44]

After emphasizing the "stupendous growth of the last 10,000 years," and "the recent spread of man," Howells states: "If we look, first of all, for that part of the world which was the hothouse of the races, we can make only one choice. All the visible footsteps lead away from Asia." [45] Similar testimony to the historicity of the Genesis account is borne out by William A. Smalley in his essay, "A Christian View of Anthropology," in *Modern Science and Christian Faith*. He says:

> The Scriptural record is of the spread of peoples from their origin in the approximate center of the great Europe, Asia-Africa land mass. The Biblical picture is so close to the best anthropological reconstructions of the original dispersion and divergences of races that it is used as the allegorical picture of scientific findings by Dr. Ruth Benedict and Miss Gene Weltfish in their population booklets combatting race prejudice, and is basic in their map.[46]

In the efforts of the integrationists to unite the various races of mankind upon a purely "secular" basis we may see an attempt to reverse the consequences of God's judgment upon mankind which He made at the Tower of Babel. Once more we are witnessing an attempt upon man's part "to make a name" for himself (Gen. 11:4), that is, trying to set himself up in opposition to God's Name, to which alone praise and glory properly belong.

At the United Nations and elsewhere godless men are seeking to erect a secular "City" or civilization that reckons little of God's grace and therefore of His law. The Word of God makes clear that all such attempts are doomed to end in catastrophe and confusion. Throughout the Bible we read first of one city, now another becoming the *type* of man's reckless defiance of God's purpose and law for humanity—Sodom and Gomorrah (Gen. 18:19); Tyre (Ezek. 26-28); and above all Babylon. Indeed, Babylon is depicted in the Bible as the great prototype of all the cities and empires of the world that despise God's grace and law. Thus at the beginning of the Bible Babylon is raised in pride and brought down in confusion, and also at the end of the Bible it is Babylon whose hour of judgment is come. The author of the Apocalypse clearly has the judgment of God upon the men of Babel in his mind when he writes: "Thus with a mighty fall shall Babylon, the great city, be cast down, and shall be found no more at all" (Rev. 18:21).

Unlike integrationists, the Bible teaches that the disunity of mankind is *not* caused by race, but by sin. *It is men's sinfulness rather than their different colored skins which divide them.* The Tower of Babel emphasizes that it is man's exaltation of himself as over against God which is the prime cause of divisions and rivalries, of which the different languages are symbolic. Men cannot speak to one another in a common tongue because they have no common interest or mutual regard.

God has appointed His own method of creating real community between men and that is by incorporating them into His own one great family, the universal Church, uniting them in one covenant of love in the blood of the Lord Jesus Christ, and speaking one common language of the Holy Spirit of God. Upon the great Day of Pentecost God's power was revealed as great enough to reverse the Babel confusion of the languages so that men became bound together in love for God and for each other in the New Covenant of grace (Acts 2:5-11). The story of the gift of tongues at Pentecost is nothing more than the Babel story in reverse.

Integrating people by the brute force of the state is therefore a violation of God's free sovereign grace in Jesus Christ—the saving grace of the shed blood of the Lamb of God by which alone men, races, and classes can be saved from the dreadful consequences of sin, including the sin of pride in one's own race and prejudice against other races. The integrationists now declare that God's appointed method of reconciling races at the foot of Christ's Cross is not sufficient or adequate. Instead of being saved by Christ alone, something more is needed, namely, miscegenation of races. Men are not to be made spiritually one in Jesus Christ, but they are to be united biologically and psychologically by the brute power of the eugenic expert and the psychiatrist assisted by the police (Col. 3:10-13).

The true Christian answer to the problem of racial and cultural conflict was provided for all Christians at the first great Council of the whole Church, held in Jerusalem and described for us in

Acts, chapter 15. Under the guidance of God the Holy Ghost, the Apostles ruled that it would be an infringement upon the Christian's newly found freedom in Christ to enforce cultural and social and racial integration between Jewish and Gentile Christians by requiring circumcision of the latter as a condition of membership of the Church. Therefore it was laid down that the Gentile Christians should continue to live according to their own historic traditions and customs, and in the conditions of the flesh in which they had been born. The Jewish Christians, with equal fervor, were to hold fast to their own Jewish laws, customs, and ceremonies, especially circumcision. Just as Jewish Christians were not saved from the power and guilt of sin by obedience to the accretions which had grown up around the Law of Moses (The Torah), but only by God's sovereign grace in Christ, so the Gentile Christians were not to be saved from sin by coming under the discipline of the Jewish ceremonial law.

In his profound study of the primitive church, *Jew and Greek*, Gregory Dix writes of the Council's decision as follows:

> The Jewish Christians at the Council of Jerusalem in A.D. 49 finally accepted the fact that the Old Israel as such had lost its Covenant and in the pathetic phrase of the Epistle to the Hebrews, "They went forth unto Jesus without the camp, bearing His reproach." The same historical situation which had forced Jesus Himself to choose between the Cross and the betrayal of the truth of the Old Covenant had speedily brought the Jewish-Christian Church to the same choice between ensuring its own rejection by Israel and a betrayal of the truth of the New Covenant. It chose His solution. . . . The Jewish Christian Church chose to be rejected and to die that this "gospel" might continue, once it was sure that "the Gospel preached among the Gentiles" was identical with "the Gospel of the circumcision." The end was swift. Jewish Christianity vanishes into obscurity with a startling suddenness in the sixties, and thereafter dies obscurely in the shadows.[47]

It was St. Paul, the great Jewish Apostle to the Gentiles, who had forced the issue. The Council, without publicly endorsing the Pauline principle, had the courage and wisdom to allow Gentile converts to be received on equal terms without imposing on them either circumcision or the Law. Gentile Christians would henceforth be accepted as full partners in the Christian Covenant without Judaizing. The Gospel of the revelation of God in Jesus Christ, cut off from its Jewish roots by the Jewish revolt, stood forth on its own merits as a third and catholic culture, to be henceforward the target alike of unconverted Jews and unconverted Gentiles, who hated it with equal intensity. Within the holy catholic and apostolic Church all races could now find their own proper place and make their own distinctive contribution in the building up of the Body of Christ.

Until the fulness of the mystery of Christ has been filled out by all peoples and races in terms of their own traditions and languages we shall not be in a position to comprehend the full glory and greatness of the Christ (Rom. 11:-1-25; Eph. 3:1-10; Col. 1:24-29). But this religious unity of the human race in Christ does not mean that one race should try to dominate all other races. It means that all races and nations must be allowed full freedom to work out their own destiny in fear and trembling before the Lord. If the religious unity of the entire human race means at the same time the destruction of all the separate spheres of life, then marriage, the family, the school, the state, and the Church would disappear as communities of a peculiar character. Then it would be enough as the godless French revolutionaries supposed, to celebrate the "Feast of Fraternization" upon the ruins of all these spheres.

If a person cannot come to Christ just as he is without one plea, if he must first become integrated before he can become a Christian, then we deny that Christ alone of His own sovereign grace is able to save us. By claiming that we have first to be integrated before we can be saved the humanists and the ecumenists have perverted and destroyed the glorious Gospel of God. If we cannot be saved even as we now are, black, white, red, or yellow, but must first lose our racial, national, and cultural and psychological identities, then Christ has been dethroned and God's grace mocked (Eph. 2:8-22; II Cor. 4:16-18).

To argue that Christian love and brotherhood requires the destruction of all racial and cultural differences between people is to deny the essence of Christlike love. Nowhere in the Gospels does

Christ teach that one's neighbor must become as we are before we can love him. If we cannot love our neighbor without first demanding that he becomes as we are and without first demanding that he commit racial and cultural suicide, then we do not really understand the meaning of Christlike love which involves accepting people as they are and not as we would like them to be (Rom. 5:6-11). After all, that is how God has accepted us.

The most dangerous fallacy to which the Anglo-Saxon democracies, under the levelling influence of apostate "liberal" and rationalist standards of justice, have succumbed since 1945, is that peace between nations and races can be forcibly brought about by internationalism and integration; that is to say, by destroying all local and national ties of loyalty to one's own family, locality, and nation. Yet a person is not more likely to live at peace with his foreign neighbors because he is devoid of natural ties of affection for his own family and nation. On the contrary, the good brother, the devoted father, and the loyal patriot are more likely to make friends with people of other lands than the person who hates his own family and fatherland.

Writing in the *Church Times* on February 28, 1966, Denis Shaw asked the question, "What do we mean by 'integration'?" He replied:

> It needs a lot of thought. Too often we mean that, with any luck, the strangers in our midst will in time become indistinguishable from ourselves—apart from the colour.
> We overlook centuries of a strange, wild history; miles of unruly rivers; an age-long war against nature; shadows of a lost mythology; the still-echoing thunder of the Prophet's wrath. . . .
> Integration must not mean the gradual imposition of anonymity. A country which, by implication, indifference or social pressure, requires her adopted children to become paltry parodies of her own true born is impoverishing the whole family.

Likewise, the Roman Catholic Archbishop William Whelan of Bloemfontein, South Africa, points out in his statement on race relations in his country that "The Church regards as immoral any policy aimed at levelling ethnic groups into an amorphous cosmopolitan mass. The Bishops of the United States have even gone so far as to say that these heterogenous racial and cultural groups have an innate right to exist" (*Times*, February 20, 1964).

The Scriptures teach that permanent and lasting peace between races and nations will never be realized until the Prince of Peace returns to rule the nations of the world. In the New Testament we are given no picture of peace on earth among the nations. On the contrary, prophecies abound of the most terrible wars among the peoples of the world before the end of history and the final consummation which transcends history. The hope of peace outside of faith and trust in the Lord Jesus Christ is alien to the New Testament. The hope of an earth in which dwells righteousness and peace is bound up with the expectation of a new heaven and a new earth. The reign of absolute peace belongs to eschatology, the realm of eternal life.

In the meantime, all that the state can hope to achieve is a relative measure of justice between its various cultural and racial groupings. As far as relations within the same nation between differing racial groups are concerned, the experience of South Africa and the Southern States of the U.S.A. shows that the government is unable to bring about an absolute and total integration within the same national territory. We also learn from these examples how essential is the dependence of the political integrating activity of the state on the leading function of justice. All that the state can be expected to do is to maintain the public legal interest and justice between the differing races within its borders.

Christian justice requires that the various racial groups within a given society and their often mutually conflicting interests should be carefully balanced against each other according to the criterion of the legal public interest. Any exploitation or discrimination against one section of the community must be considered as a tyrannical exercise of power. This implies that the different cultural positions of the ethnic groups within the body politic should also be considered, though at the same time the cultural level of underdeveloped groups should be elevated as much as possible. As Whelan says, "The public authorities have an obligation to assist the cultural and racial groups in a pluralistic state in their *distinctive* development."[48]

From this truly Christian standpoint the state must protect the freedom of cultural or racial minorities to develop in accordance with their own spiritual aspirations and values but not at the expense of the majority.

Fundamentally the question of the so-called "integration" or "segregation" of races or cultural minorities within the same nation involves the deeper question of the nature and purpose of the various structures of human society and of their relation to each other and to the Kingdom of God. It also involves the relationship of the individual to the state. Does the individual obtain his right to exist from the state as Communists suppose, or does he obtain his right to live from God as the Bible teaches? God's Word teaches that the individual's right to live comes as a gift from God, and that the various spheres of society such as the family, business, church, etc., do *not* owe their origin, existence, or structural principle to the state. They have an inner principle and cultural task all their own entrusted to them by God. Upon this sphere sovereignty given to them by God the state may not infringe. For this reason it is presumptuous and immoral for the state to dictate to its citizens how or where they shall work, eat, or play. The social basis of all law implies the competence of the legislator, but this competence must be limited by the proper correlation of all the other institutions and associations of human society which may not be infringed by the supposed absolute competence of the state. The individual does not enjoy an absolute legal competence or absolute rights, but neither does the state enjoy absolute sovereign rights in deciding, for example, on behalf of parents which school their children shall attend and which they shall not.

Integrationists are infringing upon the God-given responsibility of parents to decide which school they shall attend. The state as such has no business to interfere in the education of one's children, since children are born by reason of the natural powers of reproduction and not because of permission to procreate by the state. For this reason parents have the right to decide the kind of education their children shall receive (Deut. 6:4-9; Eph. 6:1ff.). It is contrary to God's cultural mandate to bring up their own children in accordance with their own values and custom, for the state to use schools for the political purpose of integration.

The true Christian gladly accepts all the diversities and differences which abound in the creation and in society, realizing that all these have been created after their own kind (Gen. 1:24-31) and yet they all find their ultimate unity in the sovereign will of the Creator. Rationalists and collectivists in both church and state, on the other hand, find such diversities between races, churches, and other human associations intolerable, since they are forced by their own apostasy from the Living God to find the meaning and purpose of life within the narrowed down horizons of the material universe. Since it is only within the phenomenal world that perfection can be attained, unity too must be achieved within the terms of this world at any cost, regardless of peoples' cherished feelings. Hence their apostate religious drive to achieve assimilation of races, churches, schools, etc., and to abolish all differences between men and women. As Robert T. Ingram well writes in *Essays on Segregation*:

> Integration is not an end in itself, but a supposed step toward the end of achieving heaven on earth. Integrationists, therefore, like all Utopians . . . are widely determined to remove from their path, all who obstruct their progress toward ultimate unity and heaven on earth.[49]

In short, they are determined to achieve unity at the expense of all human freedom and human diversity and difference. Integrationists and ecumenists have mistakenly identified the Kingdom of God with man's biological, psychological, political, and legal functions because they have absolutized these aspects of human existence, since they lack a true ordering principle in the Word of God.

The real road to peaceful relations between and within nations lies in an individual religious awakening on the part of ordinary people all over the world to the problem of getting on with other people— of forgiving and being forgiven; of being patient enough to try to understand others when we cannot like them; and above all of seeking God's grace and light whenever we feel only prejudice and malice. It does not lie along the road of forcible integration, or forcible segregation which an African colored bishop has well said will only land us all in Hell.

Instead of trying to reduce the races and nations of mankind to a squalid level of equality of mass cosmopolitan misery, Christians must strive to achieve the greatest possible variety in unity and differentiation of achievement, between men, races, and peoples.

As a missionary amongst the Red Indians in the Yukon the writer observed with great sorrow that the younger generation of Indians were tending to depart more and more from their own Indian customs, culture, and language. He heard old Indian grandmothers shake their heads ruefully when they admitted that many of their grandchildren could barely speak or understand their mother tongue. He was reminded of similar observations of African grandmothers living in the former Belgian Congo, made to his own parents who worked there as missionaries just before the Second World War. Where is this awful process of the industrialization of the world going to finish? Can we expect a world of mass men all thinking the same torpid thoughts and doing the same dingy things and eating and dressing alike?[50] I hardly think that was the Creator's intention when He made us of different colors, races, and languages under heaven.

In his vision of heaven the apostle St. John did not report that he saw all differences between men and races abolished. Instead he says: "I beheld, and, lo, a great multitude, which no man could number, of all nations, and kindreds and peoples and tongues stood before the throne, and before the Lamb . . . and cried with a loud voice saying: Salvation to our God which sitteth upon the throne and unto the Lamb" (Rev. 7:9-10). It is salvation the races and peoples of mankind so desperately need today and not integration by the brute force of governments and by the brainwashing techniques of the scientific elite.

(f) Civil Disobedience and the Right to Resist Tyranny

Unwilling to work for reformation of the present deformed social order, many people, especially students, are resorting to civil disobedience and violence. The present wave of demonstrations and street riots sweeping the Western world is justified by those taking

part in them on the grounds that an individual or a group is entitled
to disobey the laws of the land if he believes them to be unjust. In
support of their argument they quote with approval Henry Thoreau's essay *On the Duty of Civil Disobedience*. Thoreau had written
his essay after being imprisoned in Concord jail for refusal to pay
his taxes because he objected to the Mexican War. The war, to
Thoreau, was a hateful thing—stupid and unjust, waged for the extension of the obscene system of Negro slavery. Under the stress of
his experience in prison Thoreau was driven to examine the whole
theory of the relation of the individual to the state. As a man who
would not compromise with his conscience, he reacted to the government's resort to coercion over him by applying the counter
principle of passive resistance and civil disobedience. In the event
of a clash between political expediency and the higher moral law,
Thoreau argued that it is the duty of the individual citizen to obey
his conscience rather than the state. He went even further, and asserted the doctrine of the individual contract, which in turn implied
the doctrine of individual nullification: "No government," he said,
"can have any pure right over my person or property but what I con-
cede to it. . . . The only obligation which I have a right to assume, is
to do at any time what I think right." According to Thoreau, the
individual is the source of all moral, legal, and political obligation in
society, from which all civil power and authority are derived.[51]

For Martin Luther King, civil disobedience meant the same thing.
In his "Letter from Birmingham Jail," published in his book, *Why
We Can't Wait*, King wrote: "One may well ask, 'How can you advocate breaking some of the laws and obeying others?' I would be
the first to advocate obeying just laws. One has not only a legal but
a moral responsibility to obey just laws. Conversely, one has a
moral responsibility to disobey unjust laws. . . . A just law is a man-
made code that squares with the moral law or law of God. An unjust law is a code that is out of harmony with the moral law." [52]

For King a good end may justify the resort to evil means. "It is
right to break laws if we think that they are unfair and can get pub-
licity for a good cause by doing so." Upon this basis King advocated
disobedience of the segregation ordinances of various American

states. Because they are morally wrong they should not be obeyed. In pursuit of this policy King met his tragic death, thereby proving that civil disobedience invites a counter appeal to force, and if indulged in by everyone will soon reduce society to anarchy. While approving of King's great personal courage and his Christian stand for justice, we must reject his appeal to violence. The means one adopts to achieve a given end will always determine the nature of the end achieved. King allowed himself to be used by groups in society who exploited him for their own evil ends. Let his terrible fate be a warning from the Lord not to follow his example of playing with fire from Hell. At the same time, let us continue the struggle for justice in race relations for which he gave his life, using more Christlike methods to attain the same end for which he struggled. *It is for reformation of society that we must work, not for revolution.*

Ever since the French Revolution proclaimed the revolutionary doctrine of popular sovereignty instead of God's sovereignty summed up in the confession "no God no master," the crucial distinction between *power* and *authority* has been blurred or lost. Frightful tensions and rifts in society are bound to develop whenever the state or the general will of the majority or the party claims to be sovereign, that is, the source of both authority and power in society. Authority over men can be vested only in Almighty God, who allocates to the various separate spheres of society their own respective functions of power. All governmental authority has a divine and not a human origin which alone can keep it within bounds. What is true of governmental authority is also true of all other kinds of authority.

The police do not have authority because they carry weapons of self-defense, but because they exist to uphold the majesty of the law and maintain peace and order in society. The father does not have authority because he is bigger than his child, but because God has appointed him to that office in creation. Nor does the teacher exercise authority over his pupils because he is stronger than they, but because he acts in the place of the parents when they are at school. The authority of the government over its citizens, of parents over their children, of employers over their workers, is directly derived in each case from God alone. As the Lord told Moses from the midst of the bush that burned but was not consumed, "I AM THAT I AM" (Exod. 3:14), the source of all that exists outside himself. Apart from Him nothing could exist.

As sovereign Lord of His own creation the Lord God has only delegated to each sphere of society the authority necessary for it to carry out its own proper function. Thus God has delegated some of His authority to husbands and commanded that wives must obey them (Eph. 5:22). He has also delegated some of his authority to parents and commanded children to obey them (Exod. 20:12; Eph. 6:1).

Likewise, God has delegated to the state the power of the sword of justice so that it may restrain the evil doer. For this reason Paul teaches in the Epistle to the Romans, "Let every soul be subject unto the higher powers. For there is no power but of God" (Rom. 13:1). In other words, all civil authority has its origin in God, whether it realizes the fact or not. Of the state Dooyeweerd writes:

In the divine structural principle of this societal relationship the power of the sword is unbreakably bound up with the typical end-function of the state, that is, the maintenance of a public jural community of rulers and subjects. All the intrinsic matters of state ought to be directed by this juridical function. . . . A state where the power of the sword becomes an end in itself degenerates into an organized band of highwaymen, as Augustine and Calvin remarked.

A public community of law which, as end function, qualifies the state, is utterly different from the internal jural community of other societal relationships, such as family, school or church. In all of these the internal jural community is directed by the peculiar end function of the relationship concerned. . . .

Only in the case of the state does the jural community function as the end function, but always founded upon the territorial organization of the power of the sword. The internal community of law of the state is a community of jural government, where the government, as servant of God, does not carry the sword in vain. The government may, in accordance with the state's inner law of life, never allow itself to be led by any other point of reference than that of justice. But here is no talk of a private community of law, as in other societal relationships, but a public one, subject to the jural principle of the common good. And exactly here, in the understanding of the principle of the common good the difference between Christian and pagan or humanistic ideas of the state becomes clearly evident.[53]

Dooyeweerd then explains in *The Christian Idea of the State* that this difference between the Christian and the apostate humanist idea of the state lies in the fact that the former Christian idea "has principially broken with any absolutization of either state or individual. It alone can grasp the principle of the common good as a truly jural principle of public law because it is grounded in the confession of a supra-temporal root-community of humanity in the kingdom of Jesus Christ, and because it accepts therefore the principle of sphere-sovereignty for the temporal societal bonds." [54]

It is the state as limited by God's absolute sovereignty and not to the totalitarian state of modern society that the Christian is to be obedient. Since the authority of such a limited state is derived from God and not from the will of the majority or the will of the party, God demands that we respect and obey its officers.

In this matter of obedience to governments, Peter says: "Be subject to every ordinance of man for the Lord's sake, whether to the king as supreme or unto governors, as sent by him (I Peter 2:13-14). Civil obedience to the limited state under God is thus a fundamental moral obligation laid upon every citizen of the land, and to disobey the civil authority is to disobey God. The civil authorities are "holy servants" of God whether they believe in God or not, since they have been instituted to hold in check man's sinful tendencies. In terms of this plain teaching of Scripture, civil disobedience is revealed as a policy of the anti-Christ. Without obedience to the law-enforcing functions of government, society must inevitably collapse. For God's Word that which defines the anti-Christ, the man of sin, the godless man is precisely his will to live without any law at all (II Thess. 2:3-8).

Yet the Bible itself also teaches that there is a time to disobey the government. The divine right of kings and rulers is always qualified by that divine right to the obedience of men's hearts which is unlimited, final, and absolute. In the last analysis we must always obey God rather than the governmental, parental, or economic authority when it commands us to sin. As Peter says, "We ought to obey God rather than men" (Acts 5:29).

For example, if a drunken father tried to force his son to sin, then it would be the child's duty to disobey. Or if the government commands the Christian to sin, he must refuse to obey. When Shadrach, Meshach, and Abed-nego were commanded by King Nebuchadnezzar to fall down and worship the golden image they rightly refused. With marvellous courage they told the king, "Be it known unto thee that we will not serve thy gods, nor worship the golden image which thou hast set" (Dan. 3:18). As a result they were cast into the fiery furnace, from which God miraculously delivered them.

How terrifying is such power to the mere individual. It is usually arrayed in terrifying conformity, as in Babylon of old. All have to think the same thoughts and to act in the same way most favorable to the dictator of the day. Thus in the days of King Nebuchadnezzar, all the princes, the governors, the captains, the judges, the treasurers, and the counsellors had to conform; all except three young men who refused to fall down and worship the golden image.

In this clash between the powers of heaven and earth it is obvious that the earthly king had no idea of power except that of brute force. He, knowing his strength in this direction, found it most disturbing that there should be anyone who would attempt to resist him. This was a new experience for King Nebuchadnezzar. He could not believe his ears when it was reported to him. When finally he did understand he could not conceal the rage that welled up within him. Such opposition could not be tolerated. It must be crushed, burnt out, and destroyed.

Even so have the mighty spoken throughout all history. In a fit of rage the emperor Nero burnt thousands of Christians in the gardens of his palace. Ivan the Terrible murdered whole families to gratify his rage.

John Calvin made resistance to unjust princes not only permissible but an absolute obligation, but only when undertaken by duly constituted representatives of the people. While deprecating in the strongest terms the right of resistance on the part of "private persons," he exhorted municipal authorities, estates-general, and parliaments to call rulers to account as part of their vocation as God's magistrates. In some countries or states, he taught, there have existed magistrates specially instituted to restrain the doings of the chief magistrate. Such were certain officials of Athens, Sparta, and Rome, and such, he declared, "are possibly, nowadays, in each kingdom the three estates assembled." [55] It would, by hypothesis, be lawful for such magistrates to resist tyrannical action and, therefore, it would be their duty to do so. Failing to do so they would betray the liberty of their people.

In a letter to the French Huguenot leader, Coligny, written in 1561, Calvin applied this principle of the duty of resistance on the part of "minor magistrates" such as members of Estates-General. He had, he said, been asked beforehand, whether in view of the oppression of the "children of God" in France, active resistance would not be justified. He had answered, he declared, that it were better that all the said children of God should perish rather than that the Gospel should be dishonored by bloodshed. But he had added that if the Princes of the blood took action to maintain their legal rights and if the Parlements of France joined with them, then indeed all good subjects might lawfully aid them in arms, in defense of their legal rights, even against the legitimate sovereign.[56] This doctrine was suited to the special needs of the Huguenots. Though they were only a minority in France and could not hope to control the Estates-General, many of them were noblemen or wealthy merchants, who held the chief magistracies and controlled the highest courts of their own provinces. Calvin's doctrine of active resistance by lesser magistrates to the sovereign or supreme magistrate justified their using their local privileges in defense of their faith. John Plamenatz in *Man and Society* comments on this doctrine as follows:

> Calvin's doctrine, slightly altered to meet the needs of the Huguenots, was at bottom only the medieval theory of resistance, as we find it in Aquinas, which asserts, not a right of individual or even even popular resistance, but a right of official or privileged resistance. According to this theory, only those who already have authority have the right to resist authority. The mere citizen or subject has no such right.[57]

The first important group of political Christians to oppose absolutism were the British refugees from the persecution of Bloody Mary in the 1550's. John Knox, Bishop Ponet, and Goodman, in particular, fled to the Continent and from there urged resistance and the deposition of England's queen. They justified Wyatt's Rebellion against Mary on both biblical and constitutional grounds, appealing to the compact between ruler and people in natural law. The Geneva Bible, with its annotations, was to disseminate these ideas widely in England. Calvin himself rather guardedly followed the current, trying to moderate the more turbulent. Goodman reported that Calvin had censured his *How Superior Powers Ought to Be Obeyed* as "somewhat harsh" to rulers, but nevertheless essentially true. And in the year in which Knox left to take part in the revolution in Scotland, Calvin brought out the last edition of the *Institutes* with the famous paragraph inculcating the duty of resistance on the part of "minor magistrates." The decade closed with declarations of constitutional rights against tyrants by the Scots Assembly and a group of the French Reformed. In the *First Blast of the Trumpet against the Monstrous Regiment of Women*, John Knox declared it was the duty of the English people to depose Mary Tudor, who was persecuting the true faith. Though her title to the throne might be good by English law, that law stood for nothing against the authority of Scripture.

In terms of this Reformed doctrine of the right to resist tyranny the lesser magistrates of the Netherlands in 1581 deposed Philip of Spain on the grounds of a broken contract in natural law and justice. Philip's attempt, through Cardinal Granvelle and the Duke of Alba, to reduce the Low Countries to the status of a Spanish province met with determined opposition among all classes of society, Roman Catholics and Protestants alike. And no wonder. The number of those who were put to death for their Reformed faith in the Netherlands alone, during the reign of Charles V, has been estimated by Sarpi in his *History of the Council of Trent* as 50,000, while Grotius put it at 100,000. At least half as many perished under King Philip II. Motley points out in *The Rise of the Dutch Republic*:

Upon the 16th of Feb. 1568, a sentence of the Holy Office condemned all the inhabitants of the Netherlands to death as heretics. From this universal doom only a few persons especially named were excepted. A proclamation of the king dated ten days later, confirmed this decree of the Inquisition and ordered it to be carried into instant execution. Three millions of people, men, women and children, were sentenced to death in three lines.[58]

The Calvinist federalism or pluralism of the consequent United Provinces became the working model of free institutions to seventeenth century Europe. Neville Figgis points out in *From Gerson to Grotius* the Dutch Republic became the pioneer of liberty in modern as distinct from medieval Europe. In the age of the Roman and Anglican absolutists, Richelieu, Bousset, and Laud, the Dutch jurist Althusius stood out as the great representative Reformed political theorist, who built a rounded political system uniting popular sovereignty with the medieval Christian principles of the inherent and inalienable natural rights of communities within the state. The social community, as it existed in the thought of Althusius, is a community of communities, an assemblage of morally integrated lesser associations and groups. Its unity does not result from being permeated with sovereign law, extending from the top through all individual components of the structure. Of the profound significance of Althusius' contribution to political and social theory Dooyeweerd writes:

> It is no accident that it was a Calvinistic thinker who broke with the universalistic conception of the State in a period in which Bodin's concept of sovereignty had introduced a new version of this universalistic view. In opposition to the entire medieval-Aristotelian tradition Althusius gave evidence of taking account of the internal structural principles of society in his theory of human symbiosis.

> It was the famous jurist, Johannes Althusius, in his *Politica*, who made the following remark: "I do not call 'members of the State,' or of the universal symbiotic community, the separate single human beings, or the families, nor even the colleges according to their being constituted in a particular private and public association, but a number of provinces and districts agreeing to form one whole by mutual conjunction and communication."

The foundation of this view, which clearly contradicted the Aristotelian teleological conception of the State's parts, is to be found in the first chapter of his work. Here he summarized his anti-universalistic standpoint with respect to the inter-structural relation between the different types of social relationships as follows: "Every type of social relationships has its proper laws peculiar to it, whereby it is ruled. And these laws are different and divergent in each kind of social relationship, according to the requirement of the inner nature of each of them." This utterance may be considered the first modern formulation of the principle of internal sphere-sovereignty in the societal relationships.[59]

Summing up, we may claim that legal wrongs must be redressed by legal means. In an "open society" resort must always be made to reasoned discussion of grievances. Such legal processes may be slow, but they are still available, and any attempt to by-pass them only creates contempt for law, and, if pushed to excess, can bring about the collapse of society itself when all rights would go by the board. *The present type of civil disobedience is a far cry from the right to resist tyranny of the lesser magistrates taught by our great Reformed forebears.*

The real answer to the terrible problems now facing America is not revolution by an appeal to the guns of men but reformation by the Word of God. Let Christians work to elect men into the lesser and higher offices of government who will abide by God's great ordinances for human society, especially the great principle of sphere sovereignty. The answer to the growing bureaucratization and centralization of power in all Western states is not civil disobedience but associative pluralism which will restore to the various spheres of society their divinely given power and authority to carry out the tasks for which they were created by God himself.

Unless the nations return to obedience to God's structural principles and norms for society in all spheres they too will undergo His judgment just as the Roman, Babylonian, and Egyptian empires did in the past. It is by obedience to God's laws, not by civil disobedience to "the powers that be," that we shall be saved from the dreadful consequences of human sinfulness of which racial prejudice and discrimination are only the symptoms. To get rid of the evils which afflict our lands it is not sufficient to combat its outward symptoms, but to remove the germ. That germ is the modern belief that man's reason and will, rather than God's, are supreme in the universe. The only lasting antidote to man's inhumanity to man is belief in God as man's Creator and in the Lord Jesus Christ as his Savior.

CHAPTER NINE NOTES

1. Bernard Zylstra, *Challenge and Response* (C.L.A.C., 1960), p. 20.
2. Dooyeweerd, *op. cit.*, Vol. III, p. 177.
3. *Ibid.*
4. Bob Goudzwaard, *op. cit.*, p. 3.
5. J. N. Figgis, *Churches in the Modern State* (Cambridge, 1928), p. 58.
   Cf. M. B. Reckitt, *Maurice to Temple* (Faber & Faber, London, 1947). Bernard Zylstra, *From Pluralism to Collectivism* (Van Gorcum, 1968), p. 18ff. Of the quotation from Figgis we have just made he writes:
   "In this quotation one detects Figgis' intuitive awareness of the plurality and variety of the social structures. . . . He explicitly jumps from 'matters merely of legal theory' to 'the practical problem of securing reasonable liberty for the Church as a self-developing body.' He is thus clearly interested in the problem of freedom. . . . His defense of freedom is placed in this pluralist framework. 'More and more,' he asserted, 'it is clear that the mere individual's freedom against an omnipotent state may be no better than slavery; more and more it is evident that the real question of freedom in our day is the freedom of smaller unions to live within the whole.' "
6. F. W. Maitland, *Introduction to the Political Theories of the Middle Ages* (Cambridge, 1905), p. 100.
7. *Ibid.*, p. 99.
8. Quoted in C. K. Allen, *Law in the Making* (Oxford University Press, 1958), p. 92.
   Cf. N. Micklem, *Law and the Laws* (Sweet and Maxwell, London, 1952), p. 103ff, where he writes:
   Gierke's central thought of the reality of corporate personality, is both a political and a juristic notion which has its exact parallel in the theological conception that the Church is not an organization but an organism. On the political side this notion is patently of a totalitarian interpretation; indeed, we are bound either to say that the State is the only corporate organism or to admit a delirious hierarchy of super-personalities beyond the dream of traditional mythologies. . . . If for a generation we could drop the metaphor of the Church as the Body of Christ and could replace it with the metaphor of the Body of Christ, our theology might assume a soberer colour. There has grown up a mythology of the Church to counterbalance the mythologies of the totalitarian States. We go astray alike in

politics and in theology, when we forget that all human associations, such as a nation, a church, a university, a golf-club, a musical society or an international fellowship, are relations between men, not substantial essences.

9. Dooyeweerd, *New Critique*, Vol. III, p. 245.
10. *Ibid.*, p. 247.
11. Brunner, *op. cit.*, p. 77ff.
12. Dooyeweerd, *op. cit.*, Vol. III, p. 576.
13. Eric Lipson, *Economic History of England*, Vol. III, p. 249.
    Harold Underwood Faulkner, *American Economic History* (Harper, New York, 1957), pp. 248ff, 458ff.
14. *Ibid.*, p. 251.
15. *Ibid.*, p. 386ff.
16. W. F. de Gaay Fortman, "Aims and Purposes of the Christian Social Movement," *Free University Quarterly* (Vol. I, No. 3, July 1951), p. 165ff.
17. *Constitution and By-Laws of the Christian Labour Association of Canada* (1058 A. Albion Road, Rexdale, Ontario, Canada), p. 1.
18. Fortman, *op. cit.*, p. 164.
19. *The Rand Formula* (Reprinted from Canadian Labour Reports, Toronto, 1946), p. 46.
20. Fortman, "Industrial Relations in the Netherlands," *Delta* (Autumn, 1960), p. 3.
21. Reverend David F. Summers, *Report Re: The Request of the Reverend E. L. H. Taylor to present the matter of the Christian Labour Association of Canada to the Ontario House of Bishops.* Presented to Bishop H. R. Hunt of Toronto Diocese in June 1962, p. 9.
22. *Canadian Labour Law Reports*, Ontario High Court of Justice, May 2, 1963.
23. *Ibid.*
24. *Ibid.*
25. Fogarty, *op. cit.*, p. 388.
26. John Petrie, *The Worker Priests* (Macmillan, New York, 1956).
    Cf. Gregor, *The Church and Industrial Society* (London, 1964).
27. Horst Symanowski, *The Christian Witness in an Industrial Society* (SCM Press, London, 1965).
    E. R. Wickham, *Encounter with Modern Society* (Lutterworth Press, London, 1965).
    Harry Antonides, *The Basis of Secular Trade Unions* (C.L.A.C., Rexdale, Ont., 1965).
28. Martin Luther King, *Chaos or Community* (Hodder & Stoughton, London, 1969), p. 175.
29. Brewton Berry, *Race and Ethnic Relations* (Houghton Mifflin Company, Boston, 1966), provides the basis for our analysis of this problem, chapters 7-12. Cf. Jean Ousset, *Country, Nation, State* (Published in English from

the French edition by the Anglo-Gaelic Civic Association at 50 Crockford Park Road, Addlestone, Weybridge, Surrey).

30. Ely Chinoy, *Society* (Random House, New York, 1967), p. 179.

31. Reverend A. R. Lewis, "Rhodesia and Christian Principles," *Greengates Parish Church Magazine*, February, 1967.

32. Berry, *op. cit.*, p. 247.

33. The Des Moines *Register*, February 6, 1969.

34. Adolf Schlatter, *The Church in the New Testament Period* (S.P.C.K., London, 1961), p. 137.

35. The *Sunday Telegraph* (London, July 30, 1967), p. 12.

36. M. Steinberg, "To Be or Not to Be a Jew," *Common Ground*, Vol. I, No. 3, Spring 1941, pp. 43-50.
Cf. M. M. Gordon, *Assimilation in American Life* (Oxford University Press, 1964). Gordon distinguishes between "cultural pluralism" and "structural pluralism."

37. James B. McKee, *Introduction to Sociology* (Holt, Rinehart & Winston, 1969), p. 318.

38. H. H. Meeter, *The Basic Ideas of Calvinism*, p. 182ff.

39. C. H. Dodd, *Christianity and the Reconciliation of the Nations* (SCM Press, 1952), p. 1.

40. B. B. Caird, *Principalities and Powers* (Clarendon Press, Oxford, 1956), p. 5. Cf. Surgit Singh's essay on "Nation and Race" in *Biblical Authority for Today* (SCM Press, London, 1951), pp. 310-322. He writes:

> The Church represents, in regard to the racial question, the "earnest" (II Cor. 1:22) of something which will find its ultimate fulfilment only in the *Eschaton*, in the age to come. This does not diminish the fact that these tensions are already overcome in the Church in a real way. . . . But in so far as Christians are members of the existing world, the distinction between races and nations are not yet overcome, just as the distinction between "male and female" still plays a real role in our lives. These distinctions do not wither away, but they are now seen in a new aspect. Their validity is limited. . . .
>
> The Bible affirms the solidarity of mankind in *sin*—not only in their common origin nor in any positive values which man certainly has as the the image of God. This solidarity in sin overshadows, so to speak, the other solidarity which is not denied, but which, for this reason, can no longer provide an adequate solution . . . this very solidarity in sin provides at the same time the common possibility of being saved through Christ. This is the real eschatological solution of our problem, as promised in the Bible (p. 319ff).

41. R. Laird Harris, "Racial Dispersion," *Journal of the American Scientific Affiliation*, Vol. 7, No. 3 (Sept., 1955), p. 52.

42. William A. Smalley, "A Christian View of Anthropology," *Modern Science and Christian Faith* (2nd ed., Van Kampen Press, Wheaton, Illinois, 1950), p. 114.

43. William Howells, *Mankind So Far* (Doubleday & Co., Inc., New York, 1948), pp. 297-298.
44. *Ibid.,* p. 299. We have omitted Howells' claim that "the Grimaldi skeletons of Europe indicate that Negroes existed in the Upper Paleolithic," because A. L. Kroeber says this can no longer be sustained. *Anthropology* (Harcourt, Brace & Co., New York, 1948), pp. 104, 114, 663.
45. *Ibid.,* p. 295.
46. Smalley, *op. cit.,* p. 116.
47. Gregory Dix, *Jew and Greek* (Dacre Press, London, 1953), p. 54. Cf. Jules Isaac, *Jesus et Israel* (Paris, 1959), and his *Genese de l' Anti-Semitisme* (Paris, 1956), for an example of modern Jewish hatred of the Church. Also Vicomte Leon de Poncins, *Judaism and the Vatican* (London, 1967).
48. Reprinted by R. Bamford, in a pamphlet at 40 Swanson View, Edinburgh, 10.
49. Robert T. Ingram, editor, *Essays on Segregation* (St. Thomas Press, P.O. Box 35096, Houston, Texas, 1960), p. 6ff.
50. G. E. Simpson and J. M. Singer, "The Sociology of Race and Ethnic Relations," *Sociology Today* (Harper, New York, 1965). These authors welcome the process of industrialization as helping to achieve assimilation.
51. Quoted in *Social and Political Philosophy*, edited by J. Somerville and R. E. Santoni (Doubleday, New York, 1963), p. 283ff.
52. Martin Luther King, *Why We Can't Wait* (Harper and Row, New York, 1966), p. 25.
53. H. Dooyeweerd, *The Christian Idea of the State* (Craig Press, Nutley, N. J., 1968), p. 41f.
54. *Ibid.,* p. 44.
55. Jean Calvin, *Institute*, edited by M. Lefrance (Geneva, 1541), p. 782.; 1559 edition, Chapter XII, p. 561.
56. Jean Calvin, *Lettres Francaises*, edited by J. Bonnet (Paris, 1854), Vol. II, p. 382.
57. John Plamenatz, *Man and Society* (Longmans, London, 1967), Vol. I, p. 59.
58. Motley, *Rise of the Dutch Republic; United Netherlands* (London, 1880), Vol. II, p. 155.
59. Dooyeweerd, *The New Critique*, Vol. III, pp. 662-663. For a brilliant treatment of this subject consult Robert A. Nisbet, *Tradition and Revolt* (New York, 1968).

Chapter Ten

RESTORING MEANING TO WORK IN MODERN SOCIETY

(a) *Recovering our Integrity as Christians*

How may Christians restore meaning to work in modern society? How can workers and employers recover the will and zest to work without which our civilization must surely soon break down?

Before Christians can hope to make any impact upon modern industrial society as the social and economic church militant, it is imperative that every Christian worker and employer recover his or her personal integrity as one of Christ's new men and women, as well as a living faith in the total authority of the living Word of God over every aspect of human life. The reason why the first Christians succeeded in turning the Roman Empire "upside down" (Acts 17:6) was because their spirits had been struck as by lightning and they proclaimed a new message of the divine reformation that had already taken place in their own lives. As the apostle Paul put it: "The old things are passed away; behold they are become new" (II Cor. 5:17). Since the early Christians had been given the meaning and purpose of human life in the life, teaching, and above all the death of Jesus Christ, they no longer had any fear in their hearts of any earthly powers. Without fear or guilt they were enabled by the Holy Spirit of the Risen Christ to confront the apostate Roman Empire with the challenge to believe in Christ and to make a fresh cultural start. Since they challenged unbelievers and exposed the bankruptcy of their pagan scientific, political, and social presuppositions about man in society, they were listened to. All this was made possible because they were gripped by the powerful living Word and Spirit of God.

The Word of God became the power of God unto salvation by giving new cultural form and shape to their lives. God's Word taught them that the root of the troubles afflicting Graeco-Roman classical culture sprang from its ancient humanism and its defective logic. Writing of this Christian counterattack upon classical humanism, Charles N. Cochrane says in *Christianity and Classical Culture*:

> The Augustan Empire . . . was merely the culmination of an effort begun centuries before in Hellas, the effort to create a world which should be safe for civilization; and, from this standpoint, such originality as the emperor (Augustus Caesar) exhibited was merely one of method. In this sense, however, his settlement may well be accepted as the last and not the least impressive undertaking of what we may venture to call "creative politics."
> The history of Graeco-Roman Christianity resolves itself largely into a criticism of that undertaking and of the ideas upon which it rested; viz. that it was possible to attain a goal of permanent security, peace, and freedom through political action, especially through submission to the "virtue and fortune" of a political leader. This notion the Christians denounced with uniform vigour and consistency. To them the state, so far from being the supreme instrument of human emancipation and perfectibility, was a straight jacket to be justified at best as "a remedy for sin." To think of it otherwise they considered the grossest of superstitions.
> The Christians traced this superstition to the acceptance of a defective logic, the logic of classical "naturalism," to which they ascribed the characteristic *vitia* of the classical world. . . . It is important to notice that their revolt was not from nature; it was from the picture of nature constructed by classical science, together with its implications for practical life. And what they demanded was a radical revision of first principles as the presupposition to an adequate cosmology and anthropology. The basis for such a revision they held to lie in the *logos* of Christ, conceived as a revelation, not of "new" truth, but of truth which was as old as the hills and as everlasting. This they accepted as an answer to the promise of illumination and power extended to mankind and thus, the basis for a new physics, a new ethic and, above all, a new logic, the logic of human progress. In Christ, therefore, they claimed to possess a principle of understanding superior to anything existing in the classical world. By this claim they were prepared to stand or fall.[1]

The early Christians believed that the Scriptures alone can provide us with a true knowledge of God, of one's own selfhood, and of the great law-structures of God's creation. Such knowledge can be worked only by the Holy Spirit through the operation of God's Word upon the human heart, as the religious root and center of human existence. The Scriptures thus give us knowledge of God, knowledge of each other as persons created in His image, and knowledge of nature. Though the Bible does not give us exhaustive truth about reality, it does give us "true truth." The Word of God is the divine spiritual power which regenerates our hearts and therefore reforms our minds. It is the central ordering principle of human life and the key to all true knowledge of reality and hence the foundation of a truly human, culture economy, and society. God's Word alone can provide us with a unified field of knowledge upon which to base our theoretical and practical lives. In this way alone we obtain the truth about God, the truth about man, and the truth about nature. Thus on the basis of Scripture, while we do not have exhaustive and complete knowledge, we have true and unified knowledge. Any dualism between form and matter, between nature and grace, between nature and freedom is in principle entirely excluded. Hendrik Hart writes in *The Challenge of Our Ag*e of God's Word as follows:

> The uniqueness of the Bible is that it is an *authoritatively* inspired inscripturation of God's Word-revelation to his people. These are the scriptures which cannot be broken, which are cited by themselves as authoritative. . . . They are not themselves to be believed *in*, but to be believed. We believe in God, in His Word, *according* to the Scriptures. They are not themselves divine, though divinely inspired. The clue to the Scriptures, therefore, is that they point beyond themselves, that they need to be opened. When the Scriptures are opened to us by the Spirit of the Word, it is the Word in its directive power that comes to us in its restorative order.
>
> What we have to avoid at all cost, if biblical living is to be meaningful living, is on the one hand to undermine the full *authority* of the Bible and on the other hand to *reduce* the Word of God to a set of truths, a *collection* of infallible *propositions*. For both stand in the way of God's Word-revelation in the

Scripture. . . . Having seen the Bible primarily as the authoritative revelation of God's Word, we can also understand why it is called the canon. . . . For a canon is an authoritative rule. It has the meaning in which Paul uses it in his letter to the Galatians: Neither circumcision nor uncircumcision count but a *new creation*. Peace and mercy will be with those who walk according to this rule, this *canon of the new creation*. This is what we have in the Bible, the canon of the new creation.[2]

It is because the early Christians were gripped by this canon of the new creation that they were enabled by the Risen Christ in the power of His Holy Spirit to change the spiritual direction of the society in which they lived. This same canon alone can provide us modern Christians with the spiritual dynamic necessary to reform apostate modern industry and society. Only by returning to this canon or yardstick can we hope to rebuild modern industrial society upon a truly God-centered basis. Except the Lord build our industry we labor in vain that build. Thus the question facing us is this: Does industry today reflect biblical principles of economics and of labor relations, or purely man-centered ideas of the nature and the purpose of the economic system? Are the solutions proposed for industrial relations in harmony with God's law for human work?

The true Christian will surely be guided more in his political, social, and economic activities by a biblical motivation and an evangelical criterion of value than by a secular humanist, socialist, or capitalistic one. A person can no more avoid being religiously committed in his political and social behavior than he can avoid breathing the air around him. If he is not consciously being directed in his behavior by a Christian motivation, then he will be directed by a humanistic, communistic, or materialistic motivation, whether he is conscious of the fact or not, and whether he admits it or not.

If the Christian worker or employer really acknowledges that God rather than man or the state or the party or the dollar or the union or the bank is sovereign in this universe, then he will surely seek with all his might and main to establish God's sovereignty and dominion over every aspect of his life, political, social, economic, and industrial as well as private. God cannot be shut up within the walls of our church buildings. Do the Christian neutralists and pietists really believe that Jehovah God has abandoned the world outside the Church to Satan and the powers of darkness? If they do, they are no longer Christians but dualists, who in effect proclaim that God is not sovereign in His own cosmos. The consistent Christian believes that God's sovereignty and supremacy are at work in the life of that unbaptized world outside the Church by reason of the Lord's common grace, and for that reason the child of God, redeemed by Christ from the power and guilt of sin, cannot and must not summarily withdraw from that life in the world without committing treason against Christ the King and thus denying the Redeemer of His crown rights over the whole of His creation (John 1:1-11). If the Lord God is at work in that unregenerate world by means of his temporal conserving and restraining common grace, then the Christian's hand, too, must be put to the plow in that world in order that there also, as well as within the circle of the faithful few, the name of the Lord may ever be glorified.

If God is supreme and sovereign, His divine norms and standards of justice, truth, goodness, holiness, and love must have the final control and motivation in everything the Christian thinks, wills, and does. These norms rather than those of an apostate political, legal, social, and economic science must become the directives by which the Christian is guided by God the Holy Ghost as a citizen, as a worker, as a scientist, as a teacher, as an employer, as an artist, and as a parent; and they ALONE must constantly enlighten us in solving the problems with which we are faced in ALL areas of life.

The apostle Paul teaches that God the Father in Heaven has entrusted all power and authority upon earth to His Son through whom He now rules all things (I Cor. 15:24; Phil. 2:1-10). The risen and ascended Christ has been entrusted by the Heavenly Father with the great task of transforming not only individual lives but all cultural, legal, political, scientific, economic, and industrial life. As Lord of history and of space and time, Jesus Christ can be satisfied with nothing less than the Christian reformation and organization of human society as a whole, and it therefore becomes the bounden duty and glorious privilege and task for all Christians as Christ's Body in the world to struggle for a condition of modern society and industry which will give the maximum of opportunity for others as well as for Christians to live the full, free, and abundant life which our Lord promised (John 10:10) and to make sure that Christians are never controlled by an apostate and rebellious world, but that they direct and control that world in the strength and in the power of their sovereign God. Did not our Lord say on the Mount of Ascension, "All power is given unto me in heaven and in earth" (Matt. 28:18)?

The Word of God teaches us that our life on this planet in its integral wholeness is the service of either the one true God or of various idols and absolutizations of one or more aspects of reality. Thus the Christian's social and industrial life is one aspect of our single hearted service of the Lord. The Christian cannot avoid the duty of reforming human culture and industry after the new pattern of human relationships revealed in God's Word. All human power is derived from God, and it is the Christian's duty to use power in the service of God's Kingdom. The horror of power formation for the sake of the fulfillment of the Christian's task in the cultural development of mankind is, consequently, unscriptural. The Church itself is historically founded in power over men by means of the organized service of the Word and the Sacraments. Doubtless every power given in the hands of man implies a serious risk of abuse. But this state of affairs can only accentuate its normative meaning; it can never justify the opinion held by so many Christian pietists that power in itself is evil. The question neutralists such as Karl Barth fail to ask is this: to what ends will power in fact be used? for used it will be. Either political and economic power will be used in the service of Jesus Christ, or it will inevitably be used in the service of some idol and false god.

If the kingship of Christ is real and true, and if it is true that at our baptism we promised to fight against "the world, the flesh and the devil," ought there not be some evidence of this warfare that is going on? To restrict this warfare to the arena of the soul, to the conflict within, is certainly an unwarranted assumption made by far too many Anglo-Saxon Christians today. And, furthermore, to argue that this conflict between the two kingdoms comes to expression fully only in the individual Christian's witness and personal evangelism is an illegitimate conclusion drawn by far too many Christian pietists today. In the great and terrible warfare presently going on between Heaven and Hell and between God and Satan, the forces of darkness and of the Evil One are well organized in their struggle against God and His Christ, and not just in countries behind the Iron and Bamboo Curtains. Most modern Anglo-American-Canadian institutions and organizations that claim to be neutral—e.g., the state schools, the labor organizations, the banking houses, and great business corporations—are by that very reason and token *implicitly* if not explicitly denying Christ's claim of absolute lordship over all things. As such these institutions and organizations are serving the cause of the Anti-Christ, even if they are doing so unconsciously. To deny this is either wilful blindness or woeful ignorance of Satan's strategy and devices and of the Lord's claims and demands for surrender to His sovereignty.

If Christ is truly our King, then we His modern subjects must acknowledge that sovereignty, not only in the church building, but in the field of labor relations, education, business, banking and finance, medicine and law, communications, and government. As long as we remain in the body of our earthly flesh we are called to be the Church Militant. Only in the hereafter are we promised the rest from strife of all the saints who from their labors rest. Let us rise up and engage in battle against all the ungodly hosts presently opposed to Jehovah God and His Christ, and let us become properly organized as the Lord's mighty army instead of as a pietistic rabble.

The Christian's economic task must be concerned with the reformation of his nation's industrial and social life as an aspect of the integral renewal of our whole way of life in obedience to God's new law for human existence revealed in the Person and work of Jesus Christ. For this reason we must never think of our economic and social task as Christian workers in terms of some one particular question of this or that particular or economic issue, e.g., nationalization versus private enterprise. Christian economics and politics are eco-

nomics and politics that are based upon divinely revealed principles
of God's Word; motivated and directed by the principle of Jehovah's sovereignty over the whole of life. Christian economics and
a Christian doctrine of work take their origin in the Christian's
recognition of the total sovereignty of the Lord Jesus over the
whole of life.

For this reason it should be clear why no Christian can be satisfied
with merely voting for a labor leader in a trade union who happens
himself to be a Christian. Many English and American Christians
seem to suppose that they have done their Christian duty in a union
election when they have voted for a Christian candidate regardless
of whether or not the trade union's platform or constitution openly
acknowledges the sovereignty of Christ over its affairs. Does Mr.
Cousins or Mr. Meany or Mr. Reuther accept God's sovereignty
over British or American industry or do they trust in their own reason,
planning, and scientific methods? Does Mr. George Woodcock or
James Meany really make the Word of God the ordering principle
of his collective bargaining agreement? If the answer in both cases
is in the negative, then I do not see how any Christian worker
could vote for them, since his duty as a Christian worker requires
that he shall only support that labor union or trade association which
really seeks to apply the will of the Lord as revealed in the Holy
Scriptures in the economic and social spheres of human life.

Our glorious privilege as Christian workers is to bring to our
workshop, industry, shop, or business the blessing of Christ's redemptive concern for the world. Such Christian economic and social
action will be genuinely Christian only if it is an activity of service.
For this reason it must never be a camouflaged effort to further
merely special denominational or ecclesiastical interests. It must be
for the good of the whole economic and social body. Christian economic and social action will thus seek reform in Parliament and the
Congress, in industry and the labor unions, in the farms and the
schools so that there may come an acknowledgement of the good
and holy ordinances of the Lord in all spheres of society. Only in
this way may we expect to receive the blessings that follow obedience to God's holy ways.

(b) *The Biblical Understanding of Work in God's World*

It is plain that a wholehearted acceptance of the biblical view of man as a person created in God's image and for God's service, finding the fulfilment and satisfaction of his life relations with other persons, would have a far-reaching effect upont the conduct of modern industry. It would make it impossible to treat men solely or mainly as anonymous interchangeable units in a mechanical industrial process. It may be necessary so to treat them in certain contexts, but this would not matter if such treatment were merely incidental to a relationship in which they are regarded fundamentally as human beings. It must surely make all the difference in the way in which industry is run whether the underlying assumption is that the primary purpose is maximum production and profits, to which human beings must be subordinated and if necessary sacrificed; or that man in community is the central reality. In the latter an industrial undertaking is an association of persons cooperating in a common enterprise for the common good, in which responsibility is shared according to the capacity of each, and each is allowed his say in matters in which his experience and skill entitles him to express a judgment.

As a result of this view of man as created in God's image and for community with his fellow men, work is not looked upon in the Bible as constituting a problem. "Man goeth forth unto his work, and to his labour until the evening" (Ps. 104:23). In these words the psalmist of old takes human labor for granted as part of the natural and normal lot of mankind. That man should work for his daily bread is as much a part of the regular order of things as that the sun should rise or that lions should hunt. The Word of God does not consider that work is degrading. Unlike the ancient Greeks, who thought that working for one's living was beneath the dignity of a gentleman, the Hebrews looked upon daily work as a part of the Lord's ordering of the world, and no man was exempt from it, not even the king (I Sam. 11:5).

While Hebrew workers were often slaves, their status as such was not dishonorable, nor were their conditions of service irksome or degrading; they were often the trusted and responsible managers of their lord's household affairs or business interests. It was expected that workers would be honorably treated by their masters; the Book of the Covenant, in fact, expressly lays down directions for the treatment of Hebrew slaves. Unlike the situation in contemporary heathen polytheistic societies such as ancient Egypt and Babylon, every Hebrew worker was considered to be a legal person in his own right. As a social order grounded in God's goodness and love, Israel's primary concern was to reflect Jehovah's justice within her borders. Employers were to treat their workmen justly because the Lord was just, and because they who worshiped Him must be just. Each Israelite enjoyed his or her own rightful portion or position within the Covenant established between the Lord and Israel. The king, the priest, the firstborn, the worker, the wife, and the maid each had his *mish*p*at* or "justice," that is, a rightful and privileged place within the covenant. David gained a *mish*p*at* in the covenant by his privileged position as king, but the prophet Nathan warned him that he was uncovenanting himself by his breaking of Uriah's justice by stealing his wife Bathsheba. Everyone in Israel had a justice in the covenant; or in other words, everyone was supposed to occupy a definite status within the covenant structure of Israelite society involving both rights and obligations. Each had his *mish*p*at* to be faithfully fulfilled, secured against aggression, and restored when it was damaged. As a result of this concern for upholding justice and reflecting God's righteousness within her borders, the principle of the equality before the law of all citizens was established in Israel for the first time in human history. Unlike pagan Egyptian and Mesopotamian societies, in which a system of class legislation was in force which judged an offense quite differently according to whether it involved a royal official, a priest, or a slave, all Israelites were equal before the Covenant Law of Almighty God. As Walther Eichrodt well says:

> In this law God himself speaks to His people, and in His sight the poor man is as precious as the rich one, the member of a small tribe or of a despised family is worth just as much as the representative of an influential family or the bearer of a high office.[3]

Unlike surrounding heathen societies, capital punishment ceased to be inflicted in Israel for crimes affecting property, e.g., theft, because it was felt that the life even of a thief is worth more than the richest possessions. For the same good reason we seek in vain in the laws of ancient Israel for any sort of punishment by mutilation, by cutting off the nose or ears or like cruelties, which were often perpetrated in ancient times in the name of justice upon innocent workmen. In Israel's legal code the master of a slave pays dearly for such harm occasioned by bodily maltreatment by having to set the slave free; and the murderer of a slave "shall himself be surely put to death" (Exod. 21:12). Writing of this legal code Eichrodt says: "If we compare this with the almost unlimited power of the owner over his slave through the rest of the ancient world, then we may trace this encroachment on an otherwise unquestioned privilege to the power of the idea of the person." [4]

From another angle clear light is cast on this moral personalism of Israel's labor legislation. This may be seen in the provision made for the poor, the needy, the outcast, and the stranger within the gates. Thus the widows, orphans, and strangers, who cannot assert their rights before the law, partly because of their sex, partly on account of their youth or social insignificance, are all protected by law. In the Book of the Covenant (Ex. 21-24) it is the judge himself who is called to provide such protection. "Ye shall not afflict any widow, or fatherless child. If thou shalt afflict them in any wise, and they cry unto me, my wrath shall wax hot and I will kill you with the sword." The anger of Israel's prophets was especially aroused by the ill-treatment of Hebrew workers, especially failure to render to them their due wages. Thus Jeremiah says: "Woe unto him . . . that useth his neighbor's services without wages, and giveth him not for his work" (22:13). Protected by religious sanctions, the prophets of Israel were a reforming political force which has never been surpassed and perhaps never equalled in subsequent world-history. As direct spokesmen or heralds of the living God, they created an extraordinary atmosphere of social and political reform entirely unknown in ancient Near Eastern polytheism.

Thanks to their efforts the Lord's justice, goodness, love, and grace made themselves felt in Israel's legal and political ordering of society. For the first time in the history of mankind, workers enjoyed the protection of the rule of law, and they could expect to be treated fairly by their employers; for the equality of all the members of the nation of Israel before the Lord God, who is no respecter of persons, demanded and obtained the protection of the freedom and the security of all citizens. Such labor legislation was entirely the outcome of the Israelite faith in the sovereign lordship of the living God, who as Creator and Redeemer has chosen a people of His own, and who demands that their outer life, economic, political, and social, no less than their inward life, personal and private, should be shaped in accordance with His declared law and purpose for man in society.

Summing up, we may say that in the Bible no stigma is attached to being a worker; on the contrary, work is not looked upon as a necessary drudgery for the purpose of making a living, but as a way of life in which the nature of man should find its proper exercise and delight, and so fulfil itself to the glory of the Lord. Work is in fact thought of as a creative activity undertaken for the love of the work itself; and because man is made in God's image, he should make things for the sake of doing well a thing that is worth doing. To do one's appointed work well is to put oneself into the state in which one may receive God's blessing. Happy is the man, says the psalmist, whose labor is blessed by God, and wretched is the man, declares Isaiah, whose work is not blessed and whose labor is in vain (Ps. 128:2; Isa. 65:23). For the men of the Bible, then, work is a God-appointed "office" and service rendered by man to his Creator.

Since to labor is the common lot of mankind, it is important that men should accept it without complaining and so fulfil with cheerful obedience God's intention for man. "Hate not the laborious work, neither husbandry, which the most High hath ordained" (Ecclesiasticus 7:15 [Apocrypha]). The basic assumption of the biblical viewpoint is that work is a divine *ordinance* for man's life on earth. As such it falls within the sphere of *law* and of God's requirement for man. Work, that is to say, is a part of the divinely ordained *structure* of the world of human nature.

In his study, *The Biblical Doctrine of Work*, the Dean of York, the Very Reverend Alan Richardson, points out that the Decalogue takes work so much for granted that it commands man to rest from labor on the seventh day because it is assumed he will have worked the other six days of the week. He says:

> The very fact that the Fourth Commandment of the Decalogue is an injunction to rest from labour gives the clearest possible indication of the biblical point of view—that man is by his very nature a worker. All through the Scriptures work is regarded as a divine ordinance for human life . . . as something given by way of what we today might perhaps speak of as "natural law"; man is made that not only can he not satisfy his material needs without working but also he cannot satisfy his spiritual needs, or fulfil his function as a human being.[5]

Human work is thought of by the psalmist (Ps. 146) as man's best way of praising Jehovah.

Work is not something optional to men; it is something built into human nature, a command of the Lord laid upon every man. That is why without work a man soon deteriorates. Whether it be forced old age retirement, prolonged unemployment, or idleness and sloth, lack of work soon breaks a man into doddering pieces and no self is left to respect. This is because work is peculiarly inherent to being a man.

The Fall of Man and the invasion of God's creation by Satan and sin did not obliterate this God-given structuration of man as worker; he remains a worker even though his work now comes under the curse. Under the domination of sin work becomes labor, troublesome, tiring, frustrating under the punishing curse of weeds and sweat, sorrow and other demonic forces and influences. Outside Paradise man remains a worker, but his work is radically deformed, prone to vanity, a betrayal of his lordship over the world under the sovereign God of the Scriptures.

As a result of man's fall into sin, his cultural task and his daily work become doubly difficult. Whereas before Satan penetrated God's creation there was nothing to hinder man in his cultural task, today the earth is cursed (Gen. 3:17). The thorns and the thistles of which the Book of Beginnings speaks are types of the numberless distorting forces at work in nature which were not there originally. Instead of all things working harmoniously together, we now have soil erosion, deforestation, hunger, famine, fire, and flood.

Worse still, man's heart has itself become corrupted and God's image defaced and ruined and as a result man no longer reflects the image of God, but that of whatever false god he now chooses to worship.

Instead of serving and loving God and his neighbor, man now uses his science and technology and social institutions to exploit God's creation and his fellow man to his own selfish advantage. Again, sin has disrupted man's social life. The task which organized society must fulfil in culture by united action is hampered and often destroyed by innumerable conflicts between men, social classes, races, and nations. What one man builds up by patient statesmanship another tears down. Mankind, since sin corrupted human nature, is working at cross purposes.

In no sphere have the effects of sin been greater than in the sphere of work and of labor relations. Unless man's work in time since the Fall is redeemed by the Lord Jesus Christ, and unless it is actually and intrinsically a praising of Jehovah, work does indeed become a curse, a terrible distraction, a useless activity that ends only in the grave. As Calvin Seerveld says in his address delivered before the Christian Labour Association of Canada at Toronto on April 25, 1964:

> Those sophists who say "yet unredeemed work is not useless to civilization," have turned the truth into a lie and are ascribing what God salvages from his sinning creatures to the proud justification of man. The Bible is clear on this matter; man's work is a built-in opportunity to praise God; if his work is not genuine praise of Jehovah God borne out of faith, then it is a dead work, damned and dead. . . . Only when human work is worship of Jehovah . . . only then does work lose its human chains; only then does that narrow minded daemonic drive to get and get . . . become stilled, converted into an open-ended rush of joy. Only when Grace covers the Toil, the rising up early, the sitting up late, eating the bread you worried about providing, only under and out of Grace does work find meaning, and can a man go content.[6]

Yet, even in spite of the invasion of God's world by Satan, sin, and the forces of darkness, man is called to serve God and his neighbor. No Christian teacher did more to restore the biblical doctrine of the "calling" than Martin Luther. He rebelled against the medieval Catholic departmentalization of life by declaring that the whole "secular" realm is as much under the Lordship of Christ as the "religious." He still distinguished between "Christian" and "secular" spheres, but held that in the person of the Christian they have been conjoined. Moreover, in this world there are many offices or "callings," of which he saw three main groupings:

> Three kinds of callings are ordained by God; in them one can live with God and a clear conscience. The first is the family, the second political and secular authority, and the third the church or the ministry.[7]

We could best describe these as society, state, and church. Every Christian exists in all three at once; that is, with certain duties falling to his lot from day to day because of his relationship to other people within each sphere. It is to the Reformers that we in fact owe the crucial distinctions between church, state, and society.

Writing of this Lutheran doctrine of the "calling," Emil Brunner well says in *The Divine Imperative*:

> Nowadays the word "calling" means little more than the share of duty which falls to the lot of the individual in the whole economy of labour, in the business of earning one's living. It has become an economic conception. But even in the theological ethic it has seldom been understood in the deeper sense. How could it be otherwise when the truth of justification by faith was no longer understood? It was realized, of course, that Luther had achieved something decisive by his renewal of this conception; but men thought that the decisive element lay in the fact that through this new meaning of vocation the secular, civil, and economic forms of labour, in contrast to the ascetic monastic conception, had become hallowed once more. In so doing the very centre of Luther's ideas has been misunderstiod. Certainly this new respect for the economic, civil, and secular sphere is one of the logical results of his work. But that is only the by-product of a greater transformation.

Through the idea of the "Calling" existence in the world is revealed in its sinfulness, and at the same time it is "covered" by forgiveness, while the believer regains a good conscience with which he can take part in the action and life of the world, without feeling guilty of "compromise." To express this in a brief formula: the point is here that world pessimism is overcome, while at the same time the radical corruption of the world and the absolute character of the divine law are recognized. All that Luther cared about was to secure the *possession of a good conscience in one's Calling*, and to do away with the unsatisfactory alternatives; renunciation of the world or compromise. Therefore this idea of the Calling is full of eschatological tension and a daring which conquers the world; indeed, we might almost call it a "divine audacity"; and the reason is this: God takes over all responsibility for our action in the world which in itself is sinful, if we, on our part, will only do here and now that which the present situation demands from one who loves God and his neighbor.[8]

In this excellent statement of Brunner's we are reminded that the Bible tells us not only of God's law but also of God's grace. The glorious gospel of God in fact shows how through Jesus Christ God's law for work may be fulfilled. It is of fundamental significance that our Lord was a carpenter. In His life God's intention for man in the creation was completely fulfilled. Christians down the ages have rightly loved to dwell upon the picture of Christ as the Master-Workman of whom it was said, "He hath done all things well" (Mark 7:37). The Lord who spoke of His "yoke" as easy was also the good carpenter who knew the difference between a well-made and a badly made yoke which the oxen at the plow would have to wear. It is of the deepest significance for the biblical doctrine of work that God, when for the sake of our salvation He chose to be made man, was incarnate in a village craftsman and not in a king or statesman or general or philosopher. This was the only fitting image for the God whom the Scriptures had all along represented as himself the great and only worker in the creation. "In six days the Lord God made heaven and earth . . . and on the seventh day rested from his work" (Exod. 20:11). In this biblical doctrine of God himself the Master-Workman of the creation, we have the answer to the blasphemous Greek view that work is degrading and fit only for slaves, as well as the biblical vindication of the Christian view that work is an honorable and necessary activity of the good life. It is thus wholly appropriate that the God of our salvation, when he became man, should have been born into a working class family (John 5:17). The Almighty Lord of Heaven and earth could have been adequately revealed only by "taking the form of a servant" (Phil. 2:6). The tragedy of our age is that the working classes of the world should have turned their eyes away from the workman of Nazareth and followed the false teaching of Karl Marx.

To the world outside the Church, therefore, it is vital that Christians proclaim work as a law of God for human life, a law from which there can be no escape. At the same time, for those who have been born again from above by God's sovereign grace in Christ, work ceases to belong to the sphere of law and becomes what God intended it to be from the beginning of the world. When in Christ we are re-created and regenerated in His new creation, we are enabled to fulfil the divine intention for work, which in our own strength we could never do.

Becoming a Christian means nothing less than a complete change in the direction of one's living. It means becoming an entirely new sort of person. God's Word speaks of this as a rebirth, of "a being begotten anew," followed by a complete change in one's consciousness and subconsciousness which changes a man in the depths of his being, in what the Bible calls his heart. Only God's Spirit and sovereign grace can bring about such a fundamental change in life orientation. Once a person becomes a Christian he thinks, feels, and behaves differently from the non-Christian or unbeliever. No one saw this more clearly than Abraham Kuyper. In his *Principles of Sacred Theology* he writes:

> We speak none to emphatically, therefore, when we speak of two kinds of people. Both are human, but one is inwardly different from the other, and consequently feels a different content rising from his consciousness; thus they face the cosmos from different points of view, and are impelled by different motives. And the fact that there are now two kinds of people, occasions of necessity the fact of two kinds of human life and consciousness of life, and of two kinds of science.[9]

To which we must surely add two kinds of art, two kinds of politics, two kinds of marriage, two kinds of jurisprudence, two kinds of education, and above all, two kinds of work. For the non-Christian, work continues to remain under God's curse laid upon Adam and all his descendants: "Cursed is the ground for thy sake; and in sorrow shalt thou eat of it all the days of thy life, Thorns also and thistles shall it bring forth to thee. . . . In the sweat of thy face shalt thou eat bread, till thou return unto the ground; for out of it wast thou taken: for dust thou art, and unto dust shalt thou return" (Gen. 3:17-19). Thanks to the work of the second Adam, for the Christian work once more becomes his glad and free service. But while the Lord's curse has been alleviated by the coming of Christ, the land will always give up weeds as well as plants. Man will always have to labor to survive, although that labor will reveal itself as less of a curse as men become progressively sanctified. As the image of God becomes restored in our hearts by the indwelling spirit and presence of God's Son, so we gradually recover our God-given creativity and find joy in our daily work and find it to be good (Gen. 1:31).

But the basic truth remains: until paradise is regained and Christ returns to bring in a new heaven and a new earth, as promised in God's Word, there will always remain scarcity. This basic truth of economics is recognized by the so-called classical economists such as John Marshall, Ludwig von Mises, Roepke, Wicksteed, Robbins, Hayek, and even by such neo-classical economists as Paul A. Samuelson in his well-known textbook, *Economics*, where he writes in answer to J. K. Galbraith's thesis in *The Affluent Society* as follows:

> In *The Affluent Society*, Harvard's Galbraith has eloquently pointed out that Americans today have for the most part gone beyond the level of physiological necessity. . . . Without challenging Galbraith's thesis that the time has come to spend more on public needs and less on private needs, one may properly point out that our total product would have to become many times higher than its present level if everyone were to become able to live at the level of a moderately well-off doctor, lawyer, professor, or advertising man—to say nothing of the really well-to-do. . . . Even if the national income were divided up equally between

every man, woman and child—and it clearly cannot be—there would be only about $60 per week to go round. Therefore, while it recognizes the important germ of truth in the notion that America has become an affluent society, economics must still contend with scarcity as a basic fact of life. . . .
"Economic Scarcity" refers to the basic fact of life that there exists only a finite amount of human and nonhuman resources, which the best technical knowledge is capable of using to produce only a *limited* maximum amount of each and every good. . . .
And thus far, nowhere on the globe is the supply of goods so plentiful or the tastes of the populace so limited that every person can have more than enough of everything he might fancy.[10]

Likewise G. L. Bach recognizes in his textbook, *Economics*, that scarcity is still the basic economic problem. He writes:

Human wants are vast, perhaps infinite. Resources to fulfill these wants are limited. They are scarce. For most of the world's population—perhaps two billion people—live in abject poverty. We in the United States are rich compared to most of the world. But even we are far from rich enough to escape the ever-present need for economizing—that is, for choosing between alternatives when we would like to have both. At the individual level, few of us have all the money we want.[11]

Unfortunately this great law of scarcity in economics is not recognized by the new radical economists such as Robert Theobald in his recent work *The Guaranteed Income* and by Messers. J. N. Morgan, M. H. David, W. J. Cohen, and H. E. Brazer, who claim in *Income and Welfare in the United States*:

The U.S. has arrived at the point where poverty could be abolished easily and simply by a stroke of the pen. To raise every individual and family in the nation now below a subsistence income to the subsistence level would cost about $10 billion a year. This is less than 2 per cent of the gross national product.[12]

Regardless of the attempt of such apostate economists to climb out from under the great law of scarcity laid upon mankind as part of God's curse upon man's disobedience, it still holds good. Just as the second law of thermodynamics holds good in the world of physics and biology, so the law of scarcity holds good in the world of economics and business. It shows up constantly in the principle of diminishing returns, marginal product and utility, interest and bank rate. Like the second law of thermodynamics the law of scarcity will be suspended only when Christ shall have subdued all things unto himself, and God shall be all in all (I Cor. 15:28).

(c) *Obeying the Lord's Ordinances for Work*

What are these holy ordinances arising out of the biblical understanding of work as man's proper office and service of God?

1. The first principle is that all workers are persons created in God's holy image and, therefore, they should be treated as persons and never as functions of the economic system. Only when the workers stop feeling that they are being reduced to slaves and functions of the machines they operate may we expect to restore meaning to work.

It should by now be apparent that the principle of technical and economic rationality and present methods of so-called scientific management of men, when put into practice regardless of all other considerations, come into conflict with the real world of men and women and with their manifold and incalculable desires and purposes. The subordination of modern industry to such technical rationality and to such methods of scientific management is not a necessary and inevitable consequence of the coming of the machine. It is an act of human choice. It is within the power of men and nations to choose whether production exists for the sake of man or man exists for the sake of production. As far as God's Word is concerned, the primary purpose of industry and commerce must be to serve the community by producing goods and providing services as efficiently and profitably as possible, and no doubt technical rationality and scientific management of men may be necessary means to efficient production. But the problem which confronts industry today throughout the world is how to fulfil its primary and proper purpose without sacrificing the true ends of social living and without devaluating human labor. The workers must be given back the sense that they belong within the scheme of modern industry which their forebears previously felt in medieval and domestic industry. They must be given a share of responsibility, however humble, in that scheme. Sir George Schuster, the noted British industrialist, has expressed the conviction that "the greatest need of our modern industrial society is to make industrial employment something which *is*, and *is seen*, as an essential part of a satisfactory human life." [13] In a similar vein the late Samuel Courtauld has well and beautifully said that "the quality of the workers who leave the factory doors every evening is a more important thing than the quality of the products its delivers to the customers." [14]

Human labor must never be severed from the person of the worker. Manpower is not a mere means of production only to be considered from the point of view of greater production or profits, such as a machine, a factory building, or a patent. Labor is indissolubly connected with man, who is created in God's image and therefore called to serve and glorify his Creator in his labor. According to God's Word, man is called to have dominion over creation. The image of God is a task; man has been called upon to have dominion, and that includes both the workers and the managers.

2. Side by side with this recognition of the human dignity of the worker as created in God's image is the principle of cooperation rather than conflict in industrial life. The commandment to love one's neighbor has also its consequences for man's social and industrial life. The man who is directed by the Word of God "to love the Lord" and "his neighbor as himself" can make no compromise with the humanist doctrine of the class struggle. He must oppose those apostate socialists who would make the class struggle normative for industrial relations. Employer and worker are each other's neighbors, because they are called upon to do the same work in the same business, factory, plant, or trade. Each must have his own responsibilities. This will not be possible by way of conflict but by way of cooperation. H. Van Riessen suggests in the last chapter of *The Society of the Future* that such cooperation can take place when the industrialist keeps his workmen informed as much as possible about the running of the plant, future economic plans, and various other internal problems of organization and production.[15] Such industrial works councils have been operating successfully in the Netherlands since the end of the last war, and they go far to explain

why Dutch industry has not suffered from the wastage caused by strikes. In his article in *Delta* W. F. de Gaay Fortman on "Industrial Relations in the Netherlands" points out that:

> Any enquiry into the organizational relations between labor and management in the Netherlands will at once turn up one characteristic fact—the low number of strikes. . . . Since the liberation of the country in 1945, strikes organized by the trade unions have been infrequent. To be sure, there have been wildcat strikes spontaneous and unofficial, but even these have been less frequent than elsewhere. The Dutch worker . . . can feel at ease with the leadership given by the three large trade-union federations, which have the aim of negotiation with employers as long as possible to reach agreement. This is not to say that there is no conflict in industrial relations in the Netherlands. The struggle, however does not take place in the factories or on the docks but around what R. F. Hoxie, in his book *Trade Unionism in the United States* has termed "the mahogany table." It is carried on with the weapons of persuasion, scientific calculations, and piercing argument.[16]

What is the explanation of this happy situation existing in industrial relations in the Netherlands? The answer will surprise most Anglo-Saxon Christians who have so successfully managed to keep Jesus Christ locked up behind the doors of their churches and chapels, instead of letting Him reign in their factories and offices. Fortman answers that it is Christianity which is responsible:

> Attention must be drawn to the close links between religion and political life, religion and social life, and religion and cultural life that many in the Netherlands advocate. In virtually no other country in the world do religious and ideological movements find their expression to such a degree in corresponding organizations of employers and employees.
>
> The idea that lies at the base of the relationship is as follows: every employer's organization and every trade union starts from certain premises concerning the most desirable social order. Each of them wants to make the structure of industrial life conform to certain cherished ideals about the relation of the state to industry, about the respective responsibilities of management, capital, and labor, and about the relation of nationalized sectors of industry to private sectors. The trade unions are concerned not only with

attaining material improvements for the workers; they seek also to give them an independent, responsible place in the industrial process. Apart from this, they take an increasingly active interest in the cultural development of their members. In all this work, they start from premises of a religious or ideological nature. The patterns of society derive their forms from the philosophy of life on which they are based.

This way of thinking has led the Netherlands to the founding of Catholic and Protestant employers' organizations and trade unions alongside those which call themselves general. Given the existence of organizations with a religious base, the other, "general," organizations also tend to take on an ideological cast. In the case of the employers' organizations it is liberalism; with the trade unions, socialism or communism.

The existence of organizations split along ideological lines has come to be accepted in the Netherlands as an essential part of Dutch national life. . . . One result is that the closed shop is unknown. In labor management deliberations, the central Catholic and Protestant organizations are always drawn into the discussion along with the "general" organizations, while associations of employers or workers not federated with the central organizations also often find themselves allocated a place at the conference table. This open method has the great advantage over the closed shop system that minorities are not suppressed and that as many groups of employers and workers as possible are drawn into the consultations. If, as a consequence, negotiation sometimes becomes more difficult, from the point of view of democracy in industrial life the system has undeniable advantages.[17]

By contrast, the history of Joint Consultation given by Rodger Charles in his book on British industry, *Man, Industry and Society*, makes sorrowful reading and should cause every British Christian employer and worker in the land to bow his head in sorrowful repentance before the Lord Jesus Christ. After describing the origin and development and eventual breakdown of the Whitley Committee's Industrial Councils set up after the Great War, Charles asks why they failed. He answers:

The reasons for the failure of Whitleyism surely lie, not in any intrinsic impossibility the scheme contained, but in the unfavourable circumstances in which it was tried. Industrial relations are not something apart from, but very much a part of, our whole social and political life. To put forward proposals such as the Whitley Report embodied, at the time when macro-economic theory was so ill-developed and when the central government had so little of that care for the common good that is the essence of its true task, was asking too much. . . . As long as it was permissible for the powers-that-be to doubt the legitimate place of the unions and their collective bargaining practices in the scheme of things and to consider labor simply as an economic factor almost devoid of human needs and wants, it was not possible to reorganize industry along Whitley lines.[18]

As a Roman Catholic Christian, Rodger Charles, no doubt, is too polite to state the real reason; namely, the fact of the apostasy of the majority of Protestant Christians in Britain who have preferred to be guided in their political and economic life by humanistic categories of thinking derived from apostate laissez faire and Marxist economics rather than by the Word of God as the ordering principle of their economic and business life. Let there be no doubt of it. The deplorable situation which has prevailed and continues to prevail in British industrial relations is the direct and inevitable outcome of Protestant pietism and the abdication of all responsibility for the nation's industrial and economic affairs. Without the spirit of the Lord Jesus Christ in control of men's hearts, Anglo-American-Canadian industry is doomed to frustration, conflict, and eventual death. No wonder West Germany and Holland, which allow for Christian employer and trade unions, are today running rings around British, American, and Canadian industry with its pagan restrictive industrial practices on the part of both labor and management, with its demarcation disputes, its working to the book and go-slow policies of our so-called "neutral" trade unions, and with the price fixing and retail price maintenance of the employers' organizations.

Realizing that industrial relations are not something apart from, but very much a part of, a society's whole social and political life, the Christian worker movements upon the European Continent have been forced to widen their objectives. Along with the material improvement of the worker's position, they have also tried to bring about far-reaching changes in the social structure as a whole. Speaking of this wider objective before the Fourth Congress of the International Federation of Evangelical Workers' Associations at Copenhagen in May, 1950, W. F. de Gaay Fortman, a leading Protestant Christian trade unionist, said:

> It must be understood that the struggle for new forms of society could not be vigorously carried out until now. But today the sorest material needs of the laborer, at least in Western Europe, have been met. That is why it is possible now, more than ever before, to draw the attention of Christians to the great evil of capitalistic development: the fact that the worker no longer bears any responsibility of his own in the process of labor, and consequently has been alienated from his labor and from the community in which he performs his labor. This state of affairs now constitutes the heart of the social problem.[19]

After suggesting, as we have already suggested, that this depersonalization of the worker in modern industry is due to a number of factors, including modern techniques with their tendency towards specialization of functions and their mechanization of production, Fortman then adds:

> Besides, there is the fact that the spirit of capitalism, with its unlimited stimulation of self-interest and with its scorn of all moral considerations in the economic sphere of life, has had its destructive effect upon the working classes. Countless workers have learned the doctrine of unrestricted self-interest from their employers and how they did learn it! Then there was, in addition, the fact that society was not prepared to help the working man to utilize his leisure properly when shorter working hours were realized. This will suffice to outline the causes of the spiritual proletarisation of the working-classes.
>
> It is especially to fight this spiritual proletarisation that the Christian social movements propagate industrial democracy both in industry and factory undertaking, in the social and economic fields. The Christian social movement has adopted as its principle harmonious cooperation of capital and labor. One of these two factors should not overrule the other; together they bear the process of production and that is why they should also bear the responsibility for its progress together.
>
> The idea of cooperation on the basis of equality inevitably leads to the idea of industrial democracy. A worker is no part of a machine, but a man created by God and placed in this world with his own responsibility towards God, his family and the sev-

eral communities in which he has his task. In the social order he should find no hindrance to the acceptance of this responsibility.

A worker in these days is exposed to the temptations of a system which promises him an almost unlimited improvement of his material position but which at the same time tends to make him a slave of the totalitarian state. Resistance to this demonic system is, in my view, only possible, if the Christian social movement right now vigorously sponsors such structural changes in the social system that the worker regains his dignity as a man, bears for his part responsibility in the regulation of economic life and in so doing realizes again the significance and purpose of his labor. In opposition to the brutal destruction with which communism threatens the world, all those who recognize Jesus Christ as Lord of their life and of the world have the duty to show that the criticism of the Gospel on our social order is far more radical than the communistic criticism and that a real recovery and a real renovation of the violated social relations is not to be attained in any other way than by obedience to the Lord's commandment.

Therefore, industrial democracy is necessary in the national economic policy, in the economic relations in industry, and especially in individual plants and undertakings, for a worker carries out his work there; he spends the greater part of his life within its boundaries; and it largely defines his circumstances in life.[20]

3. A third and vital ordinance of God regarding work is that work is not primarily a thing one does to live, but the thing one lives to do.

Work is, or it should be, the full expression of the worker's faculties, the thing in which he finds spiritual, mental, and bodily satisfaction, and the means by which he offers himself in service to God and to his fellow men.

Now the implications of this are not merely that work should be performed under decent sanitary and living conditions, reasonable hours of work, and so on. That is a point even we in the English-speaking world have begun to appreciate, thanks to the efforts of a former generation of great evangelical churchmen such as Lord Shaftesbury, Oastler and Bull of Bierley, and it is all to the good.[21] But we have tended to concentrate upon such matters to the exclusion of all else.

There is, for example, the question of profits and remuneration. Apostate post-Christians have got it fixed firmly in their heads that the proper end of work is to be paid for it in terms of hard cash. As one wit has put it, we "price everything and value nothing." But, if our Christian principle is at all true, this does not follow. So long as society provides the worker with a sufficient return in real wages to enable him to carry on his work properly, then he has his reward. For his work is the measure of his life, and his satisfaction is found in the fulfilment of his own nature as a worker, and in the contemplation of the perfection of his labors. That in practice there is this satisfaction is shown by the mere fact that a man will put loving labor into some hobby which can never bring him any financial return. His satisfaction comes from looking upon what he has made and finding it very good. He is no longer bargaining with his work, but serving it. It is only when work has to be looked upon as a means to financial gain that it becomes hateful; for then instead of a friend it becomes an enemy from which tolls have to be extracted. What most workers today demand from society is that they should always get out of their work a little more than the value of the labor they give to society. By this process they persuade themselves that society is always in their debt—a Marxist conviction that piles up costs and leaves many workers with a grudge against society. Such a view of work is no doubt derived from Marx's so-called labor theory of wages.

A second consequence is that if we really believed that work is not primarily a thing one does to live but the thing one lives to do and arranged our work and our standard of values accordingly, we should stop thinking of work as something that we hasten to hurry through in order to enjoy our time off. We should look on our leisure as the period in which we are refreshed and recreated for the purpose of getting on with our work. With such a Christian attitude we would no longer tolerate conditions or regulations of any sort that prevented us from working as long and as well as our enjoyment of work demanded. We should resent any restrictions imposed by management or labor union as a gross infringement upon the liberty of the Christian worker. Such a biblical attitude would upset all our present pagan notions about hours of work, rates of work, unfair competition, seniority, and so on. We should fight as artists fight for precious time in which to get on with the job—instead of fighting for shorter time in which to fritter away precious hours. Instead of work being a drudgery it would become a delight as we sought by means of it to praise God and glorify Him in our labor. George Herbert rightly sensed this praising of Jehovah God in his wonderful hymn:

> Teach me, my God and King
> In all things thee to see
> And what I do in anything
> To do it as for thee!
>
> All may of thee partake
> Nothing can be so mean
> Which with this tincture, "for thy sake,"
> Will not grow bright and clean.
>
> A servant with this clause
> Makes drudgery divine
> Who sweeps a room, as for thy laws
> Makes that and the action fine.
>
> This is the famous stone
> That turneth all to gold
> For that which God doth touch and own
> Cannot for less be told.[22]

Our Heavenly Father stands ever ready to gather up our daily offerings of sweat and tears and to change them into "sacrifices of praise and thanksgiving"; His grace makes believing human work thanksgiving (eucharistia). As Calvin Seerveld well says:

> God's call to worship ranges the breadth of his creation; nothing is too mean for Him to stoop and save. Every Christian worker may hold on to that Biblical truth that Jehovah God works in us both the will and the deed to act out our salvation with fear and trembling and joy to his good pleasure; in whatever calling, and with however so many talents His Grace finds us. . . . My father is a seller of fish. . . . My father is in full-time service for the Lord, prophet, priest and king in the fish business. And customers who come into the store sense it. Not that we always have the

cheapest fish in town . . . not that there is no sin; But this; that little Great South Bay Fish Market . . . is not only a clean, honest place where you can buy quality fish at a reasonable price with a smile, but there is a spirit in the store, a spirit of laughter, of fun, joy, inside the buying and selling that strikes an observer. . . .

When I watch my Dad's hands, big beefy hands with broad stubby fingers . . . they could never play a piano; when I watch those hands delicately split the back of a mackerel or with a swift, true stroke fillet a flounder close to the bone, leaving all the meat together; when I know those hands dressed and peddled fish from the handlebars of a bicycle in the grim 1930's, cut and sold fish year after year with never a vacation through fire and sickness, thieves and disaster, weariness, winter cold and hot muggy summers, twinkling at work without complaint . . . struggling day in day out to fix a just price, in weakness often but always in faith consecratedly cutting up fish before the face of the Lord; when I see that, I know that God's Grace can come down to a man's hand and the flash of a scabby fish knife.[23]

It was with such a spirit that our Puritan ancestors carved America out of the bushland and scrub of the Atlantic seaboard and that Dutch Calvinists pushed back the frontiers of the sea to build up their polders. It is only such a spirit which makes work worthwhile. May the Lord give us back such a spirit.

A third consequence of such a Christian principle is that we should fight tooth and nail, not for mere employment, but for the quality of the work that we do. We should clamor to be engaged in work that is worth doing, and in which we could take a pride because it would be work for the glory of the Lord and the service of our fellow man. Workers guided by such a biblical principle would demand that the stuff and the goods they turned out of the factories would be good stuff—they would no longer be content to grab their pay packets and let the credit for their workmanship go by the board. Like the shareholders in the brewery, they would feel a sense of personal responsibility for what they produced, and clamor to know and to control what went into the beer brewed. There would be protests and strikes—not only about unjust conditions of pay and of work, but about the quality of the work demanded by the bosses, and the honesty, beauty, and usefulness of the goods produced. The greatest insult which our apostate capitalist age has offered to the workers is the end product of their labors and to force them to dedicate their lives to shoddily making things that are NOT worth making.

Of the terrible temptation to split up into sacred and secular what God has made one, Calvin Seerveld has said:

> Comes then the subtle darts of the Evil One, whether in the mouth of angel, man or snake: "Has God said that all life is to be conformed to Jesus Christ? Is there not anything indifferent to Christian conviction? Surely what God wishes is your heart, your personal commitment to Jesus Christ as your individual Saviour; this confession is what God wants. But really, sweeping the streets with a broom is sweeping the streets with a broom, whether the handle is held by a believer or unbeliever. Qua broom sweeping there is no difference. Of course, a man's behaviour and attitude and motive can be Christian or not, but not broom sweeping per se."

This line of thought may be unpremeditated but it is murder. It kills the Christian worker and leaves behind a Christian that works. Work is then no longer my work, a man is not in his working or in his work product any more, but work is turned into a kind of abstracted *qua se* mechanical function to which I seem to be locally attached as it were. Such a rootless, purely theoretical conception of the nature of work conflicts radically with the Biblical view of work and undoes the whole drive for Reformational Christian living because it separates a man's faith from his livelihood, that is makes faith something mental, "spiritual," extrinsic to his actual bodily activity. Such subtle reasoning about work per se, work-in-general, secularizes the Christian's daily walk with God as devastatingly as talk about God-in-general ruins a Christian theology. Sweeping the streets is no longer God's service or worship but simply something you do to earn a living; cutting up fish is no longer God's service, but a common naturally human busyness. It cuts the heart, the life blood out of Christian work! Christian labor, strictly speaking, is nonsense. Bodily labor is a neutral necessity, that's all.

There is no lack of Christian proponents for this evil idea. Strange bedfellows accept this barren conception of work divested of its hallelujah character. Roman catholic theory, Barth's theology, do-gooding liberals, and a wide run of Fundamentalists all agree, in varying ways for different reasons, that there is a

zone of reality not intrinsically touched, dominated, to be changed
by God's saving Grace, that there is an area of the world which
simply *is there*. These groupings sharply debate among themselves the exact dogmatic content of Christian belief and also
argue sharply among themselves just how important and what
constitutes this "other realm," and how it is to be related to
matters of salvation, but they all hold basically that certain
created states of affairs, like work, for example, are essentially
mundane.[24]

4. The fourth ordinance of the Lord God for human work is
that the so-called "secular" vocation is just as sacred as the ecclesiastical. In fact there is no secular aspect of life in which we may
safely ignore the Lord's claims upon our lives. Christians must get
it firmly into their heads that when a man or woman is called to a
particular job of "secular work," that job is as true a vocation as
though he or she had been called to the sacred ministry of Christ's
holy and catholic and apostolic Church.

Perhaps the Church should conduct a special commissioning service at which Christian workers could be empowered by God the
Holy Ghost in their chosen vocations as carpenter, electrician, truck
driver, factory worker, school teacher, nurse, etc. For the true
Christian, whether "layman" or "clergyman," everything he or she
does is an offering to God, for our Jehovah God is a jealous God
who demands the whole of our lives to be dedicated in his service.
Our God is not a mere "god" reserved for the chapel or church,
but He is the Lord of the tentmakers, the tax collectors, the fishermen, the miners, and the carpenters. All of the Christian's life is
precious to the Savior and therefore whatsoever ye do do it as unto
the Lord, whether you eat, drink, work, sleep, or play (Col. 3:23-24).

Those who laid the foundations of Western civilization had a
doctrine of work which they formulated in the Latin phrase *la-
borare est orare* (to work is to pray). Can that still be the foundation and heart of a Christian doctrine of work in modern society?
asks the Christian industrialist, Mr. Heron, in the book, *Prospect
for Christendom*:

Can a financier or a machine tender really pray at his work today? Can he practise the presence of God as he plans his next

deal or struggles against the monotony of his nut-tightening? Can he see in the thing that he is making or causing to be made something which is being made for Christ's sake? Let us admit without reservation that unless in each case the Christian can answer these questions with a simple affirmative he must, if he is logical, give up his Christianity or his activity in relation to money or to the machine.[25]

In actual fact there can take place in many forms of work—notably in the concentration of the artist upon his task, and in the process of scientific discovery, but also in craftsmanship of various kinds—an experience that is analogous to the act of prayer. As Heron does well to point out:

It is a matter of common experience that the labourer sometimes loses himself in his work and that when he does so his load is eased. There is a strong resemblance between this condition of the body absorbed in what we call work and its state in silence in what we call prayer; and the reason for the resemblance is that in both cases man is giving himself to God—in the one instance to God at work in the natural creation, in the other to God at rest in the spirit.[26]

From this it will be evident what far-reaching changes will have to be brought about in industry today before the assertion "to work is to pray" can be for many of those engaged in it anything more than a mockery. In nothing has the Church so lost her hold on reality as in her dismal failure to understand and respect the "secular" vocation. Working for God has come to be equated almost entirely with personal evangelism and witnessing for Christ. As a tragic and direct result, work and religion have become separated into two departments of life, and the "secular" every-day work of the world has become turned to purely selfish and destructive ends, while the great majority of American, British, and Canadian workers have today become completely irreligious and live as if God is dead. And then churchmen dare to express astonishment! But is such a result so really astonishing? How could any sane workman remain interested in a religion which thus appears to have no concern with nine tenths of his life. The churches' official approach to an intelligent carpenter is usually confined to exhorting him not to be drunk and disorderly in his leisure hours and to come to church on Sundays. What the churches should be telling him is that the very first demand that Jehovah God makes upon him is that he should make good tables. Let him go to church on the Lord's Day, by all means, and let him remain temperate by all means; but what use is all that if in the very center of his life and occupation he is insulting the Lord God with bad carpentry? We may rest assured that no crooked table legs or ill-fitting drawers or sloppy workmanship ever came out of the carpenter's shop at Nazareth. Nor if they did, could we really believe that they were made by the same hand that made the heavens and the earth (Gen. 1:31; Psalm 104; John 1:3).

For the same reason we must object to the usual doctrine which would confine so-called church work amongst women to organizing fetes and bazaars. The churches' official approach to wives and mothers is usually confined to exhorting them to be chaste, sober, and monogamous during the week and to attend church on Sundays, thereby implying that religion is something that goes on only in a building set aside for that purpose. What the churches should be telling wives and mothers is that the very first demand Almighty God makes upon ALL married women is that they should become good wives and better mothers. Go to church, by all means, but never forget that as a married woman she is serving God best of all when she fulfills the "office" of wife and mother to the very best of her ability.

This is not to deny the vital importance of worship. Having given to God his *worth-ship* and acknowledged His claim upon our lives in His house, we should then go out into His world to do His will on earth even as it is now done in Heaven. When asked by his mother, "Why has thou thus dealt with us," upon finding Jesus in the Temple, He replied, "I must be about my Father's business" (Luke 2:49). It is significant that no sooner had the boy Jesus declared that He must be in the things of His Heavenly Father, that He returned to Nazareth and was subject to His earthly parents. In His mother's cottage as much as when He was learning of the things of God in the Temple, He was in the things of His Father. The next eighteen years, when the Son of God was a village carpenter, are all the proof we could ask that the every day workaday routine of every one of us can be one long, unbroken act of worship of our Heavenly Father. The Christ-centered life of being in the things of our Father is indeed like a compass with its two legs. If we will strike the one leg of worship deep into our central loyalty to Christ, then the other leg of obedience can take as wide a sweep as it likes in the things of the world; for thereby it makes them our Father's business and the dominion of the Kingdom of Heaven. Thus, to Brother Lawrence of Lorraine, the monastery cook, a kitchen and an altar were as one; and to pick up a straw from the ground or to dust the cobwebs off the ceiling could be an act of adoring worship. "The time of business," he tells us, "does not with me differ from the time of prayer, and in the noise and clatter of the kitchen, when several persons are at the same time calling for different things, I possesss God in as great tranquility as if I was upon my knees at the Blessed Sacrament." We may then be in the things of our Heavenly Father by making *our* business *His* business, just as much as when we are worshiping Him in His own house. As a devout Christian housewife has written:

> Lord of all pots and pans and things, since I've not time to be
> A Saint by doing lovely things, or watching late with Thee
> Or dreaming in the dawnlight or storming Heaven's gates
> Make me a saint by getting meals, and washing up the plates.
> Although I must have Martha's hands, I may have Mary's mind
> And when I black the boots and shoes, Thy sandals Lord I find
> I think of how they trod the earth, what time I scrub the floor
> Accept this meditation, Lord, I haven't time for more
> Warm all the kitchen with Thy Love, and light it with Thy
>   peace
> Forgive me all my worrying, and make all grumbling cease
> Thou who didst love to give men food in room or by the sea
> Accept this service that I do—I do it unto Thee.[27]

(d) The Christian Answer to Automation

1. The Nature of Automation

If Christians rightly claim to have an answer to all man's problems, they must deal with the serious problem facing Western people today; namely, the silent revolution now taking place in Western Europe and North America caused by the application of scientific method and technical "know-how" to industry and commerce. Automation represents a whole new concept of manufacturing. It is taking over not only many of man's physical functions but also many of his mental functions. In his Reith Lectures Sir Leon Bagrit defined automation as follows, carefully distinguishing it from mechanization:

> Automation is that part of what I have called the "extension of man" which integrates all the sensing, thinking, and decision-making elements. . . .
> "Automation" has been, and still is, a greatly misused word, but its proper meaning, and therefore its implications, is gradually becoming better understood. Perhaps I could attempt an explanation, if not a definition, by saying that it is a concept through which a machine-system is caused to operate with maximum efficiency by means of adequate measurement, observation, and control of its behaviour. It involves a detailed and continuous knowledge of the functioning of the system, so that the best corrective actions can be applied immediately they become necessary. Automation in this true sense is brought to full fruition only through a thorough exploitation of its three major elements, communication, computation and control—the three "Cs." [28]

Bagrit then pointed out that many people today fear automation because they suppose it is going to turn them into sub-human types, into something close to robots. This is because *they confuse automation with mechanization*. While mechanization has indeed given millions of people sub-human work to do, automation does the exact opposite. Bagrit points out:

> A mass-production line is essentially a timing machine, which moves goods from place to place in a given time. In that given time a man has to be available to perform a given task. He is in fact in many ways a slave of the machine. It fixes his time and fixes his movements, and he has to produce a series of semi-intelligent mechanical motions to keep the machine fed and moving. This is what I mean by saying that mechanization is his master.
> Automation, on the contrary, by being a self-adapting and chang-

ing piece of mechanism, enables a man to work at whatever pace he wants to work, because the machine will react to him. Except in the simpler processes he is the master of the machine. The machine that forms part of an automated system is not predetermined; this kind of machine gives information and suggests a course of action, but it does not necessarily say "I won't wait." The computer produces a vast amount of information. . . . Automation is the exact opposite of mechanization. The man in charge extends his faculties but remains himself. He does not become a slave. He stays in the centre and becomes the real master.[29]

Bagrit illustrates the difference between automation and mechanization by means of an analogy. If we wanted to drink a cup of tea, following the principle of mechanization, the direction in which our hand would move and the speed at which it would do so would be completely predetermined. It would move automatically and the handle would have to be in a particular position for it to be picked up by our hand, because in mechanization there is no way of correcting any error. The cup would then move towards the place where it supposed the mouth to be. If our mouth was not there, because of some error in the operation, the machine might well pour the tea down our neck. It would not know it was doing anything wrong. This is, of course, what happened to Charlie Chaplin in the great comedy film, *Modern Times*. The machine fed him blindly because it was following a motion that was rigidly predetermined.

Automation, on the other hand, Bagrit suggests, is a system based upon what is called "feed-back." It uses sensing devices, communication mechanisms, computing or deciding elements, and control mechanisms. In the example of the teacup, if the same operation were done by automation, the eye, which is a sensing element, would communicate with the computing or brain mechanism, telling it exactly where the cup was, where the hand was, and where the mouth was. It would then continuously signal the position of the hand all the time it was moving towards the handle. The computer would calculate the necessary corrections and instruct the control mechanisms to make sure that the hand moved accurately towards the handle. In its turn, the brain would signal to the control mechanism the adjustments necessary to obtain the optimum result. At the same time another sensing device, the finger, would determine the temperature of the tea, allowing for the difference in temperature between the cup and its contents. The computing mechanism, the brain, would compare this new information with what was already stored in its memory, and then might signal back that the tea was still too hot, or it might compute the necessary delay before the tea was ready to drink. Furthermore, the eye might register that the cup was too full and that if it moved at too great a speed it would spill. The hand would then be instructed by the computer to move the cup at a pace so designed that it would arrive at its destination at the right temperature and without spilling. This is what we must understand by "automation," a process of control by communication devices which tends to produce the "optimum" result. Bagrit would prefer to have it known by the term cybernation, since it deals with the theory of commuications and control, which is what genuine automation really is.

The aims of automation include the best possible use of available resources, the production of vast quantities of manufactured material. and the doing of office work as quickly and as cheaply as possible. It has been found that it can be introduced successfully only if certain conditions exist. An enormous capital investment is necessary and the return on this investment is adequate only if production is for a mass market. The system can vary with the nature of the product, but wide variations involve radical alterations in the plant and an uneconomic delay in production. It is therefore necessary to organize flow production, that is, material at all stages passing uniformly through the production process at a steady and a rapid rate. The system cannot be introduced without the right equipment and technical expertise.

Automation is not a single, simple piece of equipment or industrial process, but rather a combination of a number of factors involving many pieces of mechanical and electronic equipment. At the present time it is being introduced into industry in special places, dealing with steps of special importance in the productive process which lend themselves to this technique. It is becoming possible to combine automated systems to produce even greater savings and efficiency of production, and eventually whole series of systems may be integrated to form fully automated factories. Such factories would employ practically no men in the ordinary way other than as managers and technicians.

Thanks to the application of this cybernation or "automation," we are now undergoing a second and even greater "industrial revolution" than the first one based upon coal and electricity. Describing what is now happening, Norbert Wiener writes in *The Human Use of Human Beings*:

> There has long been a tendency to render factories and machines automatic. Except for some special purpose, one would no longer think of producing screws by the use of the ordinary lathe, in which the mechanic must watch the progress of his cutter and regulate it by hand. The production of screws in quantity without serious human intervention is now the normal task of the ordinary screw machine. Although this does not make any special use of the process of feedback nor of the vacuum tube, it accomplishes a somewhat similar end. What the feedback and the vacuum tube have made possible is not the sporadic design of individual automatic mechanisms, but a general policy for the construction of automatic mechanisms of the most varied type. In this they have been reinforced by our new theoretical treatment of communication, which takes full cognizance of the possibilities of communication between machine and machine. It is this conjunction of circumstances which now renders possible the new automatic age.
> The existing state of industrial techniques includes the whole of the results of the first industrial revolution, together with many inventions which we now see to be precursors of the second industrial revolution. What the precise boundary between these two revolutions may be it is still too early to say. In its potential significance, the vacuum tube certainly belongs to an industrial revolution different from that of the age of power; and yet it is only at present that the true significance of the invention of the vacuum tube has been sufficiently realized to allow us to attribute the present age to a new and second industrial revolution.[30]

Thanks to this new industrial revolution, the British and North American economies are expanding at a rate unheard of in human history. More goods and services are now being produced than ever before. Science and technology are making it possible for us to have a plentiful supply of food, clothing, and other consumer goods produced by only a fraction of the labor force that was required even a few decades before. In the United States, for instance, one man on the land now produces more than enough to feed fifteen men in the cities.

2. The Social Consequences of Automation

While admitting the economic benefits brought about by automation, many people today are concerned about its social consequences, especially redundancy and unemployment. Thus the vice president of U. S. Industries, Inc., writing in *Time and Motion Study* on the "Human Side of Automation," pointed out that:

> Employment as a percentage of our labor force has dropped from 98% to about 90% or to state it another way unemployment has gone up from 2% of our labor force to almost 10%. In Britain there has been a similar economic growth yet unemployment is increasing from 1.4% to 4%. The most important factor causing this substantial reduction in both of our work forces in relation to our increased production has been automation.[31]

John Billera then went on to point out that what he called many misleading and widely broadcast myths about the effects of automation on our workers were in vogue. The first of these myths is the belief that for a number of reasons automation is not going to eliminate jobs. Yet the price of automation, he says, is written in cold and bold figures for all to read. "In the U. S. in just three years from 1955 to 1958 while productivity climbed, the number of production workers declined from 13.5 million workers to 11.9 million workers or a loss of 12%. The National Planning Association of the U. S. has made a study showing that the numbers of chronically unemployed rose from about half a million in 1953 to about two million in 1960." [31]

In a similar vein, Pope Pius XII expressed the view:

> There is no doubt that the period of transition may result in an increase of unemployment among the older workers, who are

less adapted to new training, but younger labourers as well are faced with the same danger whenever a nation is forced to hasten its steps towards automation because of its competition with other countries (March 7, 1957).[32]

Later in 1957 the Pope noted the danger of confusing technical productivity with economic productivity. Automation leads to a fantastic growth in productive capacities. But, he asked, "Will it lead to a lasting and sure attainment of conditions which will make possible the material and human well-being of every member of the population, and in which all those who contribute immediately— with their labour, their property, their capital—to the national economy will receive a return corresponding to their investment" (June 7, 1957)? [33]

The Pope was aware of the arguments that in the long run employment will rise as a result of automation. But even if this were true, he pointed out, "the fact remains that an increase in technological unemployment even for a brief period would represent in some countries a loss that could not be lightly incurred. In this area it is not at all legitimate to adopt the false principle which in the past impelled certain statesmen to sacrifice an entire generation in view of the great advantages that would accrue to succeeding ones" (June 7, 1957).[34]

The Roman Catholic priest, John F. Cronin, points out in *Labour and the Church*:

> As a social phenomenon, automation must be considered as one of the major developments of recent decades. At first there was a tendency to underestimate its impact and to consider it on a par with the technological changes of earlier years. More recently the pendulum of thought has swung to the opposite extreme and some persons despair of ever finding jobs for the workers who will ultimately be displaced by the new processes. Whether or not this despairing attitude is justified, it is clear that the false assumptions of a few years back lack validity. Automation is not like the introduction of the automobile, which displaced the horse and carriage . . . , only to create millions of new jobs directly or indirectly related to motor transport. In some fields at least automation is moving decisively in the direction of displacing far more workers than can be absorbed either by expanded pro-

duction in the automated industry or by occupations incidental
to the process of automation. Nor is it clear that displaced workers
can readily be retrained so as to find jobs in other occupations
or even other areas of the nation. Some workers are too old to
profit by retraining. Others may lack the talents for occupations
which still need workers.[35]

Fortunately there is a great deal of evidence to suggest that this
alarmist view has substantially distorted both the character and the
potential impact of automation.

First and in general, it is held by many economists that automation
is basically a continuation of, rather than a radical departure from,
the ongoing trend of technological advance as Bagrit supposes. Automation from this point of view is now considered as a gradual
development in the historical course of technological progress. While
productivity has been rising, it has been accelerating at a modest
rate. Dramatic breakthroughs in the rate of productivity increase and
peopleless plants are more fantasy than fact. It is pointed out that
productivity in manufacturing—where the alarmists have predicted
the more serious inroads on employment—has grown more slowly
in recent years than the average rate for the entire economy.

Secondly, it is pointed out that the impact of automation upon
employment has been grossly misunderstood and overstated. This
misunderstanding arose because of the historical coincidence in the
late 1950's of rising unemployment, on the one hand, and the development and expanding use of computers, on the other. While
these two developments were occurring more or less at the same
time, their causes were in fact substantially independent. The rising
unemployment rates of the late 1950's were caused primarily by a
deficiency of aggregate consumer demand, aggravated by a quite
rapid increase in the size of the labor force. If the predictions of the
alarmists are correct and automation is spreading rapidly through the
American economy, the critics point out that a growing body of displaced and unemployed workers should be evident. But this just has
not happened. On the contrary, unemployment rates, which rose to
about 7 percent in the late 1950's, have fallen significantly in the
1960's. In 1966 and 1967 the unemployment rate was below 4

percent, partially because of the stimulus to aggregate consumer demand which the 1964 tax cut provided. In short, gloomy predictions of mass technological unemployment have simply not borne fruit.

The impact of automation upon employment has been exaggerated for other reasons. In *The Myths of Automaton*,[36] Charles Silberman even argues that there is actually very little automation in existence. "No fully automated process exists for any major product in any industry in the United States. Nor is any in prospect in the immediate future."

The main reason for the modest inroads of automation is that most manipulative operations (for example, the guiding of a tool in an appropriate way by an automobile assembly-line worker) are in fact extremely difficult to automate. In addition, such important industries as agriculture, construction, and transportation are highly resistant to automation because of the large number of small, geographically dispersed firms and operations involved. This dispersion and the small size of individual operations also tend to make many service industries (merchandising, repair shops, professional services, etc.) immune to automation. And in fact, most manufacturing operations are organized on a customized "job shop" basis—the antithesis of the completely standardized, long run, production process which is conducive to automation. The inclination of the alarmists to impute the anticipated consequences of a few impressive cases of automation to the economy as a whole—to generalize upon the basis of a very small number of special cases—say the critics, has led the alarmists to give us a highly exaggerated impression of the unemployment effects of the "new technology."

Furthermore, the critics among economists argue, there is an unfortunate tendency to confuse what is technically or scientifically possible with that which is economically feasible. Many of the technologically possible uses of automation entail the substitution of very complex and expensive machines for relatively cheap labor. Unless the resulting increases in output are profitable, the substitution of expensive capital for cheap labor may simply not be worth it.

Again, it must be pointed out that there is not any theoretical reason why there should be mass unemployment on a free market. In fact, the wealthier the economy—and production is what increases real wealth—the easier it should be to employ men. This is because new opportunities become available for human labor which were not economically and socially possible in the earlier less prosperous and less productive era, e.g., the rise of the electronics, telephonic, and motor industries. Automation, if it is to be profitable for the entrepreneur, must be productive since the fantastic costs of automating an industry must be balanced by vastly increased production if the company is going to make a profit and thus stay in business.

No manufacturer would dare embark upon the costly business of automating his factory unless he can expect to increase productivity and profits by at least twenty-five percent in the first year, rising to say, forty percent after three years. At this rate he reckons he can recover the cost of the machine in a short time, say five to seven years. In these calculations the saving on wages of the operatives that the machine will replace is an essential factor. Humanitarian motives may not be entirely absent from his mind, but he will argue that it is better for a small percentage of employees to become unnecessary than for his whole business to go bankrupt. *In order to survive in today's competitive world markets the manufacturer must modernize and automate his factory; redundancy is part of the price.*

At the same time, it must be remembered that modern industry depends for its very existence upon an affluent customer society at home, so that production may be on a large enough scale for a mass market. An immediate program of total modernization, if such a thing were possible, might well reduce the labor force to a fraction of its present level, but if this meant that sixty or seventy percent of industrial workers had to subsist at the present level of unemployment benefits then the bottom would fall out of the market in consumer durables and the automated industries would go bankrupt. Too rapid modernization can prove just as fatal as too slow a movement.

Far from reducing living standards, automation should bring about a general fall in the prices of the goods produced in this way, since competition makes it essential that most of the savings be passed on to the consumer, unless, of course, the company is protected by state-enforced tariffs, state-enforced "fair trade" laws, or state-financed subsidies. This fall in prices is what the whole Western world experienced during the first industrial revolution, and there is no reason why it should not happen again if a halt is called to the present inflationary policies of all Western states.[37]

Few economists today seem to realize that inflation can exist where there is a stable price level. In fact, in a producing economy prices should normally be falling, thus permitting a wider distribution of consumer goods. If the supply of money in circulation remains constant and the supply of goods increases, the price level should drop. The most productive era of American economy was from 1870 to 1910, covering the years of America's industrial "take-off," yet the price level in these years fell by 40%. The output of goods, on the other hand, rose by 50%. Falling prices are thus not in any sense inconsistent with prosperity. The only question that concerns the economist should be the volume of production and not the price level. It is only in post-Keynesian times that economists have taken up the Social Credit cry of "stable prices and full employment through inflation." The result of this disastrous policy is exactly what we are witnessing today in Britain and the United States: inflation, outflow of gold, budget deficits, and austerity programs to fight the government-created inflation and unemployment.[38]

If automation must not be held responsible for increasing the level of unemployment, neither should it be blamed for the large number of unskilled workers in society who are being displaced by it. As automation increases, we must expect the proportion of manual, unskilled jobs to fall and the proportion of jobs requiring technical knowledge to increase. Laborers who are displaced by automation are unable to find jobs today because they have not been adequately educated for life in modern society. In his fundamental work, *The New Improved American*, Bernard Asbell has proved that the new machines have exposed the real causes of unemployment to lie in ignorance and the stupefying, dehumanizing effects of pre-automation and four hundred years of racial cruelty. Now that we have invented machines to do routine mechanical work, we must set men free from the subhuman tasks they have always performed, and train them for more demanding, more enjoyable, more human labors. As-bell claims that literacy will be forced upon us by the robots when they relieve human beings of wretched mechanical chores.[39]

In any case, Billera's argument that automation will bring about mass unemployment is just not true. In actual fact, what is occurring is a far more gradual adjustment. Most of the difficulties in the present situation are precisely about the *rate* of modernization in industry. As one set of jobs is becoming redundant and men are losing their employment, so at the same time another set of different kinds of jobs is being created. Improvements in working conditions with fewer hours of work means that more men will be required in some industries, while in other industries there will be vacancies for new kinds of jobs. For these and other reasons many industrialists and economists argue that automation and modernization will cause a shortage of jobs in the short term, but a shortage of employees in the long term.[40]

Again, it needs to be pointed out that workers who are displaced by automation are unable to find employment today because minimum wage laws have dried up the market's jobs for the less productive, less skilled worker. The unskilled laborer should not expect to receive high wages since he is unproductive. But that does not mean, as Billera and others have suggested, that he is useless to society. For those who, for various reasons, cannot be retrained for more highly skilled jobs, there are still jobs available to those who are less skilled precisely because the low productivity job cannot be economically done by an expensive and highly specialized machine. In a rapidly expanding economy, the list of services that the consumer demands gets longer and longer; as leisure time expands so the call for workers in the entertainment industries will increase. There are numerous examples of this kind of service job open to the less skilled: taxi driving, telegraph deliverers, the whole florist industry, newspapers, sales jobs of products which were before too expensive to distribute on a mass scale, e.g., swimming pools in California, golf ranges, holiday camps, motels, etc.

With the additional profitability of mass production, many firms are rapidly establishing training centers to provide opportunities for retraining of less skilled men who can service these new machines.

Action now being taken by the American and British Governments is also of great significance in this respect. The establishment of Government Training Centers and the Industrial Training Act is gradually changing the outlook of men to the question of stability of employment. A worker who had become redundant and who has made a successful adjustment in middle age to a totally new kind of job had this to say:

> In my last job I lived for five years in daily dread of becoming redundant, but when I did lose my job and got some training for a new kind of work I found it interesting and a challenge. When eventually I got a new job I realized that it was one of the best things that had happened to me and I wonder why I ever let myself get so worried.[41]

If more American and British workers would adopt this attitude towards automation then they would have far less reason to fear the future.

3. *A Christian Solution to the Social Problems of Automation*

What emerges from this discussion is the necessity for training, retraining, and mobility. Both government and industry must work together to provide facilities for retraining. As Leon Bagrit well puts it:

> Large numbers of those who become redundant as a result of automation lack skills to fit them for new jobs, and so we find ourselves faced with the paradox that, on the one hand there are numerous empty jobs, and on the other there are numerous people who remain unemployed because there is not enough retraining available. Training should be provided for every young entrant into the labour force. . . . It has been estimated that to be able to earn a living continuously, the young people now coming into the labour market may need as many as three different kinds of jobs during their lifetime. This requires not merely training in specific skills but considerable mental flexibility, so that workers are prepared and able to learn and relearn throughout the whole of their lives. We may have to provide in this country up to twelve months' training for some categories of displaced

workers. This will be a costly operation, and, whether it is in the United States or here, it will have to be paid for by the nation if undue hardship is to be avoided, either to industries, or to individuals or to local authorities.[42]

It may be argued by non-Christian capitalists and economists of the old laissez faire school of economics that society has no such responsibility towards workers displaced by automation, and that it must not therefore be expected to spend large sums on retraining programs.[43]

In reply it must be pointed out that such a view implies an acute isolation of the economic aspect of human life from the public-legal aspect. Modern neo-Liberalism especially seems to be characterized by this exaggerated isolation. The great economists Roepke, Hayek, and Von Mises have raised economic marketing relations into a world by itself, which as such has nothing to do with immediate ethical or social issues and norms. Behind this abhorrence of all governmental intervention in the business world one can detect even today a devotion to the closed view of the economic world held by the classical economists. According to Adam Smith the interplay of the purely private economic interests of the market would guarantee in an automatic manner the best possible solution for society as a whole. As Kouwenhoven says in his great Reformed thesis on *Liberty and Equality*:

> Economic thought starting from a sociological individualism was based on man as a separate and independent independent individual. Completely ignoring the sociological structures from which the economic agent acts, it is assumed that economic life went on in an amorphous society into which the economic aspect was inserted as a purely functional matter. It first disregarded the structures of individuality within which economic action takes place; it then constructed, apart from these structures, economic agents acting self-sufficiently as equal individuals, and finally—on the basis of the free association of these independent type-figures —built up an order in economic life, working by virtue of the impersonal mechanism of the market.[44]

Over against such an autonomous economic sphere Christians must stress that economic life in its "market-acts" and "market situations" reveals an individuality structure which means that it is subject not merely to economic norms but also to social and ethical norms. The economic sphere is not only mutually irreducible to any other sphere but it is indissolubly inter-related with all the other spheres. This means that the government has a God-ordained right to restore the balance in social life when this has become disrupted by automation.

The question inevitably arises, to whom does the knowledge and the skill which make the abundance of modern production belong? Does it belong only to the shareholders and to managers or to the workers. The answer to this question is fundamental, for the scientific knowledge and technical skill now being applied in industry is the most important factor in our economy today; more even than capital and investment and more important even than labor itself. For example, when a new machine is introduced to replace ten men, to whom does the product of the machine belong? Have the ten men who have become unemployed no right to share in the goods and wealth being produced with increased efficiency in the economy as a result of the new machine? Let me repeat the question: to whom does the knowledge and the skill which make the abundance of modern methods of production belong? The new managerial classes or the government or the people?

The answer is that in the first place it belongs to God. The Word of God teaches us that the earth is the Lord's and the fulness thereof and that it is from God that men derive their power to unlock the secrets of *His* universe. Man is called to be a just and faithful steward of the gifts entrusted to him, and that must include the scientific knowledge which has resulted in the tremendous technological advances of our age. Man is also called to live his life in community with his neighbor and to love his neighbor as he loves himself. This means that the benefits of automation must in love be shared by all members of society and not just by the favored few. As a Christian, this writer is convinced that the knowledge and the skill which make automation and its consequent increase in productivity possible is a part of our common national cultural and scientific heritage. This knowledge and skill belong to our entire national families, and, in equity, every ctizitzen is entitled to share in this common national cultural heritage in terms of increasing economic security, increasing economic independence, and increasing leisure as machines and automation displace the need for human labor.

Big business and big government in America, Britain, and Canada have no more right to deny the American, British, and Canadian people of the economic benefits of this common national cultural heritage in the fields of industry, agriculture, and commerce than they have any right to deny the common people the use of the highways, the courts of justice, and protection by the police against murderers and gangsters.

It should be self-evident that as automation results in increasing production with diminishing labor, the cost per unit of production should also fall and be reflected in decreasing prices and increasing real incomes. The present system of governmental restrictions on the market's pricing mechanism, including state-enforced inflation as well as the bankers' monopoly of credit with its governmentally protected fractional reserve system of issuing loans, produces the reverse results—namely, rising prices, as can be witnessed by the steadily rising price index, increasing taxation of personal and corporation incomes, and little real leisure.

Genuine democracy cannot exist unless it embraces both political and economic democracy, not in the socialist or collectivist sense, but in the sense that the people as a whole can decide what shall be produced, the conditions under which it shall be produced, and how it shall be distributed. The elaborate voting system which this requires already exists in our present economic system—the market economy of capitalism. Under this system the peoples' incomes provide their voting power. By their purchases they decide what they want produced. As Ludwig Von Mises points out:

> The customer is sovereign. . . . Businessmen are under the necessity of turning out what the consumers ask for and they must sell their wares at prices which the consumers can afford and are prepared to pay. A business operation is a manifest failure if the proceeds from the sales do not reimburse the businessman for all

he has expended in producing the product. Thus the consumers in buying at a definite price determine also the height of the wages that are paid to all those engaged in the industries. It follows that an employer cannot pay more to an employee than the equivalent of the value the latter's work, according to the judgment of the buying public, adds to the merchandise. This is the reason why the movie star gets much more than the charwoman. If he were to pay more, he would not recover his outlays from the purchasers; he would suffer losses and would finally go bankrupt. In paying wages the employer acts as a mandatory of the consumers as it were. It is upon the consumers that the incidence of the wage payments falls. As the immense majority of the goods produced are bought and consumed by people who are themselves receiving wages and salaries, it is obvious that in spending their earnings the wage earners and employees themselves are foremost in determining the height of the compensation they will get.

The buyers do not pay for the toil and trouble the worker took nor for the length of time he spent in working. They pay for the products. The better the tools are which the worker uses in his job, the more he can perform in an hour, the higher is consequently his remuneration. What makes wages rise and renders the material conditions of the wage earners more satisfactory is improvement in the technological equipment.

American wages are higher than wages in other countries because the capital invested per head of the worker is greater and the plants are thereby in the position to use the most efficient tools and machines. What is called the American way of life is the result of the fact that the United States has put fewer obstacles in the way of saving and capital accumulation than other countries.[45]

For this reason we should welcome automation as the best method of increasing productivity and thereby raising the peoples' living standards. It is not automation which is to blame for unemployment but the present financial policy of so-called easy money and credit expansion. This policy not only creates unemployment but robs the people of their hard-earned savings by inflation and lowers the purchasing power of the dollar.[46]

As regards workers who have become technologically redundant, society obviously has a responsibility to see that they are helped back into gainful employment. For this reason we suggest the following program.

(1) The school age should be raised and further education provided for all children now at school so that they can be educated for the new patterns of work which are required today because of automation. These include card punchers, computer operators, system analysts, computer programmers, and electronic engineers.

(2) Special retraining centers should be established for adult workers who have become redundant through automation.

(3) Financial inducements should be offered to encourage men to move with their families to those parts of the country where their newly acquired skills can best be used.

(4) Redundant workers should be enabled by law to draw unemployment benefits in proportion to their weekly wage, which would help to mitigate the worst features of unemployment. This would have the indirect effect of maintaining the consumer market in areas where there is a sudden rise in unemployment because of high redundancy in an industry for some special reason.[47]

The adoption of such a program would persuade workers to accept automation because they would see it as conducive to a higher material standard of life. It would show them that society cares for people even when they have become technologically redundant through no fault of their own. Then they would realize that no one is personally responsible and morally culpable just because he happens to have become unemployed through lack of the requisite skills.

(e) *The Christian Understanding of Leisure*

In the Christian view work is not only an obligation laid on man by his Creator; it also has its divinely appointed limits. Work in the Christian view may never be considered an end in itself nor the sole fulfilment of the moral being of man. As Emil Brunner says:

> There are persons on whom it is not necessary to impress the command to work; in their case it is necessary to lay emphasis upon the fact that there is also a commandment about keeping the Sabbath, as a sign that work is not an end in itself, that labour must serve man and human life, but that it must not dominate it. . . .

Only in repose does the human quality in a human being become evident, just as inhuman qualities are revealed in those who cannot rest. In the ability to rest we see whether man is still in control of his work, or whether he is *possessed* by it.[48]

No age has ever been in greater need of the reminder of the place of rest and worship in man's life than our own. Work, for millions, has become an end in itself, taking possession of all their faculties. We must remind our apostate age that the observance of the Lord's Day not only provides men with a necessary safety valve but puts their daily work in the perspective of eternity and this reduces it to its true proportions. As Brunner well writes:

> Play is a safety-valve, by means of which the superfluous steam of self-importance, self-conscious dignity, solemnity, and over-seriousness can be let off.[49]

The psalmist has told us, "Be still and know that I am God." To receive God's best gifts we need to be at rest. In his beautiful book, *Leisure the Basis of Culture*, Joseph Pieper suggests that it is not only a discarded notion of the nature of knowledge that we must recover if we are to become whole men and women again; it is also a discarded notion of the nature of leisure. In Pieper's indictment of the contemporary world, no charge is meant to be more grave than that it is a world in bondage, a world that has succumbed to the idolatry of work, of activity for its own sake. He says:

> Work is the process of satisfying the "common need"—an expression that is by no means synonomous with the notion of the "common good." The "common need" is an essential part of the "common good"; but the notion of the "common good" is far more comprehensive. . . . More and more, at the present time, "common good" and "common need" are identified; and (what comes to the same thing) the world of work is becoming our entire world; it threatens to engulf us completely, and the demands of the world of work become greater and greater, till at last they make a "total claim" upon the whole of human nature.[50]

The charge can hardly be denied, and its accuracy is reflected in the degradation of the notion of leisure. For leisure is now treated as being for the sake of work, as required simply in order to fit the worker to resume his task; and in addition, so great apparently is the fear that leisure may turn into idleness and sloth, leisure itself is now organized, every moment of it filled with activity, no matter how trivial. In the Christian past, on the contrary, the notions of idleness and sloth were closely associated with the inability to put oneself at leisure or at rest in contemplation and prayer and adoration of Almighty God, Father, Son, and Spirit.

How necessary it is to be still, especially in times of high tension. Not to know the stillness of the soul in prayer before God is comparable to being condemned to be chained, year in and year out, to the constantly grinding wheel of one's work in some great murky city, without ever getting the opportunity to

> Go down to the sea again
> To the lovely sea and sky.

Stillness induces relaxation as we all know deep down. Doctors appeal to their patients to relax, until it has become almost a modern incantation. Health cults have even been devised with nothing more by which to commend themselves than the art of relaxation. The British Medical Journal made a claim some time ago that something like 40% of the beds in the hospitals of Britain are taken up by patients suffering from various nervous disorders. And many of these are the victims of noise and the constant buzzing confusion of modern life. Is there any wonder that the human body is breaking down under the constant hammering it receives from the high tension existence of our age? Men and women are today driving themselves so that they can only come to a stop with a jerk, and that is when the damage is done.

A car mechanic was asked what was the greatest fault among modern motorists. He replied, "Driving on their brakes." What he meant by this was that drivers got the maximum speed out of their cars under all and varying circumstances and they rely on their brakes to slow down, always, they hope, just in time. But such driving always involves a jolt, and each jolt loosens some small bit or other of the car, either in the engine or the body work. Soon it begins to rattle and squeak. Is it not the same with our human bodies? Men drive themselves so hard today at their work that eventually they develop rattles and squeaks called frustration, bad tempers, jittery-ness, and so on. If only modern man would realize the tremendous therapeutic as well as spiritual value of worship. God is a Spirit and we must worship Him in spirit and in truth. Man can only nourish his spirit when he worships God. He then has to relax, and such worship of God has in itself more healing power for his frayed nerves than anything else in the world.

Again, stillness encourages reflection. How little time modern people devote to reflection. They never seem to be able to stay still a while and let their minds wander over what they are experiencing or reading. The old tramp was right after all:

> A poor life this if full of care
> We have no time to stand and stare.

"Be still and reflect upon me," saith the Lord, and then you will be restored in your inward parts and refreshed for your daily duties. As the prophet Isaiah teaches, "They that wait upon the Lord shall renew their strength; they shall mount up with wings as eagles; they shall run, and not be weary; they shall walk and not faint" (Isa. 40:31).

Let Christians today recover the art and the discipline of worship and we shall see such spiritual resources released in the world as will make the release of nuclear energy look like a firecracker. The worship of God in prayer and sacrament is the very heart of the Christian's life and the secret of any successes he may win in his great mission to the world. The worship of the One True God is not a means to a better social order; it is an end in itself. Man's chief end is in fact to glorify God and to enjoy Him forever. In seeming to do nothing for a sin-sick world, the Church of Christ by her worship of God day by day, week by week, does all for the world, or at least does that without which no human effort can ever be made perfect. All the other ministries of the Christian, when compared with this great ministry, are marginal and derivative. This liturgy or service of God in worship and prayer is central. So long as the Church calls men to worship God and provides a simple and proper vehicle for worship, it need not question its place, mission, and influence in the modern world. If the Church loses its faith in rendering God the most worthy praise that is His due and forgets to "do this in remembrance of me" on the Lord's Day; if the Church becomes thoughtless in the ordering of worship and careless in the conduct of worship, it need not look to its avocations to save it from God's judgment. It will already be dead at its heart. In the Lord's Prayer we pray first, "Our Father, who art in Heaven, Hallowed be thy name"; and then "Thy kingdom come, thy will be done on earth as it is in heaven." Before we can do any worthwhile work for God's Kingdom we must first hallow His Name.[51]

In dealing with the problems caused by automation, we must be able to distinguish between work as man's vocation to serve God and work as a mere function of the economic system. Vocation is essentially a religious term signifying the call of man by God to His service in this world. Function is a sociological term defining an individual's service to society.

The primary meaning of vocation is the call of God to the new life in Christ and to the service of His Kingdom. It is in this sense that the word is used in the New Testament. In a pre-eminent sense, vocation is a call to the Christian ministry in the service of the Word of God and the holy sacraments. But for the "lay" Christian also, God's call is first and foremost a call to serve Him in the order of redemption, but it is also a call to recapture his environment for Christ.

In view of this primary meaning of the term vocation, it might seem the better course to use it only in this sense and to speak of functions which men perform in society simply as their occupations. But this would be to deny to "secular" activities the possibility of being the fulfilment of a vocation or calling, and this would be entirely contrary to what we have said about the "world" being the place in which God is to be served. Yet it is obvious that many jobs in modern society cannot be included within a Christian definition of vocation, e.g., certain industries which are directed not to meeting men's fundamental needs but to providing them with luxuries of doubtful value or goods that are only minor embellishments of life;

and such occupations as book-making, prostitution, and the like.

Perhaps the criterion by which we can determine whether the work we are doing is a Christian vocation is that suggested by Mr. Heron—whether we can see in the thing we are making or doing something which is being made or done for Christ's sake.[52] In other words, all jobs which are meeting the real needs of human society may be considered as real "vocations" in so far as they afford an opportunity for the service of God and man. What the Christian must demand in regard to every form of work is that it should minister directly or indirectly to the satisfaction of genuine human needs, and that it should not deny or frustrate the realization of a man or woman's true manhood and womanhood as a person created in God's image and therefore responsible to God and living in love and charity with his fellows. Such a conception of work as a Christian vocation, if followed by all Christians in the English-speaking world, would result in far-reaching changes in the existing forms and structures of work in Atlantic society.

In so far as automation reduces work as a mere function it can be welcomed if it opens up new opportunities for work as vocation. Automation releases people from drudgery and boredom and thereby opens up new avenues of cultural activity for millions of people. God has entrusted to mankind the glorious task of developing not only the resources of the economic world to His honor and glory, but also of developing all the other aspects of His creation. The fulfillment of this "cultural" mandate implies that there must be opportunities available for participation in this divinely given task. It is precisely here that automation opens up a tremendous new field for human endeavor. There are numerous areas of culture and aspects of God's creation which have not even yet been touched, in any real sense, by the reformational influences of the Word of God. We have only to think of the fields of art, music, literature, and scientific research. So much has yet to be done to bring all these aspects of life into subjection to Christ's rule. Automation may well provide the necessary goods and time and leisure for such cultural activity, provided it is not regarded simply as a means of making greater profits but instead is viewed as a gift of God to be used wisely in the fulfillment of the cultural mandate. Work as vocation means that Christians, at any rate, will use the new opportunities of more leisure to engage in cultural pursuits for which previously they had little time to enjoy and develop. In this way there may well arise a whole generation devoted to glorifying God in their music, in their poetry, in their gardening, in their literature.

Already we can see that automation has freed both women and societies from the need for routine drudgery in factories and offices and given many more women than ever before not only greater domestic happiness but the opportunity to engage in voluntary social work for which they now have the time and energy. Of this development Bagrit says:

> Look at America where, through gadgetry, there has been an enormouns decrease in the time most women have to devote to their domestic chores. I doubt very much if you would find many of them looking for work in the kitchen as a way of filling in time. They discover what they consider to be more rewarding and interesting activities. . . . We find women busily buying every conceivable gadget to avoid having to do monotonous repetitive work. And as a result they have more time to devote to their children, their husbands and their homes, more time in making themselves look pretty and attractive, and more time to raising the general cultural level of their lives. . . . One valuable consequence of automation is going to be the ability to opt out of the industrial machine, and I personally believe . . . that in the long run this is likely to lead to an increase in domestic contentment. It would be a long step backwards even to attempt to "put woman back into the home," but to give her the option of going back if she prefers it seems to me to be quite different and socially valuable.[53]

Bagrit does not believe that women enjoy having to go out to work to help the husband make the budget balance at the end of the week. He says:

> I doubt if, under present conditions, women really enjoy getting up at six, preparing the family breakfast, rushing the kids off to school, and catching the bus in time to arrive for the eight o'clock shift; and, after a day's work, rushing home, cooking a dinner, and cleaning the house, while trying to maintain a decent domestic

life. Then why do so many do it? Simply because they must, if they and their families are to live at an acceptable standard. If, as a nation, we become productive enough and consequently rich enough to make the man's wage packet sufficient for the family needs, many women would prefer to go to the hairdresser rather than to the factory.[54]

This writer could not agree with Bagrit more. It is a positive disgrace that in England thousands of women have to go out to work to help their families make ends meet. In many such cases the working wives and mothers even have to work on the night shift, thereby undermining their marriages. If automation releases women and wives from having to go out to work, then we may expect to see the next generation of children being brought up instead of dragged up as they have been in England ever since their mothers went to work in the factories during the last war. The sooner women return to their peculiar office of raising and bringing up their own children, the healthier will be our society.

If used rightly then, automation may well provide the workers with new opportunities for social and cultural enrichment. Whether in fact it does so will depend on whether men use their new-found leisure to glorify God or to satisfy their own carnal lusts. However, leadership can be given in folk schools where people can be taught to recover the handicraft skills formerly enjoyed by their forebears. Training must be provided on an ever-increasing scale; more national parks, camping facilities, reasonable family hotels, community centers should be developed.

In the first Industrial Revolution most Christians stood idly by until it was too late to heal the scars which had been made upon large sections of the population, too late to expiate the sins of omission. The Church is still paying for that sin. God is now giving Christians a second chance to redeem the time, to make the days good instead of evil, to be in the vanguard rather than in the rearguard of the new cultural formation and economic organization of modern society; to be true to Christ the Redeemer of both ancient and modern civilization and to join the human race rather than to abdicate from all responsibilities for it.

In the first industrial revolution, it was only a few Protestant Christians who had any glimmering of the problem, men such as Groen van Prinsterer and Abraham Kuyper. These men realized that moralizing was not the answer. The social question arising out of the first industrial revolution required nothing less than a structural reformation of society as a whole, not a tinkering with the warped structures and institutions that had developed as a result of apostate economic individualism and collectivism. As Kuyper said:

> Only this one thing is necessary if a social question is to exist for you; that you realize the untenability of the present situation; and that you realize this untenability to be one not of incidental causes, but one involving the very basis of social association. For one who does not acknowledge this, and who thinks that the evil can be exorcised through an increase in piety, through friendlier treatment or kindlier charity, there exists possibly a religious question. This does not exist until you exercise an *architectonic* critique of human society itself and hence desire and think possible a different arrangement of the social structure.[55]

As we have seen, the Reformed philosophy of labor, industry, and society has provided modern man with the basic postulates of such a Christian structural ordering of human society in terms of the doctrine of sphere sovereignty and of the balance of authority and freedom.

Are we going to allow the second industrial revolution to be as disruptive of human society as the first proved itself to be, and are Christians going to stand by and watch the inevitable hatred grow between the new class divisions of society, or are they going to make it a new age of reconciling men and classes by reconstructing society upon God's creation norms and standards? Van Riessen warns us that a merely formal application of such biblical principles for the reconstruction and reformation of the basic structures of modern society will be useless unless such principles can be infused into the souls of men who understand them in the light of their origin and as the only means of fulfilling their divine vocation. Such creation ordinances are a mandate of creation; they come to man through the redemption of Christ. And their function is to emancipate life in keeping with the purpose of such redemption. Such principles are links in the chain of redemption, and they will function properly only if the man whom they motivate is filled with the mind and spirit of Christ. They can then become manifestations of love in compliance with the great commandment.

According to Van Riessen such creation norms become:

> . . . manifestations of reverence, not so much for man but for the calling of man, and consequently for the freedom man needs to follow his calling and to answer for his life and work to God. Such manifestations spring from a respect for *life as religion*.
>
> The distress and cultural crisis of our society can be overcome only if life is liberated. A sharp distinction must be made. Freedom is not only to be free from. Such freedom moves in a vacuum. The liberation from galling social restraints must have meaning, it must be freedom to unfold cosmic reality significantly.
>
> This brings us to the very heart of our subject. The urge toward a collectivistic social structure flows from a need for securities, for which men are willing to surrender their freedom from the restraints necessary to obtain these securities. But much more essential is the fact that men are unequal to the responsibility of this freedom of restraints, for they no longer know *why* they should be free. Through the Renaissance and humanism, life has lost its religious purpose; it is without perspectives. . . .
>
> The most profound thinker of secular positive science can delude us no longer. He leaves the question of the "why" alone, because he no longer knows a meaningful, convincing and vital answer. Modern man has lost the awareness of being called to a task by an authority beyond the cosmic horizon; he no longer knows what happens to his answer, or what his work means. As a result the anxiety of loneliness steals upon him. And man, who desires to be free "from," flees before the torturing question "why," into the shackles of collectivity.[56]

The one hope of the liberation of society from its present collectivist structures by which personal freedom has become shackled is therefore a victory over the spiritual crisis of our time. Without such a victory, which presupposes the reversal of the present trend towards complete secularization, no recovery of social life will be possible. Fundamentally this means that people recover their faith in Jesus Christ as Redeemer of the world and live out of the grace He provides. Van Riessen points out:

> The absence of the fulfilment of this condition should not prevent anybody from devoting all his energies to the recovery of society and from checking its dangerous course of development. For such recovery of society is in itself already a considerable part of the re-Christianization of social life.[57]

CHAPTER TEN NOTES

1. C. N. Cochrane, *Christianity and Classical Culture* (Oxford University Press, 1944), Preface, p. v ff.
2. Hendrik Hart, *The Challenge of Our Age*, p. 119.
3. Walther Eichrodt, "The Question of Property in the Light of the Old Testament," in *Biblical Authority for Today* (SCM Press, London, 1951), p. 261.
4. Walther Eichrodt, *Man in the Old Testament* (SCM Press, London, 1951), p. 12.
5. Alan Richardson, *The Biblical Doctrine of Work* (SCM Press, London, 1952), p. 24ff.
6. Calvin Seerveld, *Christian Workers, Unite!* (Christian Labour Association of Canada, 1965), p. 6.
7. Joseph C. McLelland, *The Other Six Days* (Burns and MacEachern, Toronto, 1959), p. 39, quoting Martin Luther.
8. Emil Brunner, *The Divine Imperative* (Lutterworth Press, London, 1949), p. 206.
9. Abraham Kuyper, *Principles of Sacred Theology* (Eerdmans, Grand Rapids, 1963), p. 154.
10. Paul A. Samuelson, *Economics*: An Introductory Analysis (McGraw-Hill, New York, 1967), p. 17.
    J. K. Galbraith, *The Affluent Society* (Houghton Mifflin, Boston, 1958).
11. G. L. Bach, *Economics*: An Introduction to Analysis and Policy (Prentice-Hall, New Jersey, 1964), p. 18.
12. J. N. Morgan, M. H. David, W. J. Cohen, and H. E. Brazer, *Income and Welfare in the United States* (McGraw-Hill, New York, 1962), pp. 3-4.
13. G. Schuster, *The Nineteenth Century Magazine* (Feb., 1949), p. 10.
14. Samuel Courtauld, *Ideals and Industry* (Cambridge, 1949), p. 35.
15. H. Van Riessen, *The Society of the Future*, p. 227ff.
16. W. F. Gaay Fortman, "Industrial Relations in the Netherlands," *Delta* (Amsterdam), p. 12.
17. *Ibid.*, pp. 3-4.

18. Rodger Charles, *Man, Industry and Society* (Sheed & Ward, New York, 1964), p. 96ff.
19. W. F. Gaay Fortman, "Aims and Purposes of the Christian Social Movement," in *The Free University Quarterly* (Vol. 1, No. 3, July, 1951, Amsterdam), p. 164.
20. *Ibid.*, p. 165.
21. K. S. Inglis, *Churches and the Working Class in Victorian Engalnd* (Routledge, Kegan and Paul, London, 1963).
22. George Herbert, *Hymns Ancient and Modern*, p. 266.
23. Seerveld, *op. cit.*, p. 8.
24. *Ibid.*, p. 11.
25. A. Heron, *Prospect for Christendom* (Faber & Faber, London, 1947), p. 116.
26. *Ibid.*, p. 117.
27. Author unknown.
28. Sir Leon Bagritt, *The Age of Automation*, The Reith Lectures (Lecture One, The BBC Listener, London, 1964), p. 744.
29. *Ibid.*, p. 744f.
30. Norbert Wiener, *The Human Use of Human Beings* (Doubleday Anchor Book, New York, 1954), p. 152ff.
31. John Billera, "The Human Side of Automation," *Time and Motion Study* (London, April, 1963), p. 29ff.
32. Quoted by John F. Cronin and Harry W. Flannery, *Labor and the Church* (Burns and Oates, London, 1965), p. 67.
33. *Ibid.*, p. 68.
34. *Ibid.*
35. *Ibid.*, p. 69.
36. Charles E. Silberman, *The Myths of Automation* (Harper & Row, New York, 1967), p. 2.
37. F. A. Hayek, *Prices and Production* (Routledge & Kegan Paul, London, 1960), p. 32ff. Cf. G. Terborgh, *The Automation Hysteria* (1966).
   Karl Brunner, "The Triple Revolution; A New Metaphysic" (*New Individualist Review*, University of Chicago, Spring, 1966).
38. Gary North, *Inflation, The Economics of Addiction* (The Pamphleteers, San Carlos, California, 1965).
   Jacques Rueff, *The Age of Inflation* (Regnery Paperback, Chicago, 1964).
   Murray Rothbard, *What Has Government Done to Our Money?* (Pine Tree Press, Colorado Springs, 1963).
39. Bernard Asbell, *The New Improved American* (McGraw-Hill, New York, 1966).
40. Yale Brozen, "Business Leadership and Technological Change" (*American Journal of Economics and Sociology*, 1954), pp. 13-30.
   Yale Brozen, "Technological Change, Ideology and Productivity" (*Politi-*

cal Science Quarterly, December, 1955), pp. 522-542.
41. Quoted by David S. Lee, *Automation and You* (Church in Wales Publications, Penarth, Glam, 1966), p. 18.
    Cf. R. S. Weiss & David Riesman, "Work and Automation: Problems and Prospects," in *Contemporary Social Problems* (Harcourt, Brace & World, New York, 1966), p. 609ff, section on Unemployment.
42. Bagrit, *op. cit.*, Lecture V, p. 929.
43. F. A. Hayek, *The Road to Serfdom* (Routledge, London, 1946).
    F. A. Hayek, *Individualism and Economic Order* (Free Press, New York, 1955).
44. A. Kouwenhoven, *Liberty and Equality* (J. Kok, Kampen, 1964), p. 253.
    K. Groen, "Dooyeweerd, and Governmental Organization of Industry," in *Jurisprudence Essays* (Kok, Kampen, 1951), p. 77ff.
    H. Dooyeweerd, *New Critique*, Vol. III, p. 446.
45. Ludwig Von Mises, *The Theory of Money and Credit* (Yale University Press, 1951), p. 103.
46. Gary North, *op. cit.*, p. 4ff.
    Don Bell, "And the Barbarians Captured the Beloved Country," in *Don Bell Reports* (August 27, September 3 and 10, 1965, Palm Beach, Florida).
    R. J. Rushdoony, *The Nature of the American System* (Craig Press, Nutley, N. J., 1959).
47. "Redundancy," Church Information Office, Westminster, London, 1962.
    G. Goodman, *Redundancy in the Affluent Society* (Fabian Society).
    L. Landon Goodman, *Man and Automation* (Pelican Book, London, 1957).
48. Emil Brunner, *The Divine Imperative*, p. 389.
49. *Ibid.*, p. 390.
50. Josef Pieper, *Leisure, the Basis of Culture* (Faber and Faber, London, 1952), p. 90.
51. Massey H. Shepherd, *The Liturgical Renewal of the Church* (Oxford University Press, New York, 1960).
    A. P. Herbert, *Liturgy and Society* (Faber & Faber, London, 1949).
52. A. Heron, *Prospect for Christendom*, p. 119.
53. Bagrit, *op. cit.*, Lecture No. VI, The Listener (Dec. 17, 1964), p. 971.
54. *Ibid.*
55. A. Kuyper, *Christianity and the Class Struggle*, pp. 39-40.
    Cf. R. K. Merton's "Social Problems and Sociological Theory," in *Contemporary Social Problems*, pp. 799-804.
56. H. Van Riessen, *op. cit.*, p. 230.
57. *Ibid.*, p. 308.

CONCLUSION

Can Christians today accept either capitalism or communism as the best and ultimate form of economic and social organization of human work and society? The writer trusts that the preceding pages of this work have made it clear that Christians can accept neither, since both forms of society are contrary to God's creational structures and norms. Instead, we have tried to show that God's Word calls all Christians in the power of their sovereign God to work for a new economic and social system which is neither capitalist nor communist, but pluralist.

Laissez-faire capitalism must be rejected because it makes the individual consumer and producer the criterion for its economic and social philosophy. Totalitarian communism must be rejected because it absolutizes the state and makes all individuals become its slaves. Both systems are contrary to God's law for man and society, and both reject God's Word as the only valid ordering principle for man's economic and social life. Both systems look upon man merely as a *function* rather than as a *person* created in God's holy image. According to God's Word men cannot thus be reduced to functions of society because man is not a functional being but a *religious* being, called to serve his Creator in all his works and to love his neighbor as himself. For the consistent Christian, life is religion, whereas for the capitalist, life is money, and for the Communist, life is politics.

Unless we understand the choice facing mankind today in these terms we shall not be able to think straight about the choice before us. Both capitalist and Communist make the error of not basing their theories of society, and thus their political and economic activities, upon the true view of man revealed in the Bible. Thus both the right-wing and the left-wing of modern politics stand revealed in their true colors as radical unbelievers who prefer to trust in their own reason, science, and planning instead of in God's Word.

God's Word refuses to accept the dilemma of collectivism versus individualism or of capitalism versus communism as being a genuine one. The Bible does not recognize any such dilemma. God's Word addresses each of us as "thou," not as an "it," and calls us unto fellowship with the living God and with our fellow men. The God and Father of the Lord Jesus Christ is the God of persons, not of things, and you cannot be a person in splendid isolation from other persons. The "individual" of laissez-faire capitalism simply does not exist in reality but only as the figment of a perverted scientistic humanism, and a false psychology.

It is only through love of God and love of each other, that is to say, through community, that we become human at all. True personality and true community are two sides of the same wonderful coin. St. John tells us "love is of God; and every one that loveth is born of God, and knoweth God. He that loveth not knoweth not God, for God is love" (I John 4:7). Love is thus the meaning of human life; indeed, it is eternal life itself. It is not the will to produce, nor the will to profit, nor the will to meaning, nor the will to sex, nor the will to power, but the will to love and to be loved that alone makes and keeps us sane and healthy human beings.

In his book, *The Great Divorce*, C. S. Lewis pictures hell as "a vast grey empty city stretching on all sides farther than the eye can reach. Why so large and empty? Because each new arrival after building his house quarrels with his neighbor and moves farther out. Everyone has the same urge. So the city is constantly expanding on the fringe. The center is abandoned streets. The whole population is on the move out to the free space beyond the suburbs where they can get away from one another. The enormous grey derelict town is a monument to the refusal of fellowship and love." [1] That sort of hell is already with us, at least in part. Far too many people, including middle-class Christians, are failing to recognize man's deep-rooted need for love, and many even try not to become involved with their neighbors. When our neighbors are doing the same thing to us, intolerable loneliness and alienation is the final outcome, and hell has already started for us. For God meant us to exist in and for love. He created us for community with himself and with each other. And we can really come alive as persons only by love of God and of each other. Death and hell are bound to exist where no love is. *When love is dead man is dead.*

As we have shown in this book, it is apostate modern man's lack of love which is today responsible for most of his mental disorders, the breakdown of community in industry, and his alienation from his fellow workers. America is dying through lack of *agape* in her industrial, political, and private life. As a result fear has gripped men's hearts. Only an emotion greater than fear can conquer fear. As St. John well says, "perfect love casts out fear."

The Christian has been commissioned at his baptism to proclaim and demand, on behalf of all, that personal and communal meaning of life which is proper to each, and to oppose everything which obscures or destroys this personal and communal significance of human life. The depersonalizing of people's lives in both capitalist and communist societies is therefore something which every true child of God will oppose. Both systems stand condemned before the divine standard of love by which Christ tells us in the great parable of the sheep and the goats we shall all be judged (Matt. 25:31-46).

At the foot of Christ's cross we learn both the measure of God's judgment upon our self-centeredness and the boundlessness of His forgiving love. God's love extends to us in all our nakedness and sin, even while we are selfish, cruel, unkind, proud, and hateful. This is the glory of Christ's cross. That it makes it possible for us to want to repent of our sinfulness and to want to live for love rather than for self. Herein lies the dynamic for Christian action and service. The cross of Christ alone can make us want an exodus from the worlds of capitalist greed and communist exploitation and manipulation of others. Such an exodus into the promised land of God's love can be undertaken only under the great captain of our salvation, the Lord Jesus Christ, who sealed the New Covenant between heaven and earth with his own precious life blood that we might be reconciled to God and to each other. Our dear Lord's death proclaims beyond all doubt not only that we have been cleansed of our sinfulness by His love, but that God's love is always more than a match for man's hateful and evil ways. But Christ has saved us that we might serve the cause of God's kingdom of love, not so we can sit back in our comfortable pews subjectively gloating over our individual salvation. Too many Christians today are willing enough to accept Christ as their own personal Savior, but they are not willing to make Him their King over every aspect of their lives. Yet in the Bible election is always seen as a call to God's service. For such Christians their religion is no longer the "unifying bond of all existence," but merely an optional frill to the more serious economic and political affairs of modern life. Such we have found to be the measure of our degeneration both as individual Christians and as the Body of Christ. The challenge of Christian action we have seen is, first, to re-discover our true identity and allegiance in modern life as God's "peculiar people" (Deut. 14:2), and secondly, to recover our sense of belonging *only* to Jesus Christ and to live for Him in all aspects of our lives.

Such a betrayal of love is inevitable as long as we think we can live as individualists or collectivists. The consistent Christian is obliged to reject capitalism because it does not recognize any need for true community or love between men and because it monetizes all human relationships and makes cash the only nexus binding men together. He will also reject communism because it absolutizes the state, which it proclaims to be man's only means of salvation from the alienation by which he is beset. But man cannot thus be saved by the state. Whenever the state tries to save man, it succeeds only in enslaving the individual. Man must never be enslaved, either by big business or by big government, not even by big church, since man in the center of his personality, in his "heart," transcends time, while as long as he remains in history he functions in a multiplicity of equally significant communities and associations. *Man has been created in the image of God, not of society.*

The biblical view of man in society alone can provide an escape from the evil snares of both individualism and collectivism, for it reveals that man is created as a person in God's image together with other men. Man's personality can develop properly only in love for

God and for his neighbor. Man has been called by his Creator to love God and his neighbor as himself. Thus the individual and the community are equally called to live in obedience to God's structural laws and norms for man in society. It is only by obedience to these norms that the present struggle between capitalism and communism will be successfully resolved. Both Eastern communism and Western capitalism equally need reforming in every aspect of their systems. Only by means of such a mighty economic and political reformation shall we be able to avoid the holocaust of nuclear warfare.

The depersonalization of modern man did not begin with the application of technology to his social and economic life, which has been falsely blamed for this terrible result, but with the progressive apostasy from the Lord Jesus Christ that has been undermining modern society since the days of the Renaissance. As we have shown, depersonalization is the inevitable outcome of secularization and of man's estrangement from that faith in God, by which alone the sovereign worth of both individual personality and true community can be founded and preserved.

In modern history this depersonalizing process has taken two main forms. At first sight the collectivist form seems to be the exact opposite of the other individualist form, and yet in fact both capitalism and communism have grown out of man's apostasy from the God of the Bible. Apostate capitalists have desired personal freedom, but they have failed to realize that the truly personal is identical with true community. So they demanded and established the freedom of the individual business entrepreneur to run his own business without interference by the state, intending that when each individual pursued his own selfish interest an "invisible hand" would bring about the well-being of everyone else. In *The Wealth of Nations* we have seen how Adam Smith secularized the old Calvinist ethic of his Scottish forebears by proclaiming the sovereignty of the individual producer and consumer and taught that economic life would be organized for the best if left to the control of the laws of supply and demand and the market. Let all economic activities be directed solely by considerations of price and competition and all would be well. Today we know where such "laissez faire" led. It led to the terrible depression of the nineteen thirties. Unrestricted, irresponsible capitalism did not lead to man's freedom but to the economic enslavement and exploitation of millions of workers, and to the despotism of the few giant cartels and monopolies.

The reaction against this godless economic system inevitably came. It was inaugurated, as we saw, by the *Communist Manifesto* of Marx and Engels in 1848, and first realized by Lenin in Soviet Russia. The totalitarian communism of Russia and Red China is the exact opposite of apostate Western individualistic liberal capitalism. As the latter pursues personal freedom detached from community and responsibility to God, so the former strives for community apart from personal freedom. As Adam Smith had secularized the Protestant ethic so Lenin and Stalin secularized the Caesar-Papism of the Russian tsars. Both capitalism and communism in fact represent the most powerful heresies ever to have inflicted the Church of God, both Western and Eastern branches. Like all heresies, they represent a partial and an incomplete truth, which is what has made them so plausible to millions of their supporters. Yet, like all heresies, because they do not reflect the whole counsel of God, both have proved destructive of true personality and community. However, totalitarian communism has proved to be far more dangerous than capitalism because it denies not only individual freedom but also any possibility of criticism and therefore of correction and reformation. The recent occupations of Hungary and Czechoslovakia show what happens to those who dare criticize the system. They are eliminated by the force of the secret police. In capitalist societies forces opposed to its godless system cannot as yet be stifled. There is therefore still some hope of a successful reformation of capitalist societies but little if any hope of the reformation of Russian and Chinese communism.

Both systems are products of one and the same apostasy; of one and the same contempt for God's Word in which true personality and community are grounded and safeguarded in Jesus Christ, the second Adam and Head of the new mankind. Thus in spite of their apparent opposition they are apostate ideological twins conceived by the spirit of eighteenth century rationalism in the womb of the

French Revolution. Marx truly recognized this fact when he predicted that communism would, as a matter of course, follow the consummation and collapse of capitalism. He believed that the communist ordering of society would inevitably develop from the control exercised by monopolist mammoth cartels and big business corporations over the organization of modern industry.

Marx did not realize the point first grasped by Lenin, that this expropriation of control from the monopolists could take place only through the violent intervention of the state. Again, it was Stalin who first realized that the total dictatorship of the state must be a permanent form of communist society, and not a transitional phase as Marx had predicted.

Given these alternatives, what can Christians do? The answer is that Christians must reject both in the name of a better and truer ordering of society. Both systems spring from the same apostate fountain of error, and both in different ways are denials of personality in community in the spirit of love.

One of the main attractions of communism has lain in its justifiable criticism of the unfair distribution of the national income and the degrading dependence of the workers upon capital, rather than in its positive program. As we saw, the communist accusation of capitalist exploitation of the workers rests upon Marx's theory of surplus value, which, reduced to its essentials, claims that the worker produces by his labor a certain value, and receives in wages less than the value he has produced.

On the basis of a Christian view of economics, we can admit that there is some truth in this argument, but we would also recognize the important role played by modern technology and capital formation. Yet we would point out that the communist cure by means of state control of all means of production, distribution, and exchange is worse than the disease it would remedy. The only result of the communist statist solution to the problem of capitalist exploitation of the worker is to make everybody equally poor, equally unfree, and equally miserable. It solves the problem of monopoly by creating the biggest concentration of the ownership of capital the world has ever seen, namely complete state control of all the instruments of production.

But there are other ways than nationalization for procuring a more just distribution both of material goods and services and of the power of the disposal of wealth. We think at once of the proper extension of that cooperation between employers and workers and of companies made more responsible to their shareholders, workers, and consumers advocated by George Goyder in *The Responsible Company*. It is not more state control of industry that is required today, but more Christ-control Once it is recognized that state control of industry is the false way because it results in the totalitarian state, then it becomes possible to entertain the *reformation* rather than the *overthrow* of capitalism, by making it more responsible than it has been. Class cooperation is the Christian answer to class conflict, and this means working for a new economic system in which both management and employees would each have its own proper and important role to play.

Acquisition by the state of the control of industry is the wrong way to remedy the social and economic injustices which are inherent in the present system of financial capitalism. The true Christian way does not consist in making the state the decisive force in economic life, but, on the contrary, in restoring to those groups and institutions their own sphere sovereignty which the centralizing trends of our century have abolished. In the Christian view of the state its essential role is precisely to guard people from being absorbed by the state and to make room for the harmonious cooperation of associations and communities prior to and outside the state— the family, the schools, churches, employers' and workers' associations, and professional organizations. The apostate humanist dogma of class conflict must be replaced by the Christian insight that employers and workers have been appointed by God to work together as fellow office bearers in God's creation, and that the well-being of the one involves the well-being of the other. Pluralism is thus the Christian answer to both capitalism and communism, since it alone can avoid the danger of depersonalization and social alienation

endemic in large-scale big business organizations and of the dictatorship endemic in state-run industries.

According to William Kornhauser in *The Politics of Mass Society*
both communist totalitarians and liberal capitalist mass-societies are
today characterized by atomized masses. But they differ in the
vulnerability of their elites to influence. The disruption of primary
group ties through sudden and extensive changes in the social
structure caused by widespread unemployment or military defeat are
among the factors he has found favoring the atomization or depersonalization of populations—one of the ingredients of totalitarianism.

It follows from Kornhauser's analysis that an essential condition for
a liberal democracy, in which both true personality and community
can be preserved, is the existence of a number of autonomous secondary associations which reduces the vulnerability of individuals
to domination by the elites either of big business or big government.
In other words, it is to the pluralist type of society to which Kornhauser turns as a protection against any trend towards totalitarianism.
He writes:

> In summary, a liberal democracy requires widespread partici-
> pation in the selection of leaders, and a large amount of self-
> governing activity on the part of non-elites. It also requires com-
> petition among leaders and would-be leaders, and considerable
> autonomy for those who win positions of leadership. The basic
> question arises, what kind of social structure will meet these
> conditions of liberal democracy? The theory of mass society
> . . . implies that social pluralism is a social arrangement which
> performs this function. A plurality of independent and limited-
> function groups supports liberal democracy by providing social
> bases of free and open competition for leadership, widespread
> participation in the selection of leaders, restraint in the application
> of pressures on leaders, and self-government in wide areas of so-
> cial life. Therefore, where social pluralism is strong, liberty and
> democracy tend to be strong; and conversely, forces which
> weaken social pluralism weaken liberty and democracy.[2]

While welcoming Kornhauser's thesis we would point out that
liberty and democracy as we have known them in the English-
speaking world have depended not only upon the existence of

autonomous sovereign spheres but upon men and women who felt themselves to be directly responsible to the living God of the Bible for the conduct of their daily lives. Obviously there can be no freedom unless the economic and cultural institutions of society are genuinely seeking to express and maintain their own authentic existence apart from the state. But here, as in the realm of personal freedom, the condition of corporate freedoms, no less than of individual freedoms, is eternal vigilance. Unless the desire to remain independent of state control exists in modern American and Canadian hearts as it once existed in Puritan and Calvinist hearts, no social institution as such can hope to resist encroachment by the leviathan state.

The conflict between the two opposing apostate ideologies of our age has for too long prevented the application of the pluralistic Christian solution to the false dilemma with which they have bedevilled mankind. It can scarcely be denied that the possibilities of such a reformational scriptural pluralism which is neither individualistic nor collectivistic have not yet been exhausted, let alone tried. In *Community and Power* Robert A. Nisbet calls for an associative pluralism which seems to this writer a good description of a viable policy for the Western world. He writes:

> Because of our single minded concentration upon the individual as the sole unit of society and upon the State as the sole source of legitimate power, we have tended to overlook the fact that freedom thrives in cultural diversity, in local and regional differentiation, in associative pluralism, and, above all, in the diversification of power.
>
> Basically, all of these are reducible, I believe, to the single massive problem of the relation of political government to the plurality of cultural associations which form the intermediate authorities of society. These are many: religious, economic, professional, local, recreational, academic, and so forth. Each of them is a structure, often large, of authorities and functions. Each of them is an organization of human purposes and allegiances related to some distinctive institutional end. Each of them is, apart from the checks provided by the existence of other and competing forms of association, potentially omni-competent in its relations to its members. . . .
>
> It is the continued existence of this array of intermediate powers in society, of this plurality of "private sovereignties" that

constitutes, above everything else, the greatest single barrier to the conversion of democracy from its liberal to its totalitarian form. . . .

To create the conditions within which autonomous *individuals* could prosper, could be emancipated from the binding ties of kinship, class, and community, was the prime objective of the old laissez-faire. To create conditions within which autonomous groups may prosper must be, I believe, the prime objective of the new laissez-faire.

I use the word create advisedly. We should not suppose that the laissez-faire individualism of the middle of the nineteenth century was the simple heritage of nature. . . . Laissez-faire, as Polanyi among others has emphasized, was *brought* into existence. It was brought into existence by the planned destruction of old customs, associations, villages and other securities; by the force of the state throwing the weight of its fast-developing administrative system in favor of the new economic elements of the population. And it was brought into existence, hardly less, by reigning systems of economic, political and psychological thought, systems which neglected altogether the social and cultural unities and settled single-mindedly on the abstract individual as the proper unit of speculation and planning. . . .

In what Frank Tannenbaum has well termed "the balance of institutional power" lie the possibilities for a harmonization of personal freedom and associative authority. "The road to personal peace," Mr. Tannenbaum writes, "is the balance of the social institutions, and a wise statesman would strengthen those institutions that seemed to be losing ground, even if he were not addicted to them; for the only way to keep peace in this world of fallible human nature is to keep all human institutions strong but none too strong; relatively weak, but not so weak as to despair of their survival. It is only thus that peaceful irritation and strife, so essential to social and individual sanity, can be maintained." . . .

Nor is there much to hope for in the way of freedom (unless such pluralism prevails). "Who says liberty, says association," declared Lammennais in the early nineteenth century, and he was echoed a generation later by Proudhon: "Multiply your associations and be free."

The liberal values of autonomy and freedom of personal choice are indispensable to a genuinely free society, but we shall achieve and maintain these only by vesting them in the conditions in which liberal democracy will thrive—diversity of culture, plurality of association, and division of authority.[3]

In other words, sphere sovereignty or economic and cultural pluralism is the answer to the needs of modern society for ordered freedom under God. Such ordered freedom has in actual historical experience, at least in the experience of Puritan democracy in England and America, been found to arise only out of a living faith in the God and Father of the Lord Jesus Christ. Our Anglo-American doctrine of the limited state grew inevitably out of the Puritan demand for freedom of conscience. The principle of religious freedom won during the English Civil War established the principle of the limitation of political authority.

Long before the English, Dutch, and American peoples gained political liberty they had achieved the liberty to worship God freely, and to govern their churches without interference from the state. The principle of congregationalism in religion meant that authority lay in the group as a whole, and not in a privileged hierarchy or elite, and that the individual had the right to follow his own conscience in his religious beliefs. This religious congregationalism of the Puritans and Baptists and Quakers was later applied to Anglo-American politics with results that had tremendous impact.[4] It led to the doctrine that political authority rested with the people, and that the government was no more than the agent of the community, ministering to its communal needs as its servants rather than its master. This freedom of conscience in religion inevitably led to the concept of basic civil rights as incorporated in the English Bill of Rights in 1689 and in the First Ten Amendments to the Constitution of the United States in 1791. This should not be surprising, for did not the Lord Christ tell us, "I am the way, the truth and the life," and that "the truth will make you free." Only as we walk in His way, believe in His truth and share in His life by the power of the Holy Spirit can we hope to remain free of domination by the apostate forces of darkness, both at home and abroad, which are now seeking to destroy the glorious liberty of the sons of God. Let us then stand fast in the freedom whereby Christ has made us free (Gal. 5:1). If the great Prince of Freedom is *for* us, who can prevail against us? Has Christ not promised His faithful followers, "In the

world ye shall have tribultaion: but be of good cheer; I have overcome the world" (John 16:33).

CONCLUSION NOTES

1. C. S. Lewis, *The Great Divorce* (G. Bless, London, 1961) p. 29.
2. William Kornhauser, *The Politics of Mass Society* (The Free Press, New York, 1959), p. 230ff.
3. R. A. Nisbet, *Community and Power* (Oxford University Press, New York, 1962), pp. 265-279).
4. William Ebenstein, C. Herman Pritchett, Henry A Turner, and Dean Mann, *American Democracy in World Perspective* (Harper and Row, New York, 1967), pp 25-29, "The Core of Free Government."

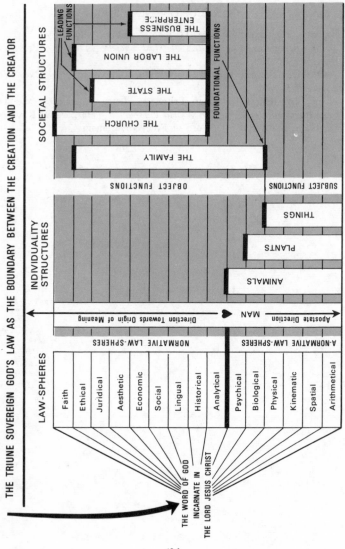

THE TRIUNE SOVEREIGN GOD'S LAW AS THE BOUNDARY BETWEEN THE CREATION AND THE CREATOR

SOCIETAL STRUCTURES

LEADING FUNCTIONS

THE BUSINESS ENTERPRISE

THE LABOR UNION

THE STATE

THE CHURCH

THE FAMILY

FOUNDATIONAL FUNCTIONS

OBJECT FUNCTIONS

SUBJECT FUNCTIONS

INDIVIDUALITY STRUCTURES

THINGS

PLANTS

ANIMALS

Direction Towards Origin of Meaning   MAN   Apostate Direction

NORMATIVE LAW-SPHERES   A-NORMATIVE LAW-SPHERES

LAW-SPHERES

Faith
Ethical
Juridical
Aesthetic
Economic
Social
Lingual
Historical
Analytical
Psychical
Biological
Physical
Kinematic
Spatial
Arithmetical

THE WORD OF GOD
INCARNATE IN
THE LORD JESUS CHRIST

626

Appendix Two

THE REFORMED ECUMENICAL SYNOD
ON CHRISTIAN ORGANIZATIONS
(Adopted in August, 1963, Grand Rapids, Mich.)

Preamble: As it is the calling of the church to let the light of the prophetic Word, entrusted to her, shine upon all spheres of life, Synod deems it desirable to formulate some directives regarding separate Christian organizations in the social and political fields. Therefore Synod declares:

1. Believers should reflect individually, in groups, and in organizations on their responsibility in the political and social fields and on the manner in which this responsibility can be discharged.

Grounds:

The church's confession and proclamation of the Kingship of Christ in all phases of life demands that believers reflect on the manner in which they are to discharge their duties in the social and political fields. Such reflection is demanded more and more in this age of constantly increasing organization of man in all kinds of alliances.

2. Although it is not possible for Synod to say that Christians must always organize on a separate basis in the social and political fields, there exists a need for greater stress on considering concerted Christian action in the above-mentioned fields.

Grounds:

a. It is the duty of the church to preach the full counsel of God, including the principles of Christian behavior in the social and political fields and not the function of the church to precsribe the details of what is or what is not Christian behavior in the social and political fields.

b. Modern developments of unchristian activity in the social, economic and political fields in which ruthless power often seems the only norm that reigns, make the question of establishing and/or joining Christian organizations a matter of great importance.

3. In the social and political fields Christians should promote the one true justice and righteousness, taught in the Word of God, and should be encouraged to organize to that end whatever and whenever it is possible.

Grounds:

a. It is God's will, as revealed in His Word and testified by His Spirit in our hearts, that justice and righteousness be established in society (Cf. Jer. 22:3; Isa. 1:17; Ps. 15:1, 2; Isa. 32:17; 33:15-17; Phil. 1:11; I John 2:29; 3:7 and 10).

b. Of all people, Christians should be the most sensitive to injustice and unrighteousness. Although the individual Christian can and should witness against these, in the increasingly complex and massive organization of society, it would seem that the Christian witness can be made more effective through Christian organizations. It should be noted that the possibility of effective Christian social and political organizations will depend to a considerable extent on the prevailing state of society as a whole and/or of local circumstances.

4. Since the contrast between the kingdom of light and of darkness is becoming more sharply defined in the sphere of social relations, and it therefore becomes increasingly difficult for Christians who have united with so-called general or neutral organizations, to give due heed to their Evangelical mandate, there is a growing need for separate organizations of believers.

Grounds:

a. Since in many countries and many situations there exists an increasing unchristian activity, appealing to ruthless power only, and not seeking a justice and fellowship that is in accord with

Scriptures, a separate Christian organization (in the social field of employers as well as of employees) will provide believers with the opportunity to exhibit their concept of society and to appeal to biblical norms.

b. Experiences with separate Christian political and social organizations in which the employee as well as the employer are viewed as God's creation, and in which harmonious cooperation between employers and employees, especially in trade unions, plays a central role, indicate that in this way the believer is enabled to make a fruitful contribution to the promotion of better social relations.

5. The purpose of separate Christian organizations must always be the service of God and fellow-men and never a matter of seeking isolation.

Ground:

Christians are the salt of the earth and the light of the world and are admonished to function as such (cf. Matt. 5:13-16).

6. With respect to the so-called general or neutral political and social organizations, believers in consultation with fellow believers who are in the same situation, must decide in the light of Holy Writ, taking into consideration the circumstances of time and place, whether they may or may not unite with such organizations, provided that the basis, aims and practice of such organizations allow them to exercise their calling in this world. It is understood, of course, that if a Christian joins such a nonchristian organization, he alone and unitedly with other Christians in the organization is in duty bound at all times to live by and advance Christian principles within the organization.

Ground:

The Christian is called upon to be obedient to Christ in every activity (cf. I Cor. 10:31). He must therefore live consistently with his confession.

7. Christians may not be members of or give aid to social and po-

litical organizations whose principles and/or whose common and regular practices conflict with biblical norms.

Ground:

To live in a manner inconsistent with biblical norms is sin, and this sin is aggravated when a Christian is aware of the contradiction and continues to ignore it (cf. James 4:12; I Thess. 5:22).

Appendix Three

PRINCIPLES AND PRACTICES OF THE CHRISTIAN LABOR ASSOCIATION OF CANADA

Principles

Principles to which the C.L.A.C. is committed are these:

1. All human beings bear the image of their Creator and must as such be treated with dignity, respect and love. Every violation of the divinely given law of love among men is a sin against God.

2. Discrimination in employment because of color, creed, race or national origin conflicts with the Biblical principle of equality of all human beings before God and the law of love toward all men.

3. The task of developing the resources of the world has been entrusted to the human race as a whole, which implies that there must be opportunities for participation in the fulfillment of that task for all members of society.

4. It has been ordered that men shall live by the fruit of their labours and that in the performance of their work they shall make use of and develop the physical and intellectual qualities with which they have been endowed; hence all men are entitled to such a reward upon their labours as will be adequate to meet their family needs and social obligations in a respectable and

honourable manner, and which will reflect also the measure of their devotion to their respective tasks.

5. Creational resources may not be exploited for personal gain or the enrichment of a group or a community, but must be developed for use in the service of all mankind.

6. Injustices among men are due, basically, to violations of divinely instituted law and order. Removal of injustices may not be sought by means of promotion of class conflict or by revolution against properly established authority—actions which are in themselves contrary to divine law—but must be promoted through reformative measures that are in harmony with divinely instituted law and order.

7. The interdependence of employers and employees, their many common interests, their obligations and responsibilities toward each other, their mutual obligations and responsibilities toward society in general and given fulfillment in obedience to the law of love, demand that there be cooperation between them in the promotion of the best interest and welfare of all concerned.

8. Employers and workers and their organizations must constantly strive for the attainment and maintenance of labour conditions in which the spiritual and the physical and moral well being of the workers is advanced; which demand conditions in which interest in the work being done and joy in the performance of it are stimulated.

9. The common bonds of interest between workers demand that there be organization among them for the purposes of protection of inherent and lawfully established rights and the promotion of their mutual welfare, through collective bargaining and the negotiation of labour agreements.

10. Workers who share in the benefits gained through the activity of an organization that represents them are socially and morally obligated to assume a just share of the obligations that are attendant upon such organized activity; provided, however, that no worker who because of a conscientious conviction cannot join the organization shall be refused employment.

11. When labour disputes arise both employers and workers must use every available means to settle their differences by means of conferences, mediation or arbitration. The use of violence against persons or property, the unlawful seizure of property, the employment of labour spies, intimidation, coercion, discrimination and all other unchristian methods for either advancing or discouraging organization, or forcing the settlement of a dispute, stand condemned.

12. All workers, whether acting individually or collectively, have the inherent right to refuse to continue work under an unjust condition, after having exhausted every reasonable means to remove the injustice by means of conference, mediation or arbitration; except that in any industry or institution or public service, where a cessation of work might endanger the life and health of the community or nation, the right to refuse to continue to work must be surrendered and all disputes settled by means of neutral arbitration.

Practices

Among practical measures which the C.L.A.C. will take to reach its objectives are these:

1. Encourage its members to render the highest grade of workmanship and service in the trades or occupations in which they are engaged and promote cooperation between workers and their employers on the basis of justice, love and mutual interests.

2. By organized activity negotiate and maintain labour contracts that will guarantee to workers adequate wages and other just labour conditions in keeping with the Christian social principles set forth in this Constitution.

3. Maintain Sunday as a day of rest and oppose all Sunday labour except that which is necessary because of natural laws and the protection of health and the public welfare; provided that the C.L.A.C. shall also protect the right of people who because of religious convictions hold their sabbath on another day of the

week, to do so and not to suffer any discrimination as a result.

4. Encourage its members to study and discuss current economic and social conditions and the bearing of Christian principles upon them.

5. Carry on propaganda through the written and spoken word for Christian economic and social principles, and for the taking of measures which will improve labour conditions and relationships and will counteract the unwholesome influence of labour groups that are inspired by communistic or other unchristian principles.

6. Bring influence to bear upon the government of municipalities, province or nation whenever important interests of labour and industry are at stake in legislative assemblies and exert legitimate influence upon administrative bodies or agencies.

7. Take practical measures to avoid labour disputes and if such disputes do arise champion methods for peaceful settlement.

8. Cooperate with organizations pursuing similar objectives whenever such action is deemed advisable and does not conflict with the Christian principles to which the C.L.A.C. is committed.

9. Assist its members in securing employment through such practical measures as are feasible, relieve as much as possible financial pressure upon its members when it is caused by involuntary unemployment, disability or old age.

10. Such activities that are in accord with C.L.A.C. principles and objectives as may be decided upon by the organization from time to time.